People, Politics, and Globalization

Annual World Bank Conference
on Development Economics—Global
2009

People, Politics, and Globalization

Edited by
Justin Yifu Lin and
Boris Pleskovic

THE WORLD BANK
Washington, D.C.

Edited by Justin Yifu Lin and Boris Pleskovic

Professional affiliations identified in this volume, unless otherwise noted, are as of the time of the conference, June 9–11, 2008.

ISBN: 978-0-8213-7722-2
eISBN: 978-0-8213-8059-8
DOI: 10.1596/978-0-8213-7722-2
ISSN: 1813-9477

Contents

Migration, Remittances, and the Transition from Foreign Aid

Higher Education and High-Technology Industry

Human Development

Political Economy

·

About This Book

The Annual World Bank Conference on Development Economics is a forum for discussion and debate of important policy issues facing developing countries. The conferences emphasize the contribution that empirical economic research can make to understanding development processes and to formulating sound development policies. Conference papers are written by researchers in and outside the World Bank. The conference series was started in 1989. Conference papers are reviewed by the editors and are also subject to internal and external peer review. Some papers were revised after the conference, to reflect the comments made by discussants or from the floor, while most discussants' comments were not revised. As a result, discussants' comments may refer to elements of the paper that no longer exist in their original form. Unless otherwise noted, participants' affiliations identified in this volume are as of the time of the conference, June 9–11, 2008.

The planning and organization of the June 2008 conference was a joint effort by the Government of South Africa and the World Bank. We gratefully acknowledge timely and valuable contributions made by the all the members of the Steering Committee and several anonymous reviewers. We would also like to thank Alan Gelb and Aehyung Kim for their insightful advice and Leita Jones, conference organizer, whose excellent organizational skills helped to ensure a successful conference. Finally, we thank the editorial staff for pulling this volume together, especially Stuart Tucker, Mark Ingebretsen, and Nora Leah Ridolfi from the Office of the Publisher.

Introduction

JUSTIN YIFU LIN AND BORIS PLESKOVIC

The Annual Bank Conference on Development Economics (ABCDE) brings fresh, innovative perspectives to key problems of development. By providing a forum in which policy makers, academics and leading researchers focus on a common theme, ABCDE plays an important role in advancing debate and shaping the international development agenda.

The 2009 ABCDE, held June 9–11, 2008, in Cape Town, South Africa, was devoted to "People, Politics, and Globalization." The program included a strong dose of empirical research on the experience of developing countries in all regions of the globe. Speakers addressed such subjects as trade and investment, higher education and high-technology industry, migration and remittances, the interaction between health and economic development, and the political economy of public expenditures.

This volume includes selected papers from the conference, as well as keynote addresses by Michael Spence, chairman of the Commission on Growth and Development and 2001 Nobel laureate for economics; Bassma Kodmani, executive director of the Arab Reform Initiative; and Sunil Kant Munjal, chairman of Hero Corporate Service Ltd., the services division of the Indian automotive concern.

Keynote Addresses

In his address "Rethinking Growth: Learning from Experience and Adapting to New Challenges," **Michael Spence** discusses the subject of sustained, high, *inclusive* growth and summarizes the findings of the Commission on Growth and Development. The commission, under Spence's chairmanship, has gathered new insights into the fundamental dynamics of sustained high growth and has identified the policy measures that appear to underpin such growth.

Justin Yifu Lin is Chief Economist and Senior Vice President for Development Economics at the World Bank. Boris Pleskovic is Research Manager for Development Economics at the World Bank.

Annual World Bank Conference on Development Economics 2009, Global
© 2010 The International Bank for Reconstruction and Development / The World Bank

Spence observes that in all of human history, only 13 economies have grown at an average annual rate of 7 percent or more for 25 years or longer—and all of these instances of sustained high growth occurred after 1950. The commission has dissected these cases to display their essential features and common characteristics, some of which derive from basic economics and others from effective government.

According to Spence, the single most important shared characteristic of the 13 high-growth economies is engagement with the global economy. Rather than generating new knowledge, these countries mastered existing knowledge and applied it in certain industries. Once they had developed a competitive advantage, they took advantage of the huge elastic demand offered by the global open economy, which allowed them to grow as quickly as they could invest.

The commission has documented that these countries also maintained macroeconomic stability and had high levels of saving, which spurred investment. Spence observes that a high national saving rate—20 percent and higher—has been common among the high-growth countries. In most cases, he notes, competitive market mechanisms, labor mobility, and rapid urbanization have been crucial.

The commission's most surprising finding, says Spence, concerns the importance of noneconomic factors, particularly political leadership and effective governance. The key factor of policy success seems to have been adherence to a consistent growth strategy. The successful economies did not all have the same type of government, but they all had political leadership that focused on improving the lives of members of society as a whole. Political leadership that focused on its own interests or on the interests of a particular group did not achieve sustained high growth. Among other ingredients of successful policy, Spence lists sustained investment in three areas: infrastructure, health and early childhood nutrition, and education.

The commission's findings do not include specific policy prescriptions. The commission did look at special challenges that face certain developing countries, including many countries in Africa. Small states, for example, have little ability to diversify their economies, and they face high costs with regard to government and public services. Countries rich in natural resources have a mixed record. Spence notes that because of the peculiar geography inherited from the colonial period, many African countries are small, many are landlocked, and although some have a rich natural resource base, others are resource poor. Middle-income countries, for their part, may experience difficulty moving from labor-intensive industry to industry fueled by knowledge, innovation, and human capital.

Bassma Kodmani presents an overview of the Middle East, juxtaposing certain grim political and economic realities against real achievements in recent years that seem to be moving the Arab region into a new era. She cites a number of long-term dangers—the Arab-Israeli conflict, the humanitarian disaster in Darfur, the war in Iraq, the depletion of water resources, and agricultural dependency—but also points to high rates of economic growth in most countries in the region and to important governance reforms. Kodmani observes, however, that reforms have slowed in the last couple of years because of reluctance to shift power decisively from government to society at large. She maintains that it is time to adopt a new democratic paradigm based on strong and accountable public institutions and on such fundamental principles as liberty, respect for human rights, the rule of law, and social justice.

Kodmani perceives a new awakening of Arab societies. Independent media have emerged and are forging horizontal links among citizens. Both the marginalized segments of society and elites are challenging governments and are launching protests. Kodmani argues that the existence of independent media has made governments much more reluctant to suppress such movements. Generally speaking, she asserts, these movements have been very positive in that they are centered on social and political issues, not issues of identity or religion, and they are calling for peaceful, gradual change through legal means. Still, she warns, major social and political unrest is possible.

In Kodmani's view, Middle Eastern society fears abrupt change and instability, and that fear is reinforced by the situation in Iraq, the threat from extremist groups such as those connected to Al Qaeda, and sectarian tensions in the region. As a consequence, political protest has generally remained peaceful, even though the space for legal protest is tightly restricted. This is true of Islamist movements, as well as secular social movements. For three decades Islamists have built social networks and have made inroads into political life, and they are now demanding a share of power. But the taking of power by force has been limited to conflict areas such as Lebanon and Palestine.

Kodmani argues that reforms in the Arab world are not sustainable without an underlying shift to a democratic paradigm. Only by recognizing this and creating a space for citizens to develop a home-grown agenda will a transition to a better future be possible. Specifically, Kodmani sees a need for a systemic approach toward reform, greater social accountability, and mechanisms for linking reform measures "from above" to the demands of society. She gives examples of two areas in which local groups have been modestly effective but foreign donors and multilateral institutions have not: security reform and gender issues. What is most important, Kodmani argues, is for Arab societies to be trusted to chart their own way, even if they choose a path with which foreign partners are not entirely comfortable.

In his keynote speech, **Sunil Kant Munjal** traces India's history of successful reform. Since 1991, India has opened with remarkable speed to the global economy, but it has followed its own unique path. Indeed, Munjal states, it could not be otherwise, as there is no precedent for a democratic country with a population of 1 billion transforming itself into an outward-facing market economy.

Munjal emphasizes the crucial role of innovation in India's miraculous progress. India, he says, has learned much along the way—mostly from its own mistakes, but also from the outside world. With respect to the latter, Munjal emphasizes the role of India's "brain bank" of overseas Indians. India, he adds, continues to need foreign capital, but most of all, it needs the knowledge and networks that accompany foreign capital.

In addition to a great capacity for low-cost innovation, Munjal observes, India has a long history as a trading nation. That history was interrupted for several decades after the country became independent in 1947, when it embraced central planning and began building dams, power plants, and steel plants. This direction may have been right at the time, says Munjal, but India held on to central planning for far too long. Only in 1991 did it make a dramatic and fateful move toward the market. Since then, India has firmly reestablished itself as a trading nation and has actively reached out to establish trade relations with many countries. Munjal gives many examples of success stories—in productivity, infrastructure development, and so forth—and cites some remarkable statistics: an average Indian today can spend twice what he or she could spend in 1985, and in the next 20 years the average Indian will be able to spend four times as much as now.

Still, Munjal remarks, many problems remain: labor regulation is still too rigid, physical infrastructure is often lacking, and red tape and corruption persist. Munjal also points to striking regional differences within India and to the failure of the central and state governments to adequately provide basic social services such as primary education and health care. He notes that the private sector has stepped in to help—in education and training; rural infrastructure, electrification, irrigation, drinking water supply, and many other areas—but that the private sector cannot be a substitute for government.

Trade and Investment

Paul Collier and **Anthony Venables** examine the economic consequences—especially the effects on trade—of the political fragmentation of Sub-Saharan Africa into 50-some states, mostly small. By contrast, in South Asia 95 percent of the population lives in just three countries: India, Pakistan, and Bangladesh.

Sub-Saharan Africa and South Asia are populated on the same scale (roughly, 1 billion people in each) and as recently as 1980 had broadly similar levels of income and human development. Since then, however, the economic performance of the two regions has diverged sharply. Africa's share of world gross domestic product (GDP) declined in the 1980s and 1990s, while South Asia's nearly doubled. In 1980 Africa's share of world exports was nearly four times that of South Asia.

Collier and Venables show that political geography has been a major factor in the regions' striking divergence over the last three decades. The political fragmentation of Sub-Saharan Africa pushes small national economies toward peasant agriculture and other economic activities in which scale is not so important. In addition, the authors observe, small markets by their nature tend to be less competitive than larger ones: monopolies, oligopolies, and rent-seeking are more common and make investment less attractive.

International borders, largely the legacy of colonialism, have led to an unequal distribution of natural advantages such as mineral wealth, coastlines, and natural harbors. Countries that are small, resource poor, or landlocked are at a tremendous economic disadvantage. Borders pose a formidable barrier to trade and labor mobility and restrict the region's ability to pool risk and absorb external shocks. Large Asian countries do not face barriers of this sort, and internal migration and urbanization have played an important role in their rapid growth.

Collier and Venables point out that whereas the rise of large industrial clusters in Asia has fueled high productivity and growth, Africa's failure to develop such clusters has had major negative effects on economic performance. The authors attribute this failure to the small size of African cities (relative to Asian cities), which derives in large part from Africa's political fragmentation.

Collier and Venables conclude that Africa would benefit greatly from political and economic integration. Previous efforts at integration have not yielded fruit in Africa, but the application of lessons from other world regions could help. The authors suggest that political and economic integration should go hand in hand; that integration is more likely to succeed if it grows from a small core of states, none of which is dominant; and that the economic agenda should be much broader than just trade policy, touching on integrated infrastructure, integrated investment and taxation rules, and so forth. Because these other areas of cooperation are much more likely to generate mutual gains than are trade agreements, their economic consequences reinforce rather than undermine the political process.

Lawrence Edwards adds to the debate on trade policy in Africa, where trade has declined dramatically over recent decades. Analyzing the effects of tariff liberalization on trade flows in Africa since 1990, Edwards paints a mixed picture. Drawing on sector-level data, he reaches three conclusions: (a) tariff liberalization has taken place in many countries, but African countries are still marginalized in terms of world trade; (b) the effect of tariff liberalization has had a very small, but positive, effect on manufacturing trade flows; and (c) tariff liberalization has had a negative effect on the manufacturing trade balance, but again the effect is very small.

Edwards presents data showing a considerable reduction in tariffs since the early 1990s. He observes, however, that African economies began from a high level and that their tariffs are still high relative to countries elsewhere in the world. He notes that other studies of trade liberalization in Africa have provided evidence of a worsening trade balance, which can lead to an external constraint on growth. Export performance in Sub-Saharan Africa showed no growth in the 1990s, and although exports have grown sharply since 2000, much of the increase is attributable to the boom in commodity prices. Edwards does, however, find some improvement in competitiveness.

Aaditya Mattoo and **Arvind Subramanian** discuss what may be a new phenomenon: "uphill skills flows"—the export of skills, embodied in highly sophisticated goods and services or foreign direct investment, from poor to wealthy countries. The authors provide evidence of a marked increase in uphill skills flows between 1991 and 2005, including such recent notable examples as the takeover of the U.K. automotive firm Jaguar by the Indian car maker Tata, Brazil's export of aircraft, and India's export of services to developed countries.

The authors provide evidence that outflows of foreign direct investment (FDI) to countries richer than the country of origin increased from 45 percent in 2003 to more than 70 percent in 2007. They find a similar pattern in the export of sophisticated, skill-intensive goods: the share rose from about 1 percent in 1980 to 10 percent in 2006. Uphill flows from China, Malaysia, and Mexico were a big part of this increase.

The authors posit some tentative hypotheses that might explain uphill skills flows. Certain countries—such as India and South Africa—may for historical reasons be following atypical development patterns that emphasize technical capabilities and give rise to pockets of skill-intensive industry. It is also possible that some firms, even in developing countries, are so productive that they succeed in entering markets in developed countries. And, trade barriers may favor uphill skills flows, as rich countries typically raise barriers against low-skill products rather than skill-intensive products.

Migration, Remittances, and the Transition from Foreign Aid

Jean-Paul Azam and **Ruxanda Berlinschi** argue that there is a trade-off between foreign aid and migration. It can be demonstrated empirically, they assert, that rich countries in fact use aid to reduce immigration from poor countries.

On the basis of a review of the literature on the economic effects of immigration, Azam and Berlinschi conclude that the effect on wages in the receiving country, whether positive or negative, is small but that remittances from migrants are now one of the main sources of external finance for developing countries. The authors point to a sizable constituency in rich countries that pressures governments to raise barriers against immigration. They then raise the questions of whether foreign aid reduces immigration and whether that is an unstated aim of foreign aid.

It has been demonstrated again and again in recent years, Azam and Berlinschi claim, that foreign aid rarely succeeds in reducing poverty or fostering growth in poor countries. The authors ask what benefits, then, bilateral donors actually get from foreign aid and suggest that reduced immigration may be one. Applying econometric methods to data from 1995–2003, they conclude that foreign aid is an effective tool for reducing migration to rich countries and that donors are in fact using aid as a policy tool for that purpose. Their further analysis shows that uncoordinated bilateral aid is just as effective as coordinated multilateral aid.

Lisa Chauvet, Flore Gubert, and **Sandrine Mesplé-Somps** analyze the impact of remittances and foreign aid on infant and child mortality. Despite the increasing magnitude of remittances (in 36 of 153 developing countries, remittances exceed official aid), there has been little examination of their relative effects on human development, as measured by infant and child mortality.

The authors' analysis of panel data on 109 developing countries and cross-country quintile-level data on 47 developing countries shows that remittances have a significant positive effect on children's health but that the effect is stronger in the richest households. The researchers discern no effect on the poorest households. When migration by physicians is included in the overall analysis of the costs and benefits of migration, the positive effects are weakened because the migration of physicians harms the overall state of children's health. The researchers also show that foreign aid to the health sector has little effect on health outcomes in developing countries.

Jinu Koola and Çağlar Özden examine the effect of migration on employment in the sending country. In their view, previous studies showing that migration decreases employment in sending countries—possibly because those who stay behind receive remittances and have less incentive to work—do not fully recognize the dynamics of migration. In fact, they argue, if workers have the opportunity to work in wealthier countries, their opportunity cost simply becomes higher. Consequently, if they do not make a high enough salary on the local market, they stop working and prepare to emigrate.

Working with panel data from two linked household surveys conducted in the Indian state of Kerala in 1998 and 2003, the authors present evidence that the drop in employment in the country of origin is more likely ascribable to the opportunities provided by migration networks that have been established in receiving countries by the migrants' families and communities. In 2003, according to the data, nearly 10 percent of Kerala's workforce—1.84 million people—was living and working in Persian Gulf countries; another million had already emigrated and had returned. Analysis of the panel data shows that social and communal networks, which can facilitate migration and lower its cost, are among the main determinants of migration.

Higher Education and High-Technology Industry

Sachi Hatakenaka examines the role that universities have played in the development of high-technology industries in a broad range of economies—the United States; Japan; Finland; Taiwan, China; the Republic of Korea; Ireland; India; Israel; and China—and draws lessons for higher education systems in other countries. In all these cases, the production of a critical mass of scientists and engineers was a prerequisite for the birth of high-technology industry, but it happened in different ways. Whereas some economies produced generic scientists and engineers, others provided specialized training with an emphasis on a narrower set of practical skills.

Hatakenaka develops an analytical framework differentiating higher education institutions along three dimensions: responsiveness to changing practical and industrial needs; the degree of commitment to fundamental science; and the level of selectivity in recruiting students and staff (in other words, whether the institution is an elite one or is, instead, open to the broader society).

Although institutions of all types have facilitated the development of high-technology industry, "responsive" institutions appear to play a much more proactive and direct role in helping such industry emerge and evolve, through a variety of modalities—education, research, spin-offs, science parks, licensing, and enrichment through international experience. Such institutions, Hatakenaka observes, do not seem to emerge naturally. In all cases, governments have played a critical role in founding them and in influencing their missions and orientation.

Hatakenaka comments that in many cases it was crucial that science and technology had a champion or champions on the national stage. Yet, she adds, in the nine economies under discussion, it has proved difficult to maintain a national commitment to science and technology over time.

Akilagpa Sawyerr and **Boubakar Barry** explore the relationship between knowledge production and economic development in the context of a strikingly different set of countries: those of Sub-Saharan Africa (excluding South Africa). Because the Sub-Saharan context differs so markedly from that of countries such as those represented in the Hatakenaka study, Sawyerr and Barry focus on small and medium-size industry. Indeed, the authors remark, the region has little industry that is truly high technology.

Sawyerr and Barry look at the supply of knowledge generated by African universities, as well as the demand for this knowledge by industry, and enumerate weaknesses in both supply and demand. The authors observe that now, as in colonial times, African industry is dominated by low-level processing of natural resources and the production of simple consumer goods. This sort of activity, unlike high technology industry, does not feel keen pressure for new knowledge and therefore does not demand industry-relevant research from African institutions. In spite of a few commendable attempts to build bridges between universities and industry, enterprises show little awareness of the importance of science and technology to competitiveness.

Moreover, on the supply side, say the authors, African universities are oriented away from science and technology and have little understanding of what industry needs. African universities do not offer proper postgraduate training in technical fields and are certainly not graduating the numbers of PhDs required for high-technology industries to take off. Generally, Sawyerr and Barry assert, universities in Sub-Saharan Africa have suffered for many years from neglect and lack of funding. Clearly, the universities are not up to the task of lifting African industry to a globally competitive level.

Sawyerr and Barry emphasize the need for a supportive public policy framework to strengthen both the supply and demand sides. They recommend that each country establish an "observatory," involving industry, government, universities, and technology institutions, to assist in understanding the issues and in building consensus. A second recommendation is to revitalize and strengthen Africa's universities. This process should include a special program for the strengthening of staff quality, as well as research and graduate study in carefully selected priority areas. To give the entire process the necessary weight and visibility, it must be championed at the highest political levels.

Human Development

Duncan Thomas comments on the close relationship between socioeconomic status and health. Poverty has been correlated with poor health again and again in studies around the world, but what to make of this correlation is still a matter of dispute. Thomas asserts that causality probably runs in both directions: poverty causes poor health, and poor health causes poverty. But, he notes, there may also be unobserved underlying factors that affect both health and socioeconomic status.

Thomas cites several recent studies showing that early childhood nutrition has a major impact on human capital formation (cognitive development, schooling, employment, and so on) and on economic productivity throughout life, beginning with school attendance. The evidence in these studies is drawn from various historical periods and from different parts of the world: contemporary rural life in Zimbabwe and Guatemala; the Spanish flu pandemic in the United States in 1918–20; malnutrition in the Netherlands during World War II; the Chinese famine of 1959–1961; and the 1974 floods in Bangladesh. Although the impact of disease is not as well researched as that of nutrition, it is nevertheless clear that successful treatment of infectious diseases is likely to have very significant positive externalities—for example, its effect on school attendance—and is in many cases inexpensive.

Markus Goldstein, Joshua Graff Zivin, and **Harsha Thirumurthy** analyze household survey data from several African countries to develop a fuller picture of the economic effects of a particular health treatment—antiretroviral therapy for adults infected with HIV. A number of studies provide compelling evidence of the efficacy of antiretroviral therapy, which has been delivered on a much larger scale in Africa in recent years.

Households with one or more adults suffering from HIV/AIDS are likely to withdraw their children from school, reduce food consumption, and increase children's labor, among other effects. Once the parent dies, the children are, of course, in an even worse position.

The authors' study clearly documents short-run benefits to the households of patients receiving antiretroviral treatment, including increased work hours, improved nutrition, and better school attendance. The research team demonstrates that the benefits from increased labor productivity alone outweigh the cost of treatment and that households in which the health of an HIV-stricken adult is improved have a much better chance of coping with poverty. According to the authors, only about 30 percent of the people in Sub-Saharan Africa who need this sort of treatment get it, which means that about 4 million persons are falling between the cracks. The study provides an added rationale for scaling up treatment programs; when viewed as investments, they offer long-term economic returns to society.

The authors observe that although the short-term effects of the therapy are large and positive, much less is known about the long-term effects. Still, it is safe to say that antiretroviral therapy can be a critical tool for avoiding large intergenerational economic effects from HIV/AIDS.

Political Economy

Using panel data from the World Bank (548 country-year estimates from 100 countries) and the International Monetary Fund's Government Finance Statistics, **Francisco Rodríguez** creates a new indicator for evaluating how the relation between poverty reduction and growth is affected by government spending and the extent to which a given country's fiscal policy favors the poor.

Rodríguez begins by asking what makes growth "inclusive." To answer this question, he grapples with two sets of issues in political economy: the conditions under which the poor can contribute to economic growth, and the conditions under which they can benefit from growth. He emphasizes the importance of evaluating not only the effect of public spending levels on the poor but also how these effects are linked to the economy's growth rate. To tackle these issues, Rodríguez develops a new measure derived directly from the effect of various fiscal policies on the level of poverty. Rather than rely on a priori theoretical assumptions, he constructs an empirically grounded estimate of how state actions affect the poor under varying economic conditions.

Rodríguez's calculations demonstrate a highly significant interaction between expenditures and changes in income, implying that government spending under conditions of growth will reduce poverty more quickly and make shared growth more likely. His empirical work shows that the optimal mix of policies will depend on a country's level of income and that certain policies which protect the poor under certain conditions may harm them if those conditions change.

Lakshmi Iyer examines the quality of public service provision in South Asian countries and provides a useful survey of the theoretical and empirical literature related to collective action and provision of public goods.

Iyer observes that school enrollment is low in developing countries generally and is lower still in South Asia. She notes, however, that rates vary widely among the countries of South Asia and even within countries: for instance, nearly every village in the Indian state of Kerala has a school, but only 39 percent of villages in Bihar have one. Moreover, educational quality varies widely across countries and within countries. Iyer cites statistics showing that on any given day 15 percent of teachers are absent in India's Maharashtra State, as are 42 percent in Jharkhand State.

Parents everywhere want their children to be educated, but not all groups are effective in demanding public services. Iyer provides empirical evidence that this is the case in South Asia: for example, access to education and other public services is better in areas with a higher population of Brahmins (the elite of India's caste system).

Among the factors that appear to limit the ability of local groups in South Asia to effectively demand public services are social heterogeneity, unequal land distribution, and small group size. Iyer's empirical analysis demonstrates that social heterogeneity, whether related to ethnicity, religion, or caste, makes groups in South Asia less able to demand adequate public services. Moreover, she contends, South Asia exhibits many of the same colonial patterns as in other parts of the world: areas with highly unequal land distribution tend to suffer from poor provision of public services.

Finally, Iyer calls attention to the remarkable rise in the number of private schools in rural areas of South Asia and asks whether private provision could be a solution to problems with quality of services. Although private schools perform better, Iyer nevertheless gives three reasons why the state must remain the provider of health and education services: (a) private schools are, so far, limited to larger and wealthier villages and do not provide universal coverage; (b) they are more expensive than public schools, and many poorer households already say they cannot afford to send their children even to public schools; and (c) a study from Pakistan suggests that private schools cannot function without teachers educated by local public schools.

Opening Address

TREVOR MANUEL

The theme of this conference, "People, Politics, and Globalization," is very appropriate. You may have seen this morning's newspaper headline, "City Refugees in Suicide Bid." Let me sketch for you the context. Three weeks ago, South Africa witnessed the horrid spectacle of poor-on-poor violence, when groups of young people in some cities turned on their neighbors, who happened to be foreign nationals. In Cape Town, fortunately, no deaths resulted, but around 10,000 people—this is a disputed number—were displaced from their homes. A group of Somalis that met with the United Nations on Saturday insisted that although they had been offered refugee status in South Africa, they would prefer to receive asylum somewhere in the Northern Hemisphere. And because the United Nations could not support them in this way, some of them chose to take the suicide route yesterday, by plunging into the sea. It is a terrible story, but it speaks to the heart of our theme.

The government has been resolute in admitting foreign nationals into South Africa as part of our commitment to African development. Many people have been displaced; Somalis have been displaced because of the failed state in their country. And the challenges of globalization are everywhere with us. Just over six years ago, we gathered at Monterrey, Mexico, to agree on a partnership that we fervently believed would alter the course of economic development into the future. African leaders endorsed this theme and introduced a program for continental transformation: the New Partnership for Africa's Development (NEPAD). Acting on these commitments, many countries moved toward more stable macroeconomic outcomes, improved their capacity to deliver services, and announced pro-growth, pro-poor economic and regulatory policies. These achievements have given many countries their first opportunity to reap the benefits of both tough economic policies and globalization.

At the time of the conference, Trevor Manuel was South Africa's Minister of Finance. He is now head of the National Planning Commission.

Annual World Bank Conference on Development Economics 2009, Global
© 2010 The International Bank for Reconstruction and Development / The World Bank

There have been significant research initiatives, such as the Commission on Global Public Goods and, just recently, the Commission for Growth and Development. And I am pleased to see with us the chair of the Commission for Growth and Development, Professor Michael Spence, and the deputy chair, Danny Leipziger. The commission has undertaken a thorough analysis of high-growth patterns between 1950 and 2005 in an attempt to understand the features of such growth, the measure of interaction between countries, and the impact on the living standards of people in high-growth countries. Among the commission's observations is the reality of growing income disparities across the world occasioned by technology change, shifting relative prices, and globalization itself. The commission report draws attention to a finding of the 2007 Pew Global Attitudes Project survey: that support for globalization is flagging, especially among citizens of developed and some developing countries.

The questions before this conference have to do with how to sustain the momentum of growth and ensure that the benefits of growth are far more inclusive than they have been to date. Emphasis should also be placed on that tangible set of global commitments that measure progress against want, the United Nations Millennium Development Goals. Our discussions are framed by the reality of rapidly rising prices for food and fuel and persistent difficulties in the financial sector. These three Fs result in a convergence that threatens to roll back many of the recent gains with respect to each of the dimensions of our theme: people, politics, and globalization.

Although this conference is not intended to conclude with a declaration, we know that the shared observations that will emerge are keenly awaited. This year will see the United Nations advance further in its discussions of food security under the Millennium Development Goals and of financing for development. None of us can afford to ignore the harsh realities that threaten to erode the gains that we have, until now, taken for granted. The moment calls for us to dig deep within ourselves and advance a new, rational set of ideas to be pursued by thinkers and policy makers everywhere.

Allow me now to introduce the brand-new chief economist of the World Bank, Justin Lin, who took up his position on June 2, 2008, and who will share with us his observations on the challenges before us.

Opening Address

JUSTIN YIFU LIN

Mr. President, Minister Manuel, Professor Spence, ladies and gentlemen: good morning. As Mr. Manuel just mentioned, I am the new chief economist of the World Bank. In effect, this is my first public lecture as chief economist. At the outset, I would like to express my sincere thanks to the government of South Africa for its hospitality and its great contribution to the conference today. I also want to take this occasion to thank the organizers of this conference. You bring a wide range of interesting topics to each of our discussions. I am pleased to welcome to the conference today the 950 participants from 70 countries. Some of them are from academia and are going to give us their insights about the process of development. But, equally important, we have many participants from the policy sectors, the private sector, and civil society. Your participation will enrich our discussions.

This is the first time that the Annual Bank Conference on Development Economics has been held in Africa. We know that Africa is at a very important stage of development. In the past decade 11 countries, representing more than half the population of Africa, enjoyed an average annual growth rate of 5.5 percent. That is the best performance since the 1970s. And, a more important number, 7 of those 11 countries are not oil exporters. This shows that Africa, like other places, is a land of hope. Certainly, it is our obligation to find a way to sustain this growth.

The title of this conference is "Politics, People, and Globalization." From my point of view, these are the three most important dimensions of economic development because people constitute the purpose of development. It is our dream to have a world free of poverty. It is also our goal to give people the freedom to choose, the opportunity for prosperity. But people are not only the end of development; they are also the means, because the world's wealth is created by people, especially people with new, good ideas.

Justin Yifu Lin is Chief Economist and Senior Vice President for Development Economics of the World Bank.
Annual World Bank Conference on Development Economics 2009, Global
© 2010 The International Bank for Reconstruction and Development / The World Bank

People alone, however, cannot create wealth. They need to have the opportunity to work, the incentive to work, and the ability to work. Whether they will have the opportunities, incentives, and abilities very much depends on the government. Mistakes can be made. In a developing country with little capital, a lot of resources, and a large population, if the government adopts a mistaken policy of encouraging the development of very capital-intensive sectors, even though its intentions are good, not enough jobs will be created for the people. Moreover, firms in those capital-intensive sectors are not going to be viable, leading to government protection, and finally generating distortions that hurt peoples' incentive to work. In that kind of situation, the best of intentions may lead to failed policies and bad results.

Mistakes can be avoided. If the government adopts a policy of building up market institutions to facilitate the country in exploring its comparative advantage it can set the stage for economic development and job creation and enable people to share the benefits of development. Even then, the government has to provide education and health services so that people will have the abilities to participate. What I like to stress is the importance of the role of the government in the process of development. As Arthur Lewis observed, looking at history, a successful country always has a very intelligent government. The government can fail by doing too much or too little, and that depends greatly on the political process in the country. So, we also need to look at politics.

In our modern world, a country cannot isolate itself. A country has a much better opportunity to prosper if it integrates itself into the world economy through the globalization process. This is demonstrated by the successful East Asian economies and by China after its transition in 1979. Certainly, globalization opens opportunities, but it also poses a new kind of challenge. These include the food crisis that we observe today and the financial turmoil that we see in the United States. In this kind of situation, a country also needs to manage the globalization process, and the global community needs to cooperate to find a new framework for integrating developing countries into the globalization process.

I am sure that the discussion in the coming two and a half days will enhance our insight on this important topic, contribute to our understanding of the nature and process of development, and enable us to approach the goal of a world without poverty.

Opening Address

THABO MBEKI

Dr. Lin, Trevor Manuel, Professor Spence, distinguished delegates, and ladies and gentlemen: I am indeed honored to welcome you to the Annual Bank Conference on Development Economics, and we are very proud to host you here in Cape Town, in South Africa, and, indeed, in Africa for the first time. I would like to think that you have among you many South African and African development economists who are engaged in a very important subject: the challenges of development on our continent.

The overarching theme of the conference is "People, Politics, and Globalization," but it is fair that what will be discussed under that topic are the three challenges of globalization, investment, and growth; human development for equitable growth; and the political economy of shared growth. These are interesting subjects.

I come among you today as one of those much-maligned human animals described as politicians. Some in this audience will, perhaps subconsciously, see in the talking head currently standing at this podium an example of what in the United States came to be known as carpetbaggers. Whatever might be the truth in this regard, I would like to say that my government and I are indeed intensely interested in the outcomes of this important conference. The simple reason is that the matters on the agenda of the conference—globalization, investment, economic growth, human development, equitable growth, and shared growth—are matters of deep interest to all Africans, and I dare say, even to whoever might fit the contemporary edition of the peculiarly African carpetbagger.

This morning I was reading a recent article by Jan-Peter Olters, who is described as a World Bank representative in Montenegro. You would never think that the World Bank would have a representative in Montenegro, but it has. Among other things, Olters wrote,

> The recognition of both globalization's inherent potential and the accompanying risk has become the starting point in the ongoing policy dialogue between national governments

---

At the time of the conference, Thabo Mbeki was president of South Africa.

Annual World Bank Conference on Development Economics 2009, Global
© 2010 The International Bank for Reconstruction and Development / The World Bank

and international financial organizations. In Robert Zoellick's words: "It is the vision of the World Bank Group to contribute to an inclusive and sustainable globalization—to overcome poverty, enhance growth with care for the environment, and create individual opportunity and hope." The World Bank's emphasis on social inclusion—apart from reasons valid in themselves—stems from global experiences that social tension and large income inequalities lead to lower rates of potential growth, weaken political cohesion, contribute to environmental degradation, and add considerable costs to societies in terms of forgone opportunities. The principal challenge of economic policy making thus consists of increasing the overall productivity of invested capital and employed labor with the instruments that governments have at their disposal: public institutions, laws, regulations, and mechanisms ensuring their rules-based application.[1]

As I read this, I remembered my own education in economics at an English university more than 40 years ago, when the economics faculty sought to drill into our heads a sound understanding of development economics. I recall that we learned to be supremely skeptical of the teachings of such economists as Peter Bauer and Milton Friedman, who, as I remember, were presented to us as what some today would characterize as "market fundamentalists," opposed to the very notion of development economics.

What was happening then and later was captured subsequently by an African public intellectual, Thandika Mkandawire, at the time director of the United Nations Research Institute for Social Development (UNRISD):

> For two decades, starting from the beginning of the mid-1970s, the status of development economics in both academia and policy circles was not enviable. . . . The "pioneers" of development economics were forced into a defensive posture as they fended off accusations of providing the intellectual scaffolding for dirigisme, which had failed, as well as of downplaying the role of the market.

> The "death" of development economics was not merely an academic "paradigm shift." It was given official sanction by the United States government. The U.S. representative to the Asian Development Bank was reported . . . to have announced that the "United States completely rejects the idea that there is such a thing as development economics." . . . Development economics became, as John Toye remarks, "an Orwellian un-thing" in the eyes of the most powerful nation. The Spartan certainty of the ascendant neoliberalism as to what was required left no room for specialized knowledge of the problems of development. Mrs. Thatcher's strident "there is no alternative" was echoed in international financial organizations through a standardized set of policies that was applicable to all economies.[2]

With regard to the Peter Bauer of my student years, Wikipedia has this to say:

> Bauer revolutionized thinking about the determinants of economic advance. Indeed, the World Bank, in its *1997 World Development Report*, reflected the point of view Bauer had been advocating for years, stating that the notion that "good advisers and technical experts would formulate good policies, which good governments would then implement for the good of society" was outdated: "The institutional assumptions implicit in this world view were, as we all realize today, too simplistic. . . . Governments embarked on fanciful schemes. Private investors, lacking confidence in public policies or in the steadfastness of leaders, held back. Powerful rulers acted arbitrarily. Corruption became endemic. Development failed, and poverty endured."

For Bauer, the essence of development was the expansion of individual choices, and the role of the state to protect life, liberty, and property so that individuals can pursue their own goals and desires. Limited government, not central planning, was his mantra. Bauer placed himself firmly in the tradition of the great classical liberals.

I must presume that this conference has convened here in Cape Town because you have made the determination that the proclamation about the death of development economics, including the apostolic pronouncements in the 1997 *World Development Report,* amount to nothing more than an opportunistic advertisement by a commercial funeral undertaker driven by the objective to maximize his or her profit, as would any self-respecting carpetbagger.

At the same time, it may be that you consider the fact that I have raised the questions I have about development economics as being somewhat arcane or archaic. Let me explain myself.

As I have already said, I have to earn my keep as an African politician. Almost by definition, and especially because I represent desperately poor communities that absolutely cannot lift themselves out of poverty without the assistance of the rich countries of our universe, I have an obligation to implement the advice of those without whose support my people cannot achieve progress and the necessary advancement toward meeting the celebrated Millennium Development Goals.

The advice I get, which I must accept, is conveyed by well-funded and immensely educated civil society organizations and a very vocal media, which together serve as the *vox populi* and therefore the *vox dei.* The message is very simple and straightforward: Long live Peter Bauer!

To celebrate Peter Bauer without this being stated explicitly, which in any case would make no sense except to the helpless and trapped cognoscenti, we are told that we must limit state intervention in the economy and expand individual choice as part of the process of the great flowering of open democratic systems and the attendant and resultant putative exponential growth and development of the economy.

We are told that, more broadly, we must aim to build a minimalist state that should focus on providing such public goods as the protection of life, liberty, property, and the environment, leaving all else to the market, except to the extent that the state must intervene as a regulator to correct the imperfect functioning of the market.

We are also told that we must create maximum space for domestic and international entrepreneurs to invest and make profits, understanding that this will release the immanent national energies that will create the wealth required to achieve the objectives stated by World Bank president Robert Zoellick: "to overcome poverty, enhance growth with care for the environment, and create individual opportunity and hope."

We are also told that we must trust and follow the advice we get from good advisers and technical experts, which, as a good government, we would then implement for the good of society, provided that what the advisers and experts advise is consistent with the preceding prescripts.

We are also told that we must always bear in mind that, given the fact of global-ization, we will fail to attract the foreign direct investment we desperately need—especially given that we are too poor to generate the investment capital needed to achieve the required rates of growth—unless we abide by the rules set by the inter-national capital markets and recognize that we are competing with other possible investment destinations.

We are told also that we must take into account the fact that the overwhelming bulk of investable capital in the world is privately owned. Foreign investment for growth and development will therefore not come from official development assis-tance funds but from private investors whose central goal is not understanding unique national public imperatives but identifying profitable business opportunities.

But above all, we must take into account the fundamental demands of the global economy: privatize, deregulate, open up to free trade.

I am confident that the development economists and other participants present here today understand very well that the prescripts I have mentioned do not fully address the overall theme and subthemes of this conference on "People, Politics, and Globalization."

The point I am making, however, is that the dominant, immediate, and material voice that bears on the African politician, including the talking head that is standing at this podium, is the voice that proclaims, insistently, Long live Peter Bauer!

There are some in organized global human society who strive to achieve preemi-nence as authentic voices of the people by claiming that, without fear or favor, they present truth to power. In many instances, many of them fail to understand that the power against which they pose as heroes and heroines is little more than a subsidiary formation in a global power system whose pinnacle funds others who pride them-selves on the claim of representing so-called civil society and enables them to devote their considerable energies to a fight that targets shadows and the powerless.

I am convinced that gathered in this hall today, at the very southern end of the African continent, are thinking human beings who will help us better understand what we need to do to liberate ourselves from poverty and underdevelopment, refus-ing to be influenced by propaganda and supposedly universal truths, which in many instances are illusions born of smoke and mirrors and intimidation.

Given the sphere of human activity in which I am inevitably and necessarily involved every day, I cannot avoid the conclusion that we are involved in titanic bat-tles on two broad fronts of an epoch-making war. One of these battles pursues the objective of winning material and, therefore, objective short- and medium-term vic-tories on the broad front of the struggle against poverty and underdevelopment in the countries of the South and globally.

The goal of the other struggle is to win a critically important subjective and pop-ular ideological and political contest, victory in which would enable all humanity to deploy the enormous human and material resources demonstrably available within global human society and so ensure the achievement of the historic objectives of development economics, as broadly defined by Nobel laureate Amartya Kumar Sen. With regard to this latter battle, I firmly believe that contemporary human society disposes of sufficient intellectual, capital, scientific, technological, innovative, and vocational skills to close the major fracture in global human society. By that, I mean poverty in the midst of plenty and a process of globalization that emphasizes and entrenches wealth inequalities rather than universal progress toward the goal of a more equal and prosperous human society.

As an African, and given the agenda you have set yourselves, I would like to suggest that you have convened here at the Cape Town International Conference Centre to consider what should be done to secure success on both the war fronts we have identified. It is for this reason that I have said that my government and I are intensely interested in the outcomes of the conference.

To have any meaning, development economics must relate not to the logical integrity of theoretical paradigms, important as this might be, but to the central task of achieving human development. Since life does not stand still to allow for philosophers to contemplate reality, this conference, even within the context of its agenda, will, I hope, consider a variety of matters that are of major importance to the peoples of Africa and other developing communities elsewhere in the world.

As you know, there are some immediate and critically important challenges we face as a country and continent, and there are questions you must help us answer.

One is: what interventions should we undertake to respond to the high and rising prices of food and fuel? Given the unavoidable inflationary impact of this price increase, which will inevitably reduce standards of living, in particular, of the poor, what immediate, medium-term, and long-term measures, including agricultural policies, should we institute to guarantee long-term and affordable food security?

What contingency measures should we take to adapt to the consequences of climate change?

How much reliance should we place on the prospects for implementing the Comprehensive African Agricultural Development Programme (CAADP) and, thus, insulating Africa from the threat of food shortages and unaffordable food prices?

Will the outcomes of the recent Global Summit of the Food and Agriculture Organization (FAO) in Rome help address these issues?

How long will the commodity boom last? How should we, as Africans, take advantage of this boom to guarantee ourselves sustainable development even when commodity prices decline?

What practical measures should be instituted globally to integrate Africa further into the world economy, other than as a producer and exporter of raw materials? How can we attract investments that will enable Africa to export greater volumes of manufactured, value-added products? What measures should we take if the global economy experiences a significant slowdown that negatively affects African exports and investment flows into Africa?

All of us recognize the critical importance of building the necessary human resource base to drive the process of sustainable African development to which we are all committed. We must therefore pose the question: what should be done to achieve this objective?

We also accept that, as can easily be demonstrated with regard to other regions of the world since the end of World War II and earlier, Africa needs the support of the developed world to achieve take-off. What should be done to strengthen this development partnership and overcome irrational and persistent Afro-pessimism? What should be done to implement the now universally accepted vision and programs of the New Partnership for Africa's Development (NEPAD), which is fundamental to the realization of the Millennium Development Goals as they relate to Africa?

We have all observed the recent exciting growth trends in Africa. For some, this may appear to be the result of the passing effects of a commodity price boom. These observers may expect African economies to slow and run into difficulty at the end of this boom, much as many countries, including South Africa, did after the boom of the 1960s and early 1970s. But I am certain that those of us who have looked more closely at Africa's development have seen evidence that the current opportunity to benefit from the commodity boom will not be frittered away, as it was before, at least not by all countries. There are various pieces of evidence that the current growth acceleration in Africa will be sustained by a number of countries, and perhaps by enough to ensure that the continental momentum is maintained.

I am certain of the capacity of the conference delegates to think independently and to carry out their own investigations relatively uninfluenced by the mass media, enabling them to understand the reality that the African continent is involved in a historical structural process focused on its sustained and progressive political, economic, and social transformation. Necessarily, development economics must be an integral part of this process. I trust that the fact that the ABCDE Conference is meeting in Africa for the first time will inspire all the participants to take it as their special obligation to intervene in the African development process so as to add impetus to our continental drive to end our condition as the wretched of the earth.

In the article that I cited earlier, Olters wrote, "The World Bank's emphasis on social inclusion—apart from reasons valid in themselves—stems from global experiences that social tension and large income inequalities lead to lower rates of potential growth, weaken political cohesion, contribute to environmental degradation, and add considerable costs to societies in terms of forgone opportunities."

You will recognize that I quoted this earlier. The African, and perhaps global, development challenge is about eradicating poverty, lessening income inequalities and other inequalities, strengthening social inclusion and political cohesion, reducing environmental degradation, and improving the capacity of individuals and society to take advantage of all opportunities to achieve development.

In his 1998 Nobel lecture, "The Possibility of Social Choice," Amartya Sen said:

> If there is a central question that can be seen as the motivating issue that inspires social choice theory, it is this: how can it be possible to arrive at cogent aggregative judgments about the society (for example, about "social welfare," or "the public interest," or "aggregate poverty"), given the diversity of preferences, concerns, and predicaments of the different individuals *within* the society? How can we find any rational basis for making such aggregative judgments as "the society prefers this to that," or, "the society should choose this over that," or "this is socially right"? Is reasonable choice at all possible, especially since, as Horace noted a long time ago, there may be "as many preferences as there are people"?[3]

This learned paragraph from a treatise by a Nobel laureate seeks to communicate the message that it is possible, in the celestial world of pure intellectual discourse, to posit a circumstance of coterminous expression of billions of different individual thoughts about the same thing, equal in number to all living human beings. At a certain level, especially within the context of an extreme solipsistic view, this is, of course, a logical possibility, but practically, within the objective world of social existence, it constitutes an impossible proposition.

Nevertheless, it offers to all of us gathered here the possibility of advancing an entirely theoretical paradigm: that we have no intellectual obligation to take any position on any of the important matters on the agenda of the conference because there are as many preferences as there are people, and therefore, there is no logical possibility of making any rational policy proposals as a conference.

The immediate reality, however, is that all of us, whatever our social circumstances, know that the poor are knocking at the gate. If this gate does not open because we who have the key are involved in the challenging effort to consider the meaning and implications of social choice theory, among other intellectual pursuits, the masses will break down the gate. They will do this to challenge us to join them practically to answer the question: what should be done to give effect to the human dignity that is due to those whom the modern social order, in all countries, does indeed define as the wretched of the earth?

I believe that is the fundamental question this Annual Bank Conference on Development Economics must strive to answer. I wish you success in your deliberations, and I formally declare this important conference open.

Thank you very much.

Notes

1. Jan-Peter Olters, "On the Agenda: Inclusive Globalization." World Bank News and Broadcast. http://go.worldbank.org/6OX5CZ3RN0. Originally published in *Monitor* (19 [911]: 32–33) April 4, 2008 as "Tema dana: globalizacija na korist svih."

2. Thandika Mkandawire, "The Need to Rethink Development Economics." Draft paper prepared for discussion at the United Nations Research Institute for Social Development (UNRISD) meeting on "The Need to Rethink Development Economics," September 7–8, 2001, Cape Town, South Africa. http://www.unrisd.org/80256B3C005BCCF9/ (httpPublications)/CE9095BA4A739828C1256BC90047D402?OpenDocument.

3. Amartya Sen, "The Possibility of Social Choice." Nobel lecture, December 8, 1998. http:// nobelprize.org/nobel_prizes/economics/laureates/1998/sen-lecture.pdf.

Keynote Address

MICHAEL SPENCE

Good morning, ladies and gentlemen. It is an honor for me to be here at this conference. I first have to apologize for my appearance. My bag and I parted company some time yesterday. There is a saying that clothes make the man. If that is true, then my name is Roberto Zagha—at least for half of my body, the better-dressed half.

What I would like to do today is to take a relatively high-speed tour of the report of the Commission on Growth and Development entitled *The Growth Report: Strategies for Sustained Growth and Inclusive Development* (CGD 2008). We have with us today the vice chairman, Danny Leipziger; the secretary, Roberto Zagha; and Trevor Manuel, South Africa's minister of finance and an important member of the commission. We have been working for just over two years. The commission members are, you will note, predominantly political or policy people, very senior, and very experienced in developing countries. There are a couple of exceptions. I am one, and Robert Solow is another. But the members' experience was intended to be an important part of the work of the commission. We focused on what we called inclusive sustained high growth. We asked two things. How does sustained high growth work; that is, what are the fundamental dynamics? What are the policies, investments, and political underpinnings that enable this kind of growth? And we defined "sustained" to mean "over several decades." We used a benchmark of 25 years or more, and we arbitrarily picked a 7 percent growth because output or income doubles every 10 years at that rate. I will talk more about the important concept of inclusiveness later.

Our primary target audience is basically political and policy leaders in developing countries. Our hope when we started this process was that we would be able to provide some useful insights and perhaps a framework that would help in setting policy priorities and developing growth strategies in the specific country context. Now,

Michael Spence is a senior fellow at the Hoover Institution and is the Philip Knight Professor Emeritus at Stanford University, both in Stanford, CA. In 2001, he was awarded the Nobel prize for economics. He is currently chairman of the Commission on Growth and Development.

Annual World Bank Conference on Development Economics 2009, Global

nobody really cares about growth as such; my family doesn't get up in the morning and think, growth is what really matters in the world. But growth does seem to be an important enabler of things people really do care about. Bassma Kodmani, in her keynote address, spoke about the importance of poverty reduction and the achievement of the Millennium Development Goals, and there are other very basic things that people care about—their families' health, and their capacity to be productively employed or to be creative, innovative, and entrepreneurial. Things like that are fundamental reasons for being interested in growth as an instrument.

We went about this in a fairly straightforward way. We asked our colleagues in institutions like the World Bank and in academic institutions to try, in a whole variety of policy areas, to give us an assessment of what we do and do not know. We discovered that there are many areas in which we lack the complete knowledge that would enable us to give confident policy advice, and we decided to talk about that. We held 12 workshops, with many members of the commission participating, and learned from them. It was a fascinating experience. We prepared a set of 25 country case studies, and we produced a relatively short commission report (CGD 2008) highlighting the essential features of growth dynamics and the key policy ingredients that seem to underpin it. We are also publishing working papers and workshop proceedings that are in-depth attempts to understand various policy areas that relate directly to growth.

We started out intending to be practical and nonideological; none of us wanted to debate some historical divide. We went into the undertaking with considerable humility, with the understanding that our knowledge of growth is not complete and that our knowledge of development—that parallel process whereby societies and economies acquire capabilities that were not there before—is even less complete. We realized that in the course of growing, countries and institutions are learning from experience and adapting; it is a process and not just the application of a static formula.

The report is therefore not a set of policy prescriptions; it is a frame of reference that attempts to get at two elements: the growth dynamics, and the leadership and policies and politics that support them. We believe very firmly that actual growth strategies have to be set at the country level and have to be context specific.

We therefore looked at countries that had actually experienced sustained high growth. Only 13 economies are in that category, and those growth episodes have all occurred post–World War II, since 1950. The countries are rather diverse in size, location, and form of government. We believe that India and Vietnam are probably pretty close to achieving sustained high growth because of growth acceleration; it is a matter of time. And there may be many more. I think that the hope in this room is that the accelerations in growth, on a much broader front, that we have witnessed in the last 5 to 10 years may actually turn into sustained high growth.

Characteristics of Sustained-High-Growth Economies

We attempted to summarize what we thought were the common characteristics of sustained high growth. The first set consists of the fundamental economics, and the second set has more to do with politics and government.

The single most important shared characteristic of the successful economies (and, of course, there are many, many differences among them) is that they are engaged with the global economy. They took advantage of its knowledge, and they benefited from the catch-up effect, the increase in both the size and the scope of potential output, that comes from not having to develop all that knowledge but being able to import it.

Second, the successful countries took advantage of the huge elastic global demand that allows a country to grow about as fast as investments can be made and areas in which the country has competitive advantage can be found. The successful countries all maintained their macroeconomic stability. Almost every time I am interviewed, I am asked whether the report is, or is intended as, an attack on the Washington consensus. And the answer is, no. There are some differences in philosophy and spirit, but there is no question that a stable macroeconomic environment and a number of other items in the Washington consensus are critical for sustaining the kind of investment that supports high growth.

The third obvious characteristic is that these economies had very high levels of saving and investment—on the order of 25 percent of gross domestic product (GDP) or more for overall saving and investment and 5 to 7 percent for the public sector component. They are also—and I think it is important to focus on the microeconomic aspects here—market economies that make use of price signals, decentralization, and incentives and in which reasonable definitions of property exist and determine resource allocation.

They are also economies in the process of structural transformation, which is a chaotic process—what Schumpeter called *creative destruction*. Therefore, there is a great deal of competition and a lot of incremental productive employment creation. Later on in the process, there is a fair amount of destruction as well, as the sectors that are the driving forces of growth become uncompetitive because of changes in incomes and relative prices.

These high-growth economies are characterized by resource mobility, especially labor mobility, and by rapid urbanization. A fair amount of the report consists of just trying to describe these trends. There are policies and investments (education, for example) that support resource mobility and policies (such as limiting competition) that interfere with it. The report talks about both.

I have learned a tremendous amount from my colleagues on the commission and from my fellow academics in the course of these two years. But what perhaps surprised me most was how important are leadership, effective political governance, and effective government. They make it possible to implement as well as develop policies. Political leadership is absolutely crucial. Difficult choices have to be made. One concerns the general approach to growth. A second has to do with a kind of consensus-building process. At saving and investment rates of 25 percent of GDP and more, very significant intertemporal choices are being made about when consumption is going to occur. That requires a credible game plan which people can sign up for, and which they *will* sign up for if they believe it will benefit their children and grandchildren. Achieving some degree of consensus and support for growth-oriented strategies is a nontrivial part of the process, not only of starting but also of sustaining growth.

We do not have complete knowledge of the impact of our policies. We need to experiment. If something is not working well, we need to stop doing it, fairly quickly. I sometimes use the metaphor of navigating with an incomplete map. The full transition from relatively poor to advanced-country income levels takes a long time (over half a century) even at high growth rates and much longer when things slow down.

Underpinnings of Growth

Without trying to summarize the report, let me give you some quick assessments of some of the things we thought were important underpinnings of sustained high growth.

Even though everybody thinks *knowledge and the catch-up effect* are important, we know less about them than we should. This is an area in which productive research could be undertaken. We do know that channels exist which are important. One is foreign direct investment. Foreign direct investment is not usually a large fraction of total investment. Its importance does not come mainly from relaxing a constraint on investment but, primarily, from the importation of productive knowledge, technology, and know-how, including knowledge of the global supply chains, that accompany the investment. There are other channels—foreign education, training, experience, and participation in a network—which are also vitally important in advanced countries that are growing by virtue of collectively generating new knowledge.

On the *demand side,* basically from a developing-country point of view, the global market is essentially limitless. On the *supply side,* in the early stages of growth you have surplus labor, meaning labor that is somewhat underemployed in traditional sectors. This combination produces a period in which you have what a theorist would call a linear growth model. You don't turn the prices against you, and you don't turn the supply, the price of labor, against you by drawing it away from the traditional sectors. Another way to think about this is that the opportunity cost in the early-stage high-growth mode of using resources in high-growth sectors is relatively low.

Leadership is crucial. The model or strategy has to be basically right. There are examples of very well-intentioned leadership that simply picked the wrong approach—for example, a closed-economy model or an import-substitution model. But communication is also terribly important.

We are often asked what form of government is most conducive to growth. Our answer is that it is not the form of government or governance that is crucial for growth. The high-growth countries exhibit a considerable variety of forms of government. What does seem to matter, and what they do seem to have in common, is a political leadership that has as one of its main objectives making the lives of pretty much everybody in the country better off. Alternatively, if you look at countries that fail or exhibit poor economic performance, it is very frequently because the government is representing either its own interests or those of some subgroup. That finding led us to believe in the crucial importance of inclusiveness.

Structural transformation and competition are, I think, pretty well understood, but a fair amount of policy in both the developing world and the developed world interferes with this kind of dynamics. There have been intellectual rationales for such policies. For example, in relatively small countries the argument would be that the country has to restrict competition in order to take advantage of scale economies. That sounds plausible, but it is a static argument, and when you look empirically, the dynamic effect of competition and of entry and exit on productivity growth is so big that it simply overwhelms the static efficiency gains. So, structural transformation that allows competition to work is important. And then the question is, what about people whose jobs may disappear? The answer is that ways have to be found to protect people in the course of transitions, but without doing so by protecting the companies they work for or the jobs that they are currently in. That is difficult but not impossible to do.

Inclusiveness is essential. Inclusiveness for us has three dimensions. One is income equality and reasonable amounts of equity. People understand that markets do not produce equitable outcomes; that is not what drives a market system. And they will accept that up to a point. But they apparently will not accept excessive income inequality. People also will not accept inequality of opportunity. Unlike ex post income equality, where people will tolerate some degree of inequality, equality of opportunity is essential, and its absence is highly toxic. Systematic exclusion on the basis of class, income, religion, ethnicity, tribal affiliation, or gender will lead to political conflict and distraction or worse. The coherence of policy and the sustained commitment that are needed for growth will be lost. It is not strictly economics that disrupts or derails the growth process. Finally, as I mentioned before, you need to protect people through the transitions, or they end up being sideswiped by the microeconomic dynamics. At a high growth rate, that happens a lot, and it is not a minor concern.

I don't believe there is a great deal of controversy about *high saving and investment rates*. What is interesting is how difficult it is to actually achieve those rates, especially on the public sector side. The pattern of government consumption's crowding out investment on the public sector side is widespread in the developing world, and so it deserves to be a focus. In China and India, saving and investment rates were high throughout the transformation. The rates in China were fairly high right at the start of the reforms, in 1980; it was not a case of rates rising once people had enough income.

Health is something people care about, quite independent of any effects on growth or productivity. But one channel seemed to us to be strikingly important for growth and equity, and that was *early childhood nutrition and stimulation*. Experts told us that a failure in this area produces a nearly permanent reduction in children's ability to acquire cognitive and noncognitive skills in school. That struck us as a very long-term problem for growth, and a deeply unfair situation that, if widespread, would materially diminish the accumulation of human capital and the growth potential of the society.

There is not much controversy about the importance of *education*, but we did focus on some issues in this area. One is that education is normally measured by years of schooling or by enrollments. That is not crazy, but years of schooling is an input, and measuring just that is not enough. According to the experts, research appears to suggest that there is extremely high variance in the output—the actual acquisition of cognitive skills and education. And so a very high priority, and not an easy task, is the improvement of the quality of education in many countries. Another issue: What do the primary, secondary, and tertiary portfolios look like at various stages of growth? Do you focus on primary first, then secondary, then tertiary? The answer appears to be, no, or only partly. That is to say you need all three, although the relative size of the investment in each component will shift as incomes rise. Generally, the share of investment going to secondary and tertiary will rise with incomes. But the key point is that the starting point is not zero. Having said that, the time path of the shares in the high-growth cases varies considerably and that seems not to impair growth. The portfolio needs to make sense and not go to the extremes, but it does not have to be optimized.

Labor markets are very complicated in developing countries, with formal and informal sectors and barriers to mobility of a wide variety of kinds. Labor markets are extremely important because problems there affect the fundamental dynamics that involve movement of labor from less productive to more productive jobs. In a surplus labor environment, the incentives for incumbents in the formal sector do not include enthusiasm for reforms that create extra competition from either the traditional or the other informal sectors. It seems to us that it is therefore often politically very difficult to reform, in a simple way, the labor market so as to expand access. And therefore, we suggest experimenting with a separate track, a different route for people who are, in many countries, trapped or cut off from the growing and more modern sectors. Sometimes that trapping occurs because of underinvestment in human capital and other factors, so I don't want to suggest that labor market rigidity is the only problem. But it is a problem that merits creative policy discussion because it is so pervasive.

Everybody knows the world is now 50 percent urban. *Urbanization* is the physical process that accompanies the structural transformation of the economy. It is chaotic, and it sometimes has ugly sides that may make people want to resist it. But resisting urbanization is not a good idea from the point of view of growth. And so the question becomes, how can urbanization be made as effective a process as possible, as unchaotic as possible? The main challenge is finding sources of finance for building the urban infrastructure that is required—sewer systems, water systems, and so on—because the normal financing mechanisms that we are used to thinking about are not available in the early stages of growth. For example, municipal bond markets do not exist in early-stage developing countries.

The notion of growing first and dealing with the local *environment*—air and water quality and the like—later struck the commission as a very bad idea. First, that approach sets off a process of capital accumulation that needs to be undone later, and it is very expensive if the wrong houses are built, the wrong industries develop, and so on. It biases the structural evolution of the economy. Second, "grow first" almost always has an adverse distributional effect. That is, the worst effects of degraded environmental conditions are felt by the poor.

On *energy*, there is a very widespread pattern (that does not include South Africa) of subsidization. This is understandable in political-economy terms, but it is a very bad strategy that is becoming worse as the cost of energy rises. The commission took a clear stance on energy subsidies, which is that they basically have to go—notwithstanding the political difficulties and the merits of an argument for maintaining subsidies for the most vulnerable parts of the population. The resources that go into energy subsidies ought to be directed toward remedying underinvestment on the public sector side, in infrastructure and education, for example. And at these energy prices, with all the other attendant problems, energy subsidies are much too costly. Furthermore, it is almost surely true that any component of a successful global program to mitigate climate change and global warming is going to have an energy-efficiency component. Commitment to a sensible approach to global climate change will require that energy subsidies disappear anyway.

We tackled things that are really controversial, complex, and unsettled. We didn't shy away from them; decision makers don't get to shy away from them. You either have a market-determined exchange rate in the global capital markets or you are managing it in some way, but it is not a choice you can put off. We tried to approach the controversies, and the divergence of opinions within the commission itself, by talking about the risks and benefits of various kinds of policy actions. I hope we have produced at least a useful guide to decision making.

Country Challenges and Transnational Cooperation

We focused on four categories of countries that we thought had important and rather specific challenges: Sub-Saharan Africa, small states, resource-rich countries, and middle-income countries. The African countries constituted one group, certainly not because they are similar, but because the continent has a very peculiar configuration and set of characteristics—many people living in landlocked countries, and many countries with large amounts of resource wealth. In Africa, effectively building out infrastructure is, for the most part, not something that can be done by a single country. We focused on small countries, defined as those with 2 million or fewer people. Small states have many problems, including lack of economic diversification and huge per capita costs of governance. They tend to solve those problems effectively when they pool resources. In resource-rich countries, resource wealth, which should be an asset, has too often turned out to be a liability in political terms. This, too, is something that could be turned around.

The middle-to-high-income transition countries are really very different in policy terms, in what drives the economy. A middle-income country is starting to be an economy whose dynamism and growth are driven mainly by capital, human capital, and knowledge-intensive sectors in the economy, including services. A necessary policy shift is to give up the growth engines inherited from the earlier stages of growth. They have to be allowed to decline and disappear, and rising incomes reduce and eliminate the comparative advantage. That turns out to be harder than it sounds. One of the most common mistakes is finding a formula that works and then following it for too long.

Trends and Policy Agendas

The report ends with some topics that I believe we all think are terribly important—global trends that affect the opportunities and strategies of developing countries. One is a clear pattern of declining enthusiasm for globalization, as measured by several surveys, including the Pew survey in October 2007. There is a lot of talk about protectionism. People attribute many of the problems they have with income distribution to globalization even when it is not the only explanation. But in general, our conclusion was that we have devoted far too little attention to things like income distribution and equity and protecting people during the transition. I don't think this problem is going to go away; in fact, it seems likely that it will get worse. It is not a closely guarded secret that the rising price of energy is, in part, driven by rapidly increasing global demand. And global demand is rising rapidly because of developing-country demand. The energy price issue is one that requires domestic policy attention in a wide range of countries, including the advanced ones.

China and India have grown quickly, and China, in particular, is big enough to have actually changed the relative price of manufactured goods. There is a widespread question in the developing world: is the old growth strategy, based on labor-intensive, optimal use of the labor asset, going to work? Some people think that it will not. The commission concluded that if the relative price of manufactured goods has gone down, perhaps the social return to the old strategy will not be as high, but that doesn't necessarily invalidate it.

In the 1980s, Bill Cline and others raised what is sometimes called the adding-up question: if everybody follows the same strategy of focusing on comparative advantage in the labor-intensive sectors in the early stages of growth, can the global economy absorb all that product? That question has been reviewed by Bill and others (see Cline 2008), and the general feeling is that it is less of a problem than people thought. But there are new versions of the question that I will come to in a minute.

Clearly—and nobody really anticipated this very effectively—we are in a period in which the relative prices of commodities in general are changing very quickly. That has caused all kinds of problems. Underlying this is a real change in the world, and it has to do with growth, not just numbers of people. The population of advanced and rapidly growing economies was about a billion 30 years ago; it is 4 billion now, and the number is rising. So, it is going to be a different world, with very different levels of demand for energy and much greater pressure on the environment.

On the food price front, the report observes that there is an emergency response problem for poor people in a wide range of countries. That has to take priority. Assuming that protecting those people from what amounts to a large effective loss of income can be accomplished fairly quickly, the balkanization that has occurred in the food markets through export restrictions and the like has to be undone. The reason is that we need the high prices and the openness of the global market to induce a very large supply response in the case of food—as in the case of energy. Nothing that I have heard or read or that the commission was aware of suggests that we are anywhere near our productive potential with respect to food. So I think if this problem is managed correctly, the supply elasticity is big enough in the long run that the problem actually might go away. That is, we could go back to a situation where the relative price of food is not so high. In the meantime, we have the food emergency and a very difficult inflation problem all over the world, and it is worse in developing countries because the poorer a country is, the larger is the fraction of GDP going to food (and, I might add, energy).

On the energy front it is a little different. Energy prices, in my judgment, are unlikely to go back to anything like the levels we saw before. (I didn't want to imply that food prices will definitely return to the old levels, but I think they could easily go down.) The elasticity of energy supply is limited, so we are going to have to bet on a large demand elasticity, drawing on energy conservation and alternative energy sources. This may be the ultimate adding-up question in the global economy. If demand does not respond to high prices, global growth will eventually slow, and the opportunities for developing countries will be substantially reduced as a result. The commission believes it would be unwise to think of what we are seeing now in terms of high price volatility as a one-time event. We are going into a world in which we will be facing relative price volatility for some time. An important part of a new growth strategy is going to have to be appropriate risk-mitigation strategies.

I will skip over demographics and aging except to note that the world (including many parts of the developing world) is getting older but the poorer parts of the developing world are getting younger. And so there are two problems: Is global growth going to slow because of the aging effect? And what is happening in the younger and poorer parts of the world? Our answer is that global growth does not necessarily have to slow down because of the aging, although policies and behavior will have to adapt to sustain growth. But in the low-growth parts of the global economy, there is a huge mismatch between where labor is available and where it is in demand. That is sometimes called the youth unemployment problem, and the commission suggests that there is no logical solution except for labor to move from excess-supply environments to high-demand locations. The implication is that we probably ought to spend some time thinking carefully about migration patterns that actually work, meaning that people are properly protected, and so on.

Many of you have thought a great deal about global warming. World carbon dioxide emissions are about 4.8 tons per capita per year. The scientists tell us that a safe per capita output would be about 2.3 tons per year. In energy-inefficient countries, the United States and Canada are at 20.6 tons per person per year. Europe with greater energy efficiency is in the 6-to-10-ton range. France is low because it has a lot of nuclear energy. China and the rest of the developing world are essentially at or below the current estimated "safe" level. But their total emissions are large because of the sizes of their populations. If growth in the global economy just stopped, we would have to reduce emissions globally by a factor of 2. But with growth in the developing world, global per capita emissions will double over the next 50 years in the absence of mitigation. So, how do we mitigate global warming and at the same time accommodate the growth of the developing world? The report begins to address this problem by suggesting ways of getting started. But a lot more work is needed to create a shared understanding of the paths we collectively need to follow to achieve safe levels of CO_2 emissions globally several decades out. This shared understanding will have to include differentiated roles for advanced and developing countries if it is going to achieve broad acceptance in the developing world.

The last section of the report deals with global governance. In brief, it says that we are increasingly interdependent in multiple dimensions, with large implications for potential financial market turmoil, infectious disease, product safety, energy prices, demand and growth, and global warming. In all of these areas there are global agendas to deal with. It is a major challenge for the next generation. It is going to be difficult; nobody has a blueprint; and in the meantime there are new and rising risks in the global economy that accompany this interdependence and that need to be addressed with a view to development strategy.

And with that I will stop. Thank you for your attention.

References

CGD (Commission on Growth and Development). 2008. *The Growth Report: Strategies for Sustained Growth and Inclusive Development.* Washington, DC: Commission on Growth and Development. http://www.growthcommission.org/index.php?option=com_content& task=view&id=96&Itemid=169.

Cline, William. 2008. "Exports of Manufactures and Economic Growth: The Fallacy of Composition Revisited." Working Paper 36, Commission on Growth and Development, Washington, DC.

Keynote Address

BASSMA KODMANI

I have chosen to speak about the challenges involved in emerging from authoritarianism in the Middle East, while maintaining security. My perspective will be one that starts from the current reality (a grim situation, constituting a regression from what seemed to be a more hopeful picture two years ago) and goes on to focus on real achievements that appear difficult to reverse and that are moving the Arab region into a new era, provided these progressive trends are protected.

The last four years have seen a convergence of serious, long-term dangers:

- The Arab-Israeli conflict exploded once more in the summer of 2006. A disaster bordering on genocide is taking place in Darfur. The war in Iraq is causing huge anxiety across the region, particularly among Iraq's neighbors.
- Water resources are being rapidly depleted. This situation carries the seeds of conflict not only between states but also within countries, as the distribution of water becomes a major new source of inequality between rich and poor.
- Among the world's regions, the Middle East is the most dependent on imports of food staples. It buys one-quarter of all cereals traded globally.

The fact that the United Nations Development Programme (UNDP) has taken human security as the central theme of its recent *Arab Human Development Report* is an indication of these mounting and converging threats. Yet, at the same time, most countries in the region are witnessing high economic growth rates. And during the past five years, the key word in the mouth of Arab leaders has been "reform."

There is much ambiguity and misunderstanding around that word. Retrospectively, we can consider the ambiguity constructive because it has allowed governments to integrate the concept into their discourse and to engage in important changes—administrative modernization, the introduction of new legislation, the

Bassma Kodmani is executive director of the Arab Reform Initiative, a network of independent research and policy institutes.

Annual World Bank Conference on Development Economics 2009, Global
© 2010 The International Bank for Reconstruction and Development / The World Bank

rationalization of some practices, and a host of measures that governments felt would yield benefits for economic growth, the country's image abroad, and foreign investments; satisfy outside partners; and renew their own control over society. Nor did "reform," as construed, require commitment by leaders to yield any of their prerogatives or to relate to their societies in a different way.

The motto of reform and good governance allowed governments and "societies" to travel some way along the road toward introducing change. But in the past two years there has been a general feeling that we are stumbling over a set of serious obstacles that we are endeavoring to identify and analyze. Were these impediments inevitable? Were they the results of circumstances, or of specific flaws in the approach?

Some of the obstacles are traceable to external factors resulting from old and new sources of insecurity over which we may have limited control. But the current stalemate is largely attributable to a reluctance on the part of governments and of some key outside players to formulate the objectives more boldly and to opt clearly for shifting some amount of power to societies.

We should not have been surprised by the resistance of old authoritarian political systems or by their resilience and capacity for adjustment, which seem to assure the ruling elites perpetuity.

I believe that the situation is ripe for formulating objectives more frankly. We need to shift to a new paradigm that states explicitly the objective of democratic transformation. This does not require agreement on the exact outcome in terms of the model of democracy desirable in each national context. The definition I want to use here is based on very basic principles. From there, we can outline a common framework and develop the practical tools that derive from it. The key principles are—in addition to building strong and accountable public institutions—respect for rights and freedoms, the rule of law, and equity and social justice. These are not new, but the emphasis here is on the interconnectedness between them. I will provide some practical considerations for making this framework operational.

To begin with, I discuss a major change that has occurred: the awakening of Arab societies. The timid progress that has been made was followed, however, by setbacks. I explore the reasons for these setbacks—fears within societies, and the top-down, government-to-government institutional approach that has been espoused so far in order to foster change. Finally, I argue that there can be no sustainable reforms without democracy. Although many believe this to be true, the debate has focused more on the definition of democracy than on which strategies to adopt, which actors to empower, and which institutions to promote.

The Awakening of Societies

A remarkable change has been the opening up of public space and the emergence of independent media. The new media—satellite television channels and, more important, local media, the Internet, and blogs—play a key role in establishing horizontal links among citizens. Such links had already existed in the social sphere (traditional civil society is strong, although not identified as such by international agencies), but not in the political sphere. Independent media are now creating those links, which are among the first conditions for political mobilization.

Societies are learning to challenge governments: they go on strike even when the law forbids strikes, and they organize demonstrations and sit-ins to protest price increases, lack of water, or loss of land. The protests are initiated by two types of actor: the poor and marginalized and the elites who give priority to political demands—constitutional reforms, free and fair elections, the abrogation of emergency laws, freedom of expression, the independence of the judiciary, and so on. Faced with such protests, governments are reluctant to suppress the movements, which they know are now covered by local and international television cameras.

There are two very positive aspects about these movements. First, the expressions of discontent and the mobilization crystallize around social and political issues and much less around issues of identity and religion. Second, these movements, whether grassroots or elite based, are calling for peaceful, gradual change through legal means and a process controlled by the state.

Governments are trying to close down these new spaces for expression and mobilization, but the protest movements are not receding. In fact, they are increasing with the deteriorating social conditions. In the face of the unbridled rise in prices of vital products, governments have come up with short-term solutions, at best. The specter of major social and political unrest is looming.

The region has to cope with economic deprivation that affects at least 80 percent of the overall Arab population. Of 320 million Arabs, only about 5 to 20 percent at most (or about 50 million) benefited from the second oil boom in the first decade of the twenty-first century. The rest are poor, and their poverty has either increased or has failed to diminish, as has begun to occur in many emerging countries of the global South. In addition to economic deprivation, social and political disenfranchisement is increasing.

These increased hardships are fueling the protest movements, but they are not the initial trigger. The reasons for the awakening are structural and will probably be difficult to reverse. Peoples' state of mind is changing. The sense of powerlessness is waning, and it is widely recognized that the change in peoples' minds is a key driver of democratic transition, as has been witnessed over the past 30 years, first in southern Europe, then in Latin America and in Eastern and Central Europe.

What Societies Fear

As unhappy as societies are with their governments, they seek to protect state institutions and the stability of the political system. Scenes of instability in their immediate environment act as a deterrent against fostering abrupt change and shape the attitudes of opposition forces. Radical groups advocating violence find little support within society. In the Arab Republic of Egypt, for example, some jihadist groups that had used violence in the past have repented and have conducted public self-criticism. It is remarkable that political protest has remained peaceful so far, even though openings for legal protest are tightly restricted.

The more we advance on the path of liberal economic development without explicit social contracts, the more vital do alternative networks of solidarity become for ever-larger numbers of vulnerable groups. These community-based support systems that help meet people's basic needs and avert social explosions are almost all faith based—Muslim (Sunni or Shia), but also Christian.

I have deliberately refrained from specifying the Islamist movements as a source of fear because Islamists are not seen as a danger by the large majority of the population. Islamists are not viewed as alien; they are a product of the social fabric, and they embody the values of the people. They have pursued a three-decade-long trajectory of building social networks and developing a political culture based on religious messages. They have evolved into political actors that are now knocking on the door of the state and demanding their share of power. When they do not get a response in the form of a political opening, they may be tempted to force their way in to conquer their share of power. But this outcome has been the exception rather than the rule; it is directly related to a context of conflict in which the movement is militarized and is leading a resistance movement. (Examples are Hezbollah in Lebanon and Hamas in Palestine, which turned their arms inward.) In other contexts, Islamists are joining multiparty coalitions, taking an active role in parliaments, and negotiating portfolios in government. This is true in Bahrain, the Arab Republic of Egypt, Jordan, Kuwait, Morocco, the Syrian Arab Republic, Tunisia, and the Republic of Yemen.

A much more serious source of fear for governments and societies alike is the threat to the stability and integrity of states as national entities that emanates from conflict situations in neighboring countries and from violent extremist groups (for example, transnational jihadists networks connected to Al Qaeda). The Iraqi situation is the most recent and the most serious source of insecurity. Countries to the south of Iraq (Saudi Arabia and the smaller Gulf states) fear a Shia state in the south of the country, while countries to the north (Syria and Turkey) fear the emergence of a Kurdish state in northern Iraq.

Despite such fears, we have not seen any serious schemes by Arab governments to address the issue of sectarian diversity within their own boundaries. Saudi Arabia has only recently announced a plan for the development of its northeastern province, where the Shia are concentrated. The budget is US$300 million—an amount that is unlikely to change the conditions of the inhabitants in any significant way or convince them that their government cares to make them equal citizens, like the rest of the population. More tragic is the behavior of Arab governments toward the crisis in Darfur and their protective attitude vis-à-vis the Sudanese government responsible for the atrocities. Arab governments have not acknowledged that sectarian coexistence is an integral part of maintaining human security, although we can clearly see that it is precisely on such issues that human security and national security intersect.

Political authorities are not regulating intercommunal relations so as to build harmonious relations between communities, and societies are not equipped or empowered to address the problem. Other institutions within society—mainly religious institutions, Christian and Muslim alike—often take on this role, for which they are intrinsically ill-equipped.

Unsustainability of Governance Reforms without Democracy

The only way out of this intricate predicament, I would argue, lies in the approach toward domestic change. We need to shift from the objective of reforms in governance to a more straightforward paradigm of democratic transformation as a way to open new options and expand the arsenal of instruments that can be mobilized. Acknowledging this will open the way for a holistic approach to change in the Arab world. There is a danger of losing a sense of the big questions that the numerous technical and institutional programs and measures collectively try to answer. With careful attention to strategies and modes of operation, we need to embark on this conceptual shift toward democratic transformation as an achievement of societies, without diluting it. Only when sharp contours are defined can we derive effective strategies.

But promoting democratic transformation is first and foremost about opening a space in which citizens can develop a home-grown agenda and about accepting the fact that societies will develop their own creative paths of transition. It may well be that international organizations and outside donors will have as much to learn from Arab experiences (once success is achieved) as they have to offer in terms of experiences with patterns of democratization. For outside players to contribute in a constructive way to such processes, a number of suggestions can be made concerning the activities to develop, the actors to involve, and the strategies to promote:

- Devise mechanisms to link measures for reforming public institutions from above with efforts to respond to demands by societies, particularly respect for rights and freedoms and for equity and social justice.
- Focus on systems of governance, on processes, and on the quality of the relationship between the ruling elite and society, rather than basing assessments on benchmarks that governments have learned to meet without changing the reality of their relation to their citizens.
- Support the establishment of monitoring tools at all stages of the process, from the drive toward and the desire for participation in decision making through the actual decision-making process, the implementation of policies, the design of guarantees for their implementation, and the assessment of their impact.
- Engage in focused research to identify areas in which the performance of public institutions can be changed through policy measures undertaken by governments and outside partner governments or institutions, as opposed to changes that can only occur through the participation of societal forces acting from below.
- Assist social groups to develop monitoring tools to track variations (negative or positive) in the status of democracy, with a view to intervening in the formulation of policies. A key area for initial efforts in this direction is to encourage groups

within societies to push their governments for access to information as a right. Legislation (freedom of information acts) and sustained pressure from citizen groups will gradually erode the culture of secrecy within most government institutions.

Practical Examples

Two concrete examples of an approach from below are described next.

Security Sector Reform

Security sector reform in the Arab world has been on the agenda of many foreign donors and multilateral institutions for the last three to five years. Yet societies are often unaware of such programs and are developing strategies of their own that remain largely disconnected from the approach taken by outside donors. The challenges in developing an indigenous agenda for security sector reform by foreign partners are threefold:

1. The current approach is strongly influenced by post-conflict situations in other parts of the world or in the Middle East itself (Palestine, Iraq, Lebanon) and is ill suited to countries that are undergoing comprehensive reform processes but are not emerging from a conflict.
2. The approach is largely technical, even though the area is one in which political considerations dominate because security institutions form the backbone of the political regimes and determine complex domestic equilibriums and, ultimately, the survival of the political systems.
3. The approach is driven from above and relies on the goodwill of governments that have learned to take what is offered by foreign partners (for example, training programs in human rights for their police forces) without linking these programs to an overall ethical code of conduct for their security institutions.

Meanwhile, societies are developing their own ways of pressuring governments concerning the behavior of security forces. In Morocco, human rights groups and groups advocating for the rule of law have seized the opportunity opened by the monarchy through the creation of the Equity and Reconciliation Commission to push for a public debate on the practices of the security institutions. The results are remarkable, as these groups have succeeded in maintaining their momentum and in opening sensitive files that have remained totally secret for several decades.

In Egypt, where the government did not initiate anything from above comparable to the Moroccan opening, a public debate on the practices of security agencies has been forced on the government thanks to independent media (newspapers and television channels), new technologies (documentation of abuses of detainees' human rights through mobile phones, blogs, and Web sites), and the work of a few filmmakers who have produced films that have been widely seen and discussed across the country. The debate is now open and ongoing. It is exposing the security sector and creating resentment within its ranks at being put in the forefront of the government's struggle against citizens, and it is forcing the government to investigate some of the most embarrassing cases of human rights violations.

Although this is a process of trial and error, societies are gradually developing strategies that amount to the beginning of what can be called a home-grown agenda for reforming the most opaque institutions of authoritarianism.

Gender Programs

Gender is arguably the area that has received the greatest attention and the most generous funding from foreign partners. Yet most programs have been focused on a small group of women in each country, often from the elite and connected with or co-opted by the first ladies. Although these programs have the blessing of the governments, they are not always successful in fostering significant change, since they rarely challenge the social order. Experience shows that female academics from the elite and scholars in general have rarely proposed alternative, more socially grounded visions of gender issues distinct from those offered by Western institutions.

The case of the Khul'a law enacted in 2002 in Egypt is one of the most telling examples of a successful home-grown strategy. The legislation was the result of a quiet 15-year struggle by a group of widely respected female and male jurists, sociologists, and civil society representatives who worked closely with religious scholars from the conservative Islamic institution Al Azhar to reach agreement on the interpretation of an old principle enshrined in Islamic sacred texts. The law amounted to a silent revolution in Egyptian society, as it allowed tens of thousands of women to obtain divorces and custody of their children, after decades of unsuccessful procedures in courts. The law was far from ideal, and the process for reaching this outcome was lengthy, but it seemed that this was the price for building a consensus and legitimacy allowing the law to be enforced. It was done by working from within society, integrating social realities and beliefs, working from Islamic sacred texts, and bringing along key actors such as the religious establishment.

A second area in need of revisiting within many donor-driven programs on gender is that these programs tend to be designed to eschew political issues, and they often promote certain rights for women specifically without integrating the larger social and political context. Although every woman in the Arab world will agree that her status as a woman needs to be improved and her rights protected, many of the most popular figures among Arab women are those active in the larger struggles for the civil and political rights of citizens. These women are members of political parties or social movements. They have constituencies and credibility to preserve, and they are often reluctant to be associated with donors' strategies, which they see as potentially weakening their own strategy—one that seeks to challenge the government in a bolder fashion. Again, we see the need to trust societies to produce their own leaders and strategies.

Conclusion

The heat around the democracy promotion agenda has receded. Now is probably the right time to say that it should not be abandoned; otherwise, foreign partner governments and organizations run the risk of being perceived as opportunists who were attracted to a fantasy of the former U.S. administration, like a noisy toy that captured their attention for a short while. The moment is probably auspicious for renewing efforts toward democratization.

But there are conditions that have to be met if these efforts are to succeed. A key requirement is to trust the societies. Gradual change toward democracy is mainly about creating a different type of relationship between a government and its citizens. Foreign donors need to constantly question their strategies to ensure that they are not increasing governments' distrust of (and sometimes contempt for) their citizens. Accountability is first and foremost to be promoted vis-à-vis the citizenry rather than foreign donors (as the recent debate on the sovereign wealth funds of the Gulf States has shown, for example).

Societies might well produce social and political models that foreign partners are not entirely comfortable with. But this is probably inevitable, and accepting the inevitable is the only way to make the best of it so as to tame radical groups and soften anti-foreign attitudes and ideas through constant engagement.

Keynote Address

SUNIL KANT MUNJAL

I am honored to be invited to address this annual conference. I consider myself fortunate to be here, for a variety of reasons. South Africa is known as the country where the founding father of the Indian nation, Mahatma Gandhi, took his first public stand. This is also the land of Nelson Mandela, who showed that peaceful protest is as powerful a tool as war for winning an argument or a case. I also count myself fortunate to be among so many economists, and all varieties of economists.

That reminds me of a story I heard the other day about an architect, a surgeon, and an economist. The surgeon said, "Look, we are the most important profession. God is a surgeon, because the very first thing God did was to extract Eve from Adam's rib." The architect said, "No. God is an architect. He made the world in seven days from complete chaos." And the economist said, "Who do you think created the chaos?"

So, you are certainly very important people. I must admit that I never studied to be an economist. I probably should have. I am told that this is the only profession where you can say "trickle-down theory" with a serious face.

The theme for this conference seems extremely apt for the world today. Certainly, for us in India it is very relevant. I was, however, surprised to get the invitation to the conference because although India is important, my understanding was that this is a conference normally addressed by government functionaries or senior economists. So I shall try not to talk just about industry but to present an overall view.

Whatever you hear about India is true—and, conversely, the exact opposite is also true at the same time. India is not a simple country by any standard. It is said that in the course of a lifetime one might just begin to understand what India is about. And that is as true for we who live in India, as well. India is a country that can launch rockets and satellites but at the same time has around 200 million people who live in

Sunil Kant Munjal is the chairman of several enterprises, including Hero Corporate Services, and is the president of the Medical College and Hospital, India. He is a member of the Prime Minister's Council of Trade and Industry in India.

Annual World Bank Conference on Development Economics 2009, Global
© 2010 The International Bank for Reconstruction and Development / The World Bank.

abject poverty. Close to half the population of Mumbai, which is considered India's big financial center, is living in shanties. We have 28 states, 22 languages officially recognized by the government of India, and thousands of dialects spoken across the nation. People in different parts of India wear different clothes, speak different languages, eat different food, and even look different. Very often, for some of us, when we travel across the country, the only common languages are cricket and Indian movies and, of course, every now and then, English.

The economic historian Angus Maddison has estimated that five centuries ago India was one of two countries in the world that accounted for nearly half of the world's gross domestic product (GDP). Attracted by India's prosperity, Columbus set out and lost his way and got to America. Who knows, if he had had a good compass, he would have probably found his way to India before the British did, and I might not be here giving this speech today. The British spent a little over 200 years in India, and they ruled India. When they arrived, India had about 21 percent of world trade and Great Britain, as it was then known, had 1 percent. In 1947, when the British left, India had 1 percent of world trade and Great Britain had 21 percent. So you can see what has happened to India. Many talk of this as the rise and fall and now the rise of India again.

Our first prime minister, Jawaharlal Nehru, said, "A moment comes which comes but rarely in history when we step out from the old into the new. When an age ends and when the soul of a nation, long suppressed, finds utterance." It did not quite happen after 1947, when India became independent. India chose as its broad philosophy a strange oxymoron, a socialist democracy. We borrowed from the Russian model of the five-year plans, and the government built power plants, steel plants, and dams. That was probably necessary at the time because no private enterprise or individual was allowed to accumulate enough wealth to invest in such projects. But the government probably did not step back quickly enough. The 20 or 30 years of this policy became a very difficult time for private enterprise.

In 1991 India made a dramatic move toward market reforms. Our current prime minister, who was then finance minister, in many ways was the leading architect of this reform program. It is popularly believed that India did not go happily toward reform. It went kicking and screaming, but we were in a situation where foreign exchange reserves were only enough for a few days of imports. In fact, India had to send out a planeload of gold as a pledge to be able to raise international currency to continue to pay for its imports. To India's credit, it has never, ever defaulted on any global commitment. I think that is saying something for a country that has gone through many crises.

What is not so well known outside is that many of the reform programs that were kicked off in 1991 had actually been discussed, debated, and written up in the 1980s—which is probably why implementation was easier than one would have imagined. Don't forget, it was a dramatic turnaround of policy from what we had had until then.

So, what has happened to the simplicities of reform in India? India's trade-to-GDP ratio has doubled over the past seven years, to almost 50 percent. As a trading nation, India is now firmly established at the top table of the World Trade Organization

(WTO), and trade agreements are currently in the pipeline with at least 10 potential partners, ranging from the Association of Southeast Asian Nations (ASEAN) to the European Union, the United States, and Canada. We already have signed agreements with Singapore, Sri Lanka, Thailand, and a host of other nations. In fact, my last trip here was when India signed what is known as the IBSA agreement between India, Brazil, and South Africa—three nations spread across different parts of the globe that are at a somewhat similar stage of evolution of their economies. All three are large, all three are complex, and all three are trying to reach across to see how we can build bridges between us. India is a keen participant in the WTO discussions (in fact, some say, too keen.

But the reality, often not recognized, is that India is a nation in which 72 percent of the people live in rural areas and 54 percent depend on agriculture as their primary source of income. Agriculture contributes less than 18 percent of GDP, so a lot of these people are just subsisting on the farming they do; it is not really trade or business for them. The government therefore finds that it has a responsibility to protect that section of the population, and it is a large number of people. (Percentages are deceptive sometimes; don't forget, this is a country of more than 1 billion people.)

We are keen to build a global world trade order, but in the meantime India, like many other nations, is reaching out rapidly and building bilateral, trilateral, and other trade relationships. Savings are now almost 35 percent of GDP, a jump of 8 percentage points in less than six years. The investment ratio stands at 36 percent, up from 22 percent in 2004, and many profess that it will rise to 50 percent in the not too distant future.

The interesting thing is not just what is happening inside India; it concerns Indians outside India. Boris Pleskovic and I were talking about how he has helped many Slovenians residing outside Slovenia to get together and build a kind of platform. If you look at how Indians have performed across the globe, you will find that among many of Fortune 500 companies, the chief executive officer level or the top tier of management will always have a few Indians. Among the major successful banks, many of the movers and shakers are Indians. In North America the largest single ethnic group of doctors is Indian.

Someone sent me an e-mail the other day that referred to NRIs, nonresident Indians. At one time NRIs was said to mean "not required Indians," but that perception is dramatically changing as India's economic situation improves. I think in many ways India is maturing as a nation, both politically and socially. It is reaching out to its people outside, trying to build a bridge. The e-mail that I mentioned said that 33 percent of the people working in Microsoft are Indians; the number at Intel is similar. The figure that surprised me was for the U.S. National Aeronautics and Space Agency (NASA), which has about 20 percent Indians, and this is really high-technology work. These individuals have gone out and done exceedingly well. So the question arises, why was it that 20 years ago Indians were doing well but India was not? It really had to do with the facilitating environment that we had built—or, rather, the nonfacilitating environment that we had built—through regulations. That is what began to change in 1991. The impact is such that I understand the national dish of the United Kingdom is now chicken tikka masala. So it is not just the doctors that we are exporting.

India is working overtime to reduce its infrastructure deficit. Some problems persist today, but we are better off than we were 10 or 15 years ago. The main problems are lack of physical infrastructure, continued red tape in decision making in government, and corruption in public life. And it is interesting, when you look around, you find that this is almost a standard feature of emerging economies. The good thing is that in spite of all its diversity, in spite of its fair share of problems and its lack of physical infrastructure, India has continued to build growth at a rate that has gotten better, decade on decade. At one time, India was known as a nation that had what was called, rather uncomplimentarily, the "Hindu growth rate" of 2.5 to 3.5 percent. Every decade since, growth has gone up by at least a couple of percentage points. As of now, we have had four years of nearly 9 percent growth, though recently issued numbers show that growth will be between 7.8 and 8.5 percent. If you are used to 9 percent and you are aiming for 9.5 percent or higher, a growth rate of 8.5 percent can be experienced as a slowdown, and it can actually begin to hurt.

Let me tell you a few more success stories, and then I will talk about what is unique about India's journey. An average Indian today can potentially spend double what he or she could spend in 1985. In the next 20 years, he or she will be able to spend four times as much as now. By the end of this decade, India is expected to have an urban population of 173 million—more than the population of several European nations put together. This is significant because urbanization rises with GDP per capita in a hockey stick fashion. And it has been seen in many economies that the moment you start to hit US$700–US$800 per capita income, the income rise is sustained and that, fortunately or unfortunately, leads to higher urbanization. Therefore, we need to focus not just on the 600,000 villages to improve rural areas but also on rapidly growing the urbanization that is required.

A large section of our workforce has become productive, much more productive, in these last 15 years. Our dependency ratio has decreased from 1.3 to 0.8. This has partially to do with the demographics of the country: 54 percent of all Indians are below age 30, and 30 percent are below age 15. Over the next 20 years or so, as the entire developed world falls short of people in the working-age group by roughly 41 million to 42 million people, India will add almost the same number to the working-age pool. So, there is a dramatic opportunity in the form of more work moving to India and more people moving out of India, but the current state of global politics prohibits that movement in many ways because of increasing concerns over security and nationalism, as we have heard in two of the sessions at this conference. Professor Spence, for example, observed that many nations, including many champions of globalization, are turning more nationalistic than they have been for a long time.

Mahatma Gandhi once said, "I do not want my house to be walled in on all sides and my windows to be stuffed. I want the cultures of all the lands to be blown about my house freely. But I refuse to be blown off my feet by any." This, in many ways, sums up the uniqueness of India. India opens itself to global influences to look at what is happening in the West and in the East, but it chooses to follow its own unique path. I suppose this is partly because no rulebook has been written for a democracy with a billion people trying to turn into a market economy. The other part is that we are a young, new economy, but we are a 5,000-to-7,000-year-old civilization, with strong likes, strong dislikes, and a very strong culture. And this has been seen by many of the global companies that came into India. Many came to India saying, "We have a standard set of products and services that is wonderfully honed to serve all the global markets," and in many cases they fell flat on their faces. They did not allow for the customers' preferences, which were engrained through many generations. McDonald's made a change in their menu for the first time, I am told, when they came to India. And they were so successful with this change that they carried out this practice in many other nations, adapting to local tastes, flavors, and recipes. There is a whole host of examples of like this.

The big move that has happened in India is that the pattern of reform is moving from the central government to the state governments. The central government backed off from many of its regular activities by stepping back, by reforming, and by reducing licensing requirements for industry and other economic activities. Many of these changes were readily adapted by state governments, as well, but not by all. In fact, in an interesting recent article an expert observed that if you draw a line approximately from the north to the south of India, between two cities he named, the areas to the left and right of the line are like two different countries. The left side, which is mostly the south, the west, and parts of northern India, is where the major growth is taking place. But although the economic numbers are high, literacy numbers are still low, and that is one of the issues that continue to dog India as a nation.

There was a wonderful session this morning on higher education, and I know some of the Indian experts who are in this audience addressed that session. At the top end, India has done exceedingly well in education; people who have gone into avionics or aeronautics or software engineering or medicine obviously must have received a good education. Yet the numbers are not nearly enough for the size of our population. Now, this was a role clearly marked out for the government. Governments are required to take care of primary education, primary health care, security, monetary policy, and the like. Nevertheless, the government has not had the wherewithal to provide sufficient education to all the people, so the private sector willy-nilly stepped in and started playing a role.

But the private sector cannot substitute for the government. There is a need for the government of the day—whichever it is. In the last 15 years we have had a series of coalition governments, with sometimes as many as 12, 14, or 18 parties in government together. These governments have been made up of parties from the extreme left to the extreme right and every color in between. The good thing is that all of them went down the same path of reform and of viewing growth as the only answer to all India's ills. The not-so-good thing is that they focused on the easy part of the reform. (I am saying easy *now*; obviously it didn't look easy when they were doing it.) Some of the work is still to be done. Also, the government did a wonderful job of trying to manage both the revenue deficit and the fiscal deficit, going as far as to write an act of parliament binding itself to improve the fiscal situation. They have done pretty well, barring the current problem that the whole world is seeing with high inflation and high prices for oil, food, and other base materials. The government also backed off from spending in some areas in which they ought to be spending—some of the major infrastructure projects. There are many private players, both Indian and global, who are building airports, ports, highways, roads, power plants, and so on in India. But it is necessary to ensure that the government remains a key player, not only in areas such as infrastructure but also in ensuring that independent regulation is set up which will allow the private sector and the new model of public-private enterprises to work well together.

In a diverse nation like India, consensus is required not just through a spectrum of political parties but also involving all sections of society. We have a very vibrant democracy. We have one of the world's freest presses. We have an active executive, judiciary, and civil society, and awareness among people in India is very high—so much so that one of our recent Nobel laureates, Professor Amartya Sen, wrote a book about it, *The Argumentative Indian*. It is said that the difference between India and China is that while in China, you make a decision today and start implementation tomorrow, in India you make a decision and the *debate* starts tomorrow—and that debate could take months or years. That is a reality we live with. The good thing is that we have learned that it is possible even with such diversity to build consensus and to take action through consensus.

Sean Casey, the very successful baseball player, said "All the world's a stage. And most of us are desperately unrehearsed." India, clearly, is one of those cases. We are learning by making our own mistakes. I doubt that we can actually learn from anybody else's, or from experts like the World Bank. Very often one hears criticism from within India that the World Bank tries to give everybody a standard prescription. The reality is that in India, a standard prescription is not going to work. And that has been proved over and over again.

It is therefore important that all international, multilateral organizations learn to work with India and with Indians, who have built this expertise of consensus. In fact, we could provide expertise to many nations on how to run an election. (We know what has happened in countries like the United States and others.) India has, of course, done a tremendous job in this area. We have elected 2.2 million representatives in what we call the *panchayati raj*—village-level local self-government. Of these representatives, more than 30 percent are women. I do not know of any nation in the world that has come anywhere close to this truly democratic exercise. So, there is a tremendous amount of strength in how India functions as a nation. Europeans, for example, can take a lesson from India in how so much diversity actually works well together and still continues to be a nation.

Our big issue is how to tackle poverty. Many people agree that our only answer is growth. Trickle-down growth, however, is not fast enough. People will not wait two generations, especially when they can see others who have become exceedingly successful, very wealthy. And India is producing many billionaires and millionaires. The poor will have patience only to some extent, which is why some of us, who would normally have objected, actively participated with the government to design four to five direct intervention programs, including programs on skill building, education, rural infrastructure, electrification, drinking water, and irrigation. These are some of the real and serious major issues that we have in India as a nation.

What we have done in India over a short period of time appears to be almost miraculous. There are many success stories that one can talk about, in telecommunications, for example. From having the highest-priced wireless service in the world, India has gone to having the lowest-priced service. In three years' time India will have 95 percent geographic wireless coverage, which will be a unique distinction across the world. Not many years ago India probably had 2.5 million telephone connections. Now it adds between 8 million and 10 million new connections every month, which is more than the population of many small nations.

We have done similar things in innovation. On the plane trip to the conference, I heard someone mention Amul, which is the brand name of a cooperative of dairy farmers. Hundreds of thousands of dairy farmers provide milk every day to this organization, which does the processing, the value adding, the distribution, and the branding. India is the world's largest producer of milk and this is our largest organization. It is made up of millions of people. And there are other examples of innovation that has taken place in a very Indian way. Jaipur Foot is an organization that makes prosthetics. It is unique in the sense that a foot which in the United States would cost US$8,000 costs US$40 when supplied by Jaipur Foot, and its functionality is at least 200–300 percent better than can be found in the best organizations and best institutions in the United States. This is just one example of how India is building a low-cost economy that can function. Of course, we realize that cost and low wages cannot be permanent advantages. Therefore, value-added productivity, efficiency, and research are the new watchwords in India. And we are conscious that we need to pursue these goals while ensuring that we do not pollute as much as many nations did while they were undergoing their development.

India's capital utility efficiency is fairly high right now. A recent McKinsey & Company report stated that for every US$1,000 spent, India is able to get 20–22 percent more than in China on the physical infrastructure that is being built. That is important because we are very short of funding. Of course, unlike the case in many countries, much of the capital for infrastructure is coming from within India. But we do need foreign capital, along with knowledge and networks. That, in fact, is our greatest need today. But India is actively investing overseas, as well. In fact, India is now the second-largest foreign investor in the United Kingdom. We are also investing in countries such as France, Germany, Italy, the United States, and a host of other places. India is uniquely positioned to serve as a lesson for many others who are attempting to dramatically change their economies. We are one of the rare economies that evolved directly from being an agrarian economy to being a service economy. More than 50 percent of India's economy is services—which is why some of us are pushing very hard to grow the manufacturing sector faster so as to be able to provide many more jobs for the millions of young Indians who are entering the job market every year.

India has been able to learn much from the rest of the world. But really, the best learning comes from making your own mistakes and at the same time being cautious when you need to be. We carried out a very calibrated opening up of the capital account, for example. Many experts across the world objected to the slow pace. But now some of them are saying, "Hey, hang on here. These guys did not suffer like some of the other economies when they went through an extreme crisis. So maybe there is something here that is being done right."

India offers a unique opportunity, to both Indians and the global population, to work in India and with India. We have learned many lessons, and we still have much to learn. But one thing we have learned is that if you have the right attitude, the right frame of mind, you are going to be able to find the right answers. I spoke of Mumbai a little while ago. Mumbai has an area called Dharavi that is probably the world's largest shantytown—certainly Asia's largest shantytown. Just now, while driving to the conference, I saw a shantytown right outside Cape Town. What was unique was that every home had a color television, most of the people living there had cell phones and other electronic gadgets, and most of them also had jobs. The India of the future that we hope to see is not one of shantytowns but of color televisions, jobs, and continuous prosperity, and concern for those around us.

Trade and Investment

Trade and Economic Performance: Does Africa's Fragmentation Matter?

PAUL COLLIER AND ANTHONY J. VENABLES

Most of the population of South Asia lives in one megacountry with a population greater than that of the whole of Sub-Saharan Africa. By contrast, the population of Sub-Saharan Africa is spread across more than 50 countries. Does this political fragmentation have economic consequences? We suggest that both private economic activity and the provision of public goods benefit from powerful scale economies that confer advantages on the South Asian model. Paradoxically, although Africa has a greater need than other regions for supranational power structures, it has made far less progress toward regional unity.

Sub-Saharan Africa and South Asia have many features in common and many that are strikingly different. They each contain roughly 1 billion people, and in 1980, their per capita incomes and human development indicator levels were broadly similar. But South Asia is dominated by India, a unified state of 1,130 million people, and Pakistan and Bangladesh, each with more than 150 million. By contrast, Africa, with a total population 60 percent the size of South Asia's, is divided into 54 states. Of these, even the largest, Nigeria, is smaller than the smallest of the big three South Asian countries and has a mere 14 percent of the region's population, whereas India contains 74 percent of the population of South Asia. About 95 percent of South Asians live in the big three, but the three largest countries of Africa account for only 28 percent of Africa's population. Indeed, the average African state has a population of only 17 million people, one-sixty-sixth the size of India's. Does this matter?

The economic performance of the two regions has diverged sharply since 1980, as illustrated in figure 1. The regions had similar gross domestic products (GDPs) in 1980, but whereas Africa's share of world GDP declined until the late 1990s, South

Paul Collier is director of the Centre for the Study of African Economies (CSAE) and professor of economics, Oxford University. Anthony J. Venables is director of the Oxford Centre for the Analysis of Resource Rich Economies (OxCarre) and professor of economics at Oxford University.

Annual World Bank Conference on Development Economics 2009, Global

FIGURE 1.
Economic Performance, Sub-Saharan Africa (upper) and South Asia (lower), 1980–2004

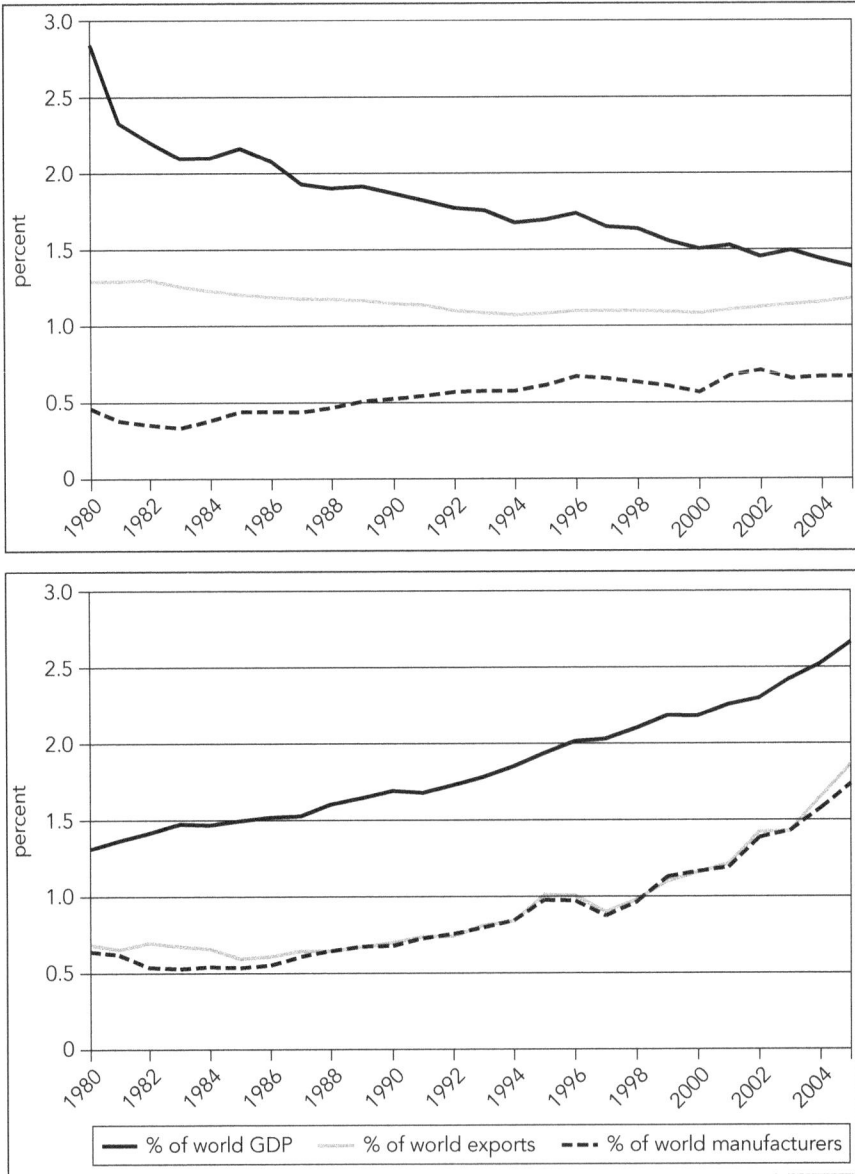

Source: *World Development Indicators 2007.*

Note: GDP, gross domestic product.

Asia's share nearly doubled during the same period. Africa's share of world exports was nearly four times that of South Asia in 1980, but—South Asia's share having risen more than twofold and Africa's having been halved in the interim—the proportions are now similar. During the same years, Africa's share of world manufacturing exports stagnated, and South Asia's more than doubled. The Sub-Saharan African data are dominated by South Africa, a single country that accounts for around 20 percent of regional GDP, and the performance of the rest of Africa is, on average, worse.

There are numerous reasons for this divergence, but in this paper we focus on one set of issues: has Africa's fragmentation into numerous small states contributed to its relatively poor performance?

The relationship between country size and economic performance has been analyzed by a number of authors, with mixed findings. Recent work by Rose on a sample of 208 economies (some, such as the Isle of Man, not independent) led him to the conclusion that an economy's population "has no significant consistent impact on its well-being" (Rose 2006, 501). By contrast, the growth literature has come up with evidence for a positive relationship between country size and growth. A 2005 article by Alesina, Spolaore, and Wacziarg provides a succinct summary of findings. The authors hypothesize that economic growth should be positively associated with country size and openness and negatively associated with the interaction of these two factors. In a sample of 104 countries, they find that these relationships are present and statistically significant. Furthermore, they are quantitatively significant: "for a country at the median level of openness ([the Republic of] Korea) the effect of multiplying the country's size by 10 would be to raise annual growth by 0.33 percentage points" (Alesina, Spolaore, and Wacziarg 2005, 1530; see also Alcalá and Ciccone 2003).

A lack of consensus in these cross-country studies is perhaps unsurprising. On various measures of per capita income, small countries are both at the top (Luxembourg and Lichtenstein) and the bottom (Burundi) of the ranking. Our approach is not to undertake aggregate cross-country studies but, rather, to investigate the impact of fragmentation into separate states in a more microfounded way. We will focus on Africa and will often compare it with South Asia and with India, in particular. Why is it that a fragmented (sub-) continent might be at a disadvantage relative to a more unified one?

Conceptually, three distinct mechanisms generate costs of fragmentation. The first is that natural advantages are likely to be unevenly distributed among countries. The second concerns the loss of scale economies, at the level of the firm, the city, and the country as a whole. The third has to do with the loss of public goods as the scale of political cooperation is reduced. We will examine each in turn.

Natural advantages such as oil deposits and natural harbors are unequally distributed across space. If a continent is politically fragmented, the likelihood that natural advantages will be unevenly distributed among countries increases. Evidently, this implies inequalities among countries. Of greater pertinence for this inquiry is that these inequalities are likely to imply inefficiencies: average income is reduced by fragmentation. This effect occurs if there are diminishing returns to having a natural advantage, in which case the aggregate benefits from nature would be greater the more equally shared are these advantages. Natural advantages may be fixed or transient, and we consider each category. As examples of fixed differences in natural advantage, we apply Collier's (2007) classification of countries into resource rich, resource scarce, coastal, and landlocked. Transient differences arise as countries experience idiosyncratic shocks, with some countries benefiting and others possibly losing. We look at the exposure to export price shocks generated by the structure of commodity exports and the fact that political fragmentation might reduce risk pooling.

Whereas the first mechanism that generates fragmentation costs arises from diminishing returns and underlying or "first-nature" unevenness, the second has to do with increasing returns and the losses stemming from the inability of small countries to gain sufficient scale to work efficiently. One context in which this matters is urbanization and the failure of Africa to develop highly productive urban centers of economic activity. Another is thick market effects and the failure of many small African economies to achieve the scale to offer predictable economic environments. The economies of scale problem is discussed in the second section, below.

The third issue concerns the provision of public goods through politically organized collective action. The free-rider problem is frequently so acute that it can only be overcome by the coercive power of a government to tax its citizens, thereby generating financing for public goods. Fragmentation of a continent into countries is, first and foremost, political fragmentation. As such, it increases the costs of providing public goods, implying that provision will be both less adequate and more expensive. This mechanism is the subject of the third section.

Uneven Distribution of Natural Endowments

The discussion begins with an examination of fixed differences in natural advantages and then turns to transient events such as shocks.

Fixed Differences in Natural Advantages

Fragmentation of a continent into countries means that geographically concentrated natural endowments such as mineral resources, coasts, and rivers are likely to be unevenly distributed among countries, and so it turns out in Africa. Table 1 shows export earnings from natural resources (as a share of GDP and per capita), together with Collier's (2007) classification of countries.

Average resource export revenues per African citizen range from several thousand dollars per capita and more than half of GDP to close to zero in resource-scarce countries, some of which, such as Burundi, Malawi, Rwanda, and Uganda, are landlocked as well.

This unequal distribution matters for two reasons. The first is that it maps into an unequal distribution of resource rents per capita. Within a country, resource rents (or at least those that find their way into public accounts) are likely to be spent throughout the country. The spending may not be spatially uniform; producing regions may be favored. (In Nigeria in 2005, federal transfers from oil revenue amounted to US$210 per capita in oil-producing states and US$70 per capita in the northwest.) But the distribution is far wider within countries than across international boundaries (i.e., zero).

The second reason is that it is not only equity that is damaged by unequal distribution of resource revenues. Since the economic impact of resource revenues is likely to be subject to diminishing returns, their unequal distribution also leads to an efficiency loss. A simple economic model makes the point. Suppose that every country

TABLE 1. "First-Nature" Geography in Sub-Saharan Africa: Natural Resource Exports and Country Classification

Country (year)	Value of exports of fuels, ores, and metals		
	As percent of GDP	Per capita (U.S. dollars)	Collier (2007) classification
Equatorial Guinea (2005)	93.92	14,591	Resource rich
Angola (2005)	72.16	1,471	Resource rich
Congo, Rep. (2005)	71.46	1,182	Resource rich
Gabon (2006)	55.90	4,071	Resource rich
Chad (2005)	44.47	258	Landlocked
Nigeria (2004)	40.94	214	Resource rich
Botswana (2005)	34.74	1,977	Resource rich
Guinea (2006)	24.40	88	Resource rich
Congo, Dem. Rep. (2006)	24.34	34	Resource rich
Mauritania (2005)	19.79	123	Newly resource rich
Mozambique (2005)	18.71	62	Newly resource rich
Zambia (2005)	18.32	116	Resource rich
Sudan (2005)	13.50	102	Newly resource rich
Côte d'Ivoire (2005)	12.52	108	Coastal
Mali (2004)	10.65	46	Landlocked
Cameroon (2005)	9.40	89	Coastal; formerly resource rich
Sierra Leone (2005)	9.40	20	Coastal
South Africa (2005)	6.81	351	Coastal
Zimbabwe (2005)	5.75	15	Landlocked
Niger (2005)	4.55	12	Landlocked
Kenya (2004)	4.52	21	Coastal
Senegal (2005)	4.30	30	Coastal
Togo (2004)	3.90	13	Coastal
Namibia (2006)	3.11	97	Coastal
Ghana (2005)	2.50	12	Coastal
Madagascar (2006)	1.70	5	Coastal
Central African Republic (2005)	1.62	5	Landlocked
Tanzania (2005)	1.58	5	Coastal
Cape Verde (2006)	0.87	19	Coastal
Swaziland (2002)	0.81	9	Landlocked
Uganda (2005)	0.66	2	Landlocked
Ethiopia (2004)	0.54	0.7	Landlocked
Burundi (2005)	0.34	0.3	Landlocked
Rwanda (2005)	0.33	0.8	Landlocked
Burkina Faso (2004)	0.31	1.2	Landlocked
Mauritius (2005)	0.17	9	Coastal
Benin (2005)	0.11	0.6	Coastal
Malawi (2005)	0.05	0.1	Landlocked
Liberia			Coastal
Guinea-Bissau (1995)	0.44	0.9	Coastal
Gambia, The (2003)	0.05	0.1	Coastal
Comoros (1997)	0.03	0.1	Coastal
Djibouti (1990)	0.01	0.1	Coastal

Source: World Development Indicators 2007.

Note: Diamond exports are included in the calculations for Angola, Botswana, the Democratic Republic of Congo, Guinea, and Zimbabwe. Gold exports are included for the Democratic Republic of Congo, Guinea, and Ethiopia. For Mali, export value of fuels, ores, and metals consists solely of gold; for Sierra Leone, it consists solely of diamonds.

FIGURE 2.
Income Loss from Uneven Distribution of Resources

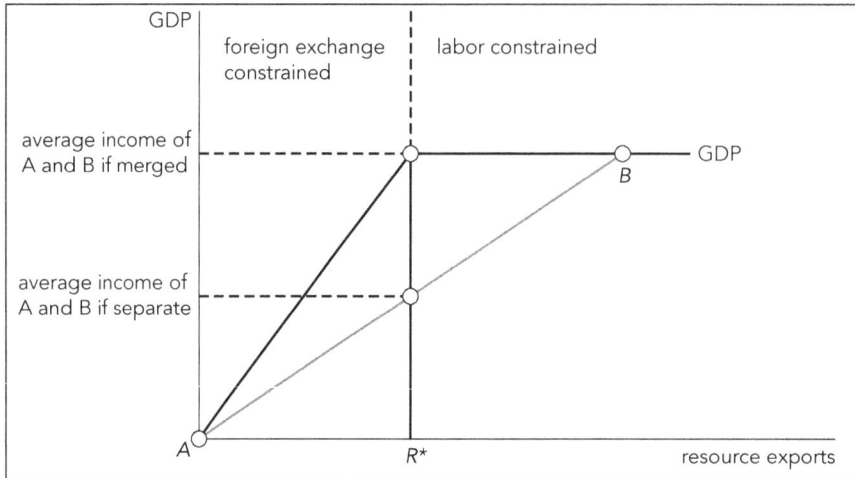

Source: Authors' elaboration.

consumes and produces a single good that is nontradable. Production of the good uses foreign exchange (imported oil or equipment) and domestic labor in fixed proportions. The only source of foreign exchange is resource revenues, and labor is in fixed supply. Real income in such an economy is illustrated in figure 2, in which resource revenue is measured on the horizontal axis. If resource exports are less than R^*, production is foreign exchange constrained, and real income is given by the upward-sloping section of the line (with slope equal to the foreign exchange content per unit of GDP). If natural resource earnings are greater than R^*, the economy is labor constrained, thus fixing income; further resource earnings beyond this point are simply accumulated as foreign assets. As a simplest case, suppose that one economy has no resource revenue (i.e., it is at point A) and another has resource revenue and is at point B. The average income of the two countries is at the midpoint between A and B. Merger of the two economies would exactly double the income, as illustrated.

This is a very clear-cut example. What insights does it provide into reality? There are two key elements to the argument. The first is that shortage of foreign exchange constrains production in economies that lack resource earnings. Many resource-scarce and landlocked African economies have extremely low shares of exports in GDP—less than 15 percent in eight of these countries. Accessing world markets has been particularly difficult for this group, and they are heavily aid dependent. If they were located within a single country, such areas would earn the resources to finance "imports" through intracountry trade. The argument must therefore turn on the fact that barriers to trade created by international borders are an order of magnitude greater than within-country trade barriers, and there is plenty of evidence that this is the case.

The classic studies of the barriers created by international borders, compared with within-country trade costs, are based on trade between Canada and the United

States. McCallum (1995) and Helliwell (1997) show that exports by Canadian provinces to other Canadian provinces are about 20 times larger than their exports to U.S. states at the same distance. According to one study, the U.S.–Canada border is 7,000 miles wide, in the sense that it chokes off trade as much as would 7,000 miles of borderless distance. African borders are generally much more difficult to navigate than is the border between the United States and Canada. Limão and Venables (2001) find that poor infrastructure is particularly important in choking off trade between African countries. The implication is that resource-scarce, landlocked regions face more acute problems in financing imports as separate nations than they would as regions of a larger country.

The second part of the argument contained in figure 2 is that at some point there are diminishing returns to resource earnings. In the example given, the economy reached full employment, and no more labor was available to produce further income. But the argument is more general. What are the sources of diminishing returns to the value of resource revenues in resource-rich African economies? Often, there are constraints on the supply of particular nontradable services, such as construction services or specific labor skills. Spending bids up the price of these inputs but does not buy additional real services. More generally, spending from resource revenues will be met by a combination of increased output and crowding out of other expenditures. The expenditures that are crowded out might be exports, giving rise to "Dutch disease."[1] Alternatively, monetary and exchange rate policy might be used to mitigate Dutch disease, in which case crowding out will affect domestic activities, quite likely investment. If these activities are particularly valuable (as would be the case if they are initially operating at a suboptimal level), crowding them out may actually reduce income.

The key point for the present argument is that the smaller are resource revenues relative to the economy as a whole, the more favorable will be the balance between increased income versus crowding out of other expenditures. If two countries are merged, the supply curve of the merged country is the horizontal sum of the supply curve of each separately, so a given increase in demand will lead to a larger quantity increase and a smaller price increase in the merged economy than in a separate one. This argument focuses on income and expenditure, but other aspects of the "resource curse" (e.g., political-economy issues) may also exhibit increasing marginal cost, possibly meaning that the benefits of resource revenue do not just flatten out with respect to resource revenue but turn negative at the margin. In this case, the citizens of *both* countries would gain from the merger and a sharing of the economic impact of revenues.

It is not just natural resources that are unequally divided between countries; access to the coast is, too. Coastal economies in developing countries are much better placed to engage in producing manufactures for world markets than are landlocked countries, and such activities are important drivers of growth (Jones and Olken 2005; Commission on Growth and Development 2008). These differential opportunities mean, once again, that the fragmentation of a region into separate countries may create both spatial inequalities and efficiency losses. A simple economic framework is helpful. Suppose that economies can produce a good in which there are diminishing returns to labor—say, in agriculture, where a fixed supply of land generates diminishing

FIGURE 3.
Returns to Labor in Coastal (C) and Landlocked (L) Economies

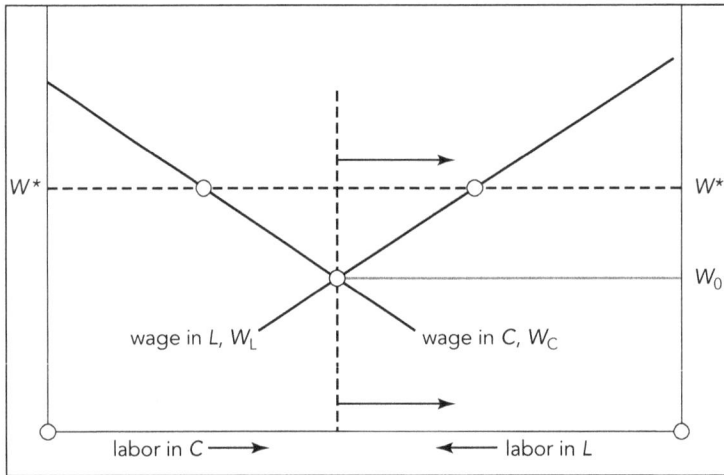

Source: Authors' elaboration.

returns. Figure 3 illustrates two such economies. The total labor force is the length of the horizontal axis, and workers are equally divided between countries, with workers in coastal economy C measured from the left-hand origin and those in landlocked economy L measured from the right. The value of marginal product of workers in each country is given by the downward-sloping lines, with the slope reflecting the diminishing returns to labor. If this were all, wages in each country would be equal (and low, W_0) at the intersection of these lines.

Suppose, however, that C, the coastal economy, can also undertake an export activity for the world market that does not run into diminishing returns. Given productivity levels, this activity can pay wage W^*. Some of the labor in the coastal economy will then move to this sector, and wages will rise until they reach W^*. Country L, however, is landlocked and is unable to access this source of employment, so it is left with wage W_0. Fragmentation into two political units means a fixed division of the labor force between countries, and the lack of migration between C and L creates inequality (the gap between W_0 and W^*), as well as a loss of efficiency and real income. Within a single economy, there would be internal migration of labor from L to C, so that the division of the total workforce would move in line with the horizontal arrows in the figure. Migrants would gain and would also bid up wages for those remaining until all workers received W^*. Although landowners (owners of the sector-specific factor) in L would lose, there is an overall real income gain from the migration equal to the shaded triangle. Furthermore, if the export activity had increasing returns to scale rather than constant returns, the expanded employment would increase productivity and the wage, raising income in both C and L.

What insights does this offer? Some Asian economies have witnessed massive migration to regions (usually, although not necessarily, coastal) that have succeeded in building up sectors supplying world markets. The best example is west-to-east migration in China. Internal migration is also important (although poorly documented) in India, both as seasonal migration and as part of rapid urbanization.

Africa has not yet developed such magnets of employment, but the analysis indicates that if it were to do so, fragmentation would prevent it from fully realizing the benefits. There have been substantial migration flows in Africa, but they have often been problematic. Even where governments permit international migration, the noncitizen status of immigrants creates opportunities for the politics of xenophobia, which increases as the stock of immigrants accumulates. Since attractive political niches at some point draw politicians willing to occupy them, the opportunity for xenophobia is unlikely to remain unexploited. In turn, this political response exposes immigrants to violence and expulsion.

The clearest instance of this depressing sequence arose from the sharp difference in natural advantage between Côte d'Ivoire and Burkina Faso. With its radically better economic opportunities stemming from its coastline and its rainfall, Côte d'Ivoire attracted massive immigration from Burkina Faso. Indeed, at one stage around 40 percent of the labor force in Côte d'Ivoire was Burkinabe. During the 1990s, this development was exploited by populist politicians and was instrumental in triggering political meltdown into coups and civil war, during which much of the migration was reversed.[2] Nigeria in the 1970s provides a second instance of the same sequence. The discovery of oil created a sharp distinction in natural advantage for Nigeria vis-à-vis Ghana. The consequence was mass migration from Ghana—at one point, around a fifth of the Ghanaian population had emigrated. Xenophobia grew in Nigeria, and when economic conditions deteriorated, the Ghanaians were formally expelled. South Africa witnessed its own backlash against immigration in 2008.

In addition to constraining migration, a further adverse effect of fragmentation can be illustrated with reference to the circumstances shown in figure 2. Owners of the specific factor in the diminishing-returns sector in the coastal country (C) suffer an income loss as production of the export activity takes off. The diminishing-returns sector is most naturally thought of as agriculture. As manufacturing expands, the agricultural sector has to compete for labor and faces higher wages. Agriculture in country C contracts, returns to land in C fall, and C comes to import agricultural goods from country L and the rest of the world. There is a likelihood that this trend will create a lobby for tariffs on agricultural imports. Although such a move would raise the real income of landowners, it would have a negative effect on total income in the coastal economy. The political economy of protectionism, however, is well understood to favor small but cohesive interests over the general interest. The import tariff would also choke off manufacturing production in the coastal economy, possibly with damaging long-run effects on development. And if the coastal economy were the primary market for the landlocked country's agricultural exports, the tariff would also damage country L. The point is, of course, that the opportunity for using an import tariff, at least against imports from country L, exists only if C and L are separate countries. Merger therefore removes a policy instrument that is likely to be misused in response to political-economy pressures. An example of manipulation of trade barriers as a result of political fragmentation is the banning of food imports from Uganda by President Daniel arap Moi of Kenya in the early 1990s in response to lobbying by business interests that were holding large stocks of food.

Time-Variant Differences in Natural Advantage: Export Volatility

The economic advantages and disadvantages of a particular location at a particular date are shaped partly by fixed geography and partly by the impact of short-run shocks. The arguments we have developed above apply to these transient effects, as well as to the permanent ones. Shocks create unevenness between areas, and the ability to spread their impact (i.e., to pool risk), with both distributional and efficiency implications, is impeded by fragmentation into national units.

Collier and Goderis (2008a, 2008b, 2009) investigate the consequences of commodity export shocks for GDP valued at constant prices. This method abstracts from the income effect accruing directly from changes in the terms of trade and focuses on the consequences for real output. The authors find that shocks have asymmetrical effects on growth: adverse shocks significantly reduce output, but positive shocks do not have significant effects. The effect of adverse shocks is substantial. For example, for a typical African country whose commodity exports are initially around 35 percent of GDP, the consequence of a 30 percent fall in export prices would be to reduce growth in the following year by 3.6 percentage points. More generally, given the frequency of shocks and their cost, it is possible to estimate the discounted present value of the output losses that they generate. Using a 3 percent discount rate, the cost for individual countries is sometimes large: for example, for Nigeria it is 13 percent of one year's GDP. Yet summed over the entire continent, country by country, the cost is modest, around 4 percentage points of one year's GDP.[3]

For this paper we investigated whether these costs would have been reduced had Africa been divided into fewer polities.[4] We examined the consequences of a United Africa, which provides an upper bound to the analysis, and of political regrouping into four regional blocs. We found that a United Africa would have reduced the costs by a mere 0.6 percentage points of the region's GDP. The gains from regional groupings are more variable, the largest being from a United West Africa, where they would amount to 1.7 percentage points of GDP.

The main reason why the effect is so limited is that the scope for risk pooling in Africa is modest. Virtually all countries are commodity exporters, and not only are the prices of most commodities highly correlated, but a single commodity, oil, dominates Africa's exports. In a United Africa, around 65 percent of commodity exports would be oil. Hence, pooling has little effect on the size of the average shock. The key potential gain therefore comes not from reducing the average size of shocks but from changing their distribution. Most African countries do not export oil, so that a United Africa would have fewer enormous shocks and more moderate-size shocks than in the distribution of country-specific shocks. Whether such redistribution matters depends on the precise relationship between the size of shocks and their costs. The original specification of the work by Collier and Goderis is linear, and the costs of a shock are thus required to be proportionate to the size of the shock. In that case, redistributions that do not affect the average make no difference.

For this paper we therefore investigated whether the true structure of costs is non-linear, rising more than proportionately with the size of the shock, as seemed inherently likely. We found little basis for a nonlinear relationship. For example, when the square of the size is added to the regression, although the coefficient is negative, it is not close to significance. We conclude that, given Africa's export structure, the scope for reducing the cost of shocks through greater political unity is modest. But, as we will argue next, Africa's export structure may itself be a consequence of political fragmentation. Manufacturing and service exports benefit from scale economies that are less important for primary commodities. If political fragmentation has frustrated these scale economies, it may have locked Africa into dependence on primary commodity exports.

Scale, Density, and Increasing Returns

The preceding section pointed to diminishing returns as a source of loss for a fragmented continent with uneven distribution of resources or of shocks. We now turn to increasing returns and the cost of opportunities forgone by small countries. We focus first on a microeconomic mechanism that we think is particularly important in many small African countries—the fact that markets are too thin to be competitive. This constitutes a major obstacle to investment, both because of high prices for capital goods and, more fundamentally, because of vulnerability to opportunistic behavior. We then discuss how the microeconomic advantages of scale combine to produce a positive relationship between city size and productivity and suggest that fragmentation has created an African city structure which is ill suited to reap these productivity effects.

Competition and the Operation of Markets

Small economies are likely to have high levels of monopoly power. That makes them bad places for new investments. Incumbent firms have little incentive to expand output or to innovate, and they have strong incentives to deter entry and innovation by newcomers. Monopoly raises the prices of many intermediate goods, as well as of final output, thereby raising costs. And, most important, monopoly creates the potential for opportunistic behavior in transactions and thereby creates a difficult business environment, even for the monopolists themselves.

Evidently, a small market is likely to be less competitive than a large one because, given some firm-level economies of scale, fewer firms will operate. The effect will be particularly pronounced in sectors that are closed to trade. For example, the typical African economy has a very highly concentrated banking sector—often, four banks dominate lending, and this is a sufficiently small number to enable collusive oligopoly. The limited nature of the market also leads to a concentration of risk: banks are exposed to a high covariance of the risk of default.

Transport is another sector that is sheltered from international competition and that is often highly cartelized. A recent study (Teravaninthorn and Raballand 2008)

TABLE 2. Relative Price of Investment

(variables in logs)

	Price of investment (all countries)	Price of investment (population < 20 million)
Real GDP per worker	−0.27	−0.30
	(−12.7)	(−8.8)
Number of workers	−0.046	−0.071
	(−3.5)	(−2.6)
N	163	83
R^2	0.50	0.50

Source: Caselli and Feyrer (2007), from Penn World Tables.

Note: GDP, gross domestic product. Numbers in parentheses are *t*-statistics.

finds that the real costs of transport services in Africa are not abnormally high but that trucking firms are able to charge exceptionally high prices. Average prices per ton-kilometer are US$0.02 in Pakistan, US$0.05 in China, US$0.08 for the run from Mombasa (Kenya) to Kampala (Uganda), and US$0.11 for the run from Doula (Cameroon) to N'Djamena (Chad). Many African economies have restrictive regulatory regimes and transport cartels. (Deregulation of the trucking industry in Rwanda has been estimated to have reduced transport prices by 75 percent.) In some cases, a major factor supporting cartelization is a treaty structure between countries designed to protect the national trucking industry from competition from neighboring countries.

Monopoly power raises relative prices, and a key relative price in an economy seeking to grow is the price of investment in relation to the price of GDP as a whole. Given the level of saving, the higher is the relative price of investment, the less physical equipment the saving will purchase. This effect is quantitatively important, as the price of investment (in relation to GDP as a whole) can be three or four times higher in developing countries than in high-income countries. Recent work by Caselli and Feyrer (2007) shows that much of the variation in the marginal physical product of capital across countries is in fact the result of this price effect.

Why is there this price difference? Part of it is attributable to the Balassa-Samuelson effect; investment has high import content, and prices of tradable goods are relatively high in low-income countries. It may also be partly the result of thin markets and monopoly power in supply of equipment and investment goods, which may be a function of country size. To investigate this relationship, we explored the impact of GDP per capita (for the Balassa-Samuelson effect) and country size (for the market power effect) on this relative price. The evidence is given in table 2, which reports the results of regressing the price of investment relative to the price of GDP on real GDP per worker and on the number of workers (used as a measure of economic size). The extremely strong dependence on output per worker is clear, and so too is the scale effect. Increasing the labor force by a factor of 20 reduces the relative price of investment by 13 percent. Restriction of the sample to countries with a labor force of less than 20 million produces a quantitatively larger effect. Recalling that India's population is

66 times larger than that of the average African country, which has a workforce of less than 10 million, the implications for differences in the price of capital are substantial.

Thin markets and the resulting monopoly power increase the price of capital goods, but they have further pernicious effects. One is that they create an incentive for incumbent firms to actively pursue strategies that deter the entry of new firms. (Strategies for entry deterrence may include the use of predatory pricing or the purchase of political influence.) From the perspective of firms that are already operating in a sector, if one firm devotes resources to keeping new entrants out of the sector, that is a public good. From the perspective of society as a whole, however, such behavior is evidently undesirable. In an industry with many existing firms, the free-riding problem implies that the returns to any one firm from such antisocial behavior are limited. But in a small market with an incumbent monopolist, all the benefits to the existing industry are internalized, and so the incentive to keep out new competitors is maximized.

Small and thin markets are unattractive places to invest because investors are vulnerable to "holdup"—opportunistic behavior by other firms with which they have to do business. Holdup refers to the possibility that once an investment has been sunk, the investor will face a monopsonistic purchaser of the output of the investment. Even if the purchaser and investor entered an agreement before the investment was undertaken, the purchaser may subsequently act opportunistically, breaking the agreement and offering a lower price. The investor will anticipate the possibility of holdup and so may not make the investment in the first place. One way to overcome the holdup problem is to make the ex ante contract legally binding, but even in countries with strong legal systems, it is often impossible to write a contract with a degree of completeness that will rule out such opportunistic behavior. The other way is to make sure that there are many alternative uses for the output of the project. This is partly a matter of the specificity of the investment (it might be a machine for making specialist parts demanded by a single manufacturer) and partly a matter of the size of the market in which the output is sold. Holdup is likelier the fewer are the people competing for the output.

This suggests that in small economies the threat of holdup may be a major deterrent to investment. In agriculture, returns to investment are reduced if there is a monopsonistic grain merchant. In manufacturing, having few potential purchasers of output deters investment. The consequence is coordination failure: there is no incentive to enter on one side of the market until the other side has more firms, and vice versa. And in a small economy, even the return to the worst option—liquidating the investment—may be reduced by thin markets for secondhand capital equipment. Distress sales are likely to be more coincident because smaller economies are less diversified, further depressing the expected price. The holdup phenomenon applies not only to goods markets but also to labor markets; the incentive to undergo training is reduced if the skill acquired can only be sold to one employer.

These arguments point to the fact that smallness does not just create static monopoly or monopsony power but also creates a fundamentally more risky business environment. Entry of new producers will be deterred by predatory behavior by incumbents and by the scarcity of outside options and the consequent vulnerability to predatory and opportunistic behavior.

Productivity and City Size

Productivity tends to be higher in large (or dense) clusters of economic activity. This is why cities form. Firms and workers locate to gain the benefits of this productivity advantage, despite the congestion costs and other diseconomies associated with large cities. A number of mechanisms drive this productivity effect. Some are narrowly technical—for example, the fact that dense activity economizes on transport costs and improves communications (and possible learning externalities) among firms, and between firms and workers. Others have to do with the impact of size on market structure and the intensity of competition, as discussed above. Still others concern political economy: a city with a large business sector is likely to have a strong business lobby, producing a business-friendly investment climate. The quantitative evidence of the productivity effect of city size comes largely from studies of cities in developed countries. Rosenthal and Strange (2004) report a consensus view that a doubling of city size is associated with a productivity increase of about 3 to 8 percent. This is a large effect: a size increase from 100,000 workers in a city to 3 million is predicted to increase productivity by more than 30 percent. Au and Henderson (2006) find even larger results for Chinese cities, where they estimate that moving from a city of 100,000 workers to one of 1.3 million workers raises productivity by 80 percent, although beyond this scale weak diminishing returns cut in.

In this section we investigate the effects of Africa's fragmentation on its city structure and argue that fragmentation has a negative impact on city size, producing a city structure that is weak compared with the structure in an integrated country such as India. We have argued elsewhere that Africa's failure to develop large clusters of economic activity has had major implications for its economic performance. Africa's failure to enter world markets for manufactured exports is best understood by looking at the location of productive clusters of activity (Collier and Venables 2007). Many Asian cities have already gained a head start in these sectors and have grown highly productive clusters, creating a barrier for new entrants. Asia's initial advantage over Africa, when Asia first penetrated the global market for manufactures in the 1980s, may have been modest. Quite probably, the reasons for Africa's initial disadvantage have evaporated; for example, in the 1980s much of coastal Africa was beset by conflict (as in Mozambique) or poor economic policies (as in Ghana). But as clusters have developed in Asia, the resulting scale economies have given that region a new and more formidable advantage. Africa may have missed the boat on industrialization, unless trade policies of the Organisation for Economic Co-operation and Development (OECD) artificially create an offsetting temporary advantage for African manufactures that pump-primes the formation of clusters.

Does the political fragmentation of Africa have any bearing on this? The obvious fact is that small countries generally have smaller cities, so some productivity benefits are forgone. We first investigate this point by employing a cross-country regression to explore the determinants of city size. We use a large dataset of world cities and take as the dependent variable the population of the *j*th-ranked city in country *i*. We work with the top five cities in each country, which yields (with some missing values for very small countries) 521 observations. The explanatory variables are

TABLE 3. Determinants of City Population

(all variables in logs)

Variable	Without regional fixed effects	With regional fixed effects	Without regional fixed effects; income per capita < US$10,000
Country population	0.639	0.70	0.731
	(23.3)	(18.9)	(13.7)
Country area	0.169	0.107	0.085
	(7.1)	(3.9)	(2.1)
GDP per capita	0.27	0.27	0.102
	(7.6)	(7.6)	(1.8)
City rank	−1.08	−1.1	−1.21
	(−25.0)	(−28.0)	(−25.0)
N	521	521	325
R^2	0.80	0.83	0.83

Note: Numbers in parentheses are t-statistics.

country population, country area, country per capita income, and the rank of the city in the country, thus,

$$\ln(population_{ij}) = a + b_1 \ln(population_i) + b_2 \ln(area_i) + b_3 \ln(income\ pc_i) + b_4 \ln(rank_j).$$

Table 3 presents results for specifications with and without regional fixed effects, for the world as a whole and for countries with per capita income of less than US$10,000. As is well known, national GDP per capita has a positive effect on city population. The city's within-country rank has a negative effect, as it must by construction. The estimated parameter in our central specification is −1.08, close to Zipf's law—the rank-size rule—which states that within countries the size of each city is inversely proportional to its rank in the city size distribution (see Gabaix and Ioannides 2004).

Of most interest for our purposes is the fact that both country population and country area are highly significant determinants of city size. The sum of the coefficients on these two variables is 0.80, indicating that a merger of two similar-size countries—producing a doubling of population and area—would lead to a 75 percent increase in the size of the largest city. To see the quantitative implications, suppose that initially there are 10 separate countries, in each of which the largest city has a population of 3 million people. Combining these countries and letting city sizes adjust in line with the regularities given in table 3 yields a largest city of 19 million and a size distribution of city population of (for the first 10 cities, in millions) 19, 9.5, 6.3, 4.7, 3.8, 3.1, 2.7, 2.4, 2.1, 1.9.

It is interesting to compare these calculations with actual city size distributions in India and Africa (table 4). Both the calculations and the actual data for India suggest that a large, integrated country, compared with Africa, has much larger cities in the top rank; slightly fewer in the upper-middle ranks (compare the numbers of Indian and African cities with populations around 3 million, as given in table 4); and many

TABLE 4. Cities with Population Greater than 1 Million, India and Sub-Saharan Africa

India		Sub-Saharan Africa	
City	Population	City and country	Population
Mumbai	21,600,000	Lagos, Nigeria	10,100,000
Delhi	21,500,000	Kinshasa, Congo, Dem. Rep.	8,200,000
Kolkata	15,700,000	Johannesburg, South Africa	7,800,000
Chennai	7,850,000	Khartoum, Sudan	5,450,000
Bangalore	7,350,000	Abidjan, Côte d'Ivoire	4,225,000
Hyderabad	7,150,000	Durban, South Africa	3,600,000
Ahmedabad	5,650,000	Kano, Nigeria	3,600,000
Pune	4,625,000	Cape Town, South Africa	3,400,000
Surat	3,875,000	Accra, Ghana	3,350,000
Kanpur	3,475,000	Ibadan, Nigeria	3,200,000
Jaipur	3,050,000	Nairobi, Kenya	3,175,000
Lucknow	2,800,000	Addis Ababa, Ethiopia	3,100,000
Nagpur	2,700,000	Dar es Salaam, Tanzania	3,000,000
Patna	2,350,000	Luanda, Angola	2,875,000
Indore	1,870,000	Dakar, Senegal	2,550,000
Vadodara	1,870,000	Pretoria, South Africa	2,450,000
Coimbatore	1,820,000	Harare, Zimbabwe	2,200,000
Bhopal	1,810,000	Douala, Cameroon	2,000,000
Ludhiana	1,730,000	Maputo, Mozambique	1,820,000
Agra	1,700,000	Antananarivo, Madagascar	1,760,000
Kochi	1,660,000	Bamako, Mali	1,730,000
Visakhapatnam	1,610,000	Lusaka, Zambia	1,720,000
Meerut	1,600,000	Yaoundé, Cameroon	1,610,000
Asansol	1,580,000	Conakry, Guinea	1,600,000
Bhubaneswar	1,560,000	Kaduna, Nigeria	1,590,000
Nashik	1,550,000	Kumasi, Ghana	1,520,000
Chandigarh	1,520,000	Kampala, Uganda	1,490,000
Varanasi	1,470,000	Lubumbashi, Congo, Dem. Rep.	1,450,000
Kolhapur	1,460,000	Mogadishu, Somalia	1,410,000
Jamshedpur	1,350,000	Brazzaville, Congo, Rep.	1,330,000
Madurai	1,350,000	Lomé, Togo	1,320,000
Rajkot	1,320,000	Ouagadougou, Burkina Faso	1,260,000
Jabalpur	1,300,000	Benin City, Nigeria	1,180,000
Dhanbad	1,290,000	Port Harcourt, Nigeria	1,170,000
Amritsar	1,270,000	Port Elizabeth, South Africa	1,150,000
Allahabad	1,230,000	Freetown, Sierra Leone	1,110,000
Vijayawada	1,220,000	Cotonou, Benin	1,090,000
Srinagar	1,180,000	Maiduguri, Nigeria	1,040,000
Shambajinagar	1,170,000		
Solapur	1,100,000		
Thiruvananthapuram	1,100,000		
Ranchi	1,090,000		
Jodhpur	1,040,000		
Guwahati	1,030,000		
Tiruchirappalli	1,010,000		
Gwalior	1,000,000		

Source: "The Principal Agglomerations of the World," City Population Web site, http://www.citypopulation.de/World.html.

more medium-size to large cities (e.g., with populations between 1 million and 2 million).

This analysis suggests that the smaller size of African cities stems in large part from the fragmentation of the region. The preceding discussion and the evidence from developed-country studies (as summarized by Rosenthal and Strange 2004) suggest that city size may have had an adverse effect on the productivity of African manufacturing. Although size is not the only determinant of urban productivity, Africa's fragmentation and consequent urban structure may have impeded the development of major international manufacturing centers of the type that contributes to the performance of high-growth economies.

Political Economy of Public Goods

Above, we considered those advantages of being a large country that arise from greater diversity and greater geographic concentration of private economic activities. We now consider those that arise from government activities. A core function of a government is to supply public goods. By definition, public goods are subject to scale economies. The distinctive aspect of public goods that ensures scale economies is that consumption is nonrival—one person's consumption does not reduce that of another person. Many public goods, however, also have more conventional scale economies: their production technology has high fixed costs that can be spread over more consumers as scale is expanded. A radio station displays both types of scale economy: listening is nonrival, and once the fixed costs of transmission have been incurred, the number of hours broadcast per day is subject to much lower variable costs.

As the number of consumers is progressively increased to the point at which it includes all the world's inhabitants, relatively few goods still have unrealized economies of scale. At some point, consumption ceases to be nonrival, and technological scale economies are exhausted. Conceptually, we can order all the goods that might potentially be provided publicly according to the minimum size at which all scale economies are realized. Along this ranking, we find first those goods that are nonrival only within the locality, then the nation, then the region, and, finally, globally.

The supply of public goods generates acute collective action problems that, except in a few cases, require coercive powers of taxation to overcome effectively. The highest level at which such powers are found is the nation. Hence, in practice, those scale economies that occur beyond the level of the nation-state are generally not realized.

The failure to realize such economies is widely lamented in discussions of the underprovision of global public goods (Barrett 2007) and regional public goods (Cook and Sachs 1999). It has a powerful corollary through its implications for differences in country size. Since there are some public goods that are global, a fortiori there must be many more for which the minimum efficient size lies somewhere within the huge population range implied by the difference between the smallest African country and India. Within this range, the smaller is the country, the fewer goods can efficiently be supplied at the level of the nation-state. This consideration is reinforced when population is replaced by GDP as the size metric. Public goods are economic activities, and the relevant metric for scale is more likely to be the size of the economy than the size of the population. Since Africa is now the poorest region, its typical national economy is even tinier than is suggested by the size of its population. The economy of Luxembourg is roughly the same size as that of the five countries of the East African Community combined.

It might seem that nations could be too large as well as too small for the efficient supply of public goods. If different communities have distinctive preferences for public goods, provision may work better if political decision units are small and so can reflect these differences. There is, however, an asymmetry. Once the optimal scale has been reached, a large state can always replicate this scale by decentralizing supply to subnational authorities. In other words, once all the scale economies have been reaped, further expansion can be under conditions of constant returns to scale. States that are too small do not have an equivalent option: a national government can choose to pass authority down, but it does not have the power to pass authority up. A large nation thus has an advantage over a small nation, and this advantage may become very pronounced by the time we reach the tiny states that are common in Africa.

We now analyze the provision of three public goods that are fundamental to prosperity: security, economic policy, and infrastructure.

Security

Security is the clearest case of a public good that is subject to scale economies far beyond the size of the typical small African state. Like radio, security benefits from both types of scale economy. Over a wide range, defense is nonrival—the same army that defends one community from rebellion can defend a proximate community. Over a very wide range, it benefits from scale economies: big armies usually defeat little armies, a proposition formalized in contest success functions. The sheer power of scale economies in security has repeatedly been revealed in the expansion of empires. Once a power gets a military advantage over its neighbors, it can expand almost without limit if it chooses to do so. Rome, the Mongol Empire, Russia, and the nineteenth-century European empires demonstrate that big is safe.

The incidence of warfare in Africa has been far higher than in India, and differences in scale in part account for this. Evidently, political union would have reduced the incidence of international war, but almost all of Africa's wars have been internal, and so the key issue is how union would have affected this risk. Statistical analysis of the risk of civil war finds that whereas population significantly increases the risk, the effect is substantially less than proportionate: a territory under a single polity has a lower risk than the combined risk for two polities were the single state split in half (Collier, Hoeffler, and Rohner 2009). The case for scale, however, is complicated by the trade-off with ethnic diversity. In general, in order to make a polity larger, it is necessary to take in additional social groups, and so diversity increases. Unfortunately, diversity heightens the risk of civil war. Were Africa to have been split into fewer countries, the adverse effect stemming from diversity might have more than offset the benefit from greater scale. The issue has recently been analyzed by

Wigstrom (2008), who has carefully investigated how mergers between neighboring African countries would affect ethnic diversity. It transpires that in some cases Africa's borders are so arbitrary that ethnic diversity would actually be *reduced* by merger. In these instances the scale and the diversity effects of political union work in the same direction, lessening the risk of civil war. Even were diversity to increase, Wigstrom finds that over a wide range, had Africa been divided into fewer independent polities, it would have had a lower risk of civil war. Although his analysis is of course hypothetical and cannot take into account many aspects of politics, it omits the consequences for peace of the economic benefits of scale discussed above. Since both the level and growth of income significantly reduce the risk of civil war, these economic effects of political union would have reinforced the effects discussed here.

The small scale of African polities not only increases the incidence of war; it increases military spending while at peace. Because large armies tend to defeat small armies, small states tend to compensate by spending a higher fraction of GDP on the military. Furthermore, although a country can increase its own security by spending more on its army, this reduces the security of neighboring countries that feel threatened. Evidently, in response to a perceived increase in threat, the neighboring country will need to increase its own military spending, producing an arms race. The essence of an arms race is that, if we think of military spending as producing security, an increase in spending by one country reduces the average productivity but increases the marginal productivity of its neighbor's spending. Collier and Hoeffler (2007) establish that neighborhood arms races have been common around the developing world. For the present paper we have used their results to simulate the reduction in average African military spending had there been a United Africa. We set the incidence of civil war equal to that estimated by Wigstrom (2008), eliminate the effect of neighborhood arms races, and set all other variables at their average actual values for the continent. The predicted level of military spending falls by a quarter, from 3.2 to 2.4 percent of GDP (calculation by Anke Hoeffler).

Good Economic Policies and Governance

A second fundamental public good is the provision of sound economic policies and accountable government. The choice between good and bad policies is typically determined by a complex mix of influences. Among them are the interests of the elite, the political power of ordinary citizens, the degree to which both elites and citizens understand basic economic issues and so grasp how their interests are best served by policies, and, finally, the capacity of the civil service to design and implement policies.

Scale may enter here through various routes. For example, the quality of the civil service can be higher in a larger society simply because it can be more selective. There is around 50 times more competition to become permanent secretary in the ministry of finance in India than in Africa, and so the quality will, on average, be higher.

Another scale effect is that, paradoxically, a larger society can be better informed about economic issues than a small one. The key reason is the scale economies in the commercial media—radio, television, newspapers, and magazines. A large market will permit more media outlets to exist than a small market will. Serious discussion of economic issues within a society is highly dependent on the existence of specialist media. India has such media, but in Africa, only South Africa comes anywhere close to providing a market in which specialist journals are viable. For example, the Indian newspaper the *Economic Times* has a circulation of 1.2 million, which is sufficient to finance a staff of economically qualified journalists. With the same density of circulation, an economics newspaper in Zambia would have a circulation of less than 10,000 and so would not be viable. Without a specialist media, discussion in the society is likely to be less sophisticated, and the pace at which social learning takes place will be slower. In effect, the society needs a critical mass of educated citizens before social learning can be rapid. This may help explain why India reformed its economic policies before Africa did.

A distinct reason why larger states may be able to reform faster is a corollary of their greater need to decentralize authority: more public goods reach the level at which decentralization is the efficient form of organization. Such decentralized authority introduces variation in strategies, and this in turn represents a source of learning. Small societies can, of course, choose to replicate the same degree of decentralization, but the increased opportunities for learning come at the expense of forgone scale economies in provision. India, with its federal structure, has clearly had a very wide range of experimentation, with some states pioneering in the provision of social services and others in encouragement of foreign investment. Indeed, the equivalent of learning can occur even if successful experiments are not copied. People and firms will choose to relocate to attractive areas, and this gradually shifts the weighted average of policies across the nation toward the most successful. Potentially, Africa's equivalent is that its division into so many nations enables policy variation at the national level. It is not clear, however, that a small country is in any better position to learn from other nations than is a large country. (India has clearly learned a great deal from China.)

A related scale effect is the switch from discretion to rules in decision making. At its best, an intimate organization can tailor each decision to the needs of the individual and the circumstance; decisions can be personalized. As the organization becomes larger, this style of decision making breaks down because micromanagement becomes overburdened and is replaced by rule-based procedures. Rule-based decisions are seldom as good as first-best discretionary decisions, but they are far better than either patronage-driven or idiosyncratic decisions. They also enable the government to have a credible commitment technology that may even dominate the best discretionary policies by providing an escape from the time-consistency problem. Hence, we might expect that public decisions in large societies lie within a narrower range than those in small societies. This is closely analogous to the difference between autocracy and democracy. Autocrats have the discretion either to be very good or very bad, whereas democracies are rule bound. Besley and Kudamatsu (2007) compared the economic outcomes for these two types of government and indeed found that democracy truncates the distribution at both extremes.

These effects of scale are plausible, but is there any evidence that they actually matter? Chauvet and Collier (2008) analyze the preconditions for policy turnaround in countries that initially had very poor economic policies and governance, using the World Bank measure of economic policy and governance, the country policy and institutional assessment (CPIA). This is a subjective, ordinal rating and thus has obvious drawbacks, but most of the controversies in economic policy concern the higher range of these ratings, and policies and governance that are very poor are often unmistakable. Chauvet and Collier define a turnaround as the passage from a rating below a very low threshold to one above a benchmark that, although substantially higher, is still modest in relation to the rating of most developing countries. The authors' universe is all low-income countries over the period 1977–2005. From this group they select those countries in which for at least four consecutive years economic policies and governance were below the threshold. They find that population size is one of the preconditions for a turnaround that is statistically significant: the larger is the population, the higher is the probability that a country that initially ranked below the threshold will achieve a sustained turnaround. Equivalently expressed, large countries appear to experience more rapid social learning.

For this paper we have used the coefficients of the Chauvet-Collier model to estimate how long India, on the one hand, and the average African country, on the other, would have taken to reform from a common initial position of poor policies to a common improved position. We create two artificial countries, "India" and "Zambia." Both are identical in all characteristics except population; all other characteristics are set at the sample mean. "India" has the population of India, and "Zambia" has the population of the average African country, both entered into the regression as logs. We set their initial CPIA scores at 2.5, indicating very poor policies, and ask how long it would take to reach a score of 3.5. Since the regression model is log-linear, the consequences of the huge differences in population are likely to be exaggerated; the regression line is trying to explain the countries within the range and is likely to fail at the extremes. Nevertheless, the predicted difference in the pace of reform is striking: "India" is predicted to bounce out of bad policies into reasonable ones in only 6 years, whereas "Zambia" is predicted to take around 60 years (calculation by Lisa Chauvet).

Infrastructure

Transport and power infrastructure are public goods with such strong scale economies that the typical African polity is too small to exhaust them. Indeed, Africa still depends on the transport infrastructure created during the period when its present polities were united into a few empires. Quite possibly, from the perspective of transport infrastructure, the key feature of colonialism was not that the empires were ruled externally but that they temporarily united Africa into a few large polities. The most obvious problem generated by political division is that many countries are landlocked. As shown by Limão and Venables (2001), the transport costs faced by landlocked countries are strongly affected by the infrastructure spending of their coastal neighbors. Evidently, these benefits to the landlocked are externalities from the perspective of the coastal countries; they are not internalized into the decision calculus, and so spending is suboptimal.

The failure to internalize costs and benefits, however, extends far more widely than the plight of the landlocked. The recent discovery of large iron ore deposits in Guinea by Rio Tinto Zinc is a telling example. The exploitation of the deposits

evidently requires investment in a mine, but the pertinent issue is the necessary investment in transport infrastructure. Fortuitously, as a legacy from the age of empires, a
railway already links the deposit with a deepwater port, Buchanan. But Buchanan is
in Liberia, and the government of Guinea does not want to find itself subject to a
holdup problem vis-à-vis the government of Liberia. It has therefore insisted that the
transport link be entirely within Guinea, which requires the construction of a new,
dedicated railway and a new deepwater port. This decision has more than doubled
the total investment needed for the project, adding around US$4 billion. Evidently,
these additional costs will be fully passed on; the government has agreed with Rio
Tinto Zinc that it will absorb them through a reduced flow of royalty payments.
Hence, the costs are ultimately borne by the people of Guinea. The decision is also
costly to the people of Liberia; in particular, the port of Buchanan loses what may
have been its key opportunity for scale economies.

The generation of electric power is also more costly if the market for power is
politically segmented. Not only is the generation of power subject to scale economies,
but noncoincident peaks in demand cannot be pooled. The resulting volatility in
demand leads to installation of capacity that is idle most of the time and to energy
rationing. Energy is a fundamental input into both resource extraction and manufacturing. The recent power cuts in South Africa are reducing investment in resource
extraction, and high energy costs risk making manufacturing uncompetitive.

Potentially, the highest costs of political division arise from the interactions
between transport and power. The resource extraction sector is highly intensive in
both, especially in Africa, where mineral deposits are often far from the coast. If, as
in Guinea, the ore is exported unprocessed, it has a low value-to-weight ratio, and so
transport costs are high. Processing would reduce weight and therefore transport
costs, but very large energy inputs are required. In Africa the obvious source of non-
exportable energy is hydropower; the key input is rainfall on high ground, something
the continent has in abundance. This nontradable energy can potentially be transmitted to resource extraction sites and used to process ore that is then cheaply trans-
ported to the coast. The exploitation of such synergies may yield huge payoffs, but
they would also entail huge investments. Unfortunately, almost all such opportunities in Africa involve crossing frontiers between sovereign states. This returns us to
the holdup problem discussed above, but with an added dimension. The holdup
problem within a state can, at least in part, be addressed by law: the difficulty is that
of writing a contract sufficiently complete to cover all eventualities. The holdup
problem between states is radically more severe because the whole domain of international law is fragile. Essentially, the concept of national sovereignty constitutes a
barrier to the enforcement of any contract entered into by states.

Policy Implications: The Need for Integration

In aggregate, Africa is less populous and poorer than India, yet it is subdivided into
around 50 independent states. We have suggested that this radical political subdivi-
sion of an already small economy has inflicted a wide range of costs on African

citizens. The benefits of smoothing, with respect to both temporary shocks and underlying natural differences, are forgone. In the private economy, manufacturing and services have the potential for large-scale economies that are frustrated by political fragmentation. This skews Africa's comparative advantage toward those sectors and modes of production in which scale is less important, notably peasant agriculture. In the public sector, the lack of scale raises the costs of a wide range of public goods and thus accentuates the problem of undersupply intrinsic to low-income economies. These losses to the private and public economies are mutually reinforcing: low private incomes reduce state revenues and compound the underprovision of public goods, while the lack of public goods further reduces private incomes.

The evident implication is that Africa needs a process of political integration. Such processes have been common in other regions; over the last two centuries many states have chosen to create legal structures at the regional level that curtailed their own sovereignty. During the nineteenth century, power within the United States gradually shifted from the individual states to the federation. This shift in the locus of decision making is even detectable in language: before the American Civil War the term "the United States of America" was treated as a plural noun, but afterward it became singular. In the 1940s, the territories of British India decided that on independence they would divide into only two large polities, India and Pakistan, instead of reverting to the many small states that had preceded colonization. During the last half-century, the European Union has gradually expanded to 27 states that have agreed to limit sovereignty across a wide range of economic decisions.

Unlike Indian politicians, African politicians chose to dissolve the federations forged by the empires: the colonial map of Africa was far less fragmented than the current configuration, with Nigeria (Africa's largest country) the sole exception. Postcolonial political fragmentation enormously increased opportunities for the political class, multiplying by 50 the number of ministers required to govern the territory.

African governments have launched many initiatives aimed at greater regional integration. These include, at the political level, the Organization for African Unity and its successor, the African Union, and, at the economic level, an array of subregional trade arrangements too numerous to list. Yet the practical achievement in terms of economic integration falls far short of other regions. This is brought out by a comparison of Burundi with California, Maharashtra (India), and Germany. Viewed as economic units, California, Maharashtra, and Germany are each over a hundred times as large as Burundi. Yet as measured by autonomy in fiscal policy, monetary policy, trade policy, exchange rate policy, and the scope for judicial appeal against the government, the government of Burundi has radically more power than the governments of the other three. Since Burundi is such a small economic unit, its citizens' need for a supranational authority is much greater than is the case for Californians, Maharashtrans, and Germans, yet they have much less resort to one.

One reason why African efforts at greater political and economic integration have to date yielded so little may be that these efforts have themselves not been integrated. The approach to political integration has been by means of a pan-African entity, the African Union, which is so diverse as to be unwieldy. For example, it includes North

Africa, which identifies more closely with the Middle East than with Africa, and it requires agreement among 53 sovereign governments for any action.

By contrast, the approach to economic integration has been too limited, predominantly involving subregional trade agreements. These deals are so numerous and uncoordinated that they are mutually incompatible: governments have signed up to commitments that simply cannot all be met. This situation generates confusion and undermines the credibility of trade policies. More fundamentally, subregional trade deals between low-income countries give rise to economic forces that are likely to create severe political tensions. As Venables (2003) shows, they generate economic divergence, with the poorest members of the integration scheme losing in relation to the least-poor members. This is in stark contrast to regional integration arrangements between high-income countries, which generate forces for convergence. Indeed, even Venables's analysis probably underestimates the forces of divergence released by regional integration among low-income countries, since it rests only on the implications of comparative advantage. The forces unleashed by the scale economies discussed above imply further forces for divergence—with, for example, the economically largest cities, such as Nairobi, Johannesburg, and Lagos, gaining at the expense of initially smaller cities in their respective regions. Hence, the politics of Africa's subregional trade schemes are almost inevitably going to be fraught.

A more promising alternative would be to learn from three aspects of successful integration in other regions. First, political and economic integration should go hand in hand; supranational entities have to acquire real sovereignty over particular domains of economic activity. For example, currently, despite the many subregional trade arrangements, each African country has been negotiating individually both with the World Trade Organization (WTO) and, for economic partnership agreements (EPAs), with the European Union. By contrast, the trade policies of each member country of the European Union are genuinely locked in common, and so negotiation at the WTO and for the EPAs is conducted by the European Commission rather than by each member country individually.

Second, integration is easier if it grows from a small core of states among which none is too dominant. In Europe integration started with just 6 countries and has progressively expanded to 27. The United States grew from a core of 13 founding states to its present total of 50. In Africa the most promising such nucleus is the East African Community (EAC), which has a core of three similarly sized states and has already added two new members. The EAC has the advantage that it is building political institutions which might acquire real sovereignty over some aspects of policy, alongside steps toward economic integration.

Third, the economic agenda should be considerably broader than trade policy. There is scope for common rules on a wide range of economic policies—for example, on investment and taxation, which would enhance credibility. There is room for the provision of common infrastructure; the East African Community used to run an integrated rail system, and power generation and distribution would be better handled at the subregional level. Unlike trade agreements, these other areas of policy cooperation are likely to generate mutual gains, so that the economic consequences will reinforce rather than undermine the political process.

Finally, we might note that the political stresses produced by poverty have tended to be perverse. What is needed is a stronger impetus toward unity, but poverty is a fertile breeding ground for xenophobia and division. During 2008, there were riots in Johannesburg against immigration from Zimbabwe, as well as de facto ethnic partition in Kenya. The vision of African unity pioneered by Kwame Nkrumah and Julius Nyerere is in need of serious revival.

Notes

The authors thank Mauro Caselli, Lisa Chauvet, Anke Hoeffler, Hyesung Kim, and Jean-Louis Warnholz for statistical analyses.

This work was supported by the BP-funded Oxford Centre for the Analysis of Resource Rich Economies (OxCarre) and by the Centre for the Study of African Economies (CSAE). This research benefited from funding by the UK Department for International Development (DFID) as part of the iiG, a research programme to study how to improve institutions for pro-poor growth in Africa and South-Asia. The views expressed are not necessarily those of DFID.

1. "Dutch disease" takes its name from the supposed effects of North Sea natural gas discoveries on the Netherlands economy.
2. See Collier (2009) for a detailed account of this sequence.
3. These output loss costs are likely to be underestimates because they omit longer-term effects. Collier and Goderis (2008a) find that unless governance is good, dependence on commodity exports has adverse effects on long-term growth. The mismanagement of volatility may be one of the routes by which poor governance has these adverse long-term effects.
4. Benedikt Goderis undertook the substantial work involved in these recalculations.

References

Alcalá, Francisco, and Antonio Ciccone. 2003. "Trade, Extent of the Market, and Economic Growth 1960–66." Economics Working Paper 765, Department of Economics and Business, Universitat Pompeu Fabra, Barcelona, Spain. http://www.econ.upf.edu/en/research/onepaper.php?id=765.

Alesina, Alberto, Enrico Spolaore, and Romaine Wacziarg. 2005. "Trade, Growth and the Size of Countries." In Handbook of Economic Growth, ed. Philippe Aghion and Steven Durlauf. Amsterdam: North-Holland.

Au, Chun-Chung, and J. Vernon Henderson. 2006. "Are Chinese Cities Too Small?" Review of Economic Studies 73 (3): 549–76.

Barrett, Scott. 2007. Why Cooperate? The Incentive to Supply Global Public Goods. Oxford, U.K.: Oxford University Press.

Besley, Timothy J., and Masayuki Kudamatsu. 2007. "Making Autocracy Work." CEPR Discussion Paper 6371, Centre for Economic Policy Research, London.

Caselli, Francesco, and James Feyrer. 2007. "The Marginal Product of Capital." Quarterly Journal of Economics 122 (2, May): 535–68.

Chauvet, Lisa, and Paul Collier. 2008. "What Are the Preconditions for Turnarounds in Failing States?" Conflict Management and Peace Science 25 (4, September): 332–48.

Collier, Paul. 2007. *The Bottom Billion: Why the Poorest Countries Are Failing and What Can Be Done about It.* Oxford, U.K.: Oxford University Press.

———. 2009. *Wars, Guns, and Votes: Democracy in Dangerous Places.* New York: Harper-Collins.

Collier, Paul, and Benedikt Goderis. 2008a. "Commodity Prices, Growth, and the Natural Resource Curse: Reconciling a Conundrum." Centre for the Study of African Economies, Oxford University, Oxford, U.K.

———. 2008b. "Structural Policies for Shock-Prone Commodity Exporters." Centre for the Study of African Economies, Oxford University, Oxford, U.K.

———. 2009. "Does Aid Mitigate External Shocks?" *Review of Development Economics* 13 (3): 429–51.

Collier, Paul, and Anke Hoeffler. 2007. "Unintended Consequences: Does Aid Promote Arms Races?" *Oxford Bulletin of Economics and Statistics* 69 (1): 1–28.

Collier, Paul, Anke Hoeffler, and Dominic Rohner. 2009. "Beyond Greed and Grievance: Feasibility and Civil War." *Oxford Economic Papers* 61 (1, January): 1–27.

Collier, Paul, and Anthony J. Venables. 2007. "Rethinking Trade Preferences: How Africa Can Diversify Its Exports." *World Economy* 30 (8, August): 1326–45.

Commission on Growth and Development. 2008. *The Growth Report: Strategies for Sustained Growth and Inclusive Development.* Washington, DC: World Bank.

Cook, Lisa D., and Jeffrey Sachs. 1999. "Regional Public Goods in International Assistance." In *Global Public Goods: International Cooperation in the 21st Century,* ed. Inge Kaul, Isabelle Grunberg, and Marc Stern. New York: United Nations Development Programme and Oxford University Press.

Gabaix, X., and Y. Ioannides. 2004. "The Evolution of City Size Distributions." In *Handbook of Urban and Regional Economics.* Vol. 4, *Cities and Geography,* ed. J. Vernon Henderson, and Jacques-François Thisse. Amsterdam: North-Holland.

Helliwell, John F. 1997. "National Borders, Trade and Migration." *Pacific Economic Review* 2 (3): 165–85.

Jones, Ben, and Ben Olken. 2005. "The Anatomy of Start-Stop Growth." NBER Working Paper 11528. National Bureau of Economic Research, Cambridge, MA.

Limão, Nuno, and Anthony J. Venables. 2001. "Infrastructure, Geographical Disadvantage, Transport Costs and Trade." *World Bank Economic Review* 15 (3): 451–79.

McCallum, John. 1995. "National Borders Matter: Canada–U. S. Regional Trade Patterns." *American Economic Review* 85 (3): 615–23.

Rose, Andrew K. 2006. "Size Really Doesn't Matter: In Search of a National Scale Effect." *Journal of the Japanese and International Economies* 20 (4, December): 482–507.

Rosenthal, S. S., and W. C. Strange. 2004. "Evidence on the Nature and Sources of Agglomeration Economies." In *Handbook of Urban and Regional Economics.* Vol. 4, *Cities and Geography,* ed. J. Vernon Henderson and Jacques-François Thisse. Amsterdam: North-Holland.

Teravaninthorn, Supee, and Gaël Raballand. 2008. *Transport Prices and Costs in Africa: A Review of the International Corridors.* Washington, DC: World Bank.

Venables, Anthony J. 2003. "Winners and Losers from Regional Integration Agreements." *Economic Journal* 113 (490, October): 747–61.

Wigstrom, Christian. 2008. "Does Size Matter?" Master of philosophy thesis, Oxford University, Oxford, U.K.

World Bank. 2007. *World Development Indicators 2007.* Washington, DC: World Bank.

Protectionist Policies and Manufacturing Trade Flows in Africa

LAWRENCE EDWARDS

It is well known that Africa's share of world trade is declining. Policy prescriptions vary widely, covering tariff liberalization, policies to facilitate output growth, and improvements in trade-related infrastructure and institutions. This study evaluates trade performance and tariff liberalization in Sub-Saharan African countries since the early 1990s. It also estimates the impact of tariff liberalization on manufacturing trade flows in Africa and other developing countries between 1990 and 2004, using sector-level data and direct measures of tariff protection. Three key results emerge. First, African countries continue to be marginalized in world trade, although there is evidence of improved competitiveness, particularly in manufacturing. Second, tariff liberalization, starting in the early 1990s, has had a positive effect on manufacturing trade flows, but its contribution to the overall growth of trade has been small. African countries are no different from other developing countries in this regard. Third, tariff liberalization in developing countries is often associated with a worsening manufacturing trade balance, but this is not necessarily so in Africa.

The marginalization of Africa in world trade is well recognized. Early evidence from a World Bank research program in the mid-1990s (Amjadi and Yeats 1995; Amjadi, Reincke, and Yeats 1996; Ng and Yeats 1996) found that Sub-Saharan Africa's share in world trade declined dramatically between the 1950s and the early 1990s, from more than 3 percent to less than 1 percent. Views on the source of this deterioration vary widely. Policy prescriptions alternatively emphasize tariff liberalization (Amjadi, Reincke, and Yeats 1996; Ng and Yeats 1996), policies to facilitate output growth (Rodrik 1997), and improvements in trade-related infrastructure and institutions (Limão and Venables 2001; Wilson, Mann, and Otsuki 2005; Djankov, Freund, and Pham 2006).

This paper focuses, in particular, on the effect of tariff liberalization on trade performance in Sub-Saharan Africa. It begins with a comparative analysis of trade flows and trade liberalization in Africa during the 1990s. This was a period of considerable

Lawrence Edwards is an associate professor at the School of Economics, University of Cape Town, South Africa.

Annual World Bank Conference on Development Economics 2009, Global

© 2010 The International Bank for Reconstruction and Development / The World Bank.

tariff reform for many developing and middle-income economies. How Africa fared relative to its counterparts is explored in some detail.

Next, the contribution of tariff liberalization to changes in manufactured exports, manufactured imports, and the trade balance in developing economies, including Africa, between 1990 and 2004 is estimated. The focus on manufacturing partly reflects data constraints but also the emphasis in the literature on the association between manufacturing and growth acceleration, externalities, learning by doing, and returns to scale. An important focus of the paper is the effect of tariff liberalization on export performance through reductions in the cost of inputs. Manufacturing goods, which are relatively import intensive and are often more dependent on processed inputs than primary products, are more suitable for such an analysis.

Where the paper makes a contribution in this field is that the empirical analysis draws on sector-level data (28 manufacturing sectors) and direct measures of tariff protection, as opposed to aggregate data and dummy variables for liberalization periods. Three key results emerge. First, African countries continue to be marginalized in world trade—even though there is evidence of improved competitiveness, particularly in manufacturing, and many countries in the region have experienced considerable tariff liberalization, despite only limited offers in the Uruguay Round of the General Agreement on Tariffs and Trade (GATT).

Second, tariff liberalization has had a statistically significant and positive effect on manufacturing trade flows in developing countries, but its contribution to overall growth in trade has been small. Africa is no different from other developing countries in this regard, although high import tariffs on intermediate and capital inputs continue to restrict exports from several countries of the continent.

Third, tariff liberalization is often associated with a worsening manufacturing trade balance in developing countries (although the evidence for Africa is weaker). The effect, however, is small, so tariff liberalization is unlikely to lead to a substantial increase in the trade deficit or to the emergence of an external constraint on growth.

The next section reviews the existing empirical literature on the effect of trade barriers on trade performance in developing economies. A comparative analysis of trade flows and trade reform in Africa and other developing economies from the early 1990s follows. Various estimates are then presented of the relationship between trade liberalization and manufactured exports, manufactured imports, and the trade balance for 50 economies, including 30 developing economies (10 in Africa), over the period 1990 to 2004. The paper concludes with a summary of the key findings and some policy recommendations.

Trade Barriers and Trade Performance in Developing Economies

In traditional trade theory, tariff barriers restrict trade flows. The effect of tariffs on imports is intuitive: by increasing the relative price of imported goods, tariffs induce consumption shifts toward domestically produced substitutes. The negative effect of import tariffs on export performance is not as well appreciated, yet as Lerner (1936) pointed out, an import tariff can have an impact on export volumes equivalent to that of an export tax. By conferring protection on import-competing sectors, import tariffs draw resources toward these sectors and away from other sectors of the economy, including those that export.

Import barriers, particularly on intermediate inputs, also raise production costs and reduce the profitability of export production. This is expected to be particularly important for exports of manufactured products, which use a high proportion of intermediate and capital goods in the production process, compared with goods produced in the primary sector. The fragmentation and global outsourcing of production processes also require that manufacturing firms be integrated into global value chains, which, in turn, necessitates cheap access to imported intermediate inputs. Tariff liberalization is therefore expected to stimulate both import and export volumes.

To some extent, these relationships are born out by the empirical evidence, including that for Africa.[1] Rodrik (1997), for example, estimates that a 10 percentage point reduction in trade taxes is associated with a 17 percentage point increase in the ratio of trade to gross domestic product (GDP) in a sample of 37 Sub-Saharan African countries over the period 1964–94. Although he emphasizes the relatively greater importance of per capita income and geography as determinants of the region's trade flows, these results suggest that, on average, taxes on international trade (exports plus imports) in the early 1990s were associated with a 12 percentage point reduction in the ratio of total trade of goods and services to GDP in Sub-Saharan African countries—a large value compared with the average trade-to-GDP ratio of 68 percent for these countries over the same period.[2]

Another relevant study is that of Santos-Paulino and Thirlwall (2004), who evaluate the effects of trade liberalization on aggregate import and export growth and the trade balance, using a pooled sample of 22 developing countries covering the mid-1970s to late 1990s. Import and export taxes, measured using collection duties, reduce import and export growth, but the effect is marginal. By far the largest impact on growth of trade volumes and the trade balance in their estimates is attributed to the dummy variable used to signify periods of trade liberalization. Africa is found to be particularly sensitive to trade liberalization, with import growth rising by 8.4 percentage points (as against an average of 6.19 percentage points for all countries) and export growth rising by a lower 3.58 percentage points (compared with 1.56 percentage points for all countries).

Liberalization is therefore associated with a worsening of the trade balance in developing countries, which can lead to an external constraint on growth. The estimates suggest that the trade balance in developing countries worsens by more than 2 percent of GDP during liberalization periods. Similar estimates (2.8 percent of GDP) are found by the United Nations Conference on Trade and Development (UNCTAD 1999), using a sample of 16 developing countries over the period 1970–95. By contrast, Parikh and Stirbu (2004) find a more mixed set of results, with the trade balance improving during liberalization in 10 of the 29 developing countries for which significant results are obtained. There is, therefore, substantial heterogeneity in the response of trade flows to liberalization across developing countries.

These studies have some serious limitations. The first is the use of a dummy variable to estimate the effect of liberalization on trade flows. This holds as well for other studies in this field (Papageorgiou, Michaely, and Choksi 1991; Greenaway and Sapsford 1994; Bleaney 1999). Trade liberalization periods are frequently accompanied by numerous other policy reforms, the effect of which will also be attributed to the dummy variable. The result may be to bias estimates of export growth from trade liberalization downward and those for import growth upward if improved confidence in the country leads to capital inflows and an appreciation of the currency, as was experienced in a number of developing countries (Bleaney 1999; UNCTAD 1999).

Dummy variables also do not adequately account for trade liberalization involving different protection instruments (tariffs, nontariff barriers, export taxes, and trade subsidies) or variations in the pace and depth of reform across countries. Definition of the commencement of the liberalization period therefore depends crucially on the definition of liberalization employed and on the aspects of the reform process that are emphasized (Santos-Paulino 2005).

A second limitation of these studies is that the mechanisms through which liberalization influences trade flows, particularly exports, are not adequately specified in the trade functions estimated. For example, the effects of lower tariffs on imports, particularly on intermediate inputs, are not included in many of the export relationships. Yet the available evidence suggests that the effect of input tariffs on export volumes can be large. Collier and Venables (2007) estimate that the waiver on the rule of origin for textile inputs for some Sub-Saharan African countries is a significant source of the quadrupling of apparel exports to the United States in response to the African Growth and Opportunity Act (AGOA). Edwards and Lawrence (2008) analyze 44 manufacturing sectors in South Africa from 1990 to 2002 and find that reductions in input costs from liberalization contributed significantly to improved export growth, particularly of noncommodity manufactures.

This leads to the third limitation. Trade liberalization has nonuniform effects across sectors of the economy. The export sector consists of heterogeneous firms and industries, and the effect of liberalization on export performance is expected to differ among them. Yet the bulk of the studies, in particular the cross-country studies, analyze aggregate export performance. It could be extremely misleading to draw implications from the aggregate cross-country studies about the likely impact of liberalization on developing economies without taking account of structural and compositional differences between countries. There is a need, therefore, to supplement the aggregate analysis with firm- or sector-level studies.

Trade Policy Reform and Trade Performance in Africa from the Early 1990s

This section evaluates Africa's export performance and trade policy reform in the 1990s. The discussion provides the background for the empirical analysis that follows.

Export Performance

The source of Africa's marginalization in world trade prior to the 1990s was two-pronged: "[Africa] experienced declining market shares for its major exports which, in turn, were of declining relative importance in world trade" (Ng and Yeats 1996, 8). To evaluate post-1990 trends, a similar decomposition is conducted using country-level data obtained from the World Development Indicators (WDI) database and product-level data from the United Nations Commodity Trade Statistics Database (Comtrade), SITC rev. 2, at the three-digit level.[3] Only countries for which data are available in both periods are included in the analysis.

Figure 1 presents a comparative perspective of merchandise exports from Sub-Saharan Africa in current prices and in constant prices between 1990 and 2006. The data are obtained from the WDI and cover 99 countries, 37 of which are in Sub-Saharan Africa. The country sample accounts for between 70 and 75 percent of the total available value of exports in each period; for Sub-Saharan Africa the figure is 93–97 percent. Sub-Saharan Africa is split into the Southern African Customs Union (SACU) and the rest of Sub-Saharan Africa (RSSA). The latter group is further sub-divided into low-income and middle-income countries.[4]

The continued marginalization of Sub-Saharan Africa in world trade during the 1990s is clearly depicted in figure 1. Export performance in all the country groupings for Sub-Saharan Africa was poor in relation to world performance during the decade, whether exports are measured in nominal or in real terms. By contrast, from 2000 on, the value of Sub-Saharan African exports (in U.S. dollars) grew sharply, and by 2006 the figure had almost tripled. Much of this growth is related to the commodity price boom. For example, the very strong export growth experienced by middle-income Sub-Saharan Africa outside the SACU is almost entirely assignable to the oil-rich countries of Equatorial Guinea and Angola, which experienced an oil price boom. Measured in volume, Sub-Saharan Africa's export performance after 2000 is substantially weaker.[5]

As a consequence, whereas Sub-Saharan Africa's share of world exports in value terms was around 2.7 percent in both 1990 and 2006, in volume terms its share declined from 2.6 to 1.6 percent over the period. The marginalization of Sub-Saharan Africa in world exports is more drastic when the region is compared with other developing countries. Sub-Saharan Africa's share of developing-country exports falls from 15.6 to 8.0 percent when current U.S. dollar values are used and from 13.8 to 5.2 percent when export volume data (in 2000 prices) are used.

The substantial heterogeneity in export performance across countries within Sub-Saharan Africa can be seen in figure 2, which presents average annual growth in merchandise export volumes by country between 1990 and 2006. In most countries of the region, export growth was relatively poor, exceeding the world average (7 percent per year) in 11 cases and the developing-country average of 11 percent per year in only 4 cases—Mozambique, Lesotho, Sudan, and Uganda.

Further insights into the source of the region's marginalization in world trade can be obtained through a more disaggregated analysis of trade flows. Table 1 presents a constant-market-shares analysis in which export growth is decomposed into changes

FIGURE 1.
Merchandise Exports: World and Sub-Saharan Africa, 1990–2006

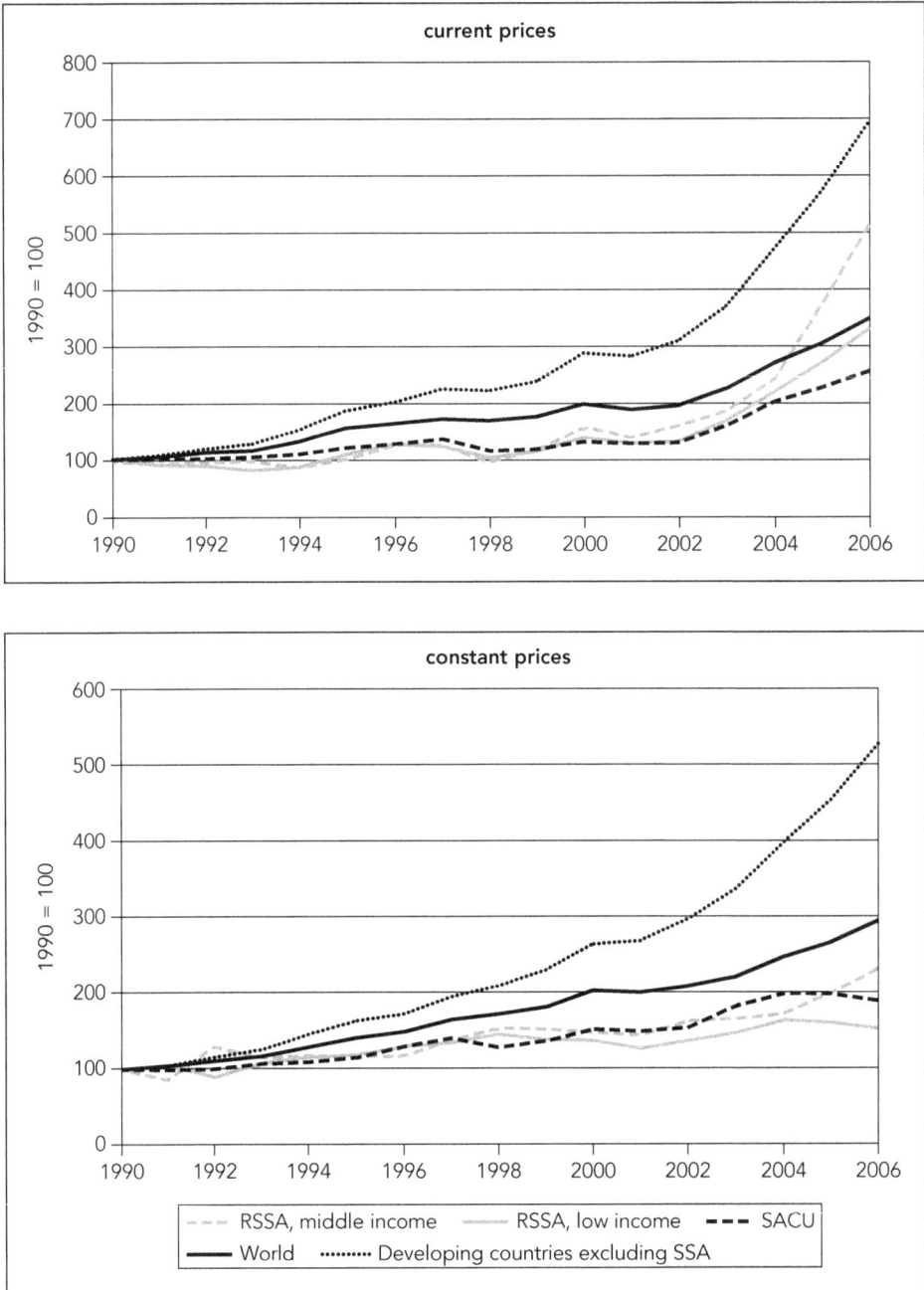

Source: Own calculations using data from World Development Indicators database.

Note: RSSA, rest of Sub-Saharan Africa; SACU, Southern African Customs Union; SSA, Sub-Saharan Africa. Export volumes are converted to values using 2000 prices in U.S. dollars.

FIGURE 2.
Average Annual Growth in Merchandise Export Volume, by Sub-Saharan
African Country, 1990–2006

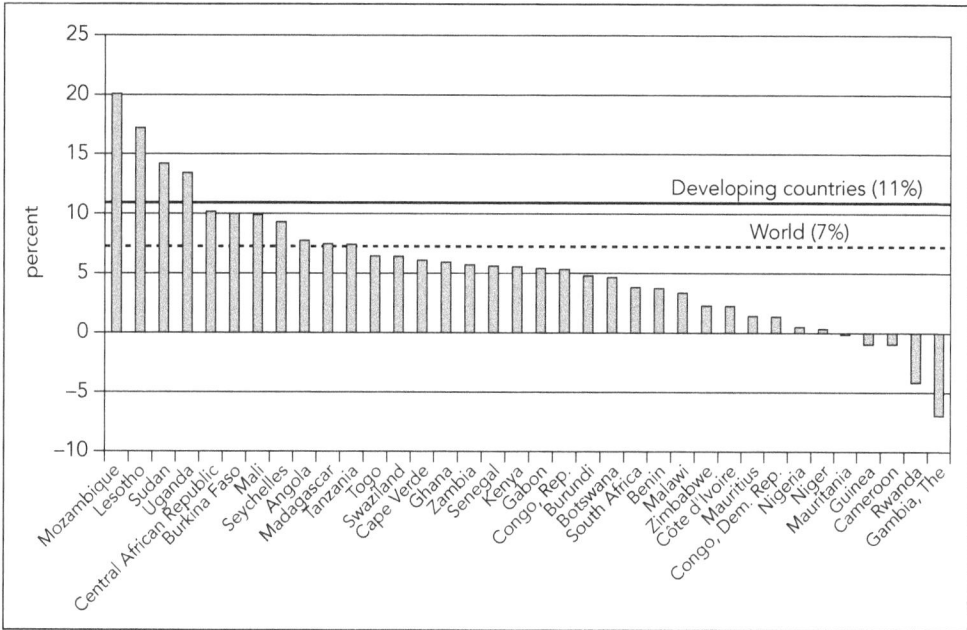

Source: Own calculations using data from World Development Indicators database.

attributable to growth in world exports, favorable or unfavorable structural concentration in products, and changes in relative competitiveness (Richardson 1971). The approach followed is similar to that of Ng and Yeats (1996). The data are drawn from UN Comtrade, and the classification is based on the three-digit-level SITC rev. 2.[6] The sample includes 89 countries, 25 of which are in Sub-Saharan Africa.

Looking first at total trade, if South Africa and Sub-Saharan Africa excluding South Africa had retained their 1990–91 market shares, the total value of exports in 2005–6 would have been 216 percent higher. Instead, the value of exports for South Africa and for Sub-Saharan Africa excluding South Africa rose by 127 and 188 percent, respectively. A substantial part of this shortfall (30 to 50 percent of initial export values) can be attributed to the region's concentration in products that grew relatively slowly during the period. For example, world trade in primary products and resource-based manufactures, which account for between 80 and 90 percent of Sub-Saharan Africa's exports, maintained a constant share in world trade, but high-technology products, of which the region exports very little, rose from 16 to 20 percent of total world trade.

Declining competitiveness, measured by declining world market share at the product level, also contributed to the shortfall for South Africa (−59 percent), but not for Sub-Saharan Africa excluding South Africa, where the competitiveness effect was positive, at 24 percent. As shown in row 5 in the table, a substantial portion (17 percentage

TABLE 1. Constant-Market-Shares Analysis: Sources of Export Growth, World Regions and Sub-Saharan Africa, 1990–91 to 2005–6

(change as percent of 1990–91 values, in U.S. dollars, except as otherwise specified)

	Developing countries	High-income (OECD)	South Africa	Sub-Saharan Africa, excluding South Africa
All products				
1. Total change	492	155	127	188
2. Product composition effect	−7	−2	−30	−52
3. Competitiveness effect	283	−58	−59	24
4. World growth effect	216	216	216	216
5. Competitiveness in growing commodities	196	−41	−38	17
Initial trade value (billions of U.S. dollars)	404	2,453	24	19
Manufacturing				
6. Total change	680	157	300	290
7. Product composition effect	−12	−2	−22	−61
8. Competitiveness effect	464	−63	99	128
9. World growth effect	222	222	222	222
10. Competitiveness in growing commodities	325	−45	64	95
Initial trade value (billions of U.S. dollars)	241	2,138	8	6

Source: Own calculations using UN Comtrade data at the three-digit Standard International Trade Classification (SITC) level and initial period shares as weights.

Note: Low-income, middle-income, and developing-country results include Sub-Saharan Africa. The decomposition is calculated as

$$\Delta q = s^0 \Delta Q + \left[\sum_i s_i^0 \Delta Q_i - s^0 \Delta Q \right] + \sum_i Q_i^1 \Delta s_i,$$

where q is total exports of the focus country, s is the export share of the focus country, Q is total exports, the subscript i refers to commodity, and the superscripts 0 and 1 refer to initial and final periods. The first term on the right-hand side is the world growth effect, the second term is the commodity effect, and the final term is the competitive effect. See Richardson (1971) for some of the shortcomings of this approach.

points) of the improved competitiveness effect for that subgroup has been driven by a restructuring of exports toward rapidly growing products.

The results for manufacturing are more positive. The world market share of South Africa and for Sub-Saharan Africa excluding South Africa rose during the period, as reflected in the 290–300 percent increase in export value compared with the 222 percent increase in world trade. Although poor product composition reduced growth, it was more than offset by improvements in competitiveness and by structural shifts toward rapidly growing products (row 10).

The trends in Sub-Saharan African trade identified by Ng and Yeats (1996) in the four decades prior to 1990 are thus only partly replicated in the subsequent period. Although exports continue to be concentrated in products with stagnant shares in

FIGURE 3.
Merchandise Exports as a Share of GDP: Country Average, by Income Group and for Sub-Saharan Africa, 1990–2006

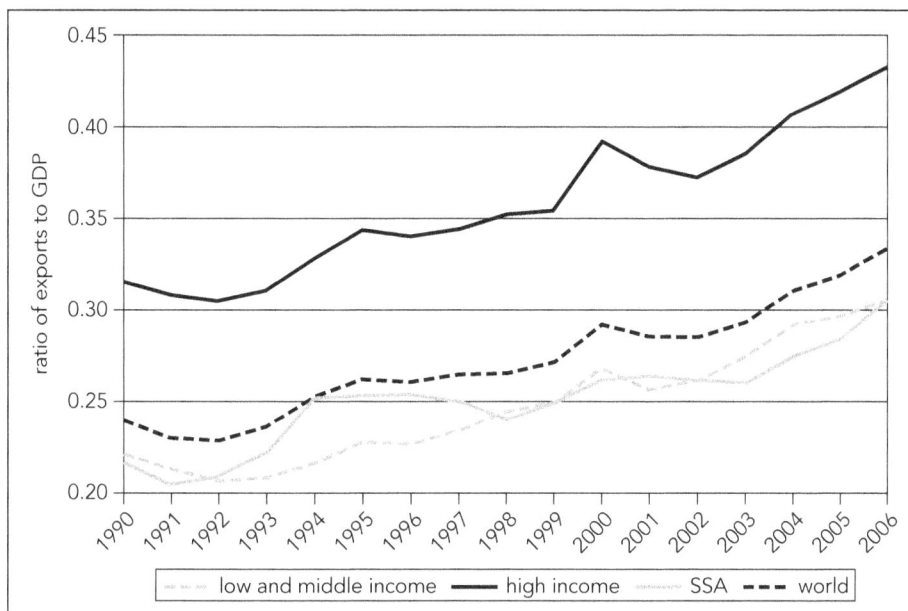

Source: Own calculations using data from World Development Indicators database.

Note: GDP, gross domestic product; SSA, Sub-Saharan Africa. The sample consists of 99 countries, 37 of which are in Sub-Saharan Africa. Values reflect the simple country average for the region or income group.

world markets, the region has managed to increase its world market share in many products, including those that are growing rapidly.

Two important caveats to this conclusion need to be highlighted. First, the world experienced a commodity price boom during the latter part of the period analyzed, and the surge had a considerable impact on the value of Sub-Saharan Africa's exports, as can be seen in figure 1. Growth in trade volumes remains relatively weak in Africa, and a fall in commodity prices, as has been experienced recently, will adversely affect Sub-Saharan Africa's share of world trade.

Second, alternative indicators, such as the ratio of exports (or trade) to domestic GDP, lead to different interpretations of the extent to which Sub-Saharan Africa is marginalized in world trade. Figure 3 presents this ratio using merchandise exports for Sub-Saharan Africa and for income-group categories. What is striking is that the level and growth of the ratio of merchandise exports to GDP for the average Sub-Saharan African country is very similar to the average for all low-income and middle-income economies between 1990 and 2006. The region's trade performance from 1990 on is no different from that of other developing countries, once bench-marked against GDP.[7] An implication is that Sub-Saharan Africa's declining share in world trade may largely be a consequence of relatively poor economic growth, as is argued by Rodrik (1997). Nevertheless, even with this indicator, the region remains less open than the world average.

Tariff Reform

Comparisons of protection across countries are fraught with difficulties. These include the lack of consistent protection data over time, problems in calculating ad valorem equivalents for non–ad valorem tariff rates and nontariff barriers, and various biases associated with the aggregation process (Anderson and Neary 1994). Nonetheless, an evaluation of protection using nominal tariff data is possible and allows for an instructive comparative analysis of trade reform across countries.

To pursue such an analysis, detailed most favored nation (MFN) and applied tariff data are obtained for 115 countries from UNCTAD's Trade Analysis and Information System (TRAINS) database for the period 1990 to 2006. The countries are made up as follows: low income, 26; lower middle income, 33; upper middle income, 31; high income countries not members of the Organisation for Economic Co-operation and Development (OECD), 14; and OECD countries, 11. The sample includes 29 African countries, some of which are North African. Only those countries in which average protection in both periods can be calculated are included.[8]

An important limitation is that the tariff rates do not include ad valorem equivalents for non–ad valorem tariff rates. This limitation mainly affects agriculture, where non–ad valorem tariffs are used extensively, but it remains an important caveat affecting the interpretation of the data.

Figure 4 shows the maximum, minimum, and simple average MFN tariff for various country groups for two periods: 1990–95 and 2004–6. The simple country average rather than the import-weighted average of the corresponding measure for the individual countries is presented. This avoids domination by any individual country—for example, South Africa in Africa, India in the low-income group, and China in the lower-middle-income group. The country-level observation is the import-weighted average tariff for the periods 1990–95 and 2004–6.

A number of observations can be drawn from the data. There has been a considerable reduction in average MFN tariffs for all income groups since the early 1990s. Low-income economies experienced relatively large decreases in the average MFN tariff, from 22 to 12.3 percent. Middle-income economies saw slightly smaller declines in MFN protection, although the initial tariffs were far lower than in low-income economies. MFN tariffs also fell in African economies, from 19 to 13 percent, despite the meager offers made in the Uruguay Round to reduce bound rates (Wang and Winters 1998). The decline in protection is roughly equivalent to that in middle-income economies but is less than in the average low-income economy.

The average change hides substantial variation in the extent of tariff liberalization across countries. As shown in figure 4, the spread of tariff rates across countries declined in almost all groups, including Africa. The narrowing of the range is greatest for low-income countries, as a result of substantial reductions in the average tariff in Bangladesh, which fell from 76 to 18.2 percent over the period.

The extent of liberalization across African economies also varies widely. Figure 5 presents the estimated percentage change in MFN tariffs for the sample of African economies. The extent of liberalization is calculated as $(t_1 - t_0)/(1 + t_0)$, where t_1

FIGURE 4.
Maximum, Minimum, and Average Country Tariff by Region and Period, Most Favored Nation (MFN) Tariffs. 1990–95 and 2004–6

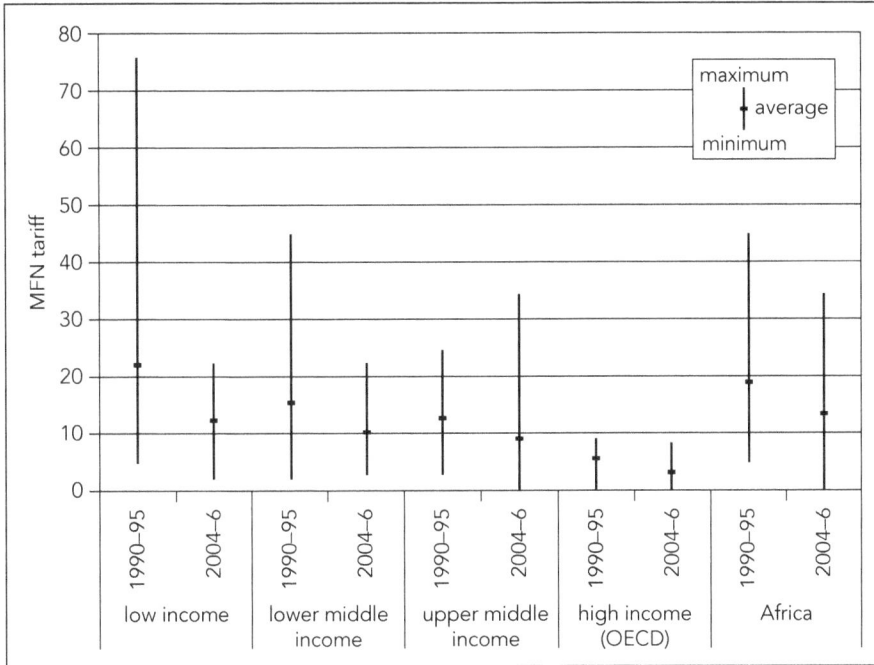

Source: UNCTAD Trade Analysis and Information System (TRAINS) database and own calculations.

Note: OECD, Organisation for Economic Co-operation and Development; UNCTAD, United Nations Conference on Trade and Development. The sample consists of 115 countries for which data are available for both periods. The Africa sample includes North African countries.

and t_0 refer to tariff rates in the final and initial periods, respectively. This is therefore an estimate of the percentage change in the tariff-inclusive border price.

Large decreases (greater than 10 percent) in the import-weighted average MFN tariff are found in Morocco, Libya, Mauritius, and Côte d'Ivoire. These economies had average protection rates in excess of 20 percent and up to 45 percent, in the case of Morocco in 1990–91. By 2004–6 average protection had fallen to 19 percent in Morocco, 12 percent in Nigeria, and less than 10 percent in the others.

Protection also rose in a number of African economies, with particularly large increases (more than 5 percent) for the Seychelles. Smaller increases were experienced in Ghana, Madagascar, and the Central African Republic. Some of this increase reflects changes in tariff rates, but shifts in the composition of import weights and the tariffication of nontariff barriers also affect the average.

Overall, more than half (16) of the 29 African economies that were studied experienced tariff reductions greater than the simple country average of all 115 countries in the sample (3.9 percent). This indicates that many African economies have opened up considerably from the early 1990s. The decline in tariffs, however, comes off a high base, and current protection rates remain relatively high. The average level of

FIGURE 5.

Change in Import-Weighted Most Favored Nation (MFN) Tariff, Selected African Countries, 1990–95 to 2004–6

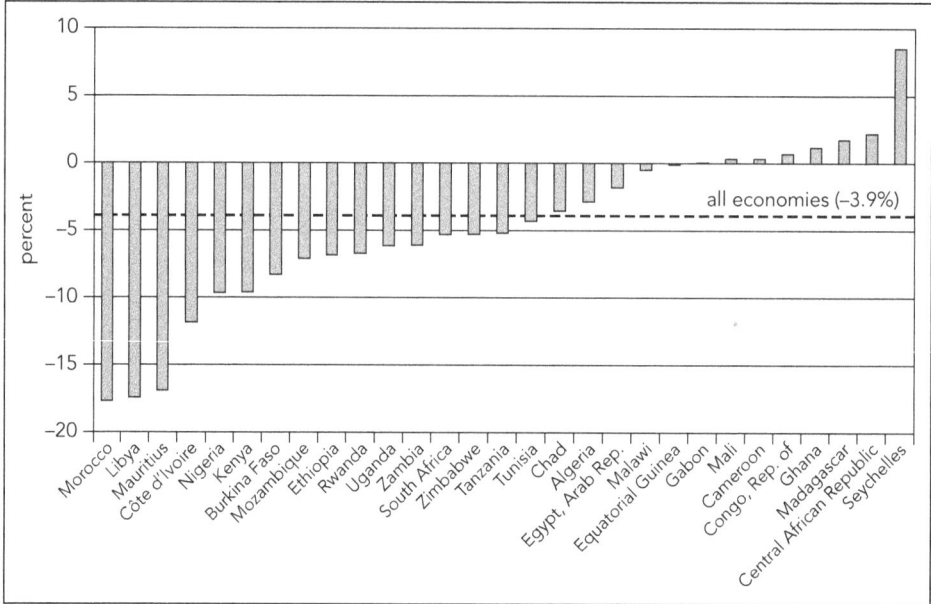

Source: UNCTAD Trade Analysis and Information System (TRAINS) database.

Note: UNCTAD, United Nations Conference on Trade and Development.

MFN protection, at 13.1 percent for African economies in 2004–6, exceeds that of low-income economies (12.3 percent), middle-income economies (9.2–10.2 percent), and OECD countries (3.1 percent); see table 2. This is also the case at the disaggregated country level. Average protection exceeds the simple country average of all low-income and middle-income economies (10.5 percent) in 19 of the 29 African economies in the sample.[9]

Up to now, the focus has been on MFN rates. Table 2 presents data on levels of and changes in applied tariffs that include preferences granted under the various preferential trade agreements. The data show more extensive liberalization from the early 1990s in response to the implementation of various preferential trade agreements during this period. Current applied rates are lower than MFN rates. The difference, however, does not appear substantial and does not alter any of the conclusions drawn on the basis of the MFN rates.

The aggregate data, again, hide considerable variation in protection at the sector level. Of particular interest for this paper is the extent to which liberalization reduces the cost of accessing key intermediate inputs. To evaluate this, table 2 presents the simple average tariff and change in tariffs on consumer, intermediate, and capital goods for Sub-Saharan Africa and by income group. The end-use categorization is based on the broad economic category (BEC) classification of the United Nations

TABLE 2. Simple Average Protection by End Use, Country Income Groups and Sub-Saharan Africa, 1990–95 and 2004–6

(percent)

	Capital goods			Consumption goods			Intermediate goods			Passenger vehicles			Total		
	1990–95	2004–6	Change	1990–95	2004–6	Change	1990–95	2004–6	Change	1990–95	2004–6	Change	1990–95	2004–6	Change
Mean import-weighted tariff, MFN															
Low income	19.4	8.6	−7.7	28.6	18.4	−7.0	20.4	11.4	−6.6	48.9	28.2	−11.1	22.1	12.3	−7.3
Lower middle income	13.2	6.7	−5.3	21.3	17.4	−2.6	13.9	8.7	−4.2	41.9	28.2	−6.5	15.3	10.2	−4.1
Upper middle income	11.5	6.0	−4.7	17.6	15.5	−1.9	10.3	6.3	−3.6	32.4	23.9	−4.9	12.6	9.2	−2.9
OECD	4.6	1.6	−2.9	9.9	5.8	−3.7	4.2	2.2	−1.9	9.4	5.7	−3.2	5.8	3.1	−2.5
Sub-Saharan Africa	16.2	8.0	−6.6	25.3	21.6	−2.5	17.2	11.1	−5.0	43.3	25.3	−11.1	19.0	13.1	−4.8
Simple average applied tariff															
Low income	18.6	8.2	−7.5	27.0	16.4	−7.4	19.3	9.7	−7.2	47.1	27.2	−10.6	21.0	10.8	−7.6
Lower middle income	12.7	6.0	−5.5	20.4	14.7	−4.0	13.3	7.1	−5.1	40.7	25.5	−7.4	14.7	8.6	−5.0
Upper middle income	11.3	4.6	−5.7	17.1	12.4	−4.2	10.1	4.4	−5.1	32.3	18.4	−9.3	12.3	7.0	−4.7
OECD	3.9	1.2	−2.6	8.0	4.4	−3.3	3.4	1.8	−1.6	9.0	4.9	−3.6	4.7	2.4	−2.2
Sub-Saharan Africa	16.1	7.7	−6.8	24.8	20.0	−3.4	16.8	9.4	−6.0	43.2	24.9	−11.3	18.7	11.8	−5.6

Source: Own calculations using data from UNCTAD Trade Analysis and Information System (TRAINS).

Note: MFN, most favored nation; OECD, Organisation for Economic Co-operation and Development; UNCTAD, United Nations Conference on Trade and Development.

Statistics Division. Passenger vehicles (BEC 51) are included as a separate item because they are both an intermediate good and a final consumer good.

The data show that the decline in tariffs from the early 1990s in African countries has been concentrated in capital and intermediate inputs. There was little liberalization of tariffs on consumer goods; they declined from 25.3 to 21.6 percent, which would have raised effective protection on consumer goods in many of the African countries sampled. Despite reductions of MFN tariffs on capital and intermediate goods, tariffs on these products remain high (8.0 and 11.1 percent, respectively). The tariffs continue to tax production and impose a barrier to exports, particularly of manufactured goods, where inputs constitute a relatively high proportion of overall production costs. The impact on Africa may be particularly large because domestic alternatives to imported inputs are not available. For example, World Bank Enterprise Survey data indicate that between 30 and 65 percent of inputs purchased by African manufacturing exporters are imported (Edwards, Rankin, and Schöer 2008). Although exporters have access to import duty rebate schemes in some African countries, utilization of these schemes by firms is low (Chandra et al. 2001; Clarke 2005).

Summary

In conclusion, Africa presents a mixed picture with regard to trade flows and liberalization from 1990 on. The share of Sub-Saharan Africa in world exports continued to decline from the 1990 level when measured in volume terms but remained stable when measured in current U.S. dollars. Although an unfavorable product concentration adversely affected export growth, there is evidence of improved competitiveness, and the region has increased its world market share in many products, including manufactured products and products that are growing rapidly in world trade. In addition, export performance in the average Sub-Saharan African economy is no different from that of other developing countries when evaluated using the ratio of merchandise exports to GDP. The results for the post-1990 period therefore differ from those found by Ng and Yeats (1996) for the period prior to the early 1990s.

In terms of protection, Sub-Saharan African economies have made reasonable progress in reducing MFN rates and simplifying their tariff structures. The extent of tariff liberalization exceeded the world average for over half of the African countries analyzed. Liberalization, however, occurred from a high initial base, and average tariffs remain relatively high, even on key intermediate and capital inputs. These may continue to pose a barrier to export growth.

Econometric Analysis of the Effect of Tariff Barriers on Manufacturing Trade in Developing Economies

This section estimates the impact of tariff liberalization from 1990 to 2004 on manufactured exports, manufactured imports, and the trade balance in African and other developing countries. The focus on manufacturing trade is restrictive in the case of

Africa, where manufacturing accounts for only 20–25 percent of exports; a high proportion of these exports is also resource based. The concentration on manufacturing in part reflects data constraints regarding the availability of tariff data for primary sectors over time. However, there are additional reasons why it is important.

Growth in manufacturing is closely associated with growth accelerations in developing countries, including those in Sub-Saharan Africa (Pattillo, Gupta, and Carey 2005; Johnson, Ostry, and Subramanian 2007). The potential for output growth in manufacturing production is often greater than for agricultural and resource-based exports, which encounter diminishing returns to scale because of limited endowments (Collier and Venables 2007). Furthermore, diversification into manufacturing production helps insulate resource-based economies from volatile natural resource prices and politically and economically disruptive rent-seeking behavior (Sachs and Warner 1999). Finally, manufactured exports are likely to grow faster than primary exports as the global economy expands because their income elasticity of demand is higher (Elbadawi 2001). As a consequence, policies to stimulate growth of manufactured exports in Sub-Saharan Africa have frequently been recommended (World Bank 2000).

This does not imply that improved economic growth cannot or should not be achieved through expansion of primary product exports, as has been done in, for example, Chile. The recent commodity price boom and growth in China provide an important opportunity for African economies to expand trade in primary commodities. Moreover, there is substantial scope for technical progress in agriculture, often more so than in manufacturing (Martin and Mitra 2001). Nevertheless, continued growth in manufactures will need to form part of the overall strategy for improving economic growth. Mayer and Fajarnes (2008), for example, show that if income growth in Sub-Saharan Africa is to achieve the Millennium Development Goals (MDGs), a ninefold increase in the region's manufactured exports will be needed.

Data

The main database used is the trade, production, and protection database produced by Nicita and Olarreaga (2006). It provides information on trade flows, various measures of tariff protection, and production for 28 three-digit ISIC rev. 2 manufacturing sectors from 1976 on.[10]

The analysis in this section draws on a sample of 30 developing countries (of which 6 are in Sub-Saharan Africa and 4 in North Africa) and 20 OECD economies over the period 1990–2004. Country selection is based on the availability of tariff data. Countries were included only if at least six years (four years for African countries) of tariff data were initially available in the period 1990–2004. To ensure as much coverage as possible, the MFN tariff data were then updated using Harmonized System (HS) six-digit-level tariff schedules obtained from the country pages on the World Trade Organization (WTO) Web site. Tariff data for South Africa for the entire period were obtained from Edwards (2005). Tariffs for missing periods that were bounded by available tariff data in the preceding and subsequent years were interpolated using simple averages. Overall, this yielded an average of 10 years of tariff data for each developing country.

The database has some important limitations (Nicita and Olarreaga 2006). It is not balanced, and data are missing for many countries in the early 1990s. The tariff data do not include estimates of ad valorem equivalents for specific and other non–ad valorem rates. This is particularly problematic for agricultural products but is expected to be less of a problem for manufacturing, on which this paper concentrates. Non-tariff barriers are also omitted. The analysis in this paper thus focuses entirely on direct tariff measures, and the potentially important effects of nontariff barriers are ignored.

Additional variables relevant for the study were included in the database. They include a consumer price index (CPI)–based real effective exchange rate (REER) index, obtained from the International Monetary Fund's *International Financial Statistics*, and updated industrial production indexes obtained from the Instat database of the United Nations Industrial Development Organization (UNIDO).[11] To capture foreign demand effects, a sector-level export-weighted foreign GDP (*gdpf*) index is calculated as

$$gdpf_{ijt} = \sum_{k}^{10} \alpha_{ij}^{k} \, GDP_{t}^{k} \tag{1}$$

where *GDP* is valued in constant 2000 prices and α_{ij}^{k} is the average share of exports of product i in country j to each of the top 10 trading partners (k) over the period 2001 to 2002.

Finally, a variable to capture the effect of tariff liberalization on the cost of production is constructed. This variable, termed input tariff cost (*tcost*), is constructed as follows:

$$tcost_{ijt} = \sum_{n} a_{ij}^{n} \, t_{nt} \tag{2}$$

where t is the tariff rate and a_{ij}^{n} is the quantity of intermediate input n used in the production of one unit of i in country j. The value of *tcost* is therefore a measure of the proportion of total costs accounted for by tariffs on intermediate inputs.

An input-output table for the United States consisting of 17 aggregated manufacturing sectors, based on the three-digit ISIC rev. 2 code, is used to calculate the input coefficients (a_{ij}^{n}). The input-output table is obtained from Nicita and Olarreaga (2006). The tariff data used to construct *tcost* are aggregated to be consistent with this classification.[12]

There are various caveats regarding the variable *tcost*. Most important, tariff protection on agricultural and mining inputs is not included because the input-output table used does not contain input shares for these sectors. This is expected to particularly affect *tcost* values for agricultural product–intensive manufacturing sectors. Measurement of protection in the agricultural sector is, however, difficult given the extensive use of nontariff barriers and specific tariffs in the sector. Protection on mining products is generally low throughout the period and is not expected to have a substantial impact on *tcost*. A second limitation is that the variable excludes duty rebates on inputs that may be granted to exporters.

Despite the limitations, this database has a number of advantages. First, it includes direct measures of tariff protection. Second, sectoral data are included, enabling a more disaggregated analysis of the effect of trade liberalization on trade flows. Third, the inclusion of *tcost* allows for an alternative specification of the export relationship that captures the effect of tariff liberalization on input costs. Finally, the database covers a period in which considerable liberalization and changes in trade flows have occurred in many economies. This variation in the data lends itself to econometric analysis.

Some of the key data related to trade flows, tariffs, and *tcost* are presented in annex table A.1. The trends in trade flows and tariff liberalization are consistent with the more detailed analysis presented earlier. Average tariffs fell in all country groups, including Africa, although tariff protection remains relatively high in that region. Tariff liberalization also reduced average production costs (*tcost*) in many countries, with particularly large decreases in the low-income country group (from 14 to 7 percent) and the lower-middle-income group (11 to 3.3 percent). The decline is reasonably widespread, with 43 of the 51 countries sampled experiencing lower production costs from liberalization. Of the 30 developing economies covered, production costs decreased in 23 between the early 1990s and 2004.

As noted earlier, manufacturing trade volumes increased for many economies from 1990 on, with relatively slower growth experienced in Africa. Aggregate import growth was also high, but it lagged export growth for low-income and lower-middle-income regions. The effect is an improvement in the real manufacturing trade balance in 21 of the 30 developing countries in the sample. The improvements in the trade balance for many of the developing countries point to a potentially important difference from the studies of Santos-Paulino and Thirlwall (2004) and UNCTAD (1999), where the trade balance worsened after liberalization.

Manufactured Exports

A simple reduced-form imperfect substitution model, as discussed by Goldstein and Khan (1985), is used to estimate the export relationship. The estimated equation takes the form:

$$\ln(x)_{ijt} = \alpha_0 + \beta_1 \ln(gdpf)_{ijt} - \beta_2 \ln(reer)_{jt} \\ + \beta_3 \ln(prod)_{ijt} - \beta_4 \ln(tcost)_{ijt} + \varepsilon_{ijt}, \quad \beta > 0, \quad (3)$$

where x denotes export volumes, *gdpf* is foreign GDP, *reer* is the real effective exchange rate, *prod* is an index of real industrial production (a proxy for productive capacity), and *tcost* is a measure of input costs associated with tariff protection. The subscripts i, j, and t represent sector, country, and time, respectively.[13]

Various methods are used to estimate the relationship. One option is to pool the data and estimate the relationship using ordinary least squares (OLS). A shortcoming of this method is that time-invariant characteristics of sectors and countries are likely to be correlated with the explanatory variables, leading to biased estimates. In an attempt to deal with this problem, two approaches are followed.

In model A, dummy variables for country ($cntry_j$), sector ($isic_i$), and year (λ_t) are included in the OLS regressions. Omitted variable bias may nevertheless persist. For example, low tariffs on mining sectors in Africa reflect a comparative advantage in these sectors arising from a relative abundance of natural resources. The high exports of these products will erroneously be attributed to the tariff variable in the estimates. Furthermore, as noted earlier, countries frequently implement other reforms, such as capital account liberalization, concurrently with tariff liberalization. To avoid these biases, model B includes country-by-sector specific effects ($cntryisic_{ij}$) and country-by-year specific effects ($ctryyear_{jt}$). The error component of equation (3) is therefore specified as

$$\varepsilon_{ijt} = \lambda_t + cntryisic_{ij} + ctryyear_{jt} + v_{ijt}. \tag{4}$$

The results for the export relationship are presented in table 3. Separate estimates are presented for the full sample of countries and for developing countries. To investigate the African trade relationship, two additional regressions are estimated. First, a dummy variable for Africa ($=1$) is interacted with the tariff variable in the developing-country regressions. Second, the export relationship is estimated for the Africa sample alone. All relationships are estimated using both mirror export data and own-country reported data. Note that in model B the *reer* variable is dropped because it correlates perfectly with $ctryyear_{jt}$.

Looking at the results for all countries (columns 1 and 5), the estimated export relationship appears to be well defined, with a high R^2 and a number of significant variables of the correct sign. Export volumes respond positively to rising foreign income, a depreciation of the real effective exchange rate, and increased domestic productive capacity. Except for the *reer*, the estimated elasticities for these variables are largely unaffected by the choice of mirror export or own-export data.

Turning to the trade liberalization variable, mirror export volumes are found to be responsive to *tcost*, and the estimated elasticity declines from -0.385 for model A (column 1) to -0.137 for model B (column 5). The latter, the preferred estimate, suggests that a 10 percent reduction in the input-weighted average manufacturing tariff raises manufactured export volumes by 1.37 percent. The results for *tcost* using own exports in model A are generally similar, but the relationship is not robust to the inclusion of the country-by-sector and country-by-year fixed effects.

The stability of the relationship across regions can be seen in the developing-country and Africa results. There is some variation in the estimated relationships across country groups and across different models. The relationship between export volumes and *reer*, foreign GDP, and industrial production in developing countries (columns 2 and 6) is generally similar to the full sample results. Rising protection, measured using *tcost*, is also found to affect export performance negatively, and the coefficients are not significantly different from those of the full sample.

TABLE 3. Determinants of Manufactured Export Performance, World, Developing Countries, and Africa

	Model A				Model B			
	All countries	Developing	Developing interaction	Africa	All countries	Developing	Developing interaction	Africa
	(1)	(2)	(3)	(4)	(5)	(6)	(7)	(8)
Mirror export data								
gdpf	0.419***	0.222***	0.223***	0.271***	1.152***	0.499	0.506	1.914***
	(0.018)	(0.023)	(0.023)	(0.045)	(0.244)	(0.313)	(0.314)	(0.526)
reer	-0.351***	-0.606***	-0.593***	-1.689***				
	(0.094)	(0.139)	(0.14)	(0.374)				
prod	0.583***	0.678***	0.674***	0.615***	0.426***	0.402***	0.402***	0.027
	(0.046)	(0.064)	(0.064)	(0.137)	(0.033)	(0.049)	(0.049)	(0.125)
tcost	-0.385***	-0.337***	-0.306***	-0.708***	-0.137***	-0.222**	-0.247**	-0.067
	(0.031)	(0.064)	(0.067)	(0.178)	(0.042)	(0.088)	(0.098)	(0.224)
Africa			-1.434***				0.131	
			(0.274)				(0.221)	
tcost*Africa			-0.156					
			(0.102)					
N	15,513	7,661	7,661	1,850	15,513	7,661	7,661	1,850
R²	0.793	0.769	0.77	0.759	0.949	0.94	0.94	0.928
F	628	338	333	101	137	97.4	97.3	56.7
Own-export data								
gdpf	0.367***	0.175***	0.176***	0.197***	1.042***	0.349	0.340	1.08*
	(0.02)	(0.026)	(0.026)	(0.058)	(0.248)	(0.326)	(0.327)	(0.62)
reer	0.072	0.041	0.043	-1.71***				
	(0.103)	(0.156)	(0.157)	(0.495)				
prod	0.523***	0.635***	0.632***	0.603***	0.341***	0.33***	0.330***	0.165
	(0.051)	(0.072)	(0.072)	(0.175)	(0.034)	(0.052)	(0.053)	(0.166)
tcost	-0.342***	-0.216***	-0.206***	-1.019***	-0.003	-0.113	-0.083	-0.27
	(0.033)	(0.071)	(0.074)	(0.244)	(0.043)	(0.094)	(0.101)	(0.333)
Africa			-1.610***				-0.224	
			(0.347)				(0.275)	
tcost*Africa			-0.068					
			(0.124)					
N	14,963	7,204	7,204	1,510	14,963	7,204	7,204	1,510
R²	0.762	0.743	0.743	0.666	0.949	0.939	0.939	0.901
F	506	274	271	52.8	132	90.9	90.8	32.3

Note: The coefficients for the various sector-, time-, and country-specific effects are not shown. Standard errors are in parentheses. *gdpf*, foreign GDP; *reer*, real effective exchange rate; *prod*, real industrial production; *tcost*, input costs associated with tariff protection.

*p < .1 **p < .05 ***p < .01

Looking at the export relationship in Africa, none of the interaction terms in columns 3 and 7 are significant, suggesting that the effect of tariff protection on exports in Africa is no different from that for other developing economies. The results for model A using the Africa sample (column 4) are also similar to those for the full sample of developing countries, although African exports of manufactured goods appear to be more than twice as sensitive to the *reer*. Lower input costs from trade liberalization are relatively strongly associated with improved export performance in the Africa sample. However, most of the results for the Africa sample become insignificantly different from zero once country-by-sector and country-by-year fixed effects are included in the model (column 8, model B), and only foreign GDP remains significant.[14]

Much of Africa's export performance therefore appears to be explained by factors other than tariff protection. This may reflect the relatively low share of manufacturing trade in total trade in African countries, as well as a dependence on resource-based products within manufacturing. Exports of resource-based products are less likely to be influenced by tariffs on inputs than are downstream products that use a relatively high proportion of manufactured inputs in the production process. Nevertheless, the results for the pooled sample of developing countries suggest that as Africa deepens its manufacturing base, continued protection, particularly on inputs, will constrain export growth.

A more detailed analysis of the contribution of tariff liberalization to export growth in developing countries from 1992–95 to 2003–4 is presented in table 4. The decomposition is based on two estimated *tcost* elasticities for developing countries: −0.222 and −0.337. Export volumes in the average developing economy grew by 110 percent over the period. Production costs associated with tariffs fell by 47 percent for the average economy, which translates roughly into an 11–16 percent increase in export volume, depending on the *tcost* elasticity selected. For the average African economy, the decline in *tcost* is associated with an increase in export volume ranging from 11 to 17 percent. This is equivalent to 14 to 20 percent of the change in total exports in the average African economy over this period. Thus, although liberalization raises export volumes, its contribution to overall export growth in the 1990s appears to be relatively small.

TABLE 4. Contribution of Tariff Liberalization to Changes in Manufactured Export Volumes, for Africa and by Income Group, 1992–95 to 2003–4

Country group	Average ln change		Estimated change in exports	
	tcost	Exports	Elasticity 1 (−0.222)	Elasticity 2 (−0.337)
Africa	−0.49	0.82	0.11	0.17
Low income	−0.73	1.12	0.17	0.25
Lower middle income	−0.47	1.18	0.11	0.16
Upper middle income	−0.28	0.99	0.06	0.09
Developing	−0.47	1.10	0.11	0.16

Note: Export and *tcost* values reflect the simple country average.

Manufactured Imports

The same estimation strategy is employed to estimate the determinants of manufactured import volumes. The estimated import equation is:

$$\ln(m)_{ijt} = b_o + \delta_1 \ln(gdp)_{jt} + \delta_2 \ln(reer)_{jt} - \delta_3 \ln(1 + tar)_{ijt} + v_{ijt}, \quad \delta > 0 \quad (5)$$

where *gdp* is domestic GDP, *reer* is the real effective exchange rate, and *tar* is the average nominal MFN tariff on output. The tariff variable is included as $(1 + tar)$ to capture the effect of tariffs on the tariff-inclusive import price. The variables *gdp* and *reer* are only defined at the country level and therefore drop out of the estimation in model B.

The estimated elasticities for the import relationship are presented in table 5. Only the results using mirror import data are presented because the results using own-country reported data are qualitatively similar. The coefficients in model A are generally of the expected signs: import volumes are negatively affected by a real depreciation of the currency, a decline in GDP, and higher tariffs. Looking more closely at the results for developing countries (columns 2 and 6), tariff protection negatively affects import volumes in both estimates, with an average elasticity of −0.74. A 10 percent increase in the tariff-inclusive price of MFN imports $(1 + tar)$ is therefore associated with a reduction in import volumes of 7.4 percent. This is a relatively inelastic response to liberalization and implies that MFN tariff liberalization from 1992–95 to 2003–4 in developing countries raised import volumes by 6 percent, on average. That figure is a small proportion of the 88 percent increase in import volumes experienced by the average developing country in this period.

African manufactured import volumes are not well explained by import tariffs. The coefficient on the interaction term in columns 3 and 7 is significant and positive. Combining the interaction coefficient with the direct coefficient on $(1 + tar)$ implies a very small negative impact (-0.3) of tariffs on import volumes for Africa in model A and a close to zero effect in model B. In the African sample estimates (columns 4 and 8), almost all the coefficients are insignificant. The exception is for the tariff variable in model A, but even this variable is insignificant once the various fixed effects are included. These results suggest that import volumes in Africa are driven by other country-specific effects not included in the regression. Why tariffs matter less for imports in Africa is unclear, but it may reflect the high dependence by African industries on imported inputs, as well as large capital inflows through foreign aid. A similarly poor import response to relative prices and import taxes in Africa is found by Santos-Paulino and Thirlwall (2004).

Manufacturing Trade Balance

The final relationship analyzed is the effect of trade liberalization on the trade balance. This relationship depends on the relative responsiveness of exports and imports to tariff protection. Much of the current literature on developing economies suggests a muted response of exports to liberalization in relation to the response in import volumes, leading to worsening trade balances (UNCTAD 1999; Santos-Paulino and Thirlwall 2004).

TABLE 5. Determinants of Manufactured Import Volumes, by Country Group and for Africa

	Model A				Model B			
	All countries (1)	Developing (2)	Developing interaction (3)	Africa (4)	All countries (5)	Developing (6)	Developing interaction (7)	Africa (8)
reer	0.544*** (0.06)	0.767*** (0.086)	0.773*** (0.086)	−0.035 (0.206)				
gdp	1.23*** (0.102)	0.757*** (0.155)	0.664*** (0.157)	0.00 (0.427)				
1 + tar	−0.513*** (0.087)	−0.714*** (0.11)	−1.121*** (0.145)	−0.931*** (0.16)	−0.478*** (0.146)	−0.765*** (0.166)	−1.450*** (0.222)	0.096 (0.262)
Africa			0.205 (0.538)					
Africa*(1 + tar)			0.808*** (0.189)				1.546*** (0.334)	
N	16,855	8,666	8,666	2,293	16,855	8,666	8,666	2,293
R^2	0.846	0.821	0.822	0.804	0.935	0.925	0.93	0.912
F	978	534	528	167	107	83	89.2	53

Note: The coefficients for the various sector-, time-, and country-specific effects are not shown. Standard errors are in parentheses. Values for reer and gdp are only defined at the country level and drop out of the estimations in model B.

*$p < .1$ ***$p < .01$

To test this effect, the following trade balance equation is estimated:

$$tb_{ijt} = b_o - \theta_1 \ln(gdp)_{jt} - \theta_2 \ln(reer)_{jt} \pm \theta_3 \ln(1 + tar)_{ijt}$$
$$+ \theta_4 \ln(gdpf)_{ijt} + \theta_5 \ln(prod)_{ijt} - \theta_6 \ln(tcost)_{ijt} + \theta_7 \ln(tot)_{ijt} + \upsilon_{ijt} \quad (6)$$

where, in addition to the variables already explained, *tb* is the log ratio of the value of exports to the value of imports, and *tot* is the terms of trade calculated as the unit value of exports relative to imports. The trade balance is expected to improve in response to a depreciation of the real exchange rate, a rise in foreign GDP, a decline in domestic consumption (proxied by domestic GDP), an improvement in the terms of trade (*tot*), or a rise in productive capacity (*prod*). Liberalization has an ambiguous effect. Rising tariffs on inputs, measured by the variable *tcost*, are expected to diminish the competitiveness of exporters and domestic producers and therefore reduce import and export volumes. Tariffs on final goods reduce imports but also reduce the incentive to produce for the export market. The sign can therefore be positive or negative.

Table 6 gives the results for the trade balance using mirror import data. The results using own data are quantitatively similar, but fewer variables are significant.

The trade balance relationship appears to be well defined, and most of the variables are significant or of the correct sign, or both. A real depreciation, for example, improves the trade balance in developing countries, including those in Africa. An exception is the terms of trade in model A, which suggests that an improvement in the terms of trade worsens the trade balance. The expected positive coefficient emerges, however, in model B.

Focusing on the tariff variables for developing countries and the full sample of countries, there is some evidence that higher input tariff costs (*tcost*) are negatively associated with the trade balance. The estimates from model A suggest that a 10 percent reduction in *tcost* is associated with an improvement in *tb* of 4.63 percent. This relationship, however, is not robust to the inclusion of the various fixed effects and is insignificant in all estimates of model B. Similar results are found for Africa.

By contrast, a positive relationship between output tariffs and the trade balance is found in both models for developing countries (and in the full sample). The preferred results from model B (column 6) suggest that a 10 percent increase in protection measured by (1 + *tar*) is associated with an increase in the value of exports relative to the value of imports in developing countries of close to 7 percent. The average decline in (1 + *tar*) during the period 1993–2004 for developing countries is 8 percent, implying that liberalization will have reduced the value of exports relative to imports for the average developing country by approximately 5 percent. This relationship, however, does not hold for African economies, as is shown by the insignificant coefficient for output tariffs in the African sample (column 8), as well as by the offsetting negative coefficient on the interaction term in column 7.

Overall, the results for developing countries are broadly consistent with those of Santos-Paulino and Thirlwall (2004), who find that tariff liberalization may have a negative impact on the trade balance. There are, nevertheless, some important differences. First, there is evidence that liberalization enhances export performance through lower input costs. Second, the effect on the trade balance is less than is suggested by

TABLE 6. Determinants of the Trade Balance, World, Developing Countries, and Africa

	Model A				Model B			
	All countries (1)	Developing (2)	Developing interaction (3)	Africa (4)	All countries (5)	Developing (6)	Developing interaction (7)	Africa (8)
gdpf	0.551***	0.328***	0.327***	0.477***	0.324**	0.454**	0.443**	0.163
	(0.016)	(0.021)	(0.021)	(0.041)	(0.153)	(0.225)	(0.225)	(0.361)
gdp	−0.863***	−1.245***	−1.155***	1.81**				
	(0.152)	(0.26)	(0.261)	(0.852)				
prod	0.480***	0.504***	0.499***	0.328***	0.354***	0.387***	0.390***	0.140
	(0.042)	(0.058)	(0.058)	(0.127)	(0.021)	(0.035)	(0.035)	(0.086)
reer	−0.784***	−0.696***	−0.687***	−1.128***				
	(0.083)	(0.129)	(0.129)	(0.335)				
(1 + tar)	0.785***	0.476**	1.272***	0.455	0.256**	0.71***	1.401***	0.106
	(0.127)	(0.189)	(0.279)	(0.266)	(0.117)	(0.184)	(0.267)	(0.275)
tcost	−0.484***	−0.463***	−0.553***	−0.782***	0.027	−0.011	−0.083	−0.160
	(0.029)	(0.069)	(0.08)	(0.174)	(0.027)	(0.072)	(0.087)	(0.16)
tot	−0.042***	−0.162***	−0.161***	−0.105***	0.021***	0.021*	0.021*	−0.004
	(0.013)	(0.018)	(0.018)	(0.038)	(0.007)	(0.012)	(0.012)	(0.024)
(1 + tar)*Africa			−1.277***				−1.339***	
			(0.344)				(0.369)	
tcost*Africa			−0.036				−0.073	
			(0.107)				(0.172)	
N	15,409	7,571	7,571	1,810	15,409	7,571	7,571	1,810
R^2	0.385	0.512	0.513	0.55	0.927	0.919	0.919	0.923
F	98.9	101	98.8	36.3	92.8	70.3	70.3	51.7

Note: The coefficients for the various sector-, time-, and country-specific effects are not shown. Standard errors are in parentheses. Values for *gdp* and *reer* are excluded from model B because their effect is captured by the *cntryyear* fixed effect.

*$p < .1$ **$p < .05$ ***$p < .01$

the authors' estimates, particularly those based on dummy variables for the trade liberalization period. Third, there does not appear to be a negative relationship between protection and the trade balance in Africa, although these estimates are generally poor.

Other Factors

The results presented indicate that tariff liberalization enhanced manufacturing trade flows in developing countries, including Africa, between 1990 and 2004, but not by much. This finding suggests a limited supply response to the changing incentives arising from tariff liberalization. There is much evidence to support this view. In a comprehensive review of economic performance in Africa, Collier and Gunning (1999) argue that distorted product and credit markets, high risk, inadequate social capital, inadequate infrastructure, and poor public services are key factors inhibiting African firms' investment responses to opportunities.

Microlevel institutions that affect the cost of exporting are also important (Johnson, Ostry, and Subramanian 2007). For example, it takes, on average, 40 days to export from a Sub-Saharan African country, but only 11 days for OECD countries. A combination of factors is responsible: excessive tariff bands, a lack of electronic documentation, undue numbers of required documents, inefficient customs systems, poor roads, port congestion, and corruption at the border (World Bank 2005). The available empirical evidence indicates that many of these factors are important determinants of Africa's export performance and firm productivity (Limão and Venables 2001; Clarke 2005; Eifert, Gelb, and Ramachandran 2005; Wilson, Mann, and Otsuki 2005; Djankov, Freund, and Pham 2006). Higher transaction costs associated with weak institutions and infrastructure facilities are found to be particularly detrimental to exports of manufactured products (Collier 2000; Elbadawi 2001; World Bank 2000).[15]

Conclusion

Sub-Saharan Africa's share of world export volumes has continued to decline since 1990. Yet there are signs of improvement. The post-2000 commodity price boom has benefited Africa, and Sub-Saharan Africa's share in the value of world exports in 2006 was equivalent to its share in 1990 despite the relatively poor growth in export volumes. There is evidence of improved competitiveness in some manufacturing sectors, and when measured relative to GDP, export performance in Sub-Saharan Africa matches that of other developing countries. There are, therefore, some important differences in the post-1990 period from the period prior to 1990 analyzed by Ng and Yeats (1996).

Some of the difference in export performance can be attributed to the progress many Sub-Saharan African countries have made in lowering tariffs since the early 1990s. The econometric estimates presented in this paper indicate that tariff liberalization stimulates manufactured export volumes in developing countries. A key mechanism through which export performance is enhanced is through decreases in the cost of production inputs.

A policy response to stimulate manufactured exports would therefore be to reduce tariffs on key production inputs. Implementation of such a policy, however, involves a number of difficulties. Whether products are inputs or final goods is not always clear cut. Lower tariffs on inputs increase effective protection in downstream sectors, which may raise the overall level of distortions in the economy. An alternative option is comprehensive liberalization that includes reductions in tariffs on final goods. For example, an across-the-board reduction in tariffs reduces input costs without leading to further increases in effective protection. Improvements in duty-drawback mechanisms available in Africa would further reduce the antiexport bias of protection.

African economies will also need to consider the possible implications of further tariff liberalization for the manufacturing trade balance. The estimates presented show that lower tariffs are associated with increased import volumes and a worsening of the manufacturing trade balance in developing countries. The growth in exports from liberalization is often exceeded by growth in imports, and if this leads to a shortage of foreign currency, the growth process may be constrained. The problem may not be as acute in Africa as in other developing countries, as the relationship between protection and the trade balance was not significant in the preferred estimates. In general, the estimated import and trade balance relationships for Africa were poor.

Nevertheless, the trade balance results suggest that liberalization policies need to be enhanced through complementary policies that stimulate export growth. For example, a depreciation of the currency is shown to have strong positive effects on the trade balance, particularly through the export channel. Although tariff liberalization is expected to depreciate the currency and thus offset some of the import effect, in many developing countries the currency appreciated in response to other reforms implemented (Bleaney 1999; UNCTAD 1999). The appropriate sequencing of reforms to minimize the possibility of unexpected currency appreciation needs to be considered. Other empirical literature indicates that improvements in trade-related infrastructure and institutions can have a substantial impact on export growth in Africa.

ANNEX TABLE A.1. Manufacturing Trade and Tariffs, Selected Countries, Early 1990s to 2004
(percent)

Income group	Share of trade, 2004	Average annual growth, 1990–2004		Average MFN tariff (import weighted)			Average tariff-related input cost		
		Imports	Exports (mirror)	1990–95	2001–4	Change	1990–95	2001–4	Change
Low income	2.1	8.3	11.7	34.2	18.7	−11.6	14.1	7.0	−50.7
Bangladesh	0.1	7.6	14.7	82.4	18.9	−34.8	43.0	12.7	−70.4
Côte d'Ivoire	0.0	3.4	2.3	23.0	10.8	−9.9	6.9	3.6	−47.6
Ghana	0.0	8.4	−0.4	11.1	13.4	2.1	4.3	7.1	64.9
India	1.1	12.1	12.6	60.7	28.5	−20.0	23.8	10.8	−54.6
Indonesia	0.7	4.6	11.7	13.9	6.1	−6.9	5.4	2.2	−59.5
Kenya	0.0	5.3	9.6	25.5	13.1	−9.9	9.4	5.7	−39.5
Uganda	0.0	6.3	7.6	16.7	6.5	−8.7	5.8	2.5	−57.6
Lower middle income	12.9	14.2	17.3	25.0	8.7	−13.1	11.1	3.3	−70.3
Algeria	0.2	5.5	−0.7	15.9	13.5	−2.0	2.7	6.1	121.3
Bolivia	0.0	7.2	7.7	9.7	9.0	−0.6	3.5	3.1	−11.7
China	9.9	17.9	18.8	30.9	8.4	−17.2	12.4	3.3	−73.4
Colombia	0.2	9.0	11.0	11.7	11.3	−0.3	4.2	4.3	2.6
Ecuador	0.1	10.8	10.9	11.0	11.0	0.0	3.8	3.6	−3.3
Egypt, Arab Rep. of	0.1	2.0	12.2	23.8	12.8	−8.9	9.8	6.2	−36.3
El Salvador	0.1	13.7	18.7	10.8	9.7	−1.0	6.0	5.9	−1.1
Morocco	0.2	7.5	8.7	59.6	25.1	−21.6	25.1	12.0	−52.4
Peru	0.1	9.6	8.8	15.8	9.4	−5.5	6.2	4.0	−34.8
Philippines	0.8	11.8	15.8	17.0	3.2	−11.8	6.8	1.2	−82.3
Sri Lanka	0.1	8.1	12.6	27.4	7.5	−15.6	13.7	2.4	−82.3
Tunisia	0.2	6.6	11.1	27.9	23.2	−3.7	11.3	10.7	−5.3
Turkey	1.1	11.9	15.3	7.9	4.8	−2.9	3.6	2.3	−36.4

(continued)

ANNEX TABLE A.1. (Continued)

Income group	Share of trade, 2004	Average annual growth, 1990–2004		Average MFN tariff (import weighted)			Average tariff-related input cost		
		Imports	Exports (mirror)	1990–95	2001–4	Change	1990–95	2001–4	Change
Upper middle income	11.6	11.5	11.5	11.9	9.5	22.1	4.2	3.2	–22.6
Argentina	0.4	17.0	7.6	12.6	13.8	1.0	3.8	4.1	6.9
Brazil	1.0	9.2	8.0	17.9	11.8	–5.2	5.4	4.3	–20.5
Chile	0.3	8.2	9.1	10.9	6.8	–3.7	4.4	2.7	–38.2
Korea, Rep. of	3.4	8.3	11.6	9.5	5.3	–3.9	3.5	1.9	–44.5
Malaysia	1.9	9.4	13.5	9.7	5.1	–4.2	4.0	2.0	–48.7
Mauritius	0.0	3.7	4.7	26.2	10.4	–12.6	11.6	5.7	–50.8
Mexico	2.8	15.7	13.4	12.1	14.9	2.5	4.6	5.6	21.1
Poland	1.1	36.3	15.2	10.5	9.8	–0.7	3.6	3.6	0.2
South Africa	0.6	8.1	8.7	16.3	8.9	–6.4	4.0	1.9	–52.2
Uruguay	0.0	7.2	3.7	9.8	13.0	2.9	3.5	4.6	32.0
OECD	73.5	6.2	5.8	6.0	3.1	–2.7	1.9	1.0	–46.4
Africa	1.4	6.2	7.5	24.6	14.1	–8.5	7.6	4.9	–35.5

Source: Updated data based on trade, production, and protection database (Nicita and Olarreaga 2006).

Note: MFN, most favored nation; OECD, Organisation for Economic Co-operation and Development.

Notes

1. See Santos-Paulino (2005) for a review of studies relating to Africa and other developing economies.

2. The calculations were based on World Development Indicators (WDI) data. The average ratio of taxes on international trade to total trade in goods and services in Sub-Saharan Africa was 10.3 percent between 1990 and 1995.

3. SITC is the Standard International Trade Classification.

4. Economies are divided according to 2006 gross national income per capita. The groups are as follows: low income, US$905 or less; lower middle income, US$906–US$3,595; upper middle income, US$3,596–US$11,115; and high income, US$11,116 or more. Developing countries include all low-income and middle-income economies.

5. These results contrast starkly with those of Morrissey and Mold (2006), who argue that African exports perform relatively well when analyzed in terms of volume.

6. Home-reported export data for most Sub-Saharan African countries are notoriously poor (Yeats 1990), and mirrored export data were used for the earlier period. Because of unreliable data over time, the following categories were excluded from the analysis: 286 (ores and concentrates of uranium); 323 (coal briquettes; coke and semicoke; lignite or peat; retort carbon); 333 (crude petroleum and oils obtained from bituminous minerals); 334 (petroleum products, refined); and 688 (uranium depleted in U235). Exports from oil-exporting economies are thus underreported.

7. The gravity models of Foroutan and Pritchett (1993) and Coe and Hoffmaister (1999) yield consistent results. Foroutan and Pritchett, for example, find that intra-African trade in manufactures in the early 1980s is unusually high in relation to that of low-income and medium-income countries, given Africa's characteristics. A recent extension of this work by Subramanian and Tamirisa (2003) finds consistent results for anglophone Africa but not for francophone Africa, which is found to trade less than predicted.

8. To maximize the number of available countries, the average for 1996–2000 instead of for 1990–95 is used for 38 of the countries, and data for 2001–3 rather than 2004–6 are used for 11 of the countries.

9. The focus on the average tariff ignores other indicators of protection. According to 2006 tariff data obtained from the WTO's *World Tariff Profiles* 2006 (WTO 2006), Sub-Saharan African countries, on average, have lower binding coverage (50.6 percent of lines versus 82 percent for all countries), higher bound rates (60 versus 35 percent); a lower proportion of lines subject to duty-free rates (15.2 versus 23.4 percent), and a higher proportion of international tariff spikes, that is, tariff lines with duties less than 15 percent (37.6 versus 20.4 percent). In other dimensions, the structure of tariffs is far simpler in Africa than in other developing economies. The average number of tariff lines is lower; there are far fewer distinct duties (51 versus 412); and the proportion of tariff lines with non–ad valorem rates is a quarter of the average for all countries (0.5 versus 2 percent).

10. ISIC stands for International System of Industrial Classification.

11. Real effective exchange rate data were not available for Argentina, Bangladesh, Brazil, the Arab Republic of Egypt, El Salvador, India, Indonesia, Kenya, the Republic of Korea, Mauritius, Mexico, Peru, Senegal, or Turkey. CPI-based REER indexes for these countries were calculated using CPI indexes, exchange rate data (from IMF, *International Financial Statistics, various years*), and bilateral export weights of the top 10 export partners.

12. The average sectoral tariff is used to calculate the production costs associated with tariff protection. An alternative approach is to calculate average tariffs on intermediate and capital goods using the broad economic categories (BEC) classification.

13. It is possible that industrial production is itself a function of exports. In an attempt to deal with possible endogeneity bias, lagged values of *prod* were included in alternative estimates. The results are largely unchanged.

14. To test the sensitivity of the results to choice of tariff variable, additional estimates were conducted using the simple average MFN tariff on output and *tcost* calculated using import-weighted applied rates that account for tariff preferences. The results using the average MFN tariff on output are poor, but those using *tcost* calculated with applied rates are similar.

15. See also Wood and Mayer (2001), who emphasize the role of endowments relative to infrastructure.

References

Amjadi, Azita, and Alexander Yeats. 1995. "Have Transport Costs Contributed to the Relative Decline of Sub-Saharan African Exports? Some Preliminary Empirical Evidence." Policy Research Working Paper 1559, International Trade Division, World Bank, Washington, DC.

Amjadi, Azita, Ulrich Reincke, and Alexander Yeats. 1996. "Did External Barriers Cause the Marginalization of Sub-Saharan Africa in World Trade?" Policy Research Working Paper 1586, International Trade Division, World Bank, Washington, DC.

Anderson, James E., and Peter Neary. 1994. "Measuring the Restrictiveness of Trade Policy." *World Bank Economic Review* 8 (2, May): 151–69.

Bleaney, Michael. 1999. "Trade Reform, Macroeconomic Performance and Export Growth in Ten Latin American Countries, 1979–95." *Journal of International Trade and Economic Development* 8 (1): 89–105.

Chandra, Vandana, Lalita Moorty, Jean-Pascal Nganou, Bala Rajaratnam, and Kendall Schaefer. 2001. "Constraints to Growth and Employment in South Africa: Evidence from the Small, Medium and Micro Enterprise Firm Survey." World Bank Informal Discussion Papers on Aspects of the South African Economy 15, Southern Africa Department, World Bank, Washington, DC.

Clarke, George. 2005. "Beyond Tariffs and Quotas: Why Don't African Manufacturers Export More?" Policy Research Working Paper 3617, World Bank, Washington, DC.

Coe, David, and Alexander Hoffmaister. 1999. "North-South Trade: Is Africa Unusual?" *Journal of African Economies* 8 (2, July): 228–56.

Collier, Paul. 2000. "Africa's Comparative Advantage." In *Industrial Development and Policy in Africa,* ed. H. Jalilian, M. Tribe, and J. Weiss. Cheltenham, U.K.: Edward Elgar.

Collier, Paul, and Jan Willem Gunning. 1999. "Explaining African Economic Performance." *Journal of Economic Literature* 37 (March): 64–111.

Collier, Paul, and Anthony J. Venables. 2007. "Rethinking Trade Preferences: How Africa Can Diversify Its Exports." *World Economy* 30 (8, August): 1326–45.

Djankov, Simeon, Caroline Freund, and Cong Pham. 2006. "Trading on Time." Policy Research Working Paper 3909, World Bank, Washington, DC.

Edwards, Lawrence. 2005. "Has South Africa Liberalised Its Trade?" *South African Journal of Economics* 73 (4): 754–75.

Edwards, Lawrence, and Robert Z. Lawrence. 2008. "South African Trade Policy Matters: Trade Performance and Trade Policy." *Economics of Transition* 16 (4): 741–68.

Edwards, Lawrence, Neil Rankin, and Volker Schöer. 2008. "South African Exporting Firms: What Do We Know and What Should We Know?" *Journal of Development Perspectives* 4 (1): 93–118.

Eifert, Benn, Alan Gelb, and Vijaya Ramachandran. 2005. "Business Environment and Comparative Advantage in Africa: Evidence from the Investment Climate Data." Working Paper 56, Center for Global Development, Washington, DC.

Elbadawi, Ibrahim A. 2001. "Can Africa Export Manufactures? The Role of Endowment, Exchange Rates, and Transaction Costs." In *Policies to Promote Competitiveness in Manufacturing in Sub-Saharan Africa,* ed. Augustin Nsouli, Kwasi Fosu, and Aristomene Varoudakis. Paris: Organisation for Economic Co-operation and Development.

Foroutan, Faezeh, and Lant Pritchett. 1993. "Intra–Sub-Saharan African Trade: Is It Too Little?" *Journal of African Economies* 2 (1): 74–105.

Goldstein, Morris, and Mohsin Khan. 1985. "Income and Price Effects in Foreign Trade." In *Handbook of International Economics,* vol. 2, ed. Ronald W. Jones, and Peter B. Kenen. Amsterdam: North-Holland.

Greenaway, David, and David Sapsford. 1994. "What Does Liberalisation Do for Exports and Growth?" *Review of World Economics* 130: 157–74.

IMF (International Monetary Fund). Various years. *International Financial Statistics.* Washington, DC: IMF.

Johnson, Simon, Jonathan Ostry, and Arvind Subramanian. 2007. "The Prospects for Sustained Growth in Africa: Benchmarking the Constraints." IMF Working Paper WP/07/52, International Monetary Fund, Washington, DC.

Lerner, Abba P. 1936. "The Symmetry between Import and Export Taxes." *Economica* 3: 306–13.

Limão, Nuno, and Anthony J. Venables. 2001. "Infrastructure, Geographical Disadvantage, Transport Costs, and Trade." *World Bank Economic Review* 15 (3): 451–79.

Martin, Will, and Devashish Mitra. 2001. "Productivity Growth and Convergence in Agriculture versus Manufacturing." *Economic Development and Cultural Change* 49 (2): 403–22.

Mayer, Jörg, and Pilar Fajarnes. 2008. "Tripling Africa's Primary Exports: What, How and Where?" *Journal of Development Studies* 44 (1): 80–102.

Morrissey, Oliver, and Andrew Mold. 2006. "Explaining Africa's Export Performance—Taking a New Look." Center for Global Trade Analysis, Department of Agricultural Economics, Purdue University, West Lafayette, IN. https://www.gtap.agecon.purdue.edu/resources/download/2643.pdf.

Ng, Francis, and Alexander Yeats. 1996. "Open Economies Work Better: Did Africa's Protectionist Policies Cause Its Marginalization in World Trade?" Policy Research Working Paper 1636, World Bank, Washington, DC.

Nicita, Alessandro, and Marcelo Olarreaga. 2006. "Trade, Production and Protection 1976–2004." *World Bank Economic Review* 21 (1): 165–71.

Papageorgiou, Demetris, Michael Michaely, and Armeane M. Choksi. 1991. *Liberalizing Foreign Trade.* Oxford: Basil Blackwell.

Parikh, Ashok, and Corneliu Stirbu. 2004. "Relationship between Trade Liberalisation, Economic Growth and Trade Balance: An Econometric Investigation." HWWA Discussion Paper 282, Hamburgisches Welt-Wirtschafts-Archiv, Hamburg.

Pattillo, Catherine, Sanjeev Gupta, and Kevin Carey. 2005. "Sustaining Growth Accelerations and Pro-Poor Growth in Africa." IMF Working Paper WP/05/195, International Monetary Fund, Washington, DC.

Richardson, J. David. 1971. "Constant-Market-Shares Analysis of Export Growth." *Journal of International Economics* 1 (2): 227–39.

Rodrik, Dani. 1997. "Trade Policy and Economic Performance in Sub-Saharan Africa." NBER Working Paper 6562, National Bureau of Economic Research, Cambridge, MA.

Sachs, Jeffrey D., and Andrew M. Warner. 1999. "The Big Rush, Natural Resource Booms and Growth." *Journal of Development Economics* 59 (1): 43–76.

Santos-Paulino, Amelia. 2005. "Trade Liberalisation and Economic Performance: Theory and Evidence for Developing Countries." *World Economy* 28 (6): 783–821.

Santos-Paulino, Amelia, and Anthony P. Thirlwall. 2004. "The Impact of Trade Liberalisation on Exports, Imports and the Balance of Payments of Developing Countries." *Economic Journal* 114 (February): F50–F72.

Subramanian, Arvind, and Natalia T. Tamirisa. 2003. "Is Africa Integrated in the Global Economy?" *IMF Staff Papers* 50 (3): 352–72.

UNCTAD (United Nations Conference on Trade and Development). 1999. *Trade and Development Report, 1999.* Geneva: United Nations.

Wang, Zhen K., and Alan L. Winters. 1998. "Africa's Role in Multilateral Trade Negotiations: Past and Future." *Journal of African Economies* 7 (Suppl. 1): 1–33.

Wilson, John S., Catherine Mann, and Tsunehiro Otsuki. 2005. "Assessing the Benefits of Trade Facilitation: A Global Perspective." *World Economy* 28 (6): 841–71.

Wood, Adrian, and Jörg Mayer. 2001. "Africa's Export Structure in a Comparative Perspective." *Cambridge Journal of Economics* 25 (3): 369–94.

World Bank. 2000. *Can Africa Claim the 21st Century?* Washington, DC: World Bank.

———. 2005. *Doing Business 2005.* Washington, DC: World Bank.

WTO (World Trade Organization). 2006. *World Tariff Profiles, 2006.* Geneva: WTO.

Yeats, Alexander. 1990. "On the Accuracy of Economic Observations: Do Sub-Saharan Trade Statistics Mean Anything?" *World Bank Economic Review* 4 (2): 135–56.

Comment on "Protectionist Policies and Manufacturing Trade Flows in Africa," by Lawrence Edwards

BEATA SMARZYNSKA JAVORCIK

Lawrence Edwards has written a useful paper that provides answers to three important questions. First, it finds that African countries continue to be marginalized in world trade. Second, it shows that own-tariff liberalization has helped African countries increase exports but that the effect has been relatively small. And third, it concludes that tariff liberalization has not worsened the trade balance in the countries considered.

Although providing those answers is valuable, the natural next step in the analysis is to examine the causes of this state of the world. In this discussion, I would like to highlight some factors that in my view are worth exploring.

Looking Back

Disappointing export performance by African economies has often been attributed to three factors: (a) geography—remote location relative to major export markets and lack of access to the sea, and thus to cheap sea transport; (b) high internal transport costs as a result of underdeveloped road and port infrastructure and to inefficiency and poor governance in the customs service; and (c) protectionism in export markets—although this last has diminished in recent years. Edwards does review in detail the arguments for why each of these factors should matter, but it would be interesting to look back and quantify to what extent each has affected Africa's export performance.

Looking Ahead

It might be even more interesting to look ahead and consider two factors that are likely to influence Africa's trade in the years to come: global production chains and ethnic networks. This discussion will focus on each factor in turn.

Beata Smarzynska Javorcik is a reader in economics at the University of Oxford and a research affiliate with the Centre for Economic Policy Research, London.

Annual World Bank Conference on Development Economics 2009, Global
© 2010 The International Bank for Reconstruction and Development / The World Bank

Global Production Chains

Technological advances in information and logistics systems, leading to a decline in transport and communication costs and accompanied by a lowering of tariffs and other barriers to trade, have changed the economic landscape facing nations, industries, and individual firms. Multinational corporations have served as the key agents in this transformation by creating international production and distribution networks that span the globe and actively interact with each other. In fact, estimates suggest that about two-thirds of all world trade in the latter half of the 1990s involved multinational corporations (UNCTAD 2002, 153).

Although so far the participation of African countries in the network trade associated with multinational corporations has been limited, participation in global production networks could create valuable opportunities for African producers, particularly in the apparel and food sectors.

It is helpful for the purpose of this discussion to follow Gereffi (1999) and classify networks into buyer-driven and producer-driven global commodity chains. Producer-driven networks are often coordinated by large multinationals. They are vertical, multilayered arrangements, usually with a direct ownership structure that includes parents, subsidiaries, and subcontractors. They tend to exist in capital- and technology-intensive sectors that are often dominated by global oligopolies, such as aircraft, automobiles, and heavy machinery.

Integration of a country into producer-driven networks usually requires significant inflows of foreign direct investment (FDI). This is illustrated in figure 1, which

FIGURE 1.
Foreign Direct Investment (FDI) and Exports of Producer-Driven-Network Products, Selected Countries, 2003
(U.S. dollars)

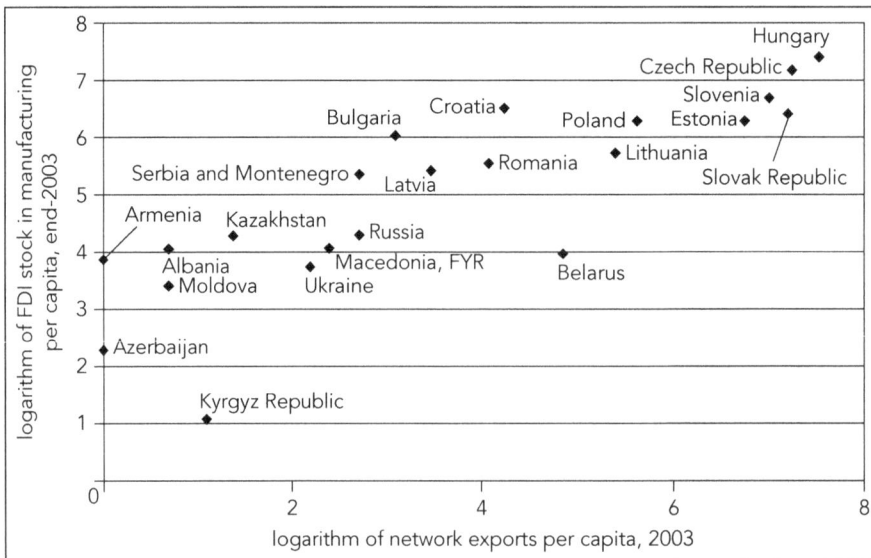

Source: Javorcik and Kaminski 2006.
Note: Macedonia, FYR, Former Yugoslav Republic of Macedonia.

depicts FDI stock and network exports (both expressed in per capita terms) in Eastern European and Central Asian countries, many of which have been very successful in joining global production chains. Given the meager success of Africa in attracting FDI inflows, producer-driven networks are likely to play a limited role in Africa's exports in the near future.

In contrast to producer-driven commodity chains, buyer-driven networks may offer greater promise to African countries. Buyer-driven networks are organized by large retailers, branded marketers, and branded manufacturers and do not necessarily require large FDI inflows. The products are designed and marketed by the buyer. They are typically labor-intensive consumer goods such as apparel, footwear, furniture, and processed food products. Buyer-driven commodity chains are characterized by highly competitive locally owned and globally dispersed production systems. Profits do not come from scale, volume, and technological advantage but, rather, from market research, design, and marketing. Buyer-driven production networks in the food and apparel sectors may be particularly relevant to African countries.

Global food markets have undergone a rapid transformation in recent years, driven by changes in consumer demand, increased concern about food safety, and the rise of modern retail systems. Two trends in the food industry during the past two decades are worth mentioning. The first is the consolidation of food retailing. In 2001 just 30 grocery retail chains jointly took in more than US$1 trillion in revenue, accounting for about 10 percent of global food sales. Within this group, the top 10 retailers constituted 57 percent of the combined total (World Bank 2005, 27). The second trend is the increasing reliance of major retail chains on their own agents for sourcing and thus the declining importance of wholesale markets. Whereas in the past wholesale and terminal markets were responsible for 20 or more percent of food sales, their share of sales in industrial countries has dropped to about 10 percent (World Bank 2005, 27).

The consolidation of food retailing has given market leaders extraordinary market and purchasing power and has resulted in a strong tendency toward global sourcing, the introduction of preferred-supplier arrangements, supply chain integration and rationalization, and lower average prices, but also lower variability in prices for contract or program suppliers (World Bank 2005). In addition, it has led to the emergence of numerous private sector codes of practice or other technical protocols that nowadays tend to play a dominant role in the market.

There are several advantages of being a supplier servicing a supermarket chain. These include higher margins than in wholesale transactions, more consistent and more predictable demand, access to detailed information on changing developments and requirements within the market, detailed guidelines for operations and good practice, and the ability to enhance one's reputation by being a supplier to a major retail chain (Jaffee 2003). In the South African context, Barrientos and Kritzinger (2004) found that producers selling fruit to U.K. and European supermarkets were able to obtain more stable outlets for their produce. For instance, most supermarkets negotiated purchases six months in advance. Moreover, producers servicing supermarkets on average received better prices than those selling on the open market.

But compliance with the standards imposed by supermarkets is costly. It requires investment in machinery and facilities (for instance, cold storage and stainless steel tables); improvements in sanitation levels, worker hygiene, and skills; and investment in obtaining a formal certification—for example, for Hazard Analysis and Critical Control Points (HACCP) systems. Such investment may be beyond the reach of smaller producers, who are often credit constrained. Supplying supermarkets may also involve an increase in variable costs, such as expenditure on microbiological testing. Timeliness is another important aspect of serving supermarket chains. If a shipment is delayed along the way and misses its vessel in the port, taking the next vessel might not be an option because the delay may result in deterioration of product quality and the shipment may no longer meet the required standard.

The apparel industry is another sector in which production is increasingly distributed across low-income countries by buyers searching for cheaper labor. As a result of Africa's preferential access to foreign markets, a significant amount of such production was moved from newly industrialized countries in Asia to Africa. Foreign direct investment from Asia, induced by the quota system of the Multifibre Arrangement (MFA) and the U.S. African Growth and Opportunity Act (AGOA), enabled rapid growth of the African apparel sector. One beneficiary was Lesotho, which, thanks to its cheap labor costs, was an ideal host for Asian capital seeking to avoid the textile quotas constraining exports from their home countries. Other African producers benefited from AGOA, which allows African countries that practice good governance and demonstrate respect for human rights to enjoy duty-free access to the U.S. market. In 2004, Sub-Saharan African exports of apparel to the United States exceeded US$1.5 billion (ILO 2005).

The expiration on January 1, 2005, of the MFA, which had set quotas on worldwide textile and apparel exports and had given preferences to many developing African countries, unleashed a new wave of Chinese sales on the world market. The ILO, in its analysis of the post-MFA environment, reported that textile and apparel exports under the AGOA fell to US$270 million in the first quarter of 2005, as against US$361 million a year earlier. The 25 percent reduction contrasts with a 19 percent increase in China's exports for the same period (ILO 2005).

After the expiration of the MFA, some Asian companies that had invested in Africa to take advantage of the quota began moving back to China in search of cheaper labor. Between January and March 2005, Kenya exported US$60 million of textile and clothing products to the United States. That was 13 percent, or US$9 million, less than the exports during the same period in 2004. Between October 2004 and May 2005, a loss of 6,000 out of 39,000 jobs was reported. In Lesotho, where the garment sector had accounted for more than 90 percent of the country's exports and was by far the largest single employer, 6,650 (out of 56,000) workers were terminated at the end of 2004, and 10,000 more were moved to short-term contracts (ILO 2005).

Are these trends in the apparel sector likely to continue, or have they already stopped? What factors can explain why some African countries have been more successful than others in becoming suppliers to large food retailers? Many African policy makers would find answers to these and related research questions useful.

Ethnic Networks

A growing literature has documented a positive link between the presence of ethnic networks and international trade. The main premise of this literature is that international transactions are plagued with informal trade barriers, in addition to formal trade barriers such as transport costs and tariffs. These informal barriers include the difficulties associated with accessing information on potential market opportunities, consumer tastes, and the trustworthiness of buyers and with the enforcement of contracts across international borders. As argued by Gould (1994), Head and Ries (1998), Rauch and Trindade (2002), and Combes, Lafourcade, and Mayer (2005), the presence of people with the same ethnic or national background on both sides of a border may alleviate these problems. Their language skills and familiarity with a foreign market can lower communication costs. They can provide valuable information about market structure, consumer preferences, business ethics, and commercial codes, and their social links may decrease the costs of negotiating and enforcing a contract. In sum, business and social networks that span international borders can help overcome many contractual and informational barriers and stimulate international transactions.

Yet the actual and potential benefits of social networks have not been examined in the African context. Do African producers find it easier to export their goods to Chinese and Indian markets not only because of product suitability but also thanks to the presence of Chinese and Indian diasporas in their countries? Have African producers been able to benefit from the presence of their nationals in industrial-country markets?

In sum, although buyer-driven production chains and ethnic networks may provide new export opportunities that can be harnessed by African producers and are thus worthy of researchers' attention, they should not divert our attention from the basics. High internal transport costs resulting from underdeveloped infrastructure and poorly functioning customs services may still be the first-order obstacle preventing African producers from exploiting new export opportunities.

References

Barrientos, Stephanie, and Andrienetta Kritzinger. 2004. "Squaring the Circle: Global Production and the Informalization of Work in the Food Sector." *Journal of International Development* 16 (1): 81–92.

Combes, Pierre-Philippe, Miren Lafourcade, and Thierry Mayer. 2005. "The Trade-Creating Effects of Business and Social Networks: Evidence from France." *Journal of International Economics* 66 (1): 1–29.

Gereffi, Gary. 1999. "International Trade and Industrial Upgrading in the Apparel Commodity Chain." *Journal of International Economics* 48 (1): 37–70.

Gould, David M. 1994. "Immigrant Links to the Home Country: Empirical Implications for U.S. Bilateral Trade Flows." *Review of Economics and Statistics* 76: 302–16.

Head, Keith, and John Ries. 1998. "Immigration and Trade Creation: Econometric Evidence from Canada." *Canadian Journal of Economics* 31 (1): 47–62.

ILO (International Labour Organization). 2005. "Promoting Fair Globalization in Textiles and Clothing in a Post-MFA Environment." Presented at the Tripartite Meeting on Promoting Fair Globalization in Textiles and Clothing in a Post-MFA Environment, Geneva.

Jaffee, Steven. 2003. "From Challenge to Opportunity. Transforming Kenya's Fresh Vegetable Trade in the Context of Emerging Food Safety and Other Standards in Europe." Agriculture and Rural Development (ARD) Discussion Paper 1, World Bank, Washington, DC.

Javorcik, Beata S., and Bart Kaminski. 2006. "Linkages between Foreign Direct Investment and Trade Flows." In *From Disintegration to Reintegration: Eastern Europe and the Former Soviet Union in International Trade,* ed. Harry Broadman. Washington, DC: World Bank.

Rauch, James, and Vitor Trindade. 2002. "Ethnic Chinese Networks in International Trade." *Review of Economics and Statistics* 84 (1, February): 116–30.

UNCTAD (United Nations Conference on Trade and Development). 2002. *World Investment Report: Transnational Corporations and Export Competitiveness.* New York and Geneva: United Nations.

World Bank. 2005. "Food Safety and Agricultural Health Standards: Challenges and Opportunities for Developing Country Exports." Report 31207, Poverty Reduction and Economic Management (PREM) Trade Unit, and Agricultural and Rural Development Department, World Bank, Washington, DC.

Crisscrossing Globalization: The Phenomenon of Uphill Skill Flows

AADITYA MATTOO AND ARVIND SUBRAMANIAN

This paper documents an unusual and possibly significant phenomenon: the export of skills embodied in goods, services, or capital from poorer to richer countries. We first present a set of stylized facts. Using a measure that combines the sophistication of a country's exports with the average income level of destination countries, we show that the performance of a number of developing countries, notably China, Mexico, and South Africa, matches that of much more advanced countries such as Japan, Spain, and the United States. Creating a new combined dataset on foreign direct investment (FDI) that covers greenfield investment as well as mergers and acquisitions, we show that flows of FDI to member countries of the Organisation for Economic Co-operation and Development from developing countries such as Brazil, India, Malaysia, and South Africa, as a share of those countries' gross domestic product, are as large as flows from countries such as Japan, the Republic of Korea, and the United States. Then, taking the work of Hausmann, Hwang, and Rodrik (2007) as a point of departure, we suggest that it is not just the composition of exports but their destination that matters. In both cross-sectional and panel regressions, using a range of controls, we find that a measure of uphill flows of sophisticated goods is significantly associated with better growth performance. These results suggest the need for a deeper analysis of whether development benefits might derive not from deifying comparative advantage but from defying it.

The phenomenon of uphill flows of capital has been subject to much scrutiny in recent years (see, for example, Bernanke 2006; Prasad, Rajan, and Subramanian 2007; Caballero, Farhi, and Gourinchas 2008). Much of this literature has focused on financial flows (or foreign savings). Indeed, Caballero and his coauthors (2008)

Aaditya Mattoo is lead economist in the International Trade Group of the World Bank's Development Economics Research Group. Arvind Subramanian is a senior fellow at the Peterson Institute for International Economics and the Center for Global Development in Washington, DC, and is senior research professor at Johns Hopkins University.

Annual World Bank Conference on Development Economics 2009, Global

attempt to explain why developing countries export savings while simultaneously importing foreign direct investment (FDI). The assumption has been that the only gravity-defying flow is finance.

But a number of recent high-profile developments raise the possibility of uphill flows in other dimensions. These flows run counter to the predictions of standard trade models in which developing countries primarily export unskilled products and are recipients of FDI. Examples are the takeover of the U.K.'s Jaguar company by a prominent Indian enterprise (Tata); the acquisition of IBM by China's Lenovo; Brazil's success in exporting small commercial aircraft to industrial countries; and the growing exports of skilled services from India and Israel to markets in member countries of the Organisation for Economic Co-operation and Development (OECD).

These developments have two things in common. The first is that skills, embodied in goods, services, or capital (in the form of entrepreneurial and managerial skills associated with FDI), are being exported. The second is that these embodied skills are exported from poorer to richer countries. On its own, the first feature, although interesting, would not necessarily run counter to the predictions of standard trade models. For example, if China were exporting sophisticated goods to and investing in Africa, that would not be inconsistent with their relative endowments. It is the movement of sophisticated goods and FDI from China to countries that have relatively more skills and capital that is noteworthy from a trade perspective. This paper is a first stab at documenting and understanding this unusual, and possibly significant, phenomenon.

How significant is the phenomenon? Figure 1 plots a measure combining the sophistication of a country's exports and the average income level of the countries that are destinations for sophisticated exports against per capita income for the years 1991 and 2005. (See the section "Consequences of Uphillness," below, for a precise definition of uphill exports.) Two features are noteworthy. First, there is an upward shift of the curve between the two time periods, suggesting that exogenous factors—perhaps technology—are increasing the propensity of countries, especially those at lower income levels, to export sophisticated goods to rich trading partners. Particularly striking is that in 2005 the performance of a number of developing countries, including China, Malaysia, Mexico, the Philippines, and South Africa, surpassed in this respect the 1991 performance of a number of industrial countries with much higher per capita incomes. Even more striking is that a few developing countries (China, Mexico, and South Africa) match the contemporary performance of Japan, Portugal, Spain, and the United States.

Figure 2 presents a similar picture for outward flows of FDI, including both mergers and acquisitions (M&A) and greenfield investments.[1] On the vertical axis are FDI outflows from selected countries to OECD countries as a share of the sending country's gross domestic product (GDP), averaged over the period 2003–07. This measure of uphill FDI flows is plotted against the sending country's per capita income. Flows of FDI to OECD countries from developing countries such as Brazil, India, Malaysia, and South Africa as a share of their GDP are as large as flows from countries such as Japan, the Republic of Korea, and the United States.

Taken together, these charts provide evidence of the "precociousness" of some developing countries in exporting skills in a manner associated with countries at much

FIGURE 1.
Exports of Sophisticated Goods by Selected Economies, 1991 and 2005

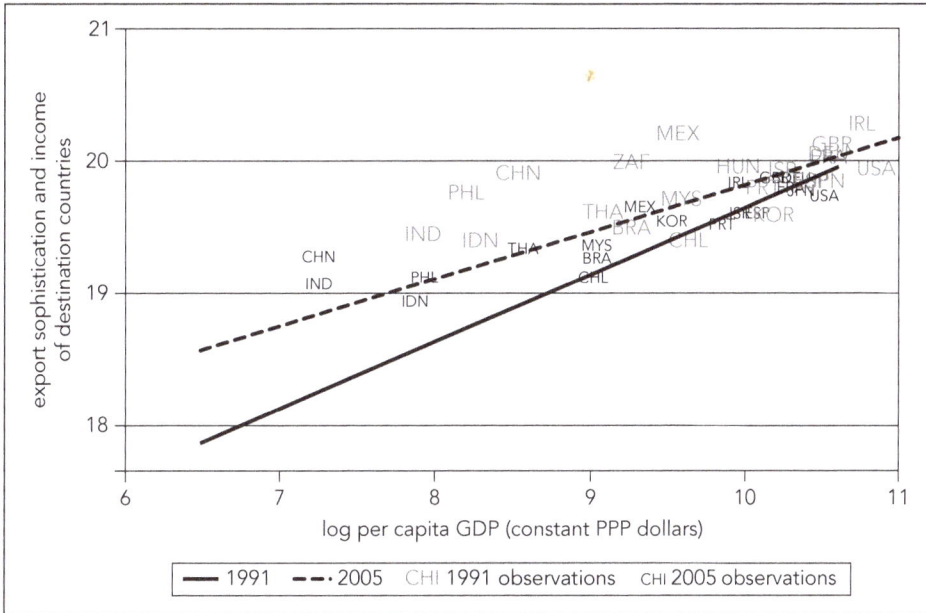

Source: United Nations Commodity Trade Statistics database (Comtrade).

Note: GDP, gross domestic product; PPP, purchasing power parity. The figure plots a measure that combines the sophistication of a country's exports and the average income level of the destination countries for these exports (see the text). The plot lines represent the fit of the relationship between this measure and per capita GDP in 1991 and 2005. The fit is based on a larger sample of countries than those identified in the figure. The country abbreviations are BRA, Brazil; CHL, Chile; CHN, China; ESP, Spain; GBR, United Kingdom; HUN, Hungary; IDN, Indonesia; IND, India; IRL, Ireland; ISR, Israel; KOR, Republic of Korea; MEX, Mexico; MYS, Malaysia; PHL, the Philippines; PRT, Portugal; THA, Thailand; USA, United States; and ZAF, South Africa.

higher levels of development. This phenomenon, of course, has not gone unnoticed. A number of studies have recently emphasized the growing sophistication of the export and production base of developing countries. For example, Schott (2007) has shown that China's export profile is becoming increasingly similar to that of many OECD countries (see also Hummels and Klenow 2005; Schott 2005). Ramamurti and Singh (2009) have documented FDI flows from developing to industrial countries.

A related literature has focused on the direction of these export flows, but in a more normative context. For example, Samuelson (2004) and Krugman (2008) have examined the consequences of growth of U.S. imports of manufactured goods produced in developing countries that compete with domestic U.S. production. There has also been some discussion in the popular press of inward flows of FDI from developing countries (for example, in connection with the Dubai Port episode), but it is primarily related to security issues. These are perspectives—even paranoid ones—on uphill flows from the top of the hill. The vast literature on the effects of global integration, through trade in goods and FDI, has focused primarily on flows to developing countries. For example, Coe, Helpman, and Hoffmaister (1997) highlighted the effect of technology diffusion through imports of capital goods on the growth of developing countries, and Lumenga-Neso, Olarreaga, and Schiff (2001)

FIGURE 2.
Defying Comparative Advantage: Foreign Direct Investment, 2003–07

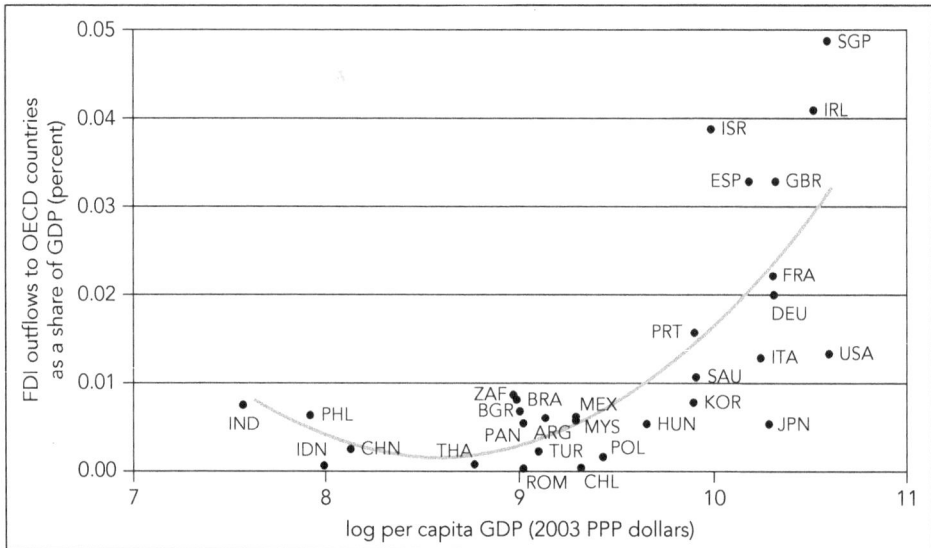

Sources: Thomson Financial SDC Platinum database and *Financial Times* FDI Intelligence database.

Note: GDP, gross domestic product; PPP, purchasing power parity. The figure plots FDI outflows from a country to OECD countries as a share of its GDP (averaged over the period 2003–07) against its per capita income. The sample comprises selected industrial and emerging-market countries. The economies shown are ARG, Argentina; BRA, Brazil; CHL, Chile; CHN, China; DEU, Germany; ESP, Spain; FRA, France; GBR, United Kingdom; HUN, Hungary; IDN, Indonesia; IND, India; IRL, Ireland; ISR, Israel; ITA, Italy; JPN, Japan; KOR, Republic of Korea; MEX, Mexico; MUS, Mauritius; MYS, Malaysia; PAK, Pakistan; PHL, the Philippines; POL, Poland; PRT, Portugal; ROM, Romania; SAU, Saudi Arabia; SGP, Singapore; THA, Thailand; TUR, Turkey; USA, United States; and ZAF, South Africa.

emphasized the impact of direct and indirect imports from industrial countries. There is also a large literature documenting the effects of inward FDI (Borensztein, De Gregorio, and Lee 1998; Haskel, Pereira, and Slaughter 2002).

Recently, Hausmann, Hwang, and Rodrik (2007) looked at the effects of the sophistication of a country's export profile on its own growth (see also Burgess and Venables 2004). In a similar vein, Feenstra and Kee (2004) examine whether diversity of export production can have productivity-enhancing effects. The effects of outward flows of FDI and skilled exports, and of the destination of these flows, have received less attention.

Why should the destination of trade and FDI flows matter? Javorcik (2004) has shown that selling to foreign-owned firms located in a country has positive upstream productivity effects because of the possibility of induced technological and managerial improvements. In principle, these benefits can also arise from sales to foreign firms located abroad. Recently, De Loecker (2007), working with microdata on Slovenian firms, has demonstrated that productivity gains are higher for firms exporting toward high-income regions. Moreover, exports of goods to high-income destinations are frequently associated with participation in global production chains that confer important benefits (Hoekman and Javorcik 2006).

In this paper we first present some new data on developing-country exports of services, goods, and FDI and assess the extent to which these are going to richer countries. We then undertake a preliminary exploration of the consequences of uphill flows of embodied skills for growth of the source country. Here, we follow closely the work of Hausmann, Hwang, and Rodrik (2007).

Data

Our focus in this paper is on the direction of flows of embodied skills. For the three areas—FDI, goods, and services—for which we present some broad data, we need to explain how we define or illustrate the flow of skills.

Our FDI data come from two sources. The Thomson Financial SDC Platinum database provides data on FDI taking the form of mergers and acquisitions. The *Financial Times* FDI Intelligence database provides similar data on greenfield investments. These databases are described in detail in the annex to this article.

Our trade data come from the United Nations World Integrated Trade Solution (WITS) database. We collected data at the five-digit level, largely because finer data— say, at the six-digit level—really become available only in the late 1980s, and we are interested in checking whether the phenomenon of uphill flows is a feature of the historical data. For computational reasons, we collected data for every five-year interval and restricted the sample to countries that together account for about 90 percent of world trade.[2]

We draw on Hausmann, Hwang, and Rodrik (2007) to characterize skill-intensive products. These authors calculate a measure called PRODY, which is a weighted sum of the per capita GDP of countries exporting a given product and, thus, represents the income level associated with each of these goods. In this paper, we define—admittedly, arbitrarily—skill-intensive products as those that are either above the median level or in the top 25th percentile of PRODY for all products defined at the five-digit level of aggregation for 1990.

Our services data come from the Balance of Payments Statistics database of the International Monetary Fund (IMF) and from the U.S. Bureau of Economic Analysis.

Stylized Facts on Uphillness

We first present some basic facts about flows of embodied skills.

Foreign Direct Investment

The share in world FDI exports of non-OECD countries for which data are available for the period 2003–07 is shown in figure 3. This share goes up from about 20 to 25 percent over the period under consideration.

These figures show how developing countries are becoming increasing exporters of FDI, but they do not indicate the direction of the flows. Figure 4 isolates the direction

FIGURE 3.
Share of Non-OECD Countries in World FDI Exports, 2003–07

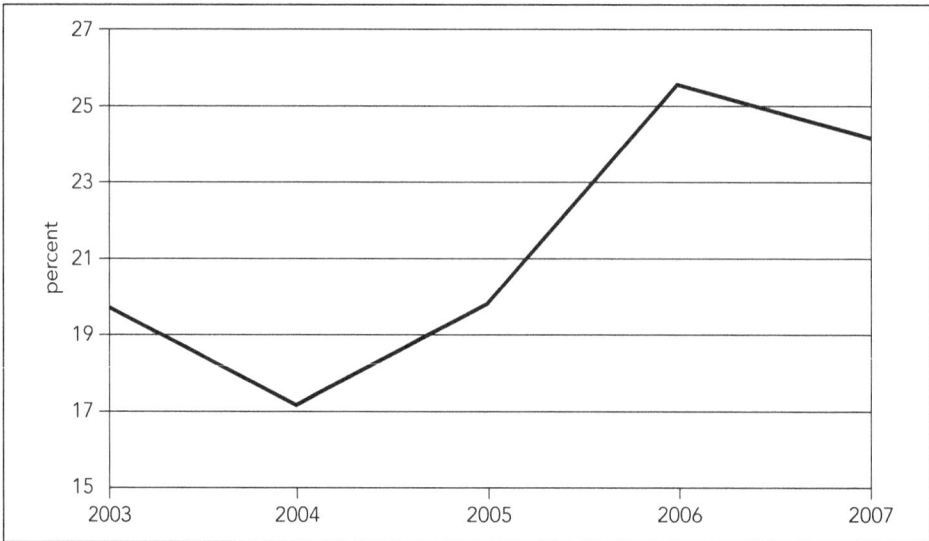

Sources: Thomson Financial SDC Platinum database and *Financial Times* FDI Intelligence database.

FIGURE 4.
Share of Non-OECD Countries in World FDI Exports to OECD Countries, 2003–07

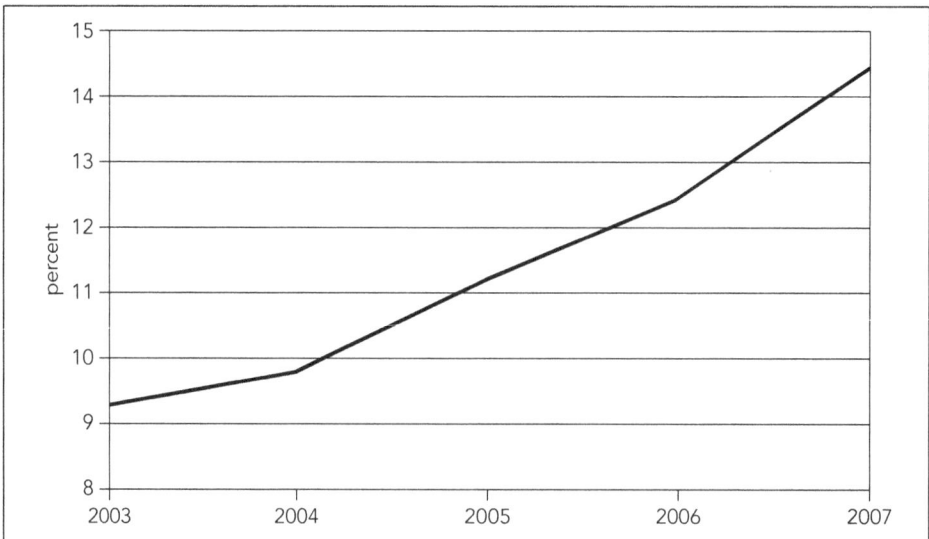

Sources: Thomson Financial SDC Platinum database and *Financial Times* FDI Intelligence database.

of flow of these skills by depicting the share of non-OECD countries in FDI exports to OECD countries and so provides a measure of uphill flows at the global level. This share increased from about 9 percent in 2003 to close to 15 percent in 2007.

Exports of Goods

We repeat this exercise for exports of sophisticated goods and find a similar pattern. The average income level of world exports of sophisticated products declined by a similar percent—about 10 percent—but over a slightly longer period (figure 5). Unlike the case of FDI, China is a big contributor to the decrease in the income of the source country for world exports of sophisticated products. Exclusion of China reduces the decline by nearly 5 percent (figure 5, panel b).

In figure 6, we calculate the uphill flows of sophisticated products from non-OECD countries. For each country, the amount of exports of sophisticated goods to richer countries as a share of the country's total sophisticated exports is the magnitude of uphill flows. These exports are added for all non-OECD countries. This share was about 1 percent in 1980; it was about 0.5 percent for highly sophisticated products (HSPs).[3] The share increased to 10 percent in 2006 (over 3 percent for HSPs).[4] As shown in figure 7, uphill flows were pronounced for China, Malaysia, and Mexico but much less so for Brazil and India.

Services

In services, we focus on exports of services other than transport and travel, that is, the category "other commercial" (in the United States, "other private") services, which includes most skill-intensive business services. Again, we find a decline, albeit slow, in the average income level of services exporters (figure 8). This trend suggests that developing countries are becoming increasingly important exporters of skilled services.

Unfortunately, bilateral data on services trade are available only for OECD countries, so it is not possible to construct measures of uphill flows analogous to those for goods and FDI.[5] However, bilateral data available for the United States show that for some developing countries (for example, India and Malaysia), services exports as a share of GDP are flowing uphill (figure 9)

Country Heterogeneity

Although the phenomenon of uphill flows appears to characterize several developing countries, there is heterogeneity across them. It is not the case, for example, that countries that see uphill flows of sophisticated exports also see uphill flows of FDI. For example, in figure 10, uphill FDI flows are plotted against uphill sophisticated exports for 22 important emerging market countries for which data are available. There seems to be little correlation between the two. Indeed, there appear to be four distinct categories: (a) countries such as Israel and Malaysia do well on both counts;

FIGURE 5.
Average Income Level of World Exports of Sophisticated Products, 1990–2006

a. Including China

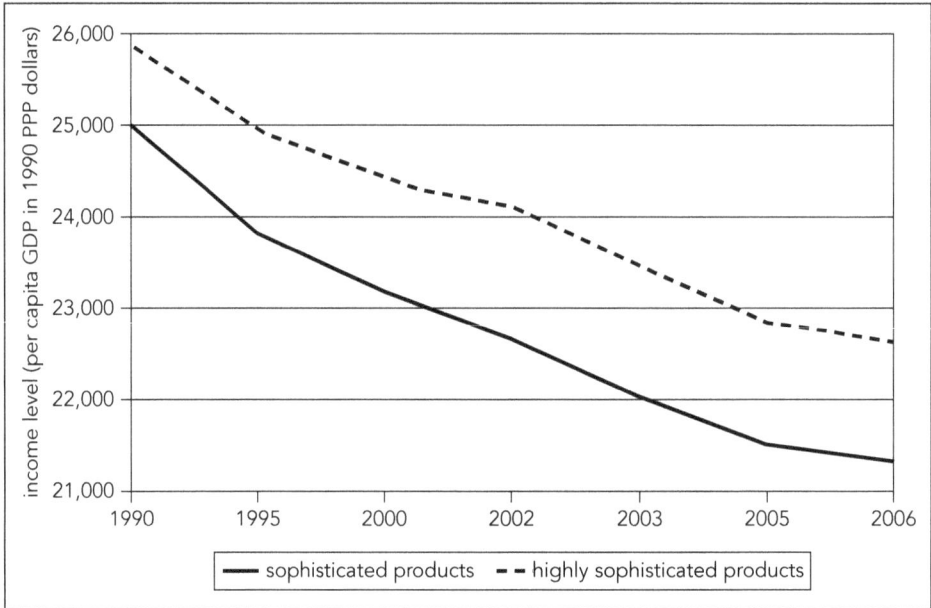

b. Excluding China

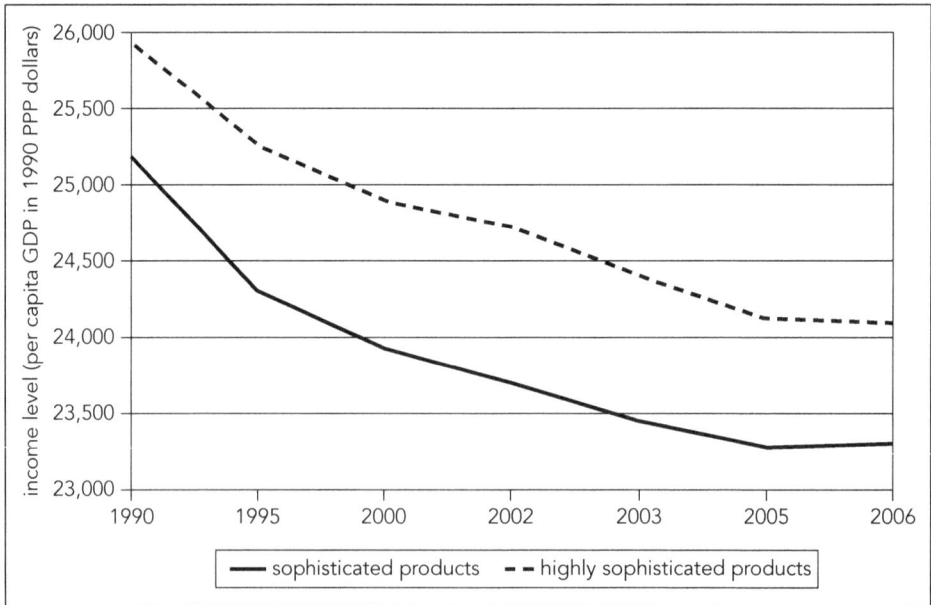

Source: United Nations Commodity Trade Statistics database (Comtrade).

Note: For definitions of sophisticated products, see note 3.

FIGURE 6.
Uphill Flows of Sophisticated Exports from Non-OECD Countries, 1990–2006

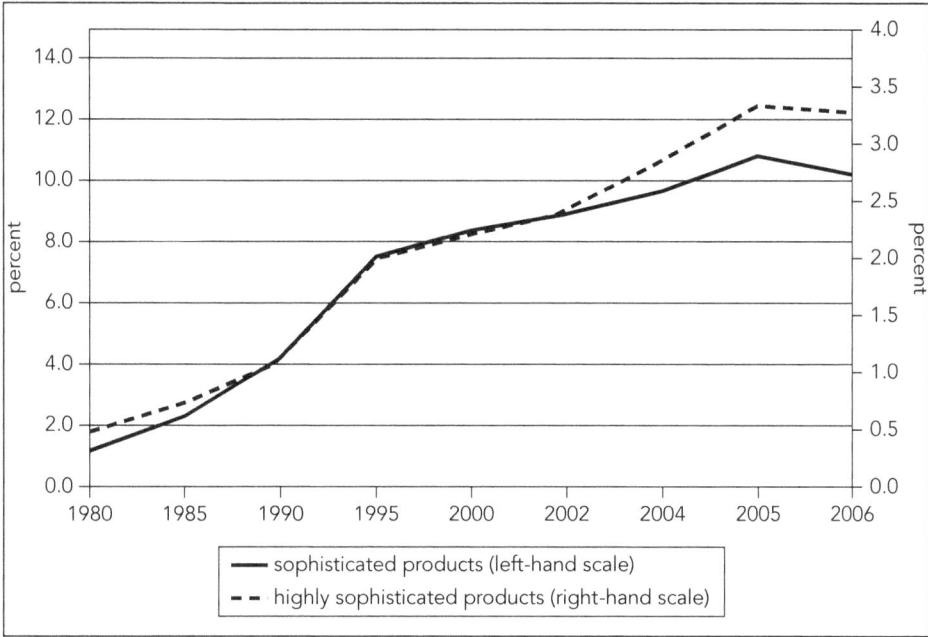

Source: United Nations Commodity Trade Statistics database (Comtrade).

Note: For each country, the measure of uphill flows is exports of sophisticated goods to countries richer than the country itself as a share of its total sophisticated exports. These are added for all non-OECD countries.

FIGURE 7.
Uphill Flows of Sophisticated Exports as a Share of Source Country GDP, 1980–2005

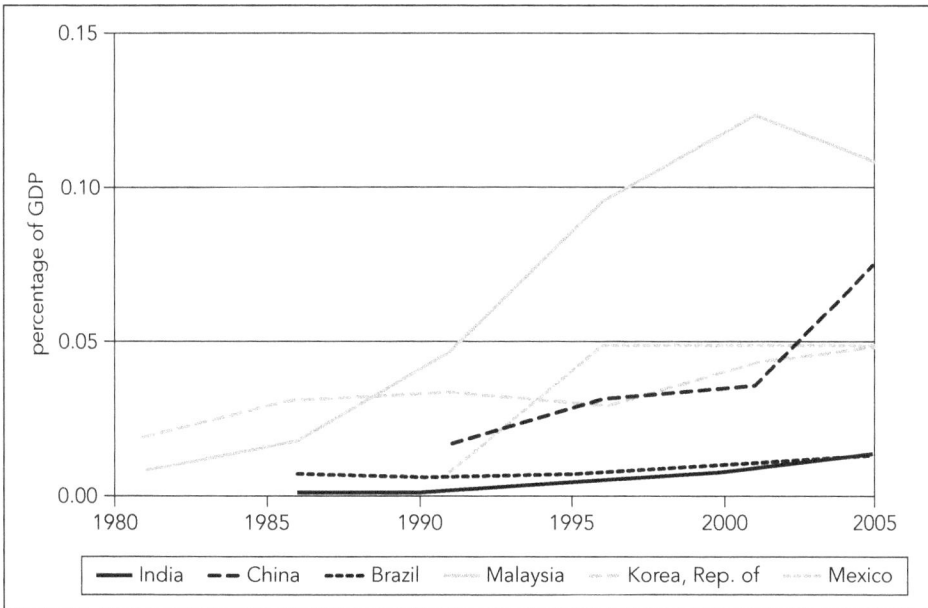

Source: United Nations Commodity Trade Statistics database (Comtrade).

Note: The measure of uphill flows is the value of exports of sophisticated products as a share of a country's GDP (all measured in current dollars).

FIGURE 8.
Average Income Level of Exporters of Other Private Services, 1995–2006

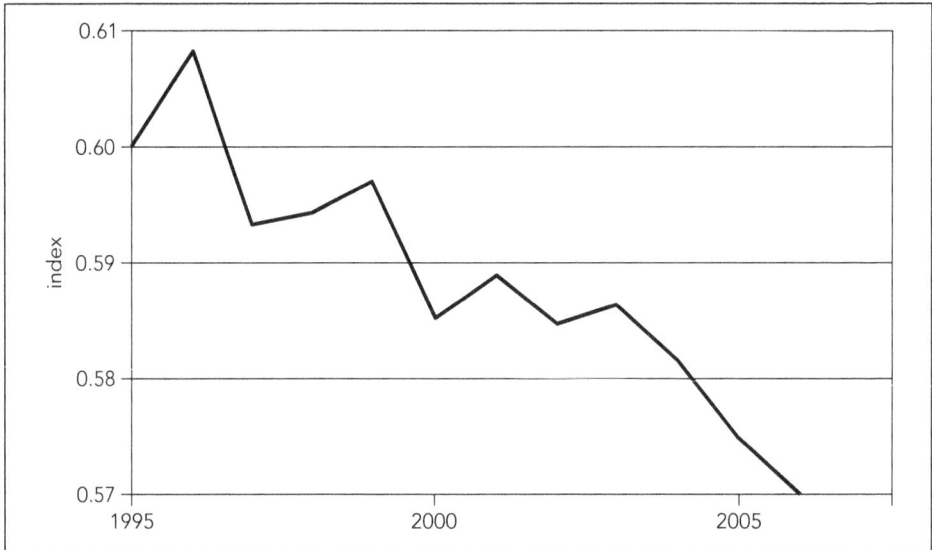

Source: IMF Balance of Payments Statistics data.

Note: The "other private services" category comprises services other than transport and travel and covers most skill-intensive business services. We compute the weighted average of per capita GDP of the exporting countries, with the weights being the share of each country in total exports of other private services.

FIGURE 9.
Exports to the United States of Other Private Services as a Share of Source Country GDP, 1992–2006

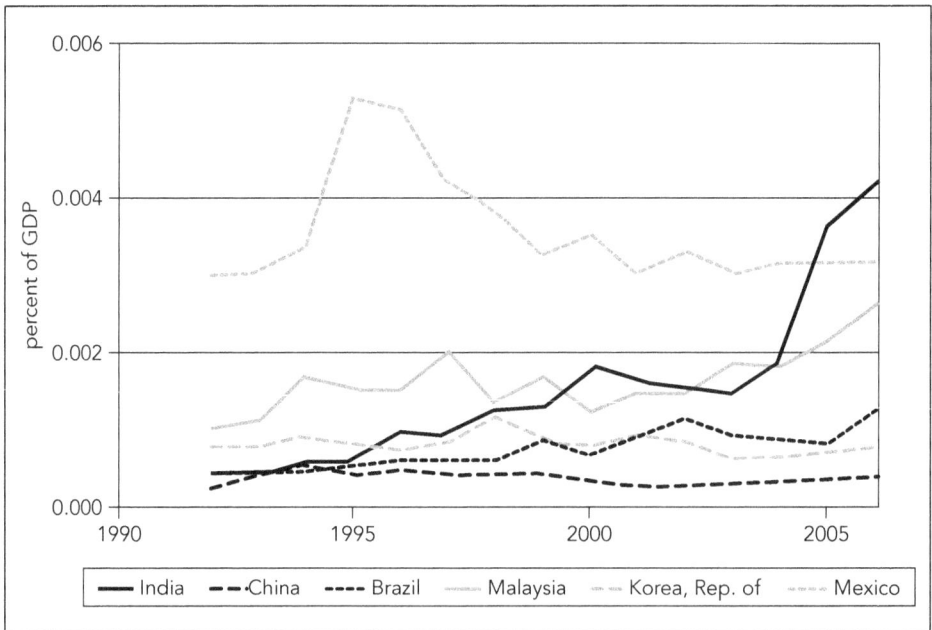

Source: U.S. Bureau of Economic Analysis.

Note: See note to figure 8.

FIGURE 10.
Uphill Flows of FDI and Exports of Sophisticated Goods, Averages for 2003–07

a. FDI

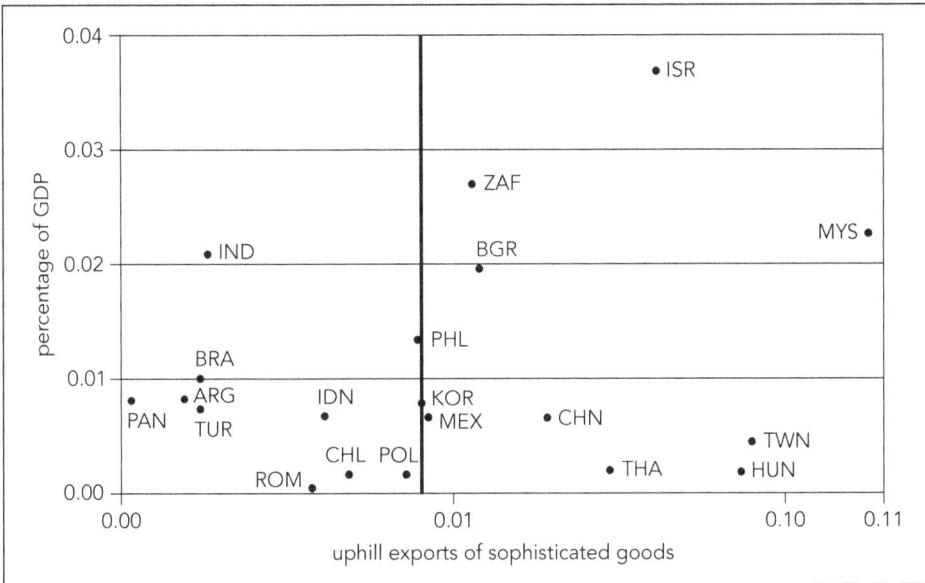

b. FDI in Manufacturing

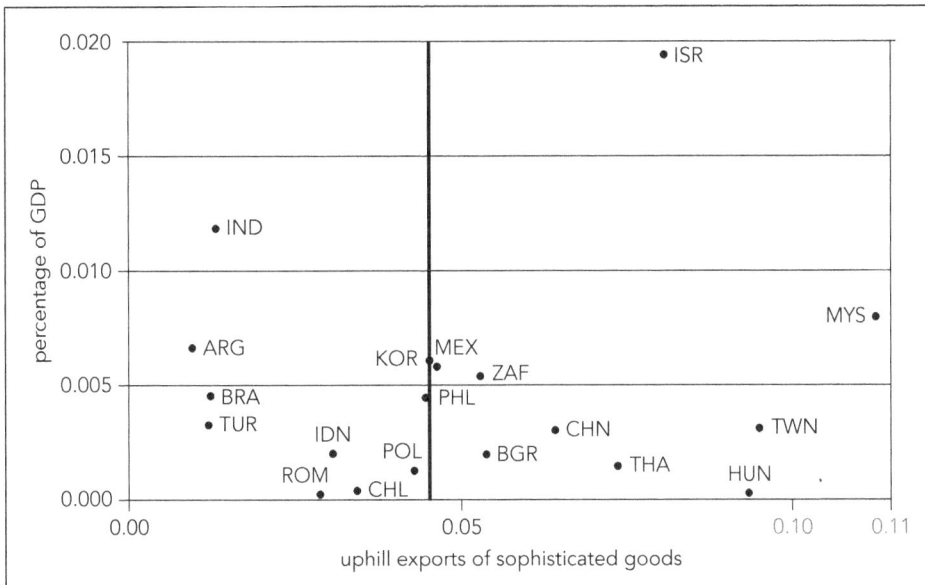

Sources: United Nations Commodity Trade Statistics database (Comtrade), Thomson Financial SDC Platinum database, and *Financial Times* FDI Intelligence database.

Note: In the first panel, uphill outflows of FDI, measured as FDI outflows of a country to countries with a higher per capita GDP purchasing power parity (PPP) than itself, and exports of sophisticated goods are expressed as a share of a country's GDP. Uphill outflows of FDI in manufacturing and exports of sophisticated goods are expressed as a share of a country's GDP. The economies shown are ARG, Argentina, BGR, Bulgaria; BRA, Brazil; CHL, Chile; CHN, China; HUN, Hungary; IDN, Indonesia; IND, India; ISR, Israel; KOR, Republic of Korea; MEX, Mexico; MYS, Malaysia; PAN, Panama; PHL, the Philippines; POL, Poland; ROM, Romania; THA, Thailand; TUR, Turkey; TWN, Taiwan, China; and ZAF, South Africa.

(b) Brazil and India have significant uphill flows of FDI but relatively small uphill exports of sophisticated goods; (c) China and some East Asian economies (Thailand and Taiwan, China) and Eastern European countries (Hungary) are exactly the opposite of Brazil and India, with large uphill export flows but limited FDI flows; and (d) some countries such as Chile, Poland, and Romania, score low on both counts.

Notwithstanding the above, success in exporting sophisticated goods could be associated with a greater likelihood of investing in manufacturing. But this does not turn out to be the case. The best examples are Brazil and India, which are not big uphill exporters of sophisticated goods but score well on FDI in manufacturing (see panel b of figure 10).

Preston Curves

How recent is this phenomenon of uphill flows? We cannot carry out meaningful historical comparisons for FDI because the data do not allow us to go so far back, but we can attempt to answer this question for exports of sophisticated goods.

To do this, we relate uphill flows to the level of per capita GDP of a country for three points in time (1986, 1996, and 2005) that are sufficiently far apart to allow changes to express themselves (figure 11). The noteworthy point that emerges is that the relationship shifts markedly upward in the most recent period for which we have data.[6] The shift implies that over time, uphill flows are becoming more common across the income spectrum. We also find that the fit of the relationship between uphill flows and income tightens over time, suggesting that higher-income countries are likely to see more uphill flows.

Consequences of Uphillness

An obvious question is, do uphill flows matter for economic growth? Hausmann, Hwang, and Rodrik (2007) have argued that the structure of exports does matter for growth. In particular, countries that produce more sophisticated goods (defined as those produced by richer countries) are shown to be more likely to grow faster. But the focus of this paper is not so much the sophistication of exports as whether a country's export pattern defies comparative advantage. As argued earlier, it would not be surprising or at odds with the predictions of the standard trade models if a poor country exported relatively sophisticated goods to countries poorer than itself. We are therefore interested not only in the sophistication of exports, but also in their destination.

To pursue this question of whether comparative advantage–defying (alternatively, "uphill") exports have growth consequences, we adopt the basic cross-national regression methodology deployed by Hausmann, Hwang, and Rodrik (2007). Our results for the pure cross-section are presented in tables 1 and 2, and the panel regressions are contained in tables 3 and 4. We calculate two measures of uphill exports. In the first, we combine the Hausmann, Hwang, and Rodrik indicator of sophistication (EXPY) with a measure of the average income level of the destination countries receiving such sophisticated exports; specifically, we add the log of the EXPY measure and the log of the average income level of destination countries, and call this UPHILL1. This is the measure used in tables 1 and 3.[7]

FIGURE 11.
Uphill Flows of Sophisticated Exports and Per Capita GDP, Selected Economies, 1986, 1996, and 2005

a. Without controls for area, population, and remoteness

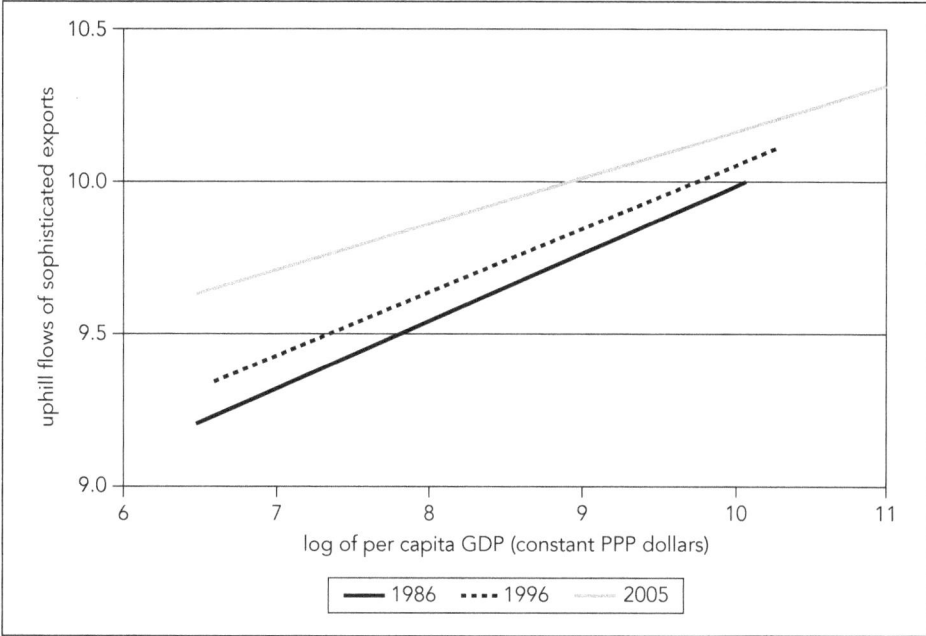

b. With controls for area, population, and remoteness

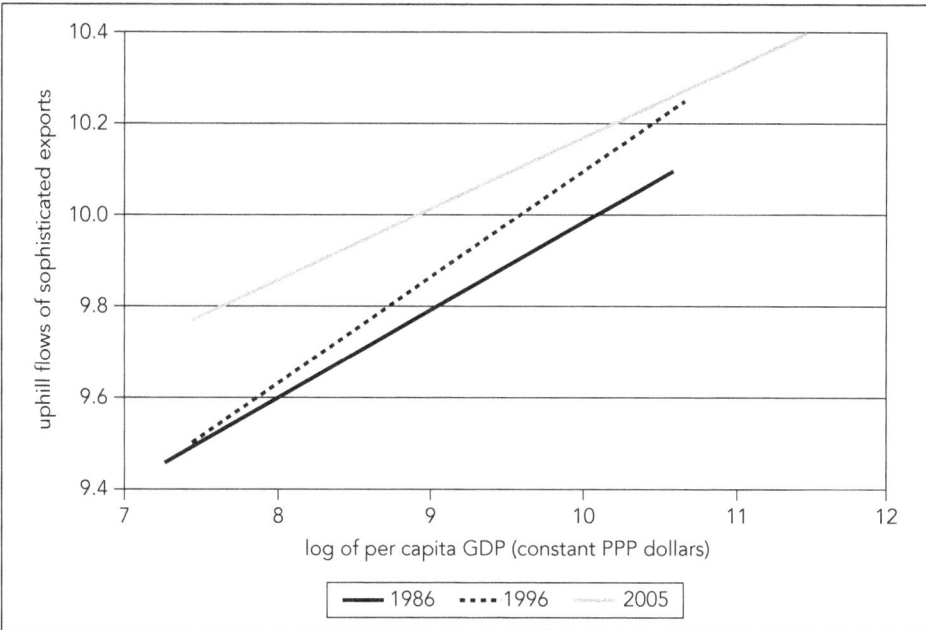

Source: United Nations Commodity Trade Statistics database (Comtrade).

Note: PPP = purchasing power parity. Uphill flows are measured as the average income level of all the destination countries that receive a country's sophisticated exports (defined here as above-median PRODY exports), where the weights are each destination country's share in total exports of the sending country. The sample is kept constant for all three periods. Panel b includes, for each year for which the relationship is plotted, controls for area, population, and remoteness, all in log terms. Remoteness, drawn from Berthelon and Freund (2008), is measured as $j \neq k$ where D is distance and there are k foreign countries.

$$remote_j = \frac{1}{\sum\limits_k^N \frac{GDP_k}{D_{ij}}}$$

TABLE 1. Growth and Uphill Flows of Sophisticated Exports: Cross-Sectional Regressions Using Scale-Free Measure of Uphill Flows

(dependent variable: annual average growth rate, 1994–2003)

Variable	(1)	(2)	(3)	(4)	(5)	(6)	(7)
Initial per capita GDP (log)	−0.013*	−0.007	−0.007	−0.003	−0.008	−0.004	−0.009
	(0.007)	(0.005)	(0.005)	(0.005)	(0.005)	(0.007)	(0.006)
Uphill flows for 1990 (median sophistication)	0.017***	0.011***					0.014*
	(0.005)	(0.003)					(0.008)
Years of primary schooling	−0.004	−0.015	−0.015	−0.003	−0.015	−0.011	−0.015*
	(0.013)	(0.009)	(0.009)	(0.011)	(0.009)	(0.010)	(0.009)
Capital stock	−0.000	0.000	−0.000	−0.001	−0.000	−0.000	0.000
	(0.006)	(0.005)	(0.005)	(0.005)	(0.005)	(0.005)	(0.005)
Institutional quality (rule of law)	0.009***	0.008***	0.008***	0.008***	0.009***	0.008***	0.008***
	(0.003)	(0.002)	(0.003)	(0.003)	(0.003)	(0.003)	(0.002)
Uphill flows for 1990 (75th percentile sophistication)			0.011***				
			(0.003)				
Uphill flows for 1990 of sophisticated relative to unsophisticated products						0.007*	
						(0.004)	
Sophistication of exports					0.013**		
					(0.006)		
Average income level of destination of sophisticated (median) exports					0.011***		
					(0.004)		
Uphill flows for 1995 (median sophistication)				0.007**			
				(0.003)			
Number of observations	58	56	56	60	56	56	55
Adjusted R²	0.260	0.321	0.303	0.224	0.308	0.205	0.328
F-test	5.60	7.19	8.33	7.01	6.01	5.80	5.00

Source: Authors' calculations.

Note: Numbers in parentheses are robust standard errors. Columns (2)–(7) exclude China and Ireland. Column (7) is an instrumental variable (IV) estimation with population and area (logs) serving as instruments for uphill flows.

*p < .1   **p < .05   ***p < .01

TABLE 2. Growth and Uphill Flows of Sophisticated Exports: Cross-Sectional Regressions, Sophisticated Exports to Richer Countries, Scaled by GDP

(dependent variable: annual average growth rate, 1994–2003)

Variable	(1)	(2)	(3)
Initial per capita GDP (log)	−0.001	−0.000	−0.000
	(0.005)	(0.005)	(0.005)
Downhill export flows of sophisticated (median)	−0.099**	−0.087**	−0.112**
products (as share of GDP)	(0.047)	(0.035)	(0.050)
Uphill export flows of sophisticated (median)	0.263***	0.122**	0.096*
products (as share of GDP)	(0.080)	(0.048)	(0.048)
Years of primary schooling	−0.001	−0.009	−0.009
	(0.017)	(0.013)	(0.013)
Capital stock	−0.003	−0.001	−0.000
	(0.006)	(0.004)	(0.004)
Institutional quality (rule of law)	0.010***	0.010***	0.010***
	(0.003)	(0.003)	(0.003)
Exports of nonsophisticated (median)			0.024
products (share of GDP)			(0.022)
Number of observations	61	59	59
Adjusted R^2	0.314	0.236	0.235
F-test	6.17	7.90	7.89

Source: Authors' calculations.

Note: Numbers in parentheses are robust standard errors. Columns (2) and (3) exclude China and Ireland.

*$p < .1$ **$p < .05$ ***$p < .01$

A particular issue with the Hausmann, Hwang, and Rodrik approach and our adaptation of it is that the measures of sophistication and uphillness are not scaled. For example, these authors' EXPY measure captures the sophistication of an economy's export basket without taking account of the importance, relative to the size of an economy, of the exports of these products. The use of a scale-free measure entails both a benefit and a limitation. The benefit is econometric; there is less endogeneity bias.

The downside is that the economic intuition is less clear. Our uphill measure, too, is scale free, capturing the importance of uphill flows in the export basket but not their economywide importance.

We accordingly calculate a second measure, which is the share of exports of sophisticated products flowing uphill as a share of GDP. We calculate uphillness by simply adding up the exports that a country sends to trading partners richer than itself. This is called UPHILL2 and is used in tables 2 and 4.

In column 1 of table 1, we present the basic results with controls for human capital, physical capital, and institutions. Our measure of uphill flows is positively signed and statistically significant at the 1 percent confidence level. We find that China and Ireland are clear outliers. So in column 2 we drop them and find that the results remain unchanged. The coefficient suggests that a 1 percent increase in uphill flows

TABLE 3. Growth and Uphill Flows of Sophisticated Exports: Panel Regressions Using Scale-Free Measure of Uphill Flows)

Variable	(1) OLS	(2) OLS	(3) OLS	(4) OLS	(5) Fixed effects	(6) IV	(7) IV
Per capita GDP (log)	−0.006**	−0.006**	−0.005**	−0.004*	0.033***	−0.015*	−0.015*
	(0.003)	(0.003)	(0.002)	(0.002)	(0.007)	(0.009)	(0.009)
Uphill flows (median sophistication)	0.011***	0.011***			0.001	0.024***	
	(0.003)	(0.003)			(0.005)	(0.009)	
Years of primary schooling	0.009**	0.009**	0.009**	0.010**	0.040**	0.013	0.012
	(0.004)	(0.004)	(0.005)	(0.005)	(0.017)	(0.020)	(0.020)
Uphill flows (75th percentile sophistication)			0.010***				0.025***
			(0.003)				(0.009)
Uphill flows of sophisticated relative to unsophisticated products				0.009***			
				(0.003)			
Number of observations	267	267	266	267	267	256	255
Adjusted R²	0.076	0.106	0.090	0.080	0.117	0.005	−0.045
F-test	7.07	4.44	4.74	3.79	7.96	3.25	2.79
Number of countries					65		

Source: Authors' calculations.

Note: IV, instrumental variable; OLS, ordinary least squares. Numbers in parentheses are robust standard errors. The instruments for uphill flows in columns (6) and (7) are population and remoteness (in logs). All columns except column (1) include time effects. Fixed effects are included only in column (5).

*p < .1   **p < .05   ***p < .01

TABLE 4. Growth and Uphill Flows of Sophisticated Exports: Panel Regressions, Sophisticated Exports to Richer Countries, Scaled by GDP

Variable	(1) Random effects	(2) Fixed effects	(3) Fixed effects	(4) Fixed effects	(5) Fixed effects
Per capita GDP (log)	0.007***	0.063***	0.063***	0.060***	0.042***
	(0.003)	(0.012)	(0.012)	(0.012)	(0.008)
Uphill export flows of	0.229***	0.231***	0.226**		
sophisticated (median) products	(0.055)	(0.085)	(0.090)		
(as share of GDP)					
Downhill export flows of	−0.024	0.056	0.063		
sophisticated (median)	(0.031)	(0.049)	(0.052)		
products (as share of GDP)					
Years of primary schooling	0.019***	0.021	0.021	0.022	0.052***
	(0.007)	(0.019)	(0.019)	(0.020)	(0.018)
Exports of nonsophisticated (median)			0.012		
products (as share of GDP)			(0.035)		
Uphill export flows of				0.264	0.489**
sophisticated (75th percentile)				(0.197)	(0.205)
products (as share of GDP)					
Downhill export flows of				0.059	0.081
sophisticated (75th percentile)				(0.127)	(0.151)
products (as share of GDP)					
Exports of				0.037	0.034
nonsophisticated (75th percentile)				(0.034)	(0.036)
products (as share of GDP)					
Number of observations	258	258	258	258	258
Number of rcode	64	64	64	64	64
R^2	0.13				
Adjusted R^2		0.288	0.285	0.271	0.171
F-test		5.92	5.19	4.82	5.59

Source: Authors' calculations.

Note: Numbers in parentheses are robust standard errors. All columns except column (1) include time effects.

*$p < .1$ **$p < .05$ ***$p < .01$

could increase growth by about 1.1 percent a year. (The partial scatterplot of this regression is shown in figure 12.) In column 3 we use the alternative measure of sophistication based on a 25th-percentile cutoff of products. In column 4 we use our uphill flow measure for 1995 instead of 1990. In column 5 we disaggregate our uphill measure into the sophistication component and the destination component and find that each is significant with the same magnitude. (The equality of the two coefficients cannot be rejected.)[8] In column 6 we subtract the destination income of countries receiving unsophisticated products from the destination income of countries receiving sophisticated products. This is a kind of validation check. In all cases the coefficient on UPHILL1 remains significant, suggesting some strong association.

FIGURE 12.
Cross-Section Regression: Scatter Plot of Growth on Uphill Flows, Selected Economies

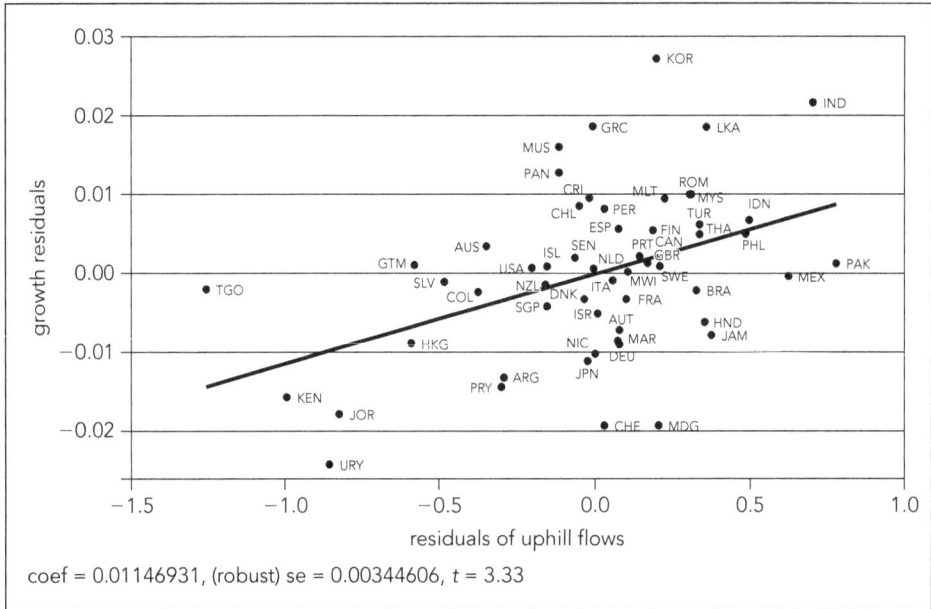

coef = 0.01146931, (robust) se = 0.00344606, t = 3.33

Source: Based on the regression in table 1, column 2.

Note: Controls include initial income, institutional quality, primary school enrollment, and capital stock. Coefficient, 0.01146931; (robust) standard error, 0.00344606; t, 3.33. The economies shown are ARG, Argentina; AUS, Australia; AUT, Austria; BRA, Brazil; CAN, Canada; CHE, Switzerland; CHL, Chile; COL, Colombia; CRI, Costa Rica; DEU, Germany; DNK, Denmark; ESP, Spain; FIN, Finland; FRA, France; GBR, United Kingdom; GRC, Greece; GTM, Guatemala; HKG, Hong Kong, China; HND, Honduras; IDN, Indonesia; IND, India; ISL, Iceland; ISR, Israel; ITA, Italy; JAM, Jamaica; JOR, Jordan; JPN, Japan; KEN, Kenya; KOR, Republic of Korea; LKA, Sri Lanka; MAR, Morocco; MDG, Madagascar; MEX, Mexico; MLT, Malta; MUS, Mauritius; MWI, Malawi; MYS, Malaysia; NIC, Nicaragua; NLD, Netherlands; NZL, New Zealand; PAK, Pakistan; PAN, Panama; PER, Peru; PHL, the Philippines; PRT, Portugal; PRY, Paraguay; ROM, Romania; SEN, Senegal; SGP, Singapore; SLV, El Salvador; SWE, Sweden; TGO, Togo; THA, Thailand; TUR, Turkey; URY, Uruguay; and USA, United States of America.

In column 7, to address the potential endogeneity of our uphill measure, we instrument for it with the log of population and log of area, as in Hausmann, Hwang, and Rodrik (2007). The first stage suggests that the instruments are reasonably but not exceptionally strong. In the second stage, the uphill measure has about the same magnitude and remains significant, albeit at the 10 percent confidence level.

Of course, there are a number of issues with our estimation method: some of our right-hand-side variables are prone to endogeneity bias despite our use of initial rather than contemporaneous values; we may be omitting other variables; and our variables could be mismeasured. Our results should therefore be interpreted at this stage as conditional associations rather than as full identifications.

In table 2, we use the UPHILL2 measure (recognizing that this may well add another layer of endogeneity bias). We introduce these measures in the cross-country regressions instead of their scale-free counterparts that we used earlier. We can either add the total share of sophisticated exports to GDP and the uphill share of that as two variables or simply use the uphill and downhill shares of sophisticated exports. We do the latter. We find that the coefficient on the share of uphill products to GDP is significant (column 1, table 2) and remains so after excluding Ireland and China (column 2). In column 3 we also control for the share of total unsophisticated exports in GDP and find that this variable is not significant and does not affect our uphill flow measure.[9]

Given the limitations of the above analysis, we turn to panel estimations in tables 3 and 4.[10] In table 3, we use the scale-free measures, and in table 4, we use the measures scaled by GDP. Instead of going through all the columns as was done above, we highlight the key findings. When we use the scale-free measures (that is, UPHILL1), we find that uphill flows are significant except when we add country fixed effects (column 5). But instrumental variable (IV) estimations (in this case, with population and remoteness of a country from the world's center of gravity as instruments) yield very strong first-stage results, with correspondingly strong and statistically significant coefficients for uphill flows in the second stage (columns 6 and 7). When we use the UPHILL2 measure (which is scaled by GDP), we find that uphill flows are statistically significant (columns 2, 3, and 5), even after adding country and time effects.

An issue we attempted to explore in greater detail was the PRODY measure. One could also try to get a measure of "sophistication" of products by, for example, using the level of education, or research and development (R&D), in the exporting country rather than per capita income. For each product, we constructed a weighted average of the exporting countries' secondary school enrollment ratio or spending on R&D as a share of GDP. The results were very similar to those from PRODY.[11] For example, in table 1, when we replaced the uphill measures based on PRODY with those based on education and R&D, the coefficient on the uphill measure was correctly signed and significant. The reason, of course, is that the income-based measure and the measures based on education and R&D are highly correlated, and the differences are not large enough to conclude that it is education, not per capita GDP, that is the more accurate measure of sophistication.

Discussion and Limitations of the Analysis

This paper is a first attempt to document a possibly new phenomenon, which we call uphill flows of skills. We presented a set of stylized facts relating to uphill flows of goods, services, and FDI and preliminary estimates of the consequences of these flows. We have not examined the determinants of these flows or elaborated on the possible channels through which these flows might have growth consequences. We offer next some suggestions with regard to these two issues.

Explaining Uphill Flows

Uphill flows raise some interesting theoretical questions. First, and most obvious, they seem to defy the prediction of the pure Heckscher-Ohlin model, where trade is determined by relative factor endowments. Second, although such flows could be seen as a manifestation of intraindustry trade, driven by economies of scale and imperfect competition, this type of trade has typically been predicted between countries at similar levels of development (Helpman and Krugman 1985).

Two possible explanations for uphill flows—one domestic and one international—suggest themselves. Within developing countries, for example, there could be atypical patterns of development as a result of historical factors and policy actions. Two good examples are India and South Africa, both of which have exhibited skill-intensive patterns of development (see Amin and Mattoo 2006; Kochhar et al. 2006). In the Indian case, this was because higher education was favored at the expense of basic education, while in South Africa, apartheid and labor market policies played a role. Recent research shows that some of these larger developing countries are investing proportionately more in technical education than are poorer or richer countries (Sequeira 2003). If such policies are then overlaid on regional disparities, it is possible for pockets to emerge within developing countries that are sufficiently endowed with skills or are sufficiently developed to explain the observed patterns of "crisscrossing globalization." In other words, the inconsistency of uphill flows with theory may be more apparent than real if we were to think of countries like China and India not as single units but as heterogeneous economic units (or regions) with widely differing relative factor endowments (Subramanian 2007).

It is also possible for the relevant heterogeneity to emerge at the firm level. For example, Melitz (2003) allows for firm-level heterogeneity in productivity and fixed costs of exporting and shows that only the most productive firms export. Helpman, Melitz, and Yeaple (2004) demonstrate, in turn, that among the firms that serve foreign markets, only the most productive engage in FDI. It is conceivable that some firms, even in developing countries, are so productive that they can incur the fixed costs of exporting and investing abroad. Furthermore, if the fixed costs of penetrating foreign markets vary across destinations—say, by per capita income of the destination country—it is possible for productivity differences across developing country firms to result in the phenomenon of "uphill" flows that we document.

External policies could be another cause of uphill flows. One factor may have been international patterns of protection, in particular, rich-country barriers against imports of less-skill-intensive products, and developing-country barriers against imports of more-skill-intensive products. Thus, the larger developing countries may have been inhibited from exploiting their natural comparative advantage by exporting less-skill-intensive products to richer countries and more-skill-intensive products to poorer countries. Put differently, if there is learning by doing, it may be that increases in uphill sophisticated exports have been possible because protection allowed domestic producers to catch up with foreign producers in terms of competitiveness.

Uphill Flows and Growth

Standard theories of trade—Heckscher-Ohlin, intraindustry, and even the new heterogeneous firm–based models—primarily see the gains from trade in static welfare rather than dynamic growth (Bernard et al. 2007). Our results are more in the spirit of endogenous growth theories, which see trade as affecting the incentives and opportunities for dynamic benefits such as technology acquisition and learning by doing.

Although a large part of the benefits of trade has traditionally been seen as access to imports and inward FDI, there is a growing recognition that exports and outward FDI may also confer important benefits.

We have not examined in any detail the channels through which uphill exports of sophisticated goods and services affect overall economic performance. One possibility is that our measure of destination may actually capture a finer degree of product differentiation, in horizontal or vertical terms. For example, Schott (2005) established that even when developing-country exports fall within the same product categories as rich-country exports, they tend to have lower unit values and may be located lower on quality ladders. In other words, what we identify as uphill flows may just be an alternative or complementary measure for product quality and sophistication. Our findings could then be seen as adding to the evidence that such quality matters for economic performance (Hausmann, Hwang, and Rodrik 2007).

Another possibility is that final exports of sophisticated goods by a country may reflect merely its comparative advantage in the final assembly stage rather than a deeper sophistication in its production processes. For example, a significant proportion of China's uphill exports of sophisticated goods contains imports of sophisticated components from rich countries. On the one hand, this could indicate that we are mismeasuring sophistication. On the other hand, our measure could capture the extent of a country's participation in modern global production chains, which confer benefits in terms of knowledge of markets, just-in-time capability, improved production technology, and so on. Thus, what we capture—imperfect though it undoubtedly is—may provide clues about an additional channel through which the impact of global integration is felt. As noted at the outset of this paper, there is now increasing evidence supporting the existence of these channels (Javorcik 2004). In principle, these benefits can also arise from sales to foreign firms located abroad.

Furthermore, uphill flows could affect growth through induced changes in economy-wide skill acquisition and, hence, in long-run endowments, creating a self-reinforcing and virtuous cycle. India again provides a relevant example. Educational attainment in India, especially at the primary and secondary levels, was disappointing until the early 1990s. In the past 15 years, however, educational indicators have improved markedly. Although greater government attention has been important, a key change has been increased demand for education because of higher returns to human capital, which in turn is a consequence of increased skill-intensive and uphill specialization. (The derived demand for skills and, hence, education is arguably a function not just of what is sold, but also to whom it is sold.) This demand has elicited a supply response, largely from the private sector, that has led to a more rapid spread of education and skills (Kremer et al. 2006).

In summary, if there are benefits from uphill flows, in some circumstances significant development benefits might derive not from deifying comparative advantage, but from defying it.

Annex. Data on Foreign Direct Investment

To what extent do we see uphill flows of foreign direct investment (FDI) in the available data, and how have these flows changed in recent years? To pursue this question, we examined merger and acquisition (M&A) FDI data from the Thomson Financial's SDC Platinum database from January 1995 to December 2007 and data on greenfield investment from the *Financial Times* FDI Intelligence, which is a private organization that compiles proprietary data on such investments.

Data Sources

The World Investment Report (WIR) database of the United Nations Conference on Trade and Development (UNCTAD) includes coverage of both total FDI and M&A inflows and outflows for each country, but the published dataset does not break down these flows on a bilateral basis—data on countries of origin are not available for inflows, and data on destination countries are not provided for outflows. Although some UNCTAD-based datasets used by other researchers have endeavored to create this bilateral breakdown, these datasets generally examine FDI stocks rather than flows and have reliable data across a broad range of countries for only a few years, generally between 2003 and 2005.

By contrast, reasonably comprehensive and highly granular coverage is available for M&A and greenfield FDI in the form of commercial financial databases. Such databases report information at the individual transaction level, enabling analysis on three principal axes: source countries of flows, destination countries of flows, and industry sectors of flows. For this analysis, the SDC Platinum database was chosen for its comprehensive dataset, including hundreds of thousands of cross-border M&A transactions from 1985 up to the present.

The FDI Intelligence database produced by the *Financial Times* has tracked greenfield foreign direct investment throughout the world since 2003. Greenfield direct investment is defined as the expansion or creation of physical facilities in any location other than the headquarters of a company. For each greenfield investment project, the database has the actual or estimated investment in dollars terms and the actual or estimated jobs created from the project. Every project is assigned to a source market and a destination market and is also disaggregated to the level of an industry sector, industry cluster, or business activity, in increasing order of disaggregation. The database is continuously updated and currently holds data on more than 78,800 projects.

For the purposes of the paper, we focused on the period 2003–07. Taken at the industry sector level, this period gives 35,045 source-destination-industry observations totaling US$4.3 trillion in value. Collapsing across industry sectors to arrive at aggregate numbers for source markets yields 9,263 bilateral greenfield investment projects over this period, for a total of 132 source markets and 184 destination markets.

Combining the greenfield FDI data with the M&A data from the Thomson Financial SDC Platinum database yields 10,457 bilateral recorded investment projects in either or both categories, with a total value over the whole period of US$7.5 trillion.

Timeframe

In seeking to examine uphill flows of FDI, we note that the years of greatest interest are evidently the most recent ones. Whereas the major East Asian countries have had a significant presence as exporters of FDI for some time, only since the turn of the millennium have the four BRIC countries (Brazil, Russia, India, and China) joined them in this regard, and only since 2002 have net FDI outflows for these four countries combined amounted to more than 2 percent of total world FDI flows. Major oil-exporting countries such as Mexico, Saudi Arabia, and the United Arab Emirates have joined these ranks even more recently. The overall period chosen for analysis for this study was thus that covering the years from 2003 to 2007, inclusive.

Data Coverage

For the purpose of M&A analysis, only completed transactions where transaction value was disclosed and recorded, and where the stake acquired in the target company met or exceeded 10 percent, were included. Accurate recording of transaction values is clearly essential to any calculation of flows, while stakes below 10 percent are considered too small to be classified as FDI under most definitions. Including only disclosed-value transactions eliminates a little over half the transactions recorded in the database, since many transactions are for unlisted companies or for other reasons do not face strict disclosure requirements. The dataset resulting from those selection criteria includes some 37,963 deals totaling US$8.4 trillion in value.

Comparison of the dataset resulting from this selection with M&A data and total FDI data provided in aggregate form in UNCTAD's WIR demonstrates that the overall transaction coverage provided by the SDC Platinum database over this time period is strong. Only between 2000 and 2002 is the total value of M&A transactions reported in the SDC database below that reported in the WIR; in those years, coverage remains above 80 percent, while in all the remaining years, the SDC dataset captures a bigger total transaction volume than that reported by the WIR.

Although the overall volume of transactions captured by the SDC-based dataset is higher than that reported by UNCTAD, for certain years and certain categories the coverage is lower. Thus, whereas—compared with UNCTAD—SDC data report higher M&A FDI inflows into OECD countries (see below for notes on country groupings) for all years except 2000–2002, the OECD outflow volumes reported are routinely lower than those reported by UNCTAD.

Country Groupings and Data Overview

OECD membership was the principal determinant used to distinguish between developed and emerging countries. Although Mexico and the Republic of Korea are now both OECD members, for the purposes of this analysis both were included in the emerging-countries grouping rather than the OECD grouping. Offshore financial centers and Mauritius were excluded from the analysis.

Notes

The authors are grateful to Brad Jensen, Dani Rodrik, Tony Venables, Daniel Xie, and, especially, our discussant Beata Javorcik for valuable comments; to Marko Klasnja and Janak Mayer for outstanding research assistance; and to Francis Ng for his generous statistical help. Janak Mayer prepared the annex to this paper. The research for this paper is supported in part by the governments of Norway, Sweden, and the United Kingdom through the Multidonor Trust Fund for Trade and Development.

1. Data for M&A and greenfield investments are from different sources, as described in the annex.

2. In subsequent work, we plan to increase the sample to cover most countries.

3. There are two definitions of sophisticated products. The first covers exports that lie above the median value of PRODY (described in the text), calculated for 1990. The second covers exports that lie in the top 25th percentile of PRODY values (highly sophisticated products, or HSPs). For each definition, we compute the weighted average per capita GDP of the exporting countries, with the weights being the share of each country in the total exports of sophisticated products.

4. Of course, this development could simply reflect the fact that richer countries, which are more likely to demand sophisticated goods, have grown faster than poorer countries. But during this period, the non-OECD countries in our sample grew substantially faster than the OECD countries.

5. It is, in principle, possible to combine OECD data and the IMF Balance of Payments Statistics to obtain an estimate of the share of exports of skilled services by developing countries directed toward OECD countries. However, significant inconsistencies in the data from those two sources prevent meaningful comparison.

6. The finding of an upward shift holds true when we estimate the relationship (a) without keeping the sample constant across time periods; (b) after controlling for a country's area, population, and remoteness from the world's center of gravity; and (c) using alternative measures of the uphillness of flows. Also, when we estimated the Preston relationships in a formal panel context, we found the coefficient on the 2005 dummy to be positive and statistically significant.

7. As a referee pointed out, in principle, it may not be necessary to make such a drastic distinction between sophisticated and unsophisticated goods. We could arrange goods along a continuum from less to more sophisticated on the basis of their PRODY values. A continuous measure of uphill exports of sophisticated goods could then be given by a weighted average of the product of the PRODY value of an export and the income level of the destination country, where the weight is exports of the product to a particular destination as a share of total exports (that is, the sum of exports of all products to all destinations). In notational form, such a measure would be

$$\sum_i \sum_j \frac{x_{ij}}{\sum_i \sum_j x_{ij}} P_i Y_j$$

where P_i is the PRODY value of product i and Y_j is the per capita income level of the destination country j. This measure is analogous to an interaction between EXPY and the average income level of all exports. It turns out to be highly correlated (0.93) with EXPY because there is relatively little variation in the average income level of all exports. We therefore use our uphill measure, which has a binary definition of sophistication and is less correlated with EXPY.

8. The equality of these components provides additional econometric justification for combining them, as we have done in UPHILL1.

9. Population and area, which were decent instruments for our UPHILL1 measure, were poor instruments for the UPHILL2 measure, precluding the possibility of instrumental variable (IV) estimations.

10. In this panel, we retained Ireland and China because they made no difference to the results.

11. The results are available from the authors on request.

References

Amin, Mohammad, and Aaditya Mattoo. 2006. "Do Institutions Matter More for Services?" Policy Research Working Paper 4032, World Bank, Washington, DC.

Bernanke, Ben S. 2006. "Global Economic Integration: What's New and What's Not?" Federal Reserve Board, Washington, DC. http://www.federalreserve.gov/boarddocs/speeches/2006/20060825/default.htm.

Bernard, Andrew B., J. Bradford Jensen, Stephen J. Redding, and Peter K. Schott. 2007. "Firms in International Trade." *Journal of Economic Perspectives* 21 (3): 105–30.

Berthelon, Matias, and Caroline Freund. 2008. "On the Conservation of Distance in International Trade." *Journal of International Economics* 75 (2): 310–20.

Borensztein, Eduardo, José De Gregorio, and Jong-Wha Lee. 1998. "How Does Foreign Direct Investment Affect Growth?" *Journal of International Economics* 45 (June): 115–35.

Burgess, Robin, and Anthony J. Venables. 2004. "Toward a Microeconomics of Growth." Policy Research Working Paper 3257, World Bank, Washington, DC.

Caballero, Ricardo J., Emmanuel Farhi, and Pierre-Olivier Gourinchas. 2008. "An Equilibrium Model of 'Global Imbalances' and Low Interest Rates." *American Economic Review* 98 (1, March): 358–93.

Coe, David T., Elhanan Helpman, and Alexander W. Hoffmaister. 1997. "North-South R&D Spillovers." *Economic Journal* 107: 134–49.

De Loecker, Jan. 2007. "Do Exports Generate Higher Productivity? Evidence from Slovenia." *Journal of International Economics* 73 (9, September): 69–98.

Feenstra, Robert, and Hiau Looi Kee. 2004. "Export Variety and Country Productivity." Policy Research Working Paper 3412, World Bank, Washington, DC.

Haskel, Jonathan E., Sonia C. Pereira, and Matthew J. Slaughter. 2002. "Does Inward Foreign Direct Investment Boost the Productivity of Domestic Firms?" NBER Working Paper 8724, National Bureau of Economic Research, Cambridge, MA.

Hausmann, Ricardo, Jason Hwang, and Dani Rodrik. 2007. "What You Export Matters." *Journal of Economic Growth* 12 (1, March): 1–25.

Helpman, Elhanan, and Paul R. Krugman. 1985. *Market Structure and Foreign Trade: Increasing Returns, Imperfect Competition, and the International Economy.* Cambridge, MA: MIT Press.

Helpman, Elhanan, Marc J. Melitz, and Stephen R. Yeaple. 2004. "Export versus FDI with Heterogeneous Firms." *American Economic Review* 94 (1, March): 300–16.

Hoekman, Bernard M., and Beata Smarzynska Javorcik, eds. 2006. *Global Integration and Technology Transfer.* Houndsmills, Basingstoke, Hampshire, U.K.: Palgrave Macmillan; Washington, DC: World Bank.

Hummels, David, and Peter Klenow. 2005. "The Variety and Quality of a Nation's Exports." *American Economic Review* 95 (3, June): 704–23.

Javorcik, Beata S. 2004. "Does Foreign Direct Investment Increase the Productivity of Domestic Firms? In Search of Spillovers through Backward Linkages." *American Economic Review* 94 (3): 605–27.

Kochhar, Kalpana, Utsav Kumar, Raghuram Rajan, Arvind Subramanian, and Ioannis Tokatlidis. 2006. "India's Pattern of Development: What Happened, What Follows?" *Journal of Monetary Economics* 53 (5, July): 981–1019.

Kremer, Michael, Nazmul Chaudhury, F. Halsey Rogers, Karthik Muralidharan, and Jeffrey Hammer. 2006. "Teacher Absence in India: A Snapshot." *Journal of the European Economic Association* 3 (2–3): 658–67.

Krugman, Paul R. 2008. "Trade and Wages Reconsidered." *Brookings Papers on Economic Activity* 2008 (1): 103–54.

Lumenga-Neso, Olivier, Marcelo Olarreaga, and Maurice Schiff. 2001. "On 'Indirect' Trade-Related Research and Development Spillovers." Policy Research Working Paper 2580, World Bank, Washington, DC.

Melitz, Marc. 2003. "The Impact of Trade on Intra-Industry Reallocations and Aggregate Industry Productivity." *Econometrica* 71 (November): 1695–725.

Prasad, Eswar, Raghuram G. Rajan, and Arvind Subramanian. 2007. "Foreign Capital and Economic Growth." *Brookings Papers on Economic Activity* 2007 (1): 153–230.

Ramamurti, Ravi, and Jitendra V. Singh. 2009. "Indian Multinationals: Generic Internationalization Strategies." In *Emerging Multinationals in Emerging Markets*, ed. Ravi Ramamurti and Jitendra V. Singh. Cambridge, U.K.: Cambridge University Press.

Samuelson, Paul A. 2004. "Where Ricardo and Mill Rebut and Confirm Arguments of Mainstream Economists Supporting Globalization." *Journal of Economic Perspectives* 18 (3): 135–46.

Schott, Peter K. 2005. "Across-Product versus Within-Product Specialization in International Trade." *Quarterly Journal of Economics* 119 (2, May): 647–78.

———. 2007. "The Relative Sophistication of Chinese Exports." *Economic Policy* 53: 5–49.

Sequeira, Tiago Neves. 2003. "High-Tech Human Capital: Do the Richest Countries Invest the Most?" *B. E. Journal of Macroeconomics, Topics in Macroeconomics* 3 (1). http://www.bepress.com/bejm/topics/vol3/iss1/art13/.

Subramanian, Arvind. 2007. "Precocious India." *Business Standard* (New Delhi), August 14. http://www.petersoninstitute.org/publications/opeds/oped.cfm?ResearchID=792.

Comment on "Crisscrossing Globalization: The Phenomenon of Uphill Skill Flows," by Aaditya Mattoo and Arvind Subramanian

BEATA SMARZYNSKA JAVORCIK

Aaditya Mattoo and Arvind Subramanian have written an enjoyable and thought-provoking paper that challenges the reader to question some basic economic theories and conventional wisdom.

In the first part of their study, the authors document a new phenomenon in which skills embodied in goods, services, or capital (in the form of entrepreneurial and managerial skills associated with foreign direct investment) flow from poor to rich countries. They call this phenomenon uphill flows. The existence of uphill flows may come as a surprise, as it appears to contradict one of the basic theorems of international trade, which predicts that developing countries, where unskilled labor is abundant and skilled labor is scarce relative to the industrial world, will specialize in unskilled labor–intensive exports.

The second part of the paper argues that there is a positive link between uphill export flows and economic growth in exporting countries. In other words, the authors contend that economic growth is affected not just by the product composition of exports (as claimed by Hausmann, Hwang, and Rodrik 2007), but also by the type of destination market.

The paper is likely to stimulate lively discussion on the link between the quality of exports and export markets and economic growth. Let me start the debate by posing a few questions under the following headings: (a) Are uphill flows real, or are they a statistical illusion? (b) Do uphill flows really contradict economic theory? (c) Uphill exports and growth: so what?

Are Uphill Flows Real, or Are They a Statistical Illusion?

There are several reasons why uphill export flows may not be "real." The first is that high skill intensity of developing country exports may simply reflect reliance of

Beata Smarzynska Javorcik is a reader in economics at the University of Oxford and a research affiliate with the Centre for Economic Policy Research, London.

Annual World Bank Conference on Development Economics 2009, Global

producers on skill-intensive imported inputs. For instance, China may import electronic components and assemble them into computers that are then exported to the United States. Although the authors would classify such exports as uphill flows, in reality they would contain little input of Chinese skilled labor. This possibility can be easily checked because China's trade statistics explicitly designate "processing imports" as imports of intermediate inputs to be used to produce products solely for export and define "processing exports" as exports that use these imported inputs. Trade figures confirm the high import content of skilled labor–intensive exports from China. For instance, in 2004 processing exports constituted 96 percent of Chinese exports of office and computing machinery. In communications equipment, the corresponding figure was 86 percent, and in medical, precision, and optical instruments, it was 76 percent (Dean and Lovely 2008).

The second reason why uphill exports may create a misleading impression is that multinational enterprises from industrial economies are responsible for a large share of export flows from developing to developed countries. In China foreign investment enterprises accounted for nearly a third of industrial output produced in 2001. In the same year, manufacture of electronic components ranked second among Chinese sectors in terms of entry of foreign investment enterprises (Amiti and Javorcik 2008). Uphill exports associated with multinational enterprises may to a large extent embody knowledge produced in the developed-country headquarters of these enterprises, rather than intangible assets created in the exporting country.

The third difficulty posed by the definition of uphill flows stems from the large differences in regional characteristics observed within developing countries, which put into question the wisdom of treating a country like China as a unit of analysis. The coastal regions of China may be more similar to developed than developing economies, so should exports from these regions really be classified as uphill flows?

Do Uphill Flows Really Contradict Economic Theory?

The recent increase in foreign direct investment (FDI) from developing to developed countries is part of the uphill flows documented by the authors. On the surface, exports of capital from capital-scarce developing countries to capital-abundant industrial countries appear to contradict economic theory. But there are three simple reasons why this contradiction may not stand up to scrutiny.

First, the apparent contradiction disappears when we reinterpret FDI undertaken by developing country firms as imports of intangible assets rather than as exports of capital. For instance, Tata's acquisition of Jaguar may be viewed as a purchase of technology and a brand name. Lenovo's acquisition of IBM production facilities may be considered a purchase of trademarks (ThinkPad), reputation, and distribution channels. Such "knowledge-sourcing" FDI, undertaken in order to import intangible assets to (relatively knowledge-scarce) developing countries, is consistent with economic theory.

Second, export of capital may be a necessary complement to export of unskilled labor–intensive or natural resource–intensive products. For example, when a large

Indian outsourcing company, WIPRO, acquired American and European consulting firms, it purchased a client base in those markets in the hope of leveraging its exports of information technology and back-office services from India. Similarly, Gazprom's acquisition of stakes in oil distribution systems seems to be a natural step complementing its oil exports.

Third, many highly publicized acquisitions undertaken in industrial countries by developing-country interests have been made by sovereign wealth funds and are not necessarily driven solely by market forces. (Political considerations may play a role.) Our economic theories simply do not apply to these cases.

Uphill Exports and Growth: So What?

The positive relationship between economic growth and uphill exports documented by the authors makes it really tempting to advise policy makers, "Export sophisticated goods to rich countries, and your country will grow faster." Yet doing so is akin to saying, "Practice bodybuilding, and you will become the next governor of California." Arnold Schwarzenegger was indeed a bodybuilder, but his highly successful Hollywood career and marriage into the Kennedy family may have been equally (if not more) important to his bid for political office.

Even if we believe in a causal link from uphill export flows to economic growth, what is a "rich-country export good"? (Sophisticated exports are defined as products that tend to be exported by rich countries.) Even if a poor country exports a good classified in the same product category as a good exported by a rich country, the two can be very different. For instance, men's cotton shirts imported by the United States from Japan are roughly 30 times as expensive as the identically classified variety originating in the Philippines (Schott 2004). Thus, ideally we would like to isolate characteristics of export goods that stimulate growth. Are such products characterized by long quality ladders? Speed of innovation? Or skill content?

Furthermore, in order to provide meaningful policy advice, we need to understand the mechanism through which a certain type of export can lead to faster economic growth. After all, saying "All you need to do to become the next governor of California is to win the election" is not terribly helpful. One possibility is that the ability to serve developed-country markets creates an incentive for developing-country producers to increase the quality of their export products. This leads to additional investment in technology and physical assets, buildup of knowledge, and knowledge spillovers. Another possibility is that sophisticated buyers in developed countries transfer knowledge to developing-country producers.

Patterns observed in Mexico after the North American Free Trade Agreement (NAFTA) came into effect are consistent with the above scenarios (Iacovone and Javorcik 2008). The data suggest that entry of Mexican producers into export markets is preceded by increased investment in physical assets. There is also evidence suggesting that high-quality products are more likely to be exported (where quality is measured as the ratio of the domestic unit value obtained by a given producer for a given product in a given time period to the average unit value of the same product observed in the same time period).

An important implication of the paper by Mattoo and Subramanian is the need for further work aiming to understand how (if at all) learning from exporting takes place. The link between uphill flows and economic growth documented in their study suggests that such learning may occur only for some types of products and export markets—which could explain why the literature on this topic has produced conflicting results.

References

Amiti, Mary, and Beata S. Javorcik. 2008. "Trade Costs and Location of Foreign Firms in China." *Journal of Development Economics* 85 (1–2): 129–49.

Dean, Judith, and Mary Lovely. 2008. "Trade Growth, Production Fragmentation, and China's Environment." NBER Working Paper 13860, National Bureau of Economic Research, Cambridge, MA.

Hausmann, Ricardo, Jason Hwang, and Dani Rodrik. 2007. "What You Export Matters." *Journal of Economic Growth* 12 (1): 1–25.

Iacovone, Leonardo, and Beata S. Javorcik. 2008. "Shipping Good Tequila Out: Investment, Domestic Unit Value and Entry of Multi-Product Plants into Export Markets." University of Oxford, Oxford, U.K.

Schott, Peter. 2004. "Across-Product versus Within-Product Specialization in International Trade." *Quarterly Journal of Economics* 119 (2, May): 647–78.

Migration, Remittances, and the Transition from Foreign Aid

The Aid-Migration Trade-off

JEAN-PAUL AZAM AND RUXANDA BERLINSCHI

This paper highlights an empirically significant trade-off between the aid flows deliv-ered by donor countries and the inflows of migrants that they receive from develop-ing countries. It draws the implications for aid policy from a simple game-theoretic model, after reviewing the recent literature on the effects and motivations of foreign aid to developing countries. The paper is part of the recent effort by economists, goaded by the dead end in which the "aid-ineffectiveness" literature had cornered itself, to discover the hidden agenda behind foreign aid.

Are migrants a blessing or a curse? In rich countries, the threat of an invasion by poor migrants from the South is evoked time and again, especially before important elec-tions. It seems that a sizable constituency exists for exerting pressure on governments with a view to inducing them to erect legal barriers against immigration. Some north-ern European countries that were once very liberal in this respect have recently wit-nessed the emergence of a National Front–type movement, with a fairly aggressive attitude toward immigration. This phenomenon can be observed even in countries where unemployment is negligible, as in the Netherlands. At the same time, there are voices cautioning that keeping migrants at bay is nothing like a free good.

Borjas (1995), for example, analyzes the benefits accruing to the receiving coun-try in a competitive general equilibrium framework. His model indicates that natives benefit from immigration because of the production complementarities that exist between immigrant workers and other factors of production and that these benefits are larger when immigrants' assets are sufficiently different from the stock of native productive inputs. A different argument is used by Ortega (2000) in a dynamic labor

Jean-Paul Azam is director of the Atelier de Recherche Quantitative Appliquée au Développement Économique (ARQADE), Toulouse School of Economics, University of Toulouse. He is a researcher with the Institut d'Economie Industrielle (IDEI) at the University of Toulouse and a senior member at the Institut Universitaire de France. Ruxanda Berlinschi is a lecturer at the Toulouse School of Economics. Comments by participants at the ABCDE conference are gratefully acknowledged. In particular, the authors thank the discussant, Melvin Ayogu. Jennifer Hunt and Devesh Kapur also offered helpful comments.

Annual World Bank Conference on Development Economics 2009, Global
© 2010 The International Bank for Reconstruction and Development / The World Bank.

market model with multiple equilibria. In this model, immigration tilts the bargaining strength in favor of firms, with a positive impact on employment and wages.

Other benefits have been identified outside the labor market. Gubert (2003) presents a striking calculation: if France accepted just 60,000 more Malian migrants, and if the new migrants had the same propensity to send remittances home as those currently living in France, total remittances would be equivalent to the aid that France is currently sending to Mali. This is a negligible number for a receiving country whose population is more than a thousand times larger than the number cited. The added migration would also help trim public expenditures, as many fewer police would be needed for tracking illegal migrants, and the French aid administration could also be cut sizably were the aid flow to be reduced correspondingly. Remittances are the key benefit that developing countries receive from the outflows of migrants that they send to rich countries every year. Klein and Harford (2005) demonstrate that remittances are now one of the main sources of external finance for developing countries, and one that is growing steadily, with a fairly smooth time profile. Remittances have become at least as important as foreign aid for many developing countries.

From this kind of calculation, it is clear that the opportunity cost of fighting immigration in rich countries is sizable. Anti-immigration constituencies must therefore perceive considerable detrimental effects on their countries to convince them to accept these costs. Yet quantitative research has found that the externalities perceived by these constituencies are difficult to confirm statistically.

This paper attempts to discover the main determinants of the inflow of migrants into rich countries, with a view toward identifying whether there are policy tools, apart from visa control, that governments of the North can (and do) use to curb immigration. The analysis is best seen as part of a research program that seeks to discover the true agenda behind foreign aid, which the so-called aid-ineffectiveness literature has shown to be different from the proclaimed goal of boosting growth and fighting poverty in the recipient country.

The next sections review studies on the effects and determinants of migration, and the aid-ineffectiveness debate is briefly discussed. In the subsequent sections a simple game-theoretic model is sketched, and several testable predictions are derived. An empirical analysis then shows that aid does indeed belong to the toolbox used by rich-country governments to control immigration. The final section contains conclusions.

Impacts of Immigration Flows

The effects of immigrant flows on host countries have been widely studied in the economics literature. Most of the research on this topic has looked at the impact on the labor market and, in particular, on the wages and employment rates of the receiving country's natives. The simplest economic model of labor market equilibrium suggests that immigration is liable to create a pecuniary externality, as an increase in the labor supply resulting from the inflow of immigrants will lead to lower wages or, in the presence of wage rigidities, to higher unemployment. In reality, this negative effect may be mitigated by adjustments in the labor market; for example, firms may move to regions where labor is becoming cheaper, thus increasing labor demand there, or natives may move away from the regions where the migrants have arrived. Moreover, in choosing their destination, migrants take into account expected future wages and possible demand shocks not observed by the econometrician (Borjas 2003). For these reasons, measuring the effect of migrants on wages is a difficult empirical exercise, and there is no general consensus on this question.

Using data from U.S. decennial censuses for 1960–90 and from the 1998–2001 current population surveys, Borjas (2003) finds that immigration has a considerable negative impact on the wages of native workers. Card (2001) shows that immigration flows in the late 1980s in U.S. cities with large immigrant populations reduced the relative employment rates of low-skilled natives by up to 1 percent and their relative wages by no more than 3 percent. Friedberg and Hunt (1995) review the existing theoretical and empirical literature on the impact of immigrants on host countries' wages and growth and conclude that the impact on natives' wages is very small. Longhi, Nijkamp, and Poot (2005), on the basis of their meta-analysis of 18 empirical studies of this type, conclude that there is a robust negative and statistically significant, but small, impact of immigrants on natives' wages and that this impact is larger in Europe than in the United States.

Other types of externality have been discussed in the context of immigration. Besides its effects on the economy, immigration also has demographic and political effects on the host countries. Given that immigrant populations are generally younger than the natives and have higher fertility rates, immigration may offer a way of decreasing the age-dependency ratio in industrial countries.

Turning to the political point of view, some countries may worry that immigrants threaten their national identity and their ethnic and cultural stability. The creation by French President Nicolas Sarkozy of a Ministry of Immigration, Integration and National Identity is a response to this type of anxiety. There are also fears of infiltration by potential terrorists or drug traffickers (Neumayer 2006). These political concerns seem to play a role at least as important as the economic impacts described above in determining decisions by immigration authorities. Neumayer (2006) shows that the poorer, the less democratic, and the more exposed to armed political conflict a country is, the more its citizens are likely to be subject to visa restrictions. The same is true for nationals of countries that were the origins of terrorist attacks.

It thus seems that migrants from the poorest countries are less welcome than migrants from rich countries. Since the poorest countries are also the most important recipients of foreign aid, it is natural to ask whether foreign aid is used to reduce immigration from them.

Other arguments against immigration are based on its effect on the source countries. One of the most important consequences of out-migration for the country of origin is the flow of remittances received by migrants' families and friends. Remittances are undoubtedly an essential means of reducing poverty and insuring the population against risks. In many developing countries, remittances are a larger and more stable source of finance than official development assistance. But remittances do not have only positive consequences. As Kapur (2004) notes, in some cases they have been an important source of funding for terrorism and civil wars. In Somalia, for example, a large proportion of the remittances supported arms purchases for rural guerrillas; in Armenia diaspora remittances boosted tough nationalist regimes and complicated efforts to solve regional conflicts; and the regime of the Democratic People's Republic of Korea has been strengthened through access to scarce foreign currency resources. Kapur also cites the creation of a culture of dependency among, and lower labor market participation by, the population that did not migrate, as well as the risk of a "Dutch disease" phenomenon if remittances are spent largely on nontradable goods such as housing and land.[1]

Some empirical findings shed light on the relative impacts of economic and other variables on public opinion in receiving countries, and on the influence of public opinion on immigration policies. Scheve and Slaughter (2001), using a direct measure of the U.S. population's preferences concerning immigration, obtained from the 1992 National Election Studies, show that less-skilled workers are significantly more likely to prefer limitation of immigrant inflows into the United States. Mayda (2006) employs individual-level survey datasets, as well as aggregate data on international migration, to study attitudes toward immigrants and how these attitudes influence migration policies. She finds that skilled individuals are more likely to be pro-immigration in countries where the relative skill composition of natives vis-à-vis immigrants is high. Other influences on attitudes toward migration are concern about the impact of immigration on crime rates, individual perceptions of the cultural effect of foreigners, racist feelings, and the size of inflows of asylum seekers. Mayda observes that countries with higher per capita gross domestic product (GDP) are, on average, less open to immigration, after allowing for the influence of individual-level variables. A study by O'Rourke and Sinnott (2006), using a cross-country dataset to investigate the determinants of individual attitudes toward immigration, indicates that these attitudes reflect economic interests, as well as nationalist sentiment. The authors show that among labor market participants, the highly skilled are less opposed to immigration than the low skilled; this effect is larger in richer countries than in poorer ones and in countries with greater equality than in countries with more inequality. Among those who are not in the labor force, noneconomic factors are much more important than economic considerations in determining attitudes toward migration.

Facchini and Mayda (2008) use a sample of 34 countries which were included in the 1995 and 2003 rounds of the International Social Survey Programme to show that voters' negative opinions toward migration explain the restrictive migration policies in place in most destination countries. They demonstrate that countries in which the median voter is more opposed to migration tend to implement more restrictive policies. Thus, it seems that besides the impact of immigrants on the economy, citizens of rich countries worry about immigrants' being a threat to security, national identity, and ethnic and cultural stability.

The Determinants of Immigration Flows

Many arguments have been advanced explaining, without necessarily justifying, why governments of the global North want to curb immigration into their countries. The key question is whether they actually do anything about it: are there policy handles that they use to reduce inflows? Visa quotas allow only an imperfect control of immigration flows. Many industrial countries have family reunification laws that lead to chain immigration, and many countries have signed asylum and refugee protection treaties that oblige them to accept some of these uprooted people. According to data from the United Nations High Commissioner for Refugees (UNHCR), about 560,000 asylum applications were received by 28 industrial countries in 2000, and about 1 million asylum seekers were awaiting a decision. Moreover, visa quotas do not reduce the number of illegal entrants, as discussed forcefully by de Haas (2006). Hatton and Williamson (2002) note that about 300,000 illegal immigrants enter the United States every year, and 400,000 to 500,000 enter Western Europe. Illegal aliens are estimated to add 10 or 15 percent to the foreign-born stock in countries of the Organisation for Economic Co-operation and Development (OECD). Thus, the visa instrument alone is not a sufficient solution if the desired immigration level is lower than the observed one or the one expected to prevail in the future if no other measure is adopted.

The rich empirical literature aimed at discovering the determinants of immigration flows has produced a good crop of convergent findings. For example, Mayda (2007), using a panel of bilateral migration flows to 14 OECD countries by country of origin between 1980 and 1995, finds that income improvements in the destination countries, as well as the share of the young population in the country of origin, have positive and significant effects on emigration rates and that distance between the countries and migration quotas have negative effects. Similar results are found by Jennissen (2003), who studied the economic determinants of net immigration in Western Europe for the period 1960–98, using net migration flows as a dependent variable. He finds that destination GDP per capita, existing migrant stock, and the educational level of the population have positive effects and that unemployment rates have a negative effect on net migration flows. Hatton and Williamson (2002) present a quantitative assessment of the economic and demographic fundamentals that drive world migration across historical periods and around the world, using data on average net immigration rates over five-year periods from 1970–75 to 1995–2000 for 80 countries. The authors find that the share of the population age 15–29 in the receiving country has a negative effect on its immigration rates and that the immigrant stock has a positive effect on net immigration. They also document that a rise in domestic income relative to the world and to the region both increase a country's net immigration. Lucas (2005) examines the causes and consequences of migration from lower-income countries. Neumayer (2005), using a panel on the annual number of asylum seekers in Western European countries by country of origin between 1982 and 1999, finds that human rights abuses, political violence, and state failure are important determinants of asylum migration and that democracy has a significant but nonlinear effect. Economic conditions in the countries of origin are also an important determinant of the number of asylum seekers coming to Western Europe. Neumayer suggests that generous development assistance and the opening of protected European markets to imports from the sending countries could ease migration pressure—a view that de Haas (2006) criticizes forcefully.

Surprisingly few quantitative studies exist on the link between aid and migration. From the above-cited literature, income differentials appear to be one of the main determinants of the supply of immigrants. Because foreign aid is a transfer that reduces, at least at the margin, these differentials, it is natural to ask whether foreign aid reduces immigration. Castles (2003) characterizes the migration policies pursued by the United Kingdom and the European Union as generally unsuccessful and claims that reducing North-South inequality is a key to effective migration management. Morrison (1982) argues that the most promising way for development assistance to influence migration in the short-to-medium run is through employment-generating activities and, in the long run, by reducing population growth and improving income distribution. In fact, for countries with very low incomes, foreign aid could actually increase emigration rates in the short run because of a possible migration-hump phenomenon. Rotte and Vogler (2000), using a panel of data on international migration to Germany from 86 countries between 1981 and 1995, study the influences of economic, demographic, and political factors on inflows to Germany and find no significant effect from aid. Berthélemy, Beuran, and Maurel (2009) estimate the two-way impact of aid and migration using cross-country data and find a positive impact of aid on migration in a simultaneous-equation system.

Searching for the Hidden Agenda behind Foreign Aid

The academic literature on foreign aid has been at times quite paradoxical. It caught the public's attention under the generic name of the "aid-ineffectiveness" literature; Easterly (2006) surveyed it in an influential review aimed at a broad audience. The aid-ineffectiveness literature shows quite consistently that foreign aid is not very successful at boosting growth and reducing poverty in recipient countries. The contributors to this body of work end up expressing severe criticism of the international community, which appears unable to pursue its proclaimed objective. The World Bank's recent slogan, "Our Dream: A World Free of Poverty," seems bound to remain just a dream. This conclusion appears to challenge the standard methodology of economics at a fundamental level. How is it that the international community has consistently spent zillions of dollars in foreign aid for nearly six decades without being "effective"? Are there no error-correction mechanisms that can put an end to this "massive waste"? But the apparent paradox only concerns a small share of the academic literature on aid and is the result of some hasty interpretation of the findings.

The Aid-Ineffectiveness Puzzle

The root cause of the turmoil is that some economists have taken at face value the declared objectives of foreign aid. The stated objective has always been to boost economic growth in the recipient country. For a long time, aid was focused on filling the "saving gap"—the allegedly insufficient national saving flow that was supposed to afflict poor countries. Collier (2007) suggests that the change in emphasis which occurred in the 1980s and 1990s, from economic growth to poverty alleviation, was the result of a public relations campaign aimed at harnessing electoral support in favor of foreign aid from all sides of the political spectrum in rich countries. Academic economists, however, soon started to blow the whistle, demonstrating that there was not much empirical support for the view that foreign aid was promoting growth in poor countries or reducing significantly the incidence of poverty.

A much-cited paper by Boone (1996) triggered a wave of debate on aid ineffectiveness by showing that no significant impact of aid on growth could be found in cross-country regressions. In a highly influential paper, Burnside and Dollar (2000) argue forcefully that in analyzing the effect of aid, due account must be taken of heterogeneity among recipient countries. The authors favor an index of the quality of macroeconomic policies as their heterogeneity parameter because their findings suggest that aid boosts growth when it is given to countries that have a sound macroeconomic policy framework. Similarly, Svensson (1999) presents cross-country regression findings showing that aid is more effective in affecting growth in more democratic countries. In the same vein, Kosack and Tobin (2006) find that foreign aid and democracy have a positive impact on economic growth and human development, provided that there is a minimum level of human capital in the recipient country.

Nevertheless, the dominant diagnosis is that, in general, with some noteworthy exceptions, aid is not boosting growth. Some authors blame the failure of aid on the misconceived approach of conditionality (see, for example, Collier 1997). A number of theorists propose clever schemes for fixing aid (see Svensson 2000, 2003; Azam and Laffont 2003). Another influential response has been to claim that aid has not been effective because there has not been enough of it—what was needed was a "big push" to lift people out of the "poverty trap." This view was forcefully supported by Sachs (2005); Collier (2007) espoused a more subtle variant.

These findings and the response that they triggered raise a more fundamental methodological issue: do they mean that aid is ineffective, or does the true agenda of aid differ from the much-publicized goals of fostering growth and alleviating poverty? The proper methodology of economics is based on revealed-preference theory: instead of trying to assess the effectiveness of foreign aid by looking at the extent to which it achieves its stated objective, we should try to infer its true agenda from its actual achievements. When people spend zillions of dollars over decades, they must certainly have achieved a measure of success that justifies the continuation of this expenditure flow. Some economists have tried to discover the hidden agenda of foreign aid by looking at the determinants of its allocation across countries. Their results suggest that the impact of foreign aid on growth and development is probably not the crucial determinant of its allocation. For example, Burnside and Dollar (2000) find that the quality of the macroeconomic policies pursued by a given country does not make the country more likely to receive more aid, although it does makes aid more "effective." Similarly, Svensson (1999) presents cross-country regression analysis showing that although aid is more effective at promoting growth in more democratic countries, those countries are not more favored as aid recipients. This finding suggests that aid allocation is governed by other considerations, hinting again that there is a hidden agenda aside from the generous drive to alleviate poverty.

Donors' Revealed Preferences

The political dimension of aid allocation is further analyzed by Alesina and Dollar (2000), who find that the colonial past and strategic alliances are the main determinants of the amount of aid received by poor countries. They also show, however, that in the time-series dimension, democratization is often followed by increased aid, although there is no significant static effect of democracy. By contrast, Berthélemy and Tichit (2004), in a panel data analysis covering 137 aid recipients and 22 bilateral donors during the period 1980–99, find a significant positive impact of the Freedom House index of civil liberty and political rights. This finding is confirmed in a later study using a different estimation method (Berthélemy 2006). The latter two studies bring out quite strongly that in allocating aid, most bilateral donors seem to be guided by their self-interest and, in particular, by their commercial relationships. Fleck and Kilby (2006a) show that commercial concerns play an important part in determining the allocation of U.S. bilateral aid across countries, particularly when the president and/or Congress are conservative. The results reported by Fleck and Kilby (2006b) suggest that the validity of such a diagnosis can be extended to the case of the World Bank, whose aid allocation behavior is significantly influenced by U.S. trade and political interests. One may wonder, however, whether trade flows are perfectly exogenous, at least as far as bilateral donors are concerned. Although most donors have formally ruled out tied aid, toward the end of the 1960 to 1997 sample period considered by Fleck and Kilby (2006a), some implicit and subtle ways of tying aid probably continued in operation. Moreover, aid helps finance the trade deficit of developing countries, and this certainly increases imports from industrial countries, which are also the main donors. This effect is even more likely toward the end of the period of analysis, as trade liberalization was a prominent feature of the reform programs supported by foreign aid under the influence of the Bretton Woods institutions. Hence, some reverse causation between aid and trade may be present, channeled by various mechanisms, so that the above findings might be misleading.

Chauvet (2002) looks at the relationship between aid allocation across countries and various kinds of "sociopolitical instabilities"—referring to events that reflect political troubles in the recipient countries. She distinguishes three types: (a) elite instability, including coups d'état, revolutions, and major government crises; (b) violent instability, including political assassinations, guerrilla warfare, and civil wars; and (c) social instability, such as strikes, demonstrations, and riots. She shows that these three types of event have different effects on the allocation of aid, depending also on the kind of aid. Instabilities of types (a) and (b) have a positive impact, suggesting that aid flows are directed to governments that are under political threat, while type (c) has a negative effect, showing that aid shies away from threats directed more specifically at the economy. These results suggest that donors give aid to recipient governments in response to political motivations, with a kind of conservative bent toward providing support to incumbent governments. Economic issues such as growth and poverty alleviation seem to play only a secondary role, in that governments facing greater "social instability"—the likely response of some constituencies to economic hardship—are somehow punished by getting less aid money. This whole line of empirical research tries to infer from the determinants of aid allocation across countries what donors are really trying to achieve, but it fails to test directly for the impact of aid on the presumed objectives.

Alesina and Weder (2002) use a slightly different empirical strategy, looking directly at the effect of aid on some potential objectives of the donors. They show that the level of corruption plaguing the recipient government does not significantly affect the allocation of aid across countries but that there is a significant effect in the other direction. Their results suggest that an increase in aid this year increases the level of corruption next year—what they call the "voracity effect." They thus conclude that donors do not care at all about corruption in the recipient country. Similarly, Azam and Delacroix (2006) and Azam and Thelen (2008) look directly at the effects of aid on some potential objectives of the donors while taking due account of reverse causation. Using such a structural econometric approach, they show that aid is effective at fighting terrorism and that donors allocate aid across countries with a view to pursuing this objective.

Our paper represents a further attempt at identifying a donor objective, by testing whether aid is actually used to reduce migration from poor countries.

Implications of the Aid-Migration Trade-off

A very simple model is sufficient for capturing the main issues raised by the potential trade-off between aid and migration when rich countries wish to use aid policy to reduce migration inflows. It is most likely that (assuming the aid is effective in the first place) there are some spillovers, insofar as the aid given by one donor might reduce simultaneously migration outflows from the recipient country in the direction of both the donor country and other destinations. This means that some free riding is bound to occur unless donors coordinate their actions. The model discussed next illustrates this point.

The Model

Assume that there are three countries in the world: two donor countries, labeled 1 and 2, whose level of affluence potentially attracts migrants, and a developing country, whose flows of migrants to each donor country are designated n_1 and n_2. The donors have the possibility of giving aid to the poor country, with a view to reducing the flow of migrants that they receive from it. Two main mechanisms can explain why aid can have a negative impact on the migration flow. First, the aid can help create an improved economic situation in the recipient country by supporting productive investments and creating jobs. Second, the aid can provide an inducement to the recipient government to try to deter out-migration, if the assistance is conditional on the adoption of policy measures aimed at reducing outflows. For example, financial incentives can be created in favor of returning migrants, thus reducing the net outflow, other things being equal, or migration-prone groups can be targeted with specific actions. In Mali and Senegal, for example, the Soninke ethnic group is the most migration prone because of the well-established diaspora that they can rely on (see Azam and Gubert 2006). A codevelopment project has been implemented with French aid money with a view to reducing migration by members of this group by developing attractive programs in their region of origin.

Let a_1 and a_2 denote aid flows from countries 1 and 2, respectively. Assume that the inflow of migrants in donor country 1 is governed by the following function:

$$n_1 = f(a_1, a_2, \theta). \tag{1}$$

We assume that the impacts of the two aid flows on n_1 are negative, reflecting the aid-migration trade-off that we want to analyze. The negative impact of a country's own aid flow is quite obvious, as discussed above, but the cross-effect deserves additional comment. If either aid flow has a positive effect on the level of economic activity and the creation of jobs that might reduce the attractiveness of migration for nationals from the developing country, then it cannot be assumed that this will affect only the outflow directed at each donor country separately; there is necessarily some spillover on the outflow to the other country. In the limit, it could be argued that only the total aid flow, $a_1 + a_2$, matters for the outflows of migrants, if the two aid flows have the same impact on the recipient economy. The more general specification embedded in equation (1), however, allows for some finer targeting by donor countries, which might devise policies that mainly affect the migration flow heading in their own individual directions. This could be done, for example, by targeting a specific ethnic group that is connected to an important diaspora in one of the donor countries. The parameter θ captures the set of the other variables that are liable in either country to affect the outflow of migrants. By permuting the subscripts 1 and 2, we can readily generate the equivalent function to equation (1) for donor country 2.

Assume then that country 1 is prepared to incur the cost of providing aid if the aid shows some effectiveness in reducing the migration flow in its direction. This is captured by assuming that country 1 seeks to minimize the following loss function:

$$\min_{a_1, n_1} L(a_1, n_1, \lambda), \tag{2}$$

which is increasing and convex in its first two arguments. This captures the facts that aid entails a cost for the donating country, by using up some fiscal revenues, and that, for whatever reason, that country's government tends to feel that its country is attracting too many migrants. The shift parameter λ captures the contextual variables that are liable to affect the government's feelings about immigration, such as elections or other political determinants. A similar function is assumed to govern the choices made by country 2.

Nash-Equilibrium Aid and Migration Flows

If the two countries determine their aid policies without any coordination between them, the aid flows and the migration flows will be determined by the Nash equilibrium of the game. This is the standard equilibrium concept in noncooperative game theory, which assumes that each player takes the other one's equilibrium choice as given.

FIGURE 1.
Nash-Equilibrium and Optimum Aid Flows

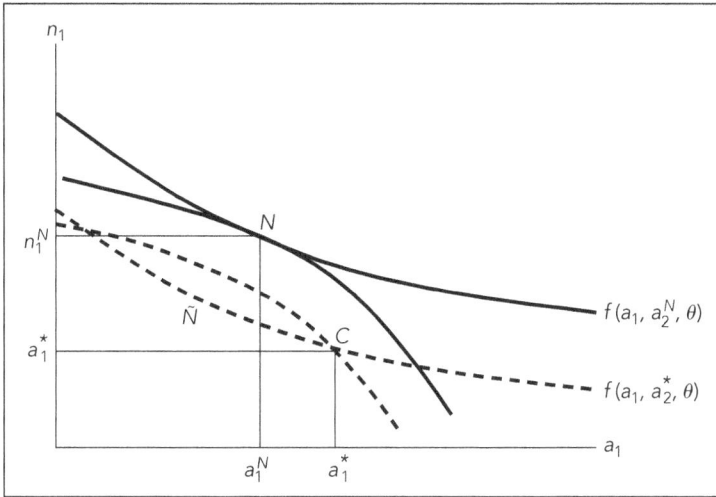

Source: Authors' elaboration.

Figure 1 describes how country 1 determines its best-response function, $a_1(a_2, \theta, \lambda)$, by minimizing equation (2), subject to the trade-off embedded in equation (1), while taking a_2, θ, and λ as given. The convex curve represents the aid-migration trade-off (equation 1), assuming that the aid flow chosen by donor 2 is at its Nash-equilibrium value, a_2^N. The assumed convexity of the curve captures the idea that aid has a decreasing marginal impact on the inflow of migrants so that even a very high aid flow would not reduce their number to zero. Then, donor 1 will choose its best-response aid flow, a_1^N, at the point where an indifference curve for the loss function (2), represented by the concave curve, is tangent to the aid-migration trade-off. The resulting point, labeled N in figure 1, is the Nash-equilibrium joint choice of aid flow a_1^N and migration inflow n_1^N made by country 1, given the equilibrium aid flow a_2^N chosen by country 2. A similar diagram could obviously be drawn for country 2.

Case for Coordinating Aid

It is easily shown that such a Nash-equilibrium point is inefficient from the point of view of the donor countries. It means that too little aid is being donated by the two donor countries because of a free-rider problem. The spillover effects of aid on migration analyzed above are likely to dilute the incentives of each donor to extend aid in order to reduce immigration. In the Nash equilibrium, each player takes the equilibrium choice of the other as given. The two players, however, could improve on this outcome by coordinating their aid decisions in order to take the spillover effects into account. The intuition for this result can be grasped by looking at the dashed lines in figure 1. Point C represents such a coordinated equilibrium outcome, as can be demonstrated by the following argument. Notice that if donor 2 increases its aid flow relative to a_2^N, the aid-migration trade-off facing donor country 1 moves downward, to a position illustrated by the dashed convex curve corresponding to $a_2^* > a_2^N$. This downward shift reflects the spillover effect of country 2's aid flow in reducing the inflow of migrants into country 1, for a given level of aid donated by country 1. Then, in the coordinated equilibrium, donor 1 will reciprocate the increased aid given by donor 2 at a point such as C, where $a_1^* > a_1^N$. Point C is located on a lower indifference curve than point N—thus corresponding to a lower value of the loss function (2)—and so donor 1 is better off in this coordinated equilibrium point than in the Nash equilibrium. This occurs even though donor 1 spends more money on aid, because it receives a lower inflow of migrants in return. A similar diagram could obviously be drawn for donor country 2.

Figure 1 also suggests that such a coordinated equilibrium requires a highly credible ability by the players to commit irreversibly in order to overcome the temptation to renege ex post. Once player 2 has engaged a_2^* so that the aid-migration trade-off has shifted downward to the dashed line $f(a_1, a_2^*, \theta)$, player 1 is tempted to reduce its own contribution by moving leftward along the trade-off in order to reach an even lower indifference curve of its loss function—for example, point $\tilde{N}$. Anticipating this, player 2 might then be deterred from increasing its own aid flow in the first place. This is the essence of the free-rider problem, which was popularized in the form of the well-known "prisoner's dilemma." Both donor countries need to have a credible way of tying their own hands if a coordinated outcome is to come about. As a matter of fact, we can observe in the real world that the donor community is expending considerable effort to make its pledged contributions credible, using methods ranging from the international definition of the Millennium Development Goals to the creation of powerful aid-dependent constituencies in their own countries (perhaps by tying aid to the advantage of some powerful firms or by creating an overstaffed aid administration). Nevertheless, unless we are prepared to assume that donor countries are coordinating perfectly their aid policies regarding the reduction of migration inflows, this free-riding problem suggests that the aid flows that we observe in the real world are probably below their optimal values.

The foregoing short theoretical analysis of the implications of the aid-migration trade-off rests heavily on the assumptions that such a trade-off does exist in the real world and that there are some spillovers such that the aid given by one country is likely to affect the inflow of migrants entering another country. The empirical exercises offered in the next section aim at testing whether these two assumptions are supported by the data.

Empirical Results

A quick look at figure 2 does not seem very promising for the aid-migration trade-off hypothesis. This figure traces the yearly flow of immigrants into, and the total official development assistance (ODA) disbursements by, the members of the OECD's

FIGURE 2.
Disbursements of Official Development Assistance (ODA) and Entry of Immigrants, DAC Countries

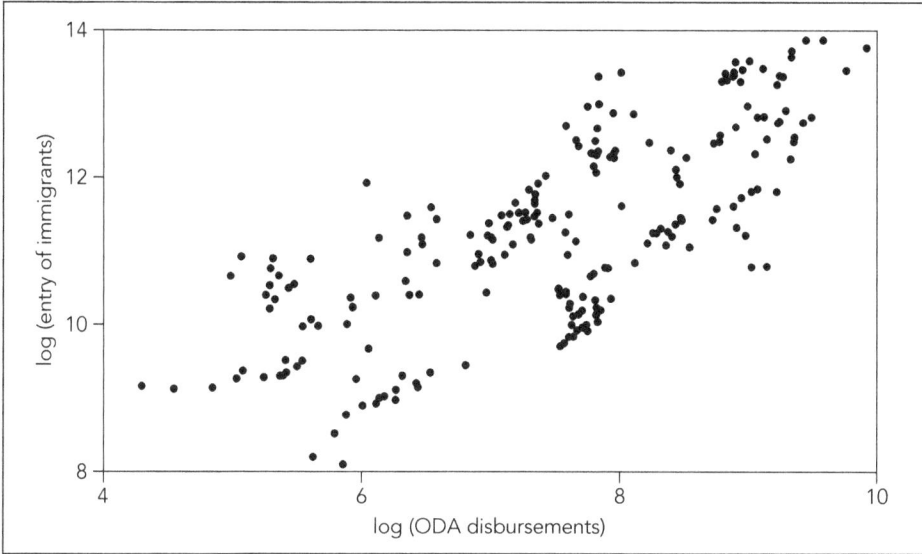

Source: OECD.Stat.

Note: DAC, Development Assistance Committee of the Organisation for Economic Co-operation and Development (OECD).

Development Assistance Committee (DAC) between 1995 and 2005. There appears to be a positive correlation between the number of immigrants coming to a donor country and the amount of foreign aid that the latter disburses. The following section shows that this first impression is seriously misleading.

Search for a Structural Equation

The positive correlation shown in figure 2 does not represent any meaningful behavioral relationship between aid and migration because it fails to control for many relevant variables. Nevertheless, Berthélemy, Beuran, and Maurel (2009) find a similar positive relationship between the two in an equation that controls for numerous variables. They cautiously explain it by referring to "policy coherence," arguing that donor countries are actively combining their aid and migration policies. Our results outlined below suggest instead that these authors face a specification problem. The model presented above implies that aid disbursements and migration inflows are jointly determined in equilibrium, as Berthélemy, Beuran, and Maurel suggest, but with different predictions.

By changing the other determinants of the migration inflow that we have captured by the parameter θ, we can generate some comparative-static predictions that are compatible with figure 2. Imagine that such an exogenous change shifts the aid-migration trade-off upward. Then it is most likely that the equilibrium points N or C will move to the northeast, that is, upward and to the right, indicating that both the aid disbursed and the migration inflow increase simultaneously. The reason for such shifts is that if more migrants are forthcoming for a given aid flow, the donor country will respond both by increasing its aid flows somewhat and by allowing a bit more migration because the marginal impact of aid on migration is decreasing. The latter effect entails an increase in the marginal cost of reducing immigration through increased foreign aid. This mental experiment suggests two things that a correct empirical analysis should take into account: (a) it is crucial to include the correct control variables in the migration equation in order to identify correctly the aid-migration trade-off, and (b) the aid flow itself is probably endogenous, and this endogeneity should also be controlled for. Because it is well known that most econometric methods for controlling for endogeneity entail a potential loss of efficiency, we first present the results without taking this problem into account. We then test whether this estimation procedure gives rise to a significant endogeneity bias in a second stage. This two-step approach allows us to perform two tests of interest with one equation—that is, to test (a) whether aid has a significant negative impact on the inflow of migrants, and (b) whether donors are actively using foreign aid as a policy response aimed at reducing the migration inflows that they face.

Because of obvious availability problems, we are working with data on the number of legal migrants when what we are really interested in is the total number of migrants. The latter is what our aid-migration trade-off is likely to govern. But because we are applying panel-data techniques, using country fixed effects, we can hope to learn a lot about total migrants from our econometric analysis. The following argument explains why.

Assume that the number of legal migrants is a random fraction of their total number, which reflects, among other things, the immigration-restriction policy enforced by the destination country. Then, because we are working with the logarithm of the number of legal migrants, the mean value of that random fraction feeds into the country fixed effect, while the deviations relative to that mean are feeding into the residuals. Formally, if n_L is the number of legal migrants and n is the total number of migrants, we can assume that:

$$n_L = \phi(G, \varepsilon)n, \tag{3}$$

where G is a set of variables that captures the immigration-restriction policy stance of the government and $0 \leq \phi(G, \varepsilon) \leq 1$ is the random share of legal migrants, depending on the exogenous shock variable ε. Then, by taking the logarithm of equation (3), we get

$$\text{Log } n_L = \text{Log } \phi(G, \varepsilon) + \text{Log } n. \tag{4}$$

Therefore, unless the restriction policy pursued by each government has changed drastically over our relatively short sample period, which spans 1995–2003, it should be well controlled for by the country fixed effects. This assumes that, with respect to immigration-restriction policy, there is more variation across countries than within

TABLE 1. Regression Results on Flows of Legal Migrants from Low-Income and Lower-Middle-Income Countries

Variable	(1)	(2)	(3)	(4)
Unemployment rate	−0.30***	−0.18***	−0.30***	−0.14**
	(0.09)	(0.08)	(0.09)	(0.08)
Social expenditures (percent of GDP)	0.32***	0.30***	0.32***	0.34***
	(0.09)	(0.09)	(0.09)	(0.10)
Log of per capita GDP	0.54	9.53***	0.54	14.80***
	(1.42)	(2.82)	(1.42)	(4.97)
Log of stock of foreign population	0.19	0.57	0.17	0.91*
	(0.57)	(0.50)	(0.59)	(0.47)
Log of official development assistance (ODA) disbursements	0.46	−3.68***	0.43	−5.15***
	(0.32)	(1.15)	(0.28)	(1.66)
Log of multilateral disbursements	—	—	0.10	−1.43
			(0.27)	(0.90)
Endogeneity bias, ODA	—	4.47***	—	5.90***
		(1.26)		(1.73)
Endogeneity bias, multilateral disbursements	—	—	—	1.50
				(0.96)
Number of observations	118	117	118	116
F-test	9.50	9.84	7.87	7.64

Source: Authors' calculations.

Note: GDP, gross domestic product. The dependent variable is the log of the inflow of migrants from low-income and lower-middle-income countries. All explanatory variables are characteristics of the destination country, and they are lagged once. The data on flow of migrants, social expenditures, stock of foreign population, ODA disbursements, and multilateral aid disbursements are taken from OECD.Stat. The data on GDP per capita and unemployment rates are taken from the *World Development Indicators*. The sample consists of the 22 donor countries of the Development Assistance Committee (DAC) of the Organisation for Economic Co-operation and Development (OECD) for 1995–2003, with the exceptions of New Zealand, for which the stock of foreign population is missing, and Australia and Canada, for which this information is available for only one point in time. Country fixed effects have been used but are not reported, to save space. Numbers in parentheses are robust standard errors. The instruments used for ODA and multilateral disbursements are the log of public expenditures on order and security, from OECD.Stat, and the percentage of right-wing members in parliament in the destination country, from "Parties and Elections," http://www.parties-and-elections.de, and Université de Sherbrooke, "World Perspective," http://perspective.usherbrooke.ca/bilan/BMEncyclopedie/BMEncycloListePays.jsp. The log of government revenues (from OECD.Stat) is added as an instrument for equation (4). Their reduced-form impacts on the aid variables are presented in annex table A.1.

*Significant at the 10 percent level.

**Significant at the 5 percent level.

***Significant at the 1 percent level.

each country over time. Then our equations explaining the logarithm of the number of legal migrants should, in fact, tell us a great deal about the total number of migrants entering each country.

Table 1 presents the results of four regression equations that explain the inflow of legal migrants from low-income and lower-middle-income countries into donor countries. This restriction is meant to capture the idea that donor countries are not viewing the inflows of migrants from other rich countries in the same way as they do inflows from poorer countries. We also performed all the estimations with the total inflows, yielding mostly similar but sometimes significantly different results. In particular, the income tax rate is significant for migrants from rich countries, but it does not matter for migrants from poorer countries.

In columns (1) and (3) of table 1, no attempt is made to control for endogeneity; that is done in columns (2) and (4). The method used for performing this control is based on the standard Hausman test and is further discussed below. All the explanatory variables are lagged once. This procedure potentially helps mitigate any remaining endogeneity problems, in particular those that might affect the various control variables, and it also provides some information about any potential time lag in the response of migration flows to changes in incentives.

Four control variables are included, of which three consistently prove highly significant. The unemployment rate is highly significant, reflecting the deterrent effect of a depressed labor market in the host country. When the probability of finding a job is low in the destination country, migrants seem to postpone their travel or even to cancel it. The social expenditures policy pursued by the target country is an important attraction factor, and it is significant in all the columns. Industrial countries that spend more on social items such as health and education are obviously more attractive to migrants than countries with a more conservative policy stance. Then, we find a strange result for per capita GDP in columns (1) and (3), where it seems to have a negligible impact on the inflow of migrants. This counterintuitive result suggests the presence of an estimation problem. Fortunately, this effect is not robust to the correction of the endogeneity bias affecting the impact of aid, as this coefficient becomes positive and significant in columns (2) and (4). It thus seems that the impacts of the business cycle and national income on immigration are fully captured by the unemployment rate and GDP per capita.

Finally, the existing stock of foreign population already residing in the country of destination is only significant at the 10 percent level in equation (4). This variable is meant to reflect the well-known network effects that play a key role in the migration process in many studies. For example, Azam and Gubert (2006) demonstrate that such an effect can explain an ethnic bias in migration. They show that two ethnic groups living in the same region of the Senegal River valley, in western Mali, and thus facing the same economic conditions, have very different migration patterns. The authors use historical evidence to document that the group with a long history of out-migration is sending a much higher fraction of its population abroad than the group without such a migration history. The established diaspora from the first group serves as a bridgehead that reduces the costs of migration for the prospective new migrants from that same group by helping them find jobs and accommodations and by providing the informal credit and insurance services that migrants' networks are known for delivering to their members. Our findings reported above suggest that such an effect is not very strong at the country level, once the impact of foreign aid is taken into account. The stock of foreign population in the destination country is probably too coarse a measure to capture this effect.

Testing for the Impact of Aid

The test variables capture the aid disbursed by the donor countries. To gain some insight into the relative effectiveness of various aid flows, we use the log of ODA disbursements by the destination country and test whether multilateral aid disbursements have a differential impact by introducing that variable in addition to ODA. Arguably, the multilateral aid variable captures a much better coordinated aid policy than ODA, which includes considerable bilateral aid. This interpretation reflects the idea that the principal donors have a say in the way the World Bank and other multilateral donor agencies determine multilateral aid disbursements and that they also have a clear opportunity to coordinate their decisions regarding these disbursements at board meetings or in the corridors. The model presented above suggests that coordinated aid flows could have some multiplier effects, as they imply a quid pro quo by other donors. It turns out that ODA disbursements represent the most significant aid variable coming out of our regressions (2) and (4), with the predicted negative sign. This is consistent with our theoretical framework, which suggests that foreign aid is probably an effective tool for reducing the inflow of migrants into rich countries. The model, however, also raises the question whether coordinated aid is a more powerful tool against immigration than uncoordinated aid. General ODA, which includes both bilateral aid and the contributions channeled through the Bretton Woods entities and other multilateral institutions, could be less effective than multilateral aid taken separately. Our findings, however, do not support the differential impact hypothesis. This suggests that, in fact, donor countries somehow manage to coordinate their bilateral and multilateral aid flows equally well.

The technique applied in columns (2) and (4) for controlling for endogeneity is derived from the standard Hausman test. Two auxiliary reduced-form equations are estimated for log of ODA and log of multilateral aid, which are assumed endogenous in the theoretical framework presented above, using the log of public expenditures on order and security, the percentage of right-wing members in parliament, and the log of government revenues (in equation 4 only) as instruments, in addition to the four exogenous variables in table 1. These variables are regarded as the contextual variables captured by λ in equation (2). The first-stage reduced-form equations are presented in annex table A.1. The residuals from these equations are then included, in addition to the aid variables themselves, in columns (2) and (4), and their estimated coefficients provide estimates of the endogeneity biases for each variable. Inclusion of these residuals in the equations provides an additional benefit, as it corrects the estimated coefficients of the aid variables themselves for the endogeneity bias that affects them in the uncontrolled equation. This justifies the discussion presented above of the estimated coefficients of these aid variables.

For the tests performed at columns (2) and (4), the residuals are obviously lagged. The corresponding estimates of the endogeneity biases are presented in table 1 under that entry. Moreover, this procedure yields the correct estimates for the coefficients of the variables themselves, as mentioned above. In column (2), where ODA only is included, we find that the latter is strongly significant, and the exogeneity assumption is rejected at the 1 percent level. The correct interpretation of this test as an endogeneity test is not immediate. The specification of the immigration function in columns (1) through (4) assumes that the inflow of migrants responds to incentives with a one-year lag. The endogeneity test performed in columns (2) and (4) assumes that the government in the donor country adjusts its aid flow in year $t - 1$ on the basis of its forecast that a component of the random shock will affect the immigration flow in year t; this forecast is presumed to be based on some information that is not available to the econometrician. For example, the government may be using a lead indicator based on the number of visa applications in year $t - 1$ that will only show up as actual migration in the subsequent year, and this is a piece of information that we have not been able to include in our estimated equations. Similarly, the government of the host country might be aware of sociological or institutional changes affecting a resident diaspora that are likely to affect the latter's ability to attract new migrants, but this is something the econometrician does not know. The reduced-form equation for aid reflects in its residuals this anticipation by the government in year $t - 1$. The latter is then necessarily correlated with the random shock occurring in year t, by construction, if our behavioral assumption correctly captures the way the donor government is forming its expectations.

The two aid variables are included in column (4). Only ODA is found to be significant and endogenous. Hence, ODA might not be worse than multilateral aid after all, suggesting that donors have found various methods for obtaining the required coordination for their other aid flows. After all, many of them have been in this line of business for about six decades, so that the aid game might safely be approximated by an infinite-horizon repeated game. It is known that this kind of setting is likely to foster cooperation between the players. Our findings thus suggest that donor countries are doing a good job of equalizing the marginal impact of each kind of aid flow, so that aggregation of flows into a single ODA variable is legitimate for econometric purposes.

In the foregoing econometric exercise, two key results seem robust: (a) foreign aid has a significant negative impact on migration inflows into donor countries, and (b) donors are actively using aid as a policy tool for reducing immigration. The third result that we tested, concerning the effectiveness of aid flows coordinated through multilateral institutions in relation to that of other aid flows, leads us to reject the view that bilateral aid is less effective.

Conclusion

This paper has investigated the assumption that donor countries employ foreign aid partly as a tool for controlling inflows of migrants. A brief theoretical analysis was used to bring out the main predictions that can be derived from such an assumption.

The model helped us identify the potential free-rider problem raised by the assumption and suggested that donors must find a coordinated equilibrium if they want to optimize the impact of their aid as a means of reducing immigration. Such a coordinated equilibrium requires donors to find a way of tying their own hands in order to make their commitment not to renege ex post on their pledged disbursements credible. We suggested that in the real world, donors are, in fact, using various mechanisms to create this credible commitment, ranging from the international definition of the Millennium Development Goals to the formation of powerful aid-dependent constituencies in their own countries. Techniques for developing the latter in the real world include, among other methods, the tying of aid to benefit powerful firms and the creation of an overstaffed aid administration. In addition, donors have created international aid institutions, such as the World Bank, whose job is precisely to coordinate at least some of the aid flows.

The empirical tests performed using a panel of data from most DAC member countries show that our assumed aid-migration trade-off is indeed supported by the data. The empirical approach used to produce these findings is based on two requirements brought out by the theoretical analysis. First, it is important to include in the estimations various control variables, which are likely to affect both immigration flows and aid disbursement flows. Second, due account must be taken of the fact that governments choose jointly the level of foreign aid that they deliver and the inmigration that they permit, so that the former must be regarded as endogenous in the econometric analysis. The findings of our econometric exercises provide robust support for these two predictions. We further tested whether the amount of aid disbursed through a coordination mechanism, which we have proxied by multilateral aid disbursements, is any more effective than the other aid flows, here captured by ODA disbursements. Our results suggest that total ODA is not performing any worse than its multilateral aid component, but this might reflect econometric problems, as these two variables are strongly correlated with one another. Our econometric exercises fail to support the view that there is a significant free-rider problem with bilateral aid flows and hence that there is significant underprovision of aid. Nevertheless, our tests of this assumption do not seem very powerful, and further investigation of this issue is warranted. In particular, a finer disaggregation of aid flows might be required to perform a convincing analysis of the free-rider problem. This points the way for future research.

Note

1. A large inflow of foreign currency drives up a country's exchange rate, which handicaps the sale of other exports and impairs the ability of domestic products to compete with imports. "Dutch disease" takes its name from the supposed effects of North Sea natural gas discoveries on the Netherlands economy.

ANNEX TABLE A.1. First-Stage Reduced-Form Equations

	Log of ODA disbursements for eq. (2)	Log of ODA disbursements for eq. (4)	Log of multilateral disbursements
Log of public expenditure on order and security	0.21*** (0.07)	0.21*** (0.08)	0.09 (0.11)
Percentage of right-wing members in parliament	−0.003 (0.002)	−0.002 (0.002)	0.01*** (0.003)
Log of government revenues		−0.06 (0.14)	−0.33* (0.19)
Unemployment rate	0.03 (0.02)	0.03 (0.02)	−0.01 (0.02)
Social expenditures (percent of GDP)	−0.009 (0.013)	−0.01 (0.01)	0.02 (0.02)
Log of per capita GDP	1.87*** (0.36)	1.95*** (0.38)	1.10*** (0.42)
Log of stock of foreign population	0.04 (0.08)	0.05 (0.09)	0.23** (0.59)
N	159	156	156
F-test	48.59	39.86	17.31

Source: Authors' calculations.

Note: GDP, gross domestic product; ODA, official development assistance.

*Significant at the 10 percent level.

**Significant at the 5 percent level.

***Significant at the 1 percent level.

References

Alesina, Alberto, and David Dollar. 2000. "Who Gives Aid to Whom and Why?" *Journal of Economic Growth* 5 (March): 33–63.

Alesina, Alberto, and Beatrice Weder. 2002. "Do Corrupt Governments Receive Less Foreign Aid?" *American Economic Review: Papers and Proceedings* 92 (4): 1126–37.

Azam, Jean-Paul, and Alexandra Delacroix. 2006. "Aid and the Delegated Fight against Terrorism." *Review of Development Economics* 10 (2): 330–44.

Azam, Jean-Paul, and Flore Gubert. 2006. "Migrants' Remittances and the Household in Africa: A Review of Evidence." *Journal of African Economies* 15 (Suppl. 2): 426–62.

Azam, Jean-Paul, and Jean-Jacques Laffont. 2003. "Contracting for Aid." *Journal of Development Economics* 70 (1): 25–58.

Azam, Jean-Paul, and Véronique Thelen. 2008. "The Roles of Foreign Aid and Education in the War on Terror." *Public Choice* 135 (3–4): 375–97.

Berthélemy, Jean-Claude. 2006. "Bilateral Donors' Interest vs. Recipients' Development Motives in Aid Allocation: Do All Donors Behave the Same?" *Review of Development Economics* 10 (2, May): 179–94.

Berthélemy, Jean-Claude, and Ariane Tichit. 2004. "Bilateral Donors' Aid Decisions—A Three-Dimensional Panel Analysis." *International Review of Economics and Finance* 13 (3): 253–74.

Berthélemy, Jean-Claude, Monica Beuran, and Mathilde Maurel. 2009. "Aid and Migration: Substitutes or Complements?" *World Development* (in press). http://dx.doi.org/10.1016/j.worlddev.2009.02.002.

Boone, Peter. 1996. "Politics and the Effectiveness of Foreign Aid." *European Economic Review* 40: 289–329.

Borjas, George J. 1995. "The Economic Benefits from Immigration." *Journal of Economic Perspectives* 9 (2): 3–22.

———. 2003. "The Labor Demand Curve *Is* Downward Sloping: Reexamining the Impact of Immigration on the Labor Market." *Quarterly Journal of Economics* 118 (4): 1335–74.

Burnside, Craig, and David Dollar. 2000. "Aid, Policies, and Growth." *American Economic Review* 90 (4): 847–68.

Card, David. 2001. "Immigrant Inflows, Native Outflows, and the Local Labor Market Impacts of Higher Immigration." *Journal of Labor Economics* 19 (1): 22–64.

Castles, Stephen. 2003. "Why Migration Policies Fail." *Ethnic and Racial Studies* 27 (2): 205–27.

Chauvet, Lisa. 2002. "Socio-Political Instability and the Allocation of International Aid by Donors." *European Journal of Political Economy* 19: 33–59.

Collier, Paul. 1997. "The Failure of Conditionality." In *Perspectives on Aid and Development*, ed. Catherine Gwinn and Joan M. Nelson. Policy Essay 22. Washington, DC: Overseas Development Council.

———. 2007. *The Bottom Billion: Why the Poorest Countries Are Failing and What Can Be Done about It*. Oxford: Oxford University Press.

de Haas, Hein. 2006. "Turning the Tide? Why 'Development Instead of Migration' Policies Are Bound to Fail." IMI Working Paper 2, International Migration Institute, Oxford.

Easterly, William. 2006. *The White Man's Burden. Why the West's Efforts to Aid the Rest Have Done So Much Ill and So Little Good*. New York: Penguin Press.

Facchini, Giovanni, and Anna Maria Mayda. 2008. "From Individual Attitudes towards Migrants to Migration Policy Outcomes: Theory and Evidence." *Economic Policy* 23 (56): 651–713.

Fleck, Robert K., and Christopher Kilby. 2006a. "How Do Political Changes Influence US Bilateral Aid Allocation? Evidence from Panel Data." *Review of Development Economics* 10 (2): 210–23.

———. 2006b. "World Bank Independence: A Model and Statistical Analysis of US Influence." *Review of Development Economics* 10 (2): 224–40.

Friedberg, Rachel M., and Jennifer Hunt. 1995. "The Impact of Immigrants on Host Country Wages, Employment and Growth." *Journal of Economic Perspectives* 9 (2): 23–44.

Gubert, Flore. 2003. "Ces immigrés qui font vivre le Mali." *Libération* 10 (February 19).

Hatton, Timothy J., and Jeffrey G. Williamson. 2002. "What Fundamentals Drive World Migration?" NBER Working Paper 9159, National Bureau of Economic Research, Cambridge, MA.

Jennissen, Roel. 2003. "Economic Determinants of Net International Migration in Western Europe." *European Journal of Population* 19 (2, June): 171–98.

Kapur, Devesh. 2004. "Remittances: The New Development Mantra?" G-24 Discussion Paper Series 29, United Nations Conference on Trade and Development (UNCTAD), New York.

Klein, Michael, and Tim Harford. 2005. *The Market for Aid*. Washington, DC: International Finance Corporation.

Kosack, Stephen, and Jennifer Tobin. 2006. "Funding Self-Sustaining Development: The Role of Aid, FDI and Government in Economic Success." *International Organization* 60 (1): 205–43.

Longhi, Simonetta, Peter Nijkamp, and Jacques Poot. 2005. "A Meta Analytic Assessment of the Effect of Immigration on Wages." *Journal of Economic Surveys* 19 (3): 451–77.

Lucas, Robert E. B. 2005. *International Migration and Economic Development: Lessons from Low-Income Countries*. Cheltenham, UK: Edward Elgar Publishing.

Mayda, Anna Maria. 2006. "Who Is against Immigration? A Cross-Country Investigation of Individual Attitudes toward Immigrants." *Review of Economics and Statistics* 88 (3): 510–30.

———. 2007. "International Migration: A Panel Data Analysis of the Determinants of Bilateral Flows." CEPR Discussion Paper 6289, Centre for Economic Policy Research, Oxford.

Morrison, Thomas K. 1982. "The Relationship of U.S. Aid, Trade and Investment to Migration Pressures in Major Sending Countries." *International Migration Review* 16 (1): 4–26.

Neumayer, Eric. 2005. "Bogus Refugees? The Determinants of Asylum Migration to Western Europe." *International Studies Quarterly* 49 (3): 389–410.

———. 2006. "Unequal Access to Foreign Spaces: How States Use Visa Restrictions to Regulate Mobility in a Globalized World." *Transactions of the Institute of British Geographers* 31 (1): 72–84.

O'Rourke, K. H., and Richard Sinnott. 2006. "The Determinants of Individual Attitudes towards Immigration." *European Journal of Political Economy* 22 (4): 838–61.

Ortega, Javier. 2000. "Pareto-Improving Immigration in an Economy with Equilibrium Unemployment." *Economic Journal* 110: 92–112.

Rotte, Ralph, and Michael Vogler. 2000. "The Effects of Development on Migration: Theoretical Issues and New Empirical Evidence." *Journal of Population Economics* 13 (3): 485–508.

Sachs, Jeffrey D. 2005. *The End of Poverty: How We Can Make It Happen in Our Lifetime*. London: Penguin Books.

Scheve, Kenneth F., and Matthew J. Slaughter. 2001. "Labor Market Competition and Individual Preferences over Immigration Policy." *Review of Economics and Statistics* 83 (1): 133–45.

Svensson, Jakob. 1999. "Aid, Growth and Democracy." *Economics and Politics* 11 (3): 275–97.

———. 2000. "When Is Foreign Aid Policy Credible? Aid Dependence and Conditionality." *Journal of Development Economics* 61 (1): 61–84.

———. 2003. "Why Conditional Aid Does Not Work and What Can Be Done about It?" *Journal of Development Economics* 70 (2): 381–402.

Comment on "The Aid-Migration Trade-off," by Jean-Paul Azam and Ruxanda Berlinschi

MELVIN D. AYOGU

Jean-Paul Azam and Ruxanda Berlinschi have highlighted an inconvenient but important concern about foreign aid to developing countries. Starting from the assumption that aid is driven by the purely altruistic motive of improving the lot of the less fortunate, the literature on the impact of aid to needy countries suggests that such assistance has been largely ineffective—yet this does not seem to have dampened the flow of aid over time. An awkward question arises: if aid is known to be ineffective but continues to be delivered, either the donors are irrational, or there are other, not yet revealed, reasons for giving. Azam and Berlinschi, on the grounds of the revealed-preference principle and empirical data, argue that part of the hidden aid agenda is to reduce the number of immigrants entering donor countries from developing countries. Although the dataset covers legal migration only and does not explicitly classify immigrants by income level, nonetheless the discussion suggests that the target groups to be discouraged are the poor and the unskilled, desperate for work. The paper thus can be viewed as part of the strand of aid literature that seeks to rescue the "aid-ineffectiveness" literature from its current embarrassment.

The Aid-Migration Theses

The authors set out to test three propositions. The first is that donor countries use foreign aid partly to control immigration from recipient countries. This is the *hidden agenda* hypothesis. By controlling for the influence of drivers of aid flows other than immigration and for drivers of immigration other than aid flows, the authors attempt to isolate the effect of aid flows on migration flows.

The second test is motivated by the insight afforded by the theoretical framework elaborated in the paper. According to this model, although donor countries that

Melvin D. Ayogu is professor of economics and dean, Faculty of Commerce, University of Cape Town, South Africa.
Annual World Bank Conference on Development Economics 2009, Global

extend bilateral aid to poor countries secretly nurture the desire to stem migration flows from the beneficiaries of their financial assistance, their actions generate an inferior outcome for themselves. The paper suggests that donors should better coordinate their efforts in order to achieve what they really desire. But it would be politically incorrect for donors to collude openly to curb the flow of migrants from the very countries that they seek to assist, particularly given that migration is a mechanism for poverty reduction, and the active espousal of such an agenda in a consortium would certainly be incompatible with the rhetoric of globalization. As a result of these implied discomforts, rich countries seek other, more subtle ways to achieve coordination at a supranational level.

The third proposition concerns the relative effectiveness of the various multilateral institutions as coordinating mechanisms for the secret desires of donor countries.

Empirical Evidence

The paper finds that aid matters significantly in curbing migration flows. The clever construction of the test for this proposition enables the authors to implicitly identify donors' true objectives. Thus, by showing the presence of reverse causation between flows of assistance and of migrants, they establish that the level of immigration affects "giving." In addition, the paper finds empirical confirmation for the second proposition: that coordinated aid is relatively more effective in curbing immigration. On the third proposition, the evidence is inconclusive, and there is as yet no established theory that marshals the relative strengths and challenges of competing alternative multilateral institutions and helps predict in rank order those that are most effective as coordinating mechanisms. (Easterly and Pfutze 2008 recently exploited the question about the ranking of aid agencies, using a set of criteria viewed as crucial for efficient aid delivery.)

Conclusion

The theme of this year's conference is rightly about people and politics, which, presumably, is what globalization is all about. Years ago, in 2000, Dani Rodrik asked whether trade can be global while politics remains local. Jurisdictional boundaries localize economic activities and define borders that then define trade as either national or international. Underpinning Rodrik's insightful analysis are concerns about likely future trends in the range of immigration policies toward people from poor countries and people with different religious and ideological persuasions. U.S. immigration policy of the recent past was an issue among Latino voters in the 2008 U.S. presidential election and, in fact, became one of the few issues on which candidates Barack Obama and John McCain were in agreement. In Europe concern is voiced about how immigration policy affects the career prospects of foreign soccer players in European leagues and what would be an appropriate policy stance on this issue. France, South Africa, and the United Kingdom have all experienced their versions of xenophobia in recent memory. In the light of the times in which we live, the issues raised by Azam and Berlinschi cannot be ignored. Their results suggest the need for more studies at the micro level, with a focus on institutions.

The authors do seem to have given us an example of aid that works. If foreign aid can generate a desired policy outcome when the agenda is hidden, why not when the objective is open? How can foreign aid be effective in furthering the hidden agenda (revealed preference) but ineffective in promoting declared objectives? And, how much can we rely on evidence from eight years of data in a history of compassionate or not-so-compassionate giving that spans more than three decades?

Perhaps the real message here is that transparency in the aid business is overdue. Easterly and Pfutze (2008) emphasized the same message. Transparency can engender the correct attribution or decomposition of aid into its various goals (hidden and covert), opening a prospect for transforming the entire aid-ineffectiveness puzzle into an understandable picture.

Finally, I have to acknowledge with a great deal of satisfaction that, as a by-product, Azam's and Berlinschi's paper provides support for the push by recipient countries for better donor coordination with a view to improving absorptive capacity (see, for instance, Birdsall, Williamson, and Deese 2002; de Renzio 2005; Ayogu 2006).

References

Ayogu, Melvin. 2006. "Can Africa Absorb More Aid?" In *Aid, Debt Relief and Development in Africa: African Development Report 2006*, ed. African Development Bank, 25–40. New York: Oxford University Press.

Birdsall, Nancy, John Williamson, and Brian Deese. 2002. *Delivering on Debt Relief: From IMF Gold to a New Aid Architecture*. Washington, DC: Center for Global Development and Institute for International Economics, http://www.iie.com.

de Renzio, Paolo. 2005. "Scaling Up versus Absorptive Capacity: Challenges and Opportunities for Reaching the MDGs in Africa." ODI Briefing Paper, London.

Easterly, William, and Tobias Pfutze. 2008. "Where Does the Money Go? Best and Worst Practices in Foreign Aid." *Journal of Economic Perspectives* 22 (2): 29–52.

Rodrik, Dani. 2000. "How Far Will International Economic Integration Go?" *Journal of Economic Perspectives* 14 (1): 177–86.

Are Remittances More Effective Than Aid for Improving Child Health? An Empirical Assessment Using Inter- and Intracountry Data

LISA CHAUVET, FLORE GUBERT, AND SANDRINE MESPLÉ-SOMPS

This paper analyzes the respective impacts of aid and remittances on human development as measured by infant and child mortality rates. Panel data on a set of 109 developing countries and cross-country quintile-level data on a sample of 47 developing countries are alternatively used. In addition to assessing the extent to which health aid and remittances contribute to reducing child health disparities between countries, the paper addresses two other questions: What is the net effect of migration, after accounting for the brain drain of health workers? What is the effective impact of aid and remittances on intracountry child health disparities? Our results tend to show that remittances significantly improve child health and that the impact of health aid is nonlinear, suggesting that aid to the health sector is more effective in the poorest countries. By contrast, medical brain drain, as measured by the expatriation rate of physicians, is found to have a harmful impact on health outcomes. The net impact of migration on human development is therefore weakened. Finally, remittances seem to be much more effective in improving health outcomes for children belonging to the richest households, whereas neither pro-poor nor antipoor effects are found for health aid.

Poverty reduction is increasingly put forward as the main objective of official development assistance (ODA) to developing countries. National leaders and the international community have pledged to meet by 2015 a series of poverty reduction targets known as the Millennium Development Goals (MDGs).[1] The pursuit of these goals calls for dramatic increases in infrastructure finance and in the provision of basic services to the population of the developing world that ODA alone cannot achieve. The Monterrey consensus, which emerged from the United Nations International Conference on Financing for Development in that city in 2002, highlighted the need

Lisa Chauvet, Flore Gubert, and Sandrine Mesplé-Somps are researchers with the Institute of Research for Development (IRD), DIAL, Paris. Flore Gubert is also associate professor at the Paris School of Economics.

Annual World Bank Conference on Development Economics 2009, Global

to find new sources of financing, and the idea that more private funds should be invested in developing countries has received strong support since then.

Given this context and an ever-increasing volume of flows from migrants, international migrant remittances have attracted considerable attention in recent years. According to the latest World Bank estimates (see Ratha et al. 2007), recorded remittances to developing countries reached US$240 billion in 2007. The actual magnitude is even larger when transfers through informal channels are taken into account. In 36 out of 153 developing countries, remittances are larger than all capital flows, public and private, and voices have already been raised here and there to call for progressive replacement of official aid by remittances.

Little is known, however, about the respective effectiveness of aid and remittances in alleviating poverty. Despite a burgeoning literature examining the impact of ODA on aggregate welfare, there exists, to our knowledge, almost no studies analyzing to what extent aid and remittances may be substitutes or how they are related to inequality and poverty reduction. Exceptions include the work of Chauvet and Mesplé-Somps (2007), who analyze the distributive impact of trade flows, foreign direct investment (FDI), official aid, and migrants' remittances using Branco Milanovic's World Income Distribution database (Milanovic 2005). The authors find that FDI increases intracountry disparities and that remittances tend to decrease them. They also find that trade and aid have a nonlinear relationship with income distribution.

The objective of our paper is to fill this knowledge gap by analyzing the respective impacts of aid and remittances on human development as measured by infant and child mortality rates. To what extent do aid and remittances help reduce child health disparities between countries? What are their respective impacts on child health disparities within countries? How do remittances compare with aid when migration costs (in the form of "brain drain") are accounted for?

We choose basic indicators of human welfare instead of a monetary measure of poverty for three reasons. First, comparable cross-country data on monetary poverty over time are extremely scarce. Second, child health figures prominently among the MDGs. Donors have committed themselves to reducing by two-thirds the mortality rate among children under age 5 (goal 4), and to this end, they have devoted an increasing share of official aid to the health sector. There is, however, very little empirical evidence on the effect of increased aid flows on health outcomes in recipient countries. Whether donors are right to prioritize the health sector in the intracountry allocation of aid is thus an unanswered question that needs to be addressed. Third, the relationship between migration and health is increasingly emphasized in the microeconomic literature, and donor agencies regularly report the success of most of their projects and programs in the health sector. It is therefore interesting to investigate whether successful health interventions from the donors' side or the migrants' side at the micro level translate into improved health outcomes at the macro level and whether Paul Mosley's micro-macro paradox also applies to the health sector (Mosley 1987).

We follow Mishra and Newhouse (2007) and use aid allocated to the health sector, instead of aggregate aid, in our empirical analyses. Our implicit assumption is that not all types of aid can reasonably be expected to affect health outcomes and that narrowing the aid variable should help us better measure the impact (if any) of official development assistance on basic indicators of human development.

Our empirical strategy relies on two econometric exercises. We first examine the respective impacts of aid, remittances, and medical brain drain on child health indicators, using panel data on a sample of 109 developing countries. We explore whether aid and remittances contribute to improving health outcomes and whether the brain drain of health workers vitiates the positive impact of remittances. This first econometric exercise raises substantial methodological issues such as measurement errors and endogeneity of our core explanatory variables, which we try to address. Keeping in mind the inherent weaknesses of this macro approach, our econometric results indicate that both remittances and health aid significantly reduce infant and child mortality rates but that the effect of health aid is nonlinear, suggesting that aid to the health sector is likely to be more effective in the poorest countries. Medical brain drain, as measured by the expatriation rate of physicians, is found to have a harmful impact on health outcomes. The net impact of migration on human development is thus diminished.

We then assess the respective effectiveness of aid and remittances in lessening health disparities within countries, using cross-country quintile-level data. The results of this second econometric exercise show that remittances are effective in reducing infant and child mortality rates, but only for the richest quintiles. This finding suggests that although remittances contribute to better mean health outcomes in recipient countries, they tend to increase intracountry health inequality. The impact of health aid, by contrast, is hardly ever significant in our within-country regressions.

The next section contains a review of the macroeconomic literature on the impacts of aid and remittances on poverty and inequality. The data, method of estimation, and results of the cross-country and intracountry analyses are presented in the subsequent two sections, followed by concluding remarks and a discussion of the policy implications of the findings.

Effects of Aid and Remittances on Poverty and Inequality: A Review of the Literature

From the early 1960s to the mid-1990s, the literature investigating the macroeconomic impact of aid focused on the link between aid and growth. The emerging picture from this literature is that aid can enhance growth but that this result is very fragile and is highly dependent on the choice of data, sample composition, and estimation methods (Roodman 2007). The adoption of the United Nations Millennium Declaration in 2000 and the obligation accepted by donors to financially support developing countries' efforts to achieve the eight Millennium Development Goals by 2015 have progressively shifted the focus from the aid-growth nexus to the relationship between aid flows and welfare or poverty indicators. This relationship is examined next, after which the effects of remittances are explored.

Poverty and Inequality Impacts of Aid

The few existing studies on the impacts of aid on poverty and inequality have adopted standard cross-country growth regression approaches, replacing growth with an indicator of welfare or poverty as the dependent variable (see, for example, Boone 1996; Mosley, Hudson, and Verschoor 2004; Gomanee, Girma, and Morrissey 2005; Gomanee et al. 2005). Because comparable cross-country data on poverty over time are extremely scarce, most studies have concentrated on the effectiveness of aid in improving human development indicators such as the infant mortality rate, the under-five mortality rate, life expectancy, and primary schooling.

In a famous paper, Boone (1996) finds no evidence that aid succeeds in improving human development indicators in recipient countries. Although aid could theoretically reduce infant mortality either through an increase in private consumption or through greater provision of public services to the poor, his results suggest that it increases the size of recipient governments but has no impact on basic measures of human development indicators. Pushing his analysis further, Boone investigates whether his result varies depending on the political regime. He finds some evidence that liberal political regimes, all else being equal, have lower infant mortality rates, which may reflect greater willingness of these systems to deliver public services to the poor.

Boone's paper has been much criticized, on two grounds. In the first place, some authors have argued that the welfare impact of aid is not direct but operates through its effect on the amount of government spending allocated to social areas. Boone's regressions would thus be inappropriately specified. Mosley, Hudson, and Verschoor (2004) estimate a system of three equations, with poverty, aid, and pro-poor expenditure as their dependent variables. They find that aid is associated with higher levels of pro-poor spending and that such spending is associated with lower poverty headcounts. Aid is also found to increase health spending, which in turn reduces infant mortality. Gomanee, Girma, and Morrissey (2005) reach the same type of conclusion, using quantile regressions. In a companion paper, however, Gomanee et al. (2005) find evidence that aid improves welfare indicators and that this effect works predominantly through direct impacts.

The second criticism is that although it may be true that aggregate aid has no impact on health, particular types of aid, including health aid, are effective in improving human development indicators (see, for example, Masud and Yontcheva 2005; Michaelowa and Weber 2007; Mishra and Newhouse 2007; Dreher, Nunnenkamp, and Thiele 2008). Mishra and Newhouse (2007), in particular, rely on a large dataset covering 118 countries between 1973 and 2004 to measure the effect of health aid on infant mortality. They estimate both ordinary least squares (OLS) regressions and a system of moment equations using the generalized method of moments (GMM) and find that increased health aid is associated with a statistically significant reduction in infant mortality. The estimated effect of health aid is small, however; since doubling health aid within a country would reduce infant mortality in the next five-year period by only 2 percent. In addition, the authors do not find any significant impact of overall aid.

Masud and Yontcheva (2005) use data on assistance from nongovernmental organizations (NGOs) and on bilateral aid to assess the effectiveness of these financial flows on two social indicators, infant mortality and adult illiteracy. Their underlying assumption is that NGOs intervene at the grassroots level and may be more effective in alleviating poverty than other types of assistance. Using an unbalanced panel of 58 countries from 1990 to 2001, they find that health expenditure per capita reduces infant mortality, as does greater NGO aid per capita. By contrast, they do not find any significant impact of total bilateral aid on infant mortality. The authors then list a number of reasons why NGO aid might work better than bilateral aid in reducing infant mortality. First, NGO aid would be allocated more toward countries with high infant mortality rates, while bilateral aid would favor countries with lower infant mortality. Second, NGOs would have more direct links to the poor and vulnerable, which would make them more efficient. Third, in line with Boone (1996), aid transiting through recipient governments could be diverted for the benefit of wealthy elites. Pushing their analysis further, the authors find no evidence of a positive impact of NGO or bilateral aid on the share of spending on health care in total expenditure.

The few existing studies examining the links between aid and aggregate welfare as measured by human development indicators do not permit clear conclusions. Some papers find no impact at all; others find evidence that aid decreases infant mortality rates, directly, or indirectly, through higher levels of pro-poor spending. This lack of consensus in the macroeconomic literature is surprising, given the number of successful health interventions financially supported by international assistance (Levine and the What Works Working Group 2004).

Poverty and Inequality Impacts of Remittances

Despite the increasing size of remittances, empirical macroeconomic evidence on the impacts of these financial flows on poverty and inequality is even scarcer than that related to aid. Here again, the scarcity of evidence stems mainly from the lack of reliable and comparable cross-country data on several of the relevant variables, such as emigration rate by country and amounts remitted, and from the absence of the long series that are required if use is to be made of the latest macroeconometric tools. Consequently, the empirical literature is confined largely to a few case studies of villages or countries based on microeconometric data (see, for example, Leliveld 1997; Lachaud 1999; Adams 2004, 2006).

At the cross-national level, to our knowledge, only four recent studies have looked at the poverty impact of remittances: Adams and Page (2005); *World Economic Outlook* (IMF 2005); Gupta, Pattillo, and Wagh (2007); and Acosta et al. (2008). Despite strong microeconomic evidence for a positive impact of remittances on education and health (see, for example, Kanaiaupuni and Donato 1999; Cox-Edwards and Ureta 2003; Hildebrandt and McKenzie 2005; Mansuri 2007), no one has ever investigated the impact of remittances on human development indicators at a macroeconomic level.

Adams and Page (2005) use a panel of 71 low-income and middle-income countries for which data on migration, remittances, poverty, and inequality are available and test whether countries that produce more international migration or receive more international remittances have less poverty. After instrumenting for the potential endogeneity of remittances, they find that a 10 percent increase in per capita official remittances leads to a 3.5 percent decline in the share of people living in poverty. Using a broader sample of 101 countries, IMF (2005) provides further evidence that remittances have an effect on poverty. The effect, however, is rather small; on average, a 2.5 percentage point increase in the ratio of remittances to gross domestic product (GDP) is associated with a less than 0.5 percentage point decrease in poverty. As argued by the authors, this (disappointing) result could stem from the fact that average income and inequality, along with remittances, are included as regressors. Since these variables are themselves likely to be influenced by remittances, the true impact of remittances on poverty could actually be larger.

Using a sample of 76 countries in which Sub-Saharan Africa is substantially represented, Gupta, Pattillo, and Wagh (2007) adopt the same methodology as that of Adams and Page (2005) and model poverty as a function of mean income, some measures of income distribution, and remittances. Their findings indicate that a 10 percent rise in remittances is associated with a decrease of about 1 percent in the incidence of poverty. In the case of Sub-Saharan Africa, however, their results suggest that the impact of poverty on migration and remittances is greater than the impact of remittances on poverty.

Finally, Acosta et al. (2008) use both cross-country and household survey data to assess the impact of remittances on growth, poverty, and inequality in Latin America. Their cross-country estimates suggest that remittances have a positive and statistically significant effect on growth, on average, but that they tend to increase the level of income inequality. For the average Latin American country, however, the effect is different; an increase in remittances tends to be associated with lower levels of inequality. Turning to the authors' microeconometric analyses, their findings suggest that the effects of remittances on poverty and inequality vary strongly across Latin American countries, depending on whether recipients are concentrated at the bottom or at the top of the distribution of nonremittance income.

In what follows, our aim is to provide additional insights into the question of whether aid and remittances, as sources of external financing, are effective in improving child health outcomes.

Impact of Aid and Remittances on Health Outcomes: A Cross-Country Analysis

This section assesses the impact of health aid and remittances on child health outcomes, using panel data on a sample of 109 countries from 1987 to 2004. (For a list of countries in the sample, see annex table A.1.) After a brief presentation of the empirical strategy and a description of the data, the results of our baseline model are discussed. The analysis is then pushed further by testing for nonlinearities in the aid-health relationship and investigating the effect of the medical brain drain on health outcomes.

Model and Data

To explore the relative impacts of aid and migration on child health indicators, we estimate a model of the following form:

$$\ln Health_{i,t} = \alpha_i + \tau_t + \beta \ln X_{i,(t-1,t-4)} + \delta \ln Remittances_{i,(t-1,t-4)} + \theta \ln Health\ aid_{i,(t-1,t-4)} + \varepsilon_{i,t}. \tag{1}$$

$Health_{i,t}$ is either the under-five mortality rate or the infant mortality rate from *World Development Indicators* (World Bank 2006). The under-five mortality rate is the probability (per 1,000 live births in a given year) that a newborn baby will die before reaching age 5, if subject to current age-specific mortality rates. The infant mortality rate is the number of infants dying before reaching age 1, per 1,000 live births.

Since our dependent variables are bounded, we use a logarithmic transformation. To ease interpretation of our results and account for potential nonlinearities, all our independent variables are also log-linearized.

We measure *Health aid_{i,t}* using aid commitments to the health sector as defined by the Country Reporting System (CRS) of the Organisation for Economic Co-operation and Development (OECD).[2] The main advantage of the CRS is that its data on aid commitments are highly disaggregated by purpose (sector). Its main disadvantage is that the data are only reliable for recent years—as reflected in figure 1 by the large underreporting of aid in the CRS data compared with data from the Development

FIGURE 1.
Total Aid, Remittances, and Health Aid, 1986–2004

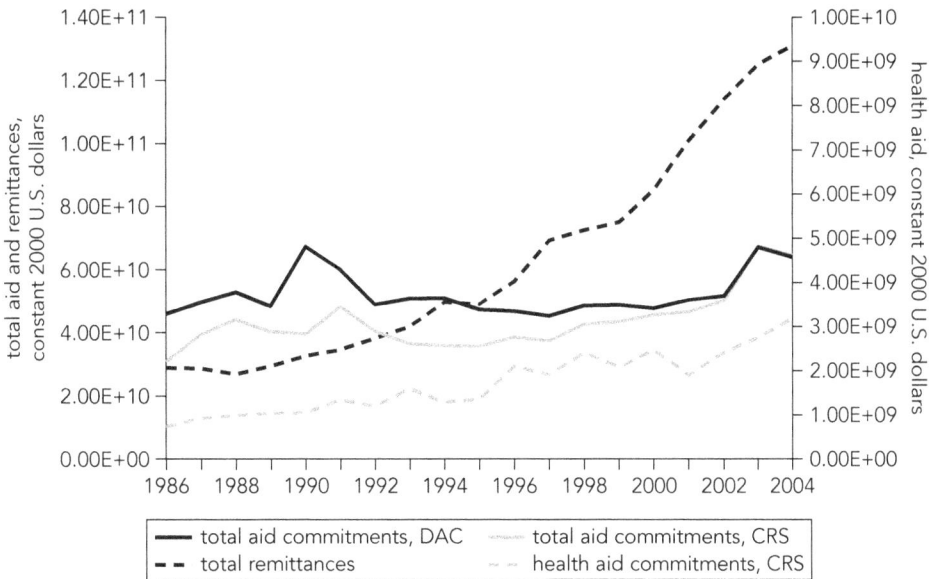

Source: Development Assistance Committee (DAC) of the Organisation for Economic Co-operation and Development (OECD); Country Reporting System (CRS), OECD; *World Development Indicators 2006* (World Bank 2006).

Assistance Committee (DAC) of the OECD. As noted by Mishra and Newhouse (2007), the extent of underreporting varies by sector, donor, and time period. Missing data are therefore omitted from the sample rather than treated as zero health aid. We restrict our sample to relatively recent observations, starting in the mid-1980s.[3] Figure 1 shows that the share of aid commitments to the health sector has gradually increased since the 1980s, when it was about 2 percent of total commitments; it is now about 5 percent. This increase in health aid reflects the switch in donors' priorities, notably, from aid for infrastructure to aid for social sectors, which reflects the adoption of the Millennium Development Goals.

The CRS also provides a disaggregation of disbursements by sector. Unfortunately, disbursements are even more underreported than commitments. As an alternative variable for *Health aid$_{i,t}$*, we proxy aid disbursements in the health sector by weighting total net disbursements with the share of health commitments in total commitments. *Health aid$_{i,t}$* is expressed in per capita constant terms, using the DAC deflator.

The term *Remittances$_{i,t}$* is defined as current transfers by migrants who are employed for more than a year in another country in which they are considered residents (World Bank 2006). We use the same deflator for remittances as for aid in order to transform this variable into per capita constant terms. As shown in figure 1, workers' remittances have been increasing in both absolute and relative terms since the mid-1980s; then, they accounted for only about 60 percent of total aid commitments, but since 2000 they have represented more than 200 percent of aid commitments, reflecting the growing importance of this financing for developing economies. The growth in remittances is partly attributable to the rise in the number of international migrants worldwide, but it also indicates that in recent years people have been shifting from informal to formal channels for sending funds. This potentially important source of measurement error is addressed in our econometric analysis. First, we include a time trend in our list of regressors in order to capture the increasing trend in remittances. Second, we control for unobservable heterogeneity among countries, hoping to account for some omitted variables that could explain simultaneously the increasing trend in remittances and the decreasing trend in child and infant mortality. Finally, this latter issue is also tackled through the instrumentation of remittances (see the next subsection).

Following the existing literature on cross-country determinants of child health outcomes, equation (1) controls for a set of relevant socioeconomic variables, $X_{i,t}$. Beginning with the work of Ravallion (1993) and Pritchett and Summers (1996), a consensus has emerged concerning the negative relationship between child mortality and national income. Female education, measured either by educational attainment or by illiteracy rates, has also been shown to be negatively correlated with child mortality (Filmer and Pritchett 1999; Anand and Bärnighausen 2004; Fay et al. 2005; McGuire 2006; Ravallion 2007). We express income per capita in purchasing power parity (PPP) constant terms (World Bank 2006) and measure female education by average years of schooling of the female population age 15 and older (Barro and Lee 2000).

Anand and Bärnighausen (2004) show that the density of human resources in the health sector is significantly correlated with child health indicators. We proxy human resources for health with the number of physicians (per 1,000 inhabitants), from Docquier and Bhargava (2007).

Other cross-country determinants of child health have been identified in the literature, such as the size of the population (Mishra and Newhouse 2007), the share of urban population (Fay et al. 2005; Masud and Yontcheva 2005; Ravallion 2007), inequality indicators (Filmer and Pritchett 1999; Fay et al. 2005; McGuire 2006; Ravallion 2007), and poverty rates (Anand and Bärnighausen 2004), but none were significant in our analysis. Two other variables—ethnic fragmentation and whether the country is predominantly Muslim—were also significantly correlated with infant mortality in Filmer and Pritchett (1999) and McGuire (2006). Both are time invariant and could not be introduced in our fixed-effects analysis.

Finally, there has been an intense debate concerning the impact of public spending on health outcomes. Because our core independent variable is health aid and the impact of health aid goes through the route of public spending, we exclude the public spending variable from our analysis. Another reason is that when public spending is introduced into the regressions, we lose half of the countries in the sample.

Equation (1) is estimated on a panel of 109 developing countries, among them 39 Sub-Saharan countries, from 1987 to 2004. (See annex table A.1 for the country list.) Child health data are for every four or five years (1990, 1995, 2000, and 2004). The right-hand-side variables are averaged over three years, from $t - 1$ to $t - 4$, and are measured in logarithms. This is true for all variables except education because the Barro and Lee (2000) database on education is for every five years and is available only up to 2000. We therefore use the 2000 level of education to explain 2004 health outcomes, and so on. We control for unobservable heterogeneity with country fixed effects, α. We also include time dummies τ_t.

Endogeneity of Aid, Remittances, and Income

There are two potential sources of endogeneity of aid and remittances to child health indicators. First, aid and remittances are given purposively, and both donors and migrants are likely to take into account the child health situation when allocating their flows. Even if aid is determined at the macro level and remittances are determined at the micro level, both are likely to reflect, to some extent, the chances of survival of children. Second, there could be some omitted variables that affect aid, remittances, and child health. For example, natural disasters are likely to induce both a deterioration of child health indicators and increased inflows of aid and remittances.

We therefore instrument health aid and workers' remittances.[4] As instruments for health aid, we use a set of variables that capture historical and cultural relationships between developing countries and donor or destination countries. These variables are more likely to be exogenous to child health than any characteristics of recipient or origin countries. Specifically, we use the total aid budget of the five main donors weighted by the cultural distance between receiving and donor or destination countries (measured by whether they have the same religion) and by the geographic distance (distance to Washington, Brussels, and Tokyo).[5] As an instrument for health aid, we use health aid lagged twice. Workers' remittances are instrumented using the ratio of broad money supply (M2) to GDP because countries that are more financially developed have been found to receive larger remittances. Income per capita is also endogenous to health indicators (Pritchett and Summers 1996; Filmer and Pritchett 1999). It is instrumented using twice-lagged income per capita.

We also suspected education to be endogenous to health indicators. We tested this hypothesis, and it turned out that the exogeneity of education could not be rejected by our test. This result is partly explained by the fact that education in $t - 5$ (or $t - 4$) is used to explain health outcomes in t.

The excludability and relevance of our instruments being legitimate concerns here, tests for their validity (Sargan test of overidentification, test of underidentification, test of weak instruments, partial R-squared) were systematically performed.[6]

Estimation of the Baseline Model

Our estimation of the baseline model proceeds in three steps. Equation (1) is first estimated with simple OLS. We then introduce country fixed effects to take into account unobservable heterogeneity in our sample. Finally aid, remittances, and income are instrumented using two-stage least squares (2SLS), including country fixed effects and time fixed effects.[7] Instrumentation equations are provided in annex table A.2.

Regressions (1) through (6) in table 1 present the estimations of the baseline model when the dependent variable is either the under-five mortality rate or the infant mortality rate. Income per capita is highly significant and tends to reduce child mortality. The impact is quite strong: the coefficients of income in regressions (3) and (6) suggest that a 1 percent increase in income reduces child mortality by around 0.59 percent and infant mortality by about 0.50 percent. The coefficients of income per capita are interestingly close to the coefficients found by Pritchett and Summers (1996) in their instrumental variables (IV) estimation of infant mortality (around 0.3), using a different set of instruments. They are even closer for the fixed-effect estimations (0.31 in Pritchett and Summers 1996).

Surprisingly, the number of physicians is not significant in table 1 except in OLS estimations. When significant, it is negative, suggesting that a larger number of doctors implies lower child and infant mortality rates. Anand and Bärnighausen (2004) find a strong impact of doctor and nurse density on various health indicators, which in their case is more robust than in our regressions. Only in OLS estimations does female education have a significant impact on child and infant mortality rates. In table 1 the negative impact of the time dummies (1990 is the omitted time dummy) reflects the decreasing trend in child and infant mortality rates over the last two decades.

Finally, aid and remittances both have a negative coefficient in regressions (1) through (6), but, contrary to Mishra and Newhouse (2007), we find no significant impact of health aid at this stage of our empirical analysis. By contrast, remittances are found to be strongly significant in most regressions, with the expected sign. When instrumented, the coefficient of remittances is multiplied more than fourfold: a 1 percent increase in remittances decreases child mortality by 0.12 percent and infant mortality by 0.10 percent.

TABLE 1. Impact of Health Aid and Remittances on Child and Infant Mortality Rates, Baseline Model

	Child mortality rate			Infant mortality rate		
	OLS	Within	2SLS	OLS	Within	2SLS
Variable	(1)	(2)	(3)	(4)	(5)	(6)
GDP per capita[a]	−0.553	−0.263	−0.595	−0.482	−0.218	−0.500
	(6.64)***	(3.03)***	(2.39)**	(6.49)***	(2.78)***	(2.26)**
Number of physicians	−0.157	−0.032	0.048	−0.107	−0.022	0.050
per 1,000 inhabitants	(3.93)***	(0.82)	(0.89)	(2.88)***	(0.62)	(1.04)
Female educational	−0.156	0.034	−0.009	−0.151	0.049	0.004
attainment	(1.97)*	(0.61)	(0.09)	(2.15)**	(0.95)	(0.05)
Dummy for missing	−0.181	0.008	−0.217	−0.170	0.038	−0.168
education variable	(1.82)*	(0.15)	(1.28)	(2.08)**	(0.81)	(1.08)
Remittances per capita[a]	−0.054	−0.031	−0.122	−0.045	−0.023	−0.104
	(2.37)**	(2.37)**	(2.97)***	(2.16)**	(2.09)**	(2.76)***
Health aid per capita[a]	−0.012	−0.012	−0.008	−0.009	−0.011	−0.000
	(0.60)	(1.26)	(0.31)	(0.44)	(1.29)	(0.01)
Year = 1995	−0.058	−0.102	0.068	−0.048	−0.094	0.081
	(1.74)*	(4.07)***	(1.29)	(1.64)	(4.16)***	(1.74)*
Year = 2000	−0.088	−0.198	0.032	−0.085	−0.189	0.037
	(2.14)**	(6.92)***	(1.27)	(2.27)**	(7.34)***	(1.68)*
Year = 2004	−0.139	−0.274		−0.139	−0.265	
	(2.94)***	(7.98)***		(3.24)***	(8.68)***	
Constant	8.704	6.360		7.872	5.669	
	(13.88)***	(9.30)***		(13.93)***	(9.19)***	
Fixed effects	No	Yes	Yes	No	Yes	Yes
Number of observations	358	358	237	358	358	237
Number of countries	109	109	86		109	86
R^2	0.75	0.57		0.72	0.57	
Sargan (p-value)			0.31			0.27
Underidentification test (p-value)			0.03			0.03
Income instrumentation F-statistic (p-value)			0.000			0.000
Aid instrumentation F-statistic (p-value)			0.100			0.100
Remittance instrumentation F-statistic (p-value)			0.000			0.000

Note: 2SLS, two-stage least squares; GDP, gross domestic product; OLS, ordinary least squares. Numbers in parentheses are robust t-statistics. All variables except the education variable are averages over three-year periods, from $t - 1$ to $t - 4$, measured in logs. In equations (1) and (4), standard errors are clustered by country.

a. Instrumented regressors in equations (3) and (5). Instruments include twice-lagged GDP per capita; twice-lagged aid; and instruments for aid and remittances in the tradition of Tavares (2003), that is, total aid budgets of the five largest donors (the United States, Japan, France, the United Kingdom, and Germany) in constant dollars, weighted by a cultural distance variable (same religion) and a geographic distance variable. The ratio of broad money supply (M2) to GDP is also included as an instrument for remittances. Tests for excludability of the instruments are available on request.

* Significant at the 10 percent level.

** Significant at the 5 percent level.

*** Significant at the 1 percent level.

Nonlinearities in the Aid-Health Relationship

As a next step in our analysis, we explore in greater detail the relationship between health aid and child health indicators. So far, we find no significant impact of health aid commitments. A relative consensus, however, has emerged in the literature: that aggregate aid disbursements affect macroeconomic outcomes such as economic growth in a nonlinear way.[8] Similarly, the impact of health aid on health outcomes may be nonlinear. The nonlinearity may be attributable to constrained absorptive capacity. Constrained absorptive capacity in the health sector may be proxied through an interaction of health aid with income per capita; health aid would be relatively more effective in richer countries because of their greater capacity to absorb aid.

To explore this kind of nonlinearity in the health-aid relationship, we estimate an equation of the following form:

$$\ln Health_{i,t} = \alpha_i + \tau_t + \beta \ln X_{i,(t-1,t-4)} + \delta \ln Remittances_{i,(t-1,t-4)}$$
$$+ \theta_1 \ln Health\ aid_{i,(t-1,t-4)} + \theta_2 \ln Health\ aid_{i,(t-1,t-4)} . \ln Income_{i,(t-1,t-4)} + \varepsilon_{i,t}, \quad (2)$$

where $\ln Health\ aid . \ln Income$ is an interaction variable of aid with income per capita. It is instrumented using the same set of instruments as those for health aid and income per capita.

The results are presented in columns (1) and (2) of table 2. The absorptive capacity hypothesis is not supported by our results. The impact of health aid is nonlinear, but the nonlinearity suggests that aid to the health sector is more effective in poorer countries. The threshold in income per capita corresponding to a switch to harmful aid is around US$4,100 per capita (in PPP). Figure 2 depicts the effect of aid on child mortality rates below and above this income threshold, respectively. The threshold is quite high and implies that most African countries belong to the decreasing part of the relationship between health aid and health outcomes. Aid increases the child mortality rate in 8 of the 35 Sub-Saharan African countries in our sample: Botswana, Cape Verde, Gabon, Mauritius, Namibia, the Seychelles, South Africa, and Swaziland. In the remaining 27 African countries, aid tends to improve child health indicators.

It is worth noting that our baseline specification implies that we capture the direct effects of aid and remittances on child health indicators. Another channel through which aid and remittances could affect health outcomes is their impact on GDP per capita. Since GDP per capita is included among our set of regressors, this indirect impact is not taken into account. Assuming that both remittances and aid tend to improve income, we therefore probably underestimate the impact of these sources of financing on child health indicators.

An alternative way of testing the constrained absorptive capacity hypothesis is to introduce the square of health aid into the regression. A quadratic relationship between health aid and health indicators would reflect marginal decreasing returns to aid: after a given threshold of aid received, an additional dollar of aid is less effective because the country no longer has the capacity to absorb it. Aid squared is never significant when introduced into any of the regressions.[9] Moreover, its sign is negative, as is that of health aid. The absence of a quadratic relationship between health aid and health outcomes confirms our previous finding of no absorptive capacity constraints

TABLE 2. Nonlinearity in the Health-Aid Relationship, Two-Stage Least Squares (2SLS) with Fixed Effects

	Child mortality rate (1)	Infant mortality rate (2)
GDP per capita[a]	−0.355	−0.264
	(1.41)	(1.16)
Number of physicians per 1,000 inhabitants	0.023	0.026
	(0.40)	(0.49)
Female educational attainment	−0.063	−0.050
	(0.53)	(0.45)
Dummy for missing education variable	−0.305	−0.255
	(1.39)	(1.26)
Remittances per capita[a]	−0.115	−0.097
	(2.72)***	(2.46)**
Health aid per capita[a]	−0.839	−0.815
	(1.87)*	(1.99)**
Health aid per capita × income per capita[a]	0.100	0.098
	(1.85)*	(1.98)**
Year = 1995	0.071	0.084
	(1.24)	(1.62)
Year = 2000	0.044	0.049
	(1.69)*	(2.09)**
Fixed effects	Yes	Yes
Number of observations	237	237
Number of countries	86	86
Sargan (p-value)	0.31	0.25
Underidentification test (p-value)	0.04	0.04
Income instrumentation F-statistic (p-value)	0.00	0.00
Aid instrumentation F-statistic (p-value)	0.10/0.12	0.10/0.12
Remittances instrumentation F-statistic (p-value)	0.00	0.00

Note: GDP, gross domestic product. Numbers in parentheses are robust *t*-statistics. All variables except the education variable are averages over three-year periods, from $t-1$ to $t-4$, measured in logs.

a. Instrumented regressors. Instruments include twice-lagged GDP per capita; twice-lagged aid; and instruments for aid and remittances in the tradition of Tavares (2003), that is, total aid budgets of the five largest donors (the United States, Japan, France, the United Kingdom, and Germany) in constant dollars, weighted by a cultural distance variable (same religion) and a geographic distance variable. The ratio of broad money supply (M2) to GDP is also included as an instrument for remittances. Tests for excludability of the instruments are available on request.

* Significant at the 10 percent level.

** Significant at the 5 percent level.

*** Significant at the 1 percent level.

on aid to the health sector. Health aid seems to be more effective where the prospects for improvements in health indicators are higher, that is, in poorer countries.

Finally, we explore whether the results using health aid disbursements are similar to those with aid commitments.[10] Regressions (1) and (3) of table 3 reproduce the baseline model; health aid disbursements are not significantly different from zero. In regressions (2) and (4), health disbursements interacted with income are significant,

FIGURE 2.
Impact of Health Aid on Child Mortality

Income per capita (PPP) less than US$4,100

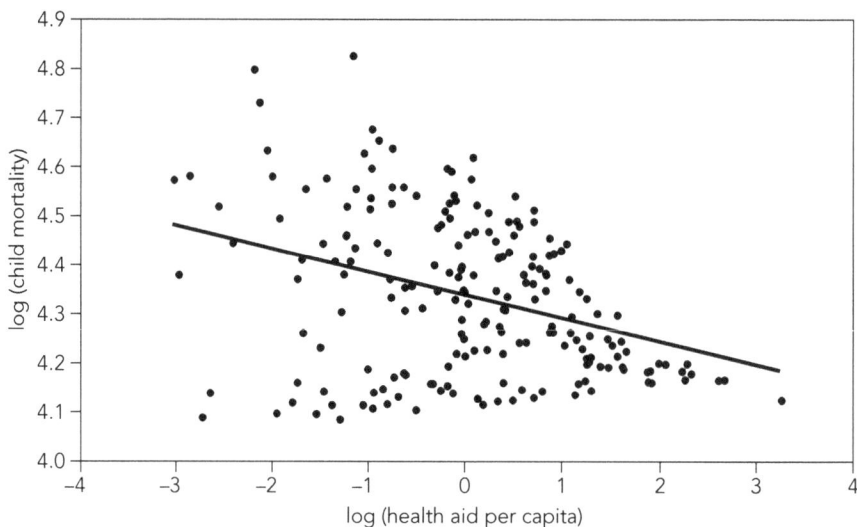

Income per capita (PPP) greater than US$4,100

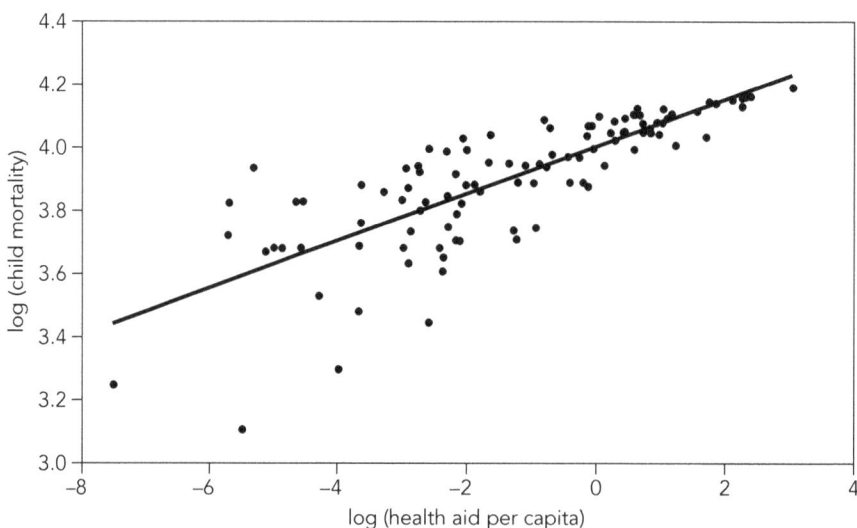

Source: Authors' calculations.

confirming our previous finding. The resulting income threshold, US$4,000, is close to the one corresponding to regressions that include commitments.

Medical Brain Drain

Our baseline model suggests that migrants' remittances help improve health outcomes in developing countries. We now turn to analysis of the counterpart of workers' remittances—the impact of the brain drain induced by migration on health outcomes

TABLE 3. Impact of Health Aid Disbursements on Health Indicators, Two-Stage Least Squares (2SLS) with Fixed Effects

	Child mortality rate		Infant mortality rate	
	(1)	(2)	(3)	(4)
GDP per capita[a]	−0.619	−0.264	−0.516	−0.176
	(2.47)**	(1.00)	(2.33)**	(0.73)
Number of physicians per 1,000 inhabitants	0.044	0.039	0.046	0.041
	(0.77)	(0.61)	(0.90)	(0.70)
Female educational attainment	−0.020	−0.134	−0.005	−0.114
	(0.19)	(1.02)	(0.05)	(0.94)
Dummy for missing education variable	−0.248	−0.445	−0.194	−0.383
	(1.36)	(1.80)*	(1.16)	(1.68)*
Remittances per capita[a]	−0.124	−0.123	−0.106	−0.104
	(2.95)***	(2.70)***	(2.74)***	(2.46)**
Health aid disbursements per capita[a]	−0.028	−0.983	−0.019	−0.937
	(0.96)	(2.25)**	(0.73)	(2.28)**
Health aid disbursements per capita × income per capita[a]		0.118		0.113
		(2.16)**		(2.20)**
Year = 1995	0.061	0.075	0.075	0.088
	(1.20)	(1.38)	(1.64)	(1.79)*
Year = 2000	0.029	0.047	0.035	0.051
	(1.17)	(1.79)*	(1.55)	(2.16)**
Fixed effects	Yes	Yes	Yes	Yes
Number of observations	233	233	233	233
Number of countries	86	86	86	86
Sargan (p-value)	0.29	0.47	0.26	0.36
Underidentification test (p-value)	0.03	0.03	0.03	0.03
Income instrumentation F-statistic (p-value)	0.00	0.00	0.00	0.00
Aid instrumentation F-statistic (p-value)	0.08	0.08/0.11	0.08/0.11	0.08/0.11
Remittances instrumentation F-statistic (p-value)	0.00	0.00	0.00	0.00

Note: GDP, gross domestic product. Numbers in parentheses are robust t-statistics. All variables except the education variable are averages over three-year periods, from $t − 1$ to $t − 4$, measured in logs.

a. Instrumented regressors. Instruments include twice-lagged GDP per capita; twice-lagged aid; and instruments for aid and remittances in the tradition of Tavares (2003), that is, total aid budgets of the five largest donors (the United States, Japan, France, the United Kingdom, and Germany) in constant dollars, weighted by a cultural distance variable (same religion) and a geographic distance variable. The ratio of broad money supply (M2) to GDP is also included as an instrument for remittances. Tests for excludability of the instruments are available on request.

* Significant at the 10 percent level.

** Significant at the 5 percent level.

*** Significant at the 1 percent level.

in developing countries. More specifically, we explore the impact of the medical brain drain. Docquier and Bhargava (2007) provide a rich dataset containing information on the expatriation rate of physicians.[11] We introduce this latter variable into our model and estimate an equation of the following form:

$$\ln Health_{i,t} = \alpha_i + \tau_t + \beta \ln X_{i,(t-1,t-4)} + \delta \ln Remittances_{i,(t-1,t-4)}$$
$$+ \gamma MedicalBrainDrain_{i,(t-1,t-4)} + \theta_1 \ln Health\ aid_{i,(t-1,t-4)} + \theta_2 \ln Health$$
$$aid_{i,(t-1,t-4)}.\ln Income_{i,(t-1,t-4)} + \varepsilon_{i,t}, \tag{3}$$

where $MedicalBrainDrain_{i,(t-1,t-4)}$ is the expatriation rate of physicians averaged over a three-year subperiod and transformed in logarithms. Health outcomes and medical brain drain may be correlated with omitted variables such as the quality of health infrastructure. We therefore instrument this variable using the same set of instruments as for aid and remittances.

Regressions (1) and (2) of table 4 present the results when medical brain drain is introduced into the analysis. The coefficient of medical brain drain is highly significant and has the expected positive sign: a 1 percent increase in the rate of expatriation of physicians increases child and infant mortality rates by around 0.5 percent. The expatriation of human resources in the health sector has a direct, harmful effect on health outcomes in developing countries.[12]

Interestingly, the medical brain drain does not really affect the impact of health aid on health outcomes. The threshold of income for which the relationship between aid and child health switches from negative to positive remains similar to that found in table 2, between US\$4,700 and US\$5,000, and the slope does not change greatly: from -0.815 it goes to about -1, suggesting that the health-improving impact of aid is not altered when the medical brain drain is taken into account.

Intracountry Empirical Assessment

In this section, we investigate the intracountry impact of aid and remittances on child health indicators by analyzing to what extent these transfers are targeted to the poorest (or are not). The discussion begins with a description of the data and the empirical strategy and ends with comments on our main findings.

Model and Data

We use the World Bank's comprehensive Health, Nutrition, and Population (HNP) database, in which development indicators from Demographic and Health Surveys (DHSs) are compiled by asset quintiles within countries (Gwatkin et al. 2007). Asset quintiles are computed using the first principal component in an analysis of the correlations between various consumer durables and other household characteristics, following a method proposed by Filmer and Pritchett (2001).

Few studies have used the HNP database to analyze the determinants of child health outcomes. To our knowledge, the first is Fay et al. (2005). Using a sample of 39 countries and a country random-effect model, the authors assert that apart from traditional variables—such as GDP per capita, assets, education, and direct health interventions—better access to basic infrastructure services has an important impact on infant and child mortality and on the incidence of stunting. Ravallion (2007) questions the robustness of their results and criticizes their empirical strategy on three points. First, the model of Fay et al. (2005) is a linear model, but a logarithmic functional form would have been more appropriate, given that the dependent

TABLE 4. Medical Brain Drain and Health Outcomes, Two-Stage Least Squares (2SLS) with Fixed Effects

	Child mortality rate (1)	Infant mortality rate (2)
GDP per capita[a]	−0.486	−0.389
	(1.77)*	(1.56)
Number of physicians per 1,000 inhabitants	0.379	0.365
	(2.50)**	(2.67)***
Female educational attainment	−0.205	−0.185
	(0.99)	(0.98)
Dummy for missing education variable	−0.536	−0.476
	(1.49)	(1.45)
Remittances per capita[a]	−0.134	(0.114
	(2.54)**	(2.35)**
Health aid per capita[a]	−1.067	−1.033
	(2.02)**	(2.14)**
Health aid per capita × income per capita[a]	0.125	0.122
	(1.99)**	(2.12)**
Medical brain drain (MBD)[a]	0.504	0.481
	(2.61)***	(2.75)***
Year = 1995	0.093	0.105
	(1.33)	(1.64)
Year = 2000	0.086	0.089
	(2.39)**	(2.75)***
Fixed effects	Yes	Yes
Number of observations	237	237
Number of countries	86	86
Sargan (p-value)	0.99	0.99
Underidentification test (p-value)	0.07	0.07
Income instrumentation F-statistic (p-value)	0.00	0.00
Aid instrumentation F-statistic (p-value)	0.10/0.12	0.10/0.12
Remittances instrumentation F-statistic (p-value)	0.00	0.00
MBD instrumentation F-statistic (p-value)	0.01	0.01

Note: GDP, gross domestic product. Numbers in parentheses are robust *t*-statistics. All variables except the education variable are averages over three-year periods, from $t-1$ to $t-4$, measured in logs.

a. Instrumented regressors. Instruments include twice-lagged GDP per capita; twice-lagged aid; and instruments for aid and remittances in the tradition of Tavares (2003), that is, total aid budgets of the five largest donors (the United States, Japan, France, the United Kingdom, and Germany) in constant dollars, weighted by a cultural distance variable (same religion) and a geographic distance variable. The ratio of broad money supply (M2) to GDP is also included as an instrument for remittances. Tests for excludability of the instruments are available on request.

* Significant at the 10 percent level.

** Significant at the 5 percent level.

*** Significant at the 1 percent level.

variables are bounded. Second, by estimating a random-effect model, the authors implicitly assume that their country fixed effects are not correlated with the regressors. This is a strong assumption because many sources of latent heterogeneity across countries are suspected. Finally, there may be a strong presumption of bias arising from the omission of within-country differences in women's schooling. Using exactly the same data but estimating a fixed-effect model that includes female education and variables in log-linear form, Ravallion (2007) fails to detect any significant impact of infrastructure access on child health outcomes. His findings suggest a significant effect of access to health care and female educational attainment on child health.[13] The study by Fielding, McGillivray, and Torres (2008) employs the same data. It examines, using a system of simultaneous equations, the relationships between four MDG-related variables (health, educational status, access to water, and access to sanitation) and aid; the authors also explore the impact of aid on these variables. They find that although aid is effective overall, the poorest subgroups within each country are typically not the primary beneficiaries of the inflows.

In what follows, we use an updated HNP database in which some countries have multiple-year data. (See annex table A.3 for a listing.) This temporal dimension of the panel makes it possible to assess the impact of country-specific variables that vary over time, such as GDP per capita, aid, and remittances, in a model that includes country fixed effects. The dataset covers 47 developing countries, of which 25 are in Sub-Saharan Africa, with five asset quintiles for each country-year, yielding a total of 380 observations.

Table 5 provides summary statistics on the main variables of interest. It suggests that there are strong within-country health disparities that are correlated with asset inequality. Households belonging to the poorest asset quintile have the highest mean infant and child mortality rates; child mortality is almost twice as high for the poorest quintile as for the richest one. A similar gap can be observed in the female school completion rate, which varies from 29.15 for the poorest quintile to 76.34 for the richest. It is worth noting that the differences in mean health indicators between the poorest and richest quintiles are always smaller than the ranges across countries within each quintile.

The intracountry model to be estimated is very similar to the cross-country model presented in the preceding section in the sense that control variables are roughly the same and are expressed in log-linear form. The baseline model may therefore be written as follows:

$$\ln Health_{j,i,t} = \alpha_i + \beta \ln X_{i,(t-1,t-4)} + \nu \ln X_{j,i,t} + \delta \ln Health\ aid_{i,(t-1,t-4)}$$
$$+ \gamma \ln Remit_{i,(t-1,t-4)} + \sum_{j=2}^{5} \varphi_j q_j + \sum_{j=2}^{5} \tau_j q_j {}^* \ln Health\ aid_{i,(t-1,t-4)}$$
$$+ \sum_{j=2}^{5} \omega_j q_j {}^* \ln Remit_{i,(t-1,t-4)} + \varepsilon_{j,i,t}, \tag{4}$$

where j is the quintile index and q_j are quintile dummy variables.[14]

Vector $X_{i,(t-1,t-4)}$ includes GDP per capita in PPP constant terms and the number of physicians per 1,000 inhabitants. These variables are averaged over three years,

TABLE 5. Summary Statistics

Variable	Mean	Standard deviation	Minimum	Maximum
Full sample (380 observations)				
Infant mortality[a]	72.13	33.75	11.90	187.70
Child mortality[b]	113.80	67.00	14.20	354.90
Female educational attainment[c]	50.44	31.94	0.50	99.80
Poorest quintile, measured by an asset index (76 observations)				
Infant mortality [a]	86.88	31.32	32.00	187.70
Child mortality[b]	140.08	62.82	39.10	297.90
Female educational attainment[c]	29.15	25.98	0.50	98.70
Second quintile (76 observations)				
Infant mortality[a]	82.62	32.71	23.80	152.30
Child mortality[b]	132.33	69.25	27.30	354.90
Female educational attainment[c]	39.24	29.75	1.00	99.50
Third quintile (76 observations)				
Infant mortality[a]	75.91	34.14	19.70	157.20
Child mortality[b]	120.08	69.44	23.50	348.30
Female educational attainment[c]	48.38	30.98	1.50	99.80
Fourth quintile (76 observations)				
Infant mortality [a]	65.64	32.17	11.90	142.00
Child mortality[b]	102.63	64.63	14.20	314.90
Female educational attainment[c]	59.09	29.71	4.80	99.60
Richest quintile (76 observations)				
Infant mortality[a]	49.58	24.51	13.80	97.20
Child mortality[b]	73.88	45.93	15.80	183.70
Female educational attainment[c]	76.34	20.13	27.00	99.80

Source: World Bank Health, Nutrition, and Population database.

a. Infant mortality is measured by the number of deaths of children under 12 months of age per 1,000 live births, based on experience during the 10 years before the survey.

b. Child mortality refers to the number of deaths of children under age 5 per 1,000 live births, based on experience during the 10 years before the survey.

c. Female educational attainment is measured by the percent of women age 15–49 years who have completed fifth grade.

from $t - 1$ to $t - 4$, and are measured in logarithms. Vector $X_{j,i,t}$ contains quintile- and time-specific female educational attainment expressed in log-linear form.

To test whether the impact of health aid and remittances differs between quintiles, ln*Healthaid* and ln*Remit* are interacted with quintile dummies q_2 to q_5, the poorest quintile being the reference. We choose not to interact quintile dummies with the other control variables such as GDP per capita. in order to limit the number of instruments when the IV specification is used. Finally, we control for quintile fixed effects ($\sum_{j=2}^{5} \tau_j q_j$), as well as for country fixed effects.

As in the cross-country analysis, endogeneity of aid, remittances, and income is controlled for using an IV specification. The education variable has also been found to be endogenous to health indicators. This is probably because education is measured by the contemporaneous school completion rate. Instruments include lagged GDP per capita, the ratio of broad money supply (M2) to GDP, lagged health aid per capita, and total aid budgets for France, Japan, the United Kingdom, and the United States in constant dollars. We also include among the instruments lagged GDP per capita and lagged health aid per capita interacted with quintiles q_2 to q_5.

Estimation Results

The intracountry impact of aid and remittances on child health is assessed using child and infant mortality rates. We proceed in two steps. First, the baseline model is estimated without including any interaction terms between health aid and remittances, on the one hand, and quintile dummies, on the other hand (table 6). We then add these interaction terms to our set of regressors (table 7). Even though controlling for endogeneity and countries' unobserved heterogeneity is likely to provide more reliable results, as in regressions (3) and (6) of table 1, tables 6 and 7 also present the results of simple OLS and fixed-effects regressions.

As suggested by table 6, the impact of our control variables is quite similar to that found using our cross-country specification. GDP per capita, for instance, tends to decrease infant and child mortality rates. The coefficient of this variable suggests that an increase of 1 percent in GDP per capita reduces child and infant mortality by about 0.6 percent. As in the previous specification, the number of physicians per 1,000 inhabitants is found to have no significant effect on child health outcomes. Female education is found to have a negative impact on the child mortality rate but not on the infant mortality rate. This result is in accordance with our previous results but not with those of Ravallion (2007), who found a significant negative impact of female education whatever child health indicators were chosen. This lack of robust impact may come about because the education variable we use is less precise than that employed by Ravallion; we use the percentage of women age 15–49 who have completed the fifth grade, whereas Ravallion (2007) uses the average number of years of female schooling.

Turning to our variables of interest, estimation results suggest that remittances and health aid have no impact at all. Adding interaction terms substantially alters the picture. As suggested by table 7, migrants' remittances are now significant, and their impact on child health outcomes is found to be stronger for the richest quintiles than for the poorest ones. Remittances and remittances interacted with quintile dummies are jointly significant in the child and infant mortality equations. The impact of remittances on health indicators for the poorest quintiles is nil (column 3), whereas it is stronger for the middle and upper classes, at about 0.11, 0.16, and 0.23 for quintiles 3, 4, and 5, respectively. Overall, this result suggests that remittances tend to increase health disparities within countries.

By contrast, neither an antipoor nor a pro-poor effect is detected for health aid. This finding contrasts with that of Fielding, McGillivray, and Torres (2008), who estimate a system of simultaneous equations on several welfare measures, including

TABLE 6. Intracountry Specification without Interaction Terms

	Child mortality rate			Infant mortality rate		
	OLS	Within	2SLS	OLS	Within	2SLS
	(1)	(2)	(3)	(4)	(5)	(6)
GDP per capita[a]	−0.272	−0.871	−0.673	−0.281	−0.868	−0.620
	(3.41)***	(5.21)***	(3.16)***	(4.52)***	(5.04)***	(2.71)***
Number of physicians	−0.157	−0.111	−0.016	−0.081	−0.065	0.034
per 1,000 inhabitants	(4.55)***	(1.61)	(0.21)	(2.82)***	(0.92)	(0.39)
Female educational attainment[a]	−0.132	0.047	−0.220	−0.100	0.052	−0.186
	(3.26)***	(2.01)**	(1.79)*	(3.08)***	(2.13)**	(1.59)
Remittances per capita[a]	−0.031	−0.036	−0.075	−0.022	−0.022	−0.076
	(1.64)	(1.30)	(1.53)	(1.34)	(0.77)	(1.56)
Health aid per capita[a]	0.027	0.053	0.048	0.023	0.047	0.045
	(0.71)	(1.72)*	(0.90)	(0.66)	(1.48)	(0.83)
Constant	7.054	11.163		6.696	10.738	
	(11.63)***	(8.84)***		(14.07)***	(8.26)***	
Fixed effects	No	Yes	Yes	No	Yes	Yes
Quintile dummies	Yes	Yes	Yes	Yes	Yes	Yes
Number of observations	380	380	370	380	380	370
R^2	0.79	0.72		0.74	0.64	
Number of countries		47	46		47	46
Underidentification test			0.01			0.01
(p-value)						
Sargan (p-value)			0.52			0.20
Income instrumentation			0.000			0.000
F-statistic (p-value)						
Female education instrumentation			0.044			0.044
F-statistic (p-value)						
Aid instrumentation F-statistic			0.000			0.000
(p-value)						
Remittance instrumentation			0.000			0.000
F-statistic (p-value)						

Note: 2SLS, two-stage least squares; GDP, gross domestic product; OLS, ordinary least squares. Numbers in parentheses are robust t-statistics. GDP per capita, number of physicians per 1,000 inhabitants, health aid per capita, and remittances are averages over three-year periods, from $t − 1$ to $t − 4$, measured in logs. Female educational attainment is measured at the same period as the outcome variable by quintile and is in logs.

a. Instrumented regressors in equations (3) and (6). Instruments include lagged GDP per capita; lagged health aid per capita; ratio of broad money supply (M2) to GDP; and total aid budgets of France, Japan, the United Kingdom, and the United States in constant dollars. Tests for excludability of the instruments are available on request.

* Significant at the 10 percent level.

** Significant at the 5 percent level.

*** Significant at the 1 percent level.

TABLE 7. Intracountry Specification with Interaction Terms

	Child mortality rate			Infant mortality rate		
	OLS	Within	2SLS	OLS	Within	2SLS
	(1)	(2)	(3)	(4)	(5)	(6)
GDP per capita[a]	−0.271	−0.867	−0.673	−0.279	−0.865	−0.620
	(3.38)***	(5.63)***	(2.72)***	(4.46)***	(5.33)***	(2.39)**
Number of physicians per	−0.156	−0.109	−0.016	−0.080	−0.063	0.034
1,000 inhabitants	(4.48)***	(1.72)*	(0.15)	(2.79)***	(0.95)	(0.31)
Female educational attainment[a]	−0.137	0.037	−0.220	−0.103	0.045	−0.186
	(3.53)***	(1.69)*	(1.49)	(3.29)***	(1.92)*	(1.39)
Remittances per capita[a]	0.017	0.015	0.035	0.022	0.024	0.011
	(0.73)	(0.56)	(0.49)	(0.99)	(0.83)	(0.16)
Remittances per capita ×	−0.033	−0.040	−0.044	−0.034	−0.040	−0.029
quintile 2[a]	(3.37)***	(2.75)***	(1.00)	(2.80)***	(2.64)***	(0.69)
Remittances per capita ×	−0.055	−0.063	−0.114	−0.052	−0.059	−0.087
quintile 3[a]	(3.64)***	(4.35)***	(3.15)***	(3.60)***	(3.84)***	(2.58)***
Remittances per capita ×	−0.074	−0.077	−0.163	−0.067	−0.070	−0.132
quintile 4[a]	(4.25)***	(5.31)***	(3.99)***	(3.84)***	(4.55)***	(3.40)***
Remittances per capita ×	−0.085	−0.076	−0.232	−0.068	−0.060	−0.187
quintile 5[a]	(3.61)***	(5.21)***	(2.98)***	(3.05)***	(3.93)***	(2.60)***
Health aid per capita[a]	−0.028	0.003	−0.073	−0.031	−0.002	−0.072
	(0.69)	(0.08)	(0.85)	(0.79)	(0.07)	(0.90)
Health aid per capita × quintile 2[a]	0.041	0.040	0.078	0.037	0.037	0.074
	(3.18)***	(1.75)*	(1.32)	(2.24)**	(1.50)	(1.28)
Health aid per capita × quintile 3[a]	0.067	0.062	0.121	0.059	0.055	0.120
	(3.11)***	(2.70)***	(2.20)**	(2.62)**	(2.26)**	(2.29)**
Health aid per capita × quintile 4[a]	0.096	0.087	0.194	0.097	0.089	0.178
	(3.35)***	(3.75)***	(2.94)***	(3.30)***	(3.63)***	(2.76)***
Health aid per capita × quintile 5[a]	0.074	0.061	0.210	0.076	0.066	0.209
	(1.95)*	(2.64)***	(2.17)**	(2.09)**	(2.69)***	(2.30)**
Constant	6.969	11.069		6.620	10.655	
	(11.43)***	(9.51)***		(13.82)***	(8.70)***	
Fixed effects	No	Yes	Yes	No	Yes	Yes
Quintile dummies	Yes	Yes	Yes	Yes	Yes	Yes
Number of observations	380	380	370	380	380	370
R^2	0.81	0.76		0.75	0.69	
Number of countries		47	46		47	46
Joint significance of aid variables	0.038	0.000	0.073	0.061	0.005	0.100
Joint significance of remittances variables	0.000	0.000	0.000	0.003	0.000	0.007
Underidentification test (p-value)			0.14			0.14
Sargan (p-value)			0.66			0.31

TABLE 7. (continued)

	Child mortality rate			Infant mortality rate		
	OLS (1)	Within (2)	2SLS (3)	OLS (4)	Within (5)	2SLS (6)
Income instrumentation F-statistic (p-value)			0.000			0.000
Female education instrumentation F-statistic (p-value)			0.000			0.000
Aid instrumentation F-statistic (p-value)			0.000			0.000
Aid × q2 instrumentation F-statistic (p-value)			0.046			0.046
Aid × q3 instrumentation F-statistic (p-value)			0.046			0.046
Aid × q4 instrumentation F-statistic (p-value)			0.046			0.046
Aid × q5 instrumentation F-statistic (p-value)			0.046			0.046
Remittances instrumentation F-statistic (p-value)			0.000			0.000
Remittances × q2 instrumentation F-statistic (p-value)			0.003			0.003
Remittances × q3 instrumentation F-statistic (p-value)			0.003			0.003
Remittances × q4 instrumentation F-statistic (p-value)			0.003			0.003
Remittances × q5 instrumentation F-statistic (p-value)			0.003			0.003

Note: 2SLS, two-stage least squares; GDP, gross domestic product; OLS, ordinary least squares; q, quintile. Numbers in parentheses are robust *t*-statistics. GDP per capita, number of physicians per 1,000 inhabitants, health aid per capita, and remittances are averages over three-year periods, from $t - 1$ to $t - 4$, measured in logs. Female educational attainment is measured at the same period as the outcome variable by quintile and is in logs.

a. Instrumented regressors in equations (3) and (6). Instruments include lagged GDP per capita; lagged health aid per capita; ratio of broad money supply (M2) to GDP; total aid budgets of France, Japan, the United Kingdom, and the United States in constant dollars; and lagged GDP per capita and lagged health aid per capita, both crossed with quintiles q2 to q5. Tests for excludability of the instruments are available on request.

* Significant at the 10 percent level.

** Significant at the 5 percent level.

*** Significant at the 1 percent level.

health outcomes, and find a significant negative impact of total aid (as a percent of GDP) on child mortality and increased effectiveness of aid for the richest quintile.

As a final step, we check whether including medical brain drain among the set of regressors changes the baseline results (table 8). The expatriation rate of physicians does not seem to have a direct significant impact, but its inclusion among the set of regressors mitigates the impact of remittances: whatever the quintile, the impact of remittances on child and infant mortality becomes indeed very low.

TABLE 8. Intracountry Specification with Medical Brain Drain, Two-Stage Least Squares Estimations

	Child mortality rate (1)	Infant mortality rate (2)
GDP per capita[a]	−0.823	−0.814
	(3.41)***	(2.71)***
Number of physicians per 1,000 inhabitants	−0.913	−1.123
	(1.55)	(1.56)
Female educational attainment[a]	0.195	0.348
	(0.65)	(0.95)
Medical brain drain[a]	−0.983	−1.268
	(1.50)	(1.61)
Remittances per capita[a]	0.115	0.114
	(1.52)	(1.18)
Remittances per capita × quintile 2[a]	−0.064	−0.055
	(1.81)*	(1.35)
Remittances per capita × quintile 3[a]	−0.126	−0.102
	(3.85)***	(2.67)***
Remittances per capita × quintile 4[a]	−0.121	−0.077
	(2.78)***	(1.53)
Remittances per capita × quintile 5[a]	−0.077	0.012
	(0.69)	(0.09)
Health aid per capita[a]	−0.116	−0.127
	(1.54)	(1.44)
Health aid per capita × quintile 2[a]	0.053	0.041
	(1.10)	(0.68)
Health aid per capita × quintile 3[a]	0.061	0.043
	(0.98)	(0.56)
Health aid per capita × quintile 4[a]	0.096	0.052
	(1.11)	(0.49)
Health aid per capita × quintile 5[a]	0.068	0.026
	(0.57)	(0.18)
Fixed effects	Yes	Yes
Quintile dummies	Yes	Yes
Number of observations	370	370
Number of countries	46	46
Joint significance of aid variables	0.557	0.804
Joint significance of remittances variables	0.001	0.080
Underidentification test (p-value)	0.67	0.67
Sargan (p-value)	0.87	0.66
Income instrumentation F-statistic (p-value)	0.000	0.000
Female education instrumentation F-statistic (p-value)	0.000	0.000
Aid instrumentation F-statistic (p-value)	0.000	0.000
Aid × q2 instrumentation F-statistic (p-value)	0.046	0.046
Aid × q3 instrumentation F-statistic (p-value)	0.046	0.046
Aid × q4 instrumentation F-statistic (p-value)	0.046	0.046
Aid × q5 instrumentation F-statistic (p-value)	0.046	0.046

TABLE 8. (continued)

	Child mortality rate (1)	Infant mortality rate (2)
Remittances instrumentation *F*-statistic (*p*-value)	0.003	0.003
Remittances × q2 instrumentation *F*-statistic (*p*-value)	0.003	0.003
Remittances × q3 instrumentation *F*-statistic (*p*-value)	0.003	0.003
Remittances × q4 instrumentation *F*-statistic (*p*-value)	0.003	0.003
Remittances × q5 instrumentation *F*-statistic (*p*-value)	0.003	0.003
Medical brain drain instrumentation *F*-statistic (*p*-value)	0.000	0.000

Note: GDP, gross domestic product; q, quintile. Numbers in parentheses are robust *t*-statistics. GDP per capita, number of physicians per 1,000 inhabitants, health aid per capita, and remittances are averages over three-year periods, from $t-1$ to $t-4$, measured in logs. Female educational attainment is measured at the same period as the outcome variable by quintile and is in logs.

a. Instrumented regressors. Instruments include lagged GDP per capita; lagged health aid per capita; ratio of broad money supply (M2) to GDP; total aid budgets of France, Japan, the United Kingdom, and the United States in constant dollars; and lagged GDP per capita and lagged health aid per capita, both crossed with quintiles q2 to q5. Tests for excludability of the instruments are available upon request.

* Significant at the 10 percent level.

*** Significant at the 1 percent level.

Conclusion

For several years it has been asserted that the achievement of the Millennium Development Goals by 2015 will require increased external financing coupled with improved targeting effectiveness in favor of the poorest population. In this context, international migrants' remittances have been increasingly put forward as a promising source of external financing. Nevertheless, empirical assessments of the respective impact of aid and remittances on aggregate welfare, measured either by poverty in monetary terms or by human development indicators, are rather scarce.

In this paper we chose to focus on two child health outcomes—under-five mortality (MDG 4) and infant mortality—in order to examine the direct impact of aid to the health sector and of remittances on these human development indicators. Given our primary focus, we do not enter the debate on the relative importance of the direct and indirect (via government pro-poor expenditure) impacts of aid. To complete our diagnosis, we push our analysis further and investigate the net impact of migration— that is, the effectiveness of migration, including the effect of the medical brain drain. We also examine the intracountry allocation of aid and migrants' remittances.

Our results for health aid are in line with the literature that examines the welfare impact of aid using cross-country data in the sense that they suggest a nonrobust relationship between aid and welfare. Although the impact of health aid is found to be significant in our cross-country regressions (but only when aid is interacted with income per capita), this result vanishes when cross-country quintile level data are used.

By contrast, and for the first time, the trade-off between the gains from migration and its costs is underlined. As suggested by our paper, the net impact of migration is rather weak when the negative effect of medical brain drain is taken into account. Moreover, remittances are found to be more beneficial for children belonging to the richest households. This result is in line with other microeconomic evidence suggesting that remittances may increase within-country inequality. It differs from the finding of Chauvet and Mesplé-Somps (2007) that remittances have a pro-poor impact.

The small estimated impact of health aid and remittances net of brain drain costs might well explain why child mortality rates have not substantially improved for three decades, as asserted by Murray et al. (2007), despite the growing volume of health aid and migrants' remittances. This does not imply that official assistance is inefficient, nor does it mean that private remittances should substitute for aid. Rather, it means that further investigation into the microlevel determinants of child mortality rates is needed to improve our understanding of the bad performance on child health outcomes in most developing countries, and in Africa in particular.

ANNEX TABLE A.1 Cross-Country Regression Sample (109 countries)

Albania*	Egypt, Arab Rep.	Madagascar	South Africa
Algeria	El Salvador	Malawi	Sri Lanka
Argentina	Equatorial Guinea*	Malaysia	St. Lucia
Armenia*	Eritrea*	Mali	St. Vincent
Azerbaijan	Ethiopia	Mauritania	Sudan
Bangladesh	Fiji	Mauritius	Swaziland
Belize*	Gabon	Mexico	Syrian Arab Republic*
Benin	Gambia, The	Moldova*	Tajikistan*
Bolivia	Georgia	Mongolia	Tanzania
Bosnia and Herzegovina	Ghana	Morocco	Thailand
Botswana	Grenada*	Mozambique	Togo
Brazil	Guatemala	Namibia	Tonga
Burkina Faso	Guinea	Nepal	Trinidad and Tobago*
Cambodia	Guinea-Bissau	Nicaragua	Tunisia
Cameroon	Guyana	Niger	Turkey
Cape Verde	Haiti	Nigeria	Uganda
Central African Republic*	Honduras	Oman*	Uruguay*
Chad*	India	Pakistan	Vanuatu
Chile*	Indonesia	Panama	Venezuela, R. B. de
China	Iran, Islamic Rep.*	Papua New Guinea	Vietnam*
Colombia	Jamaica	Paraguay	Yemen, Republic
Comoros	Jordan	Peru	Zimbabwe*
Congo, Rep.	Kazakhstan*	Philippines	
Costa Rica	Kenya	Rwanda	
Côte d'Ivoire	Kyrgyz Republic*	Samoa	
Croatia*	Lao PDR	Senegal	
Dominica*	Lebanon	Seychelles	
Dominican Republic	Lesotho	Sierra Leone	
Ecuador	Macedonia, FYR*	Solomon Islands	

* Countries excluded from the 2SLS estimations.

ANNEX TABLE A.2 Instrumentation Equations

Variable	GDP per capita	Health aid per capita	Remittances per capita
Number of physicians per 1,000 inhabitants	0.027	−0.665	0.510
	(1.050)	(−2.040)**	(1.670)*
Female educational attainment	0.019	0.582	0.204
	(0.310)	(0.780)	(0.260)
Dummy for missing education variable	−0.059	0.886	−1.425
	(−0.560)	(0.660)	(−1.130)
Year = 1995	−0.187	−0.012	−0.923
	(−2.180)**	(−0.010)	(−1.580)
Year = 2000	−0.138	0.487	−1.178
	(−1.630)	(0.600)	(−2.140)**
Twice-lagged health aid per capita	0.004	−0.244	0.074
	(0.860)	(−2.160)**	(1.680)*
Twice-lagged GDP per capita	0.289	−0.170	−0.500
	(3.630)***	(−0.310)	(−1.320)
M2/GDP	−0.054	0.093	0.738
	(−1.050)	(0.230)	(2.170)**
Total French aid budget × same religion	0.175	−0.970	3.606
	(1.030)	(−0.740)	(4.140)***
Total French aid budget × distance	0.000	0.000	0.000
	(−1.080)	(0.940)	(0.750)
Total U.K. aid budget × same religion	−0.294	0.272	−3.825
	(−1.600)	(0.160)	(−3.620)***
Total U.K. aid budget × distance	0.000	0.000	0.000
	(−1.470)	(0.940)	(1.990)**
Total German aid budget × same religion	−0.272	−1.517	−6.228
	(−1.040)	(−0.620)	(−4.090)***
Total U.S. aid budget × same religion	0.151	0.228	1.825
	(1.200)	(0.150)	(2.400)**
Total U.S. aid budget × distance	0.000	0.000	0.000
	(0.620)	(0.620)	(−3.400)***
Total Japanese aid budget × same religion	−0.146	−4.828	6.449
	(−0.590)	(−1.550)	(1.630)
Total Japanese aid budget × distance	0.000	0.000	0.000
	(1.150)	(0.360)	(1.620)
Fixed effects	Yes	Yes	Yes
Number of observations	237	237	237
F-statistic (p-value)	0.0002	0.0997	0.0000
Partial R^2 of excluded instruments	0.3139	0.1760	0.2102

* Significant at the 10 percent level.

** Significant at the 5 percent level.

*** Significant at the 1 percent level.

ANNEX TABLE A.3 Intracountry Regression Sample

Country name	Year	Country name	Year
Armenia	2000	Kyrgyz Republic	1997
Bangladesh	1996, 1999	Madagascar	1997
Benin	1996, 2001	Malawi	1992
Bolivia	1998, 2003	Mali	1995, 2001
Brazil	1996	Mauritania	2000
Burkina Faso	1993, 1999, 2003	Morocco	1992, 2003
Cambodia	1997	Mozambique	1997, 2003
Cameroon	1991, 1998, 2004	Namibia	1992, 2000
Chad	1996, 2005	Nepal	1996
Colombia	1995, 2000, 2005	Nicaragua	1997
Comoros	1996	Niger	1998
Côte d'Ivoire	1994	Nigeria	1990, 2003
Dominican Republic	1996, 2002	Peru	1996
Ethiopia	2000	Philippines	1998
Gabon	2000	Rwanda	2000
Ghana	1993, 1998, 2003	South Africa	1998
Guatemala	1995, 1998	Tanzania	1996, 1999
Guinea	1999	Togo	1998
Haiti	1994, 2000	Turkey	1993, 1998
India	1992, 1998	Uganda	1995, 2000
Indonesia	1997	Vietnam	1997, 2002
Jordan	1997	Yemen, Republic	1997
Kazakhstan	1995	Zimbabwe	1994, 1999
Kenya	1993, 1998, 2003		

Notes

1. The eight Millennium Development Goals are, in brief: (1) to halve extreme income poverty; (2) to achieve universal primary education; (3) to promote gender equality; (4) to reduce the under-five mortality rate by two-thirds; (5) to reduce the maternal mortality rate by three-quarters; (6) to reduce the incidence of AIDS; (7) to promote sustainable development and to halve the percentage of people without access to safe drinking water; and (8) to set up a global partnership for development involving more generous and more widespread official development assistance.

2. CRS data are available at the OECD Web site http://www.oecd.org/document/0/0,2340, en_2649_34447_37679488_1_1_1_1,00.html.

3. Unlike us, Mishra and Newhouse (2007) include in their sample data on health commitments covering the 1960s and 1970s.

4. Note that the introduction of country fixed effects contributes to solving, although imperfectly, the omitted variable bias.

5. Tavares (2003) and Rajan and Subramanian (2005a, 2005b) use similar instruments for aid and remittances.

6. Tests of overidentification and underidentification are reported in each table. Tests for weak instruments, excludability, and partial R-squared are available on request.

7. Following the literature on the determinants of health, and contrary to Mishra and Newhouse (2007), we do not estimate a system of moment equations using generalized method of moments (GMM) with a lagged dependent variable. The main reason is that the number of time periods is too small.

8. The kind of nonlinearity is still debated. Some authors argue that the relationship is quadratic (Hansen and Tarp 2001; Lensink and White 2001). Others claim that the impact of aid depends on economic policy (Burnside and Dollar 2000), on vulnerability to external shocks (Guillaumont and Chauvet 2001), on export price shocks (Collier and Dehn 2001), or on whether the country is tropical (Dalgaard, Hansen, and Tarp 2004).

9. Results are available from the authors on request.

10. We reran all our regressions using aggregate aid disbursements instead of health aid disbursements, but the variable was never significant, suggesting that not all types of aid affect health outcomes. Results are available on request.

11. The expatriation rate is also provided disaggregated by destination country.

12. Note that our estimations may underestimate the impact because the medical brain drain variable provided by Docquier and Bhargava (2007) measures only emigration of physicians, not that of other medical personnel such as nurses and midwives.

13. In a recent paper, Fay et al. (2007) briefly reply to Ravallion's comments.

14. We are not able to include time dummies because years vary from one country to the other and we only have one year of observation for half the sample.

References

Acosta, Pablo A., Cesar A. Calderon, Pablo R. Fajnzylber, and Humberto Lopez. 2008. "What Is the Impact of International Remittances on Poverty and Inequality in Latin America?" *World Development* 36 (1): 89–114.

Adams, Richard H. 2004. "Remittances and Poverty in Guatemala." Policy Research Working Paper 3418, World Bank, Washington, DC.

———. 2006. "Remittances and Poverty in Ghana." Policy Research Working Paper 3838, World Bank, Washington, DC.

Adams, Richard H., and John Page. 2005. "Do International Migration and Remittances Reduce Poverty in Developing Countries?" *World Development* 33 (10): 1645–69.

Anand, S., and Till Bärnighausen. 2004. "Human Resources and Health Outcomes: Cross-Country Econometric Study." *Lancet* 364: 1603–9.

Barro, Robert J., and Jong-Wha Lee. 2000. "International Data on Educational Attainment: Updates and Implications." CID Working Paper 42, Center for International Development, Harvard University, Cambridge, MA.

Boone, Peter. 1996. "Politics and the Effectiveness of Foreign Aid." *European Economic Review* 40: 289–329.

Burnside, Craig, and David Dollar. 2000. "Aid, Policies, and Growth." *American Economic Review* 90 (4): 847–68.

Chauvet, Lisa, and Sandrine Mesplé-Somps. 2007. "Impact des financements internationaux sur les inégalités des pays en développement." *Revue Economique* 58: 735–44.

Collier, Paul, and Jan Dehn. 2001. "Aid, Shocks, and Growth." Policy Research Working Paper 2688, World Bank, Washington, DC.

Cox-Edwards, Alessandra, and Manuela Ureta. 2003. "International Migration, Remittances and Schooling. Evidence from El Salvador." *Journal of Development Economics* 72 (2): 429–61.

Dalgaard, Carl-Johan, Henrik Hansen, and Finn Tarp. 2004. "On the Empirics of Foreign Aid and Growth." *Economic Journal* 114 (496): F191–F217.

Docquier, Frédéric, and Alok Bhargava. 2007. "A New Panel Data Set on Physicians' Emigration Rates (1991–2004)." Economics School of Louvain, Louvain-la-Neuve, Belgium. http://perso.uclouvain.be/frederic.docquier/filePDF/MBD1_Description.pdf.

Dreher, Axel, Peter Nunnenkamp, and Rainer Thiele. 2008. "Does Aid for Education Educate Children? Evidence from Panel Data." *World Bank Economic Review* 22 (2): 291–314.

Fay, Marianne, Danny Leipziger, Quentin Wodon, and Tito Yepes. 2005. "Achieving Child-Health-Related Millennium Development Goals: The Role of Infrastructure." *World Development* 33 (8): 1267–84.

———. 2007. "'Achieving Child-Health-Related Millennium Development Goals: The Role of Infrastructure'—A Reply." *World Development* 35 (5): 929–30.

Fielding, David, Mark McGillivray, and Sebastian Torres. 2008. "Achieving Health, Wealth and Wisdom: Links Between Aid and the Millennium Development Goals." In *Achieving the Millennium Development Goals,* ed. Mark McGillivray. Studies in Development Economics and Policy. Houndsmill, Basingstoke, Hampshire, U.K.: Palgrave MacMillan.

Filmer, Deon, and Lant Pritchett. 1999. "The Impact of Public Spending on Health: Does Money Matter?" *Social Science and Medicine* 49: 1309–23.

———. 2001. "Estimating Wealth Effects without Expenditure Data or Tears: An Application to Educational Enrolments in States of India." *Demography* 38 (1): 115–32.

Gomanee, Karuna, Sourafel Girma, and Oliver Morrissey. 2005. "Aid, Public Spending and Human Welfare: Evidence from Quantile Regressions." *Journal of International Development* 17: 299–309.

Gomanee, Karuna, Oliver Morrissey, Paul Mosley, and Arjan Verschoor. 2005. "Aid, Government Expenditure, and Aggregate Welfare." *World Development* 33 (3): 355–70.

Guillaumont, Patrick, and Lisa Chauvet. 2001. "Aid and Performance: A Reassessment." *Journal of Development Studies* 37 (6): 66–92.

Gupta, Sanjeev, Catherine Pattillo, and Smita Wagh. 2007. "Impact of Remittances on Poverty and Financial Development in Sub-Saharan Africa." IMF Working Paper 07/38, International Monetary Fund, Washington, DC.

Gwatkin, Davidson R., Shea Rutsein, Kiersten Johnson, Eldwan Suliman, Adam Wagstaff, and Agbessi Amouzou. 2007. *Socio-Economic Differences in Health, Nutrition, and Population within Developing Countries: An Overview.* Produced by the World Bank in collaboration with the government of the Netherlands and the Swedish International Development Cooperation Agency, Washington, DC.

Hansen, Henrik, and Finn Tarp. 2001. "Aid and Growth Regressions." *Journal of Development Economics* 64 (2): 547–70.

Hildebrandt, N., and David McKenzie. 2005. "The Effects of Migration on Child Health in Mexico." Policy Research Working Paper 3573, World Bank, Washington, DC.

IMF (International Monetary Fund). 2005. *World Economic Outlook, April 2005: Globalization and External Imbalances.* Washington, DC: IMF.

Kanaiaupuni, Shawn M., and Katharine M. Donato. 1999. "Migradollars and Mortality: The Effects of Migration on Infant Survival in Mexico." *Demography* 36: 339–53.

Lachaud, Jean-Pierre. 1999. "Envois de fonds, inégalité et pauvreté au Burkina Faso." *Revue Tiers Monde* 160: 793–827.

Leliveld, André. 1997. "The Effects of Restrictive South African Migrant Labor Policy on the Survival of Rural Households in Southern Africa: A Case Study from Rural Swaziland." *World Development* 25 (11): 1839–49.

Lensink, Robert, and Howard White. 2001. "Are There Negative Returns to Aid?" *Journal of Development Studies* 37 (6): 42–65.

Levine, Ruth, and the What Works Working Group. 2004. *Millions Saved: Proven Successes in Global Health.* Washington, DC: Center for Global Development.

Mansuri, Ghazala. 2007. "Migration, School Attainment and Child Labor: Evidence from Rural Pakistan." Policy Research Working Paper 3945, World Bank, Washington, DC.

Masud, Nadia, and Boriana Yontcheva. 2005. "Does Foreign Aid Reduce Poverty? Empirical Evidence from Nongovernmental and Bilateral Aid." IMF Working Paper 05/100, International Monetary Fund, Washington, DC.

McGuire, James W. 2006. "Basic Health Care Provision and Under-5 Mortality: A Cross-National Study of Developing Countries." *World Development* 34 (3): 405–25.

Michaelowa, Katharina, and Anke Weber. 2007. "Aid Effectiveness in Primary, Secondary, and Tertiary Education." Background paper for the Education for All (EFA) Global Monitoring Report 2008, *Education for All by 2015: Will We Make It?* United Nations Educational, Cultural, and Scientific Organization (UNESCO), New York. http://unesdoc.unesco.org/images/0015/001555/155559e.pdf.

Milanovic, Branco. 2005. "Can We Discern the Effect of Globalization on Income Distribution? Evidence from Household Surveys." *World Bank Economic Review* 19: 21–44.

Mishra, Prachi, and David L. Newhouse. 2007. "Health Aid and Infant Mortality." IMF Working Paper 07/100, International Monetary Fund, Washington, DC.

Mosley, Paul. 1987. *Overseas Aid: Its Defence and Reform.* Wheatsheaf Books, Brighton, U.K.

Mosley, Paul, John Hudson, and Arjan Verschoor. 2004. "Aid, Poverty Reduction and the 'New Conditionality.'" *Economic Journal* 114: F217–F243.

Murray, Christopher L., T. Laakso, K. Shibuya, K. Hill, and Alan D. Lopez. 2007. "Can We Achieve Millennium Development Goal 4? New Analysis of Country Trends and Forecasts of Under-5 Mortality to 2015." *Lancet* 370 (September 22): 1040–54.

Pritchett, Lant, and Larry Summers. 1996. "Wealthier Is Healthier." *Journal of Human Resources* 31 (4): 841–68.

Rajan, Raghuram G., and Arvind Subramanian. 2005a. "Aid and Growth: What Does the Cross-Country Evidence Really Show?" NBER Working Paper 11513, National Bureau of Economic Research, Cambridge, MA.

———. 2005b. "What Undermines Aid's Impact on Growth?" IMF Working Paper WP/05/126, International Monetary Fund, Washington, DC.

Ratha, Dilip, Sanket Mohapatra, K. M. Vijayalakshmi, and Zhimei Xu. 2007. "Remittance Trends 2007." Migration and Development Brief 3, Development Prospects Group, Migration and Remittances Team, World Bank, Washington, DC. http://siteresources.worldbank.org/EXTDECPROSPECTS/Resources/476882-1157133580628/BriefingNote3.pdf.

Ravallion, Martin. 1993. "Human Development in Poor Countries: On the Role of Private Incomes and Public Services." *Journal of Economic Perspectives* 7 (1): 133–50.

———. 2007. "'Achieving Child-Health-Related Millennium Development Goals: The Role of Infrastructure'—A Comment." *World Development* 35 (5): 920–28.

Roodman, David. 2007. "Macro Aid Effectiveness Research: A Guide for the Perplexed." Working Paper 135, Center for Global Development, Washington, DC.

Tavares, José. 2003. "Does Foreign Aid Corrupt?" *Economics Letters* 79 (1, April): 99–106.

World Bank. 2006. *World Development Indicators 2006*. Washington, DC: World Bank.

Comment on "Are Remittances More Effective Than Aid for Improving Child Health? An Empirical Assessment Using Inter- and Intracountry Data," by Lisa Chauvet, Flore Gubert, and Sandrine Mesplé-Somps

MELVIN D. AYOGU

In their paper, Chauvet, Gubert, and Mesplé-Somps investigate whether health aid or remittances matter for child health and, in particular, whether these help to reduce infant mortality. In this respect, the paper qualifies as one more aid-ineffectiveness study. The deeper issues that the authors address, however, are related to those examined in the paper by Jean-Paul Azam and Ruxanda Berlinschi, in this volume. Chauvet, Gubert, and Mesplé-Somps take note of the call for a progressive substitution of remittances for official aid. If, indeed, remittances from migrant workers prove, in general, more effective than foreign aid in alleviating poverty, the obvious next step is to promote more migration flows from poor to rich countries. The policy advice would be, do not offer aid in lieu of migration; instead, allow more migration in return for less aid—at least, those types of aid for which remittances have been found to be a superior remedy. For this reason alone, and given that the paper by Azam and Berlinschi suggests that rich countries have a hidden agenda of trading more aid for less migration (the opposite tack), this line of inquiry should be enthusiastically welcomed. The excitement of the topic, however, may have also led the authors to attempt too much with a dataset that is arguably dirty. (On the general state of aid data, see Easterly and Pfutze 2008, 30, 51.)

What the Authors Attempt to Do

Looking within and across countries, the authors investigate two key issues and attempt to tackle related interesting questions. The two main issues are (a) whether foreign aid targeted to the health care sector reduces infant (below age 1) and child (under age 5) mortality rates, and (b) whether remittances from migrant workers reduce child and infant mortality rates. Other questions concern the circumstances under which one form of intervention may be more effective than the other. If

Melvin D. Ayogu is professor of economics and dean, Faculty of Commerce, University of Cape Town, South Africa.

Annual World Bank Conference on Development Economics 2009, Global

remittances are beneficial, does it matter that they come at the expense of loss of skilled labor from migrant-sending countries? To examine this issue, the authors focus on physician expatriation and its impact. The premise is that if expatriation is harmful, the negative consequences could be set against the perceived benefits of remittances, even though not all the measured remittances accrue from expatriated physicians alone. (The latter observation would, if correct, result in an underestimation of the net effect of brain drain, if such leakages do in fact occur.) The authors also look at the impact of aid and remittances across income deciles within a country and examine the issue of absorptive capacity that has been frequently raised as a serious negative consequence of poor donor aid delivery practices. In rankings of donor best practices, excessive fragmentation and overhead costs are key factors in the rating criteria (Easterly and Pfutze 2008).

What the Authors Find

Using a panel of developing countries, the authors determine that remittances promote child health care but that health aid matters only when the relationships among child health indicators, aid, remittances, and income are taken into account. Of course, this endogeneity effect runs deeper than can be addressed by tinkering with instrumental variables. Here the authors could be picking up the consequences of existing aid practices, perhaps the effect of aid conditionality. It has been argued that the persistence of conditionality is partly attributable to its usefulness as an instrument for the pursuit of donor multiple objectives, of which only a few may be, in fact, altruistic (see Ayogu 2006 for a discussion). Recipient countries understand this larger game. One dimension of the game is the Samaritan's dilemma elaborated in Svensson (2000), according to which a quandary for the do-gooder arises because recipients behave strategically; they have no incentives for implementing poverty reduction strategies when an increasing proportion of aid is conditioned on poverty. Overall, after all the econometric adjustments, the authors find that both types of intervention (foreign aid and remittances from abroad) improve health care outcomes.

Their indirect test of absorptive capacity constraints was not so fruitful, in that it was not supported by the data. Brain drain of doctors was, however, found to be harmful to child health. Medical personnel and health aid are complementary; the lack of one depresses the other. Brain drain therefore reduces the effectiveness of aid as well as the net benefit of remittances. Remittances are found to be more effective than health aid in improving health outcomes for children from richer households. The finding of higher marginal productivity of remittances for higher-income groups may be picking up several issues, such as the fact that remittances are fungible, whereas targeted health aid is not. Remittances have the capacity to improve overall family welfare in a way that targeted health aid is unable to match. Among poor communities, remittances carry a positive feedback and a selection bias. Families that receive remittances are big fish in a small pond—even if their relatives residing overseas are little fish in a humongous pond. Therefore, selectivity bias could be confounding the interpretation of the finding that the revealed positive impact of remittances on child health discriminates with respect to income. Wealth is good for nutrition and other complementary ingredients for a healthy child, and the income flow from remittances may well add to household wealth over time.

What to Make of the Findings?

Although the authors are careful not to draw any hard recommendations from their study, they have nonetheless made clear that there are no implications here for a migration-aid trade-off. That is a prudent view; the whole question of brain drain, remittances, undocumented workers, and immigration policies in the context of a globalizing world has yet to be addressed adequately. For instance, a recent study (Clemens 2007) finds no evidence of the harmful effects of the external migration of health professionals. The more deleterious effect seems to be internal migration across sectors by professionals anxious to avoid "leaving the brain in the drain." According to the Southern African Migration Project (Crush 2008), working conditions emerge as the single most important predisposing factor for health professional emigration. Particularly influential are (a) the inequitable distribution of personnel across the public versus private and primary versus secondary health sectors, and (b) the urban-rural divide. With regard to the expatriation of physicians, analysts argue that many of the public health issues surrounding infant mortality—such as immunization and hygiene, diarrhea and dehydration, access to clean water, and other basic public health care issues—do not actually make huge demands of a physician's expertise.[1] Physicians do not appear to be as crucial as this study would seem to suggest. Drawing from the experiences of Médecins Sans Frontières (Doctors without Borders) in South Africa, it could be argued that even if the expatriation of physicians is assumed to be less than benign, the core of the primary health care problem lies in governance and in government underinvestment in clinics (Steinberg 2008, 273), rather than in the likely impact of brain drain on child health. Our view on governance is corroborated by a recent finding by Rajkumar and Swaroop (2008).

Finally there are some results that are difficult to reconcile, such as the finding that aid raises infant mortality in some African countries. Clearly, given the HIV/AIDS pandemic, it would have been advisable to control for HIV prevalence (see Deaton 2008). I am equally sympathetic regarding the data problems confronting the authors, including the problematic instrumental variables deployed. Nonetheless, aid practices such as timing of disbursements, conditionality, and the use of bilateral agencies are much more important than cultural distance and should have been used in constructing the proxy for health aid disbursements.

Note

1. I am grateful to Dr. Max Price for this insight.

References

Ayogu, Melvin. 2006. "Can Africa Absorb More Aid?" In *Aid, Debt Relief and Development in Africa: African Development Report 2006*, 25–40. New York: Oxford University Press.

Clemens, Michael. 2007. "Do Visas Kill? Health Effects of African Health Professional Emigration." Working Paper 114, Center for Global Development, Washington, DC.

Crush, Jonathan. 2008. "Southern African Migration Project SAMP. Migration Resources: Brain Drain Resources." Queen's University, Kingston, ON, Canada. http://www.queensu.ca/samp/migrationresources/braindrain/ (accessed June 8, 2008).

Deaton, Angus. 2008. "Income, Health, and Well-Being around the World: Evidence from a Gallup World Poll." *Journal of Economic Perspectives* 22 (2): 53–72.

Easterly, William, and Tobias Pfutze. 2008. "Where Does the Money Go? Best and Worst Practices in Foreign Aid." *Journal of Economic Perspectives* 22 (2): 29–52.

Rajkumar, Andrew Sunil, and Vinaya Swaroop. 2008. "Public Spending and Outcomes: Does Governance Matter?" *Journal of Development Economics* 86 (1): 96–111.

Steinberg, Johnny. 2008. *Three-Letter Plague: A Young Man's Journey through a Great Epidemic*. Johannesburg: Jonathan Ball.

Svensson, Jakob. 2000. "When Is Foreign Aid Credible? Aid Dependence and Conditionality." *Journal of Development Economics* 61: 61–84.

The Role of Emigration and Emigrant Networks in Labor Market Decisions of Nonmigrants

JINU KOOLA AND ÇAĞLAR ÖZDEN

The Indian state of Kerala is an ideal place to explore a question that is prominent in the migration literature: what role does the existence of migrant networks have in the labor market participation decisions of nonmigrant household members? Two linked statewide representative surveys in 1998 and 2003 that collected individual information about each member of 10,000 households, including members who had migrated, are used for this purpose. The analysis of the labor market participation of young men reveals interesting patterns. In cross-sectional data, young men in households with migrant members are found to be less likely to be employed, indicating that migration discourages labor market participation by nonmigrants. When, however, panel data are analyzed and individuals are followed over time, those males under age 30 are found to be more likely to migrate in the second period, taking advantage of their migrant networks. This result goes counter to the claim that migration induces unemployment or withdrawal from the labor market among family members. Rather, it suggests that young men in migrant households have a higher expectation of emigration and that they are less likely to take a job in Kerala while they prepare to emigrate.

Almost 10 percent of the labor force of Kerala State—close to 2 million people—lives and works in a Persian Gulf country. These numbers make Kerala one of the largest migrant-sending regions in the world, and an interesting place to study various aspects of emigration. This paper focuses on a paradox, created by migration, in the employment patterns seen in Kerala. Emigration there increased by around 35 percentage points between 1998 and 2003, and the unemployment rate for young males increased to 17.4 percent. Given the high unemployment rate in the face of massive emigration, the question arises: why has the exit rate of Kerala's labor force not decreased unemployment among nonmigrants in the state? More specifically, what influence does emigration have on the labor supply decisions of nonmigrant household members?

Jinu Koola and Çağlar Özden are with the Development Research Group of the World Bank.

Annual World Bank Conference on Development Economics 2009, Global
© 2010 The International Bank for Reconstruction and Development / The World Bank

Massive communal emigration rates are likely to have diverse effects on young men as they enter the labor market. The cross-sectional data show that young men in households that include migrant members and that are part of significant migrant networks are less likely to be employed. The implication is that the presence of migrants in the household or the community decreases labor market participation and supply among nonmigrant members, mainly through a higher income effect from remittances. This point has been raised many times in the literature as an undesirable consequence of migration. However, panel data that follow individuals over time indicate that these same young males are likely to migrate in the second period, taking advantage of the migration networks their families or communities have established. This finding goes counter to the previous result and indicates a more complex decision-making process by nonmigrant household members. More specifically, young men in migrant households or communities seem to have higher thresholds of entry into the Kerala labor market, since they have higher opportunity costs. And if they fail to obtain the right labor market outcomes, they simply use the network to migrate.

A unique feature of this paper is that it looks at the roles of both family networks and social networks in migration and labor market decisions. The network theory of migration states that an individual's probability of emigration increases with the size of that person's network in his or her locality (see Massey et al. 1998). Kerala's migrants, however, do not depend on the emigration experience of all the people in their *panchayat* (local jurisdiction); rather, they rely on the people they know—family, friends, and acquaintances.[1] The common characteristics of their networks are not necessarily geographic, but religious. Social contacts are determined by religion, and in Kerala, as in the rest of India, religion is a community identity that distinguishes social groups. Furthermore, the support and services provided by the network seem to be excludable and rivalrous, in that they are provided only to network members within the same geographic location.

Using religion to define a community's network, as in this paper, confers several main advantages. First and foremost, religion exogenously identifies a well-defined and well-established social group, overcoming the problem of peer effects. Religion also addresses the issue of self-selection because members of a religious group do not "choose" their religion today.[2] Another benefit of using religion and geography to identify a social group is that these variables allow for variation within localities and religious groups. Finally, religious networks provide social support and many other excludable services that are especially valuable in labor market and migration contexts.

Most of the empirical studies that have explored the relationship between migration and labor market participation by nonmigrants have focused on the role of remittances (see Hanson 2005; Amuedo-Dorantes and Pozo 2006; Kim 2007). Yet there is a gap in our understanding of how the expectation of emigration, facilitated by emigration networks and the emigration of other household members, affects the household's labor supply and demand.

One of the main determinants of migration is the social and communal network that influences the decision to migrate and helps lower migration costs. Identification of the influence of the family and the community is a key issue in this paper. The economic literature that studies migrant networks faces several empirical difficulties.

The main econometric challenge for network analysis is to identify the direction of the causal relationship between migrant networks and the migration decision, which is complicated by peer effects. Peer effects confound the interpretation of the network effect because shared community characteristics can influence the migration decision but may be unobservable (Boyd 1989; Massey, Goldring, and Durnad 1994). Manski (1993) terms this the reflection problem.

Another concern for an econometric analysis is that access to the migrant network may be endogenous to the household's own emigration experience (Taylor 1987; Orrenius 1999; McKenzie and Rapoport 2005). One way to isolate the network effect is to limit our analysis to new migrants who are temporarily exogenous to the network (Orrenius 1999; Zhao 2001).

Empirical studies of migration have attempted to address these serious econometric challenges of endogeneity in other ways, by using community fixed effects, individual-level fixed effects, or instrumental variables such as rainfall data and historical state-level migration rates (Orrenius 1999; Winters, de Janvry, and Sadoulet 2001; Munshi 2003; McKenzie and Rapoport 2005; Giles and Yoo 2007; Woodruff and Zenteno 2007). In this study, the variation afforded by religion and geography is used to help identify the relationship between migrant networks and migration.

The results in this paper have important implications for policies regarding migration and labor markets. A common view, as mentioned above, is that emigration reduces the labor market participation and supply of the family members left behind. They rely on the remittances sent by family members abroad and make the optimal leisure-labor trade-off. This is viewed as a negative outcome because lower labor supply indicates lower income levels. This paper, however, shows that the decision-making process is more complicated and intertemporal in nature. It demonstrates that although the presence of migrants in the household or the community increases the likelihood of absence from the labor market because of higher opportunity costs, the outside option turns out to be migration for the nonmigrants, not reliance on remittances indefinitely. These results imply that policies should be designed accordingly.

In the next section, the institutional setting and context for the study are outlined. Subsequent sections present the data and provide basic summary statistics for the sample population, describe the conceptual framework and empirical methodology, and set out the estimation results. The final section contains conclusions.

Linkages between Kerala and the Persian Gulf

In 2003, 1.84 million people from Kerala, or close to 10 percent of the state's total labor force, were living and working in a Persian Gulf country (Zachariah and Rajan 2004).[3] Migration is almost all temporary because of the rather restrictive immigration policies enacted by the countries of the Gulf Cooperation Council (GCC), which prohibit permanent resettlement of foreign nationals (Massey et al. 1998).

Economic linkages between Kerala and the Persian Gulf have a very long history, but the current migration began to surge in 1973 with the sudden increase in oil prices.[4] The Gulf countries, which faced a shortage of qualified local labor, sought foreign labor to satisfy their construction boom and other labor market demands. Kerala's history of trade with the region and its large surplus labor force motivated migration (Zachariah, Mathew, and Rajan 2001; see also Weiner 1982; Massey et al. 1998). By 1998, migrants from Kerala represented over 50 percent of India's total emigration to the Gulf countries (Prakash 1998). The state's geographic position, at the southwestern tip of India, with 580 kilometers of coastline, gives it privileged access to the Gulf. Its population density and literacy rates are also very high by Indian standards.[5] Thus, Kerala's unemployed but relatively well-educated labor force was attracted to the employment opportunities that the Gulf countries offered.

In a country with a Hindu-majority population (80.5 percent), Kerala is unique in that it has sizable Muslim and Christian populations (India 2001). The shares of total population are Hindu, 56.1 percent; Muslim, 24.7 percent; and Christian, 19 percent. Sufficient ethnographic data exist to suggest that social networks in Kerala have been created and are maintained within religious circles (Osella and Osella 2000; Kurien 2002). A distinguishing characteristic of Kerala's Gulf migration is its religious dimension; although Muslims make up only one-fourth of the state's total population, they represent close to half of the total emigrant population.[6] In other words, current emigrants made up 13 percent of the total Muslim population in 1998, as against only 3 percent of the Hindu population and 6 percent of the Christian population. This is the main fact used to identify migrant networks in the paper.

Data

This study uses data from two linked household surveys conducted by the Centre for Development Studies in Thiruvananthapuram, Kerala, and covering a statewide representative household sample: they are the Kerala Migration Survey (KMS) and the South Asia Migration Study (SMS). A principal advantage of this paper is that it exploits the panel nature of the survey data; half of the households canvassed in 1998 were resurveyed in 2003.

The KMS was administered to the residents of 9,995 households selected from 200 panchayats in each of Kerala's 14 districts between March and December 1998 (Zachariah, Mathew, and Rajan 2001, 64). Fifty households were selected at random from each panchayat.[7] The survey collected individual information about each member of the household, including members who had migrated, from the head of the household at the time of the household visit.

The SMS survey, conducted in 2003, was designed to replicate the KMS and used the same questionnaire and a similar sampling methodology. The primary data for the SMS were collected from 10,012 households in 225 panchayats (rather than 200 panchayats, as in 1998) in the state's 14 districts (Zachariah and Rajan 2004, 12).

Emigrant Characteristics

In the survey, current emigrants (EMIs) are categorized as those members of the household who had emigrated from Kerala and who had been living abroad at the

TABLE 1. Characteristics of Sample Populations, Kerala State, 1998 and 2003

Year and migrant category	Observations	Percent male	Mean age (years)	Mean years of education	Percent married	Percent unemployed
1998						
EMI	2,099	91	26.7[a]	8.7[a]	49[a]	26[a]
NMI	26,560	45	34.5	7.5	67	9
2003						
EMI	2,940	83	25.2[a]	9.7[a]	41[a]	33[a]
NMI	27,273	45	35.6	8.2	65	14

Source: Authors' calculations from the 1998 Kerala Migration Study (KMS) and the 2003 South Asia Migration Study (SMS), Centre for Development Studies, Thiruvananthapuram, Kerala, India.

Note: EMI, current emigrant; NMI, nonmigrant.

a. At the time of migration.

time of the survey for at least one year. Emigrants accounted for 6 percent of the total labor force in 1998 and for 8 percent in 2003. Return emigrants (REMs) are those members of the household who have returned to Kerala after living abroad. By 2003 almost one-fifth of Kerala's labor force population, or close to 3 million people, had had some sort of migration experience—they were either current emigrants or return emigrants. In this study, a nonmigrant (NMI) is a household member who was neither a current emigrant nor a return emigrant in the survey year.

The average emigrant is male, is under age 30, and has at least one more year of education than his nonmigrant counterpart (table 1).

In 1998 Muslims represented nearly one-half of the total emigrant population; Hindus accounted for about one-third and Christians, for one-fifth. One reason that Muslims are twice as likely as non-Muslims to emigrate is that the overwhelming majority of Kerala's emigrants go to the oil-rich Persian Gulf states. As table 2 shows, the shares of emigrants going to a Gulf country were 94 percent in 1998 and 88 percent in 2003. More than two-thirds of all emigrants to the Gulf went to either the United Arab Emirates (UAE) or Saudi Arabia.

The choice of destination country also varies by religion. Almost half of all Muslim emigrants went to Saudi Arabia in 2003, but only one-third of Christian or Hindu emigrants did. A large share (14 percent) of Hindu emigrants went to Oman, and a significant percentage of Christian emigrants went to Kuwait (10 percent) and the United States (8 percent). Only 1 percent of Muslim emigrants went to a country other than the Arab states of the Persian Gulf.

Waiting to Emigrate: Those Who Stay Behind

In this study, the unemployed are defined as those who are seeking a job, those who are performing unpaid household work, or those for whom a job is not required. Unemployment is higher among younger cohorts: in 1998 it was 16.7 percent for those under age 30 but only 7.5 percent for those over age 30, and in 2003 the unemployment rate of the younger cohort was double that of the older cohort (see table 3).

TABLE 2. Emigration from Kerala State, by Host Country, 1998 and 2003
(percent)

Host country	1998		2003	
	EMI	REM	EMI	REM
Saudi Arabia	38	41	27	35
United Arab Emirates	31	26	36	31
Oman	10	13	8	11
Kuwait, Republic of	5	5	6	5
Bahrain	5	6	6	6
Qatar	5	3	5	4
Total, Gulf states	94	93	88	92
United States	2	< 0.5	5	1
Southeast Asia	1	1	1	1
United Kingdom	< 0.1	< 0.1	1	< 0.5
Other	4	6	5	5
Total, other regions	6	7	12	8

Source: Authors' calculations from the 1998 Kerala Migration Study (KMS) and the 2003 South Asia Migration Study (SMS), Centre for Development Studies, Thiruvananthapuram, Kerala, India.

Note: EMI, current emigrant; REM, return emigrant. Figures may not sum to totals because of rounding.

TABLE 3. Unemployment Rate by Age and Sex, Kerala State, 1998 and 2003
(percent)

Age	1998			2003		
	Male	Female	Total	Male	Female	Total
15–19	14.3	7.0	10.7	13.3	10.6	12.0
20–24	24.5	18.0	21.3	30.4	26.9	28.7
25–29	21.2	14.1	17.8	24.0	26.6	25.3
30–34	13.7	7.3	10.7	17.5	17.4	17.3
35–39	8.7	3.6	6.3	15.0	13.3	14.2
40–44	6.1	2.9	4.6	12.3	7.0	9.7
45–49	4.8	2.7	3.8	10.3	4.5	7.4
50–54	7.5	5.6	6.6	8.5	6.2	7.4
55–59	18.3	11.3	14.5	13.8	7.9	10.8
15–60	14.2	8.8	11.6	17.4	15.0	16.22

Source: Authors' calculations from the 1998 Kerala Migration Study (KMS) and the 2003 South Asia Migration Study (SMS), Centre for Development Studies, Thiruvananthapuram, Kerala, India.

As table 3 shows, almost a quarter of males between ages 20 and 25 in 1998 and almost a third of males in the same age cohort in 2003 were unemployed. Given that emigration from Kerala is almost 90 percent male and that the average age of emigration in both years was under age 30, one might ask why the exit rate of Kerala's labor force has not decreased unemployment in the state.

One likely explanation for the high unemployment rate among young males is that they are waiting for the opportunity to emigrate and are unwilling to take a job in Kerala in the meantime. As table 4 shows, the total unemployment rate is 40 percent higher in emigrant households. Furthermore, the unemployment rate seems to increase with the number of current emigrants from the household. Table 4 also shows that the unemployment gap between emigrant and nonmigrant households is at least 5 percentage points higher for the male population.

The figures in table 5 show that the unemployment rate is highest for males between ages 15 and 29 in emigrant households. Table 6 presents the unemployment rate among males according to whether the community is above or below the mean network size (or migration prevalence ratio).

TABLE 4. Unemployment Rate for Age Group 15–60, by Number of Emigrants from the Household, Kerala State, 1998 and 2003

(percent)

Number of emigrants	Total population		Male population	
	1998	2003	1998	2003
0	10.4	14.5	12.0	14.63
1	14.6	20.0	20.0	24.44
2	19.9	24.0	28.5	29.6

Source: Authors' calculations from the 1998 Kerala Migration Study (KMS) and the 2003 South Asia Migration Study (SMS), Centre for Development Studies, Thiruvananthapuram, Kerala, India.

TABLE 5. Unemployment Rate, Males, by Age Cohort and Household Emigration Status, Kerala State, 1998 and 2003

(percent)

Household type	Age 15–29		Age 30–60	
	1998	2003	1998	2003
Nonmigrant household	14.5	23.0	9.6	13.5
Current emigrant household	28.2	26.5	17.7	27.2

Source: Authors' calculations from the 1998 Kerala Migration Study (KMS) and the 2003 South Asia Migration Study (SMS), Centre for Development Studies, Thiruvananthapuram, Kerala, India.

TABLE 6. Unemployment Rate, Males Age 15–60, by Emigrant Network Size, Kerala State, 1998 and 2003

(percent)

Community type	1998	2003
Below mean network size	12.8	16.3
Above mean network size	16.2	18.9

Source: Authors' calculations from the 1998 Kerala Migration Study (KMS) and the 2003 South Asia Migration Study (SMS), Centre for Development Studies, Thiruvananthapuram, Kerala, India.

TABLE 7. Job-Seeking Rate, Males, by Age and by Emigration Status of Household, Kerala State, 1998 and 2003

(percent)

	Age 15–29		Age 30–60	
Household type	1998	2003	1998	2003
Nonmigrant household	16.9	21.6	5.6	10.3
Current emigrant household	26.0	24.8	14.2	24.4

Source: Authors' calculations from the 1998 Kerala Migration Study (KMS) and the 2003 South Asia Migration Study (SMS), Centre for Development Studies, Thiruvananthapuram, Kerala, India.

One might assume from these findings that unemployed young males in emigrant households are simply free riders without any intention of obtaining employment. To the contrary, 90 percent of emigrants in 1998 stated that their main reason for migration was to seek employment. Indeed, the rate of job seeking is highest for young males in emigrant households. Table 7 shows that a quarter of males under age 30 in emigrant households was engaged in looking for a job at the time of the survey, as against 17 percent of young males in nonmigrant households in 1998 and 21 percent in 2003. The data do not specify whether job seekers are looking for jobs within or outside Kerala, but it is most probable, given these findings, that young males in emigrant households are likely to be seeking jobs outside the state.

Empirical Methodology

The methods used to model the behavior of those who stay behind are described in this section. The panel dataset gives us the unique opportunity to examine the situation in 2003 of those who were unemployed in 1998.

Cross-Sectional Regressions Using 1998 and 2003 Datasets

The hypothesis to be tested is that a household's migration experience and the size of the emigrant network increase the probability of unemployment among nonmigrant males. The following equation is estimated to predict whether individual i in panchayat p in time period t is employed, using a probit model:

$$\Pr(Unemployed_i) = \beta_0 + \beta_1 EMI\_hh_i + \beta_2 EMI\_Netw_p + \beta_3 EMI\_Netw_p^2 + Z_i + \varepsilon_i, \tag{1}$$

where *Unemployed* is an indicator variable equal to 1 if the individual is unemployed in year t and 0 otherwise; *EMI_hh* is a dummy variable equal to 1 if the household has at least one emigrant in year t; and *EMI_Netw* refers to what we term the geographic emigrant network and represents the proportion of adult males above age 16 who are current emigrants in year t from panchayat p.

To test the hypothesis that males in emigrant households are more likely to be job seekers, the following equation is estimated, using a probit model:

$$Pr(JobSeeker_i) = \beta_0 + \beta_1 EMI\_hh_i\ \beta_2 EMI\_Netw_p + \beta_3 EMI\_Netw_p^2 + Z_i + \varepsilon_i, \quad (2)$$

where *JobSeeker* is an indicator variable equal to 1 if the individual is seeking a job in the survey year and 0 otherwise, and all other variables are defined as before.

The sample of individuals included in these regressions is restricted to adult males between ages 15 and 60. Current emigrants and students are omitted from the sample. Equations (1) and (2) are estimated separately for males ages 15–29 and 30–60. All standard errors are clustered by household, since individuals in the same household may share similar characteristics, and all regressions are weighted.

Panel Regressions

The main question is whether the young men who were unemployed in 1998 are waiting for the opportunity to emigrate because they are seeking employment outside the state. To test this, the following regressions are estimated using panel data for the sample of males age 15–29 in 2003, excluding those who were migrants or students in 1998:

$$\begin{aligned} Pr(Employ\_Status_i) = {} & \beta_0 + \beta_1 Unemployed_i + \beta_2 EMI\_hh_i*Unemployed_i \\ & + \beta_3 EMI\_hh_i + \beta_4 EMI\_Netw_p + \beta_5 EMI\_Netw_p^2 \\ & + Z_i + \varepsilon_i. \end{aligned} \quad (3)$$

The dependent variable in this regression, *Employ_Status*, takes on three values: 1 if the individual is unemployed in 2003; 2 if the individual is employed in 2003; or 3 if the individual is an emigrant in 2003. *Unemployed* is a dummy variable equal to 1 if the individual was unemployed in 1998. *EMI_hh*Unemployed* is the interaction term if the individual was both unemployed in 1998 and a member of an emigrant household in 1998.

The following regression is then estimated for job seeking:

$$\begin{aligned} Pr(Jobseeking\_Status_i) = {} & \beta_0 + \beta_1 Jobseeker_i + \beta_2 EMI\_hh_i*Jobseeker_i \\ & + \beta_3 EMI\_hh_i + \beta_4 EMI\_Netw_p + \beta_5 EMI\_Netw_p^2 \\ & + Z_i + \varepsilon_i, \end{aligned} \quad (4)$$

where the dependent variable in this regression, *Jobseeking_Status*, takes on three values: 1 if the individual is a job seeker in 2003; 2 if the individual is employed in 2003; or 3 if the individual is an emigrant in 2003. *Jobseeker* is a dummy variable equal to 1 if the individual was a job seeker in 1998, and *EMI_hh*Jobseeker* is an interaction term if the individual was both a job seeker in 1998 and was living in an emigrant household in 1998.

In panel regressions, *EMI_hh* refers to the individual's 1998 status. The network variables refer to the individual's network in 2003. Control variables, described next, refer to the individual's 1998 status, with an additional dummy variable equal to 1 if the individual was a return emigrant in either 1998 or 2003.

Control Variables

Control variables are included in all regressions. The individual characteristics include the individual's years of schooling and years of schooling squared; age and age squared; and a binary variable equal to 1 if the individual is married or unemployed. The household-level characteristics include (a) a binary variable equal to 1 if the household has at least one return emigrant; (b) a binary variable equal to 1 if the household has at least one out-migrant; (c) a binary variable equal to 1 if there are multiple emigrants in the household; (d) family size; and (e) the number of adult males (i.e., above age 18) in the household. Family characteristics (family size and the number of adult males in the household) include the migrant, since the aim is to capture the household's "pre-emigration" state. The data do not contain information on household income. To control for that household characteristic, an income proxy, the log of the total amount of land (wet and dry) owned by the household, is included.

The panchayat-level variables included are average cost of migration for all migrants from the panchayat; average house quality of all households in the panchayat, rated on a scale of 1 to 5, with 1 being very poor and 5 being luxurious; and a binary variable equal to 1 if the panchayat is urban. The latter two variables may also proxy for the overall wealth and level of infrastructure in the panchayat.[8]

Empirical Results: Those Left Behind

The empirical results from the cross-sectional regressions described in equations (1) and (2) are presented in annex tables A.1 and A.2. The results show that the likelihood of unemployment increases for nonmigrant men between ages 15 and 60 if they live in an emigrant household. The probability of unemployment increases with the size of the emigrant network in the 1998 cross-section.

When equation (1) is estimated separately for males ages 15–29 and 30–60, the disincentive effect on employment of living in an emigrant household is found to be two times stronger for the younger cohort than for the older cohort of males in the 1998 cross-section (see table 4). Unemployment also increases significantly with the size of the emigrant network for both cross-sections.

Males in emigrant households are also more likely to be job seekers in both years, as was shown in table 5. In addition, the probability of job seeking increases with the emigrant network in the 2003 cross-section. When equation (2) is estimated separately by age cohort, the positive effect on job seeking of living in an emigrant household is found to be much stronger for younger males than for their older counterparts.

One of the main advantages of this study is the panel structure of the data. The results of the panel analysis, presented in annex tables A.3 and A.4, support the hypothesis that unemployed males are waiting for emigration and are seeking jobs outside Kerala. The probability of emigration increases for young males who were living in an emigrant household in 1998 and were also unemployed or seeking jobs in 1998. As expected, the probability of emigration increases with the size of the emigrant network.

Consistent with the theoretical literature on the determinants of unemployment and emigration, certain individual and household characteristics (years of schooling, age, marital status, employment status, family size, and number of adult males in the household) also influence the probabilities of being unemployed, seeking jobs, and emigrating.

Conclusions

The findings in this paper support the hypothesis that young males in Kerala are unemployed because they are waiting for the opportunity to emigrate and are looking for jobs outside the state. These results indicate that young men who have a higher expectation of emigration are less likely to take a job in Kerala while they prepare to emigrate. In other words, vast emigration from the state creates only "temporary" unemployment, not permanent unemployment in which nonmigrants simply rely on remittances without actively engaging in any productive activity.

One auxiliary effect from this stock of unemployed and ambitious young people is that they add (in absolute terms) to the number of highly skilled, albeit unemployed, individuals in Kerala's labor force. Emigrants are, on average, more educated than nonmigrants, and the proportion of emigrants or return emigrants with a secondary education is higher than the proportion of those with secondary education in the general population. Aspiring emigrants need higher levels of education because new policies and an increasing demand for skilled and professional workers in the Gulf countries require it. Since 1999, the United Arab Emirates no longer accepts applications for visas for unskilled workers from Bangladesh, India, or Pakistan (Zachariah and Rajan 2004). Not surprisingly, the proportion of the population with secondary or tertiary education increased by 3 percentage points between 1998 and 2003 (Zachariah and Rajan 2004). Thus, those waiting to emigrate may be a potential "brain gain" for Kerala. Still, it is a matter of concern that in 2001 almost three-fourths of the unemployed had secondary or tertiary education (Zachariah, Mathew, and Rajan 2001). According to Zachariah and Rajan (2004) the total unemployment rate in Kerala increased by 8 percentage points between 1998 and 2003, but the unemployment rate among those who had completed secondary schooling increased 15 percentage points. It is vital that the state engage these highly skilled but unemployed young people in the labor market even while they wait to emigrate.

ANNEX TABLE A.1. Probit Estimates of the Marginal Effect of Migration on Unemployment, Kerala State, 1998 and 2003

(dependent variable: unemployed persons)

	1998			2003		
	Age 15–60	Age 15–29	Age 30–60	Age 15–60	Age 15–29	Age 30–60
	(1)	(2)	(3)	(4)	(5)	(6)
EMI households	0.05	0.06	0.04	−0.04	−0.02	−0.07
	(0.02)***	(0.03)**	(0.01)**	(0.02)**	(0.03)	(0.02)***
EMI network	0.09	0.22	0.05	−0.16	−0.24	−0.08
	(0.02)***	(0.08)***	(0.02)***	(0.02)***	(0.12)**	(0.02)***
EMI network^2	0.34	0.67	0.18	−0.02	0.13	0.01
	(0.15)**	(0.34)*	(0.13)	(0.15)	(0.34)	(0.14)
REM	1.87	2.30	1.12	2.89	7.60	1.52
	(0.98)*	(2.16)	(0.84)	(0.84)***	(2.59)***	(0.66)**
Education	−0.01	−0.01	0.003	0.01	0.00	0.01
	(0.004)**	(0.01)	(0.003)	(0.004)***	(0.02)	(0.003)***
Education^2	−0.001	−0.001	−0.0002	−0.001	−0.002	−0.001
	(0.0002)***	(0.006)*	(0.0002)	(0.0002)***	(0.001)**	(0.0002)***
Married	−0.16	−0.15	−0.15	0.21	0.17	0.20
	(0.014)***	(0.021)***	(0.020)***	(0.014)***	(0.028)***	(0.020)***
Age	−0.03	0.03	−0.03	0.02	−0.19	0.01
	(0.002)***	(0.023)	(0.004)***	(0.002)***	(0.024)***	(0.004)***
Age^2	−0.0003	−0.001	−0.0004	−0.0002	0.005	−0.0002
	(0.00002)***	(0.0005)**	(0.00004)***	(0.00002)***	(0.001)***	(0.00005)***
Family size	−0.01	−0.02	0.002	0.01	0.01	0.002
	(0.002)***	(0.005)***	(0.002)	(0.002)***	(0.005)**	(0.002)
Adult males	0.02	0.03	0.004	−0.02	−0.03	−0.003
	(0.005)***	(0.01)**	(0.003)	(0.004)***	(0.01)***	(0.004)
Head	−0.04	−0.11	−0.03	0.07	0.23	0.04
	(0.01)***	(0.05)**	(0.009)***	(0.01)***	(0.03)***	(0.01)***
Head's education	0.002	0.004	0.003	−0.01	−0.02	−0.007
	(0.002)	(0.005)	(0.002)	(0.003)***	(0.006)***	(0.003)**
Land	0.02	0.04	0.01			
	(0.003)***	(0.007)***	(0.002)***			
Urban	0.01	0.03	0.01			
	(0.009)	(0.022)	(0.007)			
Number of observations	13,958	5,350	8,608	13,997	4,951	9,046
χ^2	841.96	341.55	433.26	1,094.92	293.96	563.40
Pseudo R^2	0.1851	0.1208	0.1832	0.2054	0.1338	0.2061

Source: Authors' calculations from the 1998 Kerala Migration Study (KMS) and the 2003 South Asia Migration Study (SMS), Centre for Development Studies, Thiruvananthapuram, Kerala, India.

Note: EMI, current emigrant; REM, return emigrant. Numbers in parentheses are robust standard errors.

* Significant at the 10 percent level.

** Significant at the 5 percent level.

*** Significant at the 1 percent level.

ANNEX TABLE A.2. Probit Estimates of the Marginal Effect of Migration on Job Seeking, Kerala State, 1998 and 2003

(dependent variable: job seeker)

	1998			2003		
	Age 15–60	Age 15–29	Age 30–60	Age 15–66	Age 15–30	Age 30–60
	(1)	(2)	(3)	(4)	(5)	(6)
EMI household	0.03	0.09	0.01	0.02	0.03	0.02
	(0.008)***	(0.03)***	(0.005)	(0.01)*	(0.03)	(0.009)**
EMI network	0.09	0.18	0.04	0.13	0.08	0.07
	(0.02)***	(0.08)**	(0.01)***	(0.03)***	(0.04)**	(0.02)***
EMI network^2	0.12	0.37	0.03	−0.01	−0.26	−0.01
	(0.07)*	(0.28)	(0.03)	(0.10)	(0.31)	(0.07)
REM	1.04	3.85	0.20	−2.54	−8.73	−1.11
	(0.46)**	(1.77)**	(0.21)	(0.62)***	(2.67)***	(0.38)***
Education	0.01	0.05	0.00	0.01	0.06	0.00
	(0.003)***	(0.02)***	(0.001)**	(0.005)**	(0.02)**	(0.003)
Education^2	−0.0001	−0.0006	−0.0001	−0.0002	−0.0006	−0.00
	(0.00001)	(0.001)	(0.00005)	(0.0002)	(0.001)	(0.000)
Married	−0.07	−0.12	−0.05	−0.15	−0.19	−0.12
	(0.009)***	(0.02)***	(0.01)***	(0.01)***	(0.02)***	(0.02)***
Age	−0.01	0.02	−0.00002	−0.01	0.18	0.00
	(0.001)***	(0.02)	(0.001)	(0.002)***	(0.02)***	(0.003)
Age^2	−0.00005	−0.0007	−0.0000002	−0.0006	−0.004	−0.00001
	(0.0001)***	(0.0004)*	(0.00001)	(0.00002)***	(0.001)***	(0.00003)
Family size	−0.002	−0.01	−0.0000004	−0.003	−0.01	−0.00004
	(0.001)**	(0.004)**	(0.001)	(0.001)**	(0.005)	(0.001)
Adult males	−0.0001	0.004	−0.0004	0.01	0.02	0.001
	(0.002)	(0.009)	(0.001)	(0.003)**	(0.011)**	(0.002)
Head	−0.04	−0.09	−0.01	−0.05	−0.19	−0.03
	(0.007)***	(0.04)**	(0.004)***	(0.008)***	(0.03)***	(0.006)***
Head's education	0.002	0.002	0.002	0.01	0.02	0.003
	(0.001)	(0.004)	(0.001)**	(0.002)***	(0.006)***	(0.001)**
Land	0.003	0.01	0.001			
	(0.001)**	(0.005)*	(0.001)			
Urban	−0.01	−0.02	−0.0004			
	(0.004)	(0.016)	(0.002)			
Number of observations	13,958	5,350	8,608	13,997	4,951	9,046
χ^2	683.50	317.27	376.47	944.77	388.32	474.34
Pseudo R^2	0.2798	0.1407	0.3476	0.2930	0.1632	0.3464

Source: Authors' calculations from the 1998 Kerala Migration Study (KMS) and the 2003 South Asia Migration Study (SMS), Centre for Development Studies, Thiruvananthapuram, Kerala, India.

Note: EMI, current emigrant; REM, return emigrant. Numbers in parentheses are robust standard errors.

* Significant at the 10 percent level.

** Significant at the 5 percent level.

*** Significant at the 1 percent level.

ANNEX TABLE A.3. Panel Data: Multinomial Logit Estimates of the Impact of Previous Unemployment and Migration on Current Unemployment and Migration for Males Age 15–29, Kerala State, 1998 and 2003

Dependent variable	Unemployed in 2003	External emigrant in 2003	Unemployed in 2003	External or internal migrant in 2003
	(1)	(2)	(3)	(4)
Unemployed (1998)	0.61	(0.63	0.75	−0.23
	(0.228)***	(0.401)	(0.260)***	(0.352)
EMI household (1998)	−0.21	0.45	−0.15	0.15
	(0.350)	(0.353)	(0.353)	(0.319)
Unemployed*EMI household	0.22	1.61	−0.11	1.29
	(0.646)	(0.635)**	(0.743)	(0.596)**
EMI network	1.44	20.62	1.39	11.84
	(4.182)	(6.137)***	(4.420)	(5.063)**
EMI network^2	−19.44	−45.42	−20.07	−23.95
	(16.853)	(19.047)**	(17.720)	(16.114)
REM (1998 or 2003)	−0.35	−0.04	−0.30	0.20
	(0.626)	(0.500)	(0.658)	(0.492)
Education	−0.27	0.71	−0.25	0.58
	(0.103)**	(0.327)**	(0.107)**	(0.246)**
Education^2	0.02	−0.03	0.02	−0.02
	(0.006)***	(0.017)*	(0.007)**	(0.013)*
Married	−0.44	1.14	−0.40	1.19
	(0.562)	(0.394)***	(0.657)	(0.350)***
Age	−0.09	0.95	−0.08	0.41
	(0.089)	(0.444)**	(0.033)**	(0.318)
Age^2	0.00	−0.02	0.00	−0.01
	0.61	−0.63	0.75	−0.23
Number of observations	2,117	2,117	2,053	2,053
χ^2	187.65	187.65	147.17	147.17
Pseudo R^2	0.1241	0.1241	0.1023	0.1023

Source: Authors' calculations from the 1998 Kerala Migration Study (KMS) and the 2003 South Asia Migration Study (SMS), Centre for Development Studies, Thiruvananthapuram, Kerala, India.

Note: EMI, current emigrant; REM, return emigrant. Numbers in parentheses are robust standard errors. Columns (1) and (2) refer to the multinomial logit in which the dependent variable takes on three values: 1 if unemployed, 2 if employed, or 3 if external emigrant in 2003. Columns (3) and (4) refer to the multinomial logit regression in which the dependent variable takes on three values: 1 if unemployed, 2 if employed, or 3 if external emigrant in 2003. All estimates are relative to the base outcome of employed in 2003.

* Significant at the 10 percent level.

** Significant at the 5 percent level.

*** Significant at the 1 percent level.

ANNEX TABLE A.4. Panel Data: Multinomial Logit Estimates of the Impact of Previous Job Seeking and Migration on Current Job Seeking and Migration for Males Age 15–29, Kerala State, 1998 and 2003

Dependent variable	Job seeker in 2003 (1)	External emigrant in 2003 (2)	Job seeker in 2003 (3)	External or internal migrant in 2003 (4)
Job seeker (1998)	0.38	−0.37	0.32	−0.14
	(0.246)	(0.423)	(0.302)	(0.381)
EMI household (1998)	−0.24	0.83	−0.22	0.21
	(0.378)	(0.380)**	(0.378)	(0.313)
Job seeker*EMI household	0.44	1.29	0.27	1.20
	(0.708)	(0.670)*	(0.854)	(0.636)*
EMI network	0.43	18.03	0.35	11.83
	(4.345)	(6.085)***	(4.532)	(5.064)**
EMI network^2	−15.99	−39.74	−15.67	−24.02
	(17.594)	(18.974)**	(18.235)	(16.115)
REM (1998 or 2003)	0.15	0.84	−0.15	0.25
	(0.271)	(0.367)**	(0.692)	(0.479)
Education	−0.09	0.68	−0.06	0.58
	(0.132)	(0.329)**	(0.139)	(0.242)**
Education^2	0.01	−0.03	0.01	−0.02
	(0.007)	(0.017)	(0.008)	(0.012)
Married	−0.87	1.25	−1.05	1.24
	(0.608)	(0.404)***	(0.755)	(0.349)***
Age	−0.10	0.94	−0.10	0.36
	(0.034)***	(0.440)**	(0.033)***	(0.317)
Age^2	0.00	−0.02	0.00	−0.01
	(0.001)	(0.011)*	(0.001)	(0.008)
Number of observations	2,095	2,095	2,031	2,031
χ^2	176.01	176.01	136.66	136.66
Pseudo R^2	0.1294	0.1294	0.1021	0.1021

Source: Authors' calculations from the 1998 Kerala Migration Study (KMS) and the 2003 South Asia Migration Study (SMS), Centre for Development Studies, Thiruvananthapuram, Kerala, India.

Note: EMI, current emigrant; REM, return emigrant. Numbers in parentheses are robust standard errors. Columns (1) and (2) refer to the multinomial logit in which the dependent variable takes on three values: 1 if jobseeker, 2 if employed, and 3 if external emigrant in 2003. Columns (3) and (4) refer to the multinomial logit regression in which the dependent variable takes on three values: 1 if job seeker, 2 if employed, or 3 if external emigrant in 2003. All estimates are relative to the base outcome of employed in 2003.

* Significant at the 10 percent level.

** Significant at the 5 percent level.

*** Significant at the 1 percent level.

Notes

1. Panchayats are often referred to as villages, but they are also found in cities.

2. Hinduism, Christianity, and Islam have all been established in Kerala for many centuries. Early Hinduism can be linked to the decline of Buddhism and a process of "Aryanization" in Kerala during the fifth and sixth centuries AD. The development of Islam can be traced to contacts with Arab traders in the eighth century AD. And the beginnings of Christianity are traditionally credited to Saint Thomas the apostle, in the first century AD (see Kurien 2002).

3. This figure is similar to estimations by the State Planning Board of Kerala, which determined the number of emigrants in 1997 to be 1.6 million people. The estimates presented in this section are the authors' own calculations from the Kerala Migration Study (KMS) and the South Asia Migration Study (SMS), conducted in 1998 and 2003, respectively.

4. In 1973 a conference among GCC countries led to an agreement to form an oil cartel, the Organization of the Petroleum Exporting Countries (OPEC), that drove up the price of oil. By 1974 the price of oil had quadrupled (Massey et al. 1998, 137).

5. Kerala's literacy rate, at 91 percent according to the 2001 census, is the highest among Indian states.

6. In 1998, 50 percent of Gulf emigrants were Muslim.

7. Because the number of households at the panchayat level in each sample was not adjusted to reflect the total number of households in the panchayat, observations are weighted by the percentage of the panchayat population represented by the sample households.

8. Panchayat fixed effects are not included in the probit models because inclusion of a set of panchayat dummies would induce an incidental parameters problem (see Greene 2002). An additional problem with including panchayat dummies is that the emigration prevalence rates are all measured at the panchayat level, which would make these variables perfectly collinear with the panchayat dummies.

References

Amuedo-Dorantes, Catalina, and Susan Pozo. 2006. "Migration, Remittances, and Male and Female Employment Patterns." *American Economic Review* 96 (2, May): 222–26.

Boyd, M. 1989. "Family and Personal Networks in International Migration: Recent Developments and New Agendas." *International Migration Review* 23 (3): 638–70.

Giles, John, and Kyeongwon Yoo. 2007. "Precautionary Behavior, Migrant Networks, and Household Consumption Decisions: An Empirical Analysis Using Household Panel Data from Rural China." *Review of Economics and Statistics* 89 (3, August): 534–51.

Greene, William H. 2002. *Econometric Analysis.* 5th ed. Englewood Cliffs, NJ: Prentice Hall.

Hanson, Gordon H. 2005. *Emigration, Remittances, and Labor Force Participation in Mexico.* INTAL Working Paper 28, Institute for the Integration of Latin America and the Caribbean, for the Inter-American Development Bank, Washington, DC. http://www.iadb.org/INTAL/aplicaciones/uploads/publicaciones/i_INTALITD_WP_28_2007_Hanson.pdf.

India. 2001. "Data on Religion," *Census of India 2001.* New Delhi: Office of the Registrar General. http://www.censusindia.net/.

Kim, Namsuk. 2007. "The Impact of Remittances on Labor Supply: The Case of Jamaica." Policy Research Working Paper 4120, World Bank, Washington, DC. http://econ.worldbank.org/external/default/main?pagePK=64165259&theSitePK=469372&piPK=64165421&menuPK=64166093&entityID=000016406_20070126111038.

Kurien, P. A. 2002. *Kaleidoscopic Ethnicity: International Migration and the Reconstruction of Community Identities in India.* New Brunswick, NJ: Rutgers University Press.

Manski, Charles F. 1993. "Identification of Endogenous Social Effects: The Reflection Problem." *Review of Economic Studies* 60 (3): 531–42.

Massey, Douglas S., Luis Goldring, and Jorge Durnad. 1994. "Continuities in Transnational Migration: An Analysis of Nineteen Mexican Communities." *American Journal of Sociology* 99 (6, May): 1492–1533.

Massey, Douglas S., Joaquin Arrango, Graeme Hugo, Ali Kouaouci, Adela Pellegrino, and J. Edward Taylor. 1998. *Worlds in Motion: Understanding International Migration at the End of the Millennium.* Oxford, U.K.: Clarendon Press.

McKenzie, D. J., and H. Rapoport. 2005. "Network Effects and the Dynamics of Migration and Inequality: Theory and Evidence from Mexico." Working Paper 063, Bureau for Research in Economic Analysis of Development (BREAD), Cambridge, MA.

Munshi, K. 2003. "Networks in the Modern Economy: Mexican Migrants in the US Labor Market." *Quarterly Journal of Economics* 118 (2): 549–99.

Orrenius, Pia M. 1999. "The Role of Family Networks, Coyote Prices, and the Rural Economy in Migration from Western Mexico: 1965–1994." Working Paper 9910, Federal Reserve Bank of Dallas, Dallas, TX.

Osella, F., and C. Osella. 2000. *Social Mobility in Kerala.* London: Pluto Press.

Prakash, B. A. 1998. "Gulf Migration and Its Economic Impact: The Kerala Experience." *Economic and Political Weekly* 33 (50, December 12): 3209–13.

Taylor, J. E. 1987. "Undocumented Mexico-U.S. Migration and the Returns to Households in Rural Mexico." *American Journal of Agricultural Economics* 69: 626–38.

Weiner, M. 1982. "International Migration and Development: Indians in the Persian Gulf." *Population and Development Review* 8 (1): 1–36.

Winters, P., A. de Janvry, and E. Sadoulet. 2001. "Family and Community Networks in Mexico-U.S. Migration." *Journal of Human Resources* 36 (1): 159–84.

Woodruff, C., and R. Zenteno. 2007. "Migration Networks and Microenterprises in Mexico." *Journal of Development Economics* 82 (2): 509–28.

Zachariah, K. C., and S. Irudaya Rajan. 2004. "Gulf Revisited: Economic Consequences of Emigration from Kerala; Emigration and Unemployment." Working Paper 363, Centre for Development Studies, Thiruvananthapuram, Kerala, India. http://cds.edu/download_files/363.pdf.

Zachariah, K. C., E. T. Mathew, and S. I. Rajan. 2001. "Social, Economic, and Demographic Consequences of Migration on Kerala." *International Migration* 39 (2): 43–71.

Zhao, Y. H. 2001. "The Role of Migrant Networks in Labour Migration: The Case of China." Working Paper N20001012, China Economic Research Center, Beijing University, Beijing.

Comment on "The Role of Emigration and Emigrant Networks in Labor Market Decisions of Nonmigrants," by Jinu Koola and Çağlar Özden

JEAN-LUC DEMONSANT

The paper by Koola and Özden offers new insights on the functioning of migrant networks and their impact on labor outcomes for those who stay behind. The authors present interesting empirical findings on the case of migrants from Kerala State, India, to the Arab states of the Persian Gulf. Because it is rooted in the cultural specificities of the case study and is open to sociological approaches, the paper is particularly rich and relevant for development economists eager to avoid cultural blindness in their own research. The role of networks in migration decisions offers many perspectives for research, as their functioning is complex and it is difficult to identify universal patterns.

Cultural Biases of Earlier Studies

The existing microeconomics literature on migration networks is a good example of how a focus on one geographic area can flaw the vision of development economists, in that it is clearly dominated by the case of Mexico-U.S. migration. For example, in the references to the paper by Koola and Özden, of the 10 entries on migrant networks that mention a specific destination country in the title, 8 are on Mexico. Of course, since the United States and Mexico share the longest border between a developed and a developing country, this emphasis does not come out of the blue and is perhaps legitimate. Nevertheless, the concentration on a particular case has adverse consequences for research in the field. Because theoretical economists draw their inspiration from empirical case studies, the tendency to infer general behaviors from specific cases where the context yields different outcomes is rather common. Probably more dramatic, though, is the application by policy makers of "best practices" to inappropriate situations.

Jean-Luc Demonsant is assistant professor of economics at the University of Guanajuato, Mexico.

Annual World Bank Conference on Development Economics 2009, Global

Earlier studies, working from homogenous village societies, have focused on the "quantity" rather than on the "quality" of networks. The paper by Koola and Özden remedies this deficiency by uncovering new mechanisms in play in network formation and functioning.

Religion as the Cement of Migration Networks

Departing from the existing literature on migration networks, the authors convincingly show that religious networks are more efficient than geographic ones in increasing the probability of migration of Keralites to the Gulf. In other studies, networks are usually measured by assessing the proportion of migrants from a geographic community to a given destination. By differentiating migrants according to their religion, Koola and Özden make an important point: geographic proximity is not sufficient to bond people, especially in heterogeneous societies. In Kerala, where three major religions coexist, religion is a strong identity marker.

Religious communities are a central vehicle of socialization everywhere, but particularly in poor countries, where social safety nets are incomplete or nonexistent and households must cope with a tough environment of severe poverty and shocks to economic and physical well-being. In order to face such an adverse situation, the household cannot be isolated; it needs friends and relatives to count on. As a result, the religious community is a place of exchange in the village, as it is in migration.

Indeed, economists working on networks of Mexican migrants in the United States may well become inspired by this breakthrough, as Catholicism is losing its monopoly in Mexico in favor of growing non-Catholic Christian movements. With even families now divided between Catholics and other Christians, the power of these new churches to mobilize community spirit is already indisputable.

How Do Networks Operate?

Koola and Özden find that the migration network has no spillover effect; having a network in country A increases the probability of migrating to that destination, but not to others. They conclude that the network is purely informative and is not used to finance migration; rather, experienced migrants provide referrals and circulate information about job offers, labor market conditions, and the like. The authors' main argument is that if the network financed migration, flows would not be destination specific.

I must admit that I was not fully convinced by that reasoning. Probably the difficulty is a matter of vocabulary; if "financing migration" means "paying for the trip," then it is true that migration would not be destination specific. But there are other migration costs, linked with relocation. The authors note that networks can provide "social support," and they do mention housing. For me, these kinds of support are also "economic." There are many accounts of established migrants paying the rent while the new migrant is getting settled. What about providing a safety net in case of misfortune such as unemployment or disease? The institution of rotating saving and credit associations (ROSCAs, or, in India, chit funds) has been well documented in poor rural economies but also in migrant communities, where immigrants are more likely to be at a disadvantage in the credit market. Srinivasan (1995) describes ROSCAs in Oxford run by South Asian women. There are more studies in the United States (where data availability is not such an issue) than elsewhere, but it may well be the case that there are Keralite ROSCAs in the Arab states of the Persian Gulf. Hence, without directly financing the migration, the migrant network finances the settlement of the new migrant and provides him or her with informal social security. Because settled migrants will be more in a position to lend a hand, they will be the main providers and will therefore finance this informal insurance at the time the newcomers need it the most. In turn, the new migrants will finance the next newcomers and thus form a chain of reciprocity with subsequent waves of migrants.

Religious Clustering of Minorities

Another aspect of the authors' findings is that Hindu networks have the highest impacts on both the decision to migrate and the choice of location, followed by Christian and then Muslim networks. The authors suggest that Hindus are more reliant on their networks than are the other groups. They mention that Muslims are more religiously compatible in the Arab Gulf states and that Christians have an educational advantage. I would suggest two further explanations. A first, noneconomic, one is that non-Muslims are clearly minorities in the Arab Gulf states. Religious practices are made easier when population is concentrated. The building of churches and Hindu temples, for instance, requires a minimum number of believers. Furthermore, some claim that freedom of religion would not be totally guaranteed for non-Muslims in some areas of the Gulf. The channeling effect for non-Muslims would then also be explained by the fact that a larger group is better able to defend itself.

The second, complementary, explanation stems from the network externalities. As depicted by the authors in their study on geographic network effects, the relationship between the stock of migrants in a given place and the probability of migrating is nonlinear. There are, in fact, two opposite effects: the stock of migrants reduces the relocation cost, but it increases competition on the labor market and thus decreases the incentive for migration. When the stock of migrants is still low, the positive network externality dominates; when the stock is high, the negative wage effect dominates. The authors observe that although Muslims represent only one-fourth of Kerala's population, they make up close to half of the total emigrant population in the Gulf states. The proportion is not nearly as high for Christians and Hindus, which would explain the difference in the effects: Muslim migration is at a stage at which the competition effect is very high, whereas the positive network externality still strongly dominates for both Hindus and Christians. Only longitudinal and historical data, since the 1970s, would allow us to ascertain whether this is relevant. In the results presented, with the data at hand, it appears that "own religious network" effects diminished slightly between 1998 and 2003, but the differences are not statistically significant, and five years is, anyway, too short a time to detect such a pattern.

Extended Family Networks

When one looks carefully at the regressions concerning the migration decision, it appears that for a Muslim, having relatives who are migrants is (at least) as important as having other Muslims from the same village on migration. This does not hold for Christians or Hindus. This result could be interpreted as an indication that the family is taking over from the religious network among Muslims. If there is more competition on the labor market, it becomes more costly to help new migrants because of the unemployment risk. When times are rough, family represents a safer resort. There is a large body of literature documenting how the extended family provides all kinds of insurance and protection against external events; Cox and Fafchamps (2007) offer a complete and up-to-date review. Additional information on the functioning of Keralite households would have been required in order to investigate the role of family networks, and this is beyond the scope of the paper.

Unemployment of Potential Migrants?

The authors obtain noteworthy results on employment decisions of nonmigrants. In a first econometric study, they show a standard outcome: young people are more likely to be unemployed in migrant households. Using the panel structure of the data, they show that the young unemployed in migrant households in 1998 had a higher probability of being on migration abroad in 2003. There seems, however, to be a selection bias because of an attrition problem that could potentially dampen this result. Suppose a young man was unemployed in 1998 but got married and formed a new home by 2003. Recall that in the sample regressions, persons who were between ages 10 and 24 in 1998 were between ages 15 and 29 in 2003; indeed, since students were excluded, the young persons were likely to have been between ages 14 and 24 in 1998 and therefore between ages 19 and 29 in 2003. This seems to be a reasonable marriage age range.

The bias would stem from the following issue: is this individual still present in the sample, since he cannot be traced in 2003, when he is no longer part of "the initial household"? In the data presentation the authors mention that it is the households that are resurveyed, not the household members. In reality, we do not know the situation of this particular young man in 2003. Has he found a job? Has he migrated? Leaving the parents' household and finding a job are likely to be linked. If it is the case that this young man is no longer in the sample and that he has not migrated, then the link between "unemployed in 1998" and "on migration in 2003" is biased upward. In other words, it is not to be taken for granted that unemployed young persons in migrant households are actually potential external migrants. They may still be in Kerala and may simply have left the initial household to form a new one.

Perhaps this comment is not relevant, as the issue may have been taken into account in the analysis. Nevertheless, it underscores the fact that I found no mention of the definition of "households" or "household members" in the paper. Are households mainly nuclear families, or extended ones? Concerns about change in household composition between the two dates may be quite relevant and decisive in the former case.

To conclude, research on migrant networks is a challenging field of investigation for econometricians because it is data consuming. A first-best option would be to have data on both sides: at home and for the destination country. Such a data collection process is extremely difficult to implement and is therefore expensive, but it is rewarding. I surmise that the authors would agree with me that it would definitely be of great help in better grasping the migration process. Facing a second-best situation, as development economists are trained to do, the authors fared very well in convincingly highlighting the importance of religious networks.

Finally, I have to say that this article is particularly useful and relevant for such a conference. Aimed at a large audience, from policy makers to professional and academic economists, it shows that noneconomic factors often play an important part in individuals' choices. A priori, religion has little to do with migration decisions, or at least it does not seem to be of such importance. Development economists have a tendency to overlook those issues, though times may be changing; as a recent study by Rao and Walton (2004) shows, interdisciplinarity is in the air in academia, as at the World Bank.

References

Cox, Donald, and Marcel Fafchamps. 2007. "Extended Family and Kinship Networks: Economic Insights and Evolutionary Directions." *Handbook of Development Economics*, vol. 4, ed. T. Paul Schulz and John Strauss, 3711–84. Amsterdam: North-Holland.

Rao, Vijayendra, and Michael Walton. 2004. *Culture and Public Action*. Stanford, CA: Stanford University Press.

Srinivasan, Shaila. 1995. "ROSCAs among South Asians in Oxford." In *Money-Go-Rounds: The Importance of Rotating Savings and Credit Associations for Women,* ed. Shirley Ardener and Sandra Burman. Washington, DC: Berg Publishers.

Higher Education and High-Technology Industry

The Role of Higher Education in High-Technology Industrial Development: What Can International Experience Tell Us?

SACHI HATAKENAKA

An extraordinary level of policy attention is being accorded higher education today. The reason is clear: higher education is considered one of the key factors for the development of science-based high-technology industries. This paper shows that the various types of higher education institutions play significantly different roles, which can influence the shape and nature of high-tech industry. The study further proposes a classification framework for institutions to illuminate such a difference. Drawing on experience in a variety of economies (the United States; Japan; Finland; Taiwan, China; the Republic of Korea; Ireland; Israel; China; and India), three separate dimensions are proposed for differentiating institutional characteristics: responsiveness, fundamental science orientation, and selectivity. Finally, the paper examines how the three dimensions developed in specific country contexts and suggests that early interventions for developing responsiveness may be particularly important.

Higher education commands an extraordinary level of policy attention today. The reason is clear: with the rise of knowledge economies and science-based high-technology industries, higher education is considered crucial to economic development. Experience shows that high-tech industry can emerge in highly dissimilar countries, including those with limited industrial bases or low levels of economic development such as China, India, and Ireland. It is not surprising that innovation policies to create and support high-tech industries are a priority in almost all member countries of the Organisation for Economic Co-operation and Development (OECD) and in many developing countries. Development of an appropriate higher education sector is becoming a critical component of such policies.

Sachi Hatakenaka is an independent researcher.

Annual World Bank Conference on Development Economics 2009, Global
© 2010 The International Bank for Reconstruction and Development / The World Bank

Much has been written about the role of American universities in high-tech industries and more generally in industrial development, and some studies compare the roles of U.S. institutions with those in Europe or Japan. Studies in other countries conclude that the contributions of well-trained engineers and scientists—and, by implication, higher education systems—are significant. The comparative literature on higher education describes similarities and differences among national systems, but there tends to be little emphasis on their roles in economic development.

Lester (2005), in a comparative study of several countries, argues that different types of industrial transformation require different contributions by universities. There is also an emerging literature on university-industry relationships in developing countries (Chen and Kenney 2007; Ma 2007; Wu 2007; Yusuf and Nabeshima 2007; Kroll and Leifner 2008), and the role of universities in economic development is beginning to be discussed in a more specific way (Mazzoleni and Nelson 2007; Leifner and Schiller 2008). Mazzoleni and Nelson provide an in-depth analysis of the role of public research in economic catch-up and argue for the increasing importance of such research, particularly in application-oriented sciences and engineering. They also provide a helpful overview of the nature of American research universities and their economic roles. Leifner and Schiller contribute to the debate by introducing the notion of "academic capabilities" to help with thinking about how universities contribute to the development of technological capacity. However, few studies examine how different types of higher education institutions may contribute differently to the development of high-tech industry and how institutional characteristics influence the nature of their contribution.

The objective of the paper is to fill this gap in the literature by proposing a classification framework for higher education institutions. More specifically, the paper seeks answers to three questions:

1. What are the characteristics of higher education institutions that define the nature of their contributions to high-tech industry?

2. What roles do these institutions play in the development of high-tech industry?

3. How do institutional characteristics develop?

The ultimate goal is to draw lessons for the future for higher education systems, particularly in developing countries.

This paper is based on a review of experience in a range of countries. Wherever possible, country-specific literature on higher education systems and their development is drawn on. The main emphasis is on two high-tech industrial sectors of relatively recent date: information and communications technology (ICT), both hardware and software, and biotechnology.

The point of this paper is not to fully contrast the paths taken or to examine all the contributing factors in the development of high-tech industry. That a variety of factors was behind the take-off of high-tech industry is accepted as a given. The paper focuses on the specific roles higher education has played within that context. It examines differences in capabilities for high-tech industry among countries, but only to the extent that they are related to the roles of higher education systems.

In order to explore the variety of roles played by higher education at different stages of industrial development, four sets of economies are examined:

- The United States, which has held a leading position in both sectors—ICT and biotechnology—from their very beginning

- Japan and Finland, which entered the global competition in high-tech products on a foundation of significant existing industrial capability

- A group of late developers, including the Republic of Korea and Taiwan, China, that were building industrial capability around the time these industries were born

- A group that developed high-tech industry from a much less developed industrial base (China, India, Ireland, and Israel).

The paper attempts to draw on comparative historical data, to the extent they exist, so that comparisons can be made not only geographically but also over time.

Framework for Understanding Institutional Characteristics

In this section, a framework for classifying institutions is proposed, using three dimensions that measure institutional characteristics: responsiveness, basic science orientation, and selectivity (figure 1). *Responsiveness* refers to institutions' ability and inclination to respond to changing practical and industrial needs. *Basic science orientation* measures the level of commitment to fundamental science. *Selectivity* has to do with the stringency of the criteria for recruiting students and staff and distinguishes elite institutions from those that are open to people more widely.

These three dimensions emerged in the course of the review of the various cases, but also from prior academic work. The first two dimensions, responsiveness and basic science orientation (shown in figure 2), owe much to the work of Stokes (1997),

FIGURE 1.
Three Dimensions of a Higher Education Institution

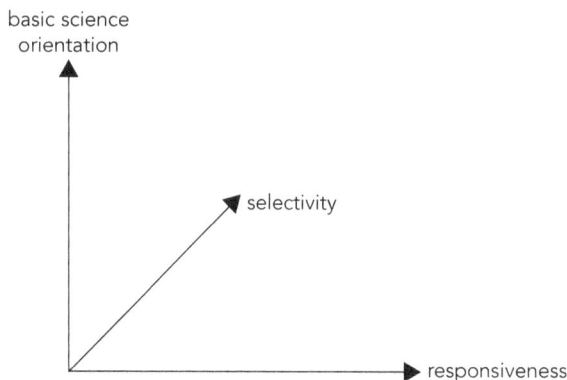

Source: Author's elaboration.

FIGURE 2.
Institutional Characteristics: Responsiveness and Basic Science Orientation

responsiveness to economic needs

	NO	YES
basic science orientation YES	basic research institutions	relevant research institutions
NO	teaching-focused institutions	practically oriented institutions

Source: Adapted from Stokes (1997).

who proposed two similar dimensions to distinguish between four different types of research orientation. Figure 2 shows the framework to differentiate between four types of institutions using these two dimensions.

The top right-hand cell is occupied by *relevant research* universities, which conduct fundamental research, but with an eye to its relevance to society. These institutions are committed to fundamental science but are also concerned about being useful, and they strive to remain responsive to socioeconomic needs. Surprisingly, not many institutions fit this category. A primary example is a group of American research universities that in their development embraced the value of relevance (Rosenberg and Nelson 1994; Geiger 2004a; Mazzoleni and Nelson 2007). When these universities became the envy of the world because of their contributions in high-tech industry such as biotechnology and ICT, the world initially looked to all American universities as if they were all the same. Over time, it became clear that even within the American system there were different types of university and that only certain research universities were proactive in industrial innovation in general and in the development of high-tech industry in particular. Some Israeli universities also appear to belong to this cell, although perhaps with less emphasis on basic science and more on applied research.

The top left-hand cell is occupied by *basic research* universities, which are driven principally by the core values of fundamental science, with little interest in or capacity for responding to external needs. This is where the classic ivory-tower universities with well-developed research capabilities belong; indeed, the great majority of research universities in the world have belonged to this cell—at least until recently, when economic relevance became a global catchphrase. These institutions value cutting-edge science, reward scientific discoveries, and encourage their academics to define actively the direction of scientific research. Scientific developments were to be independent of practical requirements, which were regarded as a "corrupting" influence on science. Indeed, until the 1990s, this cell represented what most higher education institutions aspired to be. Many Japanese national universities developed to fit into this category in spite of their origins as practically oriented universities, as is discussed next.

The bottom right-hand cell contains *practically oriented* institutions that aspire to meet the economy's needs for practical skills and knowledge. They offer courses relevant to employers and often conduct consulting and application-oriented research with and for employers. They have little interest in, or capacity for, furtherance of generic scientific knowledge or fundamental research. Examples are diverse; they range from the *grandes écoles* in France, which were designed to provide elite professional education (although some have now begun to develop basic research capacity), and many polytechnic schools and their equivalents in other countries. Ireland and Finland reformed their higher education sectors by introducing this type of institution. Historically, the Japanese national universities would have belonged to this cell at their founding, as they were established to provide key technological skills needed for national modernization, but their commitment to bring science into practice place them higher in the quadrant, in comparison with traditional trade schools, which focus on practical skills. Some Chinese universities have roots in this cell, and others appear to have moved rightward toward this cell over the last 20 years, becoming much more economically relevant. Some institutions fit this cell naturally by virtue of their emphasis on an application-oriented subject mix; engineering institutions such as the Indian Institutes of Technology are good examples.

The bottom left-hand cell is occupied by *teaching-focused* institutions, which are neither practically oriented in their teaching nor research oriented. U.S. liberal arts colleges are good examples because they are committed to offering broad curricula, with an emphasis on generic skills rather than vocational or professional content. They define their identity in terms of their commitment to teaching and conduct hardly any research. (Some teaching institutions, however, are more academically oriented.) Most universities in developing countries fall into the teaching-focused category by default simply because they do not have the resources to be active in research. In many such cases their teaching is defined according to academic discipline.

The third dimension, selectivity, differentiates further the nature of the institutions in each of the four cells. The more selective the institutions are in screening incoming students, the more elitist they are. *Grandes écoles* are differentiated from the bulk of polytechnics in that they are among the most highly selective institutions, which most polytechnics are not. Selectivity is often a system-level characteristic; some higher education systems are explicitly selective, characterized by highly competitive entrance examinations to allocate talents across institutions, as in Japan and Korea. Other systems are much less so and are based on the notion that all universities command equal status; this is the tradition in Germany and many other European countries.

As will be discussed later, selectivity appears to be an important characteristic that strengthens the roles institutions may play.

Roles of Different Types of Institution

This section describes how different types of institution contributed to the development of high-tech industry, drawing on the experiences of the countries listed above. One important observation is that none of the institutional categories appears to be necessary for the development of high-tech industry; rather, they play different roles. The footprints of university roles are sometimes visible in the shape and nature of the resulting industry, but at other times industry developed while incorporating university contributions in a way that became almost invisible.

Relevant Research Universities

It is well established that some American research universities contributed significantly to the birth and development of biotechnology and the computer industry. For instance, fundamental scientific discoveries in university laboratories and the resulting patents (such as Cohen's and Boyer's discovery of recombinant DNA technique) led to the development of biotechnology as a whole new industry with strong linkages with academic scientific research (Henderson, Orsenigo, and Pisano 1999). The early evolution of the biotechnology industry was characterized by the formation of new firms, many of which were academic spin-offs; usually, academics worked in conjunction with professional managers, backed by venture capital. The early academic inventors were labeled "star scientists" because they were key players both in basic science and in its applications. They had a special role mainly because of the significant amount of tacit knowledge associated with the original scientific discoveries (Zucker and Darby 1996; Zucker, Darby, and Brewer 1998; Zucker, Darby, and Armstrong 2002). The norms in American universities that permitted academics to become deeply engaged in commercialization—which had developed early, given their culture of striving to be useful—was crucial in this process (Henderson, Orsenigo, and Pisano 1999; Etzkowitz 2002).

American universities were also important to the development of the computer hardware and software industries, although their visibility varied over time (Rosenberg and Nelson 1994; Bresnahan and Malerba 1999; Mowery 1999). For instance, universities were actively engaged in the early development of computers in the 1940s. (During this period, European universities such as those in Manchester, Cambridge, and Berlin were as active as their American counterparts.) They were also important in the development of microcomputers, as exemplified by spin-offs from the Massachusetts Institute of Technology, Stanford University, and the University of Texas. In Europe, only Cambridge University in the United Kingdom played a similar role in microcomputers.

There is evidence that industry values the more conventional channels of contributions made by universities. One survey found that industry regarded general research findings, or instrumentation and techniques developed through research, as more important university contributions than prototypes (Cohen, Nelson, and Walsh 2002). The same survey found that publications, meetings and conferences, informal interaction, and consulting were more important than patents as mechanisms through which industry gained access to university knowledge. Furthermore, industry reported that university research was helpful in solving problems, rather than in inspiring and triggering new research. These results concern contributions made by all types of American universities, including basic research institutions. Nonetheless, it is important to note that what is valued is not so much application capabilities in universities as relevant research capability.

There is also evidence that the development of the software industry was greatly facilitated by the early establishment of computer science as a new discipline in universities (Mowery 1999). Universities contributed not only through formation of key knowledge but also through organizing and delivering education programs to supply updated skills. Indeed, American universities' ability to create and legitimate computer science as a new field was unparalleled by European or Japanese universities (Mowery 1999).

In Israel, similarly, universities supplied highly skilled human resources and served as a source of leading technologies not only in ICT but also in biotechnology and agriculture-related research (de Fontenay and Carmel 2004; Breznitz 2007). From early on, the government made significant public investments in application-oriented scientific research in universities, public research institutions, and the military. Israeli universities became well-established scientific centers early, and today Israel is high in global rankings for key metrics such as the number of publications per capita and relative citation indexes (tables 1 and 2). But they were application oriented, as well; university-industry relationships had long been well established (Breznitz 2004), and three universities ranked among the top six patent holders in the country (Trajtenberg 2001; Breznitz 2004). Israel became one of the first research and development (R&D) sites abroad for U.S. multinational companies, with Motorola establishing a research unit in 1963 (de Fonteney and Carmel 2004). The contribution of the universities tends to be overshadowed by that of the military in the narrative of Israel's

TABLE 1. Science and Engineering Articles, by Economy, 1995–2005

(number of articles, except as otherwise specified)

Economy	1995	2000	2005	Per million population	Average annual change (percent) 1995–2000	Average annual change (percent) 2000–2005	Average annual change (percent) 1995–2005
China	9,061	18,479	41,596	31	15.3	17.6	16.5
Finland	4,077	4,844	4,811	914	3.5	–0.1	1.7
India	9,370	10,276	14,608	13	1.9	7.3	4.5
Ireland	1,218	1,581	2,120	502	5.4	6.0	5.7
Israel	5,741	6,290	6,309	926	1.8	0.1	0.9
Japan	47,068	57,101	55,471	434	3.9	–0.6	1.7
Korea, Rep.	3,803	9,572	16,396	341	20.3	11.4	15.7
Taiwan, China	4,759	7,190	10,841	474	8.6	8.6	8.6
United States	193,337	192,743	205,320	678	–0.1	1.3	0.6

Source: Thomson Scientific, Science Citation Index (SCI) and Social Sciences Citation Index (SSCI), http://scientific.thomson.com/products/categories/citation/; ipIQ, Inc.; and National Science Foundation, Division of Science Resources Statistics, special tabulations, as published in *Science and Engineering Indicators 2008*; population data from World Bank database, accessed May 7, 2008; National Statistics, Taiwan, China, http://eng.stat.gov.tw/lp.asp?ctNode=2265&CtUnit=1072&BaseDSD=36.

Note: Article counts are for the set of journals covered by the SCI and SSCI. Articles are classified by year of publication and are assigned to economies on the basis of the institutional addresses listed in the article. For articles where collaborating institutions are from multiple economies, each economy receives fractional credit on the basis of the proportion of the participating institutions.

TABLE 2. Relative Prominence in Scientific Literature, Selected Economies, 1995 and 2003
(index: 1.00 indicates that an economy's share of cited literature equals its world share of scientific literature)

Rank	Economy or group	1995	2003
1	Switzerland	1.189	1.152
2	United States	1.013	1.026
5	United Kingdom	0.830	0.864
8	Finland	0.755	0.826
12	Ireland	0.662	0.764
14	Israel	0.682	0.742
15	EU-15	0.681	0.737
19	Hong Kong, China	0.438	0.672
22	Japan	0.551	0.575
24	Singapore	0.422	0.509
26	Chile	0.343	0.478
28	Korea, Rep.	0.320	0.439
29	Thailand	n.a.	0.432
30	Czech Republic	n.a.	0.417
31	Argentina	0.304	0.411
32	Slovenia	n.a.	0.409
33	South Africa	0.325	0.404
34	Taiwan, China	0.321	0.401
35	Mexico	0.349	0.385
36	Poland	0.295	0.360
37	Brazil	0.314	0.359
38	Slovak Republic	n.a.	0.339
40	Bulgaria	0.166	0.325
41	China	0.218	0.293
42	India	0.182	0.284
43	Croatia	0.257	0.281
44	Turkey	0.214	0.278
45	Saudi Arabia	0.220	0.256

Source: Thomson ISI, Science Citation Index (SCI) and Social Sciences Citation Index (SSCI), http://www.isinet.com/ products/citation/; ipIQ, Inc.; National Science Foundation, Division of Science Resources Statistics, special tabulations, *Science and Engineering Indicators 2006.*

Note: n.a., not applicable; EU-15 refers to the 15 countries of the European Union before the expansion in membership of May 1, 2004. The relative prominence of scientific literature is measured on the basis of the relative citation index of an economy, that is, the economy's share of cited literature adjusted for its share of published literature. The economy's citation of its own literature is excluded. An index of 1.00 indicates that the economy's share of cited literature equals its world share of scientific literature. An index greater than 1.00 or less than 1.00 indicates that the economy's literature is cited relatively more or less, respectively, than its share of scientific literature. Economies with a share of world publications in the cited field of less than 10 percent during the period are either excluded or are listed as n.a. In the case of cited articles with collaborating institutions from multiple economies, each economy receives fractional credit on the basis of the proportion of its participating institutions.

high-tech industry, but they have contributed to the emergence of an entrepreneurial sector, both directly and indirectly, through spin-offs and through science parks, some of which had been established as early as the 1960s (Roper and Grimes 2005).

It is no accident that the resulting high-tech industry in Israel was highly R&D-oriented and had cutting-edge technological content. This poses a sharp contrast to other emerging economies. Whereas the software industry in India and Ireland largely grew by providing software services, Israel's software industry developed on the basis of niche software products with global applications. Israel's innovation capabilities, as gauged, for example, by its patenting performance, lags behind that of Japan and the United States but is comparable with that of Finland and Taiwan, China (Trajtenberg 2001). Israel's ICT industry displays a marked concentration on upstream R&D, compared with the Finnish ICT industry, which covers a wider value chain ranging from R&D and production to marketing and distribution, or with Ireland's, which has hardly any R&D (Roper and Grimes 2005).

In summary, relevant research universities appear to contribute by

- Conducting basic research in fields pertinent to developments in industry and disseminating such knowledge through a variety of activities such as patenting and licensing, academic spin-offs, consulting, and advising

- Providing updated skills in areas relevant to industry, both in undergraduate education and in advanced research training for masters and PhDs.

Basic Research Universities

Basic research universities are characterized by an academic ethos of scientific autonomy, and it would not be surprising to find that they are less proactive than relevant research universities. Nonetheless, they are capable of supporting the development of high-tech industry with high technological content, through both research and education. One example is postwar Japan, where a group of national and some private universities developed to become basic research universities. Their contributions to the development of high-tech industry have not been very visible, and Japanese policy makers and industrialists were often critical of them because they were deemed to be less responsive than their American peers. There is, however, consistent evidence that Japanese universities' contributions are underrated and that they have played a different but "important" role as compared with their American peers (Yoshihara and Tamai 1999; Pechter and Kakinuma 1999; Kodama and Suzuki 2007). Some analysts have coined the term "receiver-active paradigm" to describe this technology transfer phenomenon; it was the technology-receiving industry, rather than the universities, that actively defined how and when technology transfer took place (Kodama and Suzuki 2007).

Indeed, Japanese companies have been extremely active in using universities to acquire new scientific knowledge. An unusual mechanism that brought university academics and industry together was industries' practice of sending their staff to universities, not for any specific education programs but, more generally, to study, sometimes for a whole year. This practice was often motivated by a desire to learn about fields of science in which industry had limited expertise (Hicks 1993; Darby and Zucker 1996). Accordingly, in biotechnology, "star scientists" worked with company employees in their university laboratories, resulting in higher levels of coauthorship than in the United States (Darby and Zucker 1996). Other researchers also find that Japanese academics' relationships with companies are equivalent to those prevailing in the United Kingdom and the United States, at least as measured by coauthorships (Pechter and Kakinuma 1999), but that companies had to be proactive in eliciting scientific and technological information from the universities (Kodama and Suzuki 2007).

Japanese universities have been much less active in directly engaging in the commercialization of science. In the early development of biotechnology, Japanese universities played a negligible role in forming new companies in Japan, in striking contrast to the visibility and dominance of academic spin-offs in the United Kingdom and the United States (Henderson, Orsenigo, and Pisano 1999). This was partly because of the unevenness of Japanese science, at least at the outset; there were literally no researchers in Japan working in genetic engineering at the time of the scientific breakthroughs (Darby and Zucker 1996). But even when they did catch up in science, universities as organizations did not permit their civil servant "star scientists" to work in the same way in new companies (Darby and Zucker 1996).

Similar passive, albeit important, roles are also evident in education. Japanese universities made a significant contribution by supplying large numbers of engineers and scientists at the undergraduate and master's levels, something that was essential for the birth and development of the electronics industry. A group of highly selective Japanese national universities with large science and engineering faculties was particularly important in producing high-caliber scientists and engineers. Companies, however, had to develop significant capability for imparting the necessary skills to graduates through extensive in-house training. A form of division of labor developed whereby universities selected students and provided general academic training, while companies carried out the necessary specialist training, even for R&D personnel.

Moreover, it was not universities that proposed massive expansion in science and engineering programs; it was government that, in response to industrial demand, planned such an expansion through funding. Indeed, Japanese universities were generally slow to respond to emerging needs for industrial skills in, for instance, new areas such as software-related engineering, semiconductors, and biotechnology (Baba, Takai, and Mizuta 1996; Darby and Zucker 1996; Mowery 1999; Kobayashi 2001). They were also slow in establishing relevant research training. Although master's programs in engineering had become commonplace by the 1980s, doctoral programs in science and engineering remained small and unattractive for industry (Clark 1995; Shimizu and Mori 2001; see also table 3). PhDs from universities were too narrowly specialized and too academically oriented for industry. Instead, industry recruited bright potential researchers with less academic training and trained them in-house, using the unique Japanese system in which doctorates were awarded by universities for dissertations that were written mainly in the companies, without detailed supervision by academics (Shimizu and Mori 2001). The companies took the extreme route of developing in-house training to cultivate doctoral-level researchers.

In summary, basic research universities can contribute to high-tech industry in developing scientific capacity and in providing scientific information, although in the

TABLE 3. Total Enrollment, Advanced Research (PhD) Programs, Selected Economies and Selected Years, 1970–2006

(numbers enrolled, except as otherwise specified)

Economy	1970	1980	1990	2000	2003	2006	Percent of total, 2006
China	—	—	—	54,038	108,737	—	—
Finland	—	—	—	19,750	19,846	22,145	7.2
India	—	—	—	55,019	65,357	36,519	—
Ireland	—	—	—	2,904	3,816	5,146	2.8
Israel	—	—	—	6,647	7,944	9,715	3.1
Japan	13,243	18,211	28,354	59,007	68,245	75,028	1.8
Korea, Rep.	—	—	—	28,924	34,712	41,055	1.3
Taiwan, China	166	673	4,437	13,822	21,658	29,839	2.3
United States	—	—	—	293,002	306,889	388,685	2.2

Source: UNESCO database accessed May 7, 2008; Education Statistics, Ministry of Education, Science and Technology, Japan; Education Statistics, Ministry of Education, Taiwan, China.

Note: —, not available. UNESCO, United Nations Educational, Scientific, and Cultural Organization.

case of Japan this required proactive work on the part of industry. Such universities can also provide large numbers of well-educated scientists and engineers, even though the graduates' training may not be fine-tuned to specific industrial technological needs. The great selectivity of Japanese universities was helpful for industry, which actively used such selectivity for identifying high-caliber talents.

Practically Oriented Institutions

Practically oriented institutions are unique in that they offer specialized engineering and science skills that are directly relevant to industrial needs. In Finland and Ireland professional institutions were created as an alternative to conventional university education, which was seen as unresponsive to industrial needs. Institutional responsiveness was particularly important when new disciplines such as computer science emerged, and it appeared to give countries a competitive edge, as was clear in the case of Ireland.

In Ireland, the government-led expansion of technically trained manpower in the 1970s and 1980s was important in attracting multinational corporations (MNCs), including ICT enterprises. The starting point was a consensus that emerged early among policy makers that technical education was essential but that universities were overly academic and that a different type of institution was needed to provide the critically needed technical manpower (White 2001). Thirteen regional technical colleges and two national institutes of higher education were established in the 1970s for this purpose, representing the bulk of expansion in the tertiary sector. They were established specifically to be responsive to economic needs, and they are known today as having well-established practices in, for instance, assessing industrial needs and obtaining industrial inputs in curricular content (Breznitz 2007).

Finland also made a decisive move to create a set of responsive institutions when it established 29 polytechnics in the 1990s. By 2000, nearly 60 percent of entrants to higher education were going to polytechnics. Although it is still early to assess the full impact of polytechnics in Finland, their early performance reviews have been positive, and there are indications that their expansion coincided with the timing of major industrial needs, particularly in telecommunications (OECD 2003). In one survey of high-tech industry in northern Finland, 47 percent of companies said that polytechnics were important, compared with 38 percent saying the same of a university with a known regional orientation, and with 10–20 percent for other universities in Finland (Juahiainen 2006).

Both Korea and Taiwan, China, invested in application-oriented research capacity in government research institutes, which had a significant part in developing domestic technological capacity within high-tech industry. The fact that such capacity was built outside universities is perhaps not surprising, given that it is faster and easier to concentrate resources in dedicated institutions. Such decisions did, however, have consequences, particularly in the case of Korea, in delaying the development of research capacity in universities, with the notable exception of the Korea Advanced Institute of Science (KAIS), discussed below.

The experience of Taiwan, China, with high-tech industry cannot be described without citing the story of the Electronic Research Service Organization (ERSO), a public research institution. ERSO is a branch of the Industrial Technology Research Institute (ITRI) and was at the heart of the economy's acquisition of technological know-how in semiconductors. ERSO orchestrated the first major technology transfer agreement, with RCA in the 1970s. It subsequently developed an integrated circuit (IC) fabrication technology and established a spin-off company that in turn was important in the diffusion of technological know-how (Wade 1990; Saxenian 2004). The industry in Taiwan, China (unlike the cases of Japan and Korea), included many small-to-medium-size enterprises that lacked the capability to undertake significant R&D in-house, and public investment in applied research was essential for their technological upgrading (Wade 1990).

The Korean experience of investing in application-oriented research capacity in government research institutes is somewhat less visible, but it has been important in building corporate research capacity. An example is the Korea Institute of Science and Technology (KIST), established in 1966 and staffed by Korean scientists and engineers brought back from abroad, one of the early efforts to reverse the brain drain. The institute was designed to undertake contract research with both industry and government and was particularly active in facilitating technology transfer from foreign firms to local firms (Mazzoleni and Nelson 2007). KIST provides an interesting and exceptional example because it later became amalgamated with the Korea Advanced Institute of Science (KAIS), a graduate-level educational institution established in the 1970s specifically to fill an important gap in Korean higher education by creating high-level skills of industrial relevance (Mazzoleni and Nelson 2007). It is thus possible, even though not common, for research capacity developed in government research institutes to contribute directly to the evolution of higher education institutions.

Teaching-Focused Institutions

In the early stage of development of high-tech industry, companies often recruited generic science and engineering graduates who were not necessarily trained in a specialization relevant to the industry. In China, India, Japan, Korea, and Taiwan, China, these graduates mainly came from teaching-focused institutions because many institutions simply had not yet developed research capacity. All these governments emphasized science and engineering. Beyond this general statement, there is a significant divergence in what happened in each case.

In Japan the government, in response to growing industrial demand in the late 1950s through the early 1960s, aggressively promoted science and engineering undergraduate programs not only in national universities but also in private universities, which were largely teaching oriented (Nakayama 1995). Most private universities in Japan had limited resources for undertaking science and engineering programs or research. It was through special government subsidies, which provided up to half of undergraduate student costs and two-thirds of the associated investment costs in science and engineering, that private universities managed to establish programs in these disciplines (Nakayama 1995). This push no doubt helped Japan produce a large number of scientists and engineers; students in these fields constituted 27–28 percent of all undergraduates in the late 1960s through the 1980s (table 4).

Korea and Taiwan, China, made earlier moves toward emphasizing science and engineering relative to their industrial development, which resulted in massive brain drains. In Korea more than a third of undergraduate enrollments were in science and engineering by the mid-1960s (table 4), and the proportion increased to over 40 percent in the subsequent period in spite of the great expansion of the higher education sector that was taking place. Korea today has one of the world's highest

TABLE 4. Undergraduate Science and Engineering Enrollments, Japan and the Republic of Korea, Including Agriculture and Excluding Medicine, Selected Years, 1960–2005

Country and indicator	1960	1965	1970	1975	1980	1985	1990	1995	2000	2005
Japan										
Number enrolled	136,818	238,596	375,598	443,180	451,904	463,336	524,201	611,351	625,371	590,549
Percent of total enrollment	23	27	28	27	26	27	26	26	25	24
Korea, Rep.										
Number enrolled	—	37,099	59,264	74,410	166,137	337,624	419,891	523,002	—	—
Percent of total enrollment	—	35	34	36	41	36	40	44	—	—

Source: Japan, MEXT, 2006; Weidman and Park 2000.

tertiary enrollment ratios, at 91 percent (table 5), and one of the highest proportions of science and engineering students (table 6). In Taiwan, China, the proportion of science and engineering enrollments was about a quarter through the early 1970s and gradually increased from the mid-1970s through the 1990s to over 40 percent (table 7). In contrast, in 2005 India's engineering students made up only 6 percent of total tertiary enrollments, and even when scientists are added, the proportion is significantly lower than for other economies, at 20 percent (see table 6). It is not that all these countries had high proportions of science and engineering in higher education.

TABLE 5. Tertiary Gross Enrollment Ratio, Selected Economies, Selected Years, 1970–2006

Economy	1970	1975	1980	1985	1990	1995	2000	2005	2006
China	0	1	2	3	3	5	8	—	22
Finland	13	28	32	34	48	70	83	92	93
India	5	5	5	6	6	7	10	11	12
Ireland	12	17	18	22	31	40	49	58	59
Israel	18	23	29	33	36	41	50	58	58
Japan	18	26	31	28	31	42	47	55	57
Korea, Rep.	7	9	15	34	39	52	73	90	91
Taiwan, China	—	—	—	—	—	39	56	82	84
United States	47	55	56	60	72	81	69	82	82

Source: UNESCO database; World Bank database accessed May 7, 2008; Education Indicators, Ministry of Education, Taiwan, China.

Note: UNESCO, United Nations Educational, Scientific, and Cultural Organization. The gross enrollment ratio is the total number of students in tertiary education, including graduate school, as a percentage of the population in the five-year age group following on from secondary school–leaving age.

TABLE 6. Total Tertiary Enrollment in Science and Engineering, Selected Countries, 2005

Economy	Enrollment			Percent of total enrollment			Science/engineering ratio
	Science	Engineering	Total	Science	Engineering	Science and engineering	
China[a]	1,443,129	5,536,123	18,352,821	8	30	38	0.3
Finland	35,468	80,827	305,996	12	26	38	0.4
India[b]	1,689,504	696,609	11,777,296	14	6	20	2.4
Ireland	22,851	19,233	186,561	12	10	23	1.2
Israel	29,967	56,812	310,937	10	18	28	0.5
Japan	118,704	668,526	4,038,302	3	17	19	0.2
Korea, Rep.	264,259	1,022,845	3,224,875	8	32	40	0.3
United States	1,537,243	1,154,971	17,272,044	9	7	16	1.3

Source: UNESCO database, accessed May 7, 2008; for China, Zhou (2005).

Note: UNESCO, United Nations Educational, Scientific, and Cultural Organization.

a. 2004.

b. 2001.

TABLE 7. Graduates in Science and Engineering, Including Agriculture and Excluding Medicine, Taiwan, China, Selected Years, 1960–95

Item	1960	1965	1970	1975	1980	1985	1990	1995
Number of graduates	1,655	2,689	7,987	19,716	25,672	37,965	50,490	82,938
Percent of total graduates	27	25	24	33	36	42	44	46

Source: Lin 2004.

One factor that appears to exert an influence going well beyond that of numbers is selectivity. China, India, Japan, Korea, and Taiwan, China, are alike in that they have highly selective institutions which recruit high-caliber students into engineering nationally and which have set high quality standards in engineering schools. Furthermore, these institutions invariably have had a significant share of their institutional profile in engineering, and in that sense their origins were closer to practically oriented institutions than to generic teaching-focused ones. At the time of the economic take-off, there was little domestic demand for graduates from these selective schools. This meant that they were cheap, high-caliber resources with training in science and technology that emerging industries could readily tap into.

Roles of Higher Education Institutions Revisited

In this section, six different kinds of involvement by higher education institutions are summarized, mainly to highlight the dependence of the nature of their participation in the economy on both institutional characteristics and the industrial context.

Education

Institutions have made diverse contributions in education. Generic teaching institutions and basic research universities produced generic scientists and engineers and left the companies to take the responsibility for developing specialized knowledge and skills. This role was particularly pronounced when the government intervened by preferentially expanding science and engineering programs. Practically oriented institutions were more proactive in keeping up with changing needs for industrial skills and supplying specialized knowledge and skills as industry evolved. Relevant research universities were able to be similarly proactive at a higher level, in their research training.

Research

Academics in relevant research universities were most proactive in conducting research and in working directly with research applications, assisted by universities' organizational capacity to promote and support consulting, patenting and licensing, and spin-offs. Basic research–oriented universities were less active in furthering industries' commercialization goals but helped companies acquire better understanding of new scientific fields, provided advice, and conducted joint research, although generally on the universities' own terms. Other institutions, such as government research institutions and practically oriented universities, helped industry acquire existing technologies through application-oriented research.

Spin-offs

University spin-offs appeared to play a visible role when there was a significant knowledge or capacity gap between universities and domestic industry. The gap could take very different forms, as demonstrated by the cases of biotechnology in the United States and ICT in China.

In the United States the knowledge gap had to do with fundamental scientific discoveries and with related tacit knowledge. In China the nature of the knowledge gap was related to established technology, which was nonetheless new to China. The highly selective nature of Chinese universities also meant that they were better positioned to assemble a group of high-caliber individuals to lead and work in new ventures than normal companies; universities in effect were able to exploit the wide capacity gap of available human resources.

Significant examples of academic spin-offs were associated with universities with relevant research capabilities. Thus, in biotechnology in the United States, academics from research universities became directly involved in spin-offs, and there were similar stories in various fields in Israel. In Ireland, where, because of lack of government funding, universities did not develop research capacity until late (Sands 2005), academic spin-offs were generally not common, but one computer science department did develop an early research capacity, with European funding, and became known for its academic spin-offs (Breznitz 2007).

A very different experience was seen in China, where universities had become active in creating enterprises since the late 1980s, even when they had little research capability. Although these enterprises are sometimes described as spin-offs, they are significantly different from the normal practice in that they are owned and managed by universities (Eun, Lee, and Wu 2006). Some of these companies have been spectacularly successful; they include three of the most successful personal computer (PC) companies, Lenovo, Founder, and Tongfang, which were created by the Chinese Academy of Sciences, Beijing University, and Tsinghua University, respectively. About 40 university enterprises are already listed on stock markets in China and Hong Kong, China (Eun, Lee, and Wu 2006).

Interestingly, the knowledge content of these spin-off companies does not often derive from significant scientific research; rather, the spin-off was the mechanism through which skilled personnel moved from universities to the commercial sector (Chen and Kenney 2007). These enterprises were a simple mechanism through which universities could contribute to industrial capabilities in an environment of very limited industrial capability (Eun, Lee, and Wu 2006). They resembled in this respect Japanese university start-ups in the early phase of industrial development (Odagiri and Goto 1996), when academics could behave as arbitragers of Western technology and were in a good position to create companies, given the underdeveloped industrial context.

It is not clear how long this practice of university enterprises will continue in China. Both the government and many universities may be going through a rethinking process, as many enterprises have not been successful and managerial responsibilities are increasingly demanding (Ma 2007; Kroll and Leifner 2008). It is likely that China's university enterprise experience was a phenomenon dictated by the specific context of underdeveloped industry and a high concentration of talent in universities.

Science Parks

Taiwan, China, provides the most visible example of a highly successful science park, which had a critical part in the development of the semiconductor industry there. In 1980 the government established a science park in Hsinchu, close to two of the island's best technical universities, and relocated ERSO to the park (Saxenian 2004). There was a certain division of labor, in that applied and relevant basic research were undertaken by ERSO, while the universities largely appeared to supply graduates as manpower to the park.

In China many high-tech zones, industrial parks, and science parks have been established close to universities by the central government and local authorities, as well as by the universities themselves. The nature of their dynamic evolution is only beginning to be documented, but the diversity in approach is already evident (Chen and Kenney 2007). The park founded by local authorities in Zhongguancun in Beijing, close to the Chinese Academy of Science as well as to Beijing and Tsinghua Universities, is considered one of the most successful in attracting multinational corporations' R&D investments. The park established by Tsinghua University on its campus has many such R&D units, as well as spin-offs from the university. An interesting variant is Shenzhen, whose high-tech industrial park has been used to attract established universities to create a virtual campus.

Licensing

Licensing is one function that seems to be linked strongly to relevant research capacity in universities, as well as to the level of development of intellectual property–related institutions in the country. In the case of the United States, the patenting practice evolved as one of many mechanisms for technology transfer from universities, predicated on huge government funding in relevant scientific research (Rosenberg and Nelson 1994; Mowery et al. 2004). An early development of professional support units such as technology-licensing offices was also important for effective technology transfer through licensing. It is increasingly clear, however, that for most U.S. universities, patenting and licensing constitute a net drain rather than a source of additional income (Thursby and Thursby 2007).

The wider acceptance of the World Trade Organization (WTO) and other international regimes related to intellectual property will undoubtedly have consequences for the paths that future developing economies can take in catching up. Although it is important for developing countries and their universities to increase their understanding of intellectual property, indiscriminate opening of technology transfer offices in universities with a view to patenting inventions may be unwarranted.

Brain Drain and Brain Circulation

Brain drain transformed into brain circulation appears to be more and more important to the introduction of high-tech industry in developing countries. This undoubtedly reflects the increasingly global nature of higher education as well as labor markets in developed countries, many of which are actively recruiting professionals from developing countries in areas of key skills shortages such as ICT. Such a brain drain can turn into brain circulation once appropriate domestic conditions are created for industrial development, when "brains" that are enriched with international experience can return to their home countries.

Indeed, one feature of high-tech development in Taiwan, China, that distinguishes it from the cases of Japan and Korea, is the visible role played by the diaspora of engineers, particularly in Silicon Valley, and the transformation of the brain drain into brain circulation linked directly to the birth of high-tech industry (Saxenian 1999, 2004, 2006; Saxenian, Motoyama, and Quan 2002). Almost 80 percent of the diaspora professionals in Silicon Valley had gone to the United States to study and remained there for work (Saxenian, Motoyama, and Quan 2002). Early generations of the diaspora were instrumental in informing the home government about Silicon Valley and its unusual dynamism, inspiring an early policy of building a similar cluster (Saxenian 2004). Hsinchu Science Park represents a Taiwanese attempt to recreate Silicon Valley, and indeed the park later became an active recipient of the returning diaspora, with 40 percent of its companies started by returnees (Wade 1990; Saxenian 2004).

It is well known that Taiwan, China, suffered a huge brain drain that started in the 1950s and lasted until the 1990s. Interestingly, the government nevertheless continued organizing programs of overseas study to complement the domestic education system. In 1975, 2,300 students were studying under government auspices; in 1986 the figure was 7,000 (Wade 1990). This was happening in the midst of the massive brain drain, which was estimated at 20 percent of all engineering graduates in the late 1970s (Hou and Gee 1993). Instead of ceasing to send students abroad, the government stepped up efforts to keep in touch with the diaspora community (Wade 1990). The benefits of this policy were finally felt in the 1990s, when the brains started to return.

China and India, too, experienced brain drain to Silicon Valley. In the survey of Silicon Valley professionals, over half of Indians and nearly 80 percent of mainland Chinese there had originally come to the United States for their education (Saxenian, Motoyama, and Quan 2002). China was able to benefit doubly from diasporas, as the Hsinchu–Silicon Valley–Shanghai nexus developed through (broadly defined) overseas Chinese engineers, including those originally from Taiwan, China (Saxenian 2006). In the early 2000s the Chinese government stepped up efforts to recruit back the overseas Chinese.

The dominance of Indian entrepreneurs in U.S. high-tech companies, and not only in Silicon Valley, is well documented (Saxenian, Motoyama, and Quan 2002;

Wadhwa et al. 2007). This highly entrepreneurial diaspora was important as a "reputational intermediary" in connecting Indian firms to client U.S. firms and in bringing American multinationals to India (Kapur 2002; Kapur and McHale 2005; Saxenian 2006).

Even during the brain drain, selectivity appears to have played a role. The competitive entrance system for higher education meant that some engineering colleges and universities had elite status, and it was largely graduates from such institutions who became critical members of the diaspora and formed vibrant alumni networks (Saxenian 2004). Such networks were important for solving technical problems, with former teachers as well as former classmates serving as important sources of technical information.

In China, India, and Taiwan, China, the brain drain was often triggered by prospects of graduate education abroad. In all three cases, graduates from the most select institutions actively pursued opportunities in graduate education abroad and succeeded in finding places, notably in good American research universities. It is easy to imagine that in their search for the best U.S. graduate schools, these graduates would have benefited from having been at elite home institutions, with active peer interactions providing information about studying abroad and with letters of recommendation from home institutions that enjoyed credibility. It is almost as though graduate schools in the United States became a natural extension of the domestic education system.

It is also interesting to observe the differing approaches taken by governments. The government of Taiwan, China, offered fellowships for study abroad even at the height of the brain drain, apparently in the belief that the economy would gain in the end. A decade later the Chinese government was doing something similar. Both valued foreign education sufficiently to send graduates abroad in the first place, but both also worked hard to bring them back. It is as if, for both, foreign institutions, particularly in the United States, functioned as a critical component of the higher education system, providing the kind of education that their domestic institutions could not offer. India, which also suffered a severe brain drain, particularly of high-caliber graduates, was somewhat hostile to the idea of expatriate Indians until much later and was also slower in orchestrating the use of expatriate brains (Saxenian 1999, 2006).

Evolution of the Universities

Although all four types of institution discussed above had some economic role in the development of high-tech industry, the "responsive" institutions in the right-hand cells of figure 2 appear to have participated much more proactively and directly in helping high-tech industry emerge and evolve. Yet such institutions do not seem to emerge naturally. In all cases government action was critical in founding them and in influencing their missions and orientations. In this section the evolution of the various types of institution in specific countries is examined to aid understanding of the underlying dynamics.

Building Responsiveness

In the *United States* the emergence of a group of responsive institutions was no accident. A whole group of American universities, the land grant colleges, was founded in the late nineteenth century with the explicit objective of serving the practical needs of the community. The federal government supported their establishment through special grants and continued to sustain their growth by funding some of their service activities, such as agricultural extension. This group was a wide mix, ranging from broad institutions such as Cornell and Purdue Universities to institutions oriented toward industrial training, such as the Massachusetts Institute of Technology. That universities could and should be useful to society became a belief shared by government, the public, and universities broadly. The responsiveness of American universities in teaching was well established in those early days, and it was their responsiveness that generated new subjects such as electrical, chemical, and aeronautical engineering (Rosenberg and Nelson 1994).

Before World War II, private foundations provided key support to some universities, helping them undertake research that was relevant and useful to society (Geiger 2004b). But it was the spectacular success with the use of science to develop key military technology during World War II that brought about a new level of commitment to "useful scientific research" by government, universities, and the public alike. Postwar government research funding was massive but also mission oriented, coming from key agencies with application interests such as defense, health, and energy (Rosenberg and Nelson 1994; Geiger 2004a). The role of the Defense Advanced Research Projects Agency (DARPA) in funding application-oriented basic research was legendary—so much so that the U.S. National Academy of Sciences has recently recommended the creation of a DARPA-like agency in energy to ensure the continued competitiveness of American science (NAS 2005).

In *Ireland* and *Finland* universities moved toward the right-hand side of figure 2, becoming more responsive over the past decades. In both cases there had been concern that universities were detached from industry and were unable to meet changing labor market needs (White 2001; OECD 2003). Both governments invested in creating a large group of practically oriented institutions, as described above, but also pushed their universities to become more economically relevant. Investments to create sizable alternatives to universities exerted pressure on universities to become more sensitive to economic needs. In Ireland the government funded the establishment of new technical programs at universities and technical institutions that were considered relevant to industry. In Finland significant public investments were made in strategic areas of R&D, with much emphasis on collaboration between companies and universities (OECD 2003; Dahlman, Routti, and Yla-Anttila 2007; Srinivas and Viljamaa 2008).

Today, Finland has a diverse university sector, with varying levels of university inclination to work with industry. Some universities with a technological orientation or regional development missions are much more active in working with industry and receive much larger shares of funding from the Finnish Funding Agency for Technology and Innovation (TEKES), which provides competitive grants for application-oriented research (Finland, Ministry of Education, 2005).

The Oulu University of Applied Sciences was important in the transformation of Oulu Province from a sleepy backwater to a vibrant high-tech center (Donnelly and Hyry 2004). Established in the 1950s with the specific mission of helping the region develop, the university has been proactive in its choice of disciplinary coverage and responsive in its educational program. An electrical engineering department was established early, well before industrial needs emerged, but the university also responded quickly to meet emerging skills shortages, for instance, in management education (Donnelly and Hyry 2004). The university's responsiveness led to the development of relevant research centers in which both basic and applied research were undertaken, often jointly with industry, and with some academic spin-offs.

In *China* the government has, since the 1980s, been taking steps to reform the higher education system. In retrospect, the measures employed have been remarkably consistent in pushing key universities toward the American relevant research university model (Ma 2007). In the science and technology reform that began in the 1980s, the role of these fields in economic development was strongly emphasized. Public research institutes were to reorient the content of their research to meet economic needs, and universities were to develop research capacity relevant to society, for the first time. The official endorsement did not mean that government funding was forthcoming for research. Although the Chinese National Science Foundation was established in 1986 to provide competitive grants for basic research projects in public research institutions, as well as in universities, university budgets had been cut and were extremely tight. Universities had strong incentives to generate their own incomes through industrial contracting (Ma 2007). This was the context in which universities began to develop a certain responsiveness to industry, through contract research and consulting and by setting up their own enterprises.

The government has also supported the emergence of elite research universities through a series of special programs, from the key university and key laboratory programs in the 1980s to the more famous Projects 211 and 985 in the 1990s, which concentrated government funding on the top 100 and top 9 universities, respectively (Ma 2007). Together with the gradual development of competitive funding for research, these initiatives resulted in strong incentives for universities to be research oriented and compete globally to become world-class institutions (Ma 2007). It is no accident that one of the first global rankings of universities was designed by a Chinese university; Chinese institutions were developing such indicators to gauge their positions in the world.

Moving away from Responsiveness

The path taken by Japanese universities provides an interesting contrast to that in the United States. The starting points in the two countries were similar in that Japan's first university, the University of Tokyo, was developed in the late nineteenth century as a critical instrument for Japan's modernization—specifically, to teach useful scientific knowledge. At the time, the university's structure of having practically oriented faculties such as engineering, agriculture, medicine, and law, along with science and literature, was highly unusual even in global terms (Bartholomew 1989). Other imperial universities were established along the lines of the Tokyo University model, and collectively they helped introduce key technologies and knowledge essential for Japan's early industrialization. University academics and graduates were critical in the birth of many of Japan's technology-oriented enterprises, such as Toyota, Toshiba, and some pharmaceutical companies (Odagiri and Goto 1996). Indeed, Japanese versions of university start-ups are visible in many corporate histories. Large companies habitually sponsored university facilities, and academics actively served as technical consultants (Hashimoto 1999). Even the largest industrial corporations had limited research facilities or capabilities in those days, and university academics undertook application-oriented research that was relevant to the companies.

After World War II, Japanese universities embarked on an evolutionary path toward becoming basic research universities and began to be somewhat removed from industrial development (Hatakenaka forthcoming). In a striking contrast to the United States, where the successful role of science in military technology had reinforced public confidence, Japanese academics moved away from the military-industrial complex (Hatakenaka 2004). When industry began to acquire foreign technology in the 1950s, universities had a minimal role in the process (Hashimoto 1999). In the 1960s, industries recruited their own researchers, often from universities, to establish corporate laboratories (Nakayama 1991), marking the beginning of a new era in which corporate research became a dominant force in industrial innovation (Nakayama 1995). In the late 1960s, student uprisings led to further criticism of university-industry relationships, and a strong sentiment for limiting such relationships prevailed (Hashimoto 1999; Hatakenaka 2004). Institutional mechanisms for working with industry remained underdeveloped under this culture of censorship; the bulk of scientists and engineers were civil servants in national universities, subject to rules that forbade them to consult with industry, and universities lacked the autonomy to create their own rules.

Although individual academics did work with industry, their modes of engagement were distinctly different from those of American universities. Relationships were formed principally by industries doing the legwork of coming to individual academics, extracting information, and making every effort to learn from the universities, in a receiver-active technical transfer model (Kodama and Suzuki 2007). There was surprisingly little interaction between universities and companies concerning the content of education (Dore and Sako 1989), and universities made little organizational effort to work with industry, until recently. Rather, companies expected universities to be no more than a selection mechanism, and they developed in-house capabilities and practices to train graduates in the needed specializations. An important consequence of this system was that Japanese universities did not learn to respond to emerging needs for industrial skills. This detachment increasingly became an issue for industry as it moved into advanced-technology fields, particularly when new industries such as computer software, semiconductors, and biotechnology developed in the 1980s (Baba, Takai, and Mizuta 1996; Darby and Zucker 1996; Kobayashi 2001). In a comparative analysis of Stanford University and the Tokyo Institute of Technology (TIT), curricular change was found to be infrequent and limited in scope at the TIT, whereas at Stanford updating took place organically and almost constantly (Harayama 2001; Hoshino,

Harayama, and Hatatani 2003). The difference appears to reflect different institutional philosophies; the TIT wished to emphasize basic core knowledge essential even in the changing environment, and Stanford had an explicit emphasis on remaining relevant to industrial needs.

The universities' lack of responsiveness was particularly pronounced in research training. Although master's programs in engineering were commonplace by the 1980s, PhD programs in science and engineering remained small and highly academic. Even when these PhD programs expanded in the 1990s, little effort was made to reform the curricular content, and 40 percent of the companies surveyed cited skills mismatch as a reason for not recruiting PhDs (Shimizu and Mori 2001). This was in some ways an inevitable and consistent development, given the corporate personnel practice of recruiting the best and brightest early and training them in-house. Indeed, a form of doctoral training developed in which industrial researchers could submit dissertations to university academics to obtain degrees when their research work was undertaken within industry (Clark 1995).

Developing a Basic Research Orientation

Developing a research capacity of whatever nature is often a difficult step in the evolution of higher education systems. In Korea universities were not very visible in the transition that Korean electronics companies made to high-tech fields such as computers and semiconductors during the 1980s. The reason was the universities' inadequately developed research capacity, a consequence of government underinvestment (Kim 1993, 2000). Korean universities were particularly underresourced in view of the rapid and massive expansion in undergraduate enrollments in the 1970s and 1980s (Kim 1993). The student-staff ratio rose from 23 in 1966 to 36 in 1985 (Kim 1993), and by 1985 nearly half of national and public university revenues came from tuition and fees (KCUE 1990). Even today, Korea's public per-student spending is strikingly low compared with that in other countries (tables 8 and 9). It was not until

TABLE 8. Public Expenditure per Tertiary-Level Student as Percent of GDP per Capita, Selected Countries, Selected Years 1999–2005

Country	1999	2000	2004	2005
China	90	—	—	—
Finland	41	39	37	35
India	—	91	94	58
Ireland	29	31	24	25
Israel	33	32	26	—
Japan	15	18	21	19
Korea, Rep.	8	—	9	—
United States	27	—	23	23

Source: UNESCO database, accessed May 7, 2008.

Note: —, not available. GDP, gross domestic product; UNESCO, United Nations Educational, Scientific, and Cultural Organization.

TABLE 9. Tertiary Education Expenditures as Share of GDP. Selected Countries, Selected Years 1999–2005

Country and type of institution	1999	2000	2004	2005
China				
Private	—	—	—	—
Public	0.4	—	—	—
Total	—	—	—	—
Finland				
Private	—	—	0.1	0.1
Public	1.7	1.7	1.7	1.7
Total	—	1.7	1.8	1.8
India				
Private	—	—	0.2	—
Public	—	0.9	1.0	—
Total	—	0.9	—	—
Ireland				
Private	—	—	—	0.2
Public	1.0	—	0.9	0.9
Total	—	—	—	1.2
Israel				
Private	—	0.9	1.0	—
Public	1.2	1.1	1.0	—
Total	—	2.0	2.0	—
Japan				
Private	0.6	0.6	0.8	0.9
Public	0.5	0.5	0.5	0.5
Total	1.1	1.1	1.3	1.4
Korea, Rep.				
Private	1.7	—	1.9	—
Public	0.4	—	0.5	—
Total	2.2	—	2.3	—
United States				
Private	—	1.7	2.0	2.0
Public	1.1	0.9	1.1	1.1
Total	—	2.6	3.1	3.0

Source: UNESCO database, accessed May 7, 2008.

Note: —, not available. GDP, gross domestic product; UNESCO, United Nations Educational, Scientific, and Cultural Organization. Figures may not sum to totals because of rounding.

the late 1990s, when government for the first time concentrated large amounts of resources in the best institutions for research and graduate education, that research performance began to improve in a significant way (Kim and Nam 2007).

Scarcity of government funding was actually beneficial from the point of view of forcing universities to develop ties with industry. Some of the quoted statistics in Korea indicate a relatively high level of engagement with industry. For instance,

TABLE 10. Academic Research and Development Financed by Industry, Selected OECD Countries, China, and Russian Federation, Selected Years, 1981–2006
(percent)

Year	France	Germany	Japan	Korea, Rep.	United Kingdom	United States	All OECD	China	Russian Federation
1981	1.3	1.8	1.0	—	2.8	4.4	2.9	—	—
1986	2.0	5.8	1.7	—	5.7	6.5	4.5	—	—
1991	4.2	7.0	2.4	—	7.8	6.8	6.0	—	—
1996	3.2	9.2	2.4	50.5	6.7	7.1	6.9	—	23.7
2001	3.1	12.2	2.3	14.3	6.2	6.5	6.4	—	26.5
2002	2.9	11.8	2.8	13.9	5.8	5.8	6.2	—	27.2
2003	2.7	12.6	2.9	13.6	5.6	5.3	6.0	35.9	27.9
2004	2.7	13.2	2.8	15.9	5.1	5.1	6.2	37.1	32.6
2005	—	—	—	15.2	—	5.2	—	36.7	29.3
2006	—	—	—	—	—	5.3	—	—	—

Source: National Science Foundation, Division of Science Resources Statistics, special tabulations, as published in Science and Engineering Indicators 2008.

Note: —, not available. OECD, Organization for Economic Co-operation and Development.

about half of university research was funded by industry in the early 1990s (Kim 2000), and one survey found that nearly half of the companies canvassed had worked with universities (Sohn and Kenney 2007). The industry share of research funding declined in the late 1990s to about 15 percent, presumably reflecting increasing levels of government funding in research (see table 10). Nevertheless, it remains higher than the 6 percent in OECD countries, indicating that industry engagement continues to be important, even if university contributions are not readily acknowledged, and in spite of the poor performance record in proactive measures such as academic spin-offs (Sohn and Kenney 2007).

Some would argue that research orientation was slow to develop in Korean universities because of the historical division of labor whereby public research institutions rather than universities were responsible for research (Lee 2000; Sohn and Kenney 2007). Similar difficulties are encountered in India, where there is a well-established group of public research institutions whose status is higher than that of the universities (Jayaram 2007). The best researchers tend to be recruited into research institutions, leaving universities in a difficult position for developing research capabilities. The fact that the research institutions have no teaching respon-sibilities makes the situation worse in that the best researchers are not contributing to the training of the next generation (Jayaram 2007).

There is no question that public research institutions can be spectacularly success-ful in the development of high-tech industry, as the experience with ERSO in Taiwan, China, shows. It is hard to imagine that similar results could have been obtained in so short a time if similar capacity had been established in a university. Still, the fact that relevant research capacity was concentrated outside universities probably repre-sents a lost opportunity for universities in Taiwan, China, as well.

Finland's experience shows that it is possible to link applied research capacity in public research institutions to universities in a productive way. When Finland made its bid to turn itself into a knowledge economy in the early 1990s, a key component of its policies was large public investment in collaborative R&D among universities, public research institutions, and companies, orchestrated by TEKES (Dahlman, Routti, and Yla-Anttila 2007).

China promoted the research role of universities early on, despite the existence of public research institutions. In the science and technology reform starting in the 1980s, the Chinese government took action both to reorient government research institutions toward becoming economically relevant and to recognize, for the first time, the research role of universities in economic development.

Concluding Remarks

This paper has argued that institutions contribute to the development of high-tech industry in different ways. It has also proposed that their roles are largely determined by characteristics which can be defined on three dimensions: their responsiveness, their basic research orientation, and their selectivity. Enhancing university characteristics along any of these three dimensions can strengthen the nature of the contributions universities make. The more responsive are the universities, the more companies can depend on universities in tailoring academia's research and education contributions to their specific needs. The more the institutions are oriented toward basic research, the better they are able to provide a sophisticated scientific base to enhance the high-technology content of industry. The more selective the universities, the less difficult it is for companies to identify appropriate talents.

The paper also introduced four key types of institutions, using the first two dimensions, responsiveness and basic research orientation. The four are basic research universities, relevant research universities, teaching-focused institutions, and practically oriented institutions. Interestingly, no single type of institution appeared to be essential for starting up high-tech industry; every one of the four types of institution was instrumental in the establishment of high-tech industry in one setting or another. In fact, different university types appear to lead to different shapes and natures of high-tech industry. For instance, the production of high-quality scientists and engineers in large numbers by teaching-focused institutions was sufficient to ensure the availability of cheap, high-caliber labor in India, leading to key production advantages.

Basic research universities help companies equip themselves with key scientific knowledge and well-trained employees in generic science and engineering. But successful companies have to be sufficiently proactive to extract appropriate scientific know-how from universities or to provide further specialized training to employees to ensure their competitiveness.

Practically oriented institutions can provide application-oriented research assistance and specialist training, as needed by industry, and can help companies reduce the costs of in-house research or training. However, they are not able to assist companies in upgrading the scientific content of their work or to provide postgraduate training in emerging fields of science. They can provide institutional support for start-ups, although these are unlikely to be characterized as science based.

Relevant research universities are characterized by their ability to be more directly involved in commercialization of scientific knowledge. These universities can also provide high-level postgraduate training in emerging fields to supply key skills for emerging industry. They tend to develop and attract appropriate ecosystems (such as venture capital and professional support services) for science-based start-ups over time.

Industrial demand for the contributions of universities is likely to become more stringent. Global competitive pressures will demand constant upgrading and redefinition of industry's competitive advantage. Universities will need to provide "higher-order" contributions, and to do so, they will need to move along at least one of the three dimensions. A good supply of cheap generic scientists and engineers may have been enough to start high-tech industry yesterday, but the growth of such industry will lead to higher wages, which in turn will demand redefinition of its competitive advantage. By enhancing responsiveness, basic research orientation, or selectivity, the power of university support to industry can be strengthened.

The paper has also proposed that moving universities along any of the dimensions requires nontrivial effort. Governments can be an important influence in orienting and guiding institutional development, in subtle or not so subtle ways.

Responsiveness does not appear to emerge naturally; in all the cases examined, some specific interventions had occurred to instill the culture of responsiveness, often at the time of founding, and often with government intervention. There is no simple recipe for encouraging institutions to become responsive. The demand to which institutions must be sensitive is often local, intangible, and ill defined. Governments may require that institutions provide new educational programs or expand existing ones, but simply following a top-down requirement does not make an institution responsive. The Korean government's central requirement of maintaining a quota for engineering programs may not have encouraged responsiveness. Indeed, it is possible that the more frequently a government interferes through regulations or even through financial incentives, the less institutions learn to be creative and strategic about what they do. In Ireland and Finland new groups of institutions were established by government from scratch in order to build responsiveness into the system.

Peer pressures and academic norms tend to push universities to become nonresponsive over time—toward becoming basic research universities or academically oriented teaching institutions. On the whole, there appear to be more cases in which institutions developed responsiveness first and then evolved toward a fundamental science orientation than vice versa. (A good example is the Massachusetts Institute of Technology; see Etzkowitz 2002.) It is probably easier to develop in that order than the other way around.

Today, economic responsiveness on the part of universities has become a global mantra. The last decade has seen an ever-increasing number of government policies seeking to push universities to develop such a dimension, and this has led to changes in academic values. For instance, it would be unusual to meet an academic in any OECD country who would contest the need for a university to be economically relevant. Notwithstanding this dynamic change, most institutions have a long way to go toward developing a full set of internal and external mechanisms that are responsive and proactive. The Japanese national universities, for example, are as collaborative with industry as are U.S, ones, but they still lag substantively in proactive commercialization as measured by metrics such as licensing and spin-offs. Indeed, in order for universities to become truly proactive, a whole new set of relationships is likely to be needed, not only with industry but also with other players, ranging from venture capital to proactive research funding bodies. It takes a full ecosystem to enhance the responsiveness of universities. One advantage that developing countries have over old economies may be the potential to develop new institutions that together can make up such a complete system.

Building a *basic research orientation* also requires serious commitment and investment, usually from government. Investments are needed not only in human capital, in the form of advanced research training, but also in infrastructure such as libraries and laboratories, as well as for direct expenses associated with research. A research orientation cannot be developed overnight, but it is difficult to change once introduced; PhD-trained academics usually gravitate toward research rather than teaching, and a sense of elitism is often associated with being research oriented—the more basic, the more elite. Active intervention is usually needed to counter the academic drift away from becoming responsive.

Selectivity is one dimension of higher education institutions that often emerges naturally as the demand for higher education expands and the competition for places increases. However, it needs to be underpinned by robust selection systems that are fair but also provide good learning incentives for future students. This is not easy, but it merits considerable attention, as selection systems can directly influence the reputational hierarchy of institutions, as well as students' learning incentives, for years to come. Some examinations inadvertently encourage students to become oriented toward test-taking tactics rather than learning, and some scoring systems give a spurious impression of accuracy.

The fact that all three dimensions are important in enabling institutions to play key roles does not mean that all institutions must be the same. Because different dimensions bring different advantages, there is a strong case for a variety of institutions, as the experience in the United States and Finland shows. It is reasonable for a national system of higher education to seek to have as much diversity as possible in terms of types of institution.

A historical legacy that the case countries share is some form of national champion of science and technology. The postwar United States was a special place in that policy makers' endorsement of the employment of science for societal benefit led to the development of a whole host of federal funding institutions that supported fundamental science, for different reasons (Geiger 2004a). Similarly, without the highest commitment from Jawaharlal Nehru, India's first postindependence leader, the country's institutes of technology would never have received the extraordinary technical assistance from the United States, the Soviet Union, and Germany that enabled them to develop their high standards. Without the commitment of Deng Xiaoping, the Chinese government would not have devoted so many resources to science and technology, which in turn helped attract the best and the brightest to the field. Such visible support of science and technology at the highest levels helped foster the commitment to science and technology within the society that led students more readily to choose to study these disciplines.

National championship of this kind is not easy to maintain. Science is expensive, and it takes a long time for its impact to be felt. It is easy for commitment to science to give way to fiscal pressures, particularly since it is never clear how much is needed. It is also not easy to cultivate and then maintain the high level of interest within the society that induces students to choose science and engineering. Many OECD countries, including Japan, the United Kingdom, and the United States, are increasingly concerned about the level of interest in science among students. Even in India, there is growing concern that fewer students are choosing a science track.

A final point for reflection is the role of governance arrangements at both the institutional level and the national level. Quality assurance considerations often lead government bodies to become overprescriptive about inputs, as well as being concerned about outputs. This is a significant dilemma in developing countries, where there is little tradition and culture concerning the quality of higher education. Attempts by governments to "control" quality on the basis of inputs can lead to institutions' becoming similar to each other and being passive in defining what they are. To make matters worse, some dimensions are easier to measure than others, which can then result in their being given undue prominence; publications and citations are established metrics for evaluating the productivity and quality of scientific research, but metrics for responsiveness are only just emerging.

Moreover, tight regulatory control by government can be a serious impediment when institutions need to respond to changing needs. Yet the desire for the system to respond to the needs of both labor markets and future students, particularly in dynamically developing countries, often pushes governments to centralize key decisions about the size and direction of the higher education system.

Institutional capacity to respond to complex change is unlikely to develop if institutions do not have autonomy in making strategic decisions. Furthermore, institutions are unlikely to be able to make good strategic decisions without appropriate governance structures and internal processes. The key for the future is to ensure that there are governance arrangements at both the institutional and the system levels that will facilitate and even encourage further evolution of higher education.

References

Baba, Y., S. Takai, and Y. Mizuta. 1996. "The User Driven Evolution of the Japanese Software Industry: The Case of Customized Software for Mainframes." In *The International Computer Software Industry: A Comparative Study of Industry Evolution and Structure,* ed. D. C. Mowery. New York: Oxford University Press.

Bartholomew, James R. 1989. *The Formation of Science in Japan.* New Haven, CT: Yale University Press.

Bresnahan, Timothy F., and Franco Malerba. 1999. "Industrial Dynamics and the Evolution of Firms' and Nations' Competitive Capabilities in the World Computer Industry." In *Sources of Industrial Leadership: Studies of Seven Industries,* ed. David C. Mowery and Richard R. Nelson. Cambridge, U.K.: Cambridge University Press.

Breznitz, Dan. 2004. "The Israeli Software Industry." In *From Underdogs to Tigers: The Rise and Growth of the Software Industry in Brazil, China, India, Ireland, and Israel,* ed. Ashish Arora and Alfonso Gambardella. Oxford, U.K.: Oxford University Press.

———. 2007. *Innovation and the State: Political Choice and Strategies for Growth in Israel, Taiwan and Ireland.* New Haven, CT: Yale University Press.

Chen, Kun, and Martin Kenney. 2007. "Universities/Research Institutes and Regional Innovation Systems: The Cases of Beijing and Schenzhen." *World Development* 35 (6): 1056–74.

Clark, Burton R. 1995. *Places of Inquiry: Research and Advanced Education in Modern Universities.* Berkeley and Los Angeles: University of California Press.

Cohen, W. M., R. R. Nelson, and J. P. Walsh. 2002. "Links and Impact: The Influence of Public Research on Industrial R&D." *Management Science* 48 (1): 1–23.

Dahlman, Carl, Jorma Routti, and Pekka Yla-Anttila. 2007. *Finland as a Knowledge Economy: Elements of Success and Lessons Learned.* Washington, DC: World Bank Institute.

Darby, Michael R., and Lynne G. Zucker. 1996. "Star Scientists, Institutions and the Entry of Japanese Biotechnology Enterprises." NBER Working Paper 5795, National Bureau of Economic Research, Cambridge, MA.

de Fontaney, Catherine, and Erran Carmel. 2004. "Israel's Silicon Wadi: The Forces behind Cluster Formation." In *Building High Tech Clusters: Silicon Valley and Beyond,* ed. Timothy Bresnahan and Alfonso Gambardella. Cambridge, U.K.: Cambridge University Press.

Donnelly, Tom, and Martti Hyry. 2004. "Urban and Regional High Technologies: The Case of Oulu." *Local Economy* 19 (2): 134–49.

Dore, Ronald P., and Mari Sako. 1989. *How the Japanese Learn to Work.* London: Routledge.

Etzkowitz, Henry. 2002. *MIT and the Rise of Entrepreneurial Science.* London: Routledge.

Eun, Jong-Hak, Keun Lee, and Guisheng Wu. 2006. "Explaining University-Run Enterprises in China: A Theoretical Framework for University-Industry Relationship in Developing Countries and Its Application to China." *Research Policy* 35: 1329–46.

Finland, Ministry of Education. 2005. "OECD Thematic Review of Tertiary Education: Country Background Report for Finland." Organisation for Economic Co-operation and Development, Paris.

Geiger, Roger. 2004a. *Research and Relevant Knowledge: American Research Universities since World War II.* New Brunswick, NJ: Transaction Publishers.

———. 2004b. *To Advance Knowledge: The Growth of American Research Universities 1900–1940.* New Brunswick, NJ: Transaction Publishers.

Harayama, Yuko. 2001. "Silicon Valley no sangyo hatten to Stanford daigaku no curriculum hensen" [Silicon Valley's Industrial Development and Curricular Change in Stanford University]. In *Daigaku kaikaku: kadai to souten,* ed. Masahiko Aoki, Akihiko Sawa, and Michio Daito, 31–66. Tokyo: Toyo Keizai Shinposha.

Hashimoto, Takehiko. 1999. "The Hesitant Relationship Reconsidered: University-Industry Cooperation in Postwar Japan." In *Industrializing Knowledge: University-Industry Linkages in Japan and the US,* ed. Lewis Branscomb, Fumio Kodama, and Richard Florida. Cambridge, MA: MIT Press.

Hatakenaka, Sachi. 2004. *University-Industry Partnerships in MIT, Cambridge and Tokyo: Storytelling across Boundaries.* New York: Routledge.

———. Forthcoming. "What's the Point of Universities? The Economic Role of Universities in Japan." *Japan Forum.*

Henderson, Rebecca, Luigi Orsenigo, and Gary P. Pisano. 1999. "The Pharmaceutical Industry and the Revolution in Molecular Biology: Interactions among Scientific, Institutional and Organizational Change." In *Sources of Industrial Leadership: Studies of Seven*

Industries, ed. David Mowery and Richard Nelson. Cambridge, U.K.: Cambridge University Press.

Hicks, Diana. 1993. "University-Industry Research Links in Japan." *Policy Sciences* 26: 361–95.

Hoshino, Yu, Yuko Harayama, and Shigeo Hatatani. 2003. "Daigaku no gaibu henka heno taio sei" [Responsiveness of Universities to External Change]. In *Sangaku Renkei,* ed. Yuko Harayama. Tokyo: Toyo Keizai Shinposha.

Hou, Chi-Ming, and San Gee. 1993. "National Systems Supporting Technical Advance in Industry: The Case of Taiwan." In *National Innovation Systems: A Comparative Analysis,* ed. Richard R. Nelson. New York: Oxford University Press.

Japan, MEXT (Ministry of Education, Culture, Science, and Technology). 2006. *Monbuka-gakutokeiyoran.* Tokyo: Ministry of Finance Press.

Jayaram, N. 2007. "Beyond Retailing Knowledge: Prospects of Research-Oriented Universities in India." In *World Class Worldwide: Transforming Research Universities in Asia and Latin America,* ed. Philip G. Altbach and Jorge Balán. Baltimore, MD: Johns Hopkins University Press.

Juahiainen, Jussi S. 2006. "Multipolis: High-Technology Network in Northern Finland." *European Planning Studies* 14 (10): 1407–28.

Kapur, Devesh. 2002. "The Causes and Consequences of India's IT Boom." *India Review* 1 (2): 91–110.

Kapur, Devesh, and John McHale. 2005. "Sojourns and Software: International Mobile Human Capital and High Tech Industry Development in India, Ireland and Israel." In *From Underdogs to Tigers: The Rise and Growth of the Software Industry in Brazil, China, India, Ireland, and Israel,* ed. Ashish Arora and Alfonso Gambardella. Oxford, U.K.: Oxford University Press.

KCUE (Korean Council for University Education). 1990. *Korean Higher Education: Its Development, Aspects and Prospects.* Seoul: KCUE.

Kim, Ki-Seok, and Sunghee Nam. 2007. "The Making of a World-Class University at the Periphery." In *World Class Worldwide: Transforming Research Universities in Asia and Latin America,* ed. Philip G. Altbach and Jorge Balán. Baltimore, MD: Johns Hopkins University Press.

Kim, Limsu. 1993. "National System of Industrial Innovation: Dynamics of Capability Building in Korea." In *National Innovation Systems: A Comparative Analysis,* ed. Richard R. Nelson. New York: Oxford University Press.

———. 2000. "Korea's National Innovation System in Transition." In *Technology, Learning And Innovation: Experiences of Newly Industrializing Economies,* ed. Limsu Kim and Richard R. Nelson. Cambridge, U.K.: Cambridge University Press.

Kobayashi, Shinichi. 2001. "Daigaku kyoiku no shokugyoteki relevance to daigaku no soshiki sekkei" [Relevance of University Education to Work and Organizational Design]. In *Daigaku kaikaku: kadai to souten,* ed. Masahiko Aoki, Akihiko Sawa, and Michio Daito. Tokyo: Toyo Keizai Shinposha.

Kodama, Fumio, and Jun Suzuki. 2007. "How Japanese Companies Have Used Scientific Advances to Restructure Their Businesses: The Receiver-Active National System of Innovation." *World Development* 35 (6): 976–90.

Kroll, Henning, and Ingo Leifner. 2008. "Spin-Off Enterprises as Means of Technology Commercialisation in a Transforming Economy—Evidence from Three Universities in China." *Technovation* 28: 293–313.

Lee, Won-Young. 2000. "The Role of Science and Technology Policy in Korea's Industrial Development." In *Technology, Learning and Innovation: Experiences of Newly Industrializing Economies,* ed. Limsu Kim and Richard R. Nelson. Cambridge, U.K.: Cambridge University Press.

Leifner, Ingo, and Daniel Schiller. 2008. "Academic Capabilities in Developing Countries: A Conceptual Framework with Empirical Illustrations from Thailand." *Research Policy* 37: 276–93.

Lester, Richard K. 2005. "Universities, Innovation, and the Competitiveness of Local Economies: Summary Report from the Local Innovation Systems Project—Phase I." MIT IPC Working Paper 05-010, Industrial Performance Center, Massachusetts Institute of Technology, Cambridge, MA.

Lin, Tin-Chun. 2004. "The Role of Higher Education in Economic Development: An Empirical Study of Taiwan Case." *Journal of Asian Economics* 15 (2): 355–71.

Ma, Wanhua. 2007. "The Flagship University and China's Economic Reform." In *World Class Worldwide: Transforming Research Universities in Asia and Latin America,* ed. Philip G. Altbach and Jorge Balán. Baltimore, MD: Johns Hopkins University Press.

Mazzoleni, Roberto, and Richard R. Nelson. 2007. "Public Research Institutions and Economic Catch Up." *Research Policy* 36 (10, December): 1512–28.

Mowery, David C. 1999. "The Computer Software Industry." In *Sources of Industrial Leadership: Studies of Seven Industries,* ed. David C. Mowery and Richard R. Nelson. Cambridge, U.K.: Cambridge University Press.

Mowery, David, Richard R. Nelson, Bhaven N. Sampat, and Arvids A. Ziedonis. 2004. *Ivory Tower and Industrial Innovation: University-Industry Technology Transfer before and after the Bayh-Dole Act.* Stanford, CA: Stanford University Press.

Nakayama, Shigeru. 1991. *Science, Technology and Society in Postwar Japan.* Japanese Studies Series. London: Kegan Paul International.

———. 1995. *Kagaku gijutsu no sengoshi.* Tokyo: Iwanami Shoten.

NAS (National Academy of Sciences). 2005. *Rising above the Gathering Storm: Energizing and Employing America for a Brighter Economic Future.* Washington, DC: National Academies Press.

Odagiri, Hiroyuki, and Akira Goto. 1996. *Technology and Industrial Development in Japan: Building Capabilities by Learning, Innovation and Public Policy.* Oxford, U.K.: Oxford University Press.

OECD (Organisation for Economic Co-operation and Development). 2003. *Reviews of National Policies for Education: Polytechnic Education in Finland.* Paris: OECD.

Pechter, Kenneth, and Sumio Kakinuma. 1999. "Co-authorship Linkages between University Research and Japanese Industry." In *Industrializing Knowledge: University-Industry Linkages in Japan and the US,* ed. Lewis Branscomb, Fumio Kodama, and Richard Florida, 102–27. Cambridge, MA: MIT Press.

Roper, Stephen, and Seamus Grimes. 2005. "Wireless Valley, Silicon Wadi and Digital Island—Helsinki, Tel Aviv and Dublin and the ICT Global Production Network." *Geoforum* 36: 297–313.

Rosenberg, Nathan, and Richard Nelson. 1994. "American Universities and Technical Advance in Industry." *Research Policy* 23: 323–48.

Sands, Anita. 2005. "The Irish Software Industry." In *From Underdogs to Tigers: The Rise and Growth of the Software Industry in Brazil, China, India, Ireland, and Israel,* ed. Ashish Arora and Alfonso Gambardella. Oxford, U.K.: Oxford University Press.

Saxenian, AnnaLee. 1999. *Silicon Valley's New Immigrant Entrepreneurs.* San Francisco: Public Policy Institute of California.

———. 2004. "Taiwan's Hsinchu Region: Imitator and Partner for Silicon Valley." In *Building High-Tech Clusters: Silicon Valley and Beyond,* ed. Timothy Bresnahan and Alfonso Gambardella. Cambridge, U.K.: Cambridge University Press.

———. 2006. *The New Argonauts: Regional Advantage in a Global Economy.* Cambridge, MA: Harvard University Press.

Saxenian, AnnaLee, Yasuyuki Motoyama, and Xiaohong Quan. 2002. *Local and Global Networks of Immigrant Professionals in Silicon Valley.* San Francisco: Public Policy Institute of California.

Shimizu, Kiyoyuki, and Kazuhiro Mori. 2001."Nihon no rikokei daigakuinkyoiku no bapponteki kaikaku" [Fundamental Reform for Graduate Schools in Japan]. In *Daigaku kaikaku: kadai to souten,* ed. Masahiko Aoki, Akihiro Sawa, and Michio Daito. Tokyo: Toyo Keizai Shinposha.

Sohn, Dong-Won, and Martin Kenney. 2007. "Universities, Clusters, Innovation Systems: The Case of Seoul, Korea." *World Development* 35 (6): 991–1004.

Srinivas, Smita, and Kimmo Viljamaa. 2008. "Emergence of Economic Institutions: Analysing the Third Role of Universities in Turku, Finland." *Regional Studies* 42 (3): 323–41.

Stokes, Donald E. 1997. *Pasteur's Quadrant: Basic Science and Technological Innovation.* Washington, DC: Brookings Institution Press.

Thursby, Jerry G., and Marie C. Thursby. 2007. "University Licensing." *Oxford Review of Economic Policy* 23 (4): 620–39.

Trajtenberg, Manuel. 2001. "Innovation in Israel 1968–1997: A Comparative Analysis Using Patent Data." *Research Policy* 30: 363–89.

Wade, Robert. 1990. *Governing the Market: Economic Theory and the Role of Government in East Asian Industrialization.* Princeton, NJ: Princeton University Press.

Wadhwa, Vivek, AnnaLee Saxenian, Ben Rissing, and Gary Gereffi. 2007. "America's New Immigrant Entrepreneurs: Part I." Duke Science, Technology and Innovation Paper 23, Master of Engineering Management Program, Pratt School of Engineering, Duke University, Durham, NC.

Weidman, John C., and Namgi Park. 2000. *Higher Education in Korea: Tradition and Adaptation.* New York: Falmer Press.

White, Tony. 2001. *Investing in People: Higher Education in Ireland from 1960–2000.* Dublin: Institute of Public Administration.

Wu, Weiping. 2007. "Cultivating Research Universities and Industrial Linkages in China: The Case of Shanghai." *World Development* 35 (6): 1075–93.

Yoshihara, Mariko, and Katsuya Tamai. 1999. "Lack of Incentives and Persisting Constraints: Factors Hindering Technology Transfer at Japanese Universities." In *Industrializing Knowledge: University-Industry Linkages in Japan and the US,* ed. Lewis Branscomb, Fumio Kodama, and Richard Florida, 348–64. Cambridge, MA: MIT Press.

Yusuf, Shahid, and Kaoru Nabeshima. 2007. *How Universities Promote Economic Growth.* Washington, DC: World Bank.

Zhou, Ji. 2005. *Higher Education in China.* Singapore: Thomson Learning.

Zucker, Lynn G., and Michael R. Darby. 1996. "Star Scientists and Institutional Transformation: Patterns of Invention and Innovation in the Formation of the Biotechnology Industry." Proceedings of the National Academy of Sciences 93 (23): 12709–116.

Zucker, Lynne G., Michael R. Darby, and Jeff S. Armstrong. 2002. "Commercializing Knowledge: University Science, Knowledge Capture and Firm Performance in Biotechnology." *Management Science* 48 (1): 138–53.

Zucker, Lynne G., Michael R. Darby, and Marilyn B. Brewer. 1998. "Intellectual Human Capital and the Birth of US Biotechnology Enterprises." *American Economic Review* 88 (1): 290–306.

Comment on "The Role of Higher Education in High-Technology Industrial Development: What Can International Experience Tell Us?" by Sachi Hatakenaka

ERIK SANDER

Over the last 20 years, technology-based multinational corporations (MNCs) and small and medium-size enterprises (SMEs) have increasingly looked to universities to undertake basic research that spawns breakthrough products for the future. This is research that companies are either not equipped to undertake themselves or are unable to fund internally, given their focus on near-term product development that has an impact on the bottom line. Concurrently, high-technology industry across the globe continues to rely on universities to produce an employee population that can be drawn on to fill company pipelines with highly skilled professionals who can contribute to the company's profitability quickly and with less postrecruitment training.

In this paper, Hatakenaka provides a strong foundation for discussing the diverse history of government-university-industry collaboration mechanisms across international borders and highlights the complex variables and key motivators affecting how these groups work together. Essentially, the particular characteristics of each university, company, and government entity are crucial to how these collaborations have grown (or have failed to grow substantially) in various settings. Whereas in some countries, such as Japan, industries have focused on the academic role of screening and providing foundational training for future long-term employees, in other countries, such as the United States, they have taken a broader viewpoint toward leveraging academic research and educational resources to build the company's technology and employee pipelines. Viewed globally, government-university-industry collaborations can be seen as a jumble of disjointed education, research, and outreach programs. Nevertheless, Hatakenaka clearly identifies the salient variables and motivational factors that determine how these collaborations have been birthed and have grown in different countries.

The themes of organizational characteristics and responsiveness arise several times in Hatakenaka's discussion of global government-university-industry collaboration

Erik Sander is director of industry programs, University of Florida College of Engineering, Gainesville.

Annual World Bank Conference on Development Economics 2009, Global

models. It can be instructive to extend and reframe these points through a brief discussion of such collaborations from the perspective of cultural barriers and issues, not only across geographic borders, but also across the cultural borders of the government, academic, and private sectors.

Support for Higher Education

One could argue that a key to understanding what drives culture and motivation within higher education is a grasp of the support mechanisms for an institute's research and education mission. In general, many U.S. universities are recognized as having built strong industrial relations through research and education programs, and so it is sensible to study the U.S. system as a baseline for understanding the broader global environment for the effect of universities on high-technology industries across borders.

As illustrated in figure 1 and discussed by Hatakenaka, U.S. university research has grown substantially since World War II, primarily in response to new government funding programs established to advance the technological and manufacturing capabilities of U.S. industry. Beginning with relatively minuscule funding levels in the 1950s, federal support of U.S. university research today spans myriad government agencies providing more than US$40 billion (in constant 2000 dollars) to assist virtually every field of scientific advancement. U.S. research-intensive universities have grown reliant on federal support, which typically funds more than 60 percent of a university's research base (NSF 2008).

Government funding agencies have their individual funding profiles; for example, whereas the Defense Advanced Research Projects Agency (DARPA) tends to fund later stages of research and is, not surprisingly, oriented toward defense applications, the National Institutes of Health (NIH) emphasizes the discovery phase. Nevertheless, the greatest part of government support for university research is targeted toward basic research, which is focused on knowledge discovery rather than on specific, predetermined market applications. The government typically seeds next-generation discoveries, some of which industry can ultimately take to market. This prevalence of government basic research funding dovetails well with university researchers' quest for basic knowledge. The result is that 75 percent of U.S. university research is defined as basic. There is a stark contrast with the profile of high-technology industry research, only 4 percent of which is categorized as basic (NSF 2008). High-technology industry is driven by market economics to direct its internal resources toward applied research and development; it is focused on meeting a specific market need through development of a product or service and its underlying technology.

As Hatakenaka rightly notes, the U.S. government funds basic research at higher education institutions to provide the foundation for fundamental technology breakthroughs for next-generation corporate products—thus establishing a key role for U.S. universities in the overall advancement of technology today and in the future. Universities in several other countries draw a much greater proportion of their funding from industry. For instance, Hatakenaka observes that industry supports more than

FIGURE 1.
Funding Sources for U.S. University Research

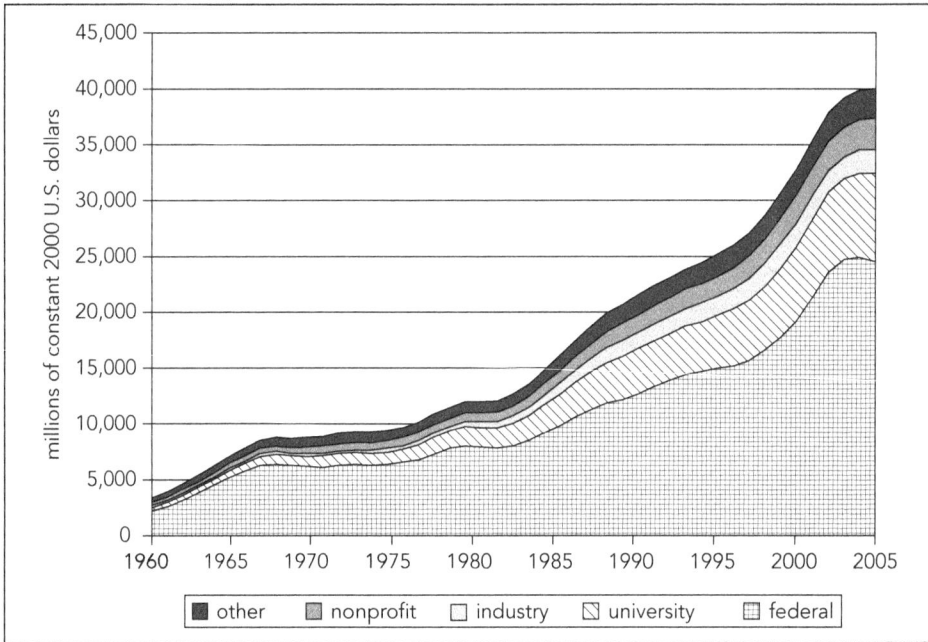

Source: NSF 2008.

30 percent of university research in China and Russia, although one could question whether this is because of greater industry involvement or less government support.

Transitioning the Valley of Death

Industry's own development of next-generation technology advances must ultimately span the continuum of basic research to applied research and development, although companies in different societies have made conscious decisions as to where they choose to focus in that spectrum. For example, Hatakenaka points out that industry in some countries, including China, has historically chosen to focus on development of new applications of existing technologies, whereas countries such as the United States have distributed resources across the entire spectrum. Whichever model of industrial product development is chosen, one common theme drives resource allocation: a market pull for the technologies being developed. This market pull, entailing a focus on customer needs in research and in product and service design and development, can produce an efficient allocation of research and development (R&D) resources, but sometimes at the cost of discovery of next-generation technologies to underpin future product lines—essentially, the basic research element.

Government-university-industry research collaborations provide an alternate means of technology development whereby the government funds next-generation,

FIGURE 2.
Bridging the Technological "Valley of Death"

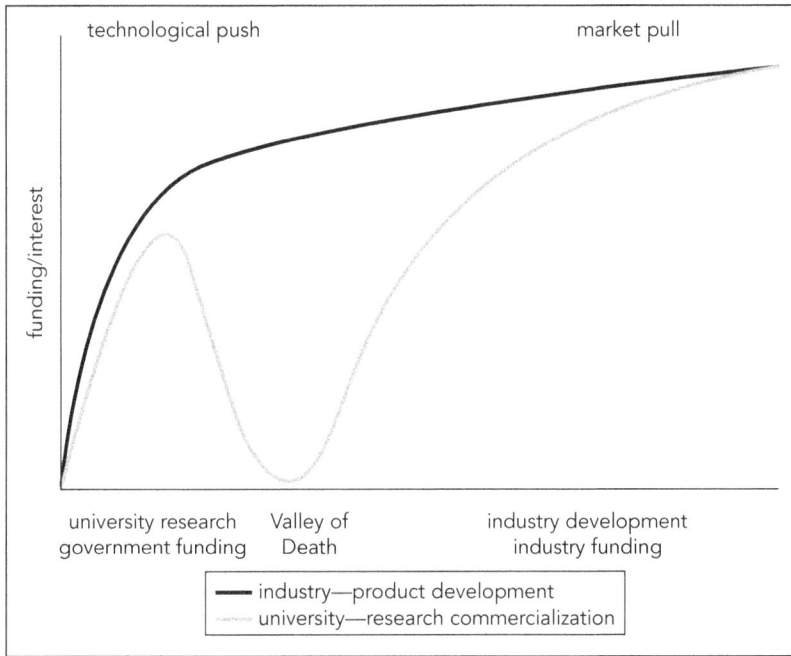

Source: Author's elaboration.

high-risk basic research in universities. Often, however, the greatest challenge is to find a home for these technologies in industry. This transition point can be difficult to negotiate because the technology is sometimes too far along for further significant government funding and university development but is not sufficiently developed and risk mitigated to attract substantial industry interest in adoption or funding.

Successful government-university-industry research collaborations require the bridging of what has been commonly termed the Valley of Death—the point in a technology's life cycle at which the research is transitioning from an academic basic research program to an applied industrial development program (figure 2). The challenge usually revolves around (a) the university's further development, and therefore risk mitigation, of the technology, perhaps to the point of a demonstrable prototype or initial clinical trials, and (b) industry's willingness to adopt earlier-stage technologies through funding and licensing.

This analytical approach can also be applied to the educational mission of higher education if one considers the output of the collaborative process to be university students/company recruits. Although most students do not fall into a true Valley of Death in the same way that university technologies may completely fail to make the transition to the private sector, there is an analogous problem of how best to fill the educational gap between the basic science knowledge of academia and the more specialized knowledge of industry. Kapur and Crowley (2008) raise an important question: is the purpose of higher education to train people for a labor force, or to train a labor force that is in turn trainable by employers? Hatakenaka points out that industry addresses the issue of educational roles through a variety of models across national borders. For instance, Japanese industry has historically relied on universities' stringent screening and selection processes for admission and basic preparation and has, for its part, focused on downstream training of employees who spend most of their careers with a single company. By contrast, U.S. technological MNCs have typically relied on universities to provide a greater share of future employees' training within the academic environment. These two models bridge the educational Valley of Death from different directions—academic and industrial. As in technology development, the salient point concerns which group takes the lead in refining the raw product (the student or new employee).

Whether research or education is under discussion, efficient bridging of the gap between academia and industry can prove critical for achieving an economic impact through production of high-value employees, products, and services. Hatakenaka makes that clear.

Bridging Cultural Barriers to Collaboration

The value perceived by all parties to these potential collaborations would seem to sow the seeds for natural partnerships between government funding sources, institutes of higher education, and high-technology industry that seek to fill product pipelines and researcher ranks in the most efficient manner possible. The question then is, why do strong government-university-industry collaborations not form more naturally across international borders? Hatakenaka makes an excellent case that this process is more complex than would appear at first glance. She identifies a number of barriers that she categorizes mostly along the lines of institutional characteristics and responsiveness.

A complementary perspective is that of a cultural spectrum spanning the wide range between institutes of higher education and MNCs, with technology SMEs often caught in the middle. Although it is dangerous to generalize, figure 3 illustrates some of the primary cultural barriers that naturally exist between the academic framework of open

FIGURE 3.
Cultural Barriers to Collaboration between Universities and Industry

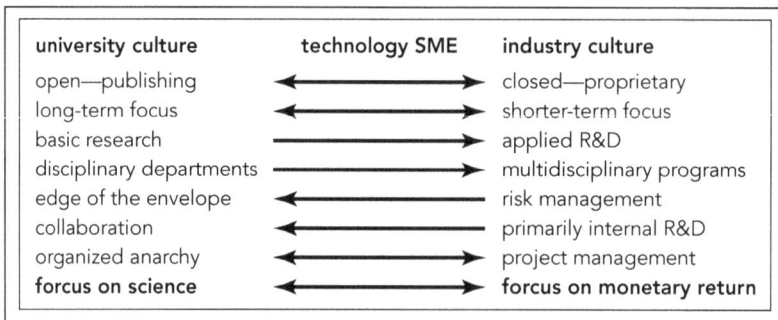

Source: Author's elaboration.

Note: SME, small and medium-size enterprise; R&D, research and development.

discourse and the more focused and proprietary company environment. It is readily seen that the cultural gaps between universities, small technology-based companies, and large industry players can be manifested in definitive ways that affect collaboration potential, such as timeframes (semesters versus weeks), focus (basic versus applied research), management (decentralized versus hierarchical and project driven), and bottom-line emphasis (discovery versus profits and shareholder value). The challenge, many times, is to overcome these cultural barriers and make full use of university, private sector, and government resources to maximize ultimate economic impact.

There are multiple avenues for higher education-industry engagement, as described by Hatakenaka, but not all universities and not all companies and governments are equipped to take advantage of them. Hatakenaka describes this relationship building in terms of responsiveness to meeting industry needs and notes that it succeeds only if it serves the university, industry, and, ultimately, the government sources that provide substantial support to the academic system. Box 1 surveys the numerous potential avenues of interaction between the industrial and academic sectors. The list is not meant to be

---

BOX 1. Pathways for Interaction between Higher Education and High-Technology Industry

Leveraging research assets
Technology licensing
Industry-sponsored research
Joint research
Facility usage agreements
Technology donations

Leveraging researcher assets
Industrial advisory boards
Faculty sabbaticals
Faculty consulting
Visiting industry researchers

Leveraging educational assets
Publications
Alumni networks
Distance education
Lifelong learning
Short courses, seminars, and conferences

Leveraging student assets
Proactive student recruitment
Student internships/cooperative education
Student scholarships

Source: Author's elaboration.

all-inclusive, but the point is that there are myriad ways in which higher education and high-technology industry can establish mutually beneficial relationships.

As Hatakenaka discusses, across national borders, industry does not engage equally with higher education institutions through all avenues, and not all academic units are equally equipped to respond fully to all high-technology companies. For instance, U.S. firms are more likely to have engaged in multiple avenues of collaboration, including technology licensing and industry-sponsored research; Japanese firms have historically not taken advantage of some of these university capabilities but have focused on others, such as student recruitment and in-house training. Even this situation is changing, as Japan is now entering an era of university spin-offs and technology commercialization catalyzed by government programs.

Global Best Practices in Public-Private Partnerships

The U.S. Science and Technology Policy Institute, with funding from the National Science Foundation (NSF), recently conducted a best practices study of government-university-industry partnerships worldwide to aid understanding of the various collaboration mechanisms (Lal et al. 2007). A team of institute personnel and various domain experts studied and visited more than 40 public-private partnerships in nine countries. The study focused on five areas of inquiry: program-level vision; center-level organization; industry partnerships; international partnerships; and engineering education. In the research domain, the study confirmed Hatakenaka's broad model of responsiveness. Even within a given country—for example, Germany—the basic research focus of, say, the Max Planck Institutes stands out in contrast to the Fraunhofer Institutes' focus on applied research in close collaboration with industry partners. In the United Kingdom, the Warwick University Manufacturing Group, which is very industrially focused and does outstanding applied research, provides another excellent example of Hatakenaka's model of responsiveness to industrial R&D needs. An outstanding mixed model is Belgium's International Microelectronics Center (IMEC), which has established a robust model of working closely with a large population of MNCs and SMEs through a multitiered association model (see figure 4).

In each of these examples, it is important to point out that the technology development spectrum discussed earlier is not isolated from the student development spectrum. Students in application-oriented academic centers typically work closely with industrial researchers and are well prepared to make significant contributions as employees of the company or industry. What is untested is whether those students are better prepared in the longer term for a broader spectrum of careers.

Conclusion

Hatakenaka provides an excellent foundation for exploring the myriad relationships among government agencies, higher education institutions, and high-technology industry across national borders. Her parsing of higher education institutions and high-technology industry by their historical interactions is exemplary and provides a

FIGURE 4.
Differences in Focus among Public-Private Partnerships, Selected Countries:
Findings from a Survey

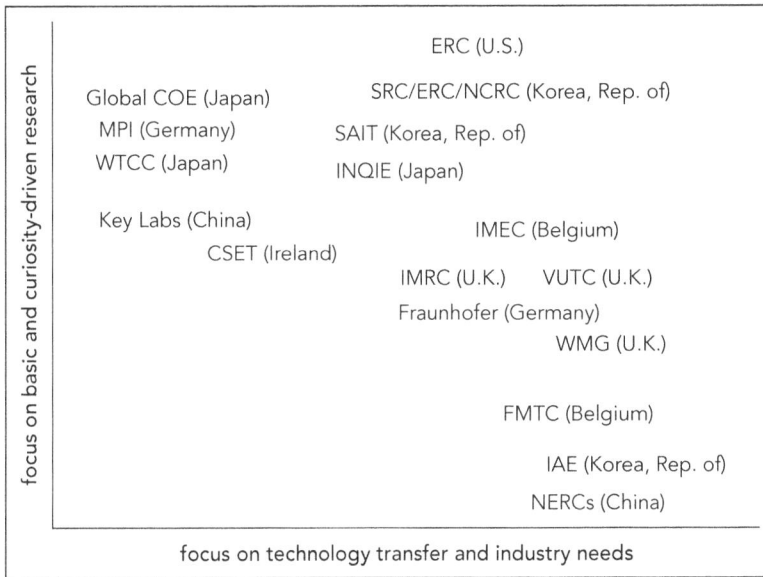

Source: Lal et al. 2007.

Note: The institutions shown in the figure are research partnerships in the countries named. The partnerships mentioned in the text are the International Microelectronics Center (IMEC), the Max Planck Institutes (MPI), the Fraunhofer Institutes (Fraunhofer), and the Warwick University Manufacturing Group (WMG).

framework for an expanded discussion of the role of higher education and high-technology industry cultures in establishing collaborative relationships. Inherent culture is a critical variable driving the influence of higher education on high-technology industry, and vice versa, and Hatakenaka rightly points out that collaborative mechanisms are varied and differ across borders. There is much that can be added to this discussion, and Hatakenaka has supplied an important first step in a field of study that has until now not gained the attention it deserves. Further studies can profoundly reshape these models of collaboration between higher education and high-technology industry to the benefit of the global economy, especially in the developing world.

References

Kapur, Devesh, and Megan Crowley. 2008. "Beyond the ABCs: Higher Education and Developing Countries." Working Paper 139, Center for Global Development, Washington, DC.

Lal, Bhavya, Craig Boardman, Nate Deshmukh Towery, Jamie Link, and Stephanie Shipp. 2007. *Designing the Next Generation of NSF Engineering Research Centers: Insights from Worldwide Practice.* Washington, DC: U.S. Science and Technology Policy Institute.

NSF (National Science Foundation). 2008. "NSF Science and Engineering Indicators." NSF, Washington, DC.

African Higher Education and Industry: What Are the Linkages?

AKILAGPA SAWYERR AND BOUBAKAR BARRY

Productive linkages between higher education and industry presuppose the existence of institutions able to prepare skilled technical personnel and to produce and transfer innovative, industry-relevant research and technology. The necessary counterpart is industry hungry for new knowledge and technology and prepared to invest in developing or acquiring it.

Weaknesses on both sides are evident in Sub-Saharan Africa. Higher education has suffered from years of neglect and underfunding and is generally considered to be oriented away from science and technology. Although there are signs of a revival, overall, higher education, particularly as regards science and technology research, is not up to the task of lifting African industry to a globally competitive level.

On the other side, high-technology industry is largely absent in the region. This paper consequently focuses on small and medium-size industry, which is important for Africa's immediate future. But given the lack of steady pressure to acquire new knowledge and technology so as to remain competitive, there is little demand from this sector for industry-relevant research by knowledge institutions.

Part of the solution to this impasse must lie in a policy framework and material interventions aimed at boosting research capacity and industrial development in priority areas while at the same time providing appropriate bridging mechanisms and supportive fiscal and other incentives. There is also scope for regional and continental collaboration to harvest economies of scale.

Massive transformations in global communication, production and management in the second half of the twentieth century placed knowledge and its applications at the center of economic and social development in all parts of the world by

Akilagpa Sawyerr is a former secretary-general of the Association of African Universities. Boubakar Barry is coordinator of the Research and Education Networking Unit, Association of African Universities. Ransford Bekoe, assistant project officer in the Office of the Secretary-General, Association of African Universities, provided substantial research support in the preparation of this paper.

Annual World Bank Conference on Development Economics 2009, Global
© 2010 The International Bank for Reconstruction and Development / The World Bank

integrating the generation and application of advanced knowledge into material and cultural production to an extent unknown in history. This evolution has given added significance to systems and institutions for knowledge production. The spectacular economic and social developments of recent decades, especially in the newly industrializing countries of Southeast Asia, have gone hand in hand with rapid and substantial expansion of higher education and skills training. Although the exact character of the nexus between knowledge production and economic and social development remains unclear, there is little doubt about its existence or about its reciprocal nature, with knowledge production and the conditions and operations of the productive sectors of economy and society influencing each other.

To introduce our examination of one aspect of this general question, we first briefly review the key features of linkages between higher education and industry and the conditions for their success. This will set the background for the examination and assessment of the specific case of Africa.

Channels and Conditions of Interaction

Although there is no reason to expect all kinds of industry to interact with the knowledge production process in exactly the same way, even in the same country, the general pathways of interaction are clear. On the side of knowledge production institutions, the contribution to industry takes a variety of forms and moves through a variety of channels (see Brennenraedts, Bekkers, and Verspagen 2006, 4).[1] The main ones are

- Preparation of well-educated technical graduates, ensuring a cadre of skilled and trainable personnel for industry, especially in the fields of science, engineering, and management
- Pursuit of fundamental as well as applications-oriented research that produces industrially relevant new knowledge, including management science
- Direct generalized transmission of research products through publications, patents, prototypes, and the like
- Direct targeted transmission through conferences, workshops, meetings, networks, and other formal and informal interactions
- Indirect transmission in the course of collaborative ventures and exchanges of personnel
- Transmission under commercial arrangements such as research contracts, licenses, and consultancies.

With regard to the provision of skilled cadres, the outcome turns, in the first instance, on the number, variety, and quality of technical graduates produced by the education and training system and available for absorption into industry as managers, skilled and semiskilled technical workers, and researchers. Equally significant for successful linkage, although often ignored, is the capacity (or otherwise) of industry to absorb the products of the universities and training institutions and put them to productive use.

For meaningful interaction around the production of knowledge and its injection into industry, there needs to be (a) a basis for interaction, namely, relevant knowledge and awareness of the need for it; (b) a disposition for productive engagement; and (c) a supportive policy framework.

Capable Knowledge Producers

In the absence of knowledge institutions with both the capability to produce usable knowledge and the orientation and ability to transfer it to industry, the supply side will be absent or weak. Thus, the higher education and training system must have the capability and flexibility to produce and supply technical graduates on a suitable scale and in fields relevant to industry and its evolving needs. Such graduates will staff the managerial and technical levels of industry and, in the case of small and medium-size industry, even provide entrepreneurial leadership. To meet the special needs of high-technology industry, these graduates must include a substantial proportion of PhDs in mathematics and the various branches of engineering to ensure high-level appreciation of emerging technologies and the possibilities for innovation.

Even more than in the supply and absorption of graduates, the linkage between higher education and industry is often perceived in the production of knowledge and its injection into production and management as a basis for technological and managerial innovation. A key condition for this is the capacity of the knowledge production centers, through cutting-edge as well as applications-oriented research, to produce usable new knowledge and new applications. Institutions that lack high-quality research capability thus have no part in such interactions. Yet the capacity to produce the relevant knowledge is not sufficient; it must be combined with the appropriate orientation and the ability to transmit knowledge to potential users. Academic institutions, through the publication of research findings, through conference presentations, and through the taking out of patents, do much of this in the normal course of their work. The critical factor is to go beyond this and engage in more deliberate and targeted transmission to industry and other potential users of the research product or, indeed, to pursue coproduction of knowledge with users. Modes of targeted transmission include workshops, meetings, networks, and other formal and informal interactions; collaborative ventures and exchanges of personnel between industry and knowledge centers; and commercial arrangements such as research contracts, licenses, and consultancies (Brennenraedts, Bekkers, and Verspagen 2006, 15–16). To help discharge this extension function effectively, institutions frequently provide special incentives to their staffs and set up specific structures, such as consultancy or commercialization units.

Receptive Industry

For its part, industry must adopt a posture of active receptiveness for there to be successful interaction. Where industry feels no need for new knowledge or technology, or is unwilling or unable to invest time or resources in its acquisition, there will be no effective demand for locally produced knowledge and technology. There must be a perception of need, recognition that the proffered or potential knowledge products will meet that need, and preparedness to invest in the acquisition of such products. In the case of skilled technical and managerial cadres, this is usually not a problem—certainly not for high-technology and medium-size enterprises, which need such cadres if they are to be minimally effective. In relation to the acquisition of knowledge, however, a distinction is usually drawn between, on the one hand, high-technology industries and enterprises engaged in the export of manufactures, which need such knowledge in order to raise their productivity and international competitiveness, and, on the other hand, small, low-technology enterprises, which do not perceive such a need. In the latter instance, the absence of a technology culture—which develops out of the pressure for constant updating and deepening of technology in order to survive competition—means that there is little disposition to invest in the acquisition of new knowledge for upgrading or adapting current technology beyond what is embodied in new machinery and equipment (World Bank 2009).

Even in the case of high-technology producers and export-oriented manufacturers, whether and under what conditions they will engage with local knowledge producers for needed knowledge depends on several factors. For local branches of transnational enterprises, the primary source of research and new technology is the parent company and its branches and affiliates, rendering marginal any local knowledge production capacity, a situation that often applies in Africa. In other instances, a good deal turns on the existence or otherwise of a technology culture, as well as the degree to which local knowledge producers are perceived as credible partners from whom to procure knowledge or with whom to collaborate in the coproduction of knowledge. As will be seen from the consideration of the case material, the lack of these preconditions constitutes a major barrier to higher education–industry linkages in Sub-Saharan Africa.

An element that runs through all discussion of higher education–industry linkages is the importance of proactiveness on both sides. Universities and research centers must provide incentives and set up structures aimed at promoting and facilitating linkages with industry, even as industry must be actively receptive. There is evidence, however, that, even though university interest is essential for engagement, successful linkages have come into being and have survived principally through the commitment of industry and its investment of time and resources in specific linkage arrangements, whether by seeking collaboration, commissioning research, setting up an incubator or a research laboratory in a university or center, receiving student interns, or releasing staff as adjuncts to institutions. Indeed, it may be stated with some force that *without vibrant industry driven by the pressure to increase productivity and lower costs in order to thrive in a fiercely competitive, usually export, market, the drive to innovate through the application of new knowledge and new technology remains weak, and recourse to knowledge institutions for support or collaboration is highly unlikely.*[2] In such conditions, the response to overtures from the knowledge institutions is bound to be lukewarm, at best. This must go a long way toward explaining why the many university-initiated measures aimed at promoting and facilitating linkages with industry have not achieved long-term success (see box 1 and the accompanying text).

BOX 1. Selected Examples of University-Industry Partnerships in Africa

Makerere University, Uganda

- The Uganda Gatsby Trust, based at Makerere's Faculty of Technology, is a not-for profit entity established in 1994 with seed funding from the Gatsby Charitable Foundation (GCF) in the United Kingdom. The trust seeks to support manufacturing and value-adding businesses with growth potential. Its activities include training courses, business development services, student internships, technology development and transfer, and a business park.
- The Makerere University Private Sector Forum serves as a platform for interaction between the university and the private sector, with the mission of encouraging support for university programs and promoting entrepreneurship training, joint research, curriculum review, technology innovation and transfer, and development of business clusters.

University of Dar es Salaam, Tanzania
The Institute of Production Innovation was founded in 1981 to carry out product innovation, transfer innovations to industry, and provide technical consultancy for enterprises.

Kwame Nkrumah University of Science and Technology, Ghana
The Technology Consultancy Centre was originally established in 1972 as a production unit of the University of Science and Technology in Kumasi. It serves as a conduit through which university research is made available to industry. Most of its clients are small and medium-size enterprises in the informal sector, and the technologies transferred are mainly in food processing, fabrication of small-scale machinery and parts, and ceramics manufacture and foundry works.

Source: Tindimubona (2000, 18, 19); UNCTAD (2003, 57, 70). For further information on the Uganda Gatsby Trust, see http://gatsbyuganda.com/; for information on the Technology Consultancy Centre, see http://www.knust.edu.gh/tcc/index.htm.

Supportive Policy Framework

A third general condition for the success of higher education–industry linkages is a supportive public policy framework. Experience shows that appropriate public policy interventions are often necessary to strengthen both the supply and demand sides and to bridge the gap between knowledge producers and industry. Such interventions take a variety of forms: for example, creating the necessary competences on the supply side, mainly through support for graduate training and research in selected priority areas in universities and research centers; establishing official structures to facilitate collaboration and information flow; and offering direct incentives to stimulate industry demand and receptivity to local knowledge workers and products. In some instances, the state has collaborated directly, in a variety of ways, with universities and industry.

The African Scene: Background

Some clarification is necessary to help frame this review of the African situation. First, the discussion is essentially limited to Sub-Saharan Africa, excluding South Africa. This is because the histories and levels of development of the Maghreb countries and South Africa are sufficiently different from the rest of Africa to make meaningful generalizations across the continent difficult for the purposes of our topic. On the other hand, even though the rest of Africa is by no means homogenous, there is enough in common to allow for reasonable generalizations.

Second, an undertaking such as this is faced with the usual difficulties of lack of adequate and consistent national and intercountry data. The problem is compounded in this instance by the virtual absence of literature dealing with the actual forms and structures of such university-industry interaction as there is, in contrast to the burgeoning literature elsewhere. In the circumstances, we have been fortunate to come across a number of country case studies that provide us with useful, if limited, material on which to proceed.

Third, given the near-absence of high-technology industry (see "Industry in Africa," below), the prevalence of small and middle-size industry, and the critical role of the latter in Africa's development, our presentation will deal primarily with such industry, concentrating on pathways between industry and knowledge production centers and the extent and potential of such linkages.

Finally, although we recognize the contribution of university-based management consulting to organizational improvement and to productivity increases, the topic does not receive direct attention in our discussion. This is largely because it is so sparsely covered in the literature.

Higher Education in Africa

As indicated above, the key conditions for effective higher education–industry linkages include (a) the capability of higher education to produce skilled technical and managerial cadres and usable knowledge and (b) the capacity and disposition of higher education institutions to transmit such knowledge to end users. To assess these conditions, it is necessary to review briefly the state of African higher education and its relationship with industry.

Capability

Most African higher education institutions, from their colonial or immediate postcolonial beginnings, have been oriented toward the liberal arts and basic sciences. This orientation, which suited the immediate postcolonial agenda of providing a cadre of leaders and workers to run the public and private sectors of the newly independent states, was, by and large, effective for the first decade or so of independence. Before the end of that period, however, a clamor arose to alter the mission of the almost exclusively public universities and training institutions to make them more development oriented. This campaign culminated in a call by Africa's higher education leaders for the transformation of the leading African universities into "developmental universities," as voiced at two major events: a United Nations–sponsored 1962 conference in Tananarive, and a workshop entitled "Creating the African University: Emerging Issues in the 1970s," organized by the Association of African Universities in Accra in 1972 (see Sawyerr 2004).[3]

In response to the changing global environment and the increasing centrality of knowledge to production and social development, the call for developmentalism became insistent, and steps were taken in many places to give it meaning. Universities of science and technology and of agriculture were established; new emphasis was placed on polytechnics and technical training; and in the early 1990s technology parks began to be set up around universities and other higher education institutions. These attempts to reorient higher education in Africa have to date met with very limited success, partly because of the persistence of the ingrained orientation and practices of the leading universities but also because of lack of complementary transformations in economy and policy.

What did change by the end of the 1980s was the profile of the typical higher education system, reshaped by an explosion of enrollments, an aging faculty, and reduced research and graduate study programs. The resulting deterioration was compounded by a combination of neglect and underfunding, as well as policy errors at both the system level and the institution level. By the late 1990s, most African universities were in dire straits, even the region's premier institutions, which had, in their prime, vied with the best in the world. (For fuller discussion of these issues and relevant references, see Sawyerr 2004; World Bank 2009.)

The situation is perhaps best captured in a set of paradoxes:

- The number of universities expanded dramatically following the wave of political independence, from 52 in 1960 to over 400 in 2000, and it continues to climb steeply, especially on the private side. Yet many countries still have only one, two, or three universities, and there is little diversity in institutional forms and functions.
- University enrollments rose fourfold between 1975 and 1985, almost tripled again during the next decade, and are still rising. Yet, with an average participation rate of barely 5 percent, pressure for expansion of enrollment is unrelenting.
- Expenditure per student as a proportion of gross national product (GNP)—that is, in relation to national wealth—is far higher in Africa than anywhere else in the world. Yet, owing to a combination of difficult economic conditions in most countries and the fact that most universities depend on public support, the provision of resources has not kept pace with enrollment.

Another problem relevant to our discussion is the aging of the faculty in virtually all universities, as senior faculty retire without being replaced at the rate required to maintain the appropriate levels of leadership of research and graduate programs. This can be seen from the following selective figures:

- Since 1990, according to the International Organization for Migration, Africa has been losing an estimated 20,000 professionals each year through migration, many of them academics.

- In 2003 Makerere University in Uganda had an estimated vacancy rate of about 40 percent, as did the Ghanaian university system.
- In Nigeria 400 professors (45 percent of the top-level professoriate) were expected to reach the mandatory retirement age in 2008.
- In South Africa 50 percent of the academic staff was over age 50 in 2004.
- Only a third of the academic staff at Makerere University held doctoral degrees as of December 2006.
- In 2008, for the first time, teaching positions at the University of Dar es Salaam were to be filled by staff with only a bachelor's degree—about 91 positions were involved.

The overall effects include

- Heavy teaching loads resulting from hugely expanded enrollments, unmatched by commensurate faculty increases or the benefit of modern teaching aids
- Involvement of academic staff in nonacademic activities as a means of supplementing low official incomes, cutting down on time for staff development and research
- The absence of mentoring by senior colleagues and the lack of a critical mass of other researchers, heightening the isolation of young researchers and reducing the scope for learning on the job.

All these have obvious implications for the quality of teaching, learning, and research.

There have, of course, been remarkable instances of coping and pockets of significant revitalization. Particularly in the last few years, there has also been a general awakening at the institutional, national, and continental levels to the need for corrective action. Nevertheless, the general situation remains problematic. This is in part because the attempt at revival has coincided with the rise of the knowledge society and the imperative of global competitiveness. The consequence is that Africa's institutions, unlike most others in the world, face a dual challenge:

- The old task of producing experts for managing the essentially primary-production economy and developing-country social conditions, and
- The new task of providing cutting-edge knowledge, advanced management, and innovation to develop and manage a modern society and economy in the context of global competitiveness.

Although this picture of degeneration in the conditions for knowledge production and innovation may appear unduly bleak, it highlights the challenges, the better to enable us to appreciate the limited capability of the higher education system to respond effectively to the needs of modern industry.

Turning directly to the matter of university-industry linkages, Sub-Saharan Africa has the lowest tertiary enrollment rate in the world, particularly in the scientific and technical fields (tables 1 and 2).

The world average gross tertiary enrollment rate is 24 percent, and that of North America and Europe is 70 percent, but in Africa it is only 5 percent. In 1995 Sub-Saharan Africa had a tertiary-level enrollment rate of 0.28 percent in technical fields; the developing-country average was 0.82 percent, and that for developed countries

TABLE 1. Tertiary Gross Enrollment Ratio (GER), 2004

Region	GER (percent)
Arab states	21
Central and Eastern Europe	54
Central Asia	25
East Asia and the Pacific	23
Latin America and the Caribbean	28
North America and Western Europe	70
South and West Asia	11
Sub-Saharan Africa	5
World (average)	24

Source: UNESCO 2006.

was 4.06 percent (table 2). From another angle, Sub-Saharan Africa, with 12 percent of the developing world's population, accounts for only 3.1 percent of the technical tertiary enrollments and 1.7 percent of the engineering enrollments in developing countries. The total number of engineers enrolled in the whole of Sub-Saharan Africa represents about 12 percent of the corresponding figure for the Republic of Korea alone. In 2002 the three universities with substantial technology programs in Uganda had approximately 1,000 students enrolled in four-year engineering degree programs; in Australia, a country with a population one-third smaller than Uganda's, the figure was 53,000.

Orientation

In a comment that captures conditions throughout Sub-Saharan Africa, a report by the United Nations Conference on Trade and Development (UNCTAD) observes, "The skill base is very weak and the educational system is generally not geared to meeting the skill needs of industrial competitiveness" (UNCTAD 2003, 16). In fairness to higher education institutions, it must be acknowledged that most are fully aware of this situation and have made efforts to improve it, through internal measures and by reaching out to industry. In many instances outreach to the productive sector has been undertaken both as an extension of the conventional objective of community service and as a means of generating income. Outreach efforts include incentives for staff to undertake industry-relevant research, accept research contracts, and provide consultancy and other services; structures to facilitate interaction with industry; technology-licensing offices to market inventions; and, in some cases, spin-off companies for the commercial exploitation of research outcomes and fuller integration into the productive sector. Some notable initiatives are Makerere University's Uganda Gatsby Trust, the University of Dar es Salaam's Institute of Production Innovation, and the Technology Consultancy Centre of the Kwame Nkrumah University of Science and Technology (see box 1). Similar examples can be found just about anywhere on the continent (World Bank 2009).

TABLE 2. Total Tertiary-Level Enrollment in Technical Subjects, 1995

Country group/country	Tertiary-level enrollment		Technical subjects			
	Total students	Percent of population	All technical subjects	Natural sciences	Mathematics/ computing	Engineering
Developing countries	35,345,800	0.82	7,021,929	2,046,566	780,930	4,194,433
Sub-Saharan Africa	1,542,700	0.28	220,660	111,500	39,330	69,830
Ghana	9,600	0.06	2,100	1,200	200	700
Kenya	31,300	0.12	4,600	3,600	—	1,000
Mauritius	5,500	0.49	500	100	100	300
South Africa	617,900	1.49	72,200	21,700	30,500	20,000
Tanzania	12,800	0.04	3,600	800	100	2,700
Uganda	27,600	0.14	2,600	800	300	1,500
Zimbabwe	45,600	0.41	9,700	2,200	800	6,700
Latin America	7,677,800	1.64	1,404,402	212,901	188,800	1,002,701
Asia	21,553,400	0.72	4,584,300	1,513,100	438,600	2,632,600
Transition economies	2,025,800	1.95	440,800	55,500	30,600	354,700
Developed countries	33,774,800	4.06	5,754,419	1,509,334	1,053,913	3,191,172

Source: UNCTAD 2003.

Note: —, not available.

In the end, these initiatives have proved neither substantial nor sustainable, for reasons to do partly with the histories and ways of work of the knowledge institutions, which make it difficult to fully integrate such initiatives within the institutions. Other factors are the state and orientation of industry, as will emerge from the discussion that follows, and the overall policy framework within which the interaction takes place, especially dependence of research projects on donor funding for survival.

Turning to the institutions, the problematic features relate to curriculum coverage and enrollment patterns, the extent and nature of research activities, and attitudes toward involvement with industry and commerce.

Curriculum and enrollment patterns. Enrollment is still heavily biased in favor of liberal arts courses, with not enough science students and even fewer in engineering and mathematics (see table 2). The roots of the problem lie largely outside the university, in that secondary schools do not turn out enough science-ready university entrants. Moreover, because the unit cost of producing science and technology (S&T) graduates is so much higher than for liberal arts graduates, most public universities and virtually all the private universities, which account for a large part of the recent institutional expansion, concentrate on non-S&T courses. The upshot is that the pool of science-trained graduates from which industry would draw its high-level technical workers is much shallower than in other regions of the world.

In addition, the teaching and learning process tends not to emphasize problem-solving skills or exposure to real-life situations. There are notable exceptions, especially in the medical schools and in those institutions where problem-based learning, community work, and industrial attachment still form part of teaching and learning. The situation in most institutions which had these programs in the past is that they are no longer affordable, especially in view of bloated enrollments, overcrowded classrooms and laboratories, and grossly inadequate staffing.

A particularly serious aspect of this situation is the absence or virtual collapse of graduate study in most universities. Although the issue affects all parts of the academic enterprise and research culture, the relevant point here is that African countries are turning out neither the numbers of PhDs in mathematics and engineering required for high-technology take-off nor enough of the holders of master's degrees needed to provide leadership in small and medium-size enterprises if African economies and societies are to be globally competitive.

This is not to say that a shortage of science graduates with problem-solving skills or PhDs is currently handicapping local industry. There is evidence to the contrary, with the arrival of the "unemployed science graduate." Although the nub of the issue appears to lie in the absorptive capacity of local industry (which we address later), the point to note is that African institutions are currently in no position to provide the depth and range of basic science and high-level problem-solving skills needed to support industrial development of the sort and at the levels required to move African societies out of poverty and into a solid competitive posture such as is demanded by the times.

Research. In the second place, there is not enough research, basic or applied, in African universities, and what does exist is of neither the type nor the quality to attract the interest of industry or to lift it to a higher level (World Bank 2009). The problem is partly attributable to the quality of human resources available at the universities and the incentives for undertaking industry-relevant research. Many faculty members do not hold PhDs and—an especially serious shortcoming in technological fields—time for research is constricted by heavy teaching loads. Issues such as the development of new products and successful linkages with industry are rarely taken into account for purposes of promotion and career advancement, creating a major disincentive to engaging in research and development (R&D) activities that do not lead to scientific publication.

A further issue concerns the relevance of such research as is undertaken. Because of the "publish or perish" syndrome, research agendas tend to focus on purely academic and narrowly scientific objectives so as to ensure publication in refereed journals, with little regard for developmental needs. This situation is compounded by undue dependence on donor funding for research, which tends not to be industry oriented. Not surprisingly, the results of such research are rarely relevant to local entrepreneurs and industries, which, as a consequence, feel no inclination to forge partnerships with local researchers or their institutions.

Attitudes. In the third place, and linked to some of the factors identified above, there is little understanding in the university setting of the ways of work and the constraints of industry, of what industry considers important, or of what it takes to prepare for and work effectively with it. In the absence of such understanding, it is virtually impossible for the two sides to act proactively in planning and undertaking collaborative work (van Zyl, Amadi-Echendu, and Bothma 2007, 2). There are, of course, attempts to get around this problem by establishing structures, including special centers, within the universities , for facilitating and promoting industrial outreach and interaction (see box 1). But by and large, this is not enough to overcome the drag of the factors mentioned above.

Finally, there is a line of thinking, particularly within the leading public universities, which holds that the role of universities is to develop knowledge through research, publication of research results, and the training of students, not to solve routine problems. In such circles, research commissioned by or targeted to industry is often regarded as "not real science." This attitude is linked to the insistence on publication in peer-reviewed journals as the basis for academic career advancement.

Industry in Africa

The basic unit of technological activity is the industrial firm, which is responsible for the acquisition, development, adaptation, and use of technology (UNCTAD 2003, 1). The firm's activities, particularly in a competitive setting, stimulate innovation in technology and its applications, which usually drives the higher education and research sector. Thus, the presence and activities of such firms are key to the technological and broader development of any society in the contemporary world. Experience shows that the factors driving technological development in such firms include competition and trade policies, governing rules and regulations, physical infrastructure, skills, and financing (UNCTAD 2003, 2). Among these, skills acquired through high-level and specialized training and knowledge generated from relevant research are major determinants of success in the new competition.

Against this background, what can we say about industrial firms and the condition and structure of industry in general in Africa, in relation to technology development and knowledge acquisition? As previously noted, the relevant data and literature are thin. We therefore rely heavily on country case studies of Kenya, Ghana, Uganda, and Tanzania published by UNCTAD in 2003. Although these four cases cannot represent the total situation on the continent, the main findings are confirmed by other studies (see, for example, World Bank 2009) and are sufficiently robust to form the basis of comments on Africa outside South Africa and the Maghreb.

By and large, African manufacturing industry, as portrayed in the case study countries, is dominated by low-level processing of natural resources and the production of simple consumer goods for local consumption. Describing a typical situation, the UNCTAD study observed,

> [Ghana's] industry structure consists mainly of a large refining industry and aluminum smelting facility, with very limited manufacturing capacity. The modern sector, largely owned by foreign companies, is concentrated on food processing and on industrial intermediaries manufactures. . . . Most of the semi-modern enterprises are relatively small-scale African-owned operations running on simple machinery and on low-level technical and managerial skills. They generally produce lower-quality goods geared to the domestic market. The informal sector is entirely African and operates on even simpler technologies. (UNCTAD 2003, 43)

Thus, rather like Africa's systems of higher education, Africa's industry has remained substantially untransformed—in this case, from its colonial raw material production and export origins. At a time when world trade has shifted strongly from resource-based to technology-based commodities, Africa has the highest proportion of resource-based exports, and its share of high-technology products is the lowest. Primary products account for over three-quarters of all exports, with two-thirds of export revenues coming from petroleum alone. The shares of engineering, food, and garment exports are relatively low, except for Mauritius (World Bank 2009). Furthermore, there is hardly any high-technology (i.e., truly R&D intensive) industry such as wireless technology, advanced biotechnology, materials science, and so on.

What industry there is consists essentially of light manufacturing, often involving simple and relatively self-contained engineering activities and agroprocessing, both largely reliant on technology embodied in simple equipment, and requiring limited skills. Not surprisingly, manufacturing value added in Sub-Saharan Africa, excluding South Africa, grew only 0.1 percent per year over the period 1990–97 and has stagnated at 0.4 percent as a share of global manufacturing value added, at a time when the developing-country share of global manufacturing exports had grown from 9.6 percent in 1980 to 26.9 percent in 2000 (UNCTAD 2003, 2, 6).

Nevertheless, as long as these medium-technology enterprises remain the most significant forms of industry in Africa, their performance will be vital to the development and competitiveness of African economies. Improvements in their productivity and coverage through engagement with local and foreign knowledge and technology sources are therefore of the first importance. That is the perspective that shapes the discussion that follows.

The key findings of the UNCTAD case studies can be summarized as follow:

- In general, industrial structure is characterized by an emphasis on low-technology products, with little evidence of technology deepening or the adaptation of foreign technologies to generate improved or new products.
- The passive importation of relatively simple technologies and their use at relatively low levels of technical efficiency, as well as the relative absence of local capital goods production and design engineering, mean that technological learning and diffusion are very limited.
- Employment of technically qualified personnel such as trained engineers is low, and in-house training is restricted to creating the basic skills needed to operate equipment and simple systems.[4]
- In general, firms show little awareness of the importance of science and technology activities and of technological capacity for ensuring industrial competitiveness. This reflects the absence of what may be termed a "technology culture." As a consequence, firms are reluctant to pay for technology services, nor do they spend enough on R&D.
- R&D spending in Sub-Saharan Africa was 0.28 percent of GNP in 1997, as against a developing country average of 0.39 and a world average of 0.92 (table 3). Indeed, formal R&D is confined to a very few large enterprises, while the bulk of R&D is conducted in public research institutions and universities, mainly with public funding. On average, in both Ghana and Kenya, for instance, the government funds 90 percent of what little R&D expenditure there is (UNCTAD 2003, 24, 49).
- Links with technology institutions are restricted to necessary, basic activities, such as mandatory certification of products or materials testing. There is very little research contracting or use of institutions to search for and adapt new foreign technologies.

TABLE 3. Research and Development (R&D), by Major Country Group, c. 1997

Country group or region	Scientists and engineers in research and development		Total R&D (percent of GNP)
	Per million inhabitants	Numbers	
Industrial market economies[a]	1,102	2,704,205	1.94
Developing economies[b]	514	1,034,333	0.39
Sub-Saharan Africa, excluding South Africa	83	3,193	0.28
North Africa	423	29,675	0.40
Latin America and Caribbean	339	107,508	0.45
Asia, excluding Japan	783	893,957	0.72
World (79–84 countries)	1,304	4,684,700	0.92

Source: UNCTAD 2003.

Note: GNP, gross national product.
a. United States, Canada, Western Europe, Japan, Australia, and New Zealand.
b. Includes the Middle Eastern oil-producing countries, Turkey, Israel, and the former socialist economies in Asia.

Considering its percentage of the world's total population, it is estimated that Africa undertakes only about a tenth of the R&D it ought to be conducting. Where R&D does occur, the research output is often prematurely abandoned and is rarely transformed into usable technologies (Massaquoi 2001, 6). Ironically, the low volume of R&D and the low rate of transformation of research results into practical use lead to low returns to R&D investment in Africa, compared with those in the developed and emerging countries, which in turn, leads to low investments, in a downward spiral.

This general absence of a technology culture is attributable, in part, to the lack of competition that would spur demand for better and more efficient technology, which in turn could stimulate science and technology institutions to create more advanced, useful, and affordable products.

Most countries have extensive public infrastructure devoted to the production of industrially useful knowledge and technology and their transmission to industry through research centers, industrial promotion units, and funding arrangements. Yet the evidence from the case studies and other sources is that, by and large, firms in Africa are unaware of the technological services or capabilities available within the official technology infrastructure and universities or regard them as irrelevant or inefficient. There are thus few links with those institutions and such facilities and resources as they have (UNCTAD 2003, 34).

For all these reasons—in particular, the generally weak skills base, the absence of a technology culture, and the resulting low inflows of high technology—most industries lack the ability to absorb sophisticated technologies, which constitute the cutting edge of industrial dynamism and competitiveness. Furthermore, especially because of the low level of in-house technological activity, firms cannot always identify their specific technological needs and so lack the necessary basis for seeking, acquiring, and absorbing essential knowledge and technology inputs through research contracting, collaborative ventures, and the like.

This situation, together with the generally weak drive for technological innovation, constitute a formidable barrier to linkages with agencies that can conduct research for or in collaboration with industry or that have the means to facilitate such research. That, we would argue, constitutes the main constraint on the provision of technology support by research and development institutions. As succinctly put in the UNCTAD study,

> Where such [in-house] capabilities are lacking, even good technology institutions can do little. (UNCTAD 2003, 33)

> Without a more dynamic technology culture in private industry, an institution such as the Kenya Industrial Research and Development Institute cannot provide much more than mundane technical services. (UNCTAD 2003, 31)

A final feature of note is that the principal industries in Africa are for the most part affiliates or subsidiaries of multinational companies established in developed countries and operate mainly in the primary sector and in services. These affiliates and subsidiaries carry out very little research on the continent, almost all the needed research being undertaken at headquarters or other locations of the parent companies. In consequence, their presence has little impact on domestic technology development (World Bank 2009).

Concluding Comment

It is difficult to bring such a wide-ranging discussion to a neat conclusion, and there is not much point in offering "recommendations." What we do instead is to suggest some initial ideas aimed at encouraging a systematic approach to what ought to be a burning national and continental issue: *the mobilization of Africa's knowledge resources in support of its sustained development in the current global dispensation*.

Given the lack of data and of basic understanding on such a crucial issue, a first step has to be the establishment, preferably in each country and certainly in each region, of a well-resourced "observatory" involving industry, government, the universities, and the technology institutions. The primary task of this body should be the thorough study and proper observation and visioning of this phenomenon, namely, that of mobilizing and applying Africa's knowledge resources, as it evolves over the coming decade. Experience elsewhere should be carefully examined and adapted to the changing African realities.

An obvious second thrust is the revitalization and strengthening of Africa's universities and the facilitation of their repositioning to provide the intellectual sinews of a new drive for African development on all fronts. The case for such a revitalization drive is now generally accepted, nationally, continentally, and among Africa's donor partners. The principal gain will be the combination of expanded access with quality and lifelong learning skills, along with the general spread of the scientific approach to all aspects of life. This will have immediate significance not only for the conditions of individual and social life but also for the quality of the labor force as a whole and, thus, for the productive sector, including industry.

The improvement of general education should be complemented by a special program for the strengthening of staff quality, research, and graduate study in carefully selected priority areas aligned with specific national industrial development objectives. The determination of priority development areas should be approached as an issue of critical national policy, involving detailed technical and sociological studies and wide consultation. In some circumstances, a subregional approach will offer the best options. Necessary intermediary arrangements, including the provision of publicly supported laboratories and other facilities, should be made, both to support priority-area research and to promote linkages to targeted industrial activities.

A crucial factor will be the stimulation of a technology culture in industry in general and especially in the targeted sectors. As appears from all that has been said above, without such a culture the demand side of the knowledge-industry interaction will remain so weak as to render the linkage anemic and unsustainable, providing no impetus to industrial innovation and competitiveness. Part of the answer will consist in the measured exposure of industry to internal and external competition. But note should also be taken of the lessons from the positive East Asian experience, as well as from Africa's not-so-positive experience: at this stage of maturity, domestic industry, exposed to unrestrained foreign competition, faces the danger of decimation, and, therefore, a policy of measured exposure must incorporate specific and targeted state support for local industry and enterprise if it is to elicit the appropriate responses (UNCTAD 2003, 4;

World Bank 2009). What is needed, drawing on East Asian experience, is a regime of carefully considered and proactive state support and incentives, aimed at building up a strong technology culture in local industry, with special emphasis on priority areas, and at raising the capacity of industry to compete locally and internationally. State-supported apprenticeships for engineers and technologists, and encouragement of firms to develop active in-house and external staff training and upgrading, can make a major contribution. Industry should be facilitated increasingly to engage with and reinforce the local knowledge and technology infrastructure, in what was known in Brazil as the "Sabato Triangle," involving close collaboration among government, universities, and industry.

To give this entire process the necessary weight and urgency, it must be championed by the highest political levels. In other countries this has been achieved by framing it as a special presidential or prime ministerial initiative. Something similar should be done in Africa.

Although the primary locus of the effort must be national, the scale of the problem, in terms of resources, skill pools, and markets, transcends national boundaries. In this connection, it is encouraging that the African Union is providing continental leadership in the revitalization of higher education. The new Second Decade for Education in Africa (2006–15), declared in 2007, includes, for the first time, a component on higher education, signaling the African Union's recognition of the vital role that higher education must play in the region's development agenda. In relation, specifically, to science and technology, this new awareness is symbolized by the Science and Technology Consolidated Plan of Action launched in 2005 by the African Union and the secretariat of the New Partnership for Africa's Development (NEPAD). This plan (NEPAD 2006) is aimed at developing and using science and technology for the socioeconomic transformation of the continent and its integration into the world economy. Although its implementation has been stalled by the failure, so far, of African leaders to reach a consensus on how to finance it, the plan is significant because, as with the declaration of the Second Decade of Education, it signals, finally, the engagement of Africa's political leadership. For its part, the African Development Bank has approved a Strategy for Higher Education, Science, and Technology aimed, among other things, at helping member countries link higher education to the productive sector.

Supplemented by appropriate national-level policies and structures, such as those outlined above, and combined with well-resourced regional nodes of strength in selected areas, these efforts provide a starting point for productive collaboration between higher education and industry nationally and across the continent.

Notes

1. We use the term "knowledge production institution," which is more general than "higher education" or "university," to emphasize that relevant knowledge production occurs outside the formal university system, although the latter remains the principal locus for research and knowledge generation.

2. An exception must be made in the case of state-sponsored research or industrial drive, as for the arms industry.

3. The Tananarive conference was sponsored by the United Nations Educational, Cultural, and Scientific Organization (UNESCO) and the United Nations Economic Commission for Africa.

4. Although the point about low employment of technically qualified personnel holds for the typical medium-to-low-technology enterprise, the situation is significantly different in the larger firms and major public enterprises and utilities, where the top engineers and managers are drawn from local graduates, occasionally with foreign postgraduate qualifications.

Bibliography

African Ministerial Council on Technology. n.d. "Flagship R&D Programmes: Building Engineering Capacity for Manufacturing." http://www.nepadst.org/platforms/engcapacity.shtml.

Ajayi, J. F. Ade, Lameck K. H. Goma, and G. Ampah Johnson. 1996. *The African Experience with Higher Education*. Accra: Association of African Universities; London: James Currey; Athens, OH: Ohio University Press.

Breier, Mignonne, and Mahlubi Mabizela. 2008. "High-Skill Requirements in Advanced Manufacturing." In *Human Resources Development Review: Education, Employment and Skills in South Africa,* ed. Andre Kraak and Karen Press, 300–21. Cape Town: HSRC Press.

Brennenraedts, Reginald, Rudi Bekkers, and Bart Verspagen. 2006. "The Different Channels of University-Industry Knowledge Transfer: Empirical Evidence from Biomedical Engineering." Working Paper 06.04, Eindhoven Centre for Innovation Studies, Eindhoven, Netherlands.

Engelhard, Rutger. 2000. *National Policy Dialogue on Research and Technology for Development. Introduction to Assessment Reports Prepared in Ghana, Senegal, Uganda and Vietnam.* Maastricht, Netherlands: European Centre for Development Policy Management.

Lorentzen, Jo Angelique Wildschut. 2008. "High-Skill Requirements in Advanced Manufacturing." *Human Resources Development Review: Education, Employment and Skills in South Africa,* ed. Andre Kraak and Karen Press, 345–64. Cape Town: HSRC Press.

Lwakabamba, Silas, and Francis Mbuza. 2004. "African Centre for Engineering and Technology Education." *Global Journal of Engineering Education* (Australia) 8 (1): 93–100.

Massaquoi, J. C. M., ed. 2001. *University-Industry Partnership for Cooperative Technology Development in Africa: Opportunities, Challenges, Strategies and Policy Issues.* Nairobi: United Nations Educational, Scientific, and Cultural Organization (UNESCO).

NEPAD (New Partnership for Africa's Development), Office of Science and Technology. 2006. *Africa's Science and Technology Consolidated Plan of Action.* Midrand, South Africa: NEPAD.

Sawyerr, Akilagpa. 2004. "Challenges Facing African Universities: Selected Issues." *African Studies Review* 47 (1): 1–59.

Scott, Alister, et al. 2001. *The Economic Returns to Basic Research and the Benefits of University-Industry Relationships: A Literature Review and Update of Findings.* Science and Technology Policy Research, Report for the U.K. Office of Science and Technology, London.

Tindimubona, Alex R. 2000. "National Policy Dialogue on Research and Technology for Development in Uganda: An Assessment." European Centre for Development Policy Management, Maastricht, Netherlands.

UNCTAD (United Nations Conference on Trade and Development). 2003. *Africa's Technology Gap: Case Studies on Kenya, Ghana, Uganda and Tanzania.* UNCTAD/ITE/IPC/Misc.13. New York: United Nations.

UNESCO (United Nations Educational, Scientific, and Cultural Organization). 2006. "Global Education Digest 2006: Comparing Education Statistics around the World." UNESCO Institute for Statistics, Montreal.

van Zyl, A., J. Amadi-Echendu, and T. J. D. Bothma. 2007. "Nine Drivers of Knowledge Transfer between Universities and Industry R&D Partners in South Africa." *South African Journal of Information Management* 9 (1, March): 1–22.

World Bank. 2009. *Accelerating Catch-up: Tertiary Education for Growth in Sub-Saharan Africa.* Directions in Development Series. Washington, DC: World Bank.

Yesufu, T. M. 1973. *Creating the African University: Emerging Issues in the 1970s.* Ibadan, Nigeria: Association of African Universities; Oxford University Press.

Comment on "African Higher Education and Industry: What Are the Linkages?" by Akilagpa Sawyerr and Boubakar Barry

SHAHID YUSUF

The paper by Sawyerr and Barry is a model of balanced exposition. It rightly starts by underscoring the axial role of knowledge for development and the increasing contribution knowledge producers can make to the pace and technological content of industrial change and to gains in productivity. The authors enumerate the pathways through which knowledge finds its way into production processes, but they stress, again rightly, that the outcomes depend on the capability of the producers to generate a stock of usable knowledge and on the efforts to disseminate this knowledge to potential users. Equally, those who can benefit from the knowledge must be active in seeking it out, and well prepared and entrepreneurial in putting it to the best possible use. Fumio Kodama has labeled firms with absorptive capacity as "receiver active" (Kodama and Suzuki 2007). The dynamism and growth of a knowledge economy depend on the initiative of both parties. To what degree this interaction between producers and users results in a virtuous economic spiral depends, according to Sawyerr and Barry, on the emergence of a technology culture that stimulates the continual deepening of knowledge, as well as unceasing efforts by industry to harness knowledge effectively for the sake of survival in a unsparingly competitive world economy.

An economy that induces the continuous production, borrowing, adaptation, and utilization of knowledge has been slow to emerge in African countries, for a variety of reasons. African universities are struggling to rise to the challenge of graduating enough engineers and scientists with skills of the requisite quality and to conduct research that can be of practical relevance. African firms, by and large, evince little desire to upgrade their technologies and diversify into areas of higher technology by fully exploiting the available supply of skills and seeking out technology from all possible sources, domestic and foreign. They are behaving passively, preferring to remain in low-technology, niche areas. As a consequence, African firms too often forgo the

Shahid Yusuf is an economic adviser at the World Bank Institute.

Annual World Bank Conference on Development Economics 2009, Global

opportunities that could be grasped through an upgrading of their workforces, through technology catch-up, and through strategies that give greater primacy to in-house applied research and to innovation.

Sawyerr and Barry conclude by calling for a determined political drive designed to strengthen the technology culture by, for example, enhancing market competition; to revitalize the universities; and to create an "observatory" composed of key stakeholders to help chart the way forward. The authors' diagnosis is balanced and well-rounded. But they never explain why African countries have been slow to evolve a technology culture, why competitive pressures impinging on African economies have been relatively weak, and why industry in African countries has remained low technology. A stab at each of these questions is surely the first step in arriving at solutions, however tentative. Absent such analysis of persistent shortcomings, the authors' recommendations, although sensible, do not go beyond the generic.

If one compares some of the Southeast Asian "tiger" economies with countries in Sub-Saharan Africa, it is apparent that Malaysia and Thailand started out from a resource base that was not different from that of several of the coastal economies in Africa. Neither of these countries had or even now possesses a technology culture. Neither has a strong tertiary education sector, and their universities are only now beginning to develop postgraduate and postdoctoral programs. Yet they have acquired substantial manufacturing capability and have absorbed the expertise to produce high-tech products. The question that arises is why Southeast Asian countries have responded differently to global competition, have integrated with global value chains, and have built an internationally competitive industrial base even though the technology culture was no stronger there than in a number of African countries. There are several possible explanations that Sawyerr and Barry could have examined. It could be, for example, that the African economies were (and remain), on balance, more closed and less politically stable than their Southeast Asian comparators and therefore attracted little foreign direct investment in manufacturing activities; that their market institutions were and are relatively weaker; that their primary and secondary education systems did not impart the basic skills required of an industrial workforce; and that the region has lacked role models such as Japan and the Republic of Korea to generate a variety of spillover and neighborhood effects. And there are other reasons, as well.

Southeast Asian countries are now attempting to build technological capabilities and deepen embryonic innovation systems, much like the African countries that are the focus of this paper. However, they have the advantage of starting from a solid manufacturing base, and one that has absorbed the advances in technology in the electronics, engineering, and transportation industries. They have also begun investing substantially in tertiary education and research. Nevertheless, the deepening of domestic technological capabilities poses severe challenges, especially for latecomers struggling to climb onto the first rung of the global market for manufactures.

The majority of countries in Sub-Saharan Africa lag far behind, and developing a competitive knowledge economy will take years of effort and investment. Sawyerr and Barry identify a broad objective, the technology culture, and they point to some of the weaknesses of African universities, which fail to emphasize problem-solving skills and are struggling to enlarge the pool of graduates with mathematics, science, and engineering skills. The authors assert that a relatively protected domestic market might explain the small appetite for technology among firms and the low investment in research and development. But all they offer by way of remedies is to call for active involvement by the state and a pan-African effort to develop science and technology skills. This is a small part of the answer that policy makers are seeking, not just in Sub-Saharan Africa but also in Asia and elsewhere. How to make government interventions more effective is the more compelling question the paper fails to address. Nor does the paper acknowledge and tackle another equally important policy question: what kinds of specific actions by firms and other nonstate actors are needed to complement the efforts of the state to embed a technology culture and to make it the foundation of an economy that derives competitive strength from innovation? Dealing with these questions in any depth would go far beyond the authors' remit, but a start at providing answers beyond the commonplace, grounded in their vast knowledge of the subject, would have augmented the contribution of the paper to policy making.

Reference

Kodama, Fumio, and Jun Suzuki. 2007. "How Japanese Companies Have Used Scientific Advances to Restructure Their Businesses: The Receiver-Active National System of Innovation." *World Development* 35 (6): 976–90.

An Arrested Virtuous Circle? Higher Education and High-Technology Industries in India

RAKESH BASANT AND PARTHA MUKHOPADHYAY

The authors provide a brief but comprehensive overview of linkages between higher education and the high-technology sector, followed by an analysis of the major linkages in India. Links outside the labor market are found to be weak—a consequence of a regulatory structure that separates research from the university and discourages good faculty from joining the university. The effect is to erode the quality of the intellectual capital necessary to generate new knowledge. In the labor market, the authors find a robust link between higher education and high-tech industry, but despite a strong private sector supply response to the growth of high-tech industry, the quality leaves much to be desired. Poor university governance may be limiting both labor market and non–labor market linkages. Industry efforts to improve the quality of graduates are promising, but overreliance on industry may compromise workforce flexibility. Addressing governance failures in higher education is necessary in order to strengthen the links between higher education and high-tech industry.

For late-industrializing countries, the creation of a high-technology industrial base is critical for development. As the links between technology and development evolve, the potential role of higher education in contributing to the creation of a high-tech industrial base is becoming a major policy focus.[1] In this context, the links between high-tech industries and higher education become crucial. The available literature has not explored these linkages adequately, especially in the context of developing countries. The aim of this paper is to explore empirically such linkages in India.

Rakesh Basant is a professor at the Indian Institute of Management, Ahmedabad. Partha Mukhopadhyay is a senior research fellow at the Center for Policy Research, Delhi. This is an extensively revised version of the paper presented at the Annual World Bank Conference on Development Economics. Rakesh Basant would like to acknowledge the support of the Observer Research Foundation, New Delhi, for part of the work reported here. The authors are also grateful to Shobha Tekumalla and Rohan Mukherjee for excellent research assistance and to Pankaj Chandra and an anonymous referee for useful comments.

Annual World Bank Conference on Development Economics 2009, Global

The next section contains a brief but comprehensive overview of linkages between higher education and the high-tech sector. This is followed by a survey of the structure of higher education in India. Empirical evidence on the major linkages in India is then examined in the context of the recent growth of high-tech industry there, and concrete examples of labor market channels in the information technology, financial services, and high-end manufacturing sectors are presented. The response of the higher education sector to developments in the labor market, and the differences in this respect between Indian states, are examined, and we argue that the response has been restricted by the nature of regulation in India. Some issues raised in earlier sections are then discussed in the context of other South Asian countries. The final sections identify policy lessons and present conclusions.

Linkages between Higher Education and High-Technology Industry

Three broad conceptual frameworks inform the analysis of the linkages between higher education and high-tech industry: the national innovation system (NIS); the triple-helix paradigm; and university-industry linkages (UILs).

The concept of NIS was developed to explain the differences in the innovative performances of industrial countries. More recently, the framework has been applied to the analysis of the experiences of developing countries, especially the newly industrializing economies of East Asia. NIS characterizes a system of interacting agents—firms, universities (including research institutions), and government agencies—that are involved in the development and commercialization of science and technology. These interactions are undertaken within national borders and encompass technical, commercial, legal, financial, and social transactions. (See Metcalfe and Ramlogan 2008 for a succinct summary of the NIS literature.) Differences in innovative performance among nation-states are ascribed to differences in the way institutions combine and interact to generate, improve, and diffuse new technologies—that is, products, processes, and practices.

The initial applications of this framework focused on nation-states, but NIS is increasingly being used to look at regional, local (cluster), and sectoral situations. It is often also employed to contextualize case studies of specific institutions—firms, universities, and state agencies. It has been suggested that the literature in this tradition has focused more on the "invention system" than on the "innovation system" and has thus accorded less importance to understanding the complementary economic processes needed to convert invention into innovation and then to diffuse the innovations (Metcalfe and Ramlogan 2008).

The triple-helix paradigm extends the NIS framework. In triple helix I, "the state encompasses industry and academia and directs relations between them." In triple helix II, the three actors are in individual and separate domains "with strong borders dividing them and highly circumscribed relations" among them. Triple helix III generates a "knowledge infrastructure . . . with each taking the role of the other and with hybrid organizations at the interface" (Etzkowitz and Leydesdorff 2000, 111). The framework thus develops a model of innovation that captures multiple reciprocal relationships among industry, university, and government which help capitalize knowledge at different stages of its development process (Etzkowitz 2003). In so doing, it focuses on the *internal transformation* of each of the helixes and the influence of one helix on the other.

The recent literature on university-industry linkages appears at first glance to be both an extension and a combination of these two frameworks, as it focuses on two of the three components of NIS and two helixes of the triple-helix system. UIL studies, however, are different, in three ways. First, UILs are typically analyzed in the context of geographically bound clusters, related to the literature on regional or cluster-specific innovation systems. In adopting this focus, they tend to deemphasize the macro linkages between the education system and industry. Second, UIL studies focus on the variety of industry-academia linkages and their measurement. Third, these studies increasingly explore the complementary economic processes that are required in order to facilitate and even push the invention-innovation-diffusion process. This exploration has led to the examination of various policy options that bring universities closer to the market and facilitate commercialization of technology developed at the university, through licensing and start-ups. Thus, the emerging focus of this work is on understanding the factors that help "traditional universities" become "entrepreneurial universities."[2]

Broadly, all three streams of literature encompass the linkages between higher education and high-tech industries, with the UIL framework giving these interactions greater attention. Nevertheless, the linkages remain largely underexplored in the context of developing countries. In particular, labor market linkages have received inadequate attention, whether in local or national contexts. This is surprising because the labor market connection between industry and academia remains the most prominent link even in developed countries, where universities contribute relatively little to patenting, licensing, and new enterprise creation except, probably, in life sciences (Hershberg, Nabeshima, and Yusuf 2007). In developing countries, such linkages are even weaker.

Conversely, industries can influence higher education institutions through a variety of channels. These relationships, again, have been little explored in developing countries, where the relative capacities of the private sector and the state differ from those in a developed country. The ability of institutions to respond positively to industry and create a virtuous feedback loop depends on the regulatory structure of higher education, especially the constraints on establishing new institutions, hiring faculty, setting salaries, and making changes in curriculum—that is, it depends on the degree of agency possessed by the institution.

The Developing-Country Context

It is useful to briefly describe the linkages between higher education and high-tech industries and how the nature of these interactions may differ in developing countries.

Linkages from Higher Education Institutions to High-Technology Industries

Consider first the links that operate from higher education institutions to high-tech industries.

1. Higher education institutions provide a common and possibly neutral platform for discussions about the broader goals of innovation policy and a forum that permits relatively open interaction between industry and government.[3] This feature may be valuable in developing countries, where the relationship between the bureaucracy and industry is often antagonistic or clientelist, either of which precludes productive dialogue. Its function may be especially important when a country is moving from one type of industry-government relationship toward another, for example, during a liberalization. We do not explore this linkage here.

2. Another mundane link is through the institutions' supply of services such as testing, training, certification, and prototype development.[4] This is especially important in developing countries, where firms are typically small and their number is relatively large. Developing skills in-house is more difficult for a small firm than for a large one; furthermore, the country's talent pool is relatively limited and is unable to meet the needs of the large number of firms. Higher education institutions such as universities can function as a common pool resource, aggregating the limited talent and making it available to all firms on a fee-for-service basis. This, again, is not an area we explore here.

3. The third link is through an ostensibly primary function of higher education, creation of knowledge, through technology licensing, industry-institution research and development (R&D) projects, and the like. Given the relatively poor state of the education infrastructure in developing countries, the predominance of state funding for higher education, and the low levels of funding of R&D by industry, this is unlikely to be a strong channel.

4. A step beyond the creation of knowledge is its commercialization through the creation of new enterprises that put to use technologies developed in the institutions by students or faculty. Often, formation of new enterprises is facilitated by science parks, incubators, and the like that are established around research-based academic institutions. The growth of high-technology industries, however, requires inputs other than those from higher education institutions. For example, if a city is to become a financial center, human skills have to be combined with urban infrastructure. Similarly, limited availability of risk capital may strongly inhibit the growth of high-tech firms.

5. Finally, and most important, higher education institutions supply talent for high-tech industries. Students trained at these institutions become part of the labor pool, which may or may not be restricted to the region. This is not true just for service sectors commonly regarded as high-tech areas, such as information technology (IT) and financial services; most types of manufacturing, too, need a certain component of high-end skills. As the higher education sector evolves, it acquires the capacity to handle more complex technologies ("deepening"), and its influence extends to more industries ("broadening").

The focus of the UIL literature has been on the creation and commercialization of knowledge and the creation of enterprises. The links through the supply of labor have, in some sense, been considered too mundane. Yet, although the former types of linkage are possibly more important in countries where growth is driven by pushing the technological frontier, the labor market link may be significant in developing countries, where the growth of high-tech industry may depend more on how quickly existing technologies can be exploited. In industries such as software, this ability may well be constrained by the supply of highly skilled labor, which will determine the cost and the pace of expansion.

Linkages from High-Technology Industries to Higher Education Institutions

The linkages that extend from high-tech industries to higher education can, again, be grouped under five broad types.

1. The first and most mundane is the supply of goods and services; for example, high-tech industry provides specialized equipment to institutions, as well as technicians to service the equipment. In developing countries, the servicing function is likely to be more important because much of the equipment may be imported and may also see much longer usage periods than in developed countries. We do not explore this link here.

2. In developing countries, where teachers are often in short supply, industry professionals may serve as teaching staff. Of course, industry also affects the supply of teachers by offering an alternative career choice for students, which could influence both the quality and the compensation of the teaching pool. This is especially true for technical and professional education, which is relevant to high-tech industries.

3. Industry can influence the curriculum by working with government or higher education institutions to effect changes in line with its own requirements. To the extent that industry is more outward-oriented than higher education institutions in developing countries, this can be a source of new ideas, but it also carries a risk of making education narrower.

4. High-tech industries can be a source of funding for higher education. Because of the stronger links between educational inputs and success in industry, alumni in these industries may be more predisposed toward giving back to the institution. Industry may also fund research projects. Given the low levels of government funding, both in general and specifically for research, and the conditionalities that restrict the use of such funding, contributions from industry can be more important in developing than in developed countries. In research, especially, the added funding from industry can be a sizable proportion of the overall research budget in universities.

5. Finally, demand for labor on the part of industry can lead to demand for new institutions and expansion of the capacity of existing institutions. Depending on the response, this can affect the structure of the higher education sector. Concentration of industry in a few areas, as is more likely in developing countries, may similarly concentrate the structure of higher education.

Higher Education in India

India has several types of higher education institutions: universities, "deemed to be universities," colleges, institutions of national importance, and postgraduate institutions

TABLE 1. Types of University-Level Institutions, by Mode of Establishment, India

Type	Central	Private	State	Total
University	20	7	209	236
Deemed-to-be university	36	59	8	103
Institute of national importance	13	0	0	13
Established by state act	0	0	5	5
Total	69	66	222	357

Source: University Grants Commission (UGC) Web site, http://www.ugc.ac.in.

(table 1).[5] Universities can be set up by an act of parliament or by the state legislature. In general, only universities, deemed-to-be universities, and institutions of national importance are authorized to grant degrees. Other postgraduate institutions and polytechnics that are recognized by specialized accreditation organizations such as the All India Council of Technical Education (AICTE) can grant postgraduate diplomas and diplomas. We next highlight some key features of the higher education system.

Funding and Fee Regulation

Institutions of national importance and public universities chartered by an act of parliament or by state legislatures are funded by states, the University Grants Commission (UGC), or both. Private universities established by state legislatures are funded privately. Central funding is directed largely to central institutions, and little of it goes to support higher education at the state level. Typically, the size of the fees that can be charged has to be justified by the institution before a quasi-judicial body in each state. Whereas the popular perception is that the share of funding from fees is low, many public universities earn a substantial portion of their operating income from fees; in engineering and technology institutions, fees range between 22,000 rupees and 72,000 rupees per year (Agarwal 2006, 177). CABE (2005) also provides evidence to this effect (see table 2). In addition, the growing number of student loans and the rising share of private colleges testify to the importance of student fees as a financing source, especially for technical and professional education.

Uniform Compensation and Automatic Promotion of Faculty

The UGC specifies a salary structure for universities that receive its funding. Compensation in the various universities is therefore nominally uniform except for minor differences in allowances. Most other publicly owned academic institutions benchmark themselves to this salary structure, which implies that faculty at these institutions also face a uniform compensation structure.[6] In addition, most institutions typically follow a pattern of time-bound automatic promotion of faculty. This is a departure from the past, when the number of senior positions was limited and recruitment to these positions was by open competition, making it possible for faculty to be promoted early by applying for positions in other institutions.

TABLE 2. Distribution of Selected Public Universities by Share of Fees in University Income, Late 1990s

<10 percent	10–30 percent	31–50 percent	>50 percent
Hyderabad	Andhra	Guru Jambeswar	Mumbai
Kalyani	Bhavnagar	Punjab	Karnataka State Open
Maharshi Dayanand	Calcutta	S. N. D. T. Women's	Kuvempu
Rabindra Bharati	Dibrugarh	Bangalore	M. D. Saraswati
Tamil	Dr Harsingh		Pune
Visva Bharati	Sri Venkateshwara		YCM Open
Anna	Calicut		
Delhi	Goa		
J. N. Vyas	Kannur		
Osmania	Karnataka		
	Kumaon		
	Mangalore		
	Mysore		
	Saurashtra		
	IGNOU		

Source: CABE (2005).

Affiliated Colleges

Undergraduate teaching mostly takes place at colleges affiliated with a university and is based on a predetermined curriculum. Affiliated colleges may offer professional education, as well. Evaluation of students is carried out externally through a universitywide examination. Autonomous colleges, accredited by the National Assessment and Accreditation Council (NAAC), also exist, but their number is not high relative to the total number of colleges. Usually, admission is based on performance on the qualifying school-leaving examination.

Separation of Teaching and Research

Currently, teaching and research are increasingly carried out at different locations because of the prevalence of specialized research institutions. The establishment of institutions in science and technology through the Council of Scientific and Industrial Research (CSIR) and the creation of social science research institutes through the Indian Council of Social Science Research (ICSSR) resulted in an exodus of research-oriented faculty from universities to these institutions, where research facilities were generally better. The consequent deterioration of the university system led to a self-reinforcing downward spiral that put the relationship between teaching and research further out of balance. One of the key adverse impacts of such a separation has been that undergraduate teaching primarily undertaken by affiliated colleges has become almost completely delinked from research (Yarnell 2006).

Specialized Institutes for Professional Education

Much professional education is provided through specialized institutes at both the undergraduate and postgraduate levels. These professional institutions may be affiliated with a university but may be independently or, often, concomitantly approved by the AICTE or other professional councils such as the Medical Council of India. They have flexibility in designing their curriculum, and student evaluation is performed in-house. Some of these entities are accredited by the National Accreditation Board (NAB). Admissions are based on highly selective nationwide or statewide competitive examinations. In some states, the increasing number of institutions has reduced the degree of selectivity overall, but the quality of the institutions varies considerably, and higher-quality institutions maintain a high level of selectivity.

Fees in private educational institutions are currently regulated through a committee headed by a former high court judge. This mechanism allows considerable variation across institutions. Some institutions, including a few that are not in the private sector, such as the Indian Institutes of Management (IIMs), are able to charge market-related fees for professional education, and these have been rising recently.[7]

Linkages between Higher Education and High-Technology Industries in India

The high-tech industry in India has seen some growth, and the share of communications and computer-related services has increased significantly in recent years (figure 1). This growth may have led to an increase in demand for skilled workers; recent studies have indicated the presence of output-skill complementarities (Berman, Somanathan, and Tan 2005; Chamarbagwala and Sharma 2008). There is some evidence for growing wage premiums for skilled workers, driven by growth in demand for skills.[8]

Developments in science and technology, and changes in global production and R&D networks, are creating new opportunities for interaction between academic institutions and firms in India. The evidence reported in Basant and Chandra (2007) suggests that some academic institutions and other entities in the cities of Pune and Bangalore have utilized these opportunities to build linkages and interact with the city clusters in a rich variety of ways. Only a few institutions, however, have the relevant knowledge base needed to undertake high-end knowledge networking activities with industrial entities. The survey data reveal a hierarchy of institutions according to the strengths of their linkages: those that undertake only teaching (linkage through the labor market); those that carry on research and teaching and provide services such as testing (linkages of all the types mentioned earlier); and those that focus on specialized research (linkages predominantly driven by knowledge generation and dissemination). Given the existence of this hierarchy, reflecting low institutional capabilities, academic institutions rarely come together to advance the linkages collectively, but many are gearing up to participate in such linkages in a more systematic manner. The experience of Pune and Bangalore broadly supports the idea

FIGURE 1.
Share of GDP, Select High-Technology Sectors, India, 1999–2000 to 2007–8

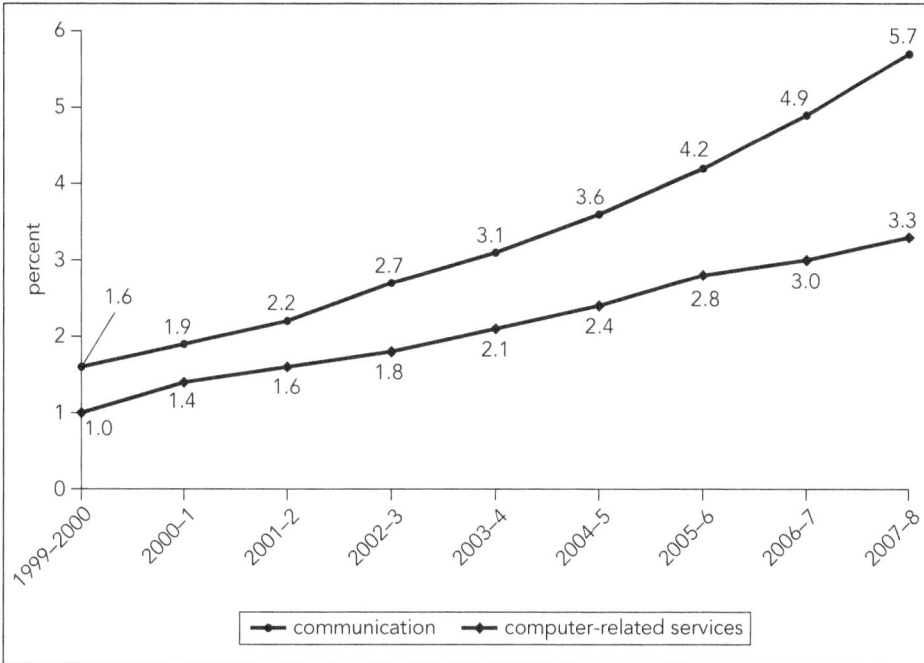

Source: Authors' computation from India, Central Statistical Organisation, *National Accounts Statistics*, various issues.
Note: GDP, gross domestic product.

that institutions (if given some autonomy) and industry coevolve to take advantage of emerging opportunities.

Linkages from Higher Education to High-Technology Industries

Higher education can contribute to high-tech industry through the creation of knowledge (as embodied in patents and publications) and by facilitating the creation of enterprises. Each form of linkage is examined below.

Creation of knowledge: Patenting and research output. Table 3 presents information from the U.S. patent database about patents issued to inventors in India, starting in 1976 (Gupta 2008). Certain broad trends are evident:

1. Patenting in India has increased over time, particularly in recent years. Indian universities, too, have increased their patenting over time in line with this trend, but their share still remains low and is in fact a little less than in 1976–80.

2. Public sector research institutions constitute most of the Indian assignees, and this share is steadily increasing—even more so than that of private firms, whose patenting is also growing. Of the public institution patents, over 80 percent is assigned to the CSIR, a network of publicly funded research laboratories around the country.[9] These laboratories do not have educational functions, reflecting the separation of teaching and research in Indian higher education.

TABLE 3. Patents Awarded to Inventors in India, by Type of Assignee, 1976–2005

	Indian assignee					Foreign assignee		
	Individual	Private firm	Public sector	University or institution	NGO	Private firm	State	University or institution
Number of patents								
1976–80	16	11	3	3	0	50	0	5
1981–85	15	10	3	1	0	34	9	4
1986–90	27	10	16	1	0	36	16	15
1991–95	31	20	35	2	0	114	8	12
1996–2000	70	90	167	13	0	272	12	20
2001–5	82	267	677	45	5	831	2	31
Total	241	408	901	65	5	1,337	47	87
Share of patents of a given assignee over time (percent)								
1976–80	6.6	2.7	0.3	4.6	0.0	3.7	0.0	5.7
1981–85	6.2	2.5	0.3	1.5	0.0	2.5	19.1	4.6
1986–90	11.2	2.5	1.8	1.5	0.0	2.7	34.0	17.2
1991–95	12.9	4.9	3.9	3.1	0.0	8.5	17.0	13.8
1996–2000	29.0	22.1	18.5	20.0	0.0	20.3	25.5	23.0
2001–5	34.0	65.4	75.1	69.2	100.0	62.2	4.3	35.6
Share of assignees as percent of total patents within a period								
1976–80	18.2	12.5	3.4	3.4	0.0	56.8	0.0	5.7
1981–85	19.7	13.2	3.9	1.3	0.0	44.7	11.8	5.3
1986–90	22.3	8.3	13.2	0.8	0.0	29.8	13.2	12.4
1991–95	14.0	9.0	15.8	0.9	0.0	51.4	3.6	5.4
1996–2000	10.9	14.0	25.9	2.0	0.0	42.2	1.9	3.1
2001–5	4.2	13.8	34.9	2.3	0.3	42.8	0.1	1.6
Total	7.8	13.2	29.1	2.1	0.2	43.3	1.5	2.8

Source: Gupta 2008.

Note: NGO, nongovernmental organization.

3. The growing number of patents issued to foreign firms (although it is a declining share, owing to the rise in patenting by domestic firms and public research laboratories) indicates that the extent of spillover from research outsourcing may be weak. This is an indirect effect of the structure of Indian higher education, in that foreign firms established research bases in India to utilize Indian researchers produced by the country's higher education system.

Gupta (2008) provides an interesting insight. Of the top 10 Indian public and private firms (excluding CSIR), which account for over half the patents, only one is in the semiconductor and IT area; the rest are in the pharmaceutical and chemical sectors. Of the top 10 foreign firms, which account for more than 40 percent of the total assignees, only 3 (including a foreign subsidiary of an Indian firm) are in pharmaceuticals and chemicals. Five are IT firms, and two, GE and Unilever, are diversified. It would thus appear that the research areas of domestic and foreign firms do not overlap significantly. Athreye and Prevezer (2008) and Athreye and Puranam (2008) provide more detailed evidence on this point; Indian involvement is much higher in chemistry-oriented sectors than in IT (table 4). The data also suggest that patenting activity has not matched industry growth in telecommunications and IT (table 4).

TABLE 4. Patent Characteristics by Patent Subclassification

Patent subclassification	Share of Indian inventors (percent)[a]	Average backward citation[b]	Average forward citation[c]	Share of Indian entities (percent)[d]
Agriculture, food chemistry	92.6	1.4	3.7	86.7
Chemical engineering	86.8	3.1	10.4	82.0
Metallurgy	86.4	4.3	8.1	80.5
Organic chemistry	87.4	1.9	5.4	73.2
Chemical and petrol industry	87.6	2.4	7.2	72.2
Biotechnology	82.8	0.6	2.5	71.4
Pharmaceuticals, cosmetics	85.7	1.9	7.4	70.6
Materials processing	79.0	36.4	49.8	66.7
Macromolecular chemistry, polymers	71.2	2.1	10.5	47.2
Control technology	71.4	7.2	15.2	36.9
Optics	58.9	19.1	33.5	36.4
Medical technology	69.2	18.8	18.4	31.3
Surface technology	63.8	13.5	28.9	21.4
Semiconductor devices	54.5	8.0	9.9	12.2
Electrical machinery	67.0	5.5	28.0	7.1
Information technology	67.5	3.3	12.8	6.3
Telecommunications	73.3	4.4	11.0	4.5
Audio-visual technology	68.6	4.4	21.1	3.9

Source: Athreye and Puranam 2008.

a. The share of Indian inventors is calculated as the proportion of the number of Indian assignees in a patent to the total number of assignees.
b. Backward citations refers to the number of patents cited by the patent in question.
c. Forward citations refers to the number of times other patents cite the patent in question.
d. Indian entities include public sector institutions, private firms, universities and institutions, and private individuals.

This raises the question of the capacity of domestic industry to benefit from spillovers, since it diminishes the likelihood that the domestic firm is receiver active in the sense described by Kodama, Kano, and Suzuki (2006). Thus, the direct generation of knowledge can largely be attributed to public research labs instead of to higher education institutions, and the indirect generation of knowledge, too, seems to be in areas where linkages to domestic industry appear low. In the case of the pharmaceutical and biotechnology industry, however—consistent with Athreye and Prevezer (2008), Athreye and Puranam (2008), and Gupta (2008)—there seems to be an indication that linkages are beginning to form (see box 1), matching the pattern in developed countries, where such linkages are concentrated in the life sciences sector.

Creation of knowledge: Publications. Even in basic research, the capacity of universities is limited and skewed. About 80 percent of the doctorates awarded in engineering were from 20 universities, and about two-thirds of the science doctorates were from 30 universities. Only about 20 universities have a fellow in one of the three science academies (Agarwal 2006). Even in social sciences, where infrastructural constraints are presumably less binding, just 26.2 percent of the 454 articles published in a leading domestic social science journal between 1998 and 2000 were from universities. Of that share, 13.9 percent came from three universities in Delhi and Mumbai, and the Indian Institutes of Management originated another 4.4 percent; that is, 70 percent of the university total was from these few institutions. Specialized research institutes and organizations accounted for more than universities, with 27.3 percent of all the articles (Chatterjee et al. 2002). Of the total publications from the 15 Indian universities most active in publishing in the areas of health and biotechnology in international peer-reviewed journals during the period 1991–2002, 20.5 percent came from one university, the Indian Institute of Science (Kumar et al. 2004). As is shown below, that institution is also the dominant player in the linkages between academia and industry, especially in the fields of pharmaceuticals and biotechnology.

Research has moved out of Indian universities and other academic institutions over the years. For many years now, the public sector research institutions have been the main centers of research activity, and universities have largely become teaching institutions.

Creation of enterprises. Apart from working in high-tech industries as employees, persons with higher education may set up enterprises in high-tech sectors. Enterprise creation as a part of UILs is still at a nascent stage in India, and relationships outside the labor market are limited to research support through consulting and other research projects. But the focus on enterprise creation is causing considerable excitement among research-oriented science, technology, and management institutions.

Conventional incubators are proliferating in India today. Virtually all the well-known technology institutions have one, and some management institutions are experimenting with the concept. Basant and Chandra (2006) analyze the emerging enterprise-creation role of academic institutions in India and the incubation models used by them. It is too early to assess the impact of these enterprise creation efforts; most have begun only within the last five years. No outstanding success has come to

---

BOX 1. University-Industry Linkages in the Biotechnology and Pharmaceutical Sectors

The Indian biotechnology and pharmaceutical industries have seen significant growth in recent years. There is ample evidence to show that links with academia have also grown, helping to create "training opportunities for in-house staff, improve access to research facilities and expensive equipment, expand clinical trial capabilities and provide access to government-sponsored research funds" (Frew et al. 2007, 408). The variety of linkages is large; partnerships may be focused on product development, drug delivery platforms, drug candidate screening, medical diagnostics, clinical trials, or data management. A few educational institutions such as the Indian Institute of Science have created new enterprises on the basis of technologies developed within the institution. Many partnerships are developing products to address India's local health needs, especially in the area of vaccines. (For descriptions of these partnerships, see, for example, Maria, Ruet, and Zerah 2003; Kumar et al. 2004; Yarnell 2006; Frew et al. 2007.)

A striking finding from a (nonexhaustive) survey of company linkages with universities and public research institutes is that relatively few institutions and firms are involved. The institutions most active in these alliances are the Indian Institute of Science (IISc), the International Centre for Genetic Engineering and Biotechnology (ICGEB), the National Institute of Immunology (NII), the All Indian Institute of Medical Sciences (AIIMS), the Indian Institute of Chemical Technology (IICT) in Hyderabad, and the Centre for Cellular and Molecular Biology (CCMB). Only one of these, the IISc, is a university; participation by other universities, which include the Jawaharlal Nehru University and the Universities of Delhi, Madurai, and Osmania, is fairly limited. Shanta Biotech, Bharat Biotech, Bharat Biotech International, Nicholas Piramal, Dr Reddy's Laboratories, and Ranbaxy are among the few firms that are active in these partnerships.

It thus appears that the linkages are still in their infancy, and it will take some time before they deepen enough to make a significant impact on technology development and diffusion. Participation of only a select set of mainly specialized research institutions highlights the quality constraints that prevent most academic institutions from contributing to these alliances and also points to the adverse effect that the separation of research and teaching may have had on the ability of Indian universities to effectively participate in such collaborations.

---

light, but many incubators can boast of moderate success. Although precise numbers are not available, many companies from technology institutions have survived the rigors of market competition after graduating from the incubators. At the moment, the most important contribution of such efforts has been to highlight the possibility of creating enterprises based on technological innovation in educational institutions. Even moderate success generates a sharper focus on technology-based entrepreneurship as a career option.

A small survey of 11 incubators (35 originally received questionnaires) reveals that 9 are publicly funded; 1 incubator is supported by alumni and another by a venture capital institution. Nine of these incubators are associated with educational institutions, but most of the incubatees are from outside the educational institution, and in eight of the incubators, all the incubatees but one are external to the institution. This is a form of UIL that is perhaps more akin to enterprise nurturing than creation. (It can be argued that this activity is part of the supply of services rather than enterprise creation.) Many incubatees have sought intellectual property (IP) protection (especially in the incubator funded by a venture capital institution), but many have not. Although in this sample most of the incubatees are "outsiders," a large proportion of the incubators in the Indian Institutes of Technology (IITs) and other nationally known institutes of technology incubate their own faculty and students—an activity that comes closer to enterprise creation in the conventional sense of the term. (See Basant and Chandra 2006 for details.)

An alternative model of enterprise creation through focused agenda-based research—as is being pursued by the TeNet group at IIT Madras (http://www.tenet. res.in)—appears to offer an interesting alternative to the conventional model. However, it requires considerable motivation on the part of the research group and the ability to address the trade-off between publication and enterprise creation. Some R&D institutions have just started to grapple with this dilemma, and the idea of enterprise creation might further sharpen the trade-off.

Linkages from High-Technology Industry to Higher Education

As mentioned earlier, industry can support higher education by providing teaching talent; pushing for curriculum reform; taking measures to improve the labor supply through assessment, certification, and registration of professionals; and directly funding institutions. We look at these linkages in the Indian context.

Supply of teachers. The number of higher education institutions has shown strong growth. This is especially true of professional institutions, most of them in the private sector. The number of teachers has not kept pace with this growth, as the number of PhDs produced indicates. Consequently, many of these institutions are staffed by part-time faculty or faculty whose experience has been more in industry than in academia. Although it is mandatory for institutions to disclose the qualifications of faculty, this information is not collated.[10] A quick survey of institution Web sites reveals, however, that a number of faculty members lack PhD degrees and that faculty size is small. In fact, even at the National Institutes of Technology, a large proportion of faculty is without PhDs.[11]

The supply of faculty members from industry, both part-timers and those embarking on a second career, is therefore a significant source of linkage. Although this practice can strengthen industry-academia links, it is possible that, given the differences in compensation, many of those who are choosing to enter academia from industry are not doing so out of choice, and their links with their former organizations may be weaker than would be initially evident.

Modifications and enhancements to curriculum. The IT industry has been in the forefront of demands for changes in the educational curriculum in India as a result of the industry perception that the quality of existing graduates is low. According to the National Association of Software and Service Companies (NASSCOM), only about 25 percent of technical graduates and 10 to 15 percent of general college graduates are currently suitable for employment in the offshore IT and business product outsourcing (BPO) industries, respectively (NASSCOM 2005).[12]

NASSCOM has signed memorandums of understanding with the UGC and the AICTE to strengthen professional education in line with the IT industry's requirements for skilled professionals. A key component is a mentorship program between a higher education institution and a firm. Some examples of these mentoring relationships are those of Zensar with VIT; Pune XANSA with Jammu University; Pixtel Technologies with the ISB Engineering College, Ghaziabad; and Pixtel Technologies with the Galgotia College of Engineering, Greater Noida. In addition, companies such as ITC InfoTech, Accenture, SUN, MindTree, Microsoft, and Patni are undertaking faculty training programs.

NASSCOM is also piloting a "finishing school" for engineering graduates who are still seeking employment. One pilot was conducted during May and June 2007 for a period of eight weeks in eight institutions, including IIT Roorkee and seven National Institutes of Technology (NITs): Khozikode, Durgapur, Kurushetra, Jaipur, Surathkal, Thiruchirapalli, and Warangal. The "finishing school" addresses both technical and soft skills development and is staffed by trained faculty and practicing IT and IT-enabled services (ITES) industry consultants. The students receive an opportunity to reinforce key basic engineering skills and, in addition, acquire industry-specific knowledge, soft skills, and management and employment skills (NASSCOM 2007).

Some NASSCOM members have intensively promoted training and supplementary education for their recruits and employees. Wipro Technologies has had an Academy of Software Excellence for over 10 years; the Infosys Campus Connect program (see box 2) is about 5 years old. The extent of remediation efforts being undertaken by the IT industry is an indication of the inappropriate training of graduating engineers from higher education institutions, at least from the point of view of the IT sector.[13] These industry initiatives are in addition to a private training industry that began to develop along with the growth of the IT sector and has now diversified into training for back-office operations, retail employment, and the like. The courses do not have a certification other than the brand name of the institute.[14] The responsibility for quality assurance therefore rests with the student.

Some pharmaceutical firms have also developed linkages with universities, for example, through continuing-education PhD programs with universities for their lab researchers.[15] These linkages, however, are restricted to a few institutions. Bhattacharya and Arora (2007) find that of seven select universities, only three (IIT Delhi, Jawaharlal Nehru University, and Delhi University) interacted actively with industry in curriculum design across departments. In two (Pune and Jadavpur) such interaction was linked to a few departments, and Hyderabad University and the Indian Institute of Science reported no such linkages. These limited relationships may become

---

BOX 2. The Infosys Campus Connect Program

Infosys, a large Indian IT services provider with over 100,000 employees, annually recruits more than 10,000 professionals. In May 2004 the company launched Campus Connect with 60 colleges, as an "industry-academia collaboration program to align engineering student competencies with industry needs" (see Infosys 2007). The program has grown rapidly, and as of March 2008, it extended to 500 colleges. It operates at present in nine cities in India and is now expanding to China, Malaysia, and Mexico. In its short history, Campus Connect has already trained 25,000 students and enhanced the skills of 2,000 faculty members.

The core of Campus Connect is the Foundation Program, a 130-classroom-hour proprietary educational supplement for a batch size of 60–75 students that is integrated with the college's academic schedule and may include industrial visits to Infosys development centers. The course material is provided by Infosys and is based on resources it uses for its induction programs, including assignments, case studies, and a student project bank that simulates live project situations adapted for academic environments. All other facilities are provided by the participating college. A companion soft skills program, delivered by alliance partners, is intended to develop students' proficiency in communications, teamwork, corporate work culture, and so on. In contrast to the foundation program, there is a charge for the soft skills program.

The college is given incentives on the basis of the performance of the number of graduates joining Infosys and is expected to pass on the cash benefits received from Infosys to faculty members and other individuals according to college-specific norms. Campus Connect also engages in such activities as facilitating faculty sabbaticals and sponsoring presentations of papers at conferences.

By aligning the skill needs of IT services with the college curriculum, Campus Connect reduces learning time and training cost after employment. Infosys does not guarantee that graduates of Campus Connect will be offered employment, nor is it incumbent on graduates to accept an offer from Infosys, should it choose to make one. Infosys thus banks on its reputation as a superior employer and its large annual recruitment to ensure that a sufficient number of Campus Connect graduates accepts Infosys offers to make its investment in the program worthwhile.

---

weaker if PhD programs begin to exit the university and move to specialized institutions, as incipient trends indicate. National laboratories rather than universities are becoming the locus of PhD research; for example, the National Chemical Laboratory may well be the largest producer of PhDs in the chemical sciences (see Yarnell 2006).

Industry participation in the curriculum is now spreading to other areas, foremost of which is vocational training, where the private sector already has a strong presence. India has many industrial training institutes (ITIs) that offer a variety of courses, including long-term courses ranging from two to three years, especially for the manufacturing sector. As part of an ongoing reform program, many industries and industry associations are now becoming involved in the management of these institutions and in improving the relevance to industry of their instruction.[16]

Although the system can be commended for allowing the growth of such initiatives by benignly neglecting to regulate them, their expansion does raise questions about the ability of the formal higher education system to respond to market demand, especially with respect to professional courses.[17]

Improvement in labor quality. In addition to modifications to curriculum, the IT industry, through NASSCOM, has undertaken other initiatives to improve the quality of the labor supply, especially for the ITES sector. The degree of selectivity in the basic educational qualification for the ITES sector, which comprises university education in all disciplines, is less than that of engineering, which is the base qualification in the IT sector. The improvement initiatives can be grouped under the heads of testing and verification.

The NASSCOM Assessment of Competence (NAC) is designed to address possible talent shortages by creating a robust and continuous pipeline of talent for the ITES industry through a standard assessment and certification program. The assessment program tests the aptitude of a candidate on seven skill sets.[18] NASSCOM has also partnered with other organizations to develop customized certification programs for frontline managers in this sector, for example, certified BPO quality analyst (CBQA) and certified BPO team leader, level 1 (CBTL-1). A test for the IT sector, NAC-Tech has also been developed. The need for such tests reflects the limited effectiveness of quality regulation with respect to educational institutions.

Labor quality is also affected by fraudulent reporting of qualifications. To facilitate more accurate verification of credentials, NASSCOM has fostered a National Skills Registry (NSR) to ensure that there is a verified database of the skill sets and talents of the human resources within the ITES industry. The NSR contains personal, academic, and employment details for IT professionals (ITPs), as entered by the individuals themselves, with associated background check information. It covers ITP employees and prospective employees in the IT and ITES industries. Every ITP registered in the NSR is identified uniquely by fingerprints, and the database includes the ITP's photograph. As of September 2009, 79 major companies and over 485,551 professionals have registered (see www.nationalskillsregistry.com).

Funding of higher education institutions. Although the government provides most of the funding for public institutions, private funding has made noticeable contributions to some. Much of this funding, however, is limited to marquee institutions such as the IITs and IIMs. On occasion, Indian industry has contributed to institutions abroad. It has been argued (for example, by Kapur and Mehta 2007) that a burgeoning trend toward private contributions may have been nipped in the bud by the government's desire to control the flows by insisting that they be channeled through a central fund, the Bharat Shiksha Kosh (India Education Fund), whose use would be determined by the central Ministry of Education. There is, however, considerable private funding of higher education through the establishment of privately owned educational institutions, which now constitute the majority of institutions in professional and technical education.

Relative Importance of Different Linkages

The creation of knowledge and the creation of enterprises are, at this time, relatively weak channels of interaction between industry and academia. The universities produce few patents, and even the generation of publications is limited and is concentrated in a few universities. As for enterprise creation, the role of educational institutions can better be described as nurturing rather than creative—facilitating existing entrepreneurs in pursuit of their goals. A select few academic institutions are collaborating with a limited number of pharmaceutical and biotechnology firms to develop technologies. In this context, the growing interest of high-tech industry, especially IT, in remedial or supplementary education and in participating in the improvement of educational institutions indicates that the strongest link at this time between higher education and high-tech industry in developing countries such as India is likely to be through the labor market.

Labor Market Linkages

To investigate the nature of the labor market linkage, we analyze unit-level data from the 61st round of the National Sample Survey (NSS) for 2004–5.[19] If the labor market links between higher education and high-tech industry are strong, one would expect that persons with higher education would have a higher propensity to be employed in high-tech industry.

Defining High-Technology Industries

Following the classification by the Organisation for Economic Co-operation and Development (OECD) of industries as low tech, medium tech, medium-high tech, and high tech, we grouped 60 manufacturing industries into three categories.[20] Stehrer and Wörz (2003), in their analysis, use four categories, according to technology level: low, medium low, medium high, and high. This grouping is not as disaggregated as the OECD's, and a comparison of the two shows that several groups categorized as medium tech by the OECD are under high tech in the other categorization. At the three-digit industry group level, reclassification of the OECD high-tech designation into medium high and high tech might be too arbitrary. Consequently, for our purposes all manufacturing industries categorized as medium-high tech in the OECD classification are considered high tech.

The "high-tech equivalent" in the services sector is categorized as financial and IT-related services. Anecdotal evidence suggests that in recent years a large proportion of persons with higher education have joined these sectors, especially those who have technical degrees. Financial intermediation, which includes banking, insurance, pension funds, and the like (Standard Industrial Classification, or SIC, codes 65–67), is treated as one of the high-tech services. The other is computer-related activities (SIC code 72), which includes software and hardware consulting. This category also captures IT outsourcing of various kinds. In accordance with this conceptualization of high-tech industry, our empirical exercise recognizes three types of high-tech industry:

- All high-tech industry (high-tech manufacturing, financial services, and IT)
- High-tech manufacturing
- High-tech services (financial intermediation and computer and computer-related activities—mainly, IT services).

Defining Higher Education

The key purpose of the exercise is to ascertain whether higher education increases the probability of being employed in the high-tech sectors. To do so, we need to define higher education. The NSS 61st round data allow us to create the following categories relating to higher education:

- *All types of higher education*: any graduate (or equivalent) qualification and above. Included are persons with a general education level of graduate or postgraduate and above, or with a technical degree or a technical diploma or certificate (graduate and above).
- *Nontechnical higher education*: graduate and above in the general education category.
- *Technical higher education*: technical degree, or graduate (and above) diploma or certificate courses.
- *Nontechnical higher education with technical nongraduate diplomas*: graduate (or above) in general education with below–graduate level technical diplomas or certificates.

Other Explanatory Variables

Apart from the level of education of the worker, several other factors may influence the probability that a worker will be employed in high-tech industry. At the individual level, we include age and gender as two control variables. At the regional or state level, apart from rural or urban place of residence, we introduce the following variables to capture the importance of high-tech employment in the region and its infrastructural characteristics:

1. *Importance of high-tech employment in the region.* If a region has a large high-tech sector, the possibility that a worker located in that region will be employed in that sector goes up. To capture this "demand" effect, we used the share of high-tech employment in total employment in the state as a variable.

2. *Infrastructural facilities.* Good infrastructure is often a prerequisite for the industrialization of a region. This is especially true for high-tech industries, which are typically infrastructure intensive. Availability of good infrastructure can facilitate

the emergence and growth of high-tech industries in a region. In that sense, it can enhance the share of high-tech employment in the region, thereby increasing the value of the high-tech employment variable defined above. However, infrastructure can have another effect by facilitating participation of workers in such industries. For example, good transportation facilities can enlarge the spatial scope of the labor market, and good telecommunications facilities can facilitate participation of workers in the hinterland, especially in the area of IT services.

The state infrastructure indexes prepared by Mohanty (2004) are used to capture this effect. The infrastructure index "reflects the degree to which a state is prepared in terms of its infrastructure to enable its population to take advantage of public services" and the associated industrial employment opportunities. The summary infrastructure index measures the overall levels of infrastructure development at the state level. The aggregate measure is based on variables that measure the supply as well as the use of infrastructural facilities in three sectors: communications, power, and transport.[21] In order to capture the relative situation of states in each of the underlying sectors, sector-specific indexes have also been used. Potentially, different segments of infrastructure can influence employment in high-tech industry differently. Thus, we have four indexes for infrastructure for each state: an aggregate summary index of infrastructure; a power infrastructure index; a telecommunications infrastructure index; and a transport infrastructure index. Both the supply and the use of each category of infrastructure have been captured in these subindexes.

Results

Table 5 shows that, on average, high-tech industries have a greater propensity to use workers with higher education. The share of workers in high-tech industries with graduate and postgraduate qualifications (both general and technical) is significantly higher than in other industries. Within high-tech sectors, high-tech services seem to be using workers with higher education more intensively than does high-tech manufacturing, especially in urban areas.[22]

TABLE 5. Share of Workers with Higher Education in High-Technology Industries
(percent)

Level of education	All high-technology industries		High-technology manufacturing		High-technology services		All industries	
	Rural	Urban	Rural	Urban	Rural	Urban	Rural	Urban
Graduate and postgraduate education	18.7	42.4	10.3	23.7	36.5	65.9	2.7	16.2
No technical education	87.1	76.8	86.6	79.2	88.3	73.9	98.6	92.6

Source: Authors' calculations based on individual-level data, National Sample Survey, Round 61.

TABLE 6. Determinants of Participation in High-Technology Industry, All Graduates

Variable	All high-technology industry		High-technology manufacturing		High-technology services	
	Marginal effect	$P > |z|$	Marginal effect	$P > |z|$	Marginal effect	$P > |z|$
Age	−0.000124	0.00	−0.000106	0.00	−0.000009	0.24
Rural dummy	−0.024291	0.00	−0.015218	0.00	−0.006815	0.00
Male dummy	0.005572	0.00	0.003227	0.00	0.001745	0.00
Infrastructure index	0.000005	0.74	0.000005	0.68	0.000001	0.92
State share of high-technology employment	0.000950	0.06	0.000412	0.24	0.000342	0.13
All graduates	0.045689	0.00	0.007687	0.00	0.034418	0.00
Nongraduate technical education	0.040615	0.00	0.026002	0.00	0.010265	0.00
Observed probability	0.019166		0.011349		0.007816	
Predicted probability	0.008276		0.005322		0.002101	
Number of observations	244,849		244,849		244,849	
Wald chi^2 (29)	3958.68		1897.17		2865.62	
Prob > chi^2	0.0000		0.0000		0.0000	
Pseudo R^2	0.1978		0.1448		0.2606	
Log pseudolikelihood	−18614.40		−13005.99		−8275.08	

Source: Authors' calculations.

Note: Estimates for state dummies have been suppressed.

In order to explore the relationship between high-tech industries and higher education more systematically, we estimate the likelihood of being employed in high-tech industries, using a probit specification. These estimated relationships assess whether the likelihood of participation in high-tech industries increases with higher education, even after controlling for some other individual- and region-specific variables.

The results presented in table 6 show that higher education has a positive and significant effect on the likelihood of a worker's participation in high-tech industries. Interestingly, nongraduate technical education also has a positive and significant effect on participation in high-tech industries, although its impact is marginally lower than that of higher education.

Within high-tech industries there are some interesting differences. In high-tech manufacturing, although the impact of higher education is positive and significant, it is somewhat lower than the effect of nongraduate technical education. The situation is just the opposite in the case of high-tech services, where higher education has a larger impact on the likelihood of being employed in the industry than does nongraduate technical education.

As expected, male workers are more likely to be engaged in such industries, and rural location affects the likelihood of working in high-tech industry adversely, other things being equal. However, it also appears that the negative effect of rural location is outweighed by the education effect. Local infrastructure does not seem to have any

TABLE 7. Determinants of Participation in High-Technology Industry, Disaggregated Education

Variable	All high-technology industry		High-technology manufacturing		High-technology services	
	Marginal effect	$P > |z|$	Marginal effect	$P > |z|$	Marginal effect	$P > |z|$
Age	−0.000121	0.00	−0.000104	0.00	0.000008	0.30
Rural dummy	−0.024286	0.00	−0.015194	0.00	−0.006846	0.00
Male dummy	0.005606	0.00	0.003201	0.00	0.001772	0.00
Infrastructure index	0.000005	0.73	0.000005	0.65	0.000001	0.91
State share of high-technology employment	0.001037	0.04	0.000455	0.18	0.000369	0.11
Nontechnical graduate	0.038146	0.00	0.003750	0.00	0.032824	0.00
Technical graduate	0.086855	0.00	0.025713	0.00	0.049432	0.00
Graduates with nongraduate technical education	0.080286	0.00	0.018771	0.02	0.055741	0.00
Nongraduate technical	0.041013	0.00	0.026084	0.00	0.010402	0.00
Observed probability	0.019166		0.011350		0.007816	
Predicted probability	0.008313		0.005296		0.002127	
Number of observations	244,849		244,849		244,849	
Wald chi^2 (31)	4033.68		1934.39		2904.67	
Prob > chi^2	0.0000		0.0000		0.0000	
Pseudo R^2	0.2002		0.1488		0.2608	
Log pseudolikelihood	−18560.63		−12945.36		−8271.93	

Source: Authors' calculations.

Note: Estimates for state dummies have been suppressed.

direct impact on a worker's participation in high-tech industries. The share of high-tech employment in total state employment does have a positive impact but is somewhat significant only when all high-tech industries are looked at together.

Disaggregation of higher education categories provides some interesting insights, as seen in table 7. The estimates suggest that the impact of technical higher education on participation in high-tech industries is higher than that of nontechnical higher education. Interestingly, when nontechnical higher education is combined with nongraduate technical education, their impact, taken together, is almost the same as that of technical higher education. Nongraduate technical education also has a positive impact, but the magnitude is less, close to that of nontechnical higher education. The impact of other variables is similar.

These results are not affected when we disaggregate the infrastructure index (results are available on request). No subsector index approaches significance, with the possible exception of the effect of power on services. It is possible that part of the impact is captured by the share of high-tech employment in total state employment insofar as good infrastructure facilitates the growth of such industries. The "commutation effect" through transport and the "local outsourcing" effect through communications are not yet visible.

Apart from highlighting the strong effect of higher education on the probability of high-tech employment, these results provide some interesting insights. The observation that graduates with nongraduate technical education are in a similar situation as technical graduates indicates that firms may have some flexibility in combining technical and nontechnical education. Furthermore, the links between higher education and high-tech employment are stronger in services than in manufacturing across most categories. As expected, nongraduate technical education helps in obtaining manufacturing jobs more than jobs in services, and nontechnical graduate education is more of a help for employment in services than in manufacturing. Services also appear relatively less gender biased than manufacturing.[23]

Response of the Higher Education Sector

The preceding analysis of the Indian labor market makes it clear that acquiring higher education, especially technical education, does help improve the chances of employment in the high-tech sector. Given the wage premium in this sector, it is natural that there will be increasing demand for higher education as the pool of the eligible population increases.[24] How has the higher education sector responded to this development?

Growth in Institutions

As figure 2 shows, the number of higher education institutions has exhibited substantial growth in recent years. The number of universities shows a sharp upward trend in figure 3, and an even more rapid rise is seen in the number of deemed-to-be universities, as shown in figure 4, with the private sector accounting for an overwhelming number in recent years.[25]

Concentration in specific states. The stock of institutions is concentrated in a few states, most of which are rich and relatively urban (table 8). Five southern states—Tamil Nadu, Kerala, Karnataka, Andhra Pradesh, and Maharashtra—and two in the north, Haryana and Punjab, have a technical institution intensity index (the share of technical institutions divided by the share of population) greater than unity. Three of these states, Maharashtra, Haryana, and Punjab, are the top three states in per capita income, and the other four occupy the sixth to ninth ranks. Five of these seven states are among the six most urbanized states in the country. (Andhra Pradesh is at the national average, and Kerala is below the national average.) Although the seven states have only 35.5 percent of the national population and 36.4 percent of the universities, they account for 48.8 percent of all nonagricultural and nonhousehold workers. Except in Andhra Pradesh, the ratio of such workers is higher than the national average.

These states account for 53.4 percent of all deemed-to-be universities, 59.3 percent of all private deemed-to-be universities, and 61.9 percent of the applications for deemed-to-be universities. They also have 74 percent of all engineering colleges and 69 percent of all medical colleges.

FIGURE 2.
Number of Colleges for Professional Education, India, 1950–2005

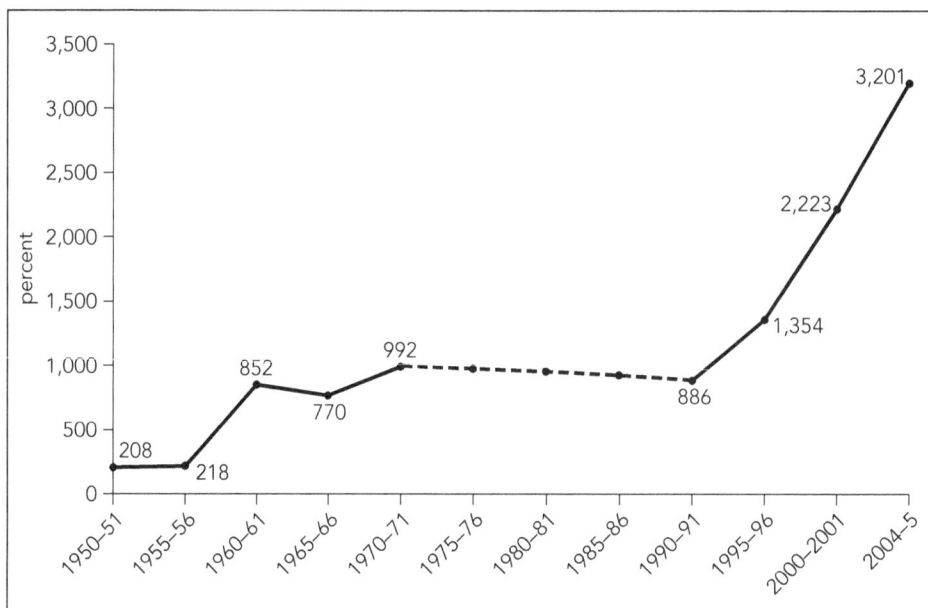

Source: India, Ministry of Human Resource Development, "Selected Educational Statistics, 2004–05."

Note: Data for the years 1975–76, 1980–81, and 1985–86 are not comparable because they include institutions other than professional colleges.

FIGURE 3.
Number of New Universities (Not Including Deemed-to-Be Universities), India, Pre-1950 and 1950–2005

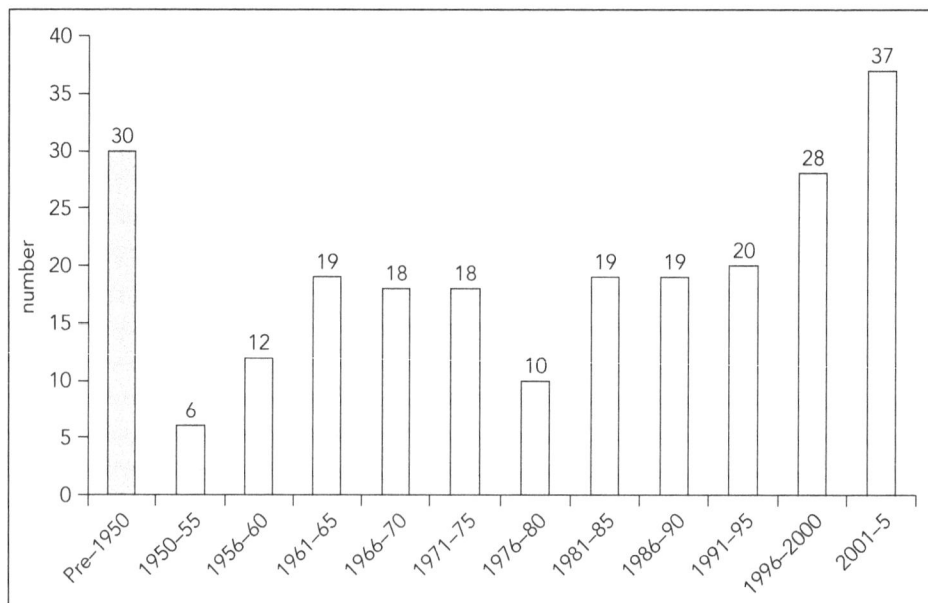

Source: Calculated from dates of establishment provided in University Grants Commission, *Annual Report 2005–06.*

FIGURE 4.
Number of New Deemed-to-be Universities, India, 1956–2009

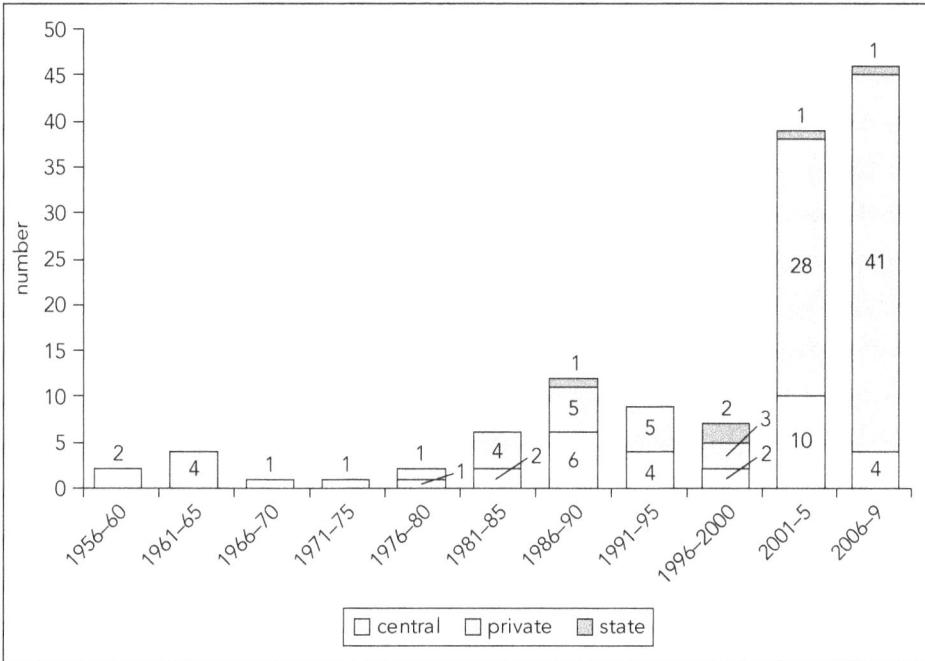

Source: Calculated from the dates of establishment provided on University Grants Commission Web site, http://www.ugc.ac.in/inside/deemeduniv.html (accessed September 9, 2009), with authors' analysis of ownership.

Rise in private participation. Most of these educational institutions are private. As table 9 shows, four of the seven states discussed above, Andhra Pradesh, Tamil Nadu, Maharashtra, and Karnataka, are in the top five states by share of private engineering colleges and among the top seven states as measured by share of private medical colleges.[26] This is consistent with an increasing trend toward private higher education institutions and enrollments in recent years. In 2000–2001 private unaided institutions constituted 42.6 percent of the total number of higher education institutions; by 2005–6 the figure was 63.21 percent. The number of private unaided institutions (universities and colleges) almost doubled in a span of four years, from 3,223 in 2000–2001 to 7,720 in 2005–6. Similarly, the share of enrollment in private unaided higher education institutions has grown from 32.89 percent in 2000–2001 (1.8 million in enrollments) to 51.53 percent in 2005–6 (3.2 million). The rise in government and private aided institutions was not as significant, according to the UGC (2005–6). The numbers are even more skewed for professional education, with the private share comprising 92 percent of engineering colleges, 64 percent of management training institutions (90 percent for hotel management), and 44 percent of medical colleges (Agarwal 2006; Prakash 2007).

TABLE 8. Number of Institutions, by State, 2004–5

State	Share of population (percent)	General colleges	Technical colleges[a]	Medical colleges[b]	Other	Technical institution Intensity index[c]
Andhra Pradesh	7.37	1,340	261	53	93	2.08
Haryana	2.05	166	69	8	35	1.83
Karnataka	5.13	930	120	172	214	2.77
Kerala	3.10	186	66	40	82	1.67
Maharashtra	9.42	1,208	177	116	128	1.52
Punjab	2.37	212	27	49	51	1.56
Tamil Nadu	6.05	445	222	97	184	2.57
Assam	2.59	317	3	7	21	0.19
Bihar	8.07	743	7	23	63	0.18
Chhattisgarh	2.02	213	2	2	32	0.10
Gujarat	4.93	507	44	57	177	1.00
Himachal Pradesh	0.59	89	3	7	24	0.83
Jammu and Kashmir	0.98	50	4	6	34	0.50
Jharkhand	2.62	117	5	8	8	0.24
Madhya Pradesh	5.88	760	60	28	209	0.73
Orissa	3.57	700	37	30	102	0.91
Rajasthan	5.50	611	39	24	113	0.56
Uttar Pradesh	16.17	1,009	69	34	702	0.31
Uttarakhand	0.83	86	2	1	28	0.18
West Bengal	7.81	374	54	19	33	0.46
Total		10,063	1,271	781	2,333	

Source: India, Ministry of Human Resource Development, "Selected Educational Statistics, 2004–5."

a. Includes technical and architecture colleges.
b. Includes Ayurvedic, homeopathic, Unani, nursing, pharmacy, etc.
c. The technical institution intensity index is the state's share of professional colleges divided by its share of population.

The surge in private engineering and technological education can be seen in the fact that whereas in 1978 the state of Andhra Pradesh had just one private engineering college and no private medical college, by 2003 it had 213 private (but only 10 government) engineering colleges, and 14 private and 14 government medical colleges. The number of private engineering colleges in Karnataka rose from 17 in 1978 to 99 in 2003; in Maharashtra, from 1 to 133; in Tamil Nadu, from 0 to 234; in Haryana, from 2 to 29; and in Uttar Pradesh, from 1 to 58. The private sector also dominates degree and diploma courses in Ayurvedic and Unani medicine, homeopathy, and physiotherapy (Powar and Bhalla 2004).

Quality of Institutions

Although the education sector has certainly responded to the growth of the high-tech sector, the quality of the response has not been as encouraging. We earlier pointed out industry's dissatisfaction with the quality of the graduates and its efforts in remedial and supplementary education. Table 10 presents data on several factors related

TABLE 9. Distribution of Technical Educational Institutions by Ownership and by State, 2003

State	Medical			Engineering		
	Number of government colleges	Number of private colleges	Share of private sector (percent)	Number of government colleges	Number of private colleges	Share of private sector (percent)
Andhra Pradesh	14	14	50.0	10	213	95.5
Haryana	1	2	66.7	7	29	80.6
Karnataka	4	22	84.6	13	99	88.4
Kerala	7	8	53.3	31	51	62.2
Maharashtra	19	18	48.6	16	133	89.3
Punjab	3	3	50.0	11	27	71.1
Tamil Nadu	12	7	36.8	16	234	93.6
Assam	3	0	0.0	3	0	0.0
Bihar	6	2	25.0	4	3	42.9
Chhattisgarh	2	0	0.0	2	9	81.8
Gujarat	8	4	33.3	9	16	64.0
Himachal Pradesh	2	0	0.0	2	3	60.0
Jharkhand	0	2	100.0	4	2	33.3
Madhya Pradesh	5	1	16.7	6	47	88.7
Orissa	3	0	0.0	6	38	86.4
Uttar Pradesh	10	2	16.7	25	58	69.9
Uttarakhand	0	2	100.0	5	4	44.4
West Bengal	7	0	0.0	15	37	71.2
Total or average	106	87	45	185	1,003	84

Source: Kapur and Mehta 2007.

to quality: the student-teacher ratio, the quality of institutions (as assessed by the NAAC), and the pass rate of graduates.

In student-teacher ratios, three of the five best states are among the seven states highlighted above, but three of the seven (Maharashtra, Punjab, and Haryana) have ratios worse than the national average, and Andhra Pradesh is close to the national average. Similarly, in the proportion of institutions rated below average, four of the seven states are among the lowest five states, but three others, Karnataka, Maharashtra, and Haryana, have a high proportion of institutions in the below-average category. As for pass rates, none of the seven states is among the top five.

Table 11 presents the pass rate for graduates by discipline. In almost none of the categories does more than one of these seven states figure in the top five in pass rates, and often none of them do. (The one exception is nursing, where two of the seven are in the top five.) Although it can be argued that this is because of the larger number of institutions and therefore a larger intake pool, the results are disturbing, especially when the other data on quality and on the employability of graduates in engineering disciplines are taken into account (table 12).

TABLE 10. Quality Indicators for Higher Education, by State

State	Student-teacher ratio[a]	Percent of colleges rated below average[b]	Percent of students passing final exams[c]	Percent gainfully employed within two years after graduating[d]
Andhra Pradesh	21	29	48	48.8
Haryana	27	59	71	
Karnataka	14	47	64	64.0
Kerala	16	11	66	94.3
Maharashtra	26	55	62	75.5
Punjab	25	17	74	54.5
Tamil Nadu	16	21	46	33.5
Assam	16	76	60	76.8
Bihar	19	64	73	62.8
Chhattisgarh	34	45	76	
Gujarat	41	34	75	62.0
Himachal Pradesh	29	42	69	
Jammu and Kashmir	18	8	79	41.2
Jharkhand	25	47	71	
Madhya Pradesh	35	55	76	52.8
Orissa	18	74	75	39.5
Rajasthan	30	61	76	74.5
Uttar Pradesh	46	52	63	87.0
Uttarakhand	40	43	77	
West Bengal	29	47	71	82.7
India	23	47	63	51.2

Source: See notes below.

a. University Grants Commission, *Annual Report 2005-06;* India, Ministry of Human Resource Development, "Selected Educational Statistics, 2004-05."
b. Quality categories used in this table are adapted from National Assessment and Accreditation Council (NAAC) grading; http://www.naacindia.org.
c. University Grants Commission, "University Development in India, Basic Facts and Figures, Examination Results—2002."
d. Institute of Applied Manpower Research (IAMR), *Manpower Profile India 2005.*

Discussion

The institutional response has been one of significant growth in recent years. The private sector is not just establishing professional colleges; it is also founding universities. Given the low number of private universities created by state acts and the much larger number of deemed-to-be universities, the preferred entry mode of the private sector appears to be by the latter route, presumably because of the considerable regulatory constraints involved in establishing a university by state act. With the approval of a large number of private deemed-to-be universities, the mix of universities is changing. If all 128 pending proposals for deemed-to-be universities were to be approved, the number of universities and deemed-to-be universities would be almost equal. The outcome, however, may not be any greater variety in curriculum and course offerings, since a number of the deemed-to-be universities are specialized institutions or engineering and technology institutions. Moreover, the UGC can be

TABLE 11. Percent of Students Passing Final Examinations, by Subject and by State

State	Computer science and applications	Engineering	Management	Medical and dental	Nursing
Andhra Pradesh	79	72	74	74	92
Haryana	85	89	71	59	—
Karnataka	88	85	79	78	100
Kerala	76	71	76	88	98
Maharashtra	97	73	47	70	90
Punjab	96	90	96	73	96
Tamil Nadu	34	77	50	70	98
Assam	98	81	85	60	66
Bihar	92	67	74	90	100
Chhattisgarh	100	86	100	77	99
Gujarat	96	92	86	77	100
Himachal Pradesh	—	83	85	78	—
Jammu and Kashmir	—	36	89	83	—
Jharkhand	100	97	100	70	—
Madhya Pradesh	88	91	56	87	96
Orissa	96	86	90	87	—
Rajasthan	88	88	57	82	88
Uttar Pradesh	62	85	87	73	—
Uttarakhand	99	98	91	—	—
West Bengal	100	94	99	95	—
India	49	79	61	75	97

Source: University Grants Commission, "University Development in India, Basic Facts and Figures, Examination Results—2002."

Note: —, not available.

overbearing in its regulation, which extends to the nomenclature of degrees. For example, in 2001 it prohibited universities from offering a bachelor's and master's degree in information technology or information sciences, insisting instead that they award bachelor of science and master of science degrees.[27]

The growth of deemed-to-be universities may have implications for the poor institutional quality of the response to the needs of high-tech industry. The regulation of higher education in India flows from the grant funding made available by the UGC, but universities theoretically have complete autonomy in their decision making. The AICTE has greater control over the institutes it regulates, but the quality and effectiveness of the regulation have come in for criticism.

Private deemed-to-be universities do not receive funding from the UGC, and as universities, they would arguably be outside the purview of the AICTE.[28] In addition, states are establishing affiliating universities, which could bypass AICTE regulation, given the concept of university autonomy. A number of technical institutions are now affiliated with a state university, which is really an affiliating organization rather than a teaching and research institution.[29] For professional disciplines like medicine and nursing, there is a single professional council that serves as regulator and accreditation agency.

TABLE 12. Percent Gainfully Employed within Two Years of Graduating,
by Engineering Discipline and by State

State	Chemical engineering	Civil engineering	Computer science	Electronics and communications	Electrical	Mechanical
Andhra Pradesh	31	56	54	57	59	36
Haryana	—	—	—	—	—	—
Karnataka	66	67	68	60	61	62
Kerala	100	82	100	100	84	100
Maharashtra	83	68	83	60	80	79
Punjab	45	45	81	58	41	57
Tamil Nadu	23	38	35	33	43	29
Assam	95	65	93	94	51	63
Bihar	67	67	—	84	77	82
Chhattisgarh	—	—	—	—	—	—
Gujarat	57	59	80	69	49	58
Himachal Pradesh	—	—	—	—	—	—
Jammu and Kashmir	29	22	95	8	50	43
Jharkhand	—	—	—	—	—	—
Madhya Pradesh	29	90	66	42	46	44
Orissa	47	40	33	36	40	41
Rajasthan	62	51	100	89	72	73
Uttar Pradesh	100	71	100	80	87	84
Uttarakhand	—	—	—	—	—	—
West Bengal	85	87	84	79	79	82

Source: Institute of Applied Manpower Research (IAMR), *Manpower Profile India 2005.*

Note: —, not available.

The system of regulation in India is thus not geared to respond to the growing role of the private sector, which appears to be reacting to a sharp spurt in demand for education. In addition, smaller foreign educational institutions are now offering distance learning courses or offsite courses through Indian educational institutions.

Overall then, in response to the growing demand, India has seen significant growth in educational institutions, led by the private sector in select states that are relatively rich. Agarwal (2006) reaches similar conclusions about the role of the private sector when he states that unaided institutions are growing rapidly and government and aided institutions are either not growing or are growing slowly. This can be seen as a progression from the situation in which the universities were largely public sector but a significant mode of undergraduate education was affiliated colleges in the private sector. The private sector has set up not just professional colleges but also universities, with deemed-to-be universities (typically small) being the preferred private entry mode. The quality of this largely private sector response is variable, in part because of the nature of regulation but also because of the inherent incentive structure in some private institutions.

Higher Education Response in Other South Asian Countries

A number of the features described above are common to other South Asian countries, such as Bangladesh, Pakistan, and Sri Lanka. The role of the government in these countries is still large, especially in Sri Lanka, but there is strong private sector growth wherever it is permitted or tolerated. Much of this growth is directed to meeting the immediate labor supply needs of the high-tech industrial and service sectors, as in India, but because of the limited size of the sectors in these countries, we do not observe the kind of feedback loop in those countries that we are beginning to see in India.

Bangladesh

At present, Bangladesh has 80 universities, of which 53 are private and 27 are public. There are 1,400 colleges providing tertiary-level education, all of which are affiliated with National University.[30] Students in these affiliated colleges make up 80 percent of all enrollment. After the enactment of the Private University Act in 1992, enrollment in private universities grew rapidly, from 8,718 students in 1998 to 35,968 in 2001 and 91,648 in 2005—nearly half of the enrollment outside National University. In public universities, the comparable figures were 67,531 students in 1998, 92,562 in 2001, and more than 115,929 in 2005. In that year there were 6,852 teachers, 5,498 officers, and 14,643 employees in public universities, and 3,487

FIGURE 5.
Distribution of Private Universities by Enrollment, Bangladesh, 2005

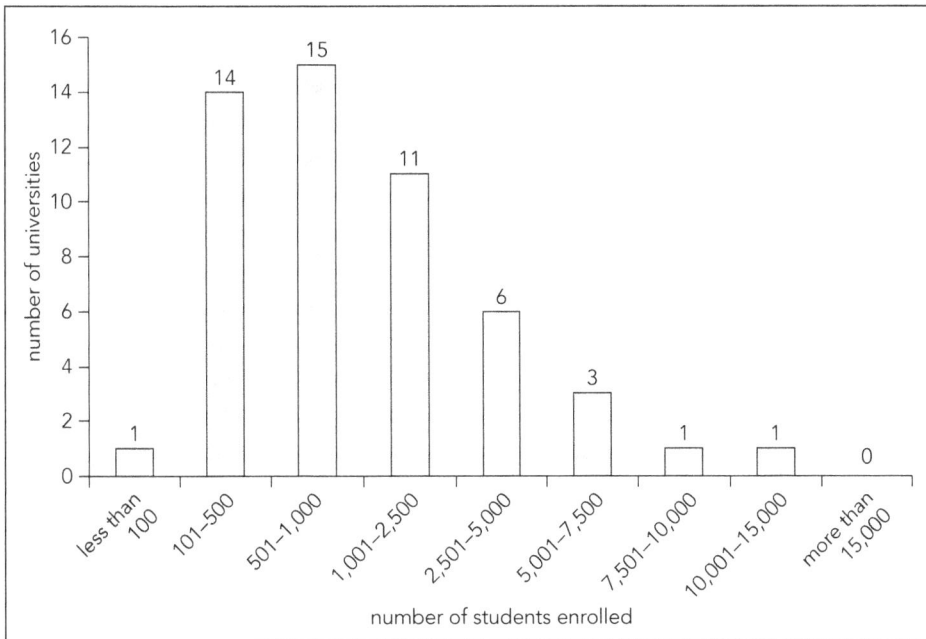

Source: BANBEIS 2006.

Note: Data are not available for all 53 private universities.

teachers, 1,299 officers, and 2,356 employees in private universities.[31] The private universities are small (see figure 5), and 46 of the total of 53 are located in the Dhaka metropolitan area. Private affiliated colleges account for more than 80 percent of enrollment in general undergraduate degree courses but for only 25 percent of the enrollment in honors courses and 17 percent in postgraduate courses. Similarly, in technical and vocational education, private offerings have been limited to the secondary and higher-secondary school levels. This indicates that the private sector is currently serving the lower end of the market.

Aminuzzaman (2007) avers that quality evaluation processes, diagnostic review, and evaluation of quality are generally absent in higher education institutions, except for administrative reviews by departmental chairmen or deans of the faculties in the public universities. Private universities do, however, have to seek mandatory approval from Bangladesh's University Grants Commission. Aminuzzaman also states that industry and corporate support, which plays an important role in research in the fields of business, science, and technology, is absent in Bangladesh. He contends that research activities in higher education are constrained by inadequate financial support and by lack of a clear research program; of facilities such as laboratories, equipment, libraries, and journals; and of faculty incentives for research, such as time-bound promotion rules. In public universities, both revenue and expenditure per student are low; 70 percent of the budget is spent on salaries, and research expenditure accounts for less than 1 percent.[32]

Pakistan

The small size of private universities is also characteristic of Pakistan, although not to as large a degree as in Bangladesh. As shown in figure 6, 36 of Pakistan's 111 universities have fewer than 1,000 students, and only 16 have more than 5,000 students. At least in principle, their university status enables them to decide their curriculum, which is more than can be said for the many private affiliated colleges in Bangladesh and India.

As in Bangladesh, private participation in Pakistan is more intensive at lower levels of education. Private institutions' share of PhD students is minuscule (3 percent of male and 2 percent of female enrollments). As shown in table 13, enrollments in private institutions are concentrated according to gender and in undergraduate education (which accounts for 18 percent of men and 9 percent of women) and postgraduate diplomas (21 percent of men and 9 percent of women). Private institutions have a large share of enrollment of postgraduate diplomas, usually in professional courses. Private participation varies regionally. In Sindh, where private institutions have the strongest presence, they account for 45 percent of the men and for 35 percent of the women enrolled.

If one excludes the Islamabad Capital Territory (ICT), 37 percent of faculty in private institutions is part time, compared with 20 percent of faculty in public institutions, as expected. In the ICT, however, the position is remarkably reversed. In private institutions, 90 percent of the faculty is full time, compared with only

FIGURE 6.
Distribution of Universities by Enrollment, Pakistan

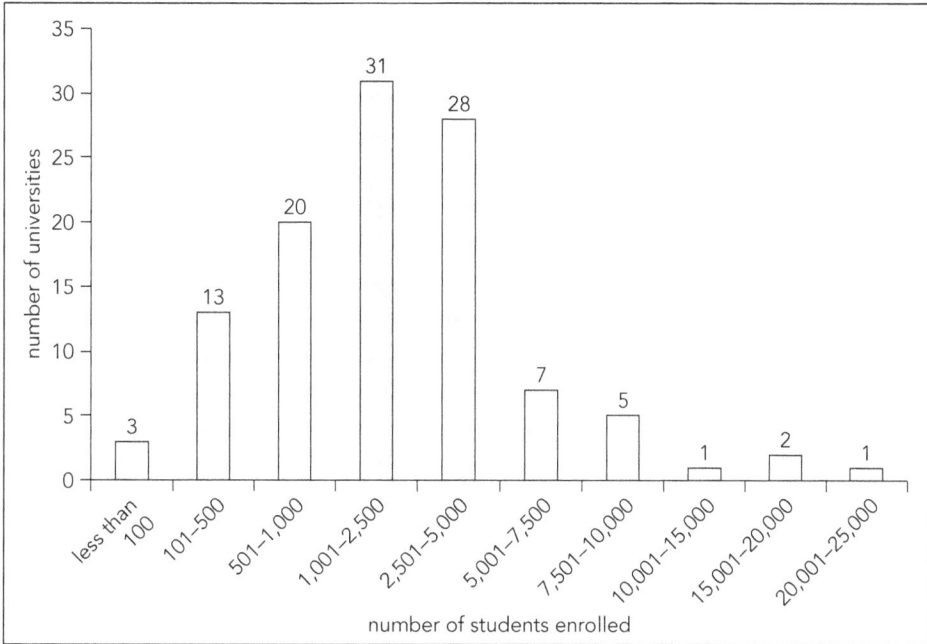

Source: Calculated from data available at Higher Education Commission, Pakistan, Web site, http://www.hec.gov.
pk/QualityAssurance/download/1319_Enrollment-in-UniversitiesDAIs-2001-06-7-2-08-websie-7-07.xls.

Table 13. Share of Private Enrollment by Educational Level, Pakistan, 2006–7
(percent of total enrollment)

Student category	Undergraduate	Postgraduate	Postgraduate (16+ years)	PhD	Postgraduate diploma
Male					
Percent	18	21	8	3	34
Number	239,274	83,264	16,433	6,659	4,560
Female					
Percent	9	9	3	2	14
Number	183,963	58,145	8,523	2,584	2,480
Average					
Percent	14	16	7	3	27
Total number	423,237	141,409	24,956	9,243	7,040

Source: Pakistan, Higher Education Commission, "Statistical Booklet on Higher Education."

11 percent in public institutions. For Pakistan as a whole, therefore, only 34 percent of the faculty in public institutions is full time, as against 68 percent in private institutions. The quality of faculty, however, varies for public and private institutions. As is shown in table 14, even among full-time faculty in private institutions, only 21 percent have a master of philosophy or a PhD degree, but 36 percent in public institutions do.

TABLE 14. Qualifications (Highest Degree) of Full-Time Faculty Members, Pakistan, 2003–4

Sector	Bachelor	Master	Master (16+ years)	Master of philosophy	PhD	Total
Number of faculty members						
Distance learning	9	110	0	22	41	182
Public	1,059	4,525	1,319	1,019	2,549	10,471
Private	1,151	1,480	508	284	540	3,963
Total	2,219	6,115	1,827	1,325	3,130	14,616
Share of sector total (percent)						
Distance learning	4.9	60.4	0.0	12.1	22.5	100.0
Public	10.1	43.2	12.6	9.7	24.3	100.0
Private	29.0	37.3	12.8	7.2	13.6	100.0
Total	15.2	41.8	12.5	9.1	21.4	100.0

Source: Pakistan, Higher Education Commission, "Statistical Booklet on Higher Education."

Note: Percentages may not sum to 100 because of rounding.

Sri Lanka

In Sri Lanka the National Policy on Education is rooted in Ordinance 31 of 1939 (significantly amended, 1945 through 1953) and in the Education Code. The Sri Lanka University Grants Commission was established in 1979 to oversee the functioning of universities. The system has gradually expanded; student intake increased from 4,950 in 1980 to 16,635 in 2006, and the country has 15 universities consisting of 78 faculties and 425 departments, with academic staff numbering 3,818. The universities are almost entirely funded by the government. Control by the national government limits the scope for experimentation and autonomy.[33] Annual enrollment in universities is about 2.4 percent of the age cohort. In addition, many professional institutes and cross-border higher education institutions offer diploma- and degree-level courses (Gamage 2007). Taking all these students together, gross enrollment in higher education in Sri Lanka is more than 12 percent of the age cohort.

Stephen (2007) identifies 19 private foreign education providers that offer 74 courses. Five sectors account for 84 percent of these course offerings: information technology (28 courses); engineering (10); business administration (10); accounting, finance, and banking (9); and tourism and hospitality (5). There are 23 representatives of universities from 12 countries. The most numerous are from Australia, the United Kingdom, New Zealand, Malaysia, and Singapore, in that order. Currently, there is no formal system of quality assurance or accreditation of diplomas and degrees awarded by cross-border educational institutions.

Given this environment, Esham (2008) finds that the common types of UIL in Sri Lanka are limited to consultancies and training programs, student internships, and informal interactions at third-party meetings such as conferences. Among departments, engineering had relatively more and humanities relatively fewer interactions. Academics and industrialists agree that the lack of established mechanisms is a key obstacle. Heavy workloads and lack of research facilities limit university capabilities, and industry continues to hold a dim view of the commercialization potential of university research and of interest among academics. In 2000, just 6 percent of patents went to public institutions, including universities, whereas individual inventors claimed 72 percent and private institutions accounted for 22 percent.

Discussion

The review of experience in Bangladesh, Sri Lanka, and Pakistan brings out a few common features. First, the extent of UIL in all three countries is low, even in Pakistan, which has demonstrated high-tech capabilities as a nation (e.g., in the nuclear industry). This finding, however, does not fully apply in certain sections of the labor market, as discussed below. Second, extensive government control of the sector persists, most so perhaps in Sri Lanka. Third, the private sector finds its niche in a variety of environments. It is reasonably quick to respond to labor market demands, as is evidenced by its behavior in the three countries, but it focuses mostly on the low-hanging fruit—for example, pass degrees and secondary professional education in Bangladesh, professional and cross-border higher education in Sri Lanka, and undergraduate and postgraduate diplomas in Pakistan. Quality is an issue in all three countries, with faculty constituting a critical constraint.

We have argued that the growth of the private education sector in India has been a response to the growth of the high-tech industry, especially the IT and ITES sectors. Arguably, the initial establishment of these industries was facilitated by the availability of high-quality skills in sufficient numbers, produced for the most part by the public education system. At the time these industries were established, in the 1990s, India may have been the preferred business location in the region for many reasons, in addition to education. The subsequent rapid increase in demand by high-tech sectors has been partly satisfied by the growth of private educational institutions of variable quality. The combination of first-mover advantages and agglomeration economies could imply that as long as the Indian supply chain continues to produce reasonably and relatively (in the context of the region) employable graduates, it would be difficult for other countries in the region to develop similar industries. Prospective investors, many of which are now domestic Indian companies, would look at the thick labor markets in Indian cities such as Bangalore, Chennai, Delhi, Hyderabad, Mumbai, Pune, and now even Kolkata and would find being there preferable to being among the initial investors in places like Dhaka, Karachi, and Colombo. Given that none of these regional countries can, at least at the moment, ensure that the supply of high-tech graduates can be maintained as the industry scales up, or that the quality of graduates will be substantially better than in India, the strength of the labor market linkage between high-tech industry and the higher education sector in India may almost act as an entry barrier for other countries in the region.[34]

Policy Implications

Our examination of the linkages between the higher education sector and high-tech industry in India (with a brief look at other countries in South Asia) indicates that links outside the labor market are rather weak, although they may be growing with the increased interest of high-tech industry in research (for example, in the pharmaceutical and biotechnology sectors in India). The linkages are more with specialized research institutions than with universities. This is not a desirable state of affairs, but it is only to be expected. The reasons, we argue, lie primarily in certain regulatory features of the system, as discussed next.

Separation of Teaching and Research

Fundamentally, Indian universities are not involved in research, which is conducted by specialized science, technology, and even social science institutions. This divorce of research from teaching is evident in our findings. The low supply of research-inclined faculty is also apparent; Banerjee and Muley (2008) put the ratio of PhDs to graduate engineers at less than 1 percent. Even within the public sector, the separation of teaching and research embodied in the establishment of specialized research institutions is "slowly depleting research-driven universities of their best faculty," according to Padmanabhan Balaram, director of IISc, Bangalore (quoted in Yarnell 2006).

Inappropriate Faculty Incentives

Universities in India have very limited autonomy with respect to faculty compensation, which is largely uniform across universities. Private universities and some specialized institutions can offer differential compensation, either in direct salary or in research support. Research-inclined students self-select into public or private laboratories (industry) or go abroad, essentially because of differences in compensation (Banerjee and Muley 2008). In addition to the level of compensation, the lack of facilities and the practice of automatic promotion undermine the faculty's research orientation. In addition, automatic promotion blunts incentives to move between universities, so that a critical mass of good faculty cannot agglomerate, leading to a suboptimal dispersion of capable faculty and adversely affecting the next generation of faculty. The absence of research-oriented, internationally visible faculty groups results in a low level of interest among researchers looking for postdoctoral opportunities. This hampers the development of the kind of research ecosystem that is critical for productive research all over the world.[35] If faculty compensation and the work environment are unattractive, quality erodes over time, affecting the very intellectual resources and capacity needed to generate new industry-relevant knowledge.

Thus, more than willingness (which could, in principle, be addressed by incentives; see box 3), it is ability that is increasingly becoming rare in universities. Given the growing opportunities available elsewhere, this has meant that good faculty is in short supply, especially in professional disciplines.[36] It is noteworthy in this context

BOX 3. Legislation to Protect and Utilize Publicly Funded Intellectual Property

Among the many shortcomings of the Indian faculty reward system is the low weight accorded to industry interfaces, except perhaps in management education. Even though it remains debatable whether the creation of new commercial knowledge and ventures should be an important objective of academic institutions, the Indian government is taking some intermediate measures to change this situation. The Protection and Utilization of Public Funded Intellectual Property (PUPFIP) Bill, a counterpart of the U.S. Bayh-Dole Act (University and Small Business Patent Procedures Act, 1980), was introduced in the Indian parliament on December 15, 2008. Under this legislation, universities and research institutions may patent the results of publicly funded research, and inventors as well as institutions will be able to receive a share of royalties and licensing fees. The researcher (inventor) is to receive a minimum of 30 percent of the royalties from the publicly funded intellectual property (PFIP), but he or she is restricted from publishing or disclosing the PFIP without a prior 30-day notice to the government. A violation will deprive the institution of future public funding and make it liable for repaying the grant with interest. This is seen as a way of supplementing the limited public budget for research and development.

A number of concerns have been raised about the effectiveness of this strategy. As Mowery et al. (2001) show, it is not clear that Bayh-Dole had a significant effect on the content of research in American universities. Data on patenting, licensing, and other types of commercialization show that the act did not facilitate technology transfer and commercialization (So et al. 2008). Furthermore, the ability of publicly funded research to address questions of limited commercial value but significant public good may be compromised if the difference between private and public research is reduced. This is especially the case in developing countries, where public benefits and commercial advantage may diverge significantly because of the low incomes of large sections of the population. As So et al. (2008, 2082) argue, "the focus on royalty returns at the expense of public goods may be misplaced."

The reason for the limited effectiveness of Bayh-Dole may be that incentives may not always act in the manner anticipated. University faculty are self-selected and are not driven primarily by monetary incentives. If increasing the commercial value of research requires limitation of its benefits, the incentives of the researcher may be adversely affected if he or she is motivated by the public benefits of the research. Here, it is the design of the incentives under the U.S. type of legislation that is called into question. Monetary incentives may, however, be more effective in developing countries. If so, the PUPFIP bill may well be more successful in India than Bayh-Dole was in the United States. Yet that success may not be in the social interest, which may be better served by an expansion of the public budget for competitively awarded research grants (see Aghion et al. 2009).

that many firms which have tried to build linkages with academia have been dissatisfied because of quality-related issues (Frew et al. 2007).[37] The result has been a downward spiral of less interaction of firms with academia and diminished ability or relevance of academia vis-à-vis industry's expectations.

Limited Autonomy of Universities

We have already stated that labor market linkages are the strongest and most widespread UIL in India. Yet, despite a vigorous response by the private sector to growth in the high-tech industry, the quality of the average graduate remains poor. This outcome is significantly driven by various problems of governance. Some of the key issues relating to the autonomy of universities are discussed next.

Reluctance to treat professional education as a commercial activity. There is extreme unwillingness to recognize even professional education as a commercial activity, and as Kapur and Mehta (2007) note, this position has been buttressed by a series of court judgments. The effort to preserve access to higher education has focused on keeping fees low rather than on expanding access to educational finance and scholarships. The inability of universities to decide their fees increases the dependence of the university on the UGC and the state government and consequentially constrains its autonomy, compromises its work environment, and limits diversity within the system.

Standardization of curriculum and affiliation of colleges. The affiliating system, under which colleges prepare students for a university-administered examination based on a uniform curriculum at the university level, fosters the existence of very large universities, reduces the colleges to teaching institutions, and limits innovation in curriculum, except to the extent allowed in autonomous colleges. To add to this, regulatory institutions such as the UGC appear to be involved in exercises to standardize the curriculum.[38] It is difficult to introduce innovations in curriculum because there are far too many colleges whose faculties would have to be retooled. Consequently, many colleges continue offering ossified content. The effect of this situation is worse when technology is changing rapidly. In such a scenario, it is nearly impossible to think of innovative multidisciplinary courses that can induce greater research orientation and leverage increasing convergence across scientific and engineering disciplines.[39]

Poor accreditation capacity. The lack of a robust accreditation system adds to the problem. The incipient accreditation bodies are all in the government sector and have limited capacity to accredit the growing number of institutions. As Agarwal (2006, 113) remarks, the current system of accreditation "serves little purpose." The reputation of institutions depends more on their selectivity in intake of students than on their curriculum and pedagogy. This makes the role of industry in signaling the quality of higher education ambiguous. Most of the courses in professional disciplines such as engineering, medicine, and management rely on entrance exams that are independent from school-leaving exams. Companies can simply leverage the stringent selection process of technical higher education and deemphasize the quality of instruction. This is especially true when the employees would have to be reskilled after recruitment—for example, in IT, where engineers from different streams enter the software sector. Such a perspective implies that the choice of employees is not overly dependent on quality and academic discipline, thereby muting industry's response to indifferent quality.

Lack of a credit and qualification framework. Credible accreditation that would allow for transferable credits, enabling students to choose their institution and pace of learning, is not yet available in India. The acquisition and especially the upgrading of skills are affected by the near-absence of a system of transferable credits, which retards the acquisition of qualifications by persons who are already employed and who do not have the opportunity for full-time study or are not continuously in one location, as would be required by the part-time courses that are currently on offer.[40]

In summary, the ability of institutions to respond positively to industry and create a virtuous feedback loop depends on the regulatory structure. Most of our findings relating to the poor state of UIL can be linked to regulatory features or to their second-order impact (see table 15). As Kapur and Mehta note:

> The most acute weakness plaguing India's higher education system is a crisis of governance. Its most visible manifestation is a crisis of faculty. The generation that was inspired by a broad commitment to the public good has retired or will do so soon. There is little likelihood of sufficient replenishment, given entrenched mediocrity in institutions with lifetime appointments, few competitive pressures and abysmal governance. The result has been the academic equivalent of Gresham's law—the bad drives out the good. The prevailing political ideological climate in which elite institutions are seen as anti-democratic, finds its natural response in political control to influence admissions policies, internal organization, and the structure of courses and funding. As quality deteriorates, students are less and less willing to pay the very resources without which quality cannot be improved. (Kapur and Mehta 2007, 49)

The solutions to enhancing both labor market and non–labor market linkages thus appear to intersect at the core issue of faculty quality. Although the indifferent quality of the private response may indicate a bigger role for regulation, the current structure of regulation has resulted in restriction of the private response at the high end while neglecting its growth at the lower end. It will be necessary to address these regulatory failures in higher education in order to strengthen the links between higher education and high-tech industry.

Concluding Observations

In this paper, we have adopted an eclectic approach to the linkages between high-tech industries and the higher education sector. Our analysis draws on the national innovation system (NIS), triple helix, and university-industry linkages (UIL) frameworks but does not situate itself solely within any one of the discourses. In the context of our initial discussion on NIS, and ignoring the financial aspects for the moment, it is useful to think of four entities: the government, industry, specialized research institutions, and universities.[41] Initially, industry, specialized institutions, and universities were embedded within the state. The first of these three to become relatively

TABLE 15. Summary of Key Findings

Finding	Feature related to regulation of higher education	Other features
Low knowledge creation	Separation of teaching and research Inappropriate faculty incentives, such as low compensation and automatic promotion, leading to poor quality of faculty	Poor facilities
Low enterprise creation	Second-order effect of low knowledge creation	Lack of venture financing
Concentration of private response in a few states	Differential entry regulation and state-level fee regulation across states	Agglomeration of industrial activity in a few states
Indifferent quality of graduates	Second-order effect of poor quality of faculty Ability to change curriculum restricted by system of college affiliation Poor accreditation system Lack of transferable credits, limiting lifelong learning	Highly selective entrance examination, making it easier for industry to tolerate poor instruction
Low involvement of industry	Second-order response to indifferent	Limited need in current competitive environment (but this is becoming less relevant) Growing ability to link with foreign research

Source: Authors' compilation.

independent was industry, through a gradual liberalization. Since then, specialized institutions have become somewhat more autonomous, but universities have arguably become less so. Meanwhile, a new class of relatively autonomous private institutions offering technical and professional education has emerged. Even the limited degree of autonomy in research and educational institutions, coupled with a relatively high degree of agency in industry, has led to many linkages between these two sectors, especially in externally oriented service and industrial sectors such as IT and pharmaceuticals, despite the difficult regulatory environment. The size of the high-tech private sector in India, particularly the IT industry, has permitted that sector to try to evolve a compensating response to regulatory obstacles. Industry associations and individual firms are working with educational institutions to provide supplementary educational inputs customized to the needs of the industry or, in the case of vocational training, of particular firms. In a research-intensive sector such as pharmaceuticals, we observe higher-level linkages between select firms and elite institutions supported by government funds such as the New Millennium Indian Technology Leadership Initiative (NMITLI). The limitations of relying on such a response can be seen in the muted participation of sectors other than IT, ITES, and pharmaceuticals. It is also evident in other countries of the region, where such a response is lacking in the absence of a large high-tech sector. Beyond this limited intersection, it is difficult to find the requisite autonomy or intellectual capability in the research and educational institutions, or even the demand from firms. In this sense, the current relationship can be seen as being at an intermediate stage between triple helix I and triple helix II, although some portions of the relationship have elements of triple helix III. It is this variegated nature of UIL that makes it difficult to adopt a single analytical metric.

Other features of the NIS can affect the linkage decisions of the actors. For example, a significant constraint in India is the absence of early-stage funding for start-ups. Most of the so-called venture capital activity in India is actually "growth funding" and takes the form of private equity. As Dhingra (2007) notes, a limited amount of true venture capital funding has just begun, but its expansion beyond well-established sectors such as IT is as yet limited. In such a situation, some firms may choose to link not to domestic educational and research institutions but to external institutions. One reason may be that external institutions come with their own linkages into the broader financial system, which are necessary for commercializing innovations.

Any success that such industry-led initiatives may have should not distract from the underlying failure in the regulation of higher education that has led to the emergence of these initiatives.[42] Not only are such responses limiting, but they may also be deeply inequitable, as industry picks the few cherries in the education system and concentrates its resources on them. There is also a risk that the production of skills will become too tailored to the current industrial structure, hindering the flexibility that is necessary for any workforce in today's globalized environment.[43]

Measured against the criterion of the need to broaden and deepen UIL, this tendency of the higher education system to narrow its focus is disturbing and may be affecting the growth of many industries. Nor does the industry engagement, except for a few instances in biotechnology and pharmaceuticals, lead to the depth of knowledge that would be needed to assimilate more complex technologies. Liberalization has made industry much more nimble in effecting structural change, but the same is not true for universities. The larger challenge is to design appropriate work environments and compensation packages that will attract talented young people to academia. This will do much to alleviate the existing constraints on the availability of research-inclined faculty in academic institutions, the effect of which is to limit the addition of value from a more intensive exchange with industry. As a consequence of the lack of appropriate faculty, the industry initiative may remain restricted to the important but still shallow level of enhancing the quality of entry-level employees. The creation of a virtuous circle seems to have been arrested by an archaic regulatory structure, with constraints on the establishment of viable new institutions, faculty recruitment and salaries, and changes in the curriculum. Many of these governance problems also permeate other South Asian countries, including Bangladesh, Pakistan, and Sri Lanka.

It is useful to benchmark the current situation to the three qualities of a world-class university proposed by Salmi (2009): (a) a "high concentration of talent" in the form of faculty, students, and researchers from around the world; (b) "abundant resources" from endowments, public resources, tuition, and competitive research funding, which enhances the pedagogy and enables advanced research to be conducted; and (c) "favorable governance features" that encourage innovation and academic freedom, foster strategic vision, and enable flexibility to allow the university to make decisions autonomously and manage resources without bureaucratic interference such as restrictions on faculty compensation.

In a separate study of European and U.S. universities, Aghion et al. (2009) find that it is extremely important to avoid endogamy in faculty—that is, recruitment of one's own graduates. Internationalization of faculty is therefore an important element of a world-class university. University autonomy and merit-based competition for research funding are also positively linked to university research output. By providing more generous stakes for research competitions, governments can induce research universities to employ their funding better, make better use of their autonomy, and respond more productively to local competition.[44] These findings broadly support the analysis in Salmi (2009), who relies on an earlier study by Aghion et al. (2008).

Each pair of the three attributes named by Salmi (2009) can produce high-quality graduates (attributes a and b), significant research (a and c), or transfer of technology (b and c), but in order to achieve all three outcomes, it is necessary that all three characteristics be present in the university. In our review, we describe a situation in India in which there are elements of (a), primarily in student quality, and elements of (b) at institutes of national importance such as the IITs, the IISc, and the IIMs, but rarely any element of (c). Consequently, India manages to produce a certain number of outstanding graduates but falls short on the goals of significant research and transfer of technology.

In conclusion, it is perhaps better to focus on how far UIL has traveled in India than on where it is currently situated. Until recently, the lack of competitive pressure in a protected, inward-looking market with government licensing meant that the private sector in India was not proactive in seeking out linkages to advance research capabilities. The bulk of research was conducted in public institutions, again with little regard for market demand. Two broad trends are combining to alter this picture. First, rising competition in recent years seems to be leading to a growing number of alliances among firms and between higher education institutions and industry, especially in globally oriented, research-intensive industries such as pharmaceuticals and biotechnology. Concomitantly, the increasing fiscal reticence of government and the push toward commercial orientation of education has meant that academic institutions are no longer financially protected. Although this trend can have deleterious consequences, especially if it is carried too far and is married to a stifling governance environment, as is the case in India, it does push some of these institutions to become more oriented toward industry, alleviating a key mindset constraint that has restricted UIL in the past.[45] As both these trends play out in the future, one can expect, in a positive scenario, more demand for UIL and, consequently, a derived demand for relief of the regulatory constraints (for example, in faculty compensation and university autonomy) that currently limit the capacity of universities to undertake cutting-edge research. To some extent, the recent suggested increase in faculty compensation addresses this problem, but it still seems unlikely that faculty compensation will be individualized to any degree. More critically, university autonomy appears to show little progress. On the other hand, in a negative scenario, industry, which is now relatively free of restrictions, may choose to cope with governance failures by exiting, perhaps to foreign academic and research institutions—a move that can have other collateral benefits such as venture funding—or by self-providing, which would usually be suboptimal. In the final analysis, research activities in industry and university are complementary and mutually reinforcing, and the success of industry-academia linkages lies in the intellectual exploitation of these complementarities.

Notes

1. This paper is confined to an instrumental view of education. Such a view is limiting; in principle, higher education must address much larger goals relating to the human condition. That project, however, seems remote, given the inability of the system to address even the instrumental issues described here.

2. For recent work in the area of UILs, see Yusuf and Nabeshima (2006) and a special issue of *World Development* on this topic (Hershberg, Nabeshima, and Yusuf 2007).

3. For example, in addition to many workshops, the Indian Institutes of Management conduct short-term management development programs for senior civil servants and offer a master's program in public policy that is well attended by civil servants.

4. One of the more commercially remunerative services supplied by higher education institutions is training, especially for management institutions. For many institutions, management education programs account for a substantial part of their revenue.

5. Deemed universities are a novel feature in India. The central government may, on the advice of the University Grants Commission (UGC), declare that any institution for higher education shall be deemed to be a university, following which all the provisions of the UGC Act (enacted with the objective of making provision for the coordination and determination of standards in universities) shall apply to that institution as if it were a university. Usually, to be a deemed university, an institution would be innovative, of a very high standard, and engaged in teaching and conducting research in chosen fields of specialization, but recently there has been a proliferation of such deemed universities. For a more detailed description of higher education in India, see Basant and Mukhopadhyay (2009).

6. The Indian Institutes of Technology (IIT), the Indian Institutes of Management (IIM), and a few other designated institutions have a slightly higher salary structure than the normal UGC scale. There are also some differences in benefits between universities funded from the central (federal) budget and those funded at the state level. In any case, nominally equivalent compensation implies variations in real compensation because differences in costs of living among locations are not fully adjusted.

7. Current fees at the more expensive Indian Institutes of Management are around US$25,000 per year.

8. For estimates, see Chamarbagwala (2006); Kijima (2006); Azam (2008); Bargain et al. (2008); and Unni and Rani (2008).

9. The data also show that within the U.S. patent database, CSIR was the dominant assignee for the health-biotechnology field, as well (Kumar et al. 2004).

10. On the disclosure requirement, see the Proforma for Mandatory Disclosure of Information about Accredited Programmes by Institutions, issued by the AICTE.

11. Some estimates, such as those by Banerjee and Muley (2008), show high percentages of faculty without PhDs at the National Institutes of Technology at Warangal (55 percent), Hamirpur (52 percent), Durgapur (44 percent), and Surat (34 percent).

12. NASSCOM is a major trade body of the IT software and services industry in India. It has about 900 members, of which nearly 150 are global companies from the United States, the United Kingdom, the European Union, Japan, China, and elsewhere. NASSCOM's member companies are in the businesses of software development, software services, and IT-enabled and business product outsourcing (BPO) services.

13. Part of the impetus for remediation programs may be the IT sector's efforts to reskill for the software industry engineers who have been trained for other specializations such as mechanical and chemical engineering.

14. Similarly, one of India's newest, better-known business schools, the Indian School of Business, is not accredited by the AICTE.

15. For example, employees at Avesthagen are encouraged to pursue doctoral studies through a collaborative program at Mysore University (Frew et al. 2007). Dr Reddy's Laboratories, Ranbaxy, and Nicholas Piramal have similar arrangements with universities for their employees (Yarnell 2006).

16. A proposal by the Confederation of Indian Industry (see CII 2007) involves the creation of institute management committees (IMCs) chaired by a person from industry who will be given financial and academic autonomy by the state governments to manage the ITIs. The central government will provide a 10-year interest-free loan of up to 25 million rupees on the basis of an institute development plan prepared by the IMC. The state government will continue to regulate admissions and fees. See also Nichenametla (2007); Mukhopadhyay (2008).

17. Sometimes even the private response is deemed inadequate by private sector clients. Reliance ADAG recently purchased NIS-Sparta, a training institution, in an effort to better control the training of its employees.

18. The skills tested by the NAC include listening and keyboard skills, verbal ability, spoken English, comprehension and writing ability, office software usage, numerical and analytical skills, and concentration and accuracy. For further details, see http://nac.nasscom.in/.

19. The analysis covers usual-status workers who report being engaged in economic activity either for the greatest part of the year (principal status) or for only part of the year (secondary status).

20. The OECD classification is based on R&D intensity in 12 OECD countries: Canada, Denmark, Finland, France, Germany, Ireland, Italy, Japan, Spain, Sweden, the United Kingdom, and the United States. The OECD high and medium-high groups have been aggregated into the high category. The detailed classification in this paper may be obtained on request from the authors.

21. In constructing the overall index, the principal-component method has been used to estimate the relative weights of the variables and the sectors. See Mohanty (2004) for details of each index.

22. It needs to be emphasized that 98.6 percent of rural workers and 92.6 percent of urban workers in all industries have no technical education.

23. A specific example is that over the period 1999–2000 to 2004–5, the NSS data show that the share of women among system analysts and programmers, which is the category of IT occupations showing the highest growth rate, rose from 6.8 to 29.7 percent.

24. For some estimates of the wage premium, see Chamarbagwala (2006); Kijima (2006); Azam (2008); Bargain et al. (2008); and Unni and Rani (2008).

25. There was a spurt in 2002, when 26 deemed-to-be-universities came into being, of which 9 were private institutions.

26. That ranking ignores two states, Jharkhand and Uttarakhand, that have 100 percent private medical colleges, but for the reason that they each have two private medical colleges but no public medical college.

27. See India, Ministry of Human Resources, Department of Higher Education, "UGC Clarification on the Recognition of BIS, BIT, MIS, MIT Degrees," http://education.nic.in/technicaledu/ugc_bis.asp.

28. In 2001, in *Bharathidasan University v. AICTE,* India's Supreme Court held that the "power to grant approval for starting new technical institutions and for introduction of new courses or programmes in consultation with the agencies concerned . . . would not cover a 'University' but only a 'technical institution.'" It is not entirely clear whether there is a distinction between universities established by state acts, such as Bharathidasan University, and deemed-to-be universities.

29. For example, the West Bengal University of Technology has 156 affiliated colleges but no faculty of its own. All appointments to the university are through deputation. The university has 17 staff members, including 4 statutory officers and support staff. See http://www.wbut.net/ (accessed September 4, 2009).

30. National University serves as an affiliating university for degree and postgraduate degree education at various colleges and institutes. Three other public universities have no regular classroom instruction. They are Bangabandhu Sheikh Mujibur Rahman Agriculture University; Bangabandhu Sheikh Mujib Medical University, the sole medical university; and Bangladesh Open University (BOU). BOU conducts 18 formal and 19 nonformal education courses. It has 12 regional centers for its 6 faculties and schools, as well as 80 local centers and 1,000 tutorials throughout the country. (Data in this section are from BANBEIS 2006.)

31. Monem (2007) finds that regular faculty in public institutions work as part-time faculty in private institutions. This could be a device used by private institutions to signal quality by emphasizing the parent institutions of the faculty.

32. Revenue and expenditure per student in public universities amount to 1,970 taka and 2,520 taka per year, respectively; the comparable figures for private universities are 16,450 taka and 15,970 taka.

33. Government policy in Sri Lanka is not to charge any fees to undergraduate and diploma-level students. The government has, however, allowed institutions to charge students for the cost of postgraduate programs, short-term training programs, contract research, and consultancy and other services. About 95 percent of the university budgets still comes from treasury funds.

34. In the case of Sri Lanka, prospects for a sufficient supply of graduates are constrained by the size of the country's labor market, but in Pakistan and Bangladesh the number of technical graduates is also limited, even though the overall size of the education sector is much larger.

35. The authors are grateful to Pratap B. Mehta for suggesting this implication. Salmi (2009) has a similar discussion on the negative effects of the separation of higher education into specialized *grande écoles* and universities in France. See also Yarnell (2006).

36. As noted in Agarwal (2006), the March 2004 report of the Board on Faculty Development of the AICTE projects a serious shortage in faculty, given the growth in the number of institutions and the increase in student intake. In fact, shortage of faculty is cited as a reason for reduction of intake in 1,346 approved engineering institutions and for the prohibition of intake in 7 institutions.

37. Maria, Ruet, and Zerah (2003) describe cases in which such partnerships were discontinued because of failure to deliver what was promised. Lack of mutual trust and low-quality infrastructure have been suggested as other constraints on linkages (Bhattacharya and Arora 2007).

38. The UGC has reiterated its belief in universities' freedom in designing the curriculum, which it describes as "fundamental" to its policies. It has said that the "impression . . . that the UGC has undertaken an exercise to design a nationally uniform curriculum . . . is not correct." It has, however, formed a committee to evolve a framework to help ensure and enhance the quality and relevance of curriculums. When this framework becomes available, it will be shared with universities, which would be free to adopt or adapt the curriculum framework (*Tribune* 2008).

39. This argument has less relevance for the AICTE and other council-approved institutions, deemed-to-be universities, or state-act universities. Efforts are being made in a few institutions, including the National Center for Biological Sciences (NCBS), the Indian Institute of Science (IISc), and the National Chemical Laboratories (NCL), to develop multidisciplinary research programs (Yarnell 2006). Given the difficulties in developing interdisciplinary courses and research programs in existing institutions, the government is experimenting with new Indian Institutes of Science Education and Research, which have a multidisciplinary curriculum at the undergraduate level, but these institutions will be limited to a minuscule number of students.

40. In 2003 the Association of Indian Universities did hold a seminar on this issue, "Threats and Opportunities in Higher Education in Context of GATS and Networking among Indian Universities and Credit Transfer with Universities in India." CABE (2005) also mentions the need for a credit system.

41. Specialized research institutions include the CSIR laboratories, the IITs and IIMs, the IISc, and the like.

42. Such coping behavior as a response to a failure of public services is common in many other sectors in India, including water, electricity, and health.

43. Wolf (2002) suggests that that investment in basic skills such as mathematics and writing may be much more relevant than investment in domain-specific skills.

44. Even external funding was found to be more efficacious if universities enjoyed autonomy and faced competition from other institutions.

45. Universities need to be autonomous not just from the government but also from industry if a critical part of their research agenda is to be self-driven and pioneering. They should therefore not become too financially dependent on either source.

References

Agarwal, Pawan. 2006. "Higher Education in India: The Need for Change." ICRIER Working Paper 180, Indian Council for Research on International Economic Relations, New Delhi.

Aghion, Philippe, Mathias Dewatripont, Caroline Hoxby, Andreu Mas-Colell, and André Sapir. 2008. *Higher Aspirations: An Agenda for Reforming European Universities*. Bruegel Blueprint Series vol. 5. Brussels: Bruegel.

———. 2009. "The Governance and Performance of Research Universities: Evidence from Europe and the U.S." NBER Working Paper 14851, National Bureau of Economic Research, Cambridge, MA.

Aminuzzaman, Salahuddin. 2007. "Overview of Quality Assurance in the Context of Bangladesh." Presented at the International Workshop on the Development of Measurements for Higher Education Quality Assurance in Bangladesh, organized by the American International University–Bangladesh (AIUB) and the Asia Pacific Quality Network (APQN), Dhaka, May 30–31. http://www.aiub.edu/StaticPages/APQN2007/Papers/aminuzzaman%20paper.doc.

Athreye, Suma, and Martha Prevezer. 2008. "R&D Offshoring and the Domestic Science Base in India and China." Working Paper 26, Centre for Globalization Research, School of Business and Management, Queen Mary University of London. http://webspace.qmul.ac.uk/pmartins/CGRWP26.pdf.

Athreye, Suma, and Phanish Puranam. 2008. "India and China: Their Role in the Global R&D Economy." Presented at the Maastricht Economic and Social Research and Training Centre on Innovation and Technology (MEIDE) Conference, Renmin University, Beijing, April 21–22. http://www.merit.unu.edu/MEIDE/papers/2008/1202480444_SA.pdf.

Azam, Mehtabul. 2008. "India's Rising Skill Premium: Role of Demand and Supply." Southern Methodist University, Dallas, TX. http://people.smu.edu/mazam/Azam-01.pdf.

BANBEIS (Bangladesh Bureau of Educational Information and Statistics). 2006. "National Education Survey (Post Primary) 2005." BANBEIS, Ministry of Education, Dhaka.

Banerjee, Rangan, and Vinayak Muley. 2008. *Engineering Education in India*. Observer Research Foundation, Delhi.

Bargain, Olivier, Sumon K. Bhaumik, Manisha Chakrabarty, and Zhong Zhao. 2008. "Earnings Differences between Chinese and Indian Wage Earners, 1987–2004." IZA Discussion Paper 3284, Institute for the Study of Labor (IZA), Bonn, Germany.

Basant, Rakesh, and Pankaj Chandra. 2006. "University-Industry Link and Enterprise Creation in India—Some Strategic and Policy Issues." In *How Universities Promote Economic Growth*, ed. Shahid Yusuf and Kaoru Nabeshima, 209–26. Directions in Development Series. Washington, DC: World Bank.

———. 2007. "Role of Educational and R&D Institutions in City Clusters: An Exploratory Study of Bangalore and Pune Regions in India." *World Development* 35 (6, June): 1037–55.

Basant, Rakesh, and Partha Mukhopadhyay. 2009. "An Arrested Virtuous Circle? Higher Education and High-Tech Industries in India." Working Paper 2009-05-01, Indian Institute of Management, Ahmedabad. http://www.iimahd.ernet.in/publications/data/2009-05-01Basant.pdf.

Berman, Eli, Rohini Somanathan, and Hong W. Tan. 2005. "Is Skill-Biased Technological Change Here Yet? Evidence from Indian Manufacturing in the 1990s." Policy Research Working Paper 3761, World Bank, Washington, DC.

Bhattacharya, S., and P. Arora. 2007. "Industrial Linkages in Indian Universities: What They Reveal and What They Imply?" *Scientometrics* 70 (2): 277–300.

CABE (Central Advisory Board of Education). 2005. "Report of the CABE Committee on Financing of Higher and Technical Education." National Institute of Educational Planning and Administration, New Delhi.

Chamarbagwala, Rubiana. 2006. "Economic Liberalization and Wage Inequality in India." *World Development* 34 (12, December): 1997–2015.

Chamarbagwala, Rubiana, and Gunjan Sharma. 2008. "Industrial Deregulation, Skill Upgrading, and Wage Inequality in India." CAEPR Working Paper 2008-002, Center for Applied Economics and Policy Research, Indiana University, Bloomington, IN.

Chatterjee, Partha, et al. 2002. "Social Science Research Capacity in South Asia." SSRC Working Paper 6, Social Science Research Council, New York. http://southasia.ssrc.org/publications/southasiareport.pdf.

CII (Confederation of Indian Industry). 2007. "Public Private Partnership for ITI Upgradation." CII Communique, July, CII, New Delhi.

Dhingra, Inderbir S. 2007. "Enhancing Innovation Finance." In *Unleashing India's Innovation: Toward Sustainable and Inclusive Growth*, ed. Mark A. Dutz. Washington, DC: World Bank.

Esham, M. 2008. "Strategies to Develop University-Industry Linkages in Sri Lanka." Research Studies on Tertiary Education Sector Study Series 4 (2007/2008), National Education Commission, Colombo.

Etzkowitz, Henry. 2003. "Innovation in Innovation: The Triple Helix of University-Industry-Government Relations." *Social Science Information* 42 (3): 293–337.

Etzkowitz, Henry, and Loet Leydesdorff. 2000. "The Dynamics of Innovation from National Systems and Mode 2 to a Triple Helix University-Industry-Government Relationship." *Research Policy* 29 (2): 109–23.

Frew, Sarah E., Rahim Rezaie, Stephen M. Sammut, Monali Ray, Abdallah S. Daar, and Peter A. Singer. 2007. "India's Health Biotech Sector at a Crossroads." *Nature Biotechnology* 25 (4, April): 403–17.

Gamage, Sujata, ed. 2007. "Linking Knowledge to Innovation in the Economy and Society: The Role of Universities in Asia." International Development Research Centre (IDRC), Ottawa.

Gupta, Anil. 2008. "Do Patents Matter: IP in Indian R&D Institutions and Universities." Presentation at the Intellectual Property Rights (IPR) Management Development Program, Indian Institute of Management, Ahmedabad.

Hershberg, Eric, Kaoru Nabeshima, and Shahid Yusuf, eds. 2007. "University-Industry Linkages and the Development of Knowledge-Intensive Clusters in Asian Cities." *World Development* 35 (6, June): 931–1098.

Infosys. 2007. "Campus Connect Program Overview." Infosys Web site, http://campusconnect.infosys.com.

Kapur, Devesh, and Pratap B. Mehta. 2007. "Indian Higher Education Reform: From Half-Baked Socialism to Half-Baked Capitalism." Presented at the Brookings–National Council on Applied Economic Research (NCAER) India Policy Forum, New Delhi, July 17–18. http://www.ncaer.org/downloads/IPF2007/kapur-mehta.pdf.

Kijima, Yoko. 2006. "Why Did Wage Inequality Increase? Evidence from Urban India 1983–99." *Journal of Development Economics* 81 (1, October): 97–117.

Kodama, Fumio, Shingo Kano, and Jun Suzuki. 2006. "Beyond Absorptive Capacity: The Management of Technology for a Proactive Corporate Strategy toward University-Industry Links." In *How Universities Promote Economic Growth*, ed. Shahid Yusuf and Kaoru Nabeshima, 241–54. Directions in Development Series. Washington, DC: World Bank.

Kumar, N. K., U. Quach, H. Thorsteinsdottir, H. Somsekhar, A. S. Daar, and P. Singer. 2004. "Indian Bio-technology—Rapidly Evolving and Industry Led." *Nature Biotechnology* 22 (December, Suppl.): 31–36.

Maria, A., J. Ruet, and M. H. Zerah. 2003. "Biotechnology in India." Centre de Sciences Humaines (CSH) and CERNA, New Delhi.

Metcalfe, Stan, and Ronnie Ramlogan. 2008. "Innovation Systems and the Competitive Process in Developing Economies." *Quarterly Review of Economics and Finance* 48 (2, May): 433–46.

Mohanty, Nirmal. 2004. "Study on State Infrastructure." Report to the 12th Finance Commission, New Delhi. http://fincomindia.nic.in/writereaddata/html_en_files/fincomnet/rpt_intra/st_infrast.doc.

Monem, Mobasser. 2007. "Higher Education in Bangladesh: Status, Issues and Prospects." Presented at seminar on "Knowledge for Development (K4D): The Role of Universities," Colombo, January 25.

Mowery, David C., Richard R. Nelson, Bhaven N. Sampat, and Arvids A. Ziedonis. 2001. "The Growth of Patenting and Licensing by U.S. Universities: An Assessment of the Effects of the Bayh-Dole Act of 1980." *Research Policy* 30 (1, January): 99–119.

Mukhopadhyay, Partha. 2008. "A PPP Model for Vocational Education: Upgrading the ITIs in India." In *India Infrastructure Report 2008: Business Models of the Future,* 3iNetwork. Delhi: Oxford University Press.

NASSCOM (National Association of Software and Service Companies). 2005. *NASSCOM-McKinsey Report: Extending India's Leadership in the Global IT and BPO Industries.* Mumbai, India: NASSCOM. http://www.nasscom.in/Nasscom/templates/NormalPage .aspx?id=4969.

———. 2007. "Finishing School for Engineering Students—NASSCOM Education Initiative." NASSCOM, Mumbai, India.

Nichenametla, Prasad. 2007. "ITI Upgrade Plan a Non-Starter." *Business Standard* (New Delhi), December 8. http:// www.rediff.com/money/2007/dec/08iti.htm.

Powar, K. B., and V. Bhalla. 2004. "Private Professional Higher Education in India." *New Frontiers in Education* 34 (2): 126–27.

Prakash, Ved. 2007. "Trends in Growth and Financing of Higher Education in India." *Economic and Political Weekly* 42 (31, August 4).

Salmi, Jamil. 2009. "The Challenge of Establishing World-Class Universities." World Bank, Washington, DC. http://portal.unesco.org/education/en/files/55825/12017990845Salmi. pdf/Salmi.pdf.

So, Anthony D., Bhaven N. Sampath, Arti K. Rai, Robert Cook-Deegan, Jerome H. Reichman, Robert Weissman, and Amy Kapczynski. 2008. "Is Bayh-Dole Good for Developing Countries? Lessons from the US Experience." *PLoS Biology* 6 (10): e262, 2078–84. http://www.plosbiology.org/article/info%3Adoi%2F10.1371%2Fjournal.pbio.0060262.

Stehrer, Robert, and Julia Wörz. 2003. "Industrial Diversity, Trade Patterns, and Productivity Convergence." WIIW Working Paper 23, Vienna Institute for International Economic Studies, Vienna. http://www.wiiw.ac.at/pdf/WP23.pdf.

Stephen. Francis M. 2007. "Relevance of Foreign Degrees, Offered Locally, and Their Contribution to the Socio-Economic Development in Sri Lanka." Research Studies on Tertiary Education Sector, Study Series 1 (2007/2008), National Education Commission, Colombo. http://www.nec.gov.lk/content/admin/-%20Rel_101.pdf.

Tribune (Chandigarh, India). 2008. "UGC Not for Uniform Curriculum." January 9. http://www.tribuneindia.com/2008/20080109/delhi.htm.

Unni, Jeemol, and Uma Rani. 2008. *Flexibility of Labour in Globalizing India: The Challenge of Skills and Technology*. New Delhi: Tulika Books.

Wolf, Alison. 2002. *Does Education Matter?* London: Penguin.

Yarnell, Amanda. 2006. "Indian Science Rising." *Chemical Engineering News* 84 (12, March 20): 12–20. http://pubs.acs.org/cen/coverstory/84/8412India.html.

Yusuf, Shahid, and Kaoru Nabeshima, eds. 2006. *How Universities Promote Economic Growth*. Directions in Development Series. Washington, DC: World Bank.

Comment on "An Arrested Virtuous Circle? Higher Education and High-Technology Industries in India," by Rakesh Basant and Partha Mukhopadhyay

Basant and Mukhopadhyay present an interesting and important view on what is happening in the higher education sector in India and its role in building and growing the high-technology industry. The authors have pieced together a story based on a variety of secondary data sources and evidence from literature. My comments on the paper will be in the form of a few questions that will, I hope, promote further understanding of the issues raised by the authors, complement their analysis, and seek a process explanation of some of their findings. The authors rue the poor linkages between higher education and high-technology industry and hold improper regulation of higher education responsible for it. They argue that among the many linkages that may exist between the higher education sector and high-technology industry, the link relating to the labor market is the most active in India, while others are weak. They note that young, male, urban graduates (and nongraduates with technical diplomas) are more likely to be working in the high-technology sector.

The paper prompts one to ask the following questions:

- Is there a hierarchy in the linkages between higher education and high technology, and does it explain the extent of linkages?

- What have been the reasons behind poor linkages?

- Is there something about the structure of higher education in India that inhibits linkages?

- Can we say something about the quality of these linkages, and does quality vary from public to private institutions?

It would indeed be interesting to know the extent of engagement in other types of linkages, independent of their strengths or weaknesses, in order to understand their

---

Pankaj Chandra is a professor of operations and technology management and director at the Indian Institute of Management Bangalore.

Annual World Bank Conference on Development Economics 2009, Global
© 2010 The International Bank for Reconstruction and Development / The World Bank

status. There appears to be a semblance of hierarchy among the identified linkages in terms of frequency of occurrence and, consequently, value in developing a knowledge economy. This hierarchy of linkages can be represented as follows (from most common to least common):

1. Supply of labor

2. Supply of services

3. Creation of enterprises

4. Neutral platform for interaction between industry and government

5. Creation of knowledge

Thus, for instance, supply of labor is the most common linkage found between higher education institutions and the high-technology sector, and linkages that facilitate creation of knowledge are the least common.

Table 1 explains various key drivers and their impact on the quality and extent of the linkage. Existing *regulations* regarding licensing of institutions bring into the sector certain types of players who desire quick returns through large-scale enrollment of students (demand for this activity is also the highest) and who have little or no interest in creation of knowledge because it is resource intensive and has a long gestation period. Consequently, the greatest impact of regulation is on the supply of labor to the high-technology sector. As one goes through the other elements of the hierarchy, the impact decreases, and there is little or no impact on or interest in working with the sector toward creation of knowledge. With increasing *autonomy*, institutions are able to set their own academic agenda so as to enhance the respect of the institution within its peer group, as well as to have an impact on the nation. This trend will have a positive effect on anything to do with knowledge generation and may see a trade-off in the form of reduced emphasis on training. One must mention that public institutions suffer from lack of autonomy as much as do private institutions in India! Similarly, when there is *competition* among institutions for resources, they will pay more attention to quality of teaching and students, as well as to research, to gain greater recognition in the market.

Just as institutions may be categorized on the basis of the above hierarchy of linkages, there is a corresponding hierarchy among high-technology firms, from those that supply goods and services to those that demand labor, those that institutionally

TABLE 1. Factors Influencing Linkages between Higher Education and High-Technology Industry and Their Impact on the Hierarchy of Linkages

Factor	Degree of impact on the hierarchy of linkages		
Regulation	High	⟶	Low
Autonomy	Low	⟶	High
Competition and markets	High	⟶	High

Source: Author's elaboration.

supply teachers, and, finally, those that supply funds for research and other activities. Thus, higher education institutions and high-technology firms are not homogenous, and it may be worthwhile to segment them appropriately and study the behavior of each segment and its performance vis-à-vis others before designing any policy intervention, as these entities' response to a common policy may vary considerably.

If we explore the linkages described in the paper further and recognize the existence of this hierarchy, a few interesting observations can be made about the linkages. The linkages may not always be as weak, but the size of the segments of different types of institution, as defined by the hierarchy, may vary. We first make a few comments on some of the observations in the paper regarding the linkages in order to explain why some may not be strong enough in India. We will examine three of the linkages identified: labor market linkages, creation of enterprises, and creation of knowledge.

Labor Market Linkages

The findings on high-technology manufacturing appear to be intuitive. From the analysis, it is apparent that high-technology services seem to dominate within all high-technology industries in terms of their propensity to hire graduates of all kinds, including nontechnical graduates. This makes one wonder if many of the industries identified as high-technology services are indeed high technology. For example, banking in India is quite manual and has low research and development (R&D) intensity. In addition, the deployment of general graduates is largely in functions that are nontechnical. Perhaps inclusion of sectors such as engineering design, animation art, and health care delivery would lead to differing findings. One may also have to segregate graduates and postgraduates to see the above effect more sharply. That may be helpful in explaining the perspective of high-technology industry, as well, in terms of the value it places on knowledge generation, as most postgraduate degrees are research oriented, especially in technical disciplines. Finally, with respect to colocation of the high-technology sector and the highly educated worker, it may be recognized that causality may be bidirectional in this case.

Creation of Enterprises

Enterprise formation through incubators is but a small fraction of all start-ups globally, and the same is true in India, where formal incubation is a rather recent phenomenon. Older incubators are to be found in technology institutions such as the Indian Institute of Technology (IIT) Bombay and the Indian Institute of Science (IISc) Bangalore. Interestingly, both these incubators support only their own students and faculty for incubation services and have had significant successes. By contrast, incubatees at the management institutions are primarily from outside the institutions. It may be worth noting that whereas incubators at management institutions focus on technology-based entrepreneurship, students and faculty at these institutions focus on innovative business models rather than technology for developing their enterprises—a clear mismatch of objectives. Another interesting hypothesis is that one of the reasons Indian incubators do not find fresh graduates may have less to do with lack of innovation in institutions than with the behavior of the middle class; most entrepreneurs who come from nonentrepreneurial families tend first to secure themselves economically through a high-paying job and then enter the world of entrepreneurship. It is no mystery, then, that many of these incubatees are not recent graduates.

Two other factors have adversely affected the formation of student- and faculty-led enterprises in the high-technology sector. First, an enterprise requires formation of a team with diverse skills—technology, marketing, finance, and so on. In India, however, science and technology institutions (as well as management institutions) are stand-alone entities, not part of a comprehensive university. As a consequence, student or faculty start-up teams remain incomplete, reducing the chances of venture funding and of success. Second, the ecosystem for nurturing high-technology entrepreneurship is not sufficiently developed. Uncertain support in the following areas adversely affects enterprise creation:

- Early financing
- Mentoring support
- Fast prototyping
- Prototyping funds
- Early market linkages

Funds made available to technical graduates to start an enterprise, and matching grants from the government, would go a long way toward promoting enterprise creation. It appears that incubation activity may be best suited for comprehensive universities that can help create an integrated support environment and provide sources of innovation. However, research parks on the campuses of stand-alone institutions may be more appropriate because they may attract slightly mature firms that might be seeking only complementary skills from such institutions.

Creation of Knowledge

Some comments are in place about the observations in the paper on the creation of knowledge as a key linkage between institutions and high-technology industry. First, an overemphasis on patents as a comprehensive indicator of knowledge creation distorts the picture for India, where patenting costs and cumbersome procedures are major deterrents to seeking a patent. On a related note, it may not be possible to assess the extent and quality of research spillovers in an industry by the share of patents awarded to foreign firms. The chemical and pharmaceutical industry, for example, is one of the largest sectors, as measured by the number of firms in the country. It should not be a surprise that it has the highest share of patents, compared with semiconductors, where the number of firms is very small. Indian firms in these sectors have been known to be working with higher education institutions to develop advanced knowledge through joint PhD programs, and they are forging strong research partnerships with select institutions, including the University Institute of Chemical Technology (UDCT), IIT Bombay, and the National Institute of Pharmaceutical Education and Research (NIPER). This is also a sector in which foreign enterprises encounter significant competition from domestic firms, explaining their low participation in institutional R&D in India (perhaps to prevent any spillover benefits to Indian firms). Research spillover occurs through movement of personnel, suppliers, and so on and may be helping domestic firms develop capabilities.

Second, it would be worthwhile to measure other indicators of the generation and quality of knowledge—for example, research contracts from industry, the value of these grants, utilization of research by industry, citation of the research in patents, joint publication, and so on, to gauge whether there has been any change in this domain over the years.

Third, without claiming that research output through the academia-industry linkage is adequate, one can argue that the mechanisms needed to translate academic research into a patent application are largely absent. For example, each year a large number of students complete dissertations, often with industry support, yet the likelihood that one of these dissertations will become the basis of a patent or industrial application is low.

Fourth, it would be useful to understand the context of knowledge creation through linkages by delineating the stage of industrial development and understanding the demand pull for research by Indian industry. This might be true for non-industry-specific knowledge, as well.

Fifth, equity and access considerations have led to the establishment of institutions in locations that are often far away from industrial clusters, providing little opportunity for linkages with high-technology industry.

In summary, observations from patenting must be seen, at best, as intermediate observations on a transiting economy that is trying to get its macro principles right! Measurement of change might be a better indicator in such a situation.

Finally, we explore whether there is something about the structure of higher education in India that inhibits linkages. Two key factors have significantly impeded formation of linkages:

1. Restrictive regulation, manifested in several areas

   - Rules governing institutions—centralization of curriculum, low compensation, licensing of institutions, and the like, leading to a weak research environment

   - Caps on endowments, resulting in low motivation to seek linkages with industry

   - High student-teacher ratios, which motivate institutions to focus more on training and less on research.

2. Proliferation of stand-alone institutions.

The aim of the underlying policies has been to improve labor-related linkages, but they may have slowed the formation of other types.

In conclusion, data-based evidence would help explain whether other linkages are weak or are simply in early stages. Two issues call for careful study: the demand pull for various linkages from the industry, and the comparison of linkages between private and public institutions. Interestingly, much of the linkage thus far has been driven by public institutions through public funds. As private industry and private institutions grow in India, their participation both in funding and in seeking innovation funds for developing new enterprises or new knowledge will become crucial for the growth of the economy.

Human Development

Health and Socioeconomic Status: The Importance of Causal Pathways

DUNCAN THOMAS

The poor tend to be in poor health. A positive association between socioeconomic status (SES) and health has been established worldwide, within specific societies, over the life course, and for a broad array of indicators of both health and SES. Experimental and nonexperimental evidence on the causal pathways that underlie this association suggests that fetal health and health in early life likely affect health and economic prosperity in later life. Some evidence suggests that changes in health during adulthood also affect work outcomes. Overall, the strongest evidence for a causal impact of health on economic success is reflected in the effect of improved nutrition on economic productivity. The evidence on other dimensions of health is more limited. Very little attention has been paid to the dynamic interplay between health and behavioral choices that shapes economic outcomes over the longer term. Recent innovations provide unparalleled opportunities for making major contributions to knowledge that could have a lasting impact on the well-being of populations around the world.

The poor tend to be in poor health. A positive association between socioeconomic status (SES) and health has been established across the globe, within specific societies, over the life course, and for a broad array of indicators of both health and SES. Interpretation of the association is at the center of a large and contentious debate.

A key issue in this debate has been isolation of the causal pathways that link health and economic prosperity. Pinning down causal pathways at the individual level is critically important from both a scientific and a policy standpoint. For example, if income growth leads to improvements in health, policy makers should take health benefits into account when allocating resources to programs that promote economic growth.

Duncan Thomas is a professor of economics at Duke University, Durham, NC, and a faculty affiliate at the Duke Global Health Institute. This paper draws extensively on collaborative work with Elizabeth Frankenberg and John Strauss, to whom the author acknowledges an enormous debt for guiding his thinking. The paper benefited from comments by T. Paul Schultz and by an anonymous reviewer.

Annual World Bank Conference on Development Economics 2009, Global

If, conversely, health contributes to economic prosperity, these benefits ought to be included in evaluations of the impact of resources allocated to the health sector—including, for example, provision of public health services, immunization, maternal and child health programs, subsidized medical care, and health insurance programs, as well as public health information campaigns and training of health personnel.

Causality likely runs in both directions. On the one hand, a family with more income is likely to invest more in its members' human capital, including health. In low-resource populations, as income increases, individuals typically invest in better diets and improved sanitation and devote more resources to health care. On the other hand, if a healthier worker is less susceptible to disease, more alert, and more energetic, he or she will probably be more productive and may work longer hours. As a result, the worker will command higher earnings. In contrast, individuals in poorer health may reduce their hours or be unable to work at all, and they may have to dip into their savings to pay for costly treatments or care.

Other, unobserved factors probably drive both health and economic prosperity. For example, part of health is inherited, as are other attributes related to economic prosperity. The role of genes, and the role the environment plays in their expression, are not fully understood. Moreover, families that choose to invest in the health of their children may also value other investments that would improve their own and their children's lives. They may make investments in other dimensions of their children's human capital, working more effectively, or saving more.

It is important to take into account factors that are not readily observed (or, more precisely, not treated as observed, in most models), for at least two reasons. First, a demonstration that health does not have a causal impact on income cannot be interpreted as indicating that the correlation between income and health should be attributed to a causal effect of income on health. The association may be attributed to these other, unobserved factors.

Second, the literature has typically referred to unobserved factors, including, for example, tastes, information, and the like. Some of these, such as information about health practices or propensities to save for the future, are amenable to measurement. Accumulation of scientific evidence on their role, if any, in behavioral choices that explain the association between health and economic prosperity is a potentially important new line of research. Moreover, some of these factors can be influenced by policy. For example, campaigns that provide information about health and the health consequences of behaviors have been successful in effecting lifestyle changes that promote better health, such as policies that discourage tobacco use.

This paper focuses on key issues involved in isolating causal pathways that link health and SES at the micro level. Rather than attempt exhaustively to describe the methods and evidence, we focus on a small number of studies to illustrate the methods that have been used in the literature and assess their contributions to knowledge. The conclusion highlights some of the lines of future inquiry in this literature that are likely to be especially profitable and describes some methodological advances that have the potential to yield new evidence that will substantially influence both science and policy design. (For more comprehensive reviews of the literature on health and development, see Strauss and Thomas 1995, 2008; Jack and Lewis 2008.)

Measurement of Health and Socioeconomic Status

The relationship between health and SES is not unidimensional. The magnitude and direction of the correlation vary with the measures of health and of SES. For example, short-term episodes of illness that have no longer-term ramifications for health or functioning may result in changes in how time is allocated (to rest and recuperation, say) and thus perhaps to earnings during the period of illness, although even this will depend on the nature of the work and the payment mechanisms. Workers paid by the piece or on an hourly or daily basis are likely to have lower earnings when sick, whereas workers with paid sick leave may not. Reallocations of time in response to episodes of illness may be temporary, and the individual may make up for lost earnings by spending more time on activities such as work when his or her health improves.

More persistent or chronic health conditions may have broader effects on SES. These conditions may result in permanent changes in earnings because of changes in time allocation or productivity, or both. The health conditions may also result in changes in consumption, savings, and wealth as individuals draw on resources for treatment or in response to reduced earnings. Conditions that affect life expectancy likely affect intertemporal preferences and therefore decisions about savings and wealth accumulation.

In practice, in many instances, whether a specific health event will turn into a chronic condition may not be immediately obvious, and the path from short-term to longer-term health difficulties may be complex. Moreover, the cumulative effect of multiple health insults may turn an apparently short-term health problem into a chronic condition. For example, the literature suggests that the deleterious consequences for day-to-day functioning of a traumatic event such as an earthquake or exposure to a violent attack are dramatically magnified when an individual has had prior exposure to traumatic events.

The impact of a health condition may also have long-reaching effects on economic and social success if the condition results in a shift in the individual's lifetime trajectory. For example, a health condition during early childhood may affect school performance, which, in turn, has lasting effects on academic achievement and economic success in later life. In other instances, behavioral responses to chronic conditions, such as change of occupation or life style, may mitigate the negative consequences for economic prosperity. Health innovations in later life can have yet other impacts on the economic security of the individual.

It is important to keep in mind that there is likely to be considerable heterogeneity not only in the magnitude and direction of the association between health and SES but also in its interpretation. These issues have received inadequate attention in the literature, partly because relatively few health measures have been used in studies relating health to SES, a shortcoming that reflects data constraints.

In recent years, the quality and quantity of data for exploring these questions have dramatically improved. There have been, and continue to be, exciting innovations in the technology for measuring a broad array of health markers, using noninvasive and minimally invasive methods that can be implemented in the field at low cost. These technologies include, for example, in-home monitors and assays of blood drops (dried on filter paper), cheek swabs, saliva, and hair, for measuring short-term and longer-term health conditions as well as DNA. These health measures have been integrated with rich administrative data, as well as with population-based socioeconomic data, many of which involve long-term longitudinal surveys that follow individuals over the life course.

In combination, these integrated data sources provide opportunities to make major advances in understanding the complex interplay between different dimensions of health and SES over the life course. In the next sections, variation over the life course will be used as an organizing principle in an assessment of the state of the field regarding the causal impact of health on socioeconomic prosperity.

Health in Early Life and Later Outcomes

Investigation of the links between health in early life, including fetal health, and later life outcomes is an active area of scientific inquiry. Research by Barker and his colleagues has highlighted the key role of maternal nutrition during pregnancy. It is thought that inadequate nutrients and oxygen during fetal development may result in adaptions in organ development to ensure survival while a fetus and possibly immediately after birth. This fetal "programming" appears to result in elevated risk of health problems throughout the entire life course (Barker 1994; Victora et al. 2008).

For example, low birthweight may result in reduced growth during infancy because the body is programmed as a fetus to survive on low levels of nutrients. This "thrifty phenotype," which develops as an adaption to adverse nutrition in utero, results in permanent metabolic and endocrine changes. These changes would be beneficial if food continued to be scarce after birth, but if food is plentiful, the same metabolic changes may be disadvantageous; they have been associated with elevated risks of obesity, dyslipidemia, and glucose intolerance in later life (Hales and Barker 1992). Thus, it is thought that being born small and thin but becoming overweight during adolescence or adulthood put an individual at greatest risk of heart disease and type 2 diabetes in later life. Furthermore, the biological literature suggests that not only does the overall nutritional status of the mother affect fetal health; the timing of nutrition and health insults also affect the growth and development of the child. For example, inadequate nutrients during the period when arteries are formed are associated with elevated risk of heart disease because of hardened arteries in midlife and later (Godfrey and Barker 2000).

Much of the experimental evidence on the longer-term effects of maternal nutrition deprivation relies on animal models. There are, however, several innovative studies that exploit quasi-experimental designs to measure the effects on humans. For example, Roseboom et al. (2001) summarize a rich body of work that examines the impact of the Dutch famine in the Netherlands on the health and mortality of prime-age adults. Toward the end of World War II, several Dutch cities that were thought to be supporting the Resistance were subjected to severe food rationing for about six months. People who were in utero during that period constitute a "treatment group" whose health in later life can be compared with that of a "control group" of people who were born at the same time in other Dutch cities and were not subjected to the same food rationing. The authors find that nutritional deprivation early in the fetal period results in an elevated risk of glucose intolerance and heart disease among adult males and females.

It is likely that maternal nutritional status is not the only factor that affects fetal outcomes. Finch and Crimmins (2004) highlight the importance of infection during the fetal period. They argue that maternal infection and stress result in inflammation that has detrimental consequences for the development of the fetus, which affects the health and well-being of the offspring through the entire life course. For example, it is thought that inflammation in utero is implicated in the development of plaque in the arteries and therefore in heart disease and that these effects are independent of diet and lifestyle choices.

Quantification of the magnitude of these effects is particularly salient for developing countries because of the coexistence of infectious diseases with the onset of the nutrition transition. On the one hand, the obesity epidemic is reaching beyond the developed countries and is spreading throughout the globe (Popkin 1993). On the other hand, levels of infection and, thus, of inflammation are much higher in poorer societies, suggesting that these populations may be carrying a particularly heavy burden of disease in the future.

A key implication of this research is that the long arm of fetal and early childhood health may extend not only to health in later life but also to economic and social prosperity through the life course. Studies have documented that low birthweight is predictive of lower school attainment and less success in the labor market. Although low birthweight likely reflects poor intrauterine growth, it is not clear that these associations can be given a causal interpretation. Low birthweight is the outcome of many factors, including low resource levels, inadequate access to health services, and maternal behaviors, all of which may be related to other investments in infants and children. To establish that variation in fetal health causes variation in economic success, it is necessary to identify changes in fetal health that are arguably exogenous and not under the direct control of parents.

This concern is addressed in some recent studies. Almond (2006) examines the longer-term effects of being conceived in late 1918, during the Spanish flu pandemic. The Spanish flu, caused by an unusually severe strain of the H1N1 virus, resulted in very high levels of morbidity and mortality. It is estimated that more than half a million people died in the United States and that about one in four people suffered from the virus (Crosby 1989). The virus was first detected in March 1918, and although the pandemic persisted to the middle of 1920, its impact on the health of the U.S. population was concentrated in the last half of 1918. Whereas influenza usually kills the youngest and oldest, the Spanish flu killed prime-age adults and fell particularly heavily on males. It has been conjectured that undetected tuberculosis among these men rendered them particularly vulnerable (Noymer and Garenne 2000).

Using data from the 1960 United States census, Almond compares the health, schooling, and labor market outcomes of people who were born in 1919 with those born before the onset of the pandemic and those born at least nine months after the

FIGURE 1.
Fetal Health, Own Education, and Socioeconomic Status (SES) of Parents, by Year of Birth, United States

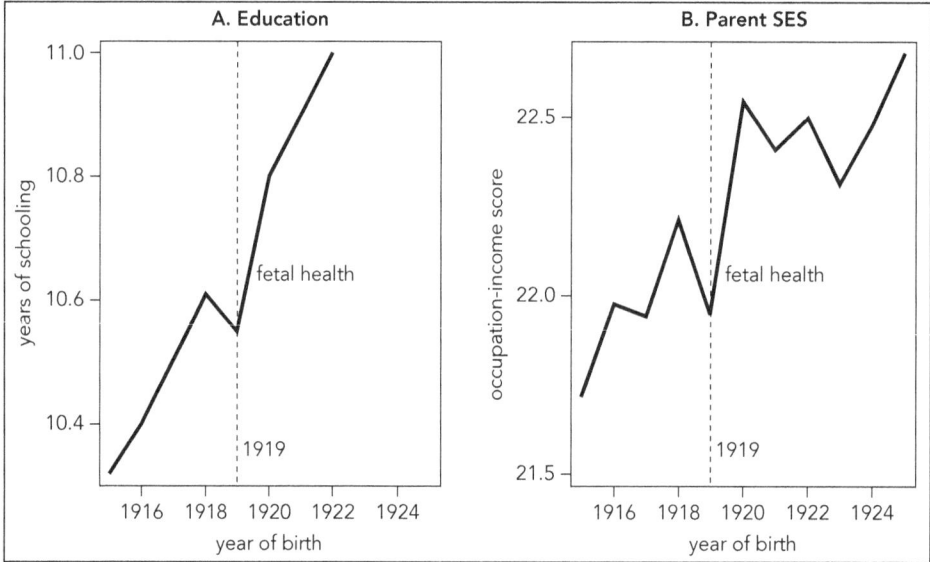

Source: Panel A, 1960 U.S. Census; panel B, 1930 U.S. Census.

Note: The 1919 cohort was age 41 at the time of the 1960 census (panel A) and age 11 at the time of the 1930 census (panel B).

pandemic ended. As shown in panel A of figure 1, he finds that, relative to other cohorts, males who were born in 1919 (and were thus in utero during the most virulent phase of the pandemic) completed significantly fewer years of schooling. They are also less likely to have graduated from high school, and at age 40 they earned less than control cohorts.

Almond attributes these effects to the impact of maternal infection on the fetus. It is possible that they reflect other influences such as higher prices for food and other goods at the time of the pandemic, lower incomes because of reduced labor supply at the time of the pandemic, or stress associated with the pandemic. It is also possible that the results reflect the impact of the pandemic on childbearing decisions of parents. The influenza virus emerged in early 1918, when soldiers were returning from World War I. Parents who chose to have children at that time may have been different from those who had recently given birth and those who delayed childbearing.

To investigate this issue, panel B of figure 1 presents an indicator of SES of parents for each cohort of births in the 1930 census. The SES index is based on an occupation-income score. It is significantly lower for children born in 1919 than for those born in 1920, suggesting either that lower SES parents were more likely to have children in 1919 than higher SES parents or that children of higher SES parents in the 1919 birth cohort were more likely to have died by age 11. The latter seems unlikely. There is a strong intergenerational correlation between education and SES, and so the fact that the 1919 birth cohort has less schooling in adulthood reflects, at least in part, differences in family background. It would seem premature to attribute the entire gap between the 1919 and other birth cohorts in economic prosperity as an adult to the impact of health insults during the fetal period resulting from the influenza pandemic. Almond also exploits variation across states in mortality attributed to the pandemic, but those estimates are potentially contaminated by behavioral responses to the pandemic. (See Thomas 2008 for a discussion.)

Related work examines the impact on human capital and economic prosperity in midlife of being born during the 1959–61 Chinese famine. Using the 1991 wave of the China Health and Nutrition Survey (CHNS), Chen and Zhou (2007) compare outcomes for cohorts born in the 1950s and 1960s. The impact of the famine is identified by using regional variation in the 1960 death rate that is attributed to the famine. The authors find that adults who were born in 1959 or 1960 and survived to 1991 would have been 3 centimeters taller if they had not been exposed to the famine. They also report reduced hours of work by individuals in this cohort. Family income per capita is lower, but the magnitude and significance of these effects differ across the cohort, depending on the specific measure of income. It is unclear how to interpret evidence on family earnings, which reflect the contributions of family members from other birth cohorts.

As with the influenza pandemic, it is possible that the estimated effects of the Chinese famine reflect the impact of income and price variation resulting from the famine. As the authors note, interpretation of the estimates is complicated by at least two additional concerns. First, location of birth is not known in the CHNS, and so the authors assume that respondents were born in the same location where they were interviewed 40 years later. This, they conjecture, is a reasonable assumption in China during the period. This concern highlights an important advantage of Almond's work, which uses census data that include information on location of birth.

Second, survivors of the famine may be selected on health and human capital. On the one hand, it is likely that the frailest individuals would have died in the harsh environment at the time of the famine—in which case the estimated effects are probably downward biased. On the other hand, there is evidence that fertility responded to the famine and that birth rates declined substantially soon after the onset of the famine. The direction of bias in this case is unclear.

One assessment of the empirical magnitude of these influences comes from a comparison of birth cohorts born around the time of the 1974 floods in Bangladesh with cohorts born before and after the floods. Flooding is commonplace in the Ganges Delta, but there had been no parallel to the severity of the 1974 floods for almost 20 years, and it is estimated that more than 20,000 people were killed by them. Table 1 presents data from the 1996 Matlab Health and Socioeconomic Survey (MHSS), which collected population-representative information on individuals living in Bangladesh's Matlab District. The fraction of the population born between 1970 and 1978 is reported in the first column for each year of birth. The substantially reduced size of the 1975 birth cohort is consistent with the idea that fetal health was affected by the floods. The second column reports differences in the fractions of males in each birth cohort who are unable to read, relative to the 1970 birth cohort. Cohorts born in 1975 are nearly 10 percentage points less likely to be illiterate than those born in the early 1970s or in the late 1970s. These are very large differences, given that about 16 percent of males born in the 1970s are unable to read. The results are very similar when we compare males who are both illiterate and innumerate, in the third column. (There is no evidence of a secular trend in literacy rates during the 1970s. By contrast, comparisons of school attainment and height are complicated by secular trends.)

The fact that the cohort of males exposed to the floods has higher levels of human capital suggests that these estimates are dominated by selection rather than by the deleterious impact of the floods on fetal health. Two additional pieces of evidence suggest that this is a legitimate interpretation of the evidence. First, the 1974 and 1976 birth cohorts are also more likely to be literate and numerate than cohorts born before or after them. The 1976 cohort was not directly exposed to the flood.

Second, by reestimating the models with a household fixed effect, it is possible to assess the extent to which families with children who were born between 1974 and 1976 and who survived to 1996 are selective on characteristics that are associated with investments in human capital. The results are shown in the last two columns of table 1. The

TABLE 1. Human Capital and Exposure to the 1974 Floods in Bangladesh: Males, by Birth Year

Year of birth	Percent of population (1)	OLS		Household fixed effects	
		Percent illiterate (2)	Percent illiterate and innumerate (3)	Percent illiterate (4)	Percent illiterate and innumerate (5)
1971	9.2	0.9	1.1	−3.2	−2.8
	(0.5)	(0.2)	(0.3)	(0.6)	(0.5)
1972	9.4	−1.7	−2.5	−0.4	−0.5
	(0.5)	(0.5)	(0.7)	(0.1)	(0.1)
1973	11.7	−1.9	−2.6	−6.1	−5.7
	(0.5)	(0.6)	(0.8)	(1.2)	(1.2)
1974	11.4	−6.3	−7.2	−3.8	−3.3
	(0.5)	(1.8)	(2.2)	(0.7)	(0.7)
1975	9.0	−9.6	−9.6	−5.2	−4.8
	(0.4)	(2.6)	(2.8)	(0.9)	(0.9)
1976	13.0	−8.4	−9.0	−3.0	−3.7
	(0.5)	(2.5)	(2.9)	(0.6)	(0.8)
1977	14.4	−0.2	−0.2	−0.2	1.7
	(0.5)	(0.0)	(0.1)	(0.0)	(0.4)
1978	12.6	−1.1	−0.6	0.5	0.6
	(0.5)	(0.3)	(0.2)	(0.1)	(0.1)
Constant		16.0	14.8	15.3	13.4
		(6.1)	(6.0)	(3.9)	(3.7)

Source: Author's calculations using data from the Matlab Health and Socioeconomic Survey on respondents born between 1970 and 1978.

Note: OLS, ordinary least squares. Number of males is 2,064. Numbers in parentheses are t-statistics. Birth year 1970 is the excluded category in regressions reported in columns (2) through (5).

differences in human capital across birth-year cohorts are substantially reduced, and there is no evidence that the 1974–76 cohorts are different from the others. We conclude that at least in the case of the Bangladesh floods, inferences about the causal effect of health insults during the fetal period need to take into account behavioral responses by parents to the floods and their aftermath.

Selective fertility, and fetal or infant mortality that is selective on characteristics related to investments in health and human capital, are potential concerns for the interpretation of results based on comparisons across cohorts. In the Chinese case, there is evidence that the number of live births declined dramatically soon after the onset of the famine. Evidence based on children born in the United States in 1919 is also potentially contaminated by selective fertility. The general point is that individuals, couples, and families are likely to take into account changes in the environment, including changes in the disease environment, when making decisions about the future.

The emerging body of literature on the health and economic impact of insults in utero is extremely important. A related line of inquiry assesses the extent to which investments in the health and well-being of reproductive-age women, especially pregnant women, contribute to the health and economic well-being of the next generation. There are other potential benefits from investments in the reproductive health of women. Greater control over fertility typically leads to fewer children ever born and, possibly, to greater investments in each child (Schultz 2008). Moreover, there may be benefits in the form of better health of reproductive-age women. Greater control over timing of births and improved health potentially improve labor market opportunities for women and the resources available to them. To the extent that these factors also elevate women's control over resources within a family, the literature suggests that further investments in the health and well-being of children, as well as in the accumulation of wealth, may result (Thomas 1990; Rubalcava, Teruel, and Thomas 2009).

These issues are explored in a series of studies that use observational data and exploit variation in the availability of reproductive health services across Indonesia. The *bidan desa,* or village midwife program, inaugurated in the mid-1990s, seeks to place a trained nurse in every village in Indonesia in an effort to reduce maternal mortality and improve birth outcomes. The cost of the midwife is absorbed by the government for the first three years, as long as the midwife remains working in the village to which she is assigned. During this time, she is encouraged to develop a private practice.

Evaluation of the program is not straightforward. Comparisons of the health of women before and after a midwife joins a community would reflect both the impact of the midwife and any other changes over time. From the outset, midwives were allocated to the poorest communities that did not already have a midwife. Comparisons of the health of females in a community that had a midwife with the health of females in a community without a midwife would therefore reflect the combined influence of the presence of the midwife and differences between the communities.

To identify the effects of the midwives, Frankenberg and Thomas (2001) suggest that if midwives focused on the health of reproductive-age females and had no direct influence on the health of males, differences between communities would be reflected in the health of males. Drawing on two waves of the Indonesia Family Life Survey (IFLS), they estimate the change in health of females in communities that did not have a midwife by the second wave and compare this change with the change among males in the same communities. This method provides an estimate of health changes in those "control communities." The difference in changes in health of females and of males in communities in which a midwife joined the community between the survey waves provides an estimate of the differential health changes in "treatment communities." Comparison of the differences in treatment communities with the differences in the control communities yields an estimate of the impact of the village midwife on the health of reproductive-age females. This estimation strategy takes into account the fact that midwives are allocated purposively to communities where they are likely to have their biggest impact. The strategy also takes into account secular changes in health within each community, as long as those changes are common for males and females. Frankenberg and Thomas (2001) focus on body mass index (BMI), an indicator of general health and nutritional status, and report a large and significant beneficial impact on the BMI of females from the introduction of a midwife into a community.

The strategy assumes that the midwife has no direct or indirect impact on the health of males. Indirect benefits may arise if women learn about better health care practices that affect other family members or if women seek advice from the midwife about the health of others in their families. If these benefits are positive, the estimated effects of the midwife will be biased downward. If, however, the presence of a midwife results in reduced resources being allocated to improving the health of males and children, the strategy would yield upward-biased estimates.

Frankenberg, Suriastini, and Thomas (2005) address this concern by examining the impact of a midwife on child health. In this case, the identification strategy combines the advantages of the longitudinal design of the IFLS with insights from the nutrition literature on the biology of linear growth. Specifically, health and nutrition interventions have their greatest impact on the length of children during the first few years of life. Eventual adult height is largely determined by around age 3 or 4. Thus, if a midwife joins a community when a child is age 5 or 6, the services provided by the midwife are unlikely to have much effect on the child's growth trajectory. In contrast, if the midwife is present from the time the child is conceived, the child will be fully exposed to the potential benefits from the midwife.

Consider a treatment community in which a midwife joins the community immediately after the first wave of the survey. Comparison of the height of children age 8 in the first wave with children the same age in the second wave provides an estimate of the changes in height that can be attributed to secular improvements and are unlikely to be associated with the presence of the midwife. In contrast, the differences between the heights of children age 3 and younger in the second wave and of children of the same age in the first wave provide an estimate of the impact of being fully exposed to the midwife relative to having no exposure to her. This difference, however, is contaminated by secular changes that might have occurred during this period. Thus, comparison of the differences in heights of young children between the waves with the differences in heights of older children between the waves (which capture secular changes) yields an estimate of the impact of the midwife on the longer-term nutritional status of young children.

It is possible that there are cohort-specific growth trajectories. To assess whether this is an important concern, an alternative strategy compares changes in heights of young children, relative to older children, in treatment communities with similar changes in heights of young and older children in control communities that never had a midwife. Furthermore, by comparing changes in the heights of older children in treatment and control communities, it is possible to evaluate the validity of the assumptions in the model. A child who is fully exposed to a midwife is almost half a standard deviation taller than a similar child who is not so exposed—a difference that is not only significant but is larger than the urban-rural gap in heights of Indonesian children. Related research shows that midwives are associated with improved birth outcomes, including increased birthweight and fewer complications at birth (Frankenberg et al. 2009). Taken as a whole, this research indicates that the introduction of improved reproductive health services in rural Indonesia has resulted in improved health of women and children.

These studies, based on observational data, are able to estimate effects that can be interpreted as causal because of the research designs, which develop credible control groups with which treatments are compared. Assessment of the impact of improved reproductive health services on economic outcomes is more tenuous with this strategy, although the evidence suggests that improved reproductive health services are associated with elevated rates of labor force participation in the market and with higher earnings among females in Indonesia.

Joshi and Schultz (2007) make further progress on this front by examining the impact of a family planning intervention that was assigned to some villages in Matlab District, Bangladesh, and not to others. Starting in 1977, family planning services, in conjunction with maternal and child health services, were provided on a door-to-door basis in treatment villages. Control villages continued to receive services at local clinics. Studies have documented large and significant declines in fertility (ICDDR,B 2004). Joshi and Schultz exploit this design to assess the impact on the health and economic prosperity of women exposed to the treatment and to measure the effects of exposure to the program on the women's children.

Drawing on survey data collected by the Matlab Health and Socioeconomic Survey (MHSS) 20 years after the initiation of the program, Joshi and Schultz report significant improvements in the health of exposed women, higher rates of employment out of the home, and greater economic productivity in those activities. The households in which these women reside are wealthier and are more likely to have access to water within the family compound. The children of exposed women are more likely to survive to age 5, and they are more likely to be immunized. There is some evidence of improved nutritional status among these children, although there are only modest gains in schooling relative to children of women in control areas.

Frankenberg and Thomas (2007) highlight the potential impact of exposure to the program on female savings and empowerment. Specifically, they exploit a feature of the MHSS, which, following the IFLS, collects information on assets at the individual level within each household. Reduced fertility associated with exposure to the family planning outreach will reduce the number of children that a woman can call on for assistance at older ages, and so there is a greater incentive to accumulate wealth over the life course to draw on in later life. Moreover, if control over assets translates into control over decisions about resource allocations, as women gain control over fertility they may also be empowered to assert themselves in other domains of the family economy. Women who were exposed to the family planning outreach treatment have significantly higher asset levels than women not in the treatment areas. Treated women tend to accumulate gold and goats—assets that are traditionally controlled by women. This is not because couples in treatment areas accumulated more assets, since males in the treatment communities did not save more than males in control communities.

The combination of data from experiments and from observational sources paints a picture in which reproductive health programs yield benefits measured not only in increased control over fertility but also in improved health and economic outcomes for women and greater accumulation of resources for the future. Furthermore, there is some evidence that the programs yield benefits in terms of improved child health. We turn next to a discussion of the evidence on the influence of child health on economic prosperity.

Child Health and Economic Success

A substantial body of literature has documented that adult height is correlated not only with improved health but also with economic prosperity, as indicated by higher rates of participation in the labor force and, among those who work, higher hourly earnings. These relationships have been established in the historical literature following pioneering work by Fogel (2004) and his collaborators, and they have also been documented in the literature on developing countries (Strauss and Thomas 1998). Adult height is largely determined during early childhood, and clearly, economic prosperity during adulthood cannot have a causal impact on linear growth during childhood. It is therefore tempting to interpret these associations as indicating a causal effect of early childhood nutrition on economic prosperity during adulthood.

That would be premature. Factors that affect early childhood growth, such as genes, parental resources, and parents' tastes for investing in the human capital of their children, might also affect economic prosperity during adulthood. In that case, height and educational attainment, and possibly cognitive achievement, would be positively correlated (Case and Paxson 2008). Genetic influences, cognition, and tastes are seldom included in empirical models that relate adult height to economic prosperity, but without taking them into account, it is difficult to interpret the associations between attained adult height and economic prosperity.

Observational studies that relate height or weight of children to school performance suffer from similar problems, although attempts have been made to treat the joint determination of child health and child schooling through an instrumental variables approach or by including family fixed effects in the models. Prices of inputs into the production of height are potential instruments; they may include (implicit or explicit) prices of local health services and prices of specific foods, relative to other prices. Estimation is complicated because child nutrition reflects both a stock and a flow component, and so the instruments necessarily capture variation in the environment to which the person was exposed during the fetal period and in the first few years of life. As noted above, the use of local variation in prices and services is complicated if allocation of programs and subsidies takes into account child health or if people move to areas because of improved services (Schultz 2002).

Alderman, Hoddinott, and Kinsey (2006) use variation in resources during the first years of life to measure the impact of early childhood nutrition on adult stature and schooling attainment. They exploit variation in resources resulting from droughts and civil war in Zimbabwe, treating this variation as a result of unanticipated shocks. It is not clear, however, that this variation is entirely unanticipated and that parents do not respond to it by, for example, moving.

The authors find that early childhood nutrition has a large and significant impact on years of completed schooling, indicating that public health interventions that ensure that infants and young children are well nourished are likely to have a direct impact on the human capital and economic prosperity of a population. (See Glewwe and Miguel 2008 for a review of this literature.)

Numerous animal experiments and some small-scale randomized interventions with children have implicated both macronutrients and several micronutrients such as iron and zinc in cognitive functioning. Some of these studies have linked supplementation to school performance or economic outcomes. (See Pollitt et al. 1993 for a review.)

Among the most influential studies of the impact of child nutrition on economic well-being is a randomized intervention conducted by the Instituto de Nutrición de Centro América y Panamá (INCAP) in four villages in rural Guatemala between 1969 and 1977. Two villages were randomly assigned to receive a treatment of a fortified drink, Atole, which was high in energy and protein and contained iron and niacin. The other two villages were provided with sugared water, Fresco. Children from birth to age 7, along with pregnant and lactating mothers, were eligible to receive the drink daily at a community center in each village. The study population was poor and undernourished. Prior to the intervention, about four of every five children age 2 in the villages were stunted (height for age z-score < 2), and about one-third exhibited wasting (weight for age z-score < 2).

Children exposed to the treatment are taller at 36 months than children in the same villages who did not receive the treatment during their first few years of life. To isolate the impact of the supplementation, these differences across cohorts are contrasted with differences across the same cohorts in control villages. This is an important result because it establishes that a nutrition intervention in early life can have long-lasting effects on the health and well-being of a population (Martorell et al. 2005).

Maluccio et al. (2006) use a similar approach to measure the impact of nutrition supplementation on cognitive achievement. In a follow-up study conducted in 2002–04, when the study subjects were adults, abstract reasoning skills were measured with a Raven's Colored Progressive Matrices test. Subjects who were exposed to the treatment during the first three years of life performed better on the test than those not exposed in early life. There is a small impact on females' completed schooling and language skills.

Related research explores the impact of the nutrition supplementation on economic productivity in adulthood. Using the same follow-up survey, Hoddinott et al. (2008) apply the same empirical strategy of comparing the cohort that was fully exposed to the supplement with earlier birth cohorts in the treatment villages and contrasting the difference in economic outcomes with the difference between the same cohorts in the control villages. They find that among males who were working and were fully exposed to the supplementation as a child, hourly earnings were 40 to 60 percent higher than they would otherwise have been. This is an extremely large effect. Elevated productivity was largely offset by reduced hours of work. Annual earnings are estimated to be about 7 percent higher among treated males relative to controls, although this difference is not significant (which may reflect inadequate power because of small sample sizes). Among females, the authors find that treated individuals tend to earn less per hour, work fewer hours, and have lower annual earnings than controls but that none of these differences is significant.

In sum, females benefit more in terms of school performance than males. Among those males who earn income, however, there is a 50 percent premium in hourly earnings for those in the treatment group relative to controls. Compensating reductions in hours of work among these males result in much smaller effects on annual earnings. There are no effects on the labor market outcomes of females. Taken together, the results are puzzling. It is possible that they reflect a complex set of choices related to schooling, marriage, and labor market participation that differs between males and females. It is also possible that the estimated effects are contaminated by attrition that differs between treatments and controls and also between males and females in ways that are related to labor market and schooling outcomes. The authors conclude that this is an unlikely explanation because they find little evidence of systematic differences between those who attrited and those who did not. These comparisons are based on observed characteristics when the respondents were young children. It is possible that there are differences between the two groups that are not observed at baseline, either because they were not measured at that time or because of changes that occurred in the lives of the respondents after the baseline.

Putting attrition aside, the results on the longer-term impact of this early child nutrition intervention suggest that improvements in the nutritional status of children in the first few years of life lead to improved human capital outcomes (as indicated by better health in later life, improved cognitive functioning, and, among females, more schooling) and elevated economic productivity among males in the labor force. Since, however, there is little evidence that annual earnings are higher among treated cohorts, the benefits of improved childhood nutrition do not appear to translate into greater economic prosperity at the aggregate level.

The bulk of the literature on the link between childhood nutrition and economic prosperity in developing countries has, appropriately, focused on undernutrition.

However, in advanced countries, rates of pediatric obesity are high, and the evidence indicates that obesity among young children is an emerging concern in developing countries passing through the nutrition transition (Popkin 1993; de Onis and Blossner 2000). Rapid changes in nutrition levels across cohorts in these countries may presage serious health problems as these children enter midlife. As noted above, the thrifty-gene hypothesis suggests that it is children who are low weight at birth but overweight in adolescence who are at greatest risk of cardiovascular disease and diabetes in later life. Low birthweight is far more common in lower-income countries and is more likely among children whose mothers were poorly nourished as children, as indicated by their height as adults (Victora et al. 2008). There is very little scientific evidence on whether and how childhood obesity affects social and economic success in later life. This is an important gap in the literature.

Although nutrition has played a central role in the literature on health and development, communicable diseases remain a leading cause of death in many low-income settings. Putting aside HIV, many of these diseases are preventable at modest cost. As an example, intestinal helminth infections, or worms, are prevalent in many parts of the developing world and can be effectively treated with readily available antihelminthic drugs. High worm loads result in iron-deficient anemia and protein-energy deficiency, which have, in turn, been associated with reduced cognitive development. The evidence from randomized trials that measure the impact on the cognitive performance of subjects receiving pharmacological interventions to treat helminth infections is inconclusive (Dickson et al. 2000).

Success in treating infectious diseases in a community is likely to have significant externality benefits. Miguel and Kremer (2004) take this as their starting point in estimating the causal effect of treating worms among school-age children, using a random assignment treatment-control design in rural Kenya. In the first year of the study, 25 primary schools were randomly assigned to receive an orally administered antihelminthic drug; those schools and an additional 25 schools received the treatment in the second year, and all 75 primary schools received the treatment in the third year. There are externality benefits: children who were not treated but who lived in the treated areas benefited from the reduced worm loads in those communities. School attendance increased substantially, as indicated by a 25 percent reduction in absenteeism after treatment in treatment areas, relative to controls. Performance on school tests, however, did not respond to the treatment. The authors conjecture that this may reflect the effects of congestion. It may also have to do with what is learned in school and what is tested in examinations—which may itself explain the high levels of absenteeism among primary school children. It is also consistent with there being little effect of helminth infection on cognition (Dickson et al. 2000).

Adult Health and Economic Success

The evidence discussed thus far suggests that health in early life likely affects schooling and economic productivity in later life. We next assess whether changes in health during adulthood affect economic prosperity.

A temporary bout of poor health is likely to be accompanied by reduced time spent working and, possibly, by lower productivity over the short run. Whether these effects translate into longer-term impacts on earnings is less clear. Individuals may compensate by allocating additional time to work when they are in better health. Family members may substitute for a member when he or she is in poor health (Thirumurthy, Graff Zivin, and Goldstein 2008). Chronic diseases and longer bouts of illness are more likely to have permanent effects on economic resources. For example, studies have documented declines in the productivity of individuals working on tea estates in Kenya during the 18 months prior to AIDS-related death or exit from the labor force (Fox et al. 2004).

Determining whether changes in adult health have a causal impact on economic and social success is a substantial challenge. Identification of the health domains that are most important and the magnitudes of their impacts on different dimensions of economic prosperity poses even greater challenges. Convincing evidence will be founded on a model of behavior that takes into account investments in health over the entire life course, expectations about future health and labor market prospects, time allocation in the short and longer runs, and the broader role of family members in these decisions.

Whereas energy supplementation during the first two or three years of life has long-term benefits, experimental studies that involve calorie supplementation of male adults indicate only modest effects on worker productivity. For example, sugarcane cutters in some villages in Guatemala were randomly assigned to receive calorie supplements, while similar workers in other villages were not. There were no differences between the productivity of the workers from the two villages (Immink and Viteri 1981). In contrast, construction workers in Kenya who were randomly given energy supplements were slightly more productive in road digging than the controls (Wolgemuth et al. 1982).

The nutrition literature has highlighted the important role that specific micronutrients play in the etiology of disease and the functioning of the human body. Iron is a good example. Iron deficiency is prevalent throughout the developing world, particularly in South and Southeast Asia, and studies have shown a causal effect of iron deficiency on reduced work capacity, suggesting that there may be a direct link between iron deficiency and economic productivity (Haas and Brownlie 2001).

Iron plays an essential role in oxidative energy production. Iron-deficiency anemia affects physical activity through two main pathways: (a) as hemoglobin levels decline, the maximum amount of oxygen the body can use (aerobic capacity) declines, and (b) as iron stores are depleted, the amount of oxygen available to muscles falls, reducing endurance and causing the heart to work harder for the same activity. Iron deficiency is also associated with, among other effects, greater susceptibility to disease, fatigue, and reduced cognitive development.

Rigorous clinical trials with animals and humans demonstrate a causal relationship between iron deficiency and reduced maximal aerobic capacity (VO_2max), which changes by about 25–30 percent as subjects are made anemic or receive adequate iron supplementation. Iron-deficient anemia is also associated with reduced endurance at below maximal work rates.

Demonstrating that iron deficiency impedes maximal capacity and endurance does not reveal the economic consequences of iron deficiency in daily life. Those consequences may be more closely aligned with energy efficiency—the amount of physiological energy required to perform a given task. In fact, evidence from randomized treatment-control studies of Chinese female cotton mill workers and Sri Lankan female tea plantation workers suggest that elevated productivity resulted in changes in time allocation. Specifically, neither study found evidence of greater productivity per hour among iron-deficient subjects who received iron supplements relative to subjects who were not supplemented, but in both cases, treated women reallocated time away from work and toward nonwork activities (Edgerton et al. 1979; Li et al. 1994). Results from a random assignment treatment-control iron supplementation study of male rubber workers, however, indicates that treated individuals who were anemic at the initiation of the study were able to tap about 20 percent more rubber after supplementation, compared with anemic controls (Basta et al. 1979). Interpretation of this result is complicated by the fact that attrition from the study exceeded 50 percent; if those subjects who did not benefit from the study were more likely to attrit, the estimated benefits would be biased upward.

The Work and Iron Status Evaluation (WISE) is designed to examine the immediate and longer-term impact of providing iron supplements to older adults in Central Java, Indonesia (Thomas et al. 2006). In this population, about one-quarter of older men and one-third of older women are iron deficient, as indicated by low hemoglobin. Older males are randomly assigned to receive a weekly iron supplement, or an identical-appearing placebo, for slightly more than a year. Everyone in the man's household is similarly assigned to treatment or control. (In the small fraction of households with more than one older male, a random male is selected to determine assignment to treatment or control for the entire household.)

Respondents who were iron deficient prior to the intervention and who were assigned to the treatment have higher levels of iron in their blood and are able to cycle longer on an ergocycle at the end of the intervention, relative to comparable control subjects. Relative to similar controls, treated subjects are more likely to be working, lose less work time to illness, are more energetic, are better able to conduct physically arduous activities, and enjoy better psychosocial health.

About half the male workers in the study are self-employed (primarily as rice farmers), and the other half are paid a time wage. There is no evidence that hours of work were affected by the treatment, for either time-wage workers or the self-employed. Among males who earned a time wage, there is no evidence of changes in productivity as indicated by hourly earnings. Of course, if their wages are set by an employer, it is not obvious that the worker will reap the benefits of greater productivity. This is not true for the self-employed; males who were iron deficient and self-employed at baseline reported 20 percent higher hourly earnings after six months of supplementation relative to similar controls. Since there was no change in their hours of work, this translates into 20 percent higher income from labor.

Wage workers who received the treatment reduced their amount of time spent sleeping by about 40 minutes per day and reallocated this time to leisure. Self-employed workers made no such adjustments. A picture emerges of iron deficiency having a causal impact on work capacity and energy needed to complete tasks. The self-employed who benefited from the treatment allocate the additional energy to their fields; they work harder, produce more, and earn more per hour of work. In contrast, wage workers were able to channel their greater energy toward reduced sleep and more time for leisure. After 12 months of supplementation, there is evidence that some of the treated iron-deficient males who were working for a time wage at baseline had shifted to self-employment or had taken an additional job.

WISE demonstrates that iron deficiency has a causal impact on time allocation and economic productivity. It also highlights the importance of taking into account behavioral responses to the experiment itself in assessing the impact of the treatment. Results from the Chinese and Sri Lankan studies reinforce this point; they indicate that iron deficiency had little impact on productivity but did affect how individuals allocated their time.

If iron supplementation improves the health and well-being of individuals, we expect that these people will be more productive not only at work but also in other domains of their lives. Furthermore, they may respond to these improvements in many ways, such as changing the nature of their work and the time spent on work. The results echo the evidence from the INCAP study indicating that treated subjects compensated for increased hourly earnings by allocating less time to work. It is critically important that all these responses are taken into account if we are to understand the impact of health improvements on economic growth. This limits the contributions to the literature of experiments that are designed to isolate specific inputs and outputs in the health and productivity relationship and do not capture the broader ramifications of the health intervention.

Health care costs have skyrocketed and have far outpaced inflation in many countries in recent decades. Much of the increase in advanced economies has been attributed to the development of technologies that improve health and extend life (Cutler 2004). At the same time, calories have become inexpensive relative to other goods (although food prices are subject to considerable variation from year to year and have increased dramatically in recent months). These changes in prices, along with differences in prices across space, provide potentially powerful sources of variation for identifying the impact of changes in the health of adults on social and economic success.

The assumptions under which identification will be valid are not obviously satisfied, at least in general. First, the relative price changes should have no direct impact on the economic prosperity of an individual. In the case of food prices, this rules out the agricultural sector, including all farmers, along with workers in food-related industries. Workers in the health sector and allied industries are similarly affected. Second, variation in prices reflects a combination of a number of factors that conspire to bring demand into line with supply in a general equilibrium. To the extent that those factors also influence economic prosperity, it will be difficult to pin down their impact on health status. This is a special challenge when relying only on temporal or spatial variation in prices. Third, measurement of markers of health in survey data that are affected by variation in prices and also affect economic success raises additional difficulties.

These issues may be sidestepped by relying on experimental or quasi-experimental variation in prices. For example, starting in 1974, subjects enrolled in the RAND Health Insurance Experiment (HIE) were randomly assigned to 1 of 14 fee-for-service health plans. About 1,800 subjects were assigned to a plan that provided free care, and 2,800 subjects were assigned to plans that varied in terms of copayments (from 25 to 95 percent of fees) and total out-of-pocket expenses. Almost three-quarters of the subjects were enrolled in the experiment for three years; the rest participated for five years.

Newhouse and the Insurance Experiment Group (1993) describe the experiment and the main results. Use of health care declined as the price increased, with subjects in the free-care group using health care services most intensively. The evidence on health outcomes is mixed. Newhouse and colleagues conclude that the health of the average person enrolled in the HIE was not adversely affected by reduced use of health services. They note, however, that the health of the poor who were sick was more improved among those who faced lower prices. For example, among the poor who were enrolled in the free-care plan, relative to other plans, mortality was lower, blood pressure improved more, vision was corrected more often, dental health was better, and the incidence of anemia was reduced more. All these indicators were measured through clinical testing or from blood samples.

In stark contrast, the self-reported general health of this group deteriorated during the period! Specifically, of 11 self-reported health indicators, 9 were reported to have worsened among those who received free care relative to those who incurred some cost when seeking health care, although only one of these differences is significant. The clinical and biomarker evidence indicates that these people were, if anything, in better health. One might suspect that, as a result of their greater exposure to the health care system, these people learned more about their health than they would have if they had used services less frequently, and it is this information that is reflected in the worse self-assessed health outcomes. These results provide a practical example of some of the difficulties associated with health measurement in population-based surveys.

Dow et al. (2008) sidestep these problems with measurement of health and examine the impact on labor outcomes of randomly assigned variation in the price of health care. They find that females who received free health care are significantly more likely to be working at the end of the intervention than females who had to pay for health services. The difference in participation rates is about 4 percentage points. Males who had not completed high school are about 8 percentage points more likely to be working if they received free care than if they paid for care (although this effect is only significant at a 10 percent size of test).

A similar experiment conducted in Indonesia involved changes in the prices of health services. To measure the impact of increased user fees, prices of basic services at public health centers were raised in randomly selected treatment districts, while prices were held constant (in real terms) in neighboring control districts. Subjects were interviewed before prices were increased in 1991 and again two years later. Paralleling the results for the HIE, respondents in the areas where prices had increased used less health care and also reported their general health as having improved relative to subjects in the control areas where prices had not been changed. However, more specific indicators of health indicated that higher prices resulted in worse health. Specifically, respondents in areas where prices increased reported that they had more difficulty doing physically demanding tasks, spent more days away from work, and had more days in bed because of illness. These results further underscore the challenges associated with health measurement.

Turning to work outcomes, in areas where health care prices increased, employment rates rose among males and females relative to those in areas where health prices did not change. These effects are largest among the least educated. The most plausible interpretation of both the HIE and Indonesian results is that the average treatment effects on labor supply indicate a causal effect of improved health on the allocation of time to the labor market.

Evidence regarding the impact of health on economic productivity in the Indonesia study is less clear. Wage growth was lower among workers in the market sector who lived in areas where health care prices were raised, relative to the control areas. The estimated effects are large (about 15 percent) but are only significant at a 10 percent size of test.

Quasi-experimental evidence supports the conclusion that health affects employment outcomes. During the 1960s and early 1970s, Canada introduced national health insurance. Taking advantage of the phased introduction of the system across provinces and occupations, Gruber and Hanratty (1995) find that employment and wages increased as workers were covered by national health insurance. The authors conclude that labor demand rose because workers were more productive, either because of increased job mobility and better matching of skills or because their health improved as a result of being covered by health insurance.

Although the introduction of national health insurance was not designed as an experiment, this study exploits the fact that some people were covered by the system earlier than others. The plausibility of the results rests crucially on the extent to which this "natural experiment" approximates random assignment. The authors provide a compelling argument in favor of this interpretation.

Designing health policy innovations so that they are phased in and rigorously evaluated during the phase-in period will not only contribute to improved policy design and implementation; it also has the potential to facilitate identification of the broader impacts of the policy innovations, beyond health care and health outcomes to economic and social indicators. It is unfortunate that this design is relatively rare.

Turning to the literature based on observational data, the challenge is to identify instruments that are, first, predictive of health status and, second, valid in the sense of not being correlated with unobserved factors that affect the economic or social outcome of interest in the model. The experimental results suggest that prices of health inputs (including foods) may satisfy the first condition for measures of productivity. Labor supply effects are harder to identify in this context because health inputs affect real wages and thus the value of time.

Studies have explored the relationship between body mass index (BMI) and labor market outcomes. BMI, which depends on net energy intake and varies over the life course, captures both longer- and shorter-run dimensions of nutrition. It is related to

VO$_2$max and thus to aerobic capacity and endurance independent of energy intake (Spurr 1983). Whether this pathway is one through which health influences productivity in an important way is not obvious, since many jobs do not require sustained physical effort. Treadmill tests suggest that excess (fat) weight affects the efficiency at which energy is transferred to work output (Cureton 1992).

Drawing on data on workers in the rural Philippines, Haddad and Bouis (1991) find no effect of BMI on earnings of agricultural workers. Using the same sample, however, Foster and Rosenzweig (1993, 1994) highlight the difficulties of observing health and argue that employers use BMI as a marker for health. They contrast workers paid by time with those paid on a piece-rate basis and find that BMI affects the wages of only time-rate workers. This suggests that it is not health (or at least robustness) that is rewarded in the labor market; rather, there is a benefit from conveying the impression of being in good health. It is not clear why employers would be consistently fooled into paying a worker more because he is heavier (but not more productive) or why employers would not learn about the productivity of workers.

Thomas and Strauss (1997) explore this issue among male and female workers in urban Brazil. With relative food prices as instruments, BMI has a positive impact on the hourly earnings of both employees and the self-employed, suggesting that BMI is more than just an easily observed marker of health used by employers. Since the effect of BMI on hourly earnings is largest among the least educated, who are the most likely to do manual labor, the authors conjecture that BMI may be a marker for strength. Similar evidence is reported for African workers by Glick and Sahn (1998) and Croppenstedt and Muller (2000). There is little empirical evidence relating BMI to labor supply, although BMI has been shown to affect the proportion of working time that is spent on very physically demanding activities by men (Pitt, Rosenzweig, and Hassan 1990; Bhargava 1994; Fafchamps and Quisumbing 1999).

Adams et al. (2003) take a different approach to evaluating the direction of causality underlying the associations between health and SES. They examine whether prior SES predicts current health status, conditional on an extensive set of information on health histories. Under the assumptions of their model, if prior SES does not predict health innovations, then a direct causal pathway from SES to health can be rejected. This is essentially a test for Granger causality. Using data for older adults in the United States, they conclude there is little evidence that SES has a causal impact on health except perhaps in the case of psychosocial health. The authors attribute the latter to the fact that Medicare does not cover mental health services. Their conclusions on the impact of health on SES are more tentative, although they generally find little evidence that health affects wealth of older adults.

The assumptions underlying these tests are not innocuous. The models include a battery of prior health indicators, each of which is the outcome of choices made over the life course. If those choices are correlated with SES, the assumptions underlying the empirical strategy will be violated. In addition, there are legitimate questions about whether the testing strategy has sufficient power to detect causal effects of SES on health in a broader class of models.

In an effort to assess the importance of this concern, Adda, Chandola, and Marmot (2003) conduct a replication using the same empirical methods with data from the United Kingdom and Sweden. They find results that are remarkably similar to those for the United States, including the evidence on psychosocial health. This is troubling because in the United Kingdom and Sweden, all health services—including mental health services—are available free of charge. The authors conclude that the testing strategy adopted by Adams et al. (2003) lacks power against plausible alternative models.

It is likely that the dynamics underlying observed health and observed SES are very complex. For example, a person's health may be in decline prior to a diagnosis of, say, heart disease, and the decline in health may result in decreased earnings because of reduced hours or lower hourly earnings. Attempts to link the diagnosis to reduced wealth are unlikely to be fruitful. Similarly, a person who perceives that his or her health is in decline and anticipates having reduced earnings in the future may choose to increase his or her labor supply and thus current earnings.

More generally, the dynamic links between health and economic prosperity have been little studied. This is an important gap in the scientific literature, for several reasons. Health is a stock that evolves over time, and prior health behaviors—and health shocks—likely influence current economic status. Virtually nothing is known about the speed with which the effects of health transitions at the individual level are transmitted to the labor market in low-income settings. Does a period of poor health (or a negative health shock) put a worker on a permanently lower wage trajectory, or do the negative consequences of ill health dissipate as health subsequently improves? The extent of catch-up likely depends on the nature of the health problem, the structure of the labor market, and the worker's characteristics, including age, education, and the extent to which the individual has a buffer of resources on which to draw in bad times.

Development of a better understanding of the dynamic interplay between health and economic prosperity is likely to shed new light on some of the mechanisms through which the two covary. Apart from the econometric advantages associated with analyses based on repeated observations of the same person over time, "natural experiments" arising from unanticipated variation in a respondent's life are likely to prove a powerful resource in this literature.

Thomas and Frankenberg (2000) provide an example. The first column of table 2, using data on males age 18–68 interviewed in the 1997 wave of the IFLS, indicates that the elasticity of wages with respect to BMI is 2.0. The results in the second column control for height, age, education, and location of residence: the elasticity is reduced to 1.0, indicating that current weight reflects, in substantial part, human capital and background characteristics. Prior BMI might serve as a control for these characteristics, and accordingly, exploiting the repeat-observation dimension of the IFLS, BMI measured in 1993 is added in column 3. Prior BMI does predict current wages, and it soaks up some of the correlation with current BMI. Controlling 1993 BMI, 1997 BMI can be interpreted as the weight gain since 1993; its effect is also positive. It is not obvious what to make of this correlation. It is possible that increased wages were spent on more energy intake (or less energy output) or that changes in both wages and weight arise because of some other unobserved factor.

To explore this further, we turn to wages measured in 1993. Column 4 essentially replicates the 1997 results reported in column 2. Wages in 1993 are related to BMI

TABLE 2. Dynamic Relationship between Body Mass Index (BMI) and Hourly Earnings of Adult Males, Indonesia Family Life Survey, 1993 and 1997

Covariates	ln(hourly earnings), 1997			ln(hourly earnings), 1993	
	BMI97 only (1)	Plus height and education (2)	BMI97and BMI93 (3)	BMI93 (4)	BMI97 and BMI93 (5)
ln(BMI) in 1997	2.03	1.03	0.82		0.35
	(0.12)	(0.10)	(0.16)		(0.17)
ln(BMI) in 1993			0.34	0.96	0.78
			(0.17)	(0.14)	(0.18)
ln(height)		2.36	2.40	2.27	2.52
		(0.34)	(0.44)	(0.40)	(0.44)
Years of education (spline)					
0–5		0.05	0.04	0.05	0.05
		(0.01)	(0.01)	(0.01)	(0.01)
6–11		0.09	0.10	0.09	0.10
		(0.01)	(0.01)	(0.01)	(0.01)
>11		0.11	0.10	0.14	0.14
		(0.01)	(0.01)	(0.01)	(0.01)
Age and location controls	No	Yes	Yes	Yes	Yes
R^2	0.06	0.29	0.30	0.30	0.30

Source: Thomas and Frankenberg 2000.

Note: Sample includes adult males age 18–68. Earnings and BMI are measured at time of each survey. Height and education are measured at baseline. Earnings, BMI, and height are specified in logarithms. Numbers in parentheses are standard errors robust to arbitrary forms of heteroskedasticity and take into account correlations resulting from survey clustering. Models 2–5 include age, specified as a linear spline, and location measured by indicators for each province and for urban sector.

in 1993 and to BMI in 1997 (column 5). BMI in 1993 remains significant. However, weight gained between 1993 and 1997 is a significant predictor of wages measured in 1993, prior to that weight change. This is compelling evidence that BMI and wages are jointly determined (or are influenced by other unobserved factors) and that the regressions in table 1 cannot be given a causal interpretation.

This evidence raises further doubts regarding the validity of the approach to identifying causal effects taken by Adams et al. (2003). We conclude that modeling the dynamics underlying the evolution of health and economic prosperity remains an important scientific endeavor.

Conclusions

The weight of the evidence indicates that fetal health and early childhood nutrition have a causal impact on human capital accumulation and economic productivity. There is some evidence indicating that changes in adult health affect labor outcomes, particularly productivity. Although the exact mechanisms underlying these relationships are not entirely clear, the most convincing evidence is distinguished by the coexistence of carefully conducted experimental studies and observational studies that have documented sizable effects of nutrition on productivity indicators. Explanations that are founded on an understanding of the underlying biological mechanisms have proved to be a powerful force in support of these conclusions.

Little attention has been paid to the behavioral response to longer-term improvements in health and productivity. The limited evidence suggests that short-term increases in productivity have little immediate impact on time allocation but that if the productivity gains persist over the longer term, individuals reduce their hours at work, as would be suggested by theory. If this turns out to be a general result, it is important.

Studies that focus exclusively on productivity and studies that focus solely on annual earnings will provide incomplete descriptions of the relationships between health and labor outcomes. By ignoring the fact that individuals choose to substitute time away from work, these studies will tend to understate the welfare gains associated with health improvements, which are not reflected in aggregate statistics of economic growth. In general, scaling estimated productivity effects to the aggregate level likely will overstate the extent to which the macro association between health and income can be attributed to a causal effect of health on economic prosperity.

A plausible argument can be, and has been, made that other dimensions of health likely affect economic prosperity. These links, however, have not been established as reliably as the links between reducing nutritional deficiencies and productivity. There is little evidence on the impact on socioeconomic success of obesity and related health conditions, of infection and inflammation, or of stress and injuries, despite the prevalence of these health concerns around the globe. And, remarkably little is known about the impact on economic prosperity of psychosocial health problems.

The cumulative effect of multiple health insults on health outcomes in later life has been highlighted in the literature on older adults in advanced economies (McEwen 2000). It has received little attention in the developing-country literature even though health insults are more frequent and potentially more damaging in lower-income societies and may take their toll in early life or midlife. It remains unclear whether wear and tear on the body resulting from health insults have implications for economic prosperity.

More generally, there is a paucity of evidence on the dynamics linking innovations in health and innovations in economic prosperity, particularly over the longer term. Studies that take into account the shorter-term and longer-term behavioral responses that accompany health innovations are few and far between.

In the literature relating health to SES, inadequate attention has been paid to the various domains of SES. The evidence discussed above suggests that the impact of particular health markers on productivity at work and on time allocation may be quite different and that these differences may only emerge over the medium or longer term. Similarly, there are likely to be distinct effects of health on education and cognition in early life and on cognitive performance in later life. The impact of health on productivity in home production, choices between consumption and savings, and intertemporal preferences are also likely to differ.

These are all critical gaps in our knowledge. The task of filling them calls for a sustained program of research that integrates the advantages of randomized treatment-control designs, phased policy interventions, and broad-purpose, longitudinal social surveys. Each of these tools, on its own, is unlikely to provide the scientific evidence necessary to make progress in the field and thereby influence policy design.

Sustained longitudinal studies that collect repeated observations on the same individual will be necessary for understanding the dynamic aspects of the links between health and SES over the short and longer terms. Broad-purpose panel surveys, in combination with the changes that will occur in the global economy, have the potential to provide a rich laboratory for understanding the links between health and economic success. Financial crises, the collapse of markets, price spikes, and natural disasters are all candidates for this research. It is often difficult, however, to separate shocks from events that might have been predicted, in which case the estimated effects of the observed change will be contaminated by behavioral responses that anticipate the change. The task of separately identifying the effects of multiple, related changes is very complex, and the level of complexity is likely to increase as the magnitude of the shock increases.

Reliance on these natural experiments alone is unlikely to suffice. Pilot studies of the impact of policy changes have the potential to yield important new insights that will improve policy design and affect the state of science. Coordination of longitudinal health and socioeconomic surveys with phased policy changes and health interventions provides opportunities for more planning in the study design and greater control over the variation that people confront.

There are good reasons for expanding the horizons of experimental studies. Specifically, measuring broader socioeconomic outcomes than is typically the case, examining behavioral responses to the treatment, and following subjects for an extended period will substantially increase the contributions of these studies. For example, an intervention that seeks to eradicate malaria in an area might not only measure its incidence before and after the intervention but also track changes in economic productivity and behavioral responses to the intervention, such as changes in work status, hours of work, time allocation, migration, expectations about the future, planning horizons, and investments. Since economic and social changes will probably take some time to emerge, subjects will need to be tracked beyond the intervention period. Taking account of the medium-term and longer-term impacts on both health and economic outcomes will provide a more comprehensive assessment of the intervention.

Randomized interventions or phased trials in parallel with large-scale panel studies have the potential to significantly affect science and policy design in cost-effective ways. A quantum leap in the breadth and quality of research in this area can be achieved by exploiting rapidly evolving technologies for health measurement in a field setting, in conjunction with innovative techniques for combining state-of-the-art survey data and administrative records on individuals, their families, and their communities.

Developing the knowledge base necessary to understand the complex linkages between health and economic prosperity is far from straightforward. Yet the challenges provide an extraordinary opportunity for health scientists, social scientists, and practitioners to collaborate to generate new knowledge that may have a lasting impact on the well-being of populations across the globe.

References

Adams, P., M. Hurd, A. Merrill, D. McFadden, and T. Ribeiro. 2003. "Healthy, Wealthy, and Wise? Tests for Direct Causal Paths between Health and Socioeconomic Status." *Journal of Econometrics* 112 (1): 3–56.

Adda, J., T. Chandola, and M. Marmot. 2003. "Socio-Economic Status and Health: Causality and Pathways." *Journal of Econometrics* 112 (1): 57–63.

Alderman, Harold, John Hoddinott, and Bill Kinsey. 2006. "Long-Term Consequences of Early Childhood Malnutrition." *Oxford Economic Papers* 58 (3): 450–74.

Almond, Douglas. 2006. "Is the 1918 Influenza Pandemic Over? Long-Term Effects of *in utero* Exposure in the Post-1940 US Population." *Journal of Political Economy* 114 (4): 672–71.

Barker, David J. P. 1994. *Mothers, Babies and Health in Later Life*. London: BMJ Publishing Group.

Basta, S. S., D. Soekirman, D. Karayadi, and N. Scrimshaw. 1979. "Iron Deficiency Anemia and the Productivity of Adult Males in Indonesia." *American Journal of Clinical Nutrition* 32: 916–25.

Bhargava, Alok. 1994. "Modeling the Health of Filipino Children." *Journal of the Royal Statistical Society,* Series A 157: 417–32.

Case, Anne, and Christina Paxson. 2008. "Stature and Status: Height, Ability and Labor Market Outcomes." *Journal of Political Economy* 116 (3, June): 499–532.

Chen, Yuyu, and Li-An Zhou. 2007. "The Long-Term Health and Economic Consequences of the 1959–61 Famine in China." *Journal of Health Economics* 26 (4): 659–81.

Croppenstedt, Andre, and Christophe Muller. 2000. "The Impact of Farmers' Health and Nutritional Status on Their Productivity and Efficiency: Evidence from Ethiopia." *Economic Development and Cultural Change* 48 (3): 475–502.

Crosby, Alfred. 1989. *America's Forgotten Pandemic: The Influenza of 1918*. Cambridge, U.K.: Cambridge University Press.

Cureton, Kirk J. 1992. "Effects of Experimental Alterations in Excess Weight on Physiological Responses to Exercise and Physical Performance." In *Body Composition and Physical Performance: Applications to the Military,* ed. B. M. Mariott and J. Grumstrup-Scott, 71–88. Washington, DC: National Academy Press.

Cutler, David. 2004. *Your Money or Your Life: Strong Medicine for America's Health Care System*. Oxford, U.K.: Oxford University Press.

de Onis, Mercedes, and Monika Blossner. 2000. "Prevalence and Trends of Overweight among Preschool Children in Developing Countries." *American Journal of Clinical Nutrition* 72 (4, October): 1032–39.

Dickson, Rumona, Shally Awasthi, Paula Williamson, Colin Demellweek, and Paul Garner. 2000. "Effects of Treatment for Intestinal Helminth Infection on Growth and Cognitive Performance in Children: Systematic Review of Randomized Trials." *British Medical Journal* 320 (June): 1697–701.

Dow, William, Paul Gertler, Robert Schoeni, John Strauss, and Duncan Thomas. 2008. "Health Care Prices, Health and Labor Outcomes: Experimental Evidence." Population Studies Center at the Institute for Social Research, University of Michigan, Ann Arbor.

Edgerton, V. R., G. W. Gardner, Y. Ohira, K. A. Gunawardena, and B. Senewiratne. 1979. "Iron-Deficiency Anemia and Its Effect on Worker Productivity and Activity Patterns." *British Medical Journal* 2: 1546–49.

Fafchamps, Marcel, and Agnes Quisumbing. 1999. "Human Capital, Productivity and Labor Allocation in Rural Pakistan." *Journal of Human Resources* 34 (2): 369–406.

Finch, Caleb, and Eileen Crimmins. 2004. "Inflammatory Exposure and Historical Changes in Human Life Spans." *Science* 305: 1736–39.

Fogel, Robert W. 2004. *The Escape from Hunger and Premature Death, 1700–2100.* Cambridge, U.K: Cambridge University Press.

Foster, Andrew, and Mark Rosenzweig. 1993. "Information Flows and Discrimination in Labor Markets in Rural Areas in Developing Countries." In *Proceedings of the World Bank Annual Conference on Development Economics, 1992: Supplement to the World Bank Economic Review and the World Bank Research Observer,* ed. Lawrence H. Summers and Shekhar Shah, 173–203. Washington, DC: World Bank.

———. 1994. "A Test for Moral Hazard in the Labor Market: Contractual Arrangements, Effort, and Health." *Review of Economics and Statistics* 76 (2): 213–27.

Fox, Matthew, Sydney Rosen, William MacLeod, Monique Wasunna, Margaret Bii, Ginamarie Foglia, and Jonathon Simon. 2004. "The Impact of HIV/AIDS on Labour Productivity in Kenya." *Tropical Medicine and International Health* 9 (3): 318–24.

Frankenberg, Elizabeth, and Duncan Thomas. 2001. "Women's Health and Pregnancy Outcomes: Do Services Make a Difference?" *Demography* 38 (2): 253–65.

———. 2007. "Family Planning, Old Age Security and Savings by Women: Experimental Evidence." Duke University, Durham, NC.

Frankenberg, Elizabeth, Wayan Suriastini, and Duncan Thomas. 2005. "Can Expanding Access to Basic Health Care Improve Children's Health Status? Lessons from Indonesia's 'Midwife in the Village' Programme." *Population Studies* 59 (1): 5–19.

Frankenberg, Elizabeth, Alison Buttenheim, Bondan Sikoki, and Wayan Suriastini. 2009. "Do Women Increase Their Use of Reproductive Health Care When It Becomes More Available? Evidence from Indonesia." *Studies in Family Planning* 40 (1, March): 27–38.

Glewwe, Paul, and Edward Miguel. 2008. "The Impact of Child Health and Nutrition on Education in Less Developed Countries." In *Handbook of Development Economics,* vol. 4, ed. T. Paul Schultz and John Strauss, 3561–846. Amsterdam: North-Holland.

Glick, Paul, and David E. Sahn. 1998. "Health and Productivity in a Heterogeneous Urban Labour Market." *Applied Economics* 30 (2): 203–16.

Godfrey, Keith, and David Barker. 2000. "Fetal Nutrition and Adult Disease." *American Journal of Clinical Nutrition* 71 (Suppl.): 1344S–52S.

Gruber, Jonathan, and Maria Hanratty. 1995. "The Labor-Market Effects of Introducing National Health Insurance: Evidence from Canada." *Journal of Business and Economic Statistics* 13 (2): 163–73.

Haas, Jere D., and Thomas Brownlie. 2001. "Iron Deficiency and Reduced Work Capacity: A Critical Review of the Research to Determine a Causal Relationship." *Journal of Nutrition* 131 (Suppl. 2): 676S–88S.

Haddad, Lawrence J., and Howarth E. Bouis. 1991. "The Impact of Nutritional Status on Agricultural Productivity: Wage Evidence from the Philippines." *Oxford Bulletin of Economics and Statistics* 53 (1, February): 45–68.

Hales, C. Nicholas, and David J. Barker. 1992. "Type 2 (Non-Insulin-Dependent) Diabetes Mellitus: The Thrifty Phenotype Hypothesis." *Diabetologia* 35: 595–601.

Hoddinott, John, John Maluccio, Jere Behrman, Rafael Flores, and Reynaldo Martorell. 2008. "Effect of a Nutrition Intervention during Early Childhood on Economic Productivity in Guatemalan Adults." *Lancet* 381: 411–16.

ICDDR,B (International Centre for Diarrhoeal Disease Research, Bangladesh), Centre for Health and Population Research. 2004. *Health and Demographic Surveillance System–Matlab,* vol. 35. Dhaka: ICDDR,B.

Immink, Maarten D. C., and Fernando E. Viteri. 1981. "Energy Intake and Productivity of Guatemalan Sugarcane Cutters: An Empirical Test of the Efficiency Wage Hypothesis, Part 1." *Journal of Development Economics* 9 (2): 251–87.

Jack, William, and Maureen Lewis. 2008. "Health Investments and Economic Growth: An Overview." Prepared for the Commission on Growth and Development. http://www.growthcommission.org/storage/cgdev/documents/ThemesPapers/jacklewis.pdf.

Joshi, Shareen, and T. Paul Schultz. 2007. "Family Planning as an Investment in Development: Evaluation of a Program's Consequences in Matlab, Bangladesh." Yale University Economic Growth Center Discussion Paper 951, New Haven, CT. http://www.econ.yale.edu/growth_pdf/cdp951.pdf.

Li, R., X. Chen, H. Yan, P. Deurenberg, L. Garby, and J. Hautvast. 1994. "Functional Consequences of Iron Supplementation in Iron-Deficient Female Cotton Workers in Beijing, China." *American Journal of Clinical Nutrition* 59 (4): 906–13.

Maluccio, John, John Hoddinott, Jere R. Behrman, Agnes Quisumbing, Reynaldo Martorell, and Aryeh D. Stein. 2006. "The Impact of Nutrition during Early Childhood on Education among Guatemalan Adults." International Food Policy Research Institute (IFPRI), Washington, DC.

Martorell, Reynaldo, Jere R. Behrman, Rafael Flores, and Aryeh Stein. 2005. "Rationale for a Follow-up Study Focusing on Economic Productivity." *Food and Nutrition Bulletin* 26 (2, Suppl. 1): S5–S14.

McEwen, Bruce. 2000. "Allostasis and Allostatic Load: Implications for Neuropsychopharmocology." *Neuropsychopharmacology* 22 (2): 108–24.

Miguel, Edward, and Michael Kremer. 2004. "Worms: Identifying Impacts on Education and Health in the Presence of Treatment Externalities." *Econometrica* 72 (1): 159–217.

Newhouse, Joseph, and the Insurance Experiment Group. 1993. *Free for All? Lessons from the RAND Health Insurance Experiment.* Cambridge, MA: Harvard University Press.

Noymer, Andrew, and Michel Garenne. 2000. "The 1918 Influenza Epidemic's Effects on Sex Differentials in Mortality in the United States." *Population and Development Review* 26 (3, September): 565–81.

Pitt, Mark, Mark Rosenzweig, and Mohammed Nasmul Hassan. 1990. "Productivity, Health, and Inequality in the Intrahousehold Distribution of Food in Low-Income Countries." *American Economic Review* 80 (December): 1139–56.

Pollitt, Ernesto, Kathleen Gorman, Patrice Engle, Raynaldo Martorell, and Juan Rivera. 1993. *Early Supplemental Feeding and Cognition.* Monographs of the Society for Research in Child Development, vol. 235. Chicago: University of Chicago Press.

Popkin, Barry M. 1993. "Nutrition Patterns and Transitions." *Population and Development Review* 19 (1): 138–57.

Roseboom, Tessa J., Jan H. P. van der Meulen, Anita Ravelli, Clive Osmond, David J. Barker, and Otto P. Blecker. 2001. "Effects of Prenatal Exposure to the Dutch Famine on Adult Disease in Later Life: An Overview." *Twin Research* 4 (5): 293–98.

Rubalcava, Luis, Graciela Teruel, and Duncan Thomas. 2009. "Investments, Time Preferences, and Public Transfers Paid to Women." *Economic Development and Cultural Change* 37 (3, April): 507–38.

Schultz, T. Paul. 2002. "Wage Gains Associated with Height as a Form of Health Human Capital." *American Economic Review* 92 (2): 349–53.

———. 2008. "Population Policies, Fertility, Women's Human Capital and Child Quality." In *Handbook of Development Economics,* vol. 4, ed. T. Paul Schultz and John Strauss. Amsterdam: North-Holland.

Spurr, G. B. 1983. "Nutritional Status and Physical Work Capacity." *Yearbook of Physical Anthropology*, 26: 1–53.

Strauss, John, and Duncan Thomas. 1995. "Human Resources: Empirical Modeling of Household and Family Decisions." In *Handbook of Development Economics,* vol. 3A, ed. J. R. Behrman and T. N. Srinivasan. Amsterdam: North-Holland.

———. 1998. "Health, Nutrition and Economic Development." *Journal of Economic Literature* 36 (2): 766–817.

———. 2008. "Health over the Life Course." In *Handbook of Development Economics,* vol. 4, ed. T. Paul Schultz and John Strauss. Amsterdam: North-Holland.

Thirumurthy, Harsha, Joshua Graff Zivin, and Marcus Goldstein. 2008. "The Economic Impact of AIDS Treatment: Labor Supply in Western Kenya." *Journal of Human Resources* 43 (3): 511–52.

Thomas, Duncan. 1990. "Intra-Household Resource Allocation: An Inferential Approach." *Journal of Human Resources* 25 (4): 635–64.

———. 2008. "The 1918 Influenza Pandemic: Longer Term Impacts." Duke University, Durham, NC.

Thomas, Duncan, and Elizabeth Frankenberg. 2000. "Dynamics of Health and Labor Market Outcomes." Duke University, Durham, NC.

Thomas, Duncan, and John Strauss. 1997. "Health and Wages: Evidence on Men and Women in Urban Brazil." *Journal of Econometrics* 77 (1, March): 159–85.

Thomas, Duncan, Elizabeth Frankenberg, Jed Friedman, Jean-Pierre Habicht, Mohammed Hakimi, Nicholas Ingwersen, Jaswadi, Nathan Jones, Christopher McKelvey, Gretel Pelto, Bondan Sikoki, Teresa Seeman, James P. Smith, Cecep Sumantri, Wayan Suriastini, and Siswanto Wilopo. 2006. "Causal Effect of Health on Labor Market Outcomes: Experimental Evidence." California Center for Population Research, Working Paper 2006-07, University of California, Los Angeles. http://papers.ccpr.ucla.edu/papers/PWP-CCPR-2006-070/PWP-CCPR-2006-070.pdf.

Victora, Cesar, Linda Adair, Caroline Fall, Pedro Hallal, Reynaldo Martorell, Linda Richter, and Hashapal Singh Sachdev. 2008. "Maternal and Child Undernutrition: Consequences for Adult Health and Human Capital." *Lancet* 371 (9609): 340–57.

Wolgemuth, June, Michael Latham, Andrew Hall, Andrew Chesher, and D. W. T. Crompton. 1982. "Worker Productivity and the Nutritional Status of Kenyan Road Construction Laborers." *American Journal of Clinical Nutrition* 36 (7): 68–78.

The Household Impacts of Treating HIV/AIDS in Developing Countries

MARKUS GOLDSTEIN, JOSHUA GRAFF ZIVIN,
AND HARSHA THIRUMURTHY

Recent data on the household impacts of providing antiretroviral therapy to HIV-infected adults permit a much fuller assessment of the economic footprint of treatment than was previously possible. Drawing on evidence from treatment programs in western Kenya and several countries of Sub-Saharan Africa, the authors discuss a range of benefits to the households of patients receiving treatment. These benefits begin with the labor market outcomes of treated patients, who are able to significantly increase their work hours within six months after they initiate treatment. In the same time period, substantial improvements take place in the nutritional status and school attendance of children in patients' households, which in turn can improve the future well-being of these children. The results demonstrate that treatment can mitigate the negative socioeconomic consequences of HIV/AIDS. The authors argue that the findings provide an added rationale for the continued scaling up of treatment programs, which should be viewed as investments that offer large, long-term economic returns to society.

Since the advent of highly active antiretroviral therapy (ART) in 1996, morbidity and mortality from HIV/AIDS have declined substantially in industrial countries.[1] Owing to the widespread availability of such treatment, HIV/AIDS is often dealt with as a chronic disease in these countries. In developing nations, access to antiretroviral therapy is growing but is still limited. In Sub-Saharan Africa, the region most affected by HIV/AIDS, the number of HIV-positive people receiving treatment rose from 100,000 in the late 1990s to nearly 2 million in 2003. Despite this

Markus Goldstein is a senior economist with the World Bank. Joshua Graff Zivin is an associate professor of economics at the University of California, San Diego, and a research associate at the National Bureau of Economic Research. Harsha Thirumurthy is an assistant professor of health economics at the University of North Carolina at Chapel Hill and a faculty fellow at the Carolina Population Center. The authors thank T. Paul Schultz, Duncan Thomas, and an anonymous referee for useful comments. This paper has also benefited from invaluable comments and suggestions by John Strauss. For the work underlying much of this paper, we are grateful for the support of the AMPATH program and the Indiana University–Moi University Partnership. Financial support for this project was received from the Economic and Social Research Council in the United Kingdom; Pfizer, Inc.; the World Bank; PEPFAR– Kenya; the Yale University Center for Interdisciplinary Research on AIDS (CIRA), through a grant from the National Institute of Mental Health to Michael Merson, MD (P30 MH 62294); the Social Science Research Council; and the Calderone Program at Columbia University.

Annual World Bank Conference on Development Economics 2009, Global

progress, only about 30 percent of the people in need of treatment currently have access to it. Since public provision of treatment remains the primary channel through which people in developing countries can access ART, expansion of donor support remains critical to achieve the international community's goal of universal access to HIV treatment (as well as prevention, care, and support) by 2010 for all who need it (Group of 8 communiqué, July 2008). According to estimates by the Joint United Nations Programme on HIV/AIDS (UNAIDS), the annual cost of achieving universal access to treatment by 2010 will be approximately US$15 billion per year—an amount much larger than current expenditures on treatment (UNAIDS 2007).

Greater support for the scaling up of treatment programs has been lacking, for a number of reasons. These include skepticism as to whether ART will generate health and economic benefits that are sizable enough to offset its costs and a related debate about how best to allocate scarce resources in developing countries (see, for example, Canning 2006). Since treatment, once initiated, must be continued for the entire duration of a person's life, there has also been concern about the wisdom and sustainability of current expenditures on ART. According to the *Economist* (2006), people who begin receiving ART today will become tomorrow's "medical pensioners" whose treatment costs will become the responsibility of the countries in which they live and the organizations that support these countries. Because evidence on the impacts of providing ART has been slow to emerge, until recently it has been impossible to evaluate treatment programs properly and assess whether expenditures on such programs may be justified on economic, as opposed to humanitarian, grounds.

In this paper we draw on recent research to describe the short-term impact of treatment on the socioeconomic outcomes of patients and households in Sub-Saharan Africa. Since the scaling up of treatment programs is a recent phenomenon, the evidence on household impacts that we present here has been largely absent in discussions of the costs and benefits of treatment. These household impacts are an important component of the benefits that stem from treatment programs, and when they are taken into consideration, it is difficult not to view treatment expenditures as investments that offer longer-term economic returns to households.

To see why treatment could induce a variety of positive changes in the well-being of households in low-income settings, it is instructive to consider how these households generally respond to health setbacks. Households in low-income settings face a great deal of health and economic risk, and their ability to cope with such risk and ensure minimum levels of food consumption and well-being is often limited. Because access to formal or informal credit and insurance against large setbacks may be lacking, some households may have to resort to extreme measures, including partial or full withdrawal of children from school, increased employment of children's labor in family farms or business enterprises, and reductions in food consumption for some or all household members. Coping with AIDS-related adult morbidity, rather than a temporary illness, is especially challenging. Individuals can expect to recover from temporary illnesses and so might be able to rely at least partially on informal credit and insurance from friends and relatives. For chronic illnesses, however, finding individuals who are willing to provide support is more difficult. Furthermore, since AIDS invariably ends in death when no treatment is available, the disease may have even larger effects on the well-being of household members, particularly children who will be left without a parent.

Longitudinal household survey data that we have collected in collaboration with a treatment program in western Kenya, along with limited evidence from other countries in Sub-Saharan Africa, suggests that ART reverses and mitigates many of the effects of HIV on the socioeconomic well-being of infected adults and their households. The starting point for these household impacts lies in the employment outcomes of adult patients who receive ART. Evidence from rural Kenya shows that after ART is initiated there is a large and immediate increase in the amount of work performed by treated patients. These increases are in contrast to the well-documented decline in productivity for HIV-infected individuals who do not have access to treatment (Fox et al. 2004). Although it is encouraging that these labor supply increases are observed in the first 6 to 12 months after initiation of treatment, we emphasize that more evidence is needed about the long-term effects of ART on the labor supply and other outcomes.

Our analysis of data from Kenya suggests that as adult patients become healthier and more productive thanks to ART, the burden on children to provide substitute labor decreases substantially. Boys work significantly less in income-generating activities, and the amount of household chores that girls perform decreases considerably. These reductions in time allocated to labor are accompanied by increased school attendance, which is likely to result in higher wages and improved health for these children in the future. ART also leads to large improvements in the nutritional status of very young children in treated patients' households—another indicator that the short-term impacts of treatment may have long-term effects on health and economic outcomes.

Although the positive effects of ART that we document here are largely private benefits realized by patients and their households, we argue that under certain conditions this evidence can provide a rationale for public support for ART. Such conditions include the existence of borrowing constraints for households in low-income settings and the externalities that may result from improved schooling outcomes. The broader socioeconomic view of the impact of ART—particularly its intergenerational effects—also suggests that cost-effectiveness analyses of ART (which typically focus on the number of patient life-years saved) may substantially underestimate the benefits of treatment. Our findings also call into question the argument that resources should be allocated to HIV prevention at the expense of treatment (Canning 2006).

The next section reviews the evidence on the clinical and immunological impacts of ART and provides an overview of existing efforts to scale up treatment programs. The empirical strategy for estimating the impact of treatment when randomized controlled trials are not feasible is then discussed. There follows a survey of unique evidence from western Kenya on socioeconomic impacts on households of patients receiving ART—from employment outcomes for treated patients, to schooling and employment outcomes for children and the nutritional status of very young children. The issue of generalizability is then examined, with reference to evidence from other settings such as South Africa and Botswana, and areas where additional research is needed are identified. The final section summarizes the policy implications that flow from these household impacts of treatment.

Effectiveness and Availability of Antiretroviral Therapy

As HIV weakens the immune system, it inevitably causes AIDS and, eventually, death, if treatment is not provided. According to a prominent study conducted in Uganda, progression to AIDS—the last stage of HIV infection—takes about nine years from the time of HIV seroconversion (Morgan et al. 2002).[2] During much of this period, most HIV-infected individuals may be unaware of their status and can be physically capable of performing all normal activities. Progression to AIDS is usually associated with substantial weight loss (wasting) and with opportunistic infections such as *P. carinii* pneumonia, Kaposi's sarcoma, and tuberculosis. In the absence of antiretroviral therapy, death usually occurs rapidly after progression to AIDS. The Ugandan study reports a median survival time of 9.2 months (Morgan et al. 2002), and an older study in Brazil documents a median survival time of 5.1 months (Chequer et al. 1992).

Highly active antiretroviral therapy (ART) has been proved to reduce the likelihood of opportunistic infections and prolong the life of HIV-infected individuals. In accordance with World Health Organization (WHO) guidelines, antiretroviral therapy is often initiated about the time that an HIV-infected individual develops AIDS (WHO 2006). After several months of treatment, patients generally become asymptomatic and have improved functional capacity. Numerous studies have shown that antiretroviral therapy dramatically reduces morbidity and mortality among HIV-infected individuals, both in industrial countries (Hammer et al. 1997; Hogg et al. 1998; Palella et al. 1998) and in developing countries (Laurent et al. 2002; Marins et al. 2003; Coetzee et al. 2004; Koenig, Leandre, and Farmer 2004; Wools-Kaloustian et al. 2006).

In Haiti patients experienced weight gain and improved functional capacity within one year after the initiation of ART (Koenig, Leandre, and Farmer 2004). A study conducted in the township of Khayelitsha, South Africa, showed that among 287 adults who received ART, 86.3 percent were still alive 24 months after treatment began (Coetzee et al. 2004). Large and significant improvements were also observed in clinical outcomes. The median weight gain was 5.0 kilograms after six months of treatment, and 9.0 kilograms after a year. CD4 cell counts—an important indicator of disease progression, with lower counts indicating weaker immune systems—increased by a median of 134 and 288 cells per microliter after 6 and 24 months of treatment, respectively. In western Kenya, where we conducted our socioeconomic study, other researchers have reported results that are strikingly similar to those from South Africa. In particular, mean increases in CD4 cell counts of 109 and 297 cells per microliter were observed at 6 weeks and 36 months, respectively, after initiation of treatment. Mortality rates in the first two to three years of ART have been low for patients whose CD4 cell counts were not too low (i.e., not less than 50) at the time of treatment initiation. Without ART, these mortality rates would undoubtedly be extremely high.

The compelling evidence that ART is effective in developing countries has accumulated just since 2003, during which time access to treatment in Sub-Saharan Africa and other HIV-affected regions of the world has grown substantially. The price of ART in developing countries is an important consideration in debates about treatment provision and in cost-benefit analyses, but that price has been falling. In 2000 first-line ART regimens cost more than US$10,000 per patient per year, and differential pricing was rarely employed by pharmaceutical companies. Beginning in 2001, widespread generic production of some antiretrovirals reduced these prices significantly, to as low as US$99 per patient-year for a commonly used first-line regimen (Medicins Sans Frontieres 2007). It should be noted, however, that the costs of improved first-line regimens (less toxic ones that have been recently recommended by the WHO), as well as second-line regimens, which are used when first-line regimens fail, are considerably more expensive. Expenditures on laboratory tests and HIV clinic operations can also be sizable. The level of such nondrug costs depends on the treatment setting and on a variety of factors that include the nature of the existing infrastructure in the area where an HIV clinic is being established and the cost of hiring additional staff.

Much like the price reductions, growth in donor support for the provision of ART has also been important in scaling up treatment to current levels. By the end of 2007, resources from the Global Fund to Fight AIDS, Tuberculosis, and Malaria; the U.S. Global AIDS Program (known as the President's Emergency Plan for AIDS Relief); and nongovernmental organizations (NGOs), as well as in-country government support, had helped nearly 2 million individuals receive ART in Sub-Saharan Africa alone. Progress, however, has been uneven among and within countries, and existing funds fall short of what is required in order to serve the nearly 5 million people who need ART. The experience with scaling up treatment in South Africa illustrates many of these issues. (For a discussion, see Nattrass 2006.)

Household Impacts of Treatment in Kenya

In collaboration with a treatment program that was among the first to scale up HIV care in Sub-Saharan Africa, we examined a cohort of patients receiving ART at a rural HIV clinic managed by the Academic Model for the Prevention and Treatment of HIV/AIDS (AMPATH). Founded in 2001 through collaboration between the Moi University School of Medicine, the Moi Teaching and Referral Hospital, and the Indiana University School of Medicine (Mamlin et al. 2004), AMPATH has been expanding HIV care and treatment at government health facilities in western Kenya. As of early 2008, more than 58,000 individuals at 21 health facilities were receiving HIV care from AMPATH, with approximately 23,000 persons clinically eligible for ART and receiving it free of charge. Details about our survey and the sample selection criteria are discussed at greater length in Thirumurthy, Graff Zivin, and Goldstein (2008). Here, we provide an overview of the survey and summarize the empirical strategy and results.

Survey Data

Our study was based at an AMPATH HIV clinic that operates within a government-run primary health care center in the town of Mosoriot. The clinic provides free HIV/AIDS medical care, including all relevant tests and ART, to infected individuals who enroll in care. The rural region that is served by the health center has a population of 35,383 individuals living in 6,643 households (Kenya 1999). Crop farming and animal husbandry are the primary economic activities of households in the survey area.

We conducted three waves of household surveys between 2004 and 2006. The data from these surveys allow us to examine how a variety of measures of socioeconomic well-being change because of ART.[3] There was an interval of roughly 6 months between the first two waves and an interval of 18 months between the second and third waves.[4] The survey questionnaires collected a range of comprehensive socioeconomic information on households and resembled those used by the World Bank's Living Standards Measurement Surveys. Questions covered demographic characteristics, health, agriculture, assets, income and employment, children's school enrollment and attendance, and time allocation to household chores. Teams of male and female enumerators interviewed the household head and spouse, and anthropometric measurements were taken of children under age 5. For in-clinic interviews, all information was obtained from the AMPATH patient.

The survey sample consists of two groups of households. The first group comprises 503 households chosen randomly from a census of all households in the clinic catchment area that did not contain an AMPATH patient (census sample households). In this sample, the HIV status of respondents is usually unknown unless the respondent self-reports having gone for an HIV test and tested HIV-positive or HIV-negative. The second group consists of 260 households enrolled in the study at the HIV clinic because they contained at least one adult HIV-positive AMPATH patient (at various stages of HIV disease). Of these 260 households, we focus here on the 200 in which, prior to wave 2, the HIV-positive patient was at a sufficiently advanced stage of the disease to begin receiving ART. (We refer to these as ART households.)[5] On completion of the first two waves of the survey, we used the AMPATH Medical Records System (AMRS), which contains electronic records of clinical and treatment-related information on all patients, to establish which patients in our sample were receiving ART and when they began receiving it. When examining the labor market outcomes of treated patients, we focus on the 191 adult ART recipients who appear in both of the first two waves of the survey. For other household-level outcomes, we focus on the children living in the patients' households.

Empirical Strategy

Estimating the effect of any intervention ideally requires experimental information from groups that do and do not receive the treatment of interest. In the absence of such data, a variety of nonexperimental techniques can be used to assess the impact of the intervention and, at the very least, determine whether the estimated impacts are likely to underestimate or overestimate the actual impacts. Since the strong evidence on the clinical effectiveness of ART makes randomized controlled trials of ART unethical, we use our longitudinal data from the cohort of ART recipients and census sample individuals to establish the household impacts of treatment.

When observing changes over time in socioeconomic outcomes for the ART recipients, an overarching concern in attributing these changes to the medical treatment is that the changes may be driven by omitted (i.e., confounding) variables that would bias estimates. Given the nature of the outcomes we study here, seasonal change associated with weather and the agricultural season is a key concern. For example, comparison of employment levels measured during the middle of the growing season with a later observation that may have occurred during harvest might suggest large labor increases as a result of treatment, whereas these effects would simply be an artifact of survey timing. For this reason, we make use of data from the census sample to control for secular trends in outcome variables within the survey region. Furthermore, to adjust for individual-specific characteristics that may be associated with average outcome levels for each individual, the regressions we estimate include individual fixed effects. This method can thus be described as a difference-in-difference strategy, in which the changes over time in the outcome variable for the ART sample (which represents the "treatment" group) are compared with changes over time for the census sample (which serves as the "comparison" group).[6]

Since clinical evidence on the impacts of ART suggest that the largest and most significant health improvements occur shortly after initiation of ART, we divide the ART sample into two groups of patients: those who were just beginning treatment at the time of the wave 1 interview (the treatment-naïve group), and those who had already been in treatment for more than 100 days as of wave 1 (treatment-nonnaïve group). In the results that follow, we document how temporal patterns in key outcomes differ for these two groups of ART recipients and their households.

Impact of ART on Treated Patients' Employment Outcomes

In many ways, the impact of ART on the employment outcomes of patients is the starting point for household impacts, since the ability of an adult to work and contribute income to the household has both income and substitution effects that may drive many decisions regarding children's employment and schooling, as well food consumption levels. Before beginning ART, adult patients at AMPATH's HIV clinic are significantly less likely to engage in income-earning activities than other adults in the clinic's catchment area. Their households are also poorer than households in the catchment area. Such comparisons are supported by the literature on the economic impacts of AIDS. Fox et al. (2004), in their study of workers at a Kenyan tea plantation, show that the onset of AIDS leads to significant reductions in productivity. As we discuss in this section, our findings suggest that treatment can substantially mitigate the employment effects of HIV/AIDS.

Our survey recorded information on two outcomes that measure an individual's employment status: (a) an indicator of participation in any economic activities during the week preceding each interview, and (b) the total number of hours worked in that week. The survey recorded this information in each wave for all household members older than age 8 and for three types of activities: wage and salaried jobs, farming on the household's owned or rented land, and nonfarm self-employed work. Our measure of market labor supply is defined as the total hours devoted to all these activities.[7]

The first indications that both the health and the employment status of patients are influenced by ART are provided in figure 1, showing the relationship between the duration of time on ART and patients' CD4 cell counts, and figure 2, showing time

FIGURE 1.
CD4 Count before and after Initiation of Antiretroviral Therapy (ART)

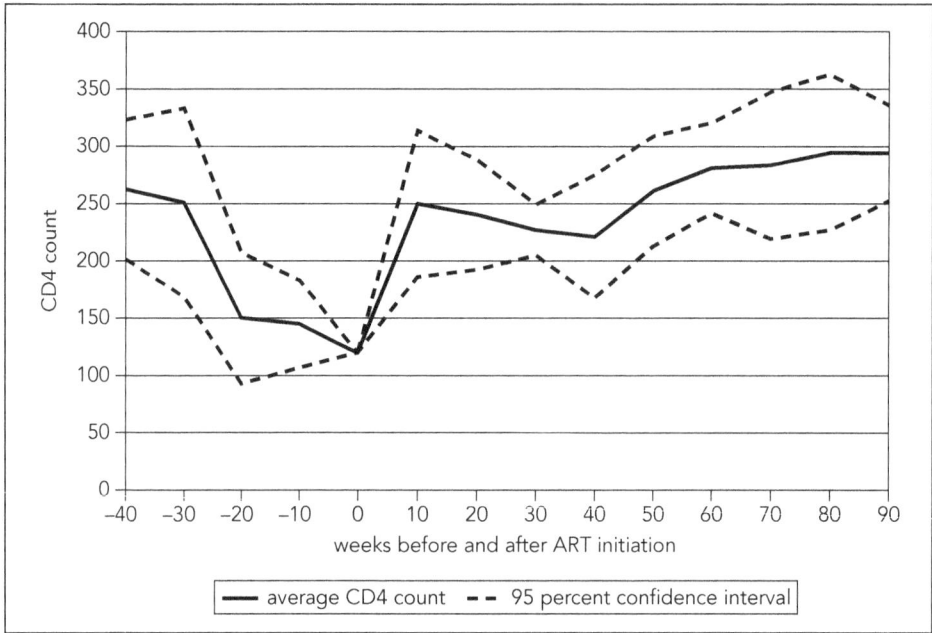

Source: AMPATH Medical Records System.

Note: The figure is generated using CD4 count data for all patients receiving ART at the Mosoriot HIV Clinic. The dashed lines indicate the 95 percent confidence intervals obtained by estimating a linear regression of individuals' CD4 counts on dummy variables for each interval, with the omitted interval being the 10 weeks prior to treatment initiation.

FIGURE 2.
Weekly Hours Worked before and after Initiation of Antiretroviral Therapy (ART)

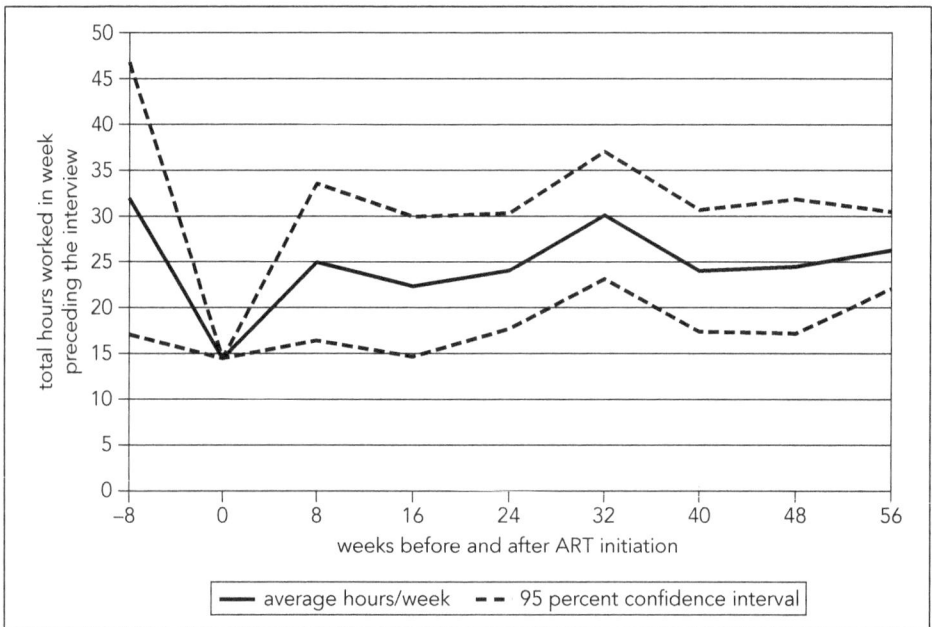

Source: Authors' survey data.

Note: The dashed lines indicate the 95 percent confidence intervals obtained from estimating a linear regression of individuals' hours worked on dummy variables for each interval, with the omitted interval being the eight weeks prior to treatment initiation. The sample consists of the 191 ART recipients who appear in both waves of the household survey data.

on ART and hours worked in the week preceding the interview. The response of CD4 cell count is highly nonlinear: at 10–20 weeks, the median count has risen to levels at which patients are generally asymptomatic (CD4 > 200). Subsequent changes are smaller and less consistent. A similar nonlinear relationship is found for patients' body mass index (not shown). The resemblance between the curves for CD4 and hours worked in the figures is striking, suggesting that the two outcomes are closely related.

When we examine the link between ART and labor market outcomes in regressions that better adjust for omitted variables, we find that ART does indeed lead to a large and significant increase in employment outcomes (table 1). These changes can be observed in just the six months between waves 1 and 2 of the survey. Controlling for various seasonal factors that are evident in both the ART sample and the census sample, adults receiving treatment are 8.5 percentage points more likely to participate in the labor force in wave 2 than in wave 1 (column 1).[8] The number of hours worked in the preceding week also increases significantly in the six months between survey waves, by 4.6 hours (column 2). In relation to the levels in wave 1, this implies a large increase in labor supply for the entire sample of ART patients: labor force participation rates rise by almost 11 percent, and weekly hours worked rise by 19 percent.

Treatment duration. As noted above, ART recipients can be divided into treatment-naïve and treatment-nonnaïve groups according to how long they have been on

TABLE 1. Impact of Antiretroviral Therapy (ART) on Labor Supply, Individual Fixed Effects

(dependent variables: labor force participation; hours worked)

	LFP	Hours	LFP	Hours
	(1)	(2)	(3)	(4)
Patient on ART * wave 2	0.085	4.575		
	(2.42)**	(1.88)*		
Treatment-naïve patient on ART * wave 2			0.170	7.860
			(3.07)***	(2.44)**
Treatment nonnaïve patient on ART * wave 2			0.015	1.920
			(0.38)	(0.69)
Constant	0.879	35.976	0.879	35.979
	(38.68)***	(16.96)***	(39.28)***	(16.98)***
Observations	2,954	2,954	2,954	2,954
R^2	0.69	0.75	0.69	0.75

Source: Authors' calculations.

Note: LFP, labor force participation. Errors are clustered at the household level for each wave. Numbers in parentheses are robust *t*-statistics. The dependent variable LFP indicates whether the individual was engaged in any labor market activity in the week preceding the interview. The dependent variable Hours is total number of hours devoted to labor market activities in the week preceding the interview. All regressions include individual fixed effects, a wave 2 indicator, and 10 month-of-interview indicators, with one month from each wave omitted to avoid collinearity with the wave 2 indicator.

*Significant at the 10 percent level.

**Significant at the 5 percent level.

***Significant at the 1 percent level.

treatment at the time of wave 1. Columns 3 and 4 of table 1 show a stronger and even more striking result. The individuals with by far the largest increase in employment outcomes between the two waves are the treatment-naïve patients who began receiving ART less than 100 days prior to the wave 1 interview. The size of these increases is substantial: over the course of six months, patients who have just initiated ART show a 17 percentage point increase in labor force participation rates and work 7.9 hours more per week. Given wave 1 employment levels of a 65.1 percent participation rate and 20.3 hours worked for this group, the estimates imply a 26 percent increase in participation rates and a 39 percent increase in number of hours worked. In contrast, the other ART recipients in our sample show no statistically significant change in outcomes between waves, suggesting that earlier employment gains are maintained through continued treatment. Thus, the story that emerges from these data is that in the first six months of ART there are large increases in labor supply, and in the second six months of ART there are no additional changes in labor supply. This temporal pattern in the labor supply response among treated patients closely resembles the health responses, as measured by body mass index (BMI) and CD4 count, reported in the next section. As is discussed there, additional follow-up is necessary in order to establish the longer-term effects of ART. The third wave of data we have collected represents one opportunity to estimate such effects (analysis is ongoing), but additional long-term studies of patients receiving ART are also necessary.

Gender differences in labor supply impacts. The survey data from each wave of the survey show that men are more likely to be engaged in market labor market activities than women. (Summary statistics are available in Thirumurthy, Graff Zivin, and Goldstein 2008.) We also find gender differences for some components of market labor supply: women are much less likely to work for a wage but are equally likely to work in a nonfarm business. This raises the question of whether the labor market impacts of ART differ according to the gender of the patient being treated. To test for such differences, we estimate the impacts separately for men and women.

Importantly, we find that for male patients in the early stages of treatment (treatment naïve in wave 1), there is no significant increase in labor force participation rates, but there is a large and significant increase of 12.7 hours in weekly labor supply between rounds (a 43 percent increase relative to average weekly hours worked in wave 1). Among male patients, therefore, those already working prior to initiation of ART are the ones who increase their labor supply after treatment. For women in the early stages of treatment, there is a large and significant increase of 21.8 percentage points in the labor force participation rate between rounds (a 35 percent increase relative to their average participation rate in round 1), but no significant increase in weekly hours worked. This is consistent with our intuition, since men have high levels of labor market participation to begin with, and most of their response to improved health takes the form of additional hours worked. For women, initial labor market participation is low, so labor supply is the natural margin for change.

It should be emphasized again that none of the results outlined above are based on a comparison of a treatment group consisting of ART recipients with a control group consisting of HIV-positive patients who require ART but do not get it. The medical literature clearly indicates that the latter group will experience continued declines in health and possibly death within 6 to 12 months. Our estimated employment impacts are likely to be *underestimates* of the full impact of treatment. This makes the size of the employment impacts described above even more striking.

Household Impacts

Households in which an adult member falls ill and becomes less able to work may be forced to rely on children to cope with the loss of income and the need for caregiving. Our research addresses whether ART, when given to adults after they develop AIDS, improves children's welfare in a manner consistent with the dramatic improvements in adult patient health. Focusing on several important aspects of children's lives, the household survey data from Kenya provide a unique opportunity to answer this question. Many of our results are discussed in greater detail in Graff Zivin, Thirumurthy, and Goldstein (2006), but we provide an overview of them here. In particular, we examine the impact of ART on the amount of time children spend working, on the amount of time they spend in school, and on measures of current nutritional status of very young children.

Information on the amount of time children spent on various activities was generally obtained from the adult respondent in each household. In order to make a comparison across activities and obtain accurate information, a recall period of seven days was chosen.

Impacts on school attendance. Turning first to the school attendance of children between ages 8 and 18, we find that between the first two waves of the study, there were large and significant increases in hours of school attended in the preceding week. The first three columns of table 2 examine the impact of ART for all children, for boys, and for girls. Children in the census sample serve as a control for other factors that may be influencing labor and schooling outcomes.

The largest increases in hours of school attended occur for children of ART recipients who were treatment naïve in wave 1. As column 1 shows, the increase in weekly hours of school attendance in the six months between waves 1 and 2 is 6.4 hours for these children, representing a 21 percent increase relative to their average attendance level in wave 1.[9] For children in households including an adult who was not treatment naïve, there is no significant change in weekly hours attended. This suggests that significant increases in attendance occur in the first six months after ART is initiated for an adult household member and remain at higher levels after six months. In columns 2 and 3, our findings indicate that there are significant increases in hours of attendance for both boys and girls in households of ART recipients who were treatment naïve in wave 1. The increase in school attendance of 8.7 hours for boys is especially large, representing a 29 percent increase relative to their average attendance level in wave 1.[10] Girls also experience a large and significant increase of 6.5 hours of school attended in the preceding week. In both cases, the increase in

TABLE 2. Impact of Antiretroviral Therapy (ART) on Children's School Attendance and Market Labor Supply, Individual Fixed Effects
(dependent variables; hours of school attended; hours worked in preceding week)

	Hours of school attended			Hours worked in preceding week		
	All children (1)	Boys (2)	Girls (3)	All children (4)	Boys (5)	Girls (6)
ART household (treatment naïve) * wave 2	6.393 (2.792)**	8.673 (3.854)**	6.513 (3.241)**	−4.475 (2.046)**	−7.452 (3.185)**	−0.812 (2.740)
ART household (treatment nonnaïve) * wave 2	1.893 (2.548)	4.902 (2.770)*	−1.035 (3.941)	−3.276 (1.996)	−7.473 (2.897)**	1.192 (2.833)
Constant	23.649 (3.097)***	23.527 (3.885)***	22.643 (4.144)***	21.776 (2.978)***	27.513 (4.019)***	13.159 (4.595)***
Observations	960	518	442	916	502	414
R^2	0.83	0.83	0.85	0.78	0.82	0.68

Source: Authors' calculations.

Note: Errors are clustered at the household level for each wave. Numbers in parentheses are robust *t*-statistics. The dependent variables are total number of hours of school attended in the week preceding the interview and total number of hours devoted to income-generating activities in that week. Observations for which school attendance was reported to be below normal because of school holidays during the week preceding the interview are excluded from the sample. The number of observations in columns 4–6 is smaller than in columns 1–3 because labor supply information is missing for 44 children. All regressions include individual fixed effects, a wave 2 indicator, and 10 month-of-interview indicators, with one month from each wave omitted to avoid collinearity with the wave 2 indicator.

*Significant at the 10 percent level.

**Significant at the 5 percent level.

***Significant at the 1 percent level.

hours of attendance occurs within roughly six months after ART initiation. There is also some evidence of prolonged increases in boys' school attendance, as those in households of ART recipients who were not treatment naïve in wave 1 experience a significant additional increase between waves 1 and 2. This more persistent effect may be attributable to the fact that boys' reductions in labor activities show a more drawn-out response to treatment, as is discussed below.

Ideally, the schooling trends of children in ART households would be compared with those of children in households where ART is needed but is not available (a counterfactual group). As we discussed for the case of patients' employment outcomes, such a comparison would reveal the "full" impact of ART on children's schooling. In the absence of such a comparison group, we rely on the literature to reveal what might happen to children's school outcomes in the absence of ART (i.e., if adult morbidity and mortality were to occur). Using longitudinal data from KwaZulu-Natal, South Africa, Case and Ardington (2006) show that children who lose a mother are significantly less likely to remain in school and complete significantly fewer years of schooling than similar-age children whose mothers are alive. The impact of paternal death on children's schooling is considerably weaker. Beegle, De Weerdt, and Dercon (2006) examine the long-term consequences drawing on longitudinal data (spanning 13 years) from the Kagera region of Tanzania. They find that maternal death results in a significant reduction in the number of years of schooling completed, as well as in lower height. There is also evidence from Kenya that children's outcomes begin to worsen even in the years prior to a parent's death, when the parent may be sick with AIDS (Evans and Miguel 2007). In light of these results, it seems likely that the impact of ART on the schooling outcomes of treated adults' children would be larger if we compared the children with a counterfactual group rather than the census sample.

These effects on school attendance imply that expenditures on ART today can yield benefits to families for years to come. Given the substantial returns to education in developing countries, these findings highlight the "investment" aspect of expenditures on ART and underscore the importance of paying attention not just to the clinical outcomes and productivity of adult patients who receive ART but also to a broader set of outcomes pertaining to the children of treated patients. They suggest that the future economic prospects of societies can be brighter if adults who are sick today are treated.

Impacts on child labor. A natural explanation for the higher school attendance levels in ART households is that these households have a lower demand for children's labor after adult patients become healthier and more productive. It therefore stands to reason that we should observe reductions in the number of hours worked by children once ART is provided. Indeed, there is strong evidence in favor of such a response within the ART households in our study.

In columns 4, 5, and 6 of table 2, we examine the responses in hours worked in labor market activities (farm, business, or wage labor). There is a large and significant reduction of 4.5 hours in the weekly hours worked for all children in households of ART recipients who were treatment naïve as of wave 1. For boys in such house-holds, the average decrease in market labor supply (7.5 hours) in the six months between waves 1 and 2 is remarkably similar to the estimated increase in weekly hours of school attendance (8.7 hours). The continued decline between waves 1 and 2 in the labor supply of boys in households of patients who were not treatment naïve in wave 1 is also accompanied by a corresponding increase in hours of school atten-dance. Thus, labor reductions for boys associated with improvements in adult patient health closely track increases in their school attendance over the corresponding time period.

The lack of any treatment effect on the market labor supply of girls should be interpreted with caution. Girls in the survey area spend significantly more time in nonmarket labor activities such as household chores and caregiving than in market activities. If girls experience decreases in their nonmarket labor supply when an adult household member becomes healthier thanks to ART, this will not be captured in the market labor supply measures reported in table 2. Indeed, in a recent paper that examines richer time allocation data from waves 1 and 3 of the survey, we find evi-dence of significant declines in the number of hours girls spend performing house-hold chores such as water and firewood collection (d'Adda et al. 2009). This result points to the importance of gathering information on multiple activities to which time is allocated, not just market labor activities.

Impacts on early childhood nutrition. As the productivity and income of treated adults increase, their households may be able to consume more food. Such a devel-opment is especially likely to affect the welfare of very young children, whose nutri-tional status is highly sensitive to changes in food consumption. Our research indicates that these children experience large and significant improvements in their nutritional status, as measured by the z-score of their weight-for-height. This is a measure of nutritional status that is sensitive to short-term growth disturbances caused by factors such as inadequate food intake (WHO 1995). Prior to the initia-tion of ART for adult patients, their children are more malnourished than other chil-dren in the clinic's catchment area. Yet this difference is completely erased within six months after ART begins, with the weight-for-height measures of children increasing by more than 0.5 standard deviations (Graff Zivin, Thirumurthy, and Goldstein 2006). The children in ART households who benefit the most are in fact those who display wasting (z-score < -2) prior to ART initiation. Such nutritional improvements at early ages have significant implications for these children's cognitive development, future school performance, and employment outcomes (Thomas and Strauss 1997; Glewwe and King 2001). These may well represent the most long-lasting gains to society from providing treatment to HIV-infected adults today.

Impacts on the elderly. The impacts of ART on the labor supply of adult patients could also have implications for the time allocation patterns of the elderly. During the periods when HIV-infected adults become sick, it is possible that elderly household members adjust their own labor supply or other activities such as caregiving. For example, in Cambodia and Thailand, Knodel (2008) has found that parents of adults who die from AIDS are more likely to provide shelter and give care to children orphaned by the adult death. An important omission from the labor supply questionnaires used in Kenya is that no information was recorded on the market labor supply of the elderly. Data were collected on the nonmarket labor supply of the elderly, and analysis of these data is ongoing. One hypothesis that remains to be tested is whether ART results in reduced labor demand for the elderly who reside in the households of treated adults. On this note, we turn to a wide range of other questions regarding the impact of ART that have yet to be addressed.

Evidence from Elsewhere and Directions for Future Research

Much of the evidence presented so far has been from a single clinic in western Kenya. Moreover, the data focus on what happens to ART recipients and their households during the short-term horizon of the first 6 to 12 months of ART. Nevertheless, additional research from other ART programs suggests that the Kenyan findings of large socioeconomic benefits from ART provision are generalizable. Two studies from southern Africa indicate that the employment effects of ART on treated patients are substantial. Studying a cohort of patients in the township of Khayelitsha, Coetzee and Nattrass (2004) find evidence of significant improvements in the labor force participation rates of ART recipients. Habyarimana, Mbakile, and Pop-Eleches (2007) examine human resource data from two mines in Botswana operated by the Debswana Diamond Company, which provides free, firm-based ART to its employees. Using data on workers' absenteeism rates, the authors find large increases in absenteeism of HIV-infected workers in the year before beginning ART. Subsequently, absenteeism rates decline rapidly. In the period from two to four years after ART initiation, treated workers have low absenteeism rates that are similar to those of other mining workers at the company. Similar evidence has been obtained from South Africa, albeit over a short time horizon of 6 to 12 months after ART initiation. Judging from the evidence from Botswana, then, it appears that the short-term impacts of ART are sustained in the medium term, as well, at least for the case of treated patients' employment. Studies that collect richer household-level information from ART recipients are greatly needed in order to learn more about the long-run impacts of ART and the generalizability of those results, particularly regarding children's health and education.

Thus far, we have viewed most of the impacts of ART through the lens of the patient's labor supply. At the same time, ART for people with AIDS (and the prospect of obtaining ART for those in the early stages of HIV infection), through its tremendous capacity to extend life, may also change people's planning horizons and lead them to undertake larger investments in the future. Indeed, such a change in perspective may be partly responsible for the human capital investments we documented earlier. Additional work on planning responses could highlight some of the other benefits of ART. For example, those who live longer may invest more in physical capital, exercise greater environmental stewardship, and engage in additional preventive health behaviors.

Many of the impacts of ART that we have documented are welfare improving, but changes in sexual behavior in response to treatment availability have the potential to erode some of these benefits. The concern is that for those individuals not in treatment (especially currently uninfected individuals), the availability of ART could result in a lower perceived cost of engaging in risky sexual behavior.[11] If this were the case, scaling up ART could pose a challenge to HIV prevention efforts. Empirical research on this topic is crucial, as the magnitude of these effects will help assess the need for companion interventions when ART is scaled up. It is reassuring that the evidence to date on the sexual behavior of ART recipients themselves indicates that ART results in reduced risky behavior and HIV transmission (Bunnell et al. 2006). In the absence of more direct evidence on community behavior, the increased provision of information and counseling to HIV-negative individuals and those of unknown status seems prudent.

In the long run, for ART to be effective and household impacts to persist, a high rate of adherence to medications is essential. Given that many treatment programs have only been functioning for a limited number of years, evidence on long-term adherence levels and household impacts is, by definition, lacking. Early evidence indicates that patients are highly adherent to ART (Orrell et al. 2003), but research on barriers to adherence is necessary (Mills et al. 2006). Similar, longitudinal studies of patients on ART are needed in order to understand the long-term household impacts of treatment.

Proper estimation of the costs of ART is another area where further work would be of value. The US$99 annual cost of first-line treatment regimens cited earlier is only one part of the overall costs; other expenditures, such as facility construction, staffing, and laboratory tests, are associated with treatment programs. These costs are likely to vary according to the locations and the socioeconomic settings in which treatment programs operate. Moreover, the sustainability of the foreign donor support that enables the establishment of some treatment programs is an important issue in light of the fact that an interruption in drug supplies for patients receiving ART could result in treatment failure and the development of drug resistance.

The Economic Rationale for Scaling Up ART

Antiretroviral therapy provides large and significant socioeconomic benefits to treated patients and their households. Although the gains from the labor productivity impacts alone outweigh the current costs of treatment (Thirumurthy, Graff Zivin, and Goldstein 2008), a more comprehensive assessment of the costs and benefits of ART is needed to underpin a thorough economic evaluation of the intervention.[12] Additional evidence from large treatment programs and over the long term is also necessary before stronger policy conclusions can be drawn. However, the improvement in patients' employment outcomes over the short term is clearly a first step in quantifying the benefits of ART, and one that is particularly large in light of the "no ART" counterfactual scenario in which rapid death would occur. The increase in patients' employment frees up children's time, and the children are then able to attend school more. In addition, some of the income derived from patients' employment pays for food that leads to improvements in child nutrition. Thus, a second step in the assessment of benefits from ART should account for the long-run investment effects of improvements in education and nutrition at this critical juncture in children's lives.

It is illuminating to consider the long-run effects, for example, of improvements in child nutrition within ART households. Without the provision of ART, children are more likely to remain malnourished, entailing costs that are highlighted by Behrman, Alderman, and Hoddinott (2004). First, malnourished children are less likely to survive into adulthood. Second, malnourished children are more likely to be susceptible to disease, which implies societal costs, given that primary health care is generally subsidized. Third, malnutrition is associated with lower educational attainment for a range of reasons, including an inability to concentrate in class. It is striking that in the absence of ART, children may be doubly cursed, as malnutrition and labor burdens will reduce both the quality and the quantity of their schooling experience. Finally, poor early childhood nutrition affects labor productivity in adulthood. Thomas and Strauss (1997), for example, show that in Brazil the height of adults, which can proxy for early childhood nutrition, is associated with higher wages. Since the provision of ART to adults improves children's nutritional status and thereby avoids these future consequences of malnutrition, the long-term benefits of ART go well beyond the increase in treated patients' incomes.

Additionally, emerging work on early childhood development drawing on neuroscience and economics may show that ART affects several outcomes for children beyond those of nutrition and schooling. In a review of early childhood development programs, Knudsen and colleagues extrapolate from animal studies to argue that "these findings, that both differences in, and disruptions of, close affinitive bonds early in life can have lifelong effects on the development of social behaviors, raise important concerns regarding the extent to which analogous early life experiences influence human development" (Knudsen et al. 2006, 10157). A growing body of neurobiological studies of children shows that severe stress, including parental death, particularly when not offset by professional assistance, can lead to long-term physical and mental health problems. (For a review, see Center on the Developing Child 2007.) Such effects are suggestive of other benefits from the provision of ART, and they deserve further investigation.

It is important to note that the impacts discussed thus far are predominantly private benefits realized by treated individuals and their immediate family members. Although our analysis suggests that treatment is a worthwhile investment for individuals and their families (uncertainty regarding the long term notwithstanding), the case for public subsidies and thus for international involvement in treatment is less obvious and is a matter for further theoretical and empirical investigation. There are four main issues that would provide justification for public support. First, borrowing constraints, which are a significant concern in low-income settings, may pose a hindrance to privatizing the market for ART, since the flows of costs and benefits occur on different time scales. (Costs are incurred during a period of sickness, and benefits are realized at least 6 to 12 months later.) Second, the provision of treatment may generate social externalities that will not factor into the decisions of private actors in the health care marketplace. For example, ART is known to reduce the transmission of HIV, and it thus imparts important benefits to the sexual partners of those receiving treatment, but by lowering the perceived costs of infection, treatment may lead to more sexually promiscuous behavior. Third, incomplete adherence to ART can lead to virologic failure and drug resistance. If a poorly adherent patient is more likely to spread a resistant strain of the disease, the social costs of such behavior are higher. Finally, in an extension of the human capital discussion above, the social returns to education may exceed private returns, and hence any intervention that improves children's education (directly, through the education effect of ART, or indirectly, through improved nutrition leading to improved educational outcomes) could provide some justification for a subsidy. This paper does not delineate the magnitude of all these factors; rather, it suggests issues for further research.

The potentially large macroeconomic impacts associated with the effects of ART that we have documented here are worth considering, particularly in countries with high HIV prevalence. The model developed by Bell, Devarajan, and Gersbach (2006) predicts drastic economic declines (e.g., a halving of household incomes in three generations' time) in the absence of interventions to address the problem of HIV/AIDS. The key to this model is the hollowing out of the human capital core that would have sustained growth. Indeed, the important assumptions of the model are supported indirectly by our evidence on the household impacts of ART. The provision of ART can thus be one of the critical tools for avoiding the potentially large intergenerational economic effects of HIV/AIDS. This consideration is a powerful argument for public support for ART, in combination with other interventions, with the aim of ensuring economic growth and efficiency (Devarajan and Goldstein 2007).

We have shown, on the basis of studies in Kenya and elsewhere, that in the first two to three years after beginning ART, patients receiving the treatment realize large socioeconomic benefits. But ART alone is not enough to stop the scourge of HIV/AIDS. The development of interventions that can effectively stem the spread of HIV/AIDS is certainly necessary, and these interventions should be scaled up when they become available. Nonetheless, short of a cure, many countries will still be faced with millions of infected individuals, many of them adults. The experience of several treatment programs in Africa indicates that ART can not only prevent the loss of this current generation of workers but can also restore their economic productivity and help prevent negative effects on the health and education of the next generation.

Notes

1. In this paper we use the terms "ART" and "treatment" to refer to highly active antiretroviral therapy (HAART), which was introduced in 1996. HAART always consists of three antiretroviral medications. Treatment for most patients begins with a first-line regimen that is usually modified over time. Generic medications that combine three medications in one pill (such as Triomune) have recently become available.

2. Conversion to HIV-positive serology normally occurs 4 to 10 weeks after transmission. The duration of the clinical latent period has been found to vary considerably, depending on the mode of transmission and age at transmission (Collaborative Group 2000). In developing countries, limited access to health care and a greater burden of other infectious diseases may expedite the progression of HIV.

3. Patients who came to the clinic from outside the clinic's catchment area were interviewed at the clinic rather than at home.

4. Our analysis of the third wave of data is ongoing, and so this paper primarily emphasizes results based on the first two waves.

5. The analysis here excludes the 60 households containing HIV-positive AMPATH patients who were in the early stages of HIV disease and were not yet sick enough to require ART, according to WHO treatment guidelines. These households are excluded because the untreated HIV-positive patients would not have experienced significant health changes during the survey period. The small sample size of these HIV households also limits our ability to use them as a control group in the data analysis. All analysis in the paper is thus restricted to the 200 households containing ART recipients and to households from the census sample.

    Included in the sample are two adults (and their household members) who were originally part of the census sample but enrolled in the AMPATH clinic and began receiving ART between waves. As is discussed in the text, several other patients in the ART sample initiated ART between waves.

6. A key assumption of the difference-in-difference approach is that there are no time-varying characteristics that differ between the ART sample and the census sample and that are also correlated with trends in the outcome variables of interest.

7. Information on labor supply of household members was typically provided by the household head, except in the case of clinic interviews at which the patient provided all information about the household.

8. The coefficient of the variable "Patient on ART * wave 2" indicates how much the outcome variable changed between wave 1 and wave 2 for patients on ART, after controlling for time trends with data from the census sample.

9. Average hours attended are 30.47 for children in households with adult ART recipients who were treatment naïve in wave 1 or who began treatment shortly after wave 1.

10. Average hours attended are 30.15 for boys in households with adult ART recipients who were treatment naïve in wave 1 or who began treatment shortly after wave 1.

11. This is considerably less of a concern for those on ART, since the drugs significantly reduce infectivity.

12. It should be noted that calculating the impact of ART on household income using the estimated impacts on labor supply is difficult because it is not obvious which is the appropriate wage rate to use. Those with HIV may not be able to obtain average local wage rates if they are less productive (if their health has not been fully restored, or even after their health has been restored) or if they encounter HIV-related stigma and discrimination.

References

Beegle, Kathleen, Joachim De Weerdt, and Stefan Dercon. 2006. "Orphanhood and the Long-Run Impact on Children." *American Journal of Agricultural Economics* 88: 1266–72.

Behrman, Jere, Harold Alderman, and John Hoddinott. 2004. "Hunger and Malnutrition." Challenge Paper Summary prepared for the Copenhagen Consensus, Copenhagen. May 24. http://www.copenhagenconsensus.com/Admin/Public/DWSDownload.aspx?File=Files%2FFiler%2FCC%2FPress%2FUK%2FCPHunger%5B1%5D.pdf.

Bell, Clive, Shantayanan Devarajan, and Hans Gersbach. 2006. "The Long-Run Economic Costs of AIDS: A Model with an Application to South Africa." *World Bank Economic Review* 20: 55–89.

Bunnell, Rebecca, et al. 2006. "Changes in Sexual Behavior and Risk of HIV Transmission after Antiretroviral Therapy and Prevention Interventions in Rural Uganda." *AIDS* 20: 85–92.

Canning, David. 2006. "The Economics of HIV/AIDS in Low-Income Countries: The Case for Prevention." *Journal of Economic Perspectives* 20: 121–42.

Case, Anne, and Cally Ardington. 2006. "The Impact of Parental Death on School Outcomes: Longitudinal Evidence from South Africa." *Demography* 43: 401–20.

Center on the Developing Child. 2007. "A Science-Based Framework for Early Childhood Policy: Using Evidence to Improve Outcomes in Learning, Behavior, and Health for Vulnerable Children." Center on the Developing Child, Harvard University, Cambridge, MA. http://www.developingchild.harvard.edu/content/publications.html.

Chequer, P., et al. 1992. "Determinants of Survival in Adult Brazilian AIDS Patients, 1982–1989." *AIDS* 6: 483–87.

Coetzee, Celeste, and Nicoli Nattrass. 2004. "Living on AIDS Treatment: A Socio-Economic Profile of Africans Receiving Antirctroviral Therapy in Khayelitsha, Cape Town." CSSR Working Paper 04/71, Centre for Social Science Research, Cape Town.

Coetzee, David, et al. 2004. "Outcomes after Two Years of Providing Antiretroviral Treatment in Khayelitsha, South Africa." *AIDS* 18: 887–95.

Collaborative Group (Collaborative Group on AIDS Incubation and HIV Survival Including the CASCADE EU Concerted Action). 2000. "Time From HIV-1 Seroconversion to AIDS and Death before Widespread Use of Highly-Active Antiretroviral Therapy: A Collaborative Re-Analysis." *Lancet* 355: 1131–37.

d'Adda, Giovanna, Markus Goldstein, Joshua Graff Zivin, Mabel Nangami, and Harsha Thirumurthy. 2009. "ARV Treatment and Time Allocation to Household Tasks: Evidence from Kenya." *African Development Review* 21 (1): 180–208.

Devarajan, Shantayanan, and Markus Goldstein. 2007. "The Case for Public Action on AIDS Orphans." Paper prepared for the Joint Learning Initiative on Children and AIDS, World Bank, Washington, DC.

Economist. 2006. "Look to the Future: The War against AIDS." August 19.

Evans, David, and Edward A. Miguel. 2007. "Orphans and Schooling: A Longitudinal Analysis." *Demography* 44: 35–57.

Fox, Matthew P., et al. 2004. "The Impact of HIV/AIDS on Labour Productivity in Kenya." *Tropical Medicine and International Health* 9: 318–24.

Glewwe, Paul, and Elizabeth M. King. 2001. "The Impact of Early Childhood Nutritional Status on Cognitive Development: Does the Timing of Malnutrition Matter?" *World Bank Economic Review* 15 (1): 81–113.

Graff Zivin, Joshua S., Harsha Thirumurthy, and Markus Goldstein. 2006. "AIDS Treatment and Intrahousehold Resource Allocations: Children's Nutrition and Schooling in Kenya." NBER Working Paper 12689, National Bureau of Economic Research, Cambridge, MA.

Habyarimana, James, Bekezela Mbakile, and Cristian Pop-Eleches. 2007. "HIV/AIDS, ARV Treatment and Worker Absenteeism: Evidence from a Large African Firm." Columbia University, New York.

Hammer, Scott M., et al. 1997. "A Controlled Trial of Two Nucleoside Analogues plus Indinavir in Persons with Human Immunodeficiency Virus Infection and CD4 Cell Counts of 200 per Cubic Millimeter or Less." *New England Journal of Medicine* 337: 725–33.

Hogg, Robert S., et al. 1998. "Improved Survival among HIV-Infected Individuals Following Initiation of Antiretroviral Therapy." *Journal of the American Medical Association* 279: 450–54.

Kenya, Central Bureau of Statistics. 1999. *Kenya 1999 Population and Housing Census.* Nairobi: Central Bureau of Statistics.

Knodel, John E. 2008. "Poverty and the Impact of AIDS on Older Persons: Evidence from Cambodia and Thailand." *Economic Development and Cultural Change* 56 (2): 441–75.

Knudsen, Eric, James Heckman, Judy Cameron, and Jack Shonkoff. 2006. "Economic, Neurobiological, and Behavioral Perspectives on Building America's Future Workforce." *Proceedings of the National Academy of Sciences* 103 (27): 10155–62.

Koenig, Serena P., Fernet Leandre, and Paul E. Farmer. 2004. "Scaling-up HIV Treatment Programmes in Resource-Limited Settings: The Rural Haiti Experience." *AIDS* 18: S21–S25.

Laurent, Christian, et al. 2002. "The Senegalese Government's Highly Active Antiretroviral Therapy Initiative: An 18-Month Follow-up Study." *AIDS* 16: 1363–70.

Mamlin, Joe, Sylvester Kimaiyo, Winstone Nyandiko, and William Tierney. 2004. *Academic Institutions Linking Access to Treatment and Prevention: Case Study.* Geneva: World Health Organization.

Marins, Jose Ricardo P., et al. 2003. "Dramatic Improvement in Survival among Adult Brazilian AIDS Patients." *AIDS* 17: 1675–82.

Medicins Sans Frontieres. 2007. *Untangling the Web of Price Reductions.* Geneva: Medicins Sans Frontieres.

Mills, Edward J., et al. 2006. "Adherence to HAART: A Systematic Review of Developed and Developing Nation Patient-Reported Barriers and Facilitators." *PloS Med* 3 (11): e438.

Morgan, Dilys, et al. 2002. "HIV-1 Infection in Rural Africa: Is There a Difference in Median Time to AIDS and Survival Compared with That in Industrialized Countries?" *AIDS* 16: 597–603.

Nattrass, Nicoli. 2006. "South Africa's 'Rollout' of Highly Active Antiretroviral Therapy: A Critical Assessment." *Journal of Acquired Immune Deficiency Syndrome* 43 (5): 618–23.

Orrell, C., D. R. Bangsberg, M. Badri, and R. Wood. 2003. "Adherence Is Not a Barrier to Successful Antiretroviral Therapy in South Africa." *AIDS* 17: 1369–75.

Palella, Frank J., et al. 1998. "Declining Morbidity and Mortality among Patients with Advanced Human Immunodeficiency Virus Infection." *New England Journal of Medicine* 338: 853–60.

Thirumurthy, Harsha, Joshua Graff Zivin, and Markus Goldstein. 2008. "The Economic Impact of AIDS Treatment: Labor Supply in Western Kenya." *Journal of Human Resources* 43 (3, Summer): 511–52.

Thomas, Duncan, and John Strauss. 1997. "Health and Wages: Evidence on Men and Women in Urban Brazil." *Journal of Econometrics* 77 (1, March): 159–85.

UNAIDS (Joint United Nations Programme on HIV/AIDS). 2007. *Financial Resources Required to Achieve Universal Access to HIV Prevention, Treatment, Care and Support.* Geneva: UNAIDS.

WHO (World Health Organization). 1995. *Physical Status: The Use and Interpretation of Anthropometry—Report of a WHO Expert Committee.* World Health Organization Technical Report 854. Geneva: WHO. http://whqlibdoc.who.int/trs/WHO_TRS_854.pdf.

———. 2006. *Antiretroviral Therapy for HIV Infection in Adults and Adolescents: Recommendations for a Public Health Approach—2006 Revision.* Geneva: WHO.

Wools-Kaloustian, Kara, et al. 2006. "Viability and Effectiveness of Large-Scale HIV Treatment Initiatives in Sub-Saharan Africa: Experience from Western Kenya." *AIDS* 20: 41–48.

Comment on "Health and Socioeconomic Status: The Importance of Causal Pathways," by Duncan Thomas, and "The Household Impacts of Treating HIV/AIDS in Developing Countries," by Markus Goldstein, Joshua Graff Zivin, and Harsha Thirumurthy

T. PAUL SCHULTZ

One goal of health economics is to clarify how to achieve improvements in health at the least private and social cost. But several issues arise. The first is that determining how to measure health status is not a simple task. Health has many facets. The common indicators of mortality and morbidity are generally measured poorly and with much systematic error in low-income countries. Furthermore, they cannot be decomposed reliably by cause or disease or readily linked to individuals who exhibit different biological and economic endowments, opportunities, and health-related behaviors.

The second problem is to evaluate how public policies affect health outcomes over time. Health production functions are difficult to estimate in high-income countries and are rarely assessed in low-income countries unless the policy inputs or health treatments are administered in a social experiment—in which case the inputs are not associated with the confounding biological and economic endowments of individuals and their lifetime health-related behaviors.

The third challenge is to estimate the social value of the measured health outcome and the social cost of delivery of the health policy inputs. Needless to say, assignment of social values to health and to its distribution in the population involves issues of ethics, as well as of economics and politics, that go far beyond our discussion here. One among many methods for assigning a private economic value to health measures is to assess the effect of a health outcome on individuals' productive potential. This approach is parallel to the human capital framework that has been employed to clarify the economic consequences of education as a factor raising individual productivity. The increasing availability of multipurpose household surveys and censuses that collect the socioeconomic and health characteristics of a representative population provides a basis for estimating in some contexts the effect of health human capital on individual productivity or observed wage rates. There are many reasons to expect

T. Paul Schultz is Malcolm K. Brachman Professor Emeritus of Economics at Yale University, New Haven, CT.

Annual World Bank Conference on Development Economics 2009, Global

that health policy variations affecting the accumulation of health human capital will be associated with the individual's endowments before the policy treatment and with the persisting patterns of health-related behaviors. Given these sources of individual heterogeneity, such as genetic diversity and variation in socioeconomic status—which are likely to be associated with who receives heath policy treatments—little can be learned about the causal effect of the policy treatment on health outcomes from the direct association of the two unless the policy is prescribed in a random experiment or unless strong assumptions are maintained regarding the functioning of program institutions and individual and family behavior.

This is the dilemma that faces applied health economics, and it appears to me even more serious in developing countries than in developed ones, although conceptually similar. We tend to be guided by medical knowledge derived from clinical experiments in carefully monitored situations that do not allow an economic assessment of the cost of scaling up the specified medical treatment to a field program at a regional or national level. Nor do these clinical experiments provide the economist with a basis on which to evaluate the economic productivity effects of the health improvements and, hence, their private income effects.

Another dilemma for public health policy evaluations is that interventions are believed to have social externalities on the health of other individuals who do not experience the policy treatment.[1] It is generally believed that preventive health care for infectious and parasitic diseases creates such spillover social benefits, which partly justifies the production of such goods in the public sector.

The papers in the session on human development provide insights into the issues described above. Duncan Thomas draws attention to areas in which knowledge about what produces health and about the consequences of health for income growth, or, as he terms it, "prosperity," has been mounting rapidly. Let me summarize some of his observations and then note where our perspectives differ slightly. First, evidence has recently accumulated showing that the nutritional and physical condition and development of the pregnant woman and her fetus set into motion long-lasting effects on the child, related not only to lifespan but also to the child's cognition, school attainment, earnings, and disability-free years of life that may be potentially applied to productive work. These life-course outcomes are likely to add up to greater productive potential and tend to be associated with higher market income—although, as Thomas notes, this did not necessarily hold in his iron supplement social experiment.

This body of evidence on health and development is generated by research conducted in many disciplines, using disparate data and methods and creating plenty of puzzling paradoxes and loose ends. The types of research, with the associated problems, include the following:

1. *Historical accidents or natural experiments,* in which a treatment appears to occur at a specific time or location or to a specific group and the effects can be followed as the members of relevant cohort live out their lives. Examples include the Spanish flu epidemic and the radioactive rainfall on Sweden after the Chernobyl nuclear reactor accident.

2. *Social experiments*, in which treatments are randomly allocated among people, households, or communities. The treated and comparison populations are followed to minimize attrition and to document consequences accumulating over time.
3. *Assessment of technical and behavioral relationships* between, on the one hand, preconditions or risk factors and, on the other hand, outcomes affected by family and institutional behavior and constrained by biology and technology. Inference of causal effects typically requires the researcher to impose debatable identifying assumptions.
4. *Findings from randomized animal studies*, which may be arguably relevant to human development.

Because studies linking health to outcomes are complicated, and many mechanisms may be consistent with observed empirical regularities, it is generally desirable to distinguish how specific pathways relate socioeconomic characteristics to health and to subsequent individual and family outcomes. New biological markers are helping to quantify some of these biological indicators in large representative household surveys. Thomas cites several examples to illustrate what can be learned from these data and methods, and what the limitations are of even well-designed research programs:

1. The experience of survivors from the cohort born in China during the famine of 1959–60 may show how malnutrition stunts and scars a cohort and affects its members' capacities as adults. But some of the cohort—probably individuals who were less healthy, on average—die as a result of the stress of the famine, and this culling changes the composition of the surviving cohort and should be taken into account. Thomas also notes that fertility tends to decline during a famine, which may further change the socioeconomic composition of those born because fertility is a choice—as is migration to mitigate the conditions of the famine.
2. A parallel behavioral change in fertility associated with the flood in Bangladesh in 1974 makes it difficult to ascertain how the health crisis caused by the flood affected the educational attainment of the cohort born near the time of the flood.
3. Social programs in rural Indonesia stationed midwives in poor villages in the 1990s, but evaluation of the local health effects of the program requires careful comparisons among suitable groups. Because midwives' presence directly benefits only the health of women and children, not men, a comparison of how gender differences in health evolve in communities that receive midwives and those that do not offers Thomas a convincing basis for evaluating this health intervention.

A similar approach in Matlab District, Bangladesh, followed a family planning and child and maternal health social experiment that began in 1977. By 1996, program villages exhibited much lower fertility, lower child mortality, and improved health among women of childbearing age, compared with the control villages, but the health of men was not affected (Schultz 2009). The benefits of the Matlab program for health and productivity are therefore expected to be specific by age and sex. The monthly earnings of women working in the paid labor force are indeed shown to be one-third higher for women age 25–54 in the program treatment villages in 1996, whereas wages are no different for men, controlling for their schooling and age. Nor are there distinguishable program effects on wages of males or females age 15–24, even when adjusted for sample selection bias of wage earners, where household landholdings are specified to raise home productivity and thereby identify the model of selection into the paid labor force.

The increased wage rate of women in the program villages in Matlab comes about because women who presumably have been enabled to avoid unwanted childbearing are more productive in paid jobs. But because the households in the program villages also accumulate more household assets and have fewer children to perform house-hold chores, the women actually choose to increase their participation in household production, even though their wage opportunities in the market are now greater. An economist might hypothesize that the value of home productivity of women must have increased even more than their market wages, to dominate the attractiveness of the higher wage rates women receive in the paid labor force.

Foster and Rosenzweig (2007) note a similar pattern in rural India, where the Green Revolution increased agricultural yields differentially across the country between 1970 and 2000. Household incomes have consequently increased, and women's wages have risen since 1982, during a period when birthrates declined and schooling increased. But the adult women who are reducing their birthrates are not turning to the paid labor force; rather, they may be reallocating their time from child care to home production. In the longer run, I would expect the labor productivity of women in market employment in rural South Asia to increase more rapidly than labor productivity in home production, but this will not necessarily occur immedi-ately or in all countries experiencing the common features of the demographic tran-sition, even when the aggregate economy experiences robust growth, as has India's since the 1990s.

Thomas argues that it is important, in evaluating how health affects prosperity, to understand how long-term gains in health and productivity affect labor supply. Econ-omists have conceptualized workers' labor supply response to an increase in their wages as a combination of an income effect, which favors the demand for leisure or less work, and a substitution effect associated with the increased opportunity cost of leisure, which favors a reduction in the demand for leisure or a tendency to work more.[2] When individual labor supply is embedded in a family model of coordinated labor supply, the wages of other family members also enter the equation with their own combinations of income and cross-substitution effects. In the rural Indian and Bangladesh studies, it is likely that the increasing wages of husbands have con-tributed to wives' reallocation of time from child care to home production, as the husbands' cross-wage effects tend to have a negative influence on wives' supply of time for working in the labor market.

Another of Thomas's arguments regarding health is also reflected in the labor supply literature. A short-run fluctuation in health and productivity as a result of control of an acute infectious illness is expected to exert a more positive effect on current labor supply than would a long-term or permanent change in health—for example, reduction of the disabling effects of chronic illness, which brings with it a lifetime improvement in wage opportunities and hence a larger gain in lifetime wealth that encourages workers to consume more leisure and work fewer hours.

The Work and Iron Status Evaluation (WISE), a social experiment Thomas and his colleagues planned and implemented in central Java, illustrates how increased health and productivity resulting from provision of a randomized iron supplement brought about improvements in objective and subjective health status and led male wage earners to reallocate time from sleep to leisure—perhaps because they were paid on an hourly basis and thus did not receive increased wages from their employers. Self-employed males, who realized financial gains of 15 percent from their enhanced productivity, received more income but still worked about the same amount of time as before. Wage earners who received the iron supplements were more likely to shift over time to self-employment, where they could expect to realize the financial benefit from their decreased anemia and increased productivity per hour worked.[3]

Further study of family labor supply behavior in developing countries is needed, especially that of women as they adjust their time allocation to the declining levels of fertility observed worldwide and to what I expect to be a period of improving health status of women relative to men. Design of public policies in the labor market and social welfare systems that assist women in their reallocation of time could be significant factors in reducing poverty and increasing total income. Targeting family planning and reproductive health programs to those women and young children who have the most to gain from this package of information, services, and supplies might represent a form of health human capital investment with relatively high long-term internal rates of return, as documented in Matlab. But more prospective experimental and pilot programs must be evaluated before any generalizations can be drawn in this regard. Conversely, there are probably many parts of the world where the fertility of the upper and middle classes does not respond substantially to family planning subsidies or does not suggest that a market failure is being mitigated by this public intervention. The challenge is to define the context in which returns are suitably high for publicly subsidized social welfare programs.

In their paper, Goldstein, Graff Zivin, and Thirumurthy estimate the benefits from an antiretroviral (ARV) drug therapy that was prescribed to HIV/AIDS patients in western Kenya when their CD4 counts collapsed to levels at which their immune systems were unlikely to sustain their capacity to work. With the recent drop in the cost of these drugs and the increase in donor funding for ARV treatment programs, it is appropriate to ask, what are the health and economic consequences of these programs for those treated, under the conditions prevailing in rural Africa? It is not ethically acceptable to provide therapy for a random sample of AIDS patients. An alternative approach to evaluation is to collect representative data on the population from which the patients come and then to construct a comparison of how patients' CD4 count and their labor supply and other household behaviors change over time for individuals after they enter ARV therapy, as well as how this change compares with that occurring at the same time in the same community within the representative sample (that is, to control for variation by age, sex, and season). Using relatively small samples, the authors are able to document that the medical indicator of disease remission improves within two months; patients' work hours increase 39 percent; and work hours by children in patients' households decrease (significantly, in the case of boys), while children of both genders reallocate more hours to attending school. Although the concluding claims of the authors to have evaluated the economic costs and benefits of ARV programs are somewhat overstated, their evaluation methodology is promising and deserves to be replicated in other settings where the costs of scaling up the program can be more thoroughly assessed.

Notes

1. Thus, provision of deworming medicine in randomly selected schools in Kenya led to reduced burdens of these parasites on children from neighboring school districts and on other children within the district who did not undergo the treatment (because they did not attend school the day the medicine was available or because their families did not complete the permission form allowing them to participate in the medical treatment).

2. The balance of the offsetting income and substitution effects allows a labor economist to account for own-wage responses in either sign within this framework: a positive labor supply response to a rise in wages by women results when the substitution effect dominates the income effect, whereas a negative (uncompensated) labor supply response for men occurs because the income effect weighted by initial hours worked by the man dominates his substitution effect, accounting in the extreme case for a backward-bending labor supply relationship with respect to male wages.

3. One might argue that the value of home production is largely omitted from national income and product accounts because of the difficulty of valuing the product, and the same is, of course, true of leisure. But the welfare gains from the increased value of leisure, efficiency of sleep, and productivity at work are nonetheless clear, even if national income and product accounts do not capture all of them.

References

Foster, Andrew D., and Mark R. Rosenzweig. 2007. "Does Economic Growth Reduce Fertility? Rural India, 1971–1999." In *India Policy Forum, 2006–07*, ed. Suman Bery, Barry Bosworth, and Arvind Panagariya. New Delhi: National Council of Applied Economic Research (NCAER); Washington, DC: Brookings Institution Press; New Delhi: Sage Publications India.

Schultz, T. Paul. 2009. "How Does Family Planning Promote Development? Evidence from a Social Experiment in Matlab Bangladesh—1977–1996." Presented at the annual meeting of the Population Association of America, Detroit, MI, April 30. http://paa2009.princeton.edu/download.aspx?submissionId=90065.

Comment on "The Household Impacts of Treating HIV/AIDS in Developing Countries," by Markus Goldstein, Joshua Graff Zivin, and Harsha Thirumurthy

JOHN STRAUSS

In this paper, Goldstein, Graff Zivin, and Thirumurthy summarize their excellent article published in the *Journal of Human Resources* (Thirumurthy, Graff Zivin, and Goldstein 2008). That work is quite important because it represents the best scientific study to date of the impact of antiretroviral (ARV) therapy on HIV patients' labor supply and the spillover effects on the labor supply of other household members, notably children. The authors find that the therapy has a large effect on HIV patients' hours worked, which rise back toward what they were before the patients became so ill. The impacts are much larger for patients in the first six months of ARV treatment. The authors also find a large effect on increased blood CD4 counts, indicating that the ARV medication is working. An important finding is that these impacts on CD4 counts and on labor supply occur almost immediately after treatment has begun and last for the six months' portion of the study that is reported. Also of importance are the spillover effects—the increased time at school and decreased labor time of children who had been taking care of HIV-infected parents.

In addition to providing a simplified summary of their journal article, the authors advocate the scaling up of ARV treatment programs such as the one they study in rural Kenya. Here, important issues of public economics arise that the authors have not considered carefully enough, as discussed below.

To begin with, I summarize the scientific issues in the conference paper. Adequately assessing the impacts of ARV on labor supply poses a challenge. Experiments are not possible in this case because of ethical concerns about controls not receiving treatment. The authors use hospital data from the Academic Model for the Prevention and Treatment of HIV/AIDS (AMPATH), an organization in western Kenya, on HIV-positive patients undergoing ARV treatment. In addition, they conduct several waves of surveys of these patients to obtain information on the labor supply of the respondents and others in their households. Unfortunately, they do not have available

John Strauss is professor of economics at the University of Southern California.

Annual World Bank Conference on Development Economics 2009, Global
© 2010 The International Bank for Reconstruction and Development / The World Bank

data on these patients prior to treatment, but they do know how long the treatments have been going on.

Of course, those persons who seek treatment constitute a very select group of the HIV-positive population, which would lead to bias if their characteristics were simply compared with a control group. The authors recognize this and instead use first differences over a six-month period during which they collected data prospectively. The first difference eliminates additive, unobserved, time-invariant individual characteristics that may be responsible for those patients' seeking care in the first place.

The difficult part is to find a plausible treatment group. The authors use a sample made up of individuals in the area who are not registered in the AMPATH medical system. Of course, some of these persons will be HIV positive, while most will be HIV negative. They will differ in their underlying characteristics, since the HIV-positive persons are not yet receiving treatment. These controls, too, were interviewed over time, and a difference over a six-month time period is taken for them as well. The authors then use a difference-in-difference specification to examine the impact on labor supply of being on ARV treatment. As mentioned, the difference-in-difference specification will eliminate time-invariant unobservables that may cause selection bias, but it will not eliminate time-varying unobservables. If, for instance, there are differential trends over time between treatments and controls, or there exist time-varying shocks that affect both treatment status and labor supply (say, from unanticipated side effects of the ARV drugs), this would not be accounted for by the difference-in-difference estimator. Overall, though, the results in this study seem quite plausible and are certainly far more reliable than those from other studies to date.

One of the important results reported in the paper is the existence of gender differentials associated with treatment. (These differences are explored in much more detail in the longer *Journal of Human Resources* version.) The results on labor force participation show up only for women, not men—perhaps not surprisingly, since it is female labor force attachment that is usually suspect, more than men's. The impact on hours is greater for men, although part of the reason is probably that female work in home production is not taken into account. Schooling hours rise for both boys and girls, but work declines only for boys (again, perhaps because home production work is not counted).

Finally, the *Journal of Human Resources* version reports on impacts on earnings, which are also strong and positive. These estimates are probably biased upward, however, because the value of labor hours is evaluated at mean market wages, whereas the market wages of these still-sick workers are likely to be below mean wages. In addition, it may be the more productive workers in the population who contract HIV, or it may be the less productive ones; the authors provide no data on this, and evidence from other studies is mixed on this point (see Strauss and Thomas 2008). In addition, household income will not rise as much as does the treated individual's income if the labor supply of other members falls, as the authors demonstrate happens, at least for boys. What is more useful to think about than labor income is full income, which should rise by the value of the increase in nonsick time for the treated respondents. The paper claims that the rise in full income is equal to US$350 per year, about the same as the current costs for first-line ARV drugs plus laboratory tests (although less than the costs of second-line drugs, should they be needed). But, as explained below, the stated costs are not complete, and so a proper benefit-cost calculation is not performed in this research.

One drawback of the results is that people are followed for only six months. The study went on for two years, but the authors do not use the extra 18 months of data. Indeed, it would be extremely useful if the authors could go back and reinterview the respondents after more time has elapsed.

The science in the study is good, in my view, and the micro results are plausible and convincing. However, the public economics in the second part of the paper are problematic.

The first issue, which the authors now realize but did not in an earlier version of this paper, is that the benefits they calculate are private benefits. There are no social externalities in these results. That is not to say that social externalities may not exist; they may indeed. Examples that come to mind are the possibilities that transmission rates of HIV may slow because some HIV-positive persons are taking ARVs (of course, their sexual behavior may respond in perverse ways to the treatment, offsetting any such benefit) and that more people may decide to be tested for HIV because of treatment being available. Unfortunately the science behind both scenarios is limited, and the authors' results say nothing about these mechanisms. (See Glick 2005 for a nice survey on HIV testing.)

The real issue is that in practice, ARV drugs are being given free of charge by organizations such as AMPATH, yet the fact that the benefits are in large part private indicates that there should be scope to charge patients, at least in the interests of economic efficiency. Goldstein, Graff Zivin, and Thirumurthy argue against such a policy on grounds of potential credit market constraints, but their own results belie this rationale because the impacts occur so rapidly after the start of treatment—within the first six months. One might assert that there should be a price schedule that increases with time from the initiation of treatment, but to argue for continued free access seems extreme in light of the authors' results. It is still possible, and perhaps likely, that an optimal pricing schedule would not recover the full cost—certainly not, if positive externalities do exist—but the optimal price will surely not be zero. Although it may not be interpreted in this way, this pricing argument is really good news for equity if implemented carefully because a limited ARV budget can extend to more HIV-positive patients if existing patients can successfully begin to pay part of the costs.

A second key issue that must be considered before thinking of scaling up the ARV effort is the ability to scale up while maintaining the same level (or even close to the same level) of service quality. In western Kenya, the group that runs the hospitals providing the ARV treatments, AMPATH, is a collaboration by the medical schools of the University of Indiana and the University of Nairobi. Hence, the quality of the administrative staff running the programs is very high—much higher than would presumably be the case if the Kenyan Ministry of Health were operating the system.

Issues of corruption, of waste, and of favoritism of treatment that would likely have to be dealt with in a publicly run system may not have to be considered for AMPATH, or at least to a much smaller degree. Presumably, it is much easier for AMPATH to staff the system with high-quality medical staff than it would be for the government. To illustrate the problem, during my recent visit to a hospital very much like the AMPATH system in rural southeastern Uganda, a manager explained that a key difficulty was in attracting high-quality medical staff, even though the hospital was private and foreign run. One reason was that the area was so isolated. The hospital had set up and was supplying free satellite Internet access for staff, to make living in that area more agreeable. In this regard AMPATH may have some advantages because population densities are higher in rural Kenya than in other parts of rural Sub-Saharan Africa and there are towns and cities in the area that offer some amenities.

The ability of AMPATH to deliver services and attain high rates of proper intakes of medicine may be high. (It is claimed to be more than 80 percent, but the data on which that claim is based are not absolutely accurate.) Whether a publicly run system would be able to achieve the same level is unclear. If not, then of course the worries about emerging ARV-resistant types of HIV would be at issue.

These private-public distinctions are important because where delivery is in private or nongovernmental organization hands, as with AMPATH, the full costs are undoubtedly far higher than they would be under a public system. It is highly doubtful that the authors have data on all the costs, many of which would originate in Bloomington, Indiana. As an aside, in the case of the Ugandan hospital I visited, 100 percent of capital costs and more than 80 percent of operating costs, including all the costs of the ARV drugs, were borne by foreign sources. Continued foreign aid is certainly essential to the sustainability of AMPATH-like centers.

Concerning the evaluation of the social benefits and costs of ARV, the best discussion is still found in the World Bank report *Confronting AIDS* (World Bank 1997). Although the costs of ARV have dropped phenomenally since 1997, when *Confronting AIDS* was published, the economic arguments contained in that volume are still the starting place for any serious economic evaluation of the trade-offs involved.

Nevertheless, Goldstein, Graff Zivin, and Thirumurthy have made an essential contribution to the evaluation of ARV treatment. As noted, the analysis is not complete as a benefit-cost study or as an assessment of the ability to scale up this intervention and pass a benefit-cost test. The study does, however, raise interesting and valuable issues of the pricing of ARV treatment and thus of the ability to perhaps reach many more HIV-infected patients than might have been thought possible.

References

Glick, Peter. 2005. "Scaling Up HIV Voluntary Counseling and Testing in Africa: What Can Evaluation Studies Tell Us about Potential Prevention Impacts?" *Evaluation Review* 29 (4): 331–57.

Strauss, John, and Duncan Thomas. 2008. "Health over the Life Course." In *Handbook of Development Economics,* vol. 4, ed. T. Paul Schultz and John Strauss. Amsterdam: North-Holland.

Thirumurthy, Harsha, Joshua Graff Zivin, and Markus Goldstein. 2008. "The Economic Impact of AIDS Treatment: Labor Supply in Western Kenya." *Journal of Human Resources* 43 (3, Summer): 511–52.

World Bank. 1997. *Confronting AIDS: Public Policies in a Global Epidemic.* World Bank Policy Research Report. New York: Oxford University Press.

Political Economy

When Is Public Expenditure Pro-Poor?

FRANCISCO RODRÍGUEZ

Studies of the progressivity of government spending often assume that certain types of expenditure (e.g., for education and health) deliver the largest benefits to the poor. But the extent to which different types of expenditure can be pro-poor is likely to vary significantly for countries at different levels of development. To deal with that issue, this paper develops a new indicator of the progressivity of fiscal policies. The measure is obtained by empirically assessing the effect of different types of expenditure on poverty and on the income elasticity of poverty reduction, using a panel of 387 growth spells derived from the World Bank's PovcalNet database. It is then used to evaluate the extent to which countries' fiscal policies are pro-poor and to test different political-economy theories of the determination of fiscal policies. The results indicate that whereas richer economies have more pro-poor fiscal policies, policies in more unequal, less financially developed, and more open economies are likely to be less pro-poor.

What makes for shared growth? How do some countries develop arrangements in which the poor benefit from and contribute to the growth process? Why are some development processes inclusive, while others appear to be driven by the actions and self-interest of particular groups?

Providing an answer to these questions requires that two distinct sets of issues be addressed. One concerns the conditions under which the poor can contribute to economic growth. A well-established strand of the political-economy literature considers that participation by the poor in the political process tends to increase the pressures on governments to enact distortionary policies that end up harming growth prospects (Alesina and Rodrik 1994; Persson and Tabellini 1994). However, the links between political-economy models, redistribution, and growth are complex, and

Francisco Rodríguez is head of research at the Human Development Report Office of the United Nations Development Programme. The author thanks Maria Eugenia Boza, Robert Bates, Andrew Donaldson, and Eduardo Zambrano for helpful discussions and Madalina Ursu and Mark Purser for superb research assistance.

Annual World Bank Conference on Development Economics 2009, Global

the exact effect of greater political participation is likely to depend on the precise workings of the political system, including the role that economic resources play in influencing politics (Bénabou 1996; Rodríguez 2004). The existence of credit constraints may imply that the poor have unexploited high-productivity investment opportunities, so that redistributing resources to them can generate high rates of growth as the returns from these investments are realized (Galor and Zeira 1993). Furthermore, the participation of the poor in the political process may be necessary to stave off the emergence of radical revolutionary movements, the effects of which can be much more harmful to an economy than those of the moderate redistribution likely to emerge under voting in a democratic system (Acemoglu and Robinson 2006).

A second set of issues has to do with the conditions under which the poor can benefit from growth. Several theories of political economy, going back at least to Meltzer and Richard (1981), have studied the conditions under which the political equilibrium will deliver high amounts of redistribution. The classic prediction is that more unequal societies will tend to have higher redistribution. Other theories have stressed, as alternative determinants of redistribution, the role of economic development in fostering the growth of the state and the need for social insurance, as a result of an economy's integration into world markets.

Empirically, both of these literatures are hampered by lack of clarity as to the appropriate measure of pro-poor policies. The standard approach is to regress a set of public policies, such as government expenditures, on a set of demographic and political determinants that stand in for different political-economy theories (see, e.g., Shelton 2007). It is assumed that government expenditures, or certain types of government expenditure, are inherently redistributive and that the predictions of political-economy models can therefore be evaluated by studying the effect of certain variables (e.g., inequality and openness) on these expenditures.

The relationship between public policies and redistribution, however, is likely to differ significantly from country to country. European countries tend to carry out significant amounts of redistribution through their social security systems. In contrast, in many developing countries the social security system covers only the formal sector, which tends to be made up of relatively better off individuals. Similarly, government action is likely to affect not only the level of poverty but also the responsiveness of poverty to economic growth. A government that heavily invests in public redistributive spending but finances that spending with the fiscal dividends of an economic expansion may be able to reduce poverty substantially while the expansion lasts. If, however, the economy enters a contraction and fiscal resources dry up, the ensuing contraction in public programs may end up significantly harming the poor. To understand how the poor can share in economic growth, one must accordingly evaluate not only the effects of spending levels on the poor but also how these effects are linked to the economy's growth rate.

This paper tackles these issues by developing a new measure of the benefits that the poor derive from social policies. The measure is derived directly from an assessment of the effects of different fiscal policies on the level of poverty. By regressing the change in poverty on the levels, differences, and interactions of various types of government expenditure, we can construct an empirically grounded estimate of how the actions of the state affect the poor under different economic conditions. Using these results, we develop an index of the extent to which a government's policies benefit the poor. The index is based not on a priori assumptions but, rather, on the observed relationships between public spending and the evolution of poverty. This measure can then be used to evaluate key questions in the shared growth debate, such as: To what extent are pro-poor policies consistent with economic growth? How relevant are existing political-economy theories to an understanding of the determinants of pro-poor policies?

Government action on poverty reduction does not operate only through government expenditure. Governments can impose regulations that make it more or less difficult for the poor to access credit or enter markets; they can design social programs efficiently or in ways that invite rent-seeking; and they can allow or attempt to change conditions that lead to discrimination against disadvantaged groups. The paper does not attempt to characterize the stance of the whole of government policies; instead, it centers on the effects that two key variables, the level and the composition of government expenditures, have on poverty reduction and its association with growth.

In the next section, we introduce our theoretical framework and present our key estimating equations. We then discuss our data and results. The final section presents concluding comments and discusses possible directions for further research.

Estimation Framework

The basis for our estimation exercise will be a set of regressions of the form:

$$\Delta p_t = \alpha_1 + \alpha_2 \Delta y_t + \beta X_t, \tag{1}$$

where p_t is the logarithm of the poverty rate, y_t is the logarithm of mean income, and X_t is a set of control variables. The estimate of α_2 in this regression is known as the income elasticity of poverty reduction; it captures the percentage change in poverty rates resulting from a 1 percent change in mean income. Bourguignon (2003) has shown that this elasticity is governed by an identity linking the poverty rate, the level of income, and the degree of income inequality. He suggests that this can be controlled for by adding the change in income inequality as a right-hand-side variable:

$$\Delta p_t = \alpha_1 + \alpha_2 \Delta y_t + \alpha_3 \Delta G_t + \beta X_t, \tag{2}$$

where G_t is an indicator of inequality, such as the Gini coefficient.

Our interest lies in understanding the effect that public expenditures have on this relationship. A number of natural possibilities come to mind. The first is simply to introduce the level of public expenditures in this regression. Thus, for example, one could hypothesize that for every percentage point of gross domestic product (GDP) devoted to public expenditures, one would expect to see a decline of α_4 percent in the poverty rate, yielding the specification:

$$\Delta p_t = \alpha_1 + \alpha_2 \Delta y_t + \alpha_3 \Delta G_t + \alpha_4 E_t, \tag{3}$$

where E_t denotes the ratio of government expenditures to GDP. Note that since it is natural to expect that expenditures may also affect inequality, it may make sense to supplement estimation of this relationship with a separate equation for the determination of inequality. Perhaps a more natural hypothesis would be that increases in public expenditures would lead to declines in poverty:

$$\Delta p_t = \alpha_1 + \alpha_2 \Delta y_t + \alpha_3 \Delta G_t + \alpha_4 E_t + \alpha_5 \Delta E_t. \tag{4}$$

An additional class of hypotheses would explore the determinants of heterogeneity across countries in the responsiveness of poverty reduction to growth. For example, we may be interested in evaluating the sensitivity of the income elasticity of poverty to the level of public expenditure. This hypothesis would capture the idea, for example, that if a country devotes x percent of GDP to government spending, the poor will benefit more from economic growth than if it did not do so. In that case, equation (4) would become:

$$\Delta p_t = \alpha_1 + \alpha_2 \Delta y_t + \alpha_3 \Delta G_t + \alpha_4 E_t + \alpha_5 \Delta E_t + \alpha_6 E_t \Delta y_t. \tag{5}$$

These specifications are motivated purely by intuitive concerns: it seems reasonable to expect that at a given level of income and inequality, higher levels of pro-poor spending would lead to faster declines in the poverty rate. Only some of these specifications, however, will map neatly into a theory of the determination of poverty. For example, if $\beta = 0$, equation (2) will easily integrate out to:

$$p_t = c + \alpha_1 t + \alpha_2 y_t + \alpha_3 G_t. \tag{6}$$

If, in addition, we set $\alpha_1 = 0$, we have a linear version of the identity between poverty, income, and inequality derived by Bourguignon (2003) and Kraay (2004). Similarly, if we believe that there is a complementarity between government spending and mean income in the determination of poverty such that poverty is a decreasing function of the product of y_t and E_t, our natural representation of poverty would be:

$$p_t = c + \alpha_1 t + \alpha_2 y_t + \alpha_3 G_t + \alpha_4 E_t + \alpha_5 E_t y_t, \tag{7}$$

which would generate the following equation in differences:

$$\Delta p_t = \alpha_1 + \alpha_2 \Delta y_t + \alpha_3 \Delta G_t + \alpha_4 \Delta E_t + \alpha_5 \Delta (E_t y_t). \tag{8}$$

Note the contrast between equation (8) and equation (5): if expenditures and output are multiplicative complements in the poverty function, then the appropriate control in a regression in differences is $\Delta(E_t y_t)$ and not $E_t \Delta y_t$. The reason is simple: if expenditures increase the effect of output on poverty, it must be the case that output increases the effect of expenditures on poverty by the same magnitude.[1] Thus, it is incorrect to control only for the interaction between the levels of one variable and the changes in the other—at least, if what one has in mind is a theory such as equation (7).

Given that equations (7) and (8) are simply different expressions of the same theory, one may ask why it makes sense to estimate the equation in differences instead of in levels. Put another way, why concentrate on estimating the effect of changes in income on changes in poverty (and suffer the inevitable loss in information that comes from first-differencing), if one can simply estimate the relationship between levels of poverty and levels of income in the cross-country data? To a certain extent, this question parallels the discussion of whether to evaluate theories of development by studying growth rates or levels of GDP. In this paper, we follow the conventional approach of concentrating on the equation in differences. An argument in favor of this approach comes from the belief that there is a large component of time-invariant country-specific factors that help determine poverty levels and that will drop out on first-differencing. Another consideration is that the change in poverty as a result of economic growth is the focus of considerable attention by policy makers—much more so than the existence of differences in poverty levels between poorer and richer economies.[2] Nevertheless, it is useful to remember that some equations in differences will have corresponding tractable formulations in levels, a fact that we appeal to below.

We close with a caveat. It is common to find estimates in the literature of equation (1) and its variants that are given a causal interpretation. There is nothing in the specification of poverty elasticity estimates to ensure that they are not contaminated by reverse causation or omitted variable bias. Indeed, it is not hard to come up with a story in which the reduction of poverty generates the necessary social conditions to enable high economic growth, so that α_2 fails to capture the effect of growth on poverty. One school of thought treats estimation of these equations as cross-national extensions of an accounting relationship in which causality is not as important as the strength of the association. It is essential to bear these points in mind as we discuss the role that social expenditures play in this relationship.

Data and Evidence

The analysis employs data on income distributions, poverty rates, and mean income taken from the World Bank's PovcalNet database, which contains 548 country-year estimates for 100 countries. Most of these estimates are national, although in some cases they correspond to only urban or rural areas. The national estimates are used except for three cases (Argentina, China, and India) for which there are no national-level estimates available: in those cases, urban data are used. For 13 countries there is just one observation, and these cases are lost on first-differencing, leaving 387 spells of growth for 87 economies. The purchasing power parity (PPP)–adjusted US$2 per day poverty rate is used to construct the dependent variable.

The data on expenditures come from the Government Finance Statistics (GFS) database of the International Monetary Fund (IMF 2006a, 2006b), and the data on output are from the IMF's International Financial Statistics (IFS) database (IMF 2006c). Building this series (as well as the other expenditure series in the database) requires that data from the GFS Historical Statistics, which cover the 1972–90 period, be linked with those for the 1990–2006 period. This is done using the guidelines set out in Wickens (2002); the post-1990 expenditure series is combined with the sum of the pre-1990 current expenditure and capital transfer series. All series are expressed net of interest payments. A set of analogous linking rules is employed to construct series for the share of alternative components of expenditures. Indicators of the share of environmental expenditure in total spending can also be built, but these series are only available after 1990 and thus are of limited use.

The GFS database lists data for a large number of spending categories. Since the data (and degrees of freedom) are limited, five expenditure indicators are constructed: (a) core social spending, for education, health, and housing (generally considered the most pro-poor type of expenditure); (b) noncore social spending (spending commonly classified under the rubric "social" but that tends to benefit the middle class), representing the sum of expenditure on recreation, culture and religion, and social protection; (c) economic spending, which covers support to agriculture, fuels and energy, mining, transport, communications, and other productive sectors; (d) security expenditures, which consist of defense spending plus protection of public order; and (e) spending on general public services, including unclassified expenditures.

The rest of our data consist of control variables that are common in the cross-country literature.

Estimation

Table 1 presents our initial elasticity estimates of equation (1). Regressing the log difference of poverty on the log difference of incomes gives us an elasticity estimate of −2.55, which is well in line with the values found in most of the existing literature. In column (2) we add the change in the Gini coefficient and find a significantly positive coefficient (increases in inequality leading to increases in poverty rates), as was found by Bourguignon (2003).

Our key purpose in this paper is to evaluate how the relationship between growth and poverty reduction is affected by government spending. Thus, it seems natural to include an interaction in this equation between the level of government expenditures as a percent of GDP and the change in incomes. A negative coefficient would indicate that increasing government expenditures would lower the income elasticity of poverty reduction. If the elasticity is negative, this would imply that higher government spending increases the sensitivity of poverty to incomes. We also introduce the expenditure variable in levels in this equation for two reasons: (a) to make sure that any estimated interaction is not simply capturing a levels effect, and (b) to test the hypothesis that higher levels of spending lead to faster poverty reduction, as in equation (3).

The result of this exercise is shown in column (3). The interaction between expenditures and the change in incomes is highly significant and in fact makes the coefficient on the change in incomes term insignificant. There is a moderate increase in explanatory power.[3] The estimates indicate that a low-spending country such as Argentina ($E = 0.16$) would have an income elasticity of poverty reduction of only −1.4, while a relatively high-spending country such as Tunisia ($E = 0.35$) would have one of −3.27. Figure 1 shows the partial association between the interaction term and poverty reduction, highlighting the fact that the relationship is not driven by outliers.

TABLE 1. Elasticity Estimates with Aggregate Expenditure Interactions

	Dependent variable: log change in poverty rate								Dependent variable: change in Gini coefficient			
	(1)	(2)	(3)	(4)	(5)	(6)	(7)	(8)	(9)	(10)	(11)	(12)
Change in log incomes	-2.5548 (0.3238)***	-2.5541 (0.2871)***	0.2618 (0.7103)	-5.1558 (1.4511)***	-4.2664 (1.4343)***	-4.8041 (0.6797)***	-4.8421 (0.6799)***	-5.0037 (1.0305)***	-1.1743 (1.4118)	-0.7834 (4.6109)	2.5367 (4.2384)	2.5574 (2.2808)
Change in Gini		0.0619 (0.0112)***	0.0555 (0.0145)***	0.0526 (0.0126)***	0.0405 (0.0116)***	-0.3167	-0.3187 (0.0615)***	-0.3403 (0.1005)***				
Expenditures/GDP			0.0948 (0.3889)	0.0359 (0.3582)	0.295 (0.3397)	0.2535 (0.3019)				0.8997 (3.7501)	2.0513 (4.2018)	2.1074 (4.2131)
Expenditures/GDP* change in log incomes			-10.2687 (2.9358)***	-4.6261 (2.6070)*	-5.3338 (2.2452)**					2.6507 (14.8046)	-3.728 (14.2356)	
Gini * change in log incomes				0.0985 (0.0255)***	0.0867 (0.0266)***							
Change in expenditures/GDP					-0.138 (0.6303)	10.3402 (3.5524)***	10.2914 (3.5853)***	11.349 (3.9863)***			0.6827 (6.6576)	18.4327 (29.2377)
Change in (expenditures/ GDP * log income)						-2.2053 (0.7472)***	-2.1878 (0.7489)***	-2.3486 (0.7782)***				-3.695 (6.0562)
Change in Gini * log income						0.0766 (0.0137)***	0.077 (0.0137)***	0.0812 (0.0209)***				
Constant	0.086 (0.0318)***	0.0608 (0.0253)**	0.0215 (0.0787)	0.0161 (0.0732)	-0.0517 (0.0696)	-0.0261 (0.0652)	0.0343 (0.0215)	0.0344 (0.0084)***	0.7005 (0.3361)**	0.5075 (1.0700)	-0.0343 (1.1754)	-0.0535 (1.1765)
Method	Random	Random	Random	Random	Random	Random	Random	Fixed	Random	Random	Random	Random
Number of observations	387	387	249	249	237	237	237	237	405	260	244	244
Number of countries	87	87	62	62	61	61	61	61	90	65	63	63
R^2	0.53	0.64	0.64	0.71	0.68	0.75	0.75	0.76	0	0	0.01	0.01

Source: Author's calculations.

Note: GDP, gross domestic product. Numbers in parentheses are robust standard errors.

* Significant at the 10 percent level.

** Significant at the 5 percent level.

*** Significant at the 1 percent level.

FIGURE 1.
Poverty Reduction and the Interaction between Growth and Government Expenditures

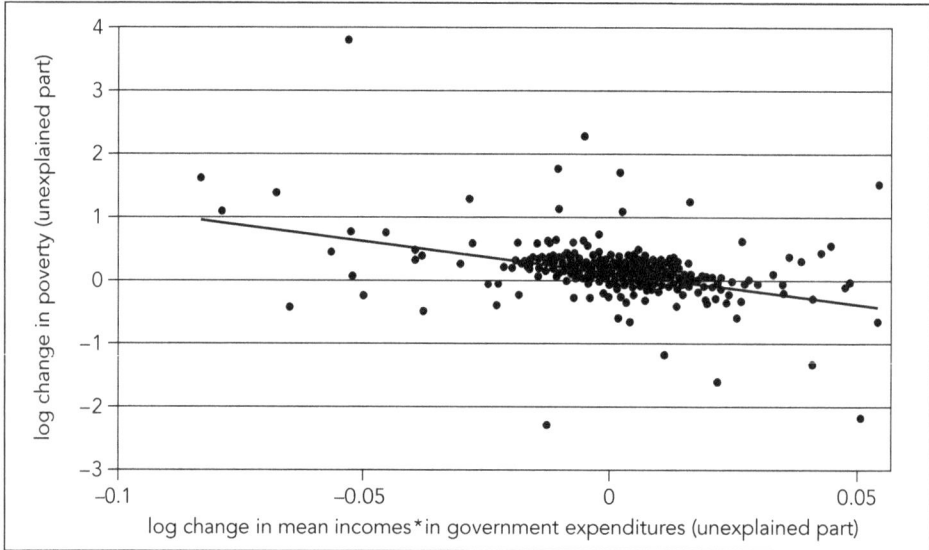

Source: Author's elaboration.

Note: Coefficient = −10.268702; standard error = 2.9358033; $t = 3.5$.

Does this mean that high government spending is unequivocally good for the poor? Not necessarily. What this result shows is that government spending will lead growth to translate into a faster rate of poverty reduction and thus make shared growth more likely. But the greater responsiveness of poverty to growth is a double-edged sword, as it also implies that poverty will increase more rapidly during an economic contraction. To continue with the above examples, Tunisia's high level of government spending has enabled it to share the benefits of its high growth more broadly, but the fact that poverty is less responsive to growth in Argentina has para-doxically diminished the increase in poverty that could result from that country's negative growth.

A reasonable alternative hypothesis is that exogenous reductions in poverty allow for the empowerment of poor individuals, thus permitting the generation of a polit-ical coalition that supports expansion of expenditure. The existence of such a chan-nel of causation could contaminate the estimates in table 1 and offer a reasonable alternative interpretation of the estimated relationship. Note, however, that it is more difficult—although certainly not impossible—to come up with a reverse causation story to account for the significance of the nonlinear interaction terms. Finding appropriate instruments for the composition of government expenditures in cross-national data that are exogenous and have no direct effect on poverty is a worthwhile yet daunting task that we will not attempt to carry out here. It is therefore important to keep in mind that the estimated relationship is best interpreted as an empirical association that may embody a causal effect.

Ravallion (1997) has suggested that high-inequality countries have a lower income elasticity of poverty reduction. This implies that there is an additional interaction between inequality and the change in incomes that is absent from our current specification, and it may be that the interaction between expenditures and income changes is really proxying for the inequality-growth interaction. In column (4), we introduce the interaction suggested by Ravallion and find that it is indeed significant. The expenditure-growth interaction does remain significant (at 10 percent), although the coefficient falls by more than half.

If the level of poverty depends on the level of spending, it may be more natural to expect that the change in poverty would depend on the change in spending levels, as in equation (8). Column (5) adds a term for the change in the ratio of expenditures to GDP. The term is not significant, although the significance of the expenditure-growth interaction increases somewhat. But remember also that equation (8) suggests that the correct specification corresponding to a theory of a multiplicative complementarity between income levels and expenditure would include a control for $\Delta(E_t y_t)$ and not just for $E_t \Delta y_t$. The same reasoning applies to the inequality-growth interaction: if poverty depends on $G_t y_t$, the change in poverty over time will depend on $\Delta G_t y_t$ and not just on $G_t \Delta y_t$. Column (6) corrects our specification to include both of these terms. They are now highly significant, as is the change in expenditures. The level of expenditures is insignificant and can be dropped with little consequence for the explanatory value of the model (column 7).

We adopt the equation in column (7)—which is simply equation (8)—as our preferred specification for the calculations below. We estimate it using a random-effects specification to make the fullest available use of limited data, but in fact the random-effects and fixed-effects specifications do not differ much, as is seen in column (8).

The effects of spending on poverty may not be limited, however, to those captured by the coefficients of this equation. As was pointed out in the preceding section, expenditure levels could also have a direct effect on inequality. Since equation (8) shows that the change in poverty depends on the change in inequality, one could reasonably expect expenditures to have an effect on inequality that would thus turn into an indirect effect on poverty. The last four columns of table 1 evaluate this hypothesis. Somewhat surprisingly, we find little evidence of an effect of government spending on inequality, whether through the level of spending, an interaction with growth, or the change in spending. We conclude that for the purposes of studying the effects of spending on poverty reduction, we may reasonably treat the evolution of inequality as given.

Although our results are interesting, they arise from the use of a very gross aggregate variable, the ratio of total government expenditures to GDP. One would expect the results of these exercises to vary considerably once one splits spending into its diverse categories. Intuitively, one might expect certain categories of spending to be very pro-poor and thus to have significant effects on the level of poverty. Thus, in table 2 we repeat the same exercise as in table 1 but now disaggregate spending into the five broad categories outlined above.

Using the more disaggregated category certainly has a cost in terms of data, cutting the number of countries in our baseline estimation from 87 to 35 and the number of

TABLE 2. Elasticity Estimates with Disaggregated Expenditure Interactions

	Dependent variable: log change in poverty rate						Dependent variable: change in Gini coefficient			
	(1)	(2)	(3)	(4)	(5)	(6)	(7)	(8)	(9)	(10)
Change in log incomes	−0.8773	−3.2761	−2.1459	−3.5593	−3.4353	−2.9958	−1.1743	−1.1566	6.8834	6.316
	(0.7232)	(1.5649)**	(1.7969)	(0.7669)***	(0.7831)***	(0.9343)***	(1.4118)	(6.7991)	(5.0768)*	(3.0361)**
Change in Gini	0.1001	0.0968	0.082	−0.1652	−0.1608	−0.1254				
	(0.0158)***	(0.0156)***	(0.0181)***	(0.0839)**	(0.0875)*	(0.1003)				
Core social expenditures	−0.8226	−0.8898	−2.4239	−0.8752				9.3114	−0.6791	4.6812
	(1.3363)	(1.3226)	(1.4292)*	(1.5285)				(12.8660)	(12.1725)	(13.4530)
Security expenditures	−0.8668	−0.9458	−0.2704	−2.4448				−0.3037	−2.2799	−12.9095
	(1.4169)	(1.4178)	(1.7455)	(2.4897)				(15.0925)	(16.3538)	(22.5874)
Noncore social expenditures	0.0358	0.1089	0.5009	0.4696				2.3957	4.5895	3.0914
	(0.5352)	(0.5044)	(0.5112)	(0.4319)				(4.2420)	(3.3404)	(3.4493)
Economic expenditures	0.494	0.0478	1.9214	1.7311				10.5237	4.5407	3.9804
	(2.0369)	(2.0479)	(1.7523)	(1.7131)				(12.4974)	(11.9018)	(11.7981)
General public services expenditures	0.0894	0.0074	−0.172	−0.3664				4.4134	3.47	2.4276
	(0.6475)	(0.6605)	(0.7522)	(0.6845)				(5.6415)	(5.2104)	(4.9211)
Core social * change in log incomes	1.9173	−3.6017	3.9135					76.742	88.0434	
	(7.9692)	(8.8173)	(10.1859)					(74.8895)	(62.6340)	
Security * change in log incomes	16.2709	20.3399	15.0488					−2.316	−49.2495	
	(6.1797)***	(6.3809)***	(8.7650)*					(72.1827)	(59.8871)	
Noncore social * change in log incomes	−16.5971	−12.5239	−16.855					8.1004	−32.9004	
	(4.1369)***	(5.4417)**	(6.2949)***					(31.7541)	(24.9727)	

	(1)	(2)	(3)	(4)	(5)	(6)	(7)	(8)
Economic * change in log incomes	−18.0479	−14.0308	−9.314				−85.8622	−48.8116
	(9.7402)*	(10.5009)	(8.7396)				(61.7035)	(57.6475)
General public services * change in log incomes	−13.25	−9.6335	−11.4674				22.2797	−17.2893
	(4.8565)***	(6.1762)	(6.2874)*				(35.4100)	(33.8482)
Gini * change in log incomes		0.0504	0.0258					
		(0.0271)*	(0.0273)					
Change in core social			1.8713	−17.4229	−16.9055	−16.5891	−7.6823	−264.9578
			(2.9534)	(21.2341)	(21.9875)	(25.0460)	(31.7128)	(156.5816)*
Change in security			1.905	−54.5502	−31.6595	−46.6339	26.7218	17.4727
			(4.0094)	(30.7477)*	(17.0442)*	(27.2844)*	(46.4360)	(331.9344)
Change in noncore social			−0.0252	55.5169	53.4657	59.0382	15.0017	170.4482
			(1.8189)	(14.3171)***	(13.7825)***	(17.6290)***	(22.9907)	(101.8455)*
Change in economic			−1.5441	57.8221	55.9247	80.8525	−19.7443	197.4234
			(1.6009)	(20.8527)***	(18.5307)***	(34.5515)**	(13.4343)	(124.6522)
Change in general public services			1.878	7.9887	7.5074	12.7277	6.1131	57.3078
			(1.0369)*	(13.8647)	(13.6307)	(17.1037)	(13.8169)	(88.7869)
Change in (log incomes * core social)				3.8214	3.5584	3.9026	49.9037	
				(4.1839)	(4.3603)	(4.6321)	(31.3756)	
Change in (log incomes * security)				10.0766	5.6142	8.4365	−0.2951	
				(5.8383)*	(3.4697)	(4.7707)*	(63.3242)	
Change in (log incomes * noncore social)				−10.6088	−10.2238	−11.3004	−30.8816	
				(2.6154)***	(2.5340)***	(3.2739)***	(18.7931)	
Change in (log incomes * economic)				−11.4232	−10.9861	−15.4307	−41.1765	
				(4.0530)***	(3.6386)***	(6.4208)**	(22.2285)*	

(continued)

429

TABLE 2. Elasticity Estimates with Disaggregated Expenditure Interactions (continued)

	Dependent variable: log change in poverty rate						Dependent variable: change in Gini coefficient			
	(1)	(2)	(3)	(4)	(5)	(6)	(7)	(8)	(9)	(10)
Change in (log incomes * general public services)				−1.3744 (2.6088)	−1.3385 (2.5512)	−2.2175 (3.1368)				−10.1701 (17.0372)
Change in (log incomes * Gini)				0.0467 (0.0172)***	0.0461 (0.0179)**	0.0392 (0.0205)*				
Constant	0.0711 (0.0877)	0.0846 (0.0855)	0.0395 (0.0871)	0.0302 (0.0736)	−0.0052 (0.0284)	−0.0025 (0.0334)	0.7005 (0.3361)**	−0.6489 (0.7489)	−0.4247 (0.6734)	−0.1771 (0.7008)
Method	Random	Random	Random	Random	Random	Fixed	Random	Random	Random	Random
Number of observations	153	153	140	140	140	140	405	164	147	147
Number of countries	35	35	33	33	33	33	90	38	35	35
R^2	0.85	0.85	0.85	0.85	0.85	0.86	0	0.04	0.16	0.17
Joint significance tests (p-values)										
Spending levels	0.90	0.84	0.62	0.75				0.30	0.76	0.92
Spending levels * change in log incomes	0.00	0.00	0.00							
Changes in spending levels			0.04	0.00	0.00	0.00		0.61	0.58	
Changes in (spending levels * log incomes)				0.00	0.00	0.00			0.39	0.22

Source: Author's calculations.

Note: Numbers in parentheses are robust standard errors.

* Significant at the 10 percent level.

** Significant at the 5 percent level.

*** Significant at the 1 percent level.

growth spells from 387 to 153. Nonetheless, our smaller sample still covers all the major developing regions. Included are 13 countries in Eastern Europe and Central Asia, 10 in Latin America, 5 in the Middle East and North Africa, 4 in East Asia, and 2 in South Asia. Lesotho is the only country in Sub-Saharan Africa remaining in the sample. Since the data maintain their breadth in coverage, we are confident that our results are not purely attributable to any regional effects.

As with our results in table 1, we do not find effects of the level of spending on poverty reduction in columns (1)–(4). Indeed, the joint significance tests for the levels variables have very high p-values (0.62–0.90), indicating that these variables contribute almost nothing to the regressions. The interactions between spending levels and changes in income, however, are jointly highly significant in all specifications, regardless of whether we include the level of spending multiplied by the time difference of spending (columns 1–3) or the more appropriate time difference in the product of income and spending levels (columns 4–6). We also find that the changes in spending levels are jointly highly significant in all specifications in which they enter (columns 3–6).

Let us consider our preferred specification. Somewhat surprisingly, the change in core social spending is not significantly related to poverty reduction or to the income elasticity. This is unexpected because the categories that make up this spending are often seen as highly pro-poor. The signs of the coefficients do indicate that an increase in core social spending reduces the poverty rate, while it diminishes the sensitivity of poverty to growth. Spending on security, by contrast, does appear to reduce poverty significantly while at the same time making poverty less responsive to income changes. (Both effects are significant at the 10 percent level.) This is a striking result even if it is only borderline significant, as it is often assumed that security expenditures are highly regressive; the finding surely merits greater exploration. But a great part of the action comes from the effects of noncore social spending and economic spending. Both of these increase the level of poverty but also increase the sensitivity of poverty to growth. (All effects for these two variables are significant at 1 percent.) Spending on general public services has an insignificant and numerically small effect on the change in poverty, both directly and through the multiplicative interaction. Also consistent with the results of table 1, we find no evidence of significant effects of spending on change in inequality, suggesting that we can treat the evolution of inequality as given.

Construction of Indicator

To interpret these effects more carefully, recall that, as we showed in equations (5) and (8), our preferred specifications have a representation in levels, which can be expressed succinctly as:

$$p_t = c + \alpha_1 t + \alpha_2 y_t + \alpha_3 G_t + \alpha_{41} E_{t11} + \cdots + \alpha_{4n} E_{tn} + \alpha_{11} E_{t11} y_t + \cdots + \alpha_{5n} E_{tn} y_t, \quad (9)$$

so that the effect of a particular category of spending on the level of poverty is given by:

$$\frac{dp_t}{dE_{ti}} = \alpha_{4i} + \alpha_{5i} y_t < 0.$$

In the case of core social and security spending, where $\alpha_{5i} > 0$, this implies:

$$-\frac{\alpha_{4i}}{\alpha_{5i}} > y_t.$$

For both categories, the threshold levels of log income correspond, respectively, to monthly incomes of US\$116 and US\$281 (in 1993 PPP-adjusted dollars). Thus, core social spending is pro-poor only in the poorest 44.9 percent of countries, while security is pro-poor in the poorest 86.7 percent of countries. Note, however, that only the coefficient on security spending is estimated with a reasonable degree of precision, so that the other estimate must be interpreted with caution.

In the case of the remaining three categories—noncore social, economic, and general public services spending—a similar logic shows that they will be pro-poor only when:

$$-\frac{\alpha_{4i}}{\alpha_{5i}} < y_t.$$

For these three categories, the threshold levels of income correspond to US\$187, US\$162, and US\$273, or, respectively, the richest 32.7, 37.8, and 13.3 percent of countries. The coefficient of general public services spending, however, is not significant and should be interpreted cautiously.

Using these coefficients, we can now go on to evaluate the appropriateness of fiscal policies in different countries by estimating the contribution that government spending makes to poverty reduction. Applying equation (9), we can calculate the contribution of government expenditure to poverty reduction as the difference between the predicted level of poverty given the country's level of expenditure and the predicted level of poverty that the model would yield if all its expenditure values were set to zero:

$$\Delta\hat{p}_t = \Delta\hat{p}_t - \Delta d\hat{p}_t|_{E_{t1}} \cdots {}_{=E_{tn}=0} = \alpha_{41}E_{t1} + \cdots + \alpha_{4n}E_{tn} + \alpha_{51}E_{t1}y_t + \cdots + \alpha_{5n}E_{tn}y_t.$$

(10)

Table 3 shows the result of this exercise, which we have carried out using both the results of table 1 (aggregate expenditures) and those of table 2 (disaggregated expenditures). The former has the advantage of being available for a larger number of countries, while the latter has the benefit of using the full information on spending on diverse categories. Fortunately, we find that the correlation between the two indexes is reasonably high (0.76). Figure 2 illustrates how, although some differences exist, both indexes seem to be telling a consistent story.

Although the results shown in table 3 are not unexpected, there are some surprises. The countries with the highest amounts of poverty reduction attributable to fiscal policy tend to be in Eastern Europe. To a large extent, this is a result of these countries' high levels of government expenditure, coupled with the fact that they are relatively wealthy (among developing nations) and spend significantly on the types of expenditure that are good for relatively rich countries, such as social security. Indeed, the estimates suggest that for Slovenia, government expenditures lowered the level of

TABLE 3. Poverty Reduction Impact of Expenditures, by Country, Average 1977–2005

Country	Aggregate expenditures	Disaggregated expenditures	Country	Aggregate expenditures	Disaggregated expenditures
Slovenia	1.2886	1.7656	Georgia	0.1099	−0.0276
Czech Republic	0.8960	0.6049	Guatemala	0.0465	
Hungary	0.8399	0.7725	Thailand	0.0455	−0.0626
Slovak Republic	0.7972	0.4698	Honduras	0.0401	
Uruguay	0.7969	1.4173	Ukraine	−0.0386	−0.9320
Croatia	0.7616	0.6486	Philippines	−0.0554	
Poland	0.6355	0.6160	Moldova	−0.0665	−0.9410
Panama	0.5869	0.0931	Botswana	−0.0778	
Brazil	0.5811	0.8151	Vietnam	−0.1050	
Bulgaria	0.5425	0.3288	Côte d'Ivoire	−0.1128	
Chile	0.5249	0.4398	Lesotho	−0.1148	−0.5922
Belarus	0.5200	0.4417	Azerbaijan	−0.1216	−0.2316
Jordan	0.4867		Haiti	−0.1391	
Namibia	0.4798		Cameroon	−0.1411	
Malaysia	0.4687	0.2694	Bangladesh	−0.1452	
Tunisia	0.4500	0.1097	Sri Lanka	−0.1458	−0.9879
Iran, Islamic Rep. of	0.4090	0.2105	Egypt, Arab Rep. of	−0.1507	−0.4199
Estonia	0.4076	0.0929	Kenya	−0.1551	
Colombia	0.3715		Indonesia	−0.1796	−0.4030
Latvia	0.3558	0.0522	Nepal	−0.1819	
Argentina	0.3542	0.5404	India	−0.2115	
Trinidad and Tobago	0.3532	−0.0614	Sierra Leone	−0.2259	
Turkey	0.3286	−0.0134	Mongolia	−0.2316	−0.9227
Morocco	0.3109	0.0566	Burkina Faso	−0.2744	
Romania	0.3091	0.0057	Ghana	−0.3058	
Costa Rica	0.2801	0.0114	Pakistan	−0.3404	0.7553
Algeria	0.2679		Madagascar	−0.3545	
Dominican Republic	0.2396	0.1337	Gambia, The	−0.3715	
Venezuela, R.B. de	0.2373	−0.1187	Rwanda	−0.3777	
Lithuania	0.2021	−0.2044	Nicaragua	−0.3883	−0.5844
Paraguay	0.1861		Nigeria	−0.4221	
Albania	0.1735	−0.2490	Mali	−0.4445	
Bolivia	0.1709	−0.1381	Swaziland	−0.5302	
Yemen, Republic of	−0.0004		Uganda	−0.5649	
Peru	0.1661		Burundi	−0.6152	−1.1004
Kazakhstan	0.1541	−0.2005	Zambia	−0.8489	

Source: Author's calculations.

poverty by a whopping 129 log points. In contrast, in almost half of the sample we find that government expenditures do not contribute to poverty reduction.[4]

Although the most pro-poor countries tend to be in Eastern Europe, while the less pro-poor tend to be in Africa, there are some notable exceptions. Uruguay, Panama, and Brazil are among the 10 countries with most pro-poor fiscal policies, while

FIGURE 2.
Correlation between Pro-Poor Spending Indicators

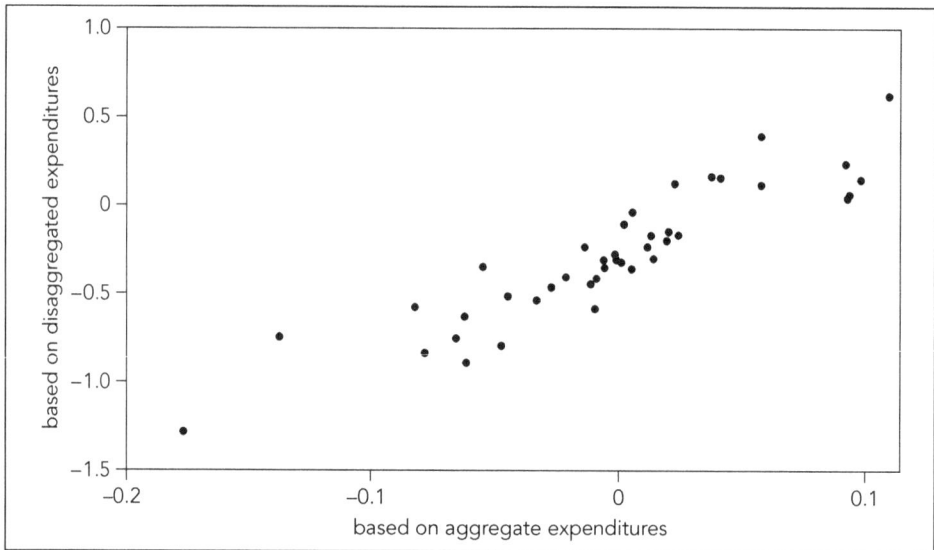

Source: Author's elaboration.

another Latin American country, Nicaragua, is in the bottom 10. Somewhat surprisingly, Indonesia and India rank 55th and 57th, respectively, out of 72 countries, indicating that they have scope for substantial improvements in poverty through a reorganization of fiscal priorities.

Determinants of Pro-Poor Spending

What makes some countries embrace pro-poor fiscal policies while others do not? Although it is difficult to give a complete answer to this question, given the constraints of cross-country data work, our results allow us to study the correlates of pro-poor spending and to examine the patterns arising in cross-national correlations and their consistency with different political theories of government spending. In tables 4 and 5, we present a set of panel regressions evaluating these predictions.

Perhaps one of the best-established theories of government spending hypothesizes that the size of government grows with the level of income (Wagner 1890). We consistently find that income level is a strong explanator of pro-poor spending, with the coefficient significant at 1 percent in all the specifications shown in tables 4 and 5. We also find a strong correlation between the trade-to-GDP ratio and pro-poor spending. The sign of the association, however, differs from that suggested by Rodrik (1998): whereas he hypothesized that the demand for social insurance would grow with openness, we find that increases in the trade-to-GDP ratio are associated with

TABLE 4. Determinants of Pro-Poor Policies, Random-Effects Regressions

(dependent variable: expected decline in poverty attributable to spending policies)

	(1)	(2)	(3)	(4)	(5)	(6)	(7)	(8)	(9)	(10)	(11)	(12)	(13)	(14)	(15)
Mean income	−0.5507 (0.0272)***	−0.5566 (0.0286)***	−0.5331 (0.0268)***	−0.5324 (0.0258)***	−0.552 (0.0335)***	−0.5337 (0.0257)***	−0.4812 (0.0310)***	−0.492 (0.0293)***	−0.4779 (0.0308)***	−0.4901 (0.0293)***	−0.5281 (0.0242)***	−0.5184 (0.0282)***	−0.4862 (0.0280)***	−0.5396 (0.0289)***	−0.5468 (0.0287)***
Trade/GDP	0.0009 (0.0003)***	0.0009 (0.0003)***	0.0011 (0.0003)***	0.001 (0.0003)***	0.001 (0.0003)***	0.001 (0.0003)***	0.0014 (0.0003)***	0.0014 (0.0003)***	0.0015 (0.0004)***	0.0014 (0.0003)***	0.0011 (0.0003)***	0.0012 (0.0003)***	0.0012 (0.0003)***	0.0014 (0.0003)***	0.0011 (0.0003)***
Liquid liabilities/GDP			−0.0007 (0.0004)*	−0.0007 (0.0003)**	−0.0007 (0.0004)*	−0.0007 (0.0004)*	−0.0007 (0.0004)*	−0.0007 (0.0004)*	−0.0007 (0.0004)*	−0.0007 (0.0004)*	−0.0007 (0.0004)**	−0.0009 (0.0004)**	−0.0006 (0.0004)	−0.001 (0.0004)**	−0.0011 (0.0004)**
Gini coefficient				0.0031 (0.0014)**	0.0031 (0.0013)**	0.0029 (0.0013)**	0.0022 (0.0017)	0.0021 (0.0017)	0.0023 (0.0019)	0.0023 (0.0018)	0.0028 (0.0013)**	0.0022 (0.0014)	0.0015 (0.0016)	0.0002 (0.0013)	0.0001 (0.0012)
Percent of urban population					0.0013 (0.0008)										
Democracy (polity)						0.0013 (0.0008)									
Economic freedom							0.0434 (0.0364)								
Executive constraints								0.003 (0.0080)							
Expropriation risk									−0.0197 (0.0166)						
Degree of capitalism										−0.0056 (0.0157)					

(continued)

TABLE 4. Determinants of Pro-Poor Policies, Random-Effects Regressions (*continued*)

(dependent variable: expected decline in poverty attributable to spending policies)

	(1)	(2)	(3)	(4)	(5)	(6)	(7)	(8)	(9)	(10)	(11)	(12)	(13)	(14)	(15)
Ethnolinguistic fractionalization											0.0532 (0.0548)				
Percent of population over age 65												−0.0135 (0.0079)*			
Percent of population under age 15												−0.0024 (0.0035)			
Primary exports as percent of GDP													0.2456 (0.0912)***		
Latin America and the Caribbean														0.0608 (0.0425)	0.0508 (0.0428)
Africa														−0.0699 (0.0539)	−0.0796 (0.0552)
Asia														−0.0496 (0.0487)	−0.0605 (0.0506)
East Asia and Pacific														−0.0301 (0.0411)	−0.0235 (0.0387)

	(1)	(2)	(3)	(4)	(5)	(6)	(7)	(8)	(9)	(10)	(11)	(12)	(13)	(14)
Eastern Europe													−0.1603 (0.0494)***	−0.165 (0.0489)***
1980s														0.0691 (0.0163)***
1990s														0.1178 (0.0142)***
2000–2008														0.13 (0.0183)***
Constant	2.5405 (0.1300)***	2.4005 (0.1211)***	2.2733 (0.1080)***	2.3107 (0.1173)***	2.2949 (0.1123)***	1.9227 (0.2211)***	2.1098 (0.1107)***	2.1669 (0.1475)***	2.1194 (0.1154)***	2.2366 (0.1052)***	2.4037 (0.2084)***	1.9265 (0.1143)***	2.4592 (0.1293)***	2.4233 (0.1274)***
Number of observations	317	311	309	309	302	239	239	228	239	309	309	235	309	309
Number of countries	73	73	73	73	72	53	53	48	53	73	73	51	73	73

Source: Author's calculations.

Note: GDP, gross domestic product. Numbers in parentheses are robust standard errors.

* Significant at the 10 percent level.

** Significant at the 5 percent level.

*** Significant at the 1 percent level.

TABLE 5. Determinants of Pro-Poor Policies, Fixed-Effects Regressions
(dependent variable: expected decline in poverty attributable to spending policies)

	(1)	(2)	(3)	(4)	(5)	(6)	(7)	(8)
Mean income	−0.5931	−0.5917	−0.5378	−0.5376	−0.5416	−0.5347	−0.5315	−0.5523
	(0.0717)***	(0.0675)***	(0.0531)***	(0.0535)***	(0.0524)***	(0.0514)***	(0.0541)***	(0.0516)***
Trade/GDP		0.0019	0.0021	0.0021	0.002	0.0019	0.0021	0.0017
		(0.0007)***	(0.0007)***	(0.0007)***	(0.0008)***	(0.0006)***	(0.0007)***	(0.0007)**
Liquid liabilities/GDP			−0.0008	−0.0008	−0.0008	−0.0008	−0.0007	−0.0009
			(0.0005)	(0.0005)	(0.0005)	(0.0006)	(0.0005)	(0.0006)
Gini coefficient				−0.0009	−0.001	−0.0011	−0.0016	−0.0011
				(0.0015)	(0.0014)	(0.0015)	(0.0015)	(0.0014)
Urban population as percent of total					0.0012			
					(0.0024)			
Democracy (polity)						0.0013		
						(0.0006)**		
Percent of population over age 65							0.0408	
							(0.0236)*	
Percent of population under age 15							0.0082	
							(0.0062)	
1980s								0.0722
								(0.0145)***
1990s								0.1074
								(0.0133)***
2000s								0.1146
								(0.0225)***
Constant	2.7614	2.6159	2.3737	2.4101	2.3793	2.4134	1.8719	2.4204
	(0.3536)***	(0.3122)***	(0.2383)***	(0.2375)***	(0.2557)***	(0.2382)***	(0.4439)***	(0.2228)***
Observations	317	311	309	309	309	302	309	309
Number of countries	73	73	73	73	73	72	73	73
R^2	0.61	0.64	0.64	0.64	0.64	0.64	0.65	0.65

Source: Author's calculations.

Note: GDP, gross domestic product. Numbers in parentheses are robust standard errors.

* Significant at the 10 percent level.   ** Significant at the 5 percent level.   *** Significant at the 1 percent level.

lower levels of pro-poor spending. In column (3) we add a measure of financial development, capturing the idea that there may be complementarities between the action of the public sector to help the poor and the availability of well-functioning credit markets. Here, indeed, we do find that the level of financial development is associated with poverty reduction, although the coefficient is generally significant only at 10 percent. In column (4) we introduce one of the classic explanatory variables: median-voter theories of politics predict a positive association between inequality and redistribution (Meltzer and Richard 1981). In contrast, we find a negative association between inequality and pro-poor spending, in line with the predictions of Bénabou (1996, 2005) and Rodríguez (2004).

A number of variables that are commonly used in the political-economy literature appear not to enter significantly. One could expect that more urbanized economies would have more extensive working-class organizations and would thus be able to pressure for more pro-poor spending, but this prediction is not borne out in our data. Similarly, median-voter theories tend to predict that democracy should be associated with more redistribution (Boix 2003), but we fail to find an effect. Nor do we find an association between our measure of pro-poor spending and institutional measures such as the degree of economic freedom, executive constraints, the degree of capitalism, expropriation risk, or ethnolinguistic fractionalization. We do find some weak evidence that the age composition of the population is associated with pro-poor spending, with older populations spending less on redistribution. We also find somewhat stronger evidence of an association between the share of primary exports in GDP and redistribution, although other controls for resource abundance (not shown) do not deliver consistent results. Our last two columns show that the inequality effect seems to disappear once we control for regional dummies, although the openness, financial development, and income effects survive. We find that Eastern European countries, after taking into account their level of income, openness, financial depth, and inequality, exhibit higher levels of redistribution than other countries. (The omitted region is the Middle East and North Africa.) Our last column shows that the degree of progressivity of spending appears to be declining over time (the omitted period is the 1970s). Table 5 shows that similar results are present in fixed-effects regressions (although some of the variables in table 4 are time invariant and thus drop out of this specification), but the only effects that seem to consistently survive are the income and openness effects.

Conclusions

This paper has explored the determinants of pro-poor spending. In contrast to other works, which assume a priori that some types of expenditures are pro-poor and others are not, we empirically derive our measure of progressivity of spending from the empirical identification of the effect of different fiscal policies on the poor. Our specification takes into account the fact that the level of expenditures should not just affect poverty but should also influence the responsiveness of poverty to growth, thereby affecting the extent to which growth is shared. Our results show that the optimal mix of polices will depend on a country's level of income and that certain policies that protect the poor under some conditions (e.g., high economic growth) may end up being harmful to the poor if those conditions change. Some of our results are close to what one would reasonably expect. Social spending is beneficial to the poor in the poorest countries, while noncore social spending such as social security and recreation seems to benefit the poor only in countries that are well above the average level of income. However, we also find the association between core social spending and poverty to be statistically weak, an effect that is surprising and that may reflect the need for further examination of subdivisions of this category. (For example, spending on higher education, which is included, is rarely pro-poor.) The fact that some of the results do not accord with received notions about the progressivity of expenditure categories suggests that it is necessary to explore further the microeconomic evidence on the links between these categories and poverty reduction.

We find that Eastern European countries tend to be following the most pro-poor strategies. Being relatively rich, they can redistribute using mechanisms such as social security systems, to which they indeed devote significant resources. We find that the mix of government expenditures in African countries tends to be detrimental to the welfare of the poor. Countries such as Brazil, Panama, and Uruguay are strong performers in terms of poverty reduction, but other countries whose poverty reduction record is generally considered strong, such as India and Indonesia, do not come out well in our indicator.

Our indicator also provides new evidence as to the necessary political conditions for sharing growth. We find that richer countries tend to be more pro-poor, even though the poor make up a smaller group of the population in these countries. We also find that openness and inequality are negatively associated with pro-poor policies, contrary to the conventional wisdom. Financial development, by contrast, seems to be positively correlated with pro-poor fiscal policies.

Notes

1. This is simply a consequence of Young's theorem, which states that for any twice differentiable function $f(x, y)$, it must be that $f_{xy} = f_{yx}$.
2. If the poverty rate is a nonlinear function of y, then the average effect in equation (7) of y_t may be very different from the marginal effect of an increment in y, and policy makers may be much more interested in the latter than in the former.
3. If we run the same regression as in column (2) but restrict it to the sample in column (3), we get an R^2 of 0.58, so that adding in the level and interaction expression increases the R^2 by 0.06.
4. This does not mean that they should be zero. As we saw above, there are always some types of expenditure that will be poverty reducing even for very poor countries.

References

Acemoglu, Daron, and James Robinson. 2006. *Economic Origins of Dictatorship and Democracy.* Cambridge, U.K.: Cambridge University Press.

Alesina, Alberto, and Dani Rodrik. 1994. "Distributive Politics and Economic Growth." *Quarterly Journal of Economics* 109 (2, May): 465–90.

Bénabou, Roland. 1996. "Inequality and Growth." *NBER Macroeconomics Annual,* ed. Ben S. Bernanke and Julio J. Rotemberg, 11–92. Cambridge, MA: National Bureau of Economic Research.

———. 2005. "Inequality, Technology and the Social Contract." In *Handbook of Economic Growth,* ed. Philippe Aghion and Steven Durlauf, vol. 1, 1595–1638. Amsterdam: North-Holland.

Boix, Carles. 2003. *Democracy and Redistribution.* Cambridge, U.K.: Cambridge University Press.

Bourguignon, Francois. 2003. "The Growth Elasticity of Poverty Reduction: Explaining Heterogeneity across Countries and Time Periods." In *Inequality and Growth: Theory and Policy Implications,* ed. Theo S. Eicher and Stephen J. Turnovsky. Cambridge, MA: MIT Press.

Galor, Oded, and Joseph Zeira. 1993. "Income Distribution and Macroeconomics." *Review of Economic Studies* 60 (1): 35–52.

IMF (International Monetary Fund). 2006a. "Government Finance Statistics Database and Browser." CD-ROM. International Monetary Fund, Washington, DC.

———. 2006b. "Historical Government Finance Statistics Database and Browser." CD-ROM. International Monetary Fund, Washington, DC.

———. 2006c. "International Financial Statistics Database." International Monetary Fund, Washington, DC.

Kraay, Aart. 2004. "When Is Growth Pro-Poor? Cross-Country Evidence." IMF Working Paper 04/47, International Monetary Fund, Washington, DC.

Meltzer, Allan, and Scott Richard. 1981. "A Rational Theory of the Size of Government." *Journal of Political Economy* 89: 914–27.

Persson, Torsten, and Guido Tabellini. 1994. "Is Inequality Harmful for Growth?" *American Economic Review* 84 (3, June): 600–21.

Ravallion, Martin. 1997. "Can High Inequality Developing Countries Escape Absolute Poverty?" *Economics Letters* 56 (1): 51–57.

Rodríguez, Francisco. 2004. "Inequality, Redistribution, and Rent-Seeking." *Economics and Politics* 16 (3, November): 287–320.

Rodrik, Dani. 1998. "Why Do More Open Economies Have Bigger Governments?" *Journal of Political Economy* 106 (5): 997–1032.

Shelton, Cameron A. 2007. "The Size and Composition of Government Expenditure." *Journal of Public Economics* 91 (11–12): 2230–60.

Wagner, Adolph. 1890. *Finanzwissenschaft.* Leipzig.

Wickens, Tobias. 2002. *Classification of GFSM 1986 Data to the GFSM 2001 Framework.* Washington, DC: International Monetary Fund.

The Political Economy of Public Service Provision in South Asia

LAKSHMI IYER

Access to education and health facilities varies considerably across the countries and regions of South Asia. This paper surveys the theoretical and empirical literature on collective action and public goods provision. The role of group influence, heterogeneity within groups, and group size is explored in detail. The paper then discusses the impact of committed leaders on public goods provision, together with the factors involved in sustaining that impact, and examines how these insights can be applied in analyzing issues related to the quality of public goods provision. The growing role of the private sector in providing basic education services in South Asia is briefly surveyed.

Basic health and education remain remarkably scarce in developing countries. In 2007 more than one-third of the children in developing countries were not enrolled in school, and a quarter of the children were not immunized. South Asia lagged behind the developing-country average, with a combined gross enrollment ratio of 60 percent and an immunization rate of 65 percent (UNDP 2007, tables 1 and 6). The situation varies by country—primary school enrollment rates in South Asia range from 97 percent in Sri Lanka to 68 percent in Pakistan—and considerable regional differences exist within countries. In India nearly every village in Kerala State has access to a school, but only 39 percent of villages in Bihar do. In 2005, 57 percent of children in Pakistan's Punjab Province were enrolled in primary school; the figure for Balochistan was 34 percent. Rates of full immunization varied from 76 percent in Punjab to 48 percent in Balochistan (Pakistan 2007). In Nepal access to schools is tenfold better in the best districts than in the worst. (See Banerjee, Iyer, and Somanathan 2008 for a broader range of within-country comparisons of the availability of public goods.) By contrast, Sri Lanka presents a case of relative equality in

Lakshmi Iyer is an assistant professor of business administration at the Harvard Business School. The author thanks Shanta Devarajan, Asim Khwaja, Karthik Muralidharan, and participants at the ABCDE, Cape Town, for helpful comments and suggestions.

Annual World Bank Conference on Development Economics 2009, Global
© 2010 The International Bank for Reconstruction and Development / The World Bank

educational attainment: the fraction of the population completing secondary school varies across districts from 35 to 41 percent (Sri Lanka 2006, table 14.2b).

We should note that simply providing access to a school or enrolling a child in school is not enough to ensure an educated population. The quality of the services provided at these physical facilities is quite low in many South Asian countries and regions. A nationally representative survey found that 25 percent of primary school teachers in India and 16 percent of those in Bangladesh are likely to be absent on any given day and that 40 percent of health workers in India and 35 percent of those in Bangladesh are likely to be absent (Chaudhury et al. 2006). In Pakistan a detailed study of schools in Punjab found that teachers in government schools are absent approximately four days a month and that by the end of the third class (grade), just over 50 percent of children had mastered the mathematics curriculum for class 1 (Andrabi et al. 2007). The quality of service provision also varies considerably within countries: teacher absenteeism in India ranges from 15 percent in Maharashtra to 42 percent in Jharkhand (Kremer et al. 2005, table 2).

Interestingly, the quality of service provision appears to be correlated with physical access. For instance, states in India where fewer villages have access to schools have worse rates of teacher attendance (figure 1). Furthermore, the variation in physical access to health and education facilities is not simply a matter of different preferences; data from India again show that the same places have worse access to both health and education facilities (figure 2). In all South Asian countries, governments

FIGURE 1.
Quality and Quantity of Education Services across Indian States

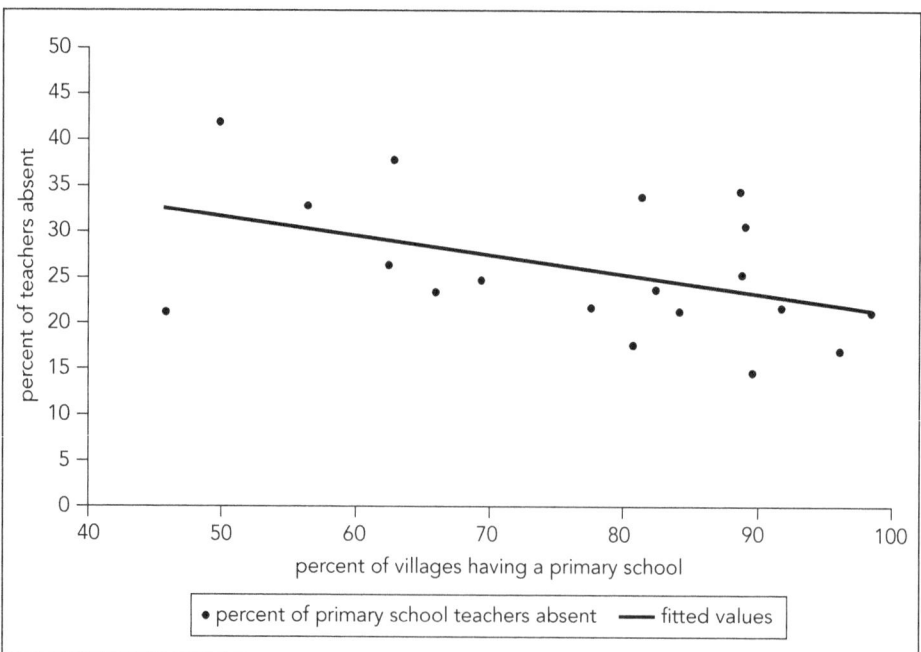

Source: India 2001; Kremer et al. 2005.

Note: Dots represent individual states.

FIGURE 2.
Access to Health and Educational Facilities across Indian States

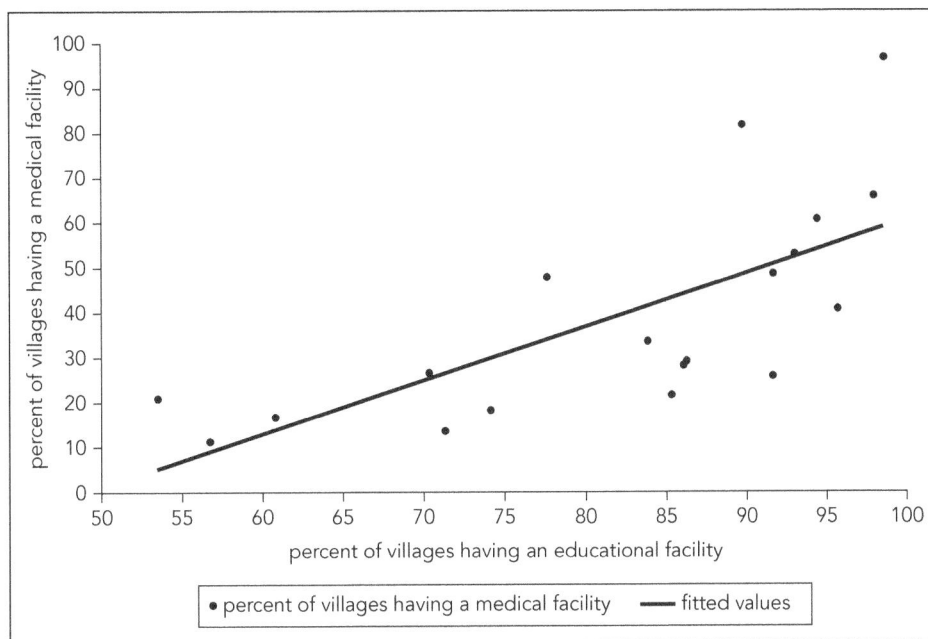

Source: India 2001.

Note: Dots represent individual states.

have the primary responsibility for providing these services to their citizens. Why, then, are some regions relatively more successful in obtaining these services for their residents, while other areas within the same country lag behind?

In this paper, I review theoretical models of physical public goods provision, as well as the empirical evidence for the channels hypothesized in this literature. Most of these models focus on the physical provision of health and education facilities. I consider two classes of explanations: "bottom-up" accounts that concentrate on the ability of local communities to successfully obtain public goods from the state, and "top-down" factors emphasizing unilateral policy interventions undertaken by committed leaders. In this sense, I abstract away from the policy maker–provider relationship discussed in detail in *World Development Report 2004* (World Bank 2004), subsuming the provider-type decision under the second class of factors. The analysis in this paper can be applied both to the relationship between citizens and service providers and to the relationship between citizens and policy makers, as long as the electoral process does not automatically result in better service provision. The analysis takes a purely positive point of view; that is, it describes which factors matter in practice rather than attempting to suggest specific types of public service delivery for specific contexts.

I then consider whether similar factors can explain the variations in the quality of public goods, highlighting some recent field experiments aimed at improving health and education outcomes. In the final section, I turn to the issue of whether purely private provision of these goods can be the solution to failures of public provision.

Theories of Collective Action

Citizens in South Asia value education and health services. The *Public Report on Basic Education in India* (PROBE Team 1999) surveyed parents in the four states of India with the lowest enrollment ratios. Virtually all parents (98 percent) felt that it was important for a boy to be educated, and 89 percent of parents also felt that it was important for a girl to be educated. A survey of 10,000 voters in 1996 revealed that public amenities were listed as the "main problem faced by people like you" by one-fifth of the respondents—the second biggest concern after poverty (Center for the Study of Developing Societies 1996). Surveys in Pakistan confirm that parents care deeply about their children's education (Andrabi et al. 2007, 6). Why do some communities manage to articulate these demands well enough to obtain these public services from the state, while others do not succeed in doing so?

The standard model of public goods provision assumes that the provision of a public good depends on the total effort exerted by all the individuals in a group but that an individual's costs of participating in group activities are privately incurred. This model has been traditionally applied to the analysis of the provision of local schools or health facilities funded by local taxes. In such cases, the benefit is having a local school for the children, and the private cost is the tax paid to obtain it.

This model is also appropriate where such infrastructure is financed by the government but local communities have to coordinate to extract resources from the state and to make sure these resources are then used to build the relevant infrastructure. The benefit is, again, the building of a local school, and the private cost is the cost of participating in community actions such as organizing local meetings, writing to state officials, monitoring the spending of local funds, meeting with the local elected representative, and publicizing the activities of state officials.[1] Such efforts are necessary because the electoral process may not automatically result in better access to health and education. Keefer and Khemani (2005) survey three major sources of political market imperfections: lack of information among voters about the performance of politicians; lack of credibility of political promises to citizens; and social polarization that leads to resources being targeted toward specific social groups. The evidence from several countries shows that there is at most a weak link between expenditures on public services and the actual level of services received by the local community (World Bank 2004, 35–38), suggesting that "public goods" such as information gathering and monitoring are underprovided at the local level.

In this theoretical framework, individuals in a community first decide on the level of effort (or the costs) they would be willing to incur toward getting a local school. The probability of obtaining the school depends on the overall effort mobilized by the community relative to a preset threshold (in the local financing model) or relative to the effort mobilized by other communities (in a setting in which several communities are competing for limited state resources). Undertaking individual effort is costly and entails rising marginal costs for the agent. Each person in the group makes his or her choice independent of the others, and therefore there is an incentive to free ride on other people's effort. For instance, if I expect others in my community to bear the fixed cost of setting up a school, I have every incentive to contribute zero effort or cost toward the project.

This simple framework generates several comparative statics predictions for the impact of community characteristics on the provision of education and health facilities. The main implications involve the role of group influence, heterogeneity within groups, and group size.

Group Influence

Communities that are inherently more powerful in demanding public goods are more likely to get them. This difference in political influence usually arises because certain groups have historically been advantaged in terms of income or political connections. Examples of such privileged groups include whites in South Africa during the apartheid years, high castes in India through most of its history, and large landowners in Brazil. A corollary is that institutional changes which increase the political influence of certain groups should result in members of that group having greater access to public goods.

Heterogeneity within Groups

The theory generates ambiguous predictions, depending on the type of heterogeneity that is present within the group. First, members of a group might have heterogeneous preferences concerning the type or nature of the public good, depending on their demographic or locational characteristics. In the local school example, one can easily imagine individuals within a community having considerably different preferences about the provision of a primary versus a high school (depending on the age of the individual's child); choice of the language of instruction; whether the school should provide a school bus (which would depend on the location of the individual's residence); whether the students should have school uniforms; the length of the school day; and other details of the curriculum. The theory implies that groups with very heterogeneous preferences concerning public goods will typically make lower individual contributions toward those public goods.

If land and labor markets are well functioning, rational economic behavior would imply that households would migrate to form more homogeneous communities where all members share the same tastes concerning public good provision. This is the insight of a classic paper implying that citizens have the option to "vote with their feet" to obtain better public goods (Tiebout 1956). Such migration results in better provision of public goods through two channels. First, it generates competition across jurisdictions to retain residents and hence creates better incentives for local governments. Second, free riding is likely to be minimized in a completely homogenous community, since each resident has migrated to a community that provides his or her desired level or type of public good.

In most developing countries, migration rates are typically low, and hence we do not expect the Tiebout mechanism to be a significant channel for obtaining public goods. Migration rates in South Asia are particularly low: the Indian census of 2001 reveals that 96 percent of India's people live in the state of their birth.[2] Some reasons for these extremely low migration rates may be differences in language and culture across state boundaries, the costs involved in leaving established social networks, the relative paucity of infrastructure such as roads, and dysfunctional land markets that might make it difficult to buy or sell property.

A second type of heterogeneity could lie in the benefits the public good confers on residents. For instance, farmers with large plots of land have more to gain from an irrigation canal; families with several children have more to gain from a local public school than single-child families; and people with preexisting medical conditions might derive more benefit from a local health center. In many cases the rich will have less to gain from public provision of education and health, since they are the ones who can best access private provision of such services. Analyzing the theoretical implications of such inequality can become quite complicated, especially if a private "exit option" is available to some households (see, among others, Bardhan, Ghatak, and Karaivanov 2007; Das and Khwaja 2005). Greater inequality of benefits can make people less likely to contribute toward a public good, but this effect can be reversed at high levels of inequality: if one person expects to gain almost all the benefits (e.g., if there is only one farmer in the whole area), he will be motivated to bear the whole cost.

Third, a group can be socially heterogeneous in terms of religion, language, caste, or ethnicity, and this can lead to differences in preferences concerning public goods. (For example, each person may want the medium of instruction in the school to be his or her mother tongue.) It can also lead directly to less effective collective action because of increased communication costs across social categories, less trust, or a lower degree of altruism toward members of a different social category. Conversely, socially homogeneous groups may also be able to monitor their members' contributions toward the public good and use social sanctions to achieve high contributions. Channels such as these predict worse outcomes when society is divided into several different social groups. An alternative possibility is that social tensions are maximized when there are two large groups rather than several small groups, in which case increasing heterogeneity might even help achieve greater social cohesion.

In sum, the theoretical framework predicts that groups with heterogeneous preferences will make lower contributions toward the public good. The predictions for the impact of economic and social heterogeneity are more nuanced.

Group Size

Larger group size has two possible effects. First, although having a large number of people in the group does exacerbate the free-rider problem, a large group has the potential to mobilize more effort at a lower cost (since the costs for each individual are convex). The net effect is therefore uncertain and depends on whether the increase in the free-rider problem outweighs the resource advantage of large groups. If the public good does not deteriorate with a large number of users (i.e., if congestion effects are small), the resource advantage effect is likely to dominate. Examples of such public goods include public health campaigns such as malaria eradication and AIDS awareness. Second, if the large number of users means that individual benefits from the public good are reduced (e.g., if the same irrigation canal is to be used by a larger number of farmers), the free-rider effect is exacerbated, and so larger groups are likely to generate lower contributions. These comparisons assume that the scale of the project being considered remains the same, but larger communities might choose projects of a different scale or scope. Extending the analysis to incorporate these factors would bring an added layer of complexity to the model.

Empirical Evidence on Collective Action and Public Goods

In this section, I survey the empirical evidence on the determinants of collective action postulated by the theoretical framework: the power of certain groups, group heterogeneity, and group size.

Group Influence

There is considerable evidence from South Asia that groups with historical political advantages are able to obtain better public goods for themselves. Banerjee and Somanathan (2007) conducted an analysis on the availability of education, health, and other infrastructure across all the states of India, using census data at the level of the parliamentary constituency. They found that areas with a higher population of Brahmans, the elite priestly caste in India's caste system, have better access to primary, middle, and secondary schools, post offices, and piped water. These are, in fact, exactly the goods we would expect the Brahman caste to value most, given the caste's traditional deep involvement in education and written knowledge and the caste pollution norms that prohibit Brahmans from sharing water with lower castes. In the case of infrastructure for which Brahmans would not be expected to have a special preference, such as electricity connections, health centers, and roads, the study does not find any significant correlation between the presence of Brahmans and the provision of such services.[3] On a more local level, village-level surveys found that households that belong to the same community as the village head are more likely to obtain access to public housing funds, public toilets, and water and electricity connections (Besley, Pande, and Rao 2005).

Do institutional reforms that affect the political advantage of different groups result in corresponding changes in access to public services? To illustrate, the Indian Constitution provides for the reservation of a number of electoral constituencies for members of the Scheduled Castes and Scheduled Tribes.[4] In these constituencies, only members of the targeted communities are allowed to contest elections, and so this provision significantly increases the political influence of these communities. It turns out that reserving electoral constituencies for Scheduled Caste candidates results in greater access to primary schools for members of that community. Such an impact is not observed for Scheduled Tribe communities (Krishnan 2007). Between 1971 and 1991, areas with higher Scheduled Castes populations experienced a rapid expansion in access to various types of infrastructure, while areas with higher Scheduled Tribe populations do not show such increases (Banerjee and Somanathan 2007).

One reason for this difference may be that Scheduled Castes have been able to mobilize politically, creating parties such as the Bahujan Samaj Party (BSP) that cater specifically to their interests. Another possibility is that Scheduled Tribes tend to live in remote isolated areas where it is costly to provide infrastructure. There is some evidence that such political reservations work well only if the context is conducive. A detailed survey of teacher attendance in the schools of Uttar Pradesh found that having a Scheduled Caste village head in fact reduces teacher attendance (Pandey 2006). This is probably because most teachers are not from the Scheduled Caste communities, and, hence, teacher absence is a type of "noncooperation" in heterogeneous communities. I explore further evidence on the impact of social heterogeneity below.

Another major political reform in India has been the decentralization of power to village-level *panchayats* following the 73rd Amendment to the Constitution in 1992. Reservations for village-head positions for Scheduled Castes and Scheduled Tribes were put in place, similar to the reservation policies for state and national electoral constituencies. The amendment also required that a certain fraction of the village-head positions be reserved for women; the villages that are reserved under this scheme are chosen at random in each election, providing an excellent natural experiment setting for evaluating the impact of strengthening women's political voice.

Increasing the political voice of women does help them gain access to the goods they most value. A detailed survey of villages in the Birbhum District of West Bengal State found that having a woman head increased the provision of goods which women valued, such as drinking water and roads (Chattopadhyay and Duflo 2004). Some of the results again sound a cautionary note regarding the importance of the social context. For instance, female village heads were widely perceived by village residents as less competent, even though they did no worse than men on any objective measure of performance. Results from further studies indicate that such social bias may be decreasing as voters are more exposed to women leaders (Beaman et al. forthcoming).

Heterogeneity within Groups

Several studies find that social or ethnic heterogeneity is associated with reduced contributions for public projects and lower levels of access. The pioneering study in this empirical literature was an analysis of expenditure patterns across cities in the United States that found that cities with racially diverse populations spent a lower share of their budget on schools, roads, and garbage collection and a greater share on health services and police (Alesina, Baqir, and Easterly 1999). It is in fact not clear whether this reflects different preferences, difficulties of collective action in heterogeneous communities, or perhaps the fact that cities which provide more health and police services attract a more diverse population. A related paper finds some evidence for the Tiebout migration hypothesis. The United States witnessed a dramatic consolidation of school districts (jurisdictions) over the course of the twentieth century: the number of jurisdictions decreased by a factor of 12. This decline, however, was much more marked in areas where the population became more racially homogeneous, suggesting strong support for the notion that people migrate to form homogeneous communities. Where the population is not homogeneous, people prefer to retain separate communities providing their own preferred type of school (Alesina, Baqir, and Hoxby 2004).

Direct evidence on the role of social heterogeneity in public goods contributions comes from experimental results, where subjects participate in a variety of public goods "games" that simulate real-life situations. Interestingly, subjects in most of these experiments display a much lower level of free riding than is predicted by economic theory. (For a detailed survey of the experimental literature, see Ledyard 1995.) There is no consensus on the impact of introducing heterogeneity across agents. Heterogeneity in the distribution of benefits across agents raises contribution levels (Cardenas, Stranlund, and Willis 2002), while introducing heterogeneity in the perceived status of participants tends to decrease contribution levels (Anderson, Mellor, and Milyo 2008).

Real-life results are similar to the experimental ones, suggesting that different types of heterogeneity matter in different ways. Asim Khwaja conducted a detailed survey of project maintenance across communities in Baltistan, northwest Pakistan, and found that inequality of benefits has a very nonlinear relationship with project maintenance undertaken by the community; residents with more assets (land) benefit more from these project maintenance expenditures. At low levels of asset inequality, project maintenance decreases with increasing inequality, while at high levels of inequality, further increases in inequality actually lead to better maintenance (Khwaja 2009). This is consistent with the theoretical prediction outlined earlier. A similar nonlinear relationship is seen in the operation of sugar cooperatives in Maharashtra, with high prices more likely to be maintained when the number of big farmers is either very small or very large (Banerjee et al. 2001).

Several papers have documented the long-run impact of historical patterns of inequality and lack of social cohesion. In a comparative study of New World economies, Stanley Engerman and Kenneth Sokoloff found that places where the climate was suited to the cultivation of plantation crops such as sugar (e.g., Brazil and Haiti) or places which had extractive industries (e.g., Mexico and Peru) had colonial institutions under which a small elite owned most of the productive resources. The elite in these high-inequality areas managed to capture a disproportionate share of political power, as well. These countries ended up having much lower investments in public education, as well as a delayed transition to democracy and universal suffrage compared with initially more equal places such as the United States and Canada, precisely because policy moves such as democratization or widespread public education would likely threaten the economic and political dominance of the elites (Engerman and Sokoloff 2000, 2005).

In the context of South Asia, we find a similar perpetuation of colonial-era heterogeneity. Abhijit Banerjee and Lakshmi Iyer compared development paths across the districts of India according to whether they had a historically unequal distribution of land. This variation stems from the differing land tenure systems implemented by the British colonial rulers: areas in which a small number of landlords was assigned the primary responsibility for land revenue collection ended up having an economically and politically powerful elite class, compared with nonlandlord areas where taxes were effectively collected directly from the peasant. Even though landlords were formally abolished in the 1950s, the study found that the formerly landlord-controlled areas lag behind the nonlandlord areas in the provision of education and health facilities. The authors' explanation is that in landlord areas there is a much greater social and economic distance between the elites and the masses, making it difficult to effectively coordinate public action to obtain public goods (Banerjee and Iyer 2005). Some evidence for this noncooperation hypothesis is seen in the greater incidence of violent crimes, such as murder and armed robbery, in landlord areas. Preliminary results from Pakistan also suggest a similar pattern of landlord-dominated areas having worse outcomes in terms of public service provision (Cheema and Siddiqui 2008).

Many studies document a negative effect of social heterogeneity on public goods provision. Parents whose children attended ethnically heterogeneous schools in Kenya contributed less to school fund-raising drives (Miguel and Gugerty 2005). In India areas with a higher degree of caste and religious heterogeneity had significantly lower levels of access to schools, transport services, wells, health services, and electricity connections (Banerjee, Iyer, and Somanathan 2005). In Nepal social heterogeneity is associated with increased firewood collection (and, consequently, worse maintenance of common forest resources), while economic inequality is positively associated with forest maintenance (Baland et al. forthcoming).

Why does social heterogeneity have a negative effect on collective action? As discussed earlier, there are three potential mechanisms: social heterogeneity may reduce the degree of altruism or trust among members of the community, increase the costs of communication, or lessen the ability of members to enforce social contribution norms. A series of public goods experiments in Uganda explicitly tested these various channels (Habyarimana et al. 2007). The authors found that the impact of social heterogeneity mainly works through the third channel; that is, members of the same social group are more likely to be able to find each other through their social networks, which gives them an edge in monitoring social contributions.

Group Size

Relatively little empirical evidence exists on the effect of group size on the provision of public goods. Theoretically, the impact is ambiguous, depending on how much the free-riding problem increases with group size. Experimental evidence by Isaac and Walker (1988) suggests that free riding increases in large groups mainly because the marginal benefits of the group activity diminish, specifically because of congestion effects in the public project. Once these congestion effects are controlled for, free riding does not increase appreciably with group size.

Larger villages in India were significantly more likely, in 1971, to have access to almost every type of infrastructure, and they were more likely to increase their access

TABLE 1. Availability of Public Goods, by Village Size, Selected Indian States, 2001

(percent of villages in state with specified service)

Village population category	Kerala			Andhra Pradesh, Karnataka, and Tamil Nadu		
	Primary school	Middle school	Medical facility	Primary school	Middle school	Medical facility
All villages	98	92	97	83	43	54
Less than 500	33	0	33	53	8	25
500–999	n.a.	n.a.	n.a.	91	33	38
1,000–1,999	80	30	60	97	52	60
2,000–3,999	88	44	63	99	74	83
4,000–5,999	95	72	89	100	88	94
6,000–7,999	96	69	91	100	94	97
Greater than 8,000	100	97	99	100	97	99

Source: Author's calculations from India (2001).

Note: n.a., not applicable. Kerala has no villages in the 500–1,000 population category.

to middle schools, health facilities, and phone connections between 1971 and 1991 (Banerjee and Somanathan 2007). Table 1 illustrates the impact of village size by comparing the state of Kerala, which leads India's states in provision of health and education facilities to its residents, with the neighboring states of Andhra Pradesh, Karnataka, and Tamil Nadu. In 2001, 98 percent of Kerala's villages had a primary school, 92 percent had a middle school, and 97 percent had a medical facility. The corresponding figures for the other three states were 83, 43, and 54 percent, respectively. It turns out, however, that Kerala's villages are much larger than those in the other three states: 85 percent of villages in Kerala have populations greater than 8.000, and the number with fewer than 2,000 people is very low. In contrast, 72 percent of the villages in the neighboring states have fewer than 2,000 people, and only 2 percent have populations greater than 8,000 (table 2). When access to education and health facilities is compared by village-size category, there does not seem to be any advantage for Kerala. Although this evidence is suggestive, it is certainly not conclusive because we do not know why villages are so much larger in Kerala (is it merely a function of local geography?) or whether village sizes have changed over time in response to the provision of public goods.

The relevance of collective action factors in determining the supply of public goods is subject to two main caveats. First, in many countries, including those of South Asia, the provision of education and health services is the responsibility of the state, and hence the actions of committed leaders can have a direct effect on these outcomes, over and above the effect of local community characteristics. Second, the evidence suggests that the impact of community characteristics (village size, caste and religious heterogeneity, and the presence of disadvantaged communities) is diminishing over time (Banerjee and Somanathan 2007). In particular, a considerable convergence took place among Indian regions in public goods provision between 1971 and

TABLE 2. Village Size Categories, Selected Indian States, 2001
(percent of villages in each size category)

Village population	Kerala	Andhra Pradesh, Karnataka, and Tamil Nadu
Less than 500	0.4	29.2
500–999	0.0	19.8
1,000–1,999	0.7	23.5
2,000–3,999	3.5	17.8
4,000–5,999	4.8	5.6
6,000–7,999	5.0	2.1
Greater than 8,000	85.6	2.0
Total	100.0	100.0

Source: Author's calculations from India (2001).

1991, a development that Banerjee and Somanathan attribute to specific policies of the Indian government aimed at equalizing access. Can top-down interventions by particular leaders make a difference?

The Role of the State: Ideology, History, and Sustainability

When asked how Kerala had succeeded in ensuring widespread literacy, the state's minister of education cited several reasons aside from local collective action: "A long tradition of public action, strong support for Leftist political movements, benevolent rulers such as the royal family of Travancore, and strong social reform movements against practices such as untouchability."[5]

This comment highlights three key factors: commitment by leaders, policy competition, and conditions for long-term sustainability.

1. *Committed leaders* matter. As early as 1817, Regent Gauri Parvathi Bai of Travancore State declared, "The state should defray the entire cost of the education of its people in order that there might be no backwardness in the spread of enlightenment among them, that by diffusion of education they might become better subjects and public servants and that the reputation of the state might be enhanced thereby." This remarkable announcement was followed by the setting up of schools in each district of Travancore State over the next few decades and by state commitments to health care. The *Travancore Administrative Report* for 1901 records 809 students in the Maharaja's High School, of whom 800 had received vaccinations. The students came from both the priestly Brahman caste and the lower castes and from a wide range of occupational groups, suggesting that the state was also active in removing barriers to social cohesion. In contrast, the British colonial state set up the first English school in British Malabar (the northern region of the modern Kerala State) only in 1848.

Travancore was not the only place with a committed ruler. Sayajirao III, the ruler of Baroda (in present-day Gujarat State) from 1875 to 1939, declared that education was "absolutely necessary for the realization of my ambitions and wishes for the future of my people." The state ordered that schools be provided in all villages which could produce 16 children willing to attend; Sayajirao was also the first to introduce compulsory education in certain areas, in 1892. It took the British more than 20 years to introduce a similar law in the neighboring Central Provinces. It is important to note that the rulers mentioned here were hereditary kings with little direct pressure from their subjects for the provision of such facilities. This effect is also not limited to the specific rulers mentioned here: in general, areas of India that were ruled by native rulers have better access to schools and health centers than areas ruled by British administrators (Iyer 2007).

2. The presence of committed actors can help spur *policy competition.* In addition to keeping social reform on the political agenda, it is possible that the strong presence of Communist parties in Kerala forced competing parties to make a similar commitment to public services.

The history of education in Sri Lanka (known as Ceylon until 1972) is illustrative in this regard. (The discussion here is based on Sri Lanka, Ministry of Education, 2004.) Before the colonial period, education had traditionally been provided by Buddhist monks. The arrival of the Portuguese and then the Dutch led to the setting up of several missionary schools during the sixteenth, seventeenth, and eighteenth centuries. During the period of direct British colonial rule (1796–1931), the colonial government also established a few schools. In the mid-nineteenth century, Buddhist, Hindu, and Muslim communities started their own religious schools to give their children an alternative to the Christian schools. This increase in the number of schools led to a 42 percent literacy rate for men as early as 1901. By comparison, the literacy rate for men in the state of Travancore, the highest in India, was only 21 percent at that time. Thus, competing (religious) ideologies appear to have advanced the cause of access to education. A cross-country analysis finds a similar result: competition among missionaries resulted in better education outcomes across former colonies in Africa, irrespective of the religious denomination of the missionaries themselves (Gallego and Woodberry 2006).

Following the end of direct British colonial rule and the institution of universal suffrage in 1931, Sri Lanka adopted several major education initiatives, in 1942. These were heavily influenced by the views of C. W. W. Kannangara, the country's first minister of education. They included free education from kindergarten through university, instruction in the mother tongue of the student, the setting up of 53 high-quality central schools for secondary education throughout the country, the institution of a scholarship program, and the establishment of the University of Ceylon. It should be noted that Kannangara faced considerable opposition from the elites before the measures were passed. These initiatives have contributed to a literacy rate of over 90 percent in Sri Lanka and to a secondary school completion rate of 40 percent in 2001.

3. The *long-term sustainability* of the original initiative is a critical factor, but little is known about what determines it. Did education continue to receive prominence in Kerala because of the commitment of successive rulers in the states of Travancore and Cochin, or because of the influence of social reform movements in Kerala that

were specifically aimed at increasing the access of lower castes to public facilities (Ramachandran 1997)? Why is Gujarat not among the leading states of India in public goods provision, even though it had had an extremely committed ruler in the past? What factors prompted the Sri Lankan state to continue its long-term commitment to education after the colonial period and the 1942 reforms?

One possibility is that a higher initial level of literacy might change the effectiveness of local collective action, by lowering the costs of demanding public goods or by increasing social cohesion. In this context, it is interesting to note that literacy rates across Indian districts in 1961 are significant predictors of access to a range of public goods in 1991 (Banerjee and Iyer 2008). By contrast, an initial provision of deworming drugs in Kenya proved extremely difficult to sustain over the longer term. This suggests that specific measures are needed to galvanize local collective action; simply providing a public good is not sufficient for sustainability (Kremer and Miguel 2007).

Can governments undertake measures to increase social cohesion and hence make collective action more effective? Some indications are provided by comparing the contrasting experiences of Kenya and Tanzania: local ethnic heterogeneity is negatively correlated with the quality of schools in Kenya's Busia, but the two are positively correlated in the nearby Meatu region in Tanzania (Miguel 2004). A plausible reason is that whereas after independence, the Kenyan leadership played up tribal loyalties for political reasons, and little effort was put into building a Kenyan identity, Tanzania's leadership laid considerable emphasis on creating a single Tanzanian identity. The importance of such feedback mechanisms between initial top-down initiatives and later bottom-up processes has not yet been explored in much detail, in either the theoretical or the empirical literature.

Quality of Public Services

The theoretical framework described earlier can also be applied to analysis of the factors affecting the quality of public services. As long as some private cost is incurred by the user in verifying or enforcing the quality of service (e.g., going to the health center to check whether the nurse is present, or filing a complaint with school authorities if the teacher is not doing a good job), the same insights would apply. The implications of the framework would be that people who have political advantages will enjoy a higher quality of public goods provision but that the impact of group size and group heterogeneity is ambiguous.

The empirical evidence has highlighted many of the same factors as important determinants of public goods quality. For instance, schools located in areas of India that were under the landlord-based land tenure system are much more likely to have higher rates of teacher absenteeism (Pandey 2006). The importance of bottom-up factors is highlighted by the observation that teacher absence is lower in schools in which the Parent Teacher Association (PTA) has met in the preceding three months (Kremer et al. 2005). It is important to note that this result is not driven solely by links between the teacher and the local community: teachers from the local community are not less likely to be absent, and the mere existence of a PTA does not help to reduce absenteeism. This evidence clearly suggests a role for the kind of community action modeled earlier.

Given the failures of community action to ensure service delivery in many cases, what means can be used to rectify the situation? Duflo, Hanna, and Ryan (2008) report the results of an experiment in which teachers in a randomly chosen subset of schools in Rajasthan were offered a bonus if they proved their presence in school by photographing themselves with their students. This scheme reduced teacher absence in those schools by half—a huge improvement. Increased teacher presence also led to improved student learning outcomes. It should be noted that this approach does not focus on improving local collective action, and in this sense, it is a top-down method of intervention. Olken (2007) found a similar result in Indonesia, where increased centralized auditing dramatically improved the quality of roads built by local village committees.

The latter study is unusual because it included an explicit comparison of top-down auditing with more bottom-up community monitoring. The study found that making it easier for citizens to monitor local road building had very little effect on the quality of roads. A similar result was found in a study in Rajasthan (Banerjee, Deaton, and Duflo 2004). Members of the local community were given strong incentives to monitor the presence of nurses at the local health center. They did keep track of whether the nurse was present, but in the absence of any effective sanctioning mechanism, there was no impact on absence of service providers.[6] An innovative experiment in Andhra Pradesh was explicitly designed to improve teacher accountability: public school teachers were given bonuses if their students improved their test scores. This initiative significantly improved student learning outcomes, mainly by inducing greater instructional effort on the part of the teacher (Muralidharan and Sundararaman 2006).

Is Private Provision the Solution?

In recent years, many countries of South Asia have witnessed a dramatic rise in the number of private schools in rural areas. In Pakistan the number of private schools increased from 32,000 to 47,000 between 2000 and 2005; in 2005 one in three primary school students was enrolled in a private school (Andrabi et al. 2007). In India 28 percent of the rural population had access to a private school in 2003, and 15 percent of all students were estimated to be studying in private schools (Muralidharan and Kremer 2008). In Bangladesh a nongovernmental organization (NGO), BRAC, is one of the biggest suppliers of primary schooling: its nonformal primary education program, which covers the same competencies as the government schools, grew from 22 one-room schools in 1985 to 49,000 schools in 2004, accounting for about 11 percent of the primary school children in the country. By contrast, in Sri Lanka, where the public school system is working well, only 4 percent of all students are enrolled in private or religious schools (Sri Lanka, Ministry of Education, 2007).

Private schools perform better than public schools on many dimensions. Teacher absence is considerably less, and student learning outcomes are significantly better (Muralidharan and Kremer 2008; Andrabi et al. 2007). Can the entry of such non-state actors into the education sector be the answer to the substantial failings in the public education system that were documented earlier, as well as to the difficulties in improving local collective action?

There are three reasons why the state still needs to be a major force in the provision of health and education services on a large scale. First, private schools do not provide universal service: they are more likely to be located in larger villages, as in India, or in richer villages and richer settlements within villages, as in Pakistan. In both India and Pakistan, they are much more likely to exist when teacher absenteeism in the public school system is high. Second, private schools are more expensive for the students than are public schools. In Pakistan, the average annual cost of a private primary school is 3,563 rupees, more than seven times the public school cost of 479 rupees. The cost of schooling is a significant deterrent to enrollment: 25 percent of boys and 22 percent of girls cite the cost of schooling as their reason for not going to school, and 18 percent of boys and 15 percent of girls cite it as their reason for dropping out of primary school (Pakistan 2007, tables 2.20, 2.23, and 2.24). Both the location and the cost of private schools limit the access of the poorest households to such facilities. We should note, however, that the total social costs of private schools are in fact lower than those of public schools (Andrabi et al. 2007). This suggests that increasing the ability of households to access these schools—for instance through education vouchers—can be an effective policy tool for improving learning outcomes. In general, such combinations of public and private action in providing education and health services deserve more detailed attention, both in the academic literature and in policy making.

Third, an intriguing study from Pakistan suggests that an initial investment by the state may be needed for private schools to be viable. The main advantage of private schools is that they are able to hire local teachers for much lower wages than those paid to government schoolteachers, who typically enjoy civil service protection. Where do private schools find teachers with at least minimal levels of education? Andrabi, Das, and Khwaja (2007) find that these teachers are the products of prior investments by the state in expanding access to public education in rural areas. This is consistent with the timing of the recent rise in private schools. Over time, it may be possible for the private school system to generate its own teachers and thus become self-sustaining.

Conclusions

This paper has documented the shortfalls in the delivery of health and education services across South Asia. A key feature of the data is that there are large gaps in service delivery even within specific countries. I surveyed two classes of explanations for such underprovision. The first broad class focuses on the factors that might make local demand insufficient or ineffective in ensuring provision of services. These are the factors that make collective action more or less difficult; they include the influence of certain politically advantaged groups, group heterogeneity, and group size. We saw that in many cases the theoretical framework yielded ambiguous predictions. The empirical evidence, on the whole, suggests that (a) the political influence of the group matters significantly in obtaining the group's preferred goods; (b) groups which are socially heterogeneous are less effective in obtaining public goods, and results for groups which are economically heterogeneous vary; and (c) larger groups are likely to be more effective in obtaining desired public goods.

The second class of explanations focused on factors that might affect the supply of public goods, irrespective of demand conditions. Several experiences suggest that committed leaders can make a big difference in providing public goods, that competition among motivated agents can be a significant force, and that top-down interventions may not be self-sustaining. We know relatively little about how to effectively promote collective action or about other channels for making an initial intervention sustainable. These remain fruitful avenues for theoretical and, especially, empirical work.

Notes

1. This framework is based on the theoretical model in Banerjee, Iyer, and Somanathan (2008).
2. The Indian migration rate contrasts with the figures in developed countries. For instance, 40 percent of the U.S. population resides in a state other than the birth state.
3. Although caste pollution norms might apply to contact in health centers as well, it is very likely that the service providers (e.g., doctors) would be from the upper castes.
4. The Scheduled Castes are communities that have historically been at the bottom of the Hindu caste hierarchy; Scheduled Tribes include communities that have traditionally been outside the Hindu caste system.
5. Author's interview with M.A. Baby, minister of education and culture, Kerala, September 2006.
6. Banerjee and Duflo (2006) survey a number of other studies aimed at reducing absences of service providers.

References

Alesina, Alberto, Reza Baqir, and William Easterly. 1999. "Public Goods and Ethnic Divisions." *Quarterly Journal of Economics* 114 (4): 1243–84.

Alesina, Alberto, Reza Baqir, and Caroline Hoxby. 2004. "Political Jurisdictions in Heterogeneous Communities." *Journal of Political Economy* 112: 348–96.

Anderson, Lisa R., Jennifer M. Mellor, and Jeffrey Milyo. 2008. "Inequality and Public Good Provision: An Experimental Analysis." *Journal of Socio-Economics* 37 (3, June): 1010–28.

Andrabi, Tahir, Jishnu Das, and Asim Ijaz Khwaja. 2007. "Students Today, Teachers Tomorrow? Identifying Constraints on the Provision of Education." Working Paper, Kennedy School of Government, Harvard University, Cambridge, MA. http://ksghome.harvard. edu/~akhwaja/papers/teachersstudentssept07.pdf.

Andrabi, Tahir, Jishnu Das, Asim Ijaz Khwaja, Tara Vishwanath, Tristan Zajonc, and the LEAPS Team. 2007. "Pakistan—Learning and Educational Achievements in Punjab Schools (LEAPS): Insights to Inform the Education Policy Debate." World Bank, Washington, DC. http://leapsproject.org/assets/publications/LEAPS_report.pdf.

Baland, Jean Marie, Pranab Bardhan, Sanghamitra Das, Dilip Mookherjee, and Rinki Sarkar. Forthcoming. "The Environmental Impact of Poverty: Evidence from Firewood Collection in Rural Nepal." *Economic Development and Cultural Change.* http://people.bu.edu/dilipm/publications/nepaledccsept083.pdf.

Banerjee, Abhijit, and Esther Duflo. 2006. "Addressing Absence." *Journal of Economic Perspectives* 20 (1, Winter): 117–32.

Banerjee, Abhijit, and Lakshmi Iyer. 2005. "History, Institutions and Economic Performance: The Legacy of Colonial Land Tenure Systems in India." *American Economic Review* 95 (4): 1190–1213.

———. 2008. "Colonial Land Tenure, Electoral Competition and Public Goods in India." Harvard Business School Working Paper 08-062, Cambridge, MA.

Banerjee, Abhijit, and Rohini Somanathan. 2007. "The Political Economy of Public Goods: Some Evidence from India." *Journal of Development Economics* 82 (2): 287–314.

Banerjee, Abhijit, Angus Deaton, and Esther Duflo. 2004. "Health Care Delivery in Rural Rajasthan." *Economic and Political Weekly* 39 (9): 944–49.

Banerjee, Abhijit, Lakshmi Iyer, and Rohini Somanathan. 2005. "History, Social Divisions and Public Goods in Rural India." *Journal of the European Economic Association* 3 (2–3): 639–47.

———. 2008. "Public Action for Public Goods." In *Handbook of Development Economics,* vol. 4, ed. T. Paul Schultz and John Strauss. Amsterdam: North-Holland.

Banerjee, Abhijit, Dilip Mookherjee, Kaivan Munshi, and Debraj Ray. 2001. "Inequality, Control Rights and Rent Seeking: Sugar Cooperatives in Maharashtra." *Journal of Political Economy* 109 (1): 138–90.

Bardhan, Pranab, Maitreesh Ghatak, and Alexander Karaivanov. 2007. "Wealth Inequality and Collective Action." *Journal of Public Economics* 91 (9): 1843–74.

Beaman, Lori, Raghabendra Chattopadhyay, Esther Duflo, Rohini Pande, and Petia Topalova. Forthcoming. "Powerful Women: Does Exposure Reduce Bias?" *Quarterly Journal of Economics* 124 (4). Draft available at http://ksghome.harvard.edu/~rpande/Research,%20Working%20Papers.htm.

Besley, Timothy, Rohini Pande, and Vijayendra Rao. 2005. "Participatory Democracy in Action: Survey Evidence from South India." *Journal of the European Economic Association* 3 (2–3): 648–57.

Cardenas, Juan Camilo, John Stanlund, and Cleve Willis. 2002. "Economic Inequality and Burden-Sharing in the Provision of Local Environmental Quality." *Ecological Economics* 40 (3): 379–95.

Center for the Study of Developing Societies. 1996. "National Election Studies." Center for the Study of Developing Societies, New Delhi. http://www.lokniti.org/dataunit.htm.

Chattopadhyay, Raghbendra, and Esther Duflo. 2004. "Women as Policy Makers: Evidence from a Randomized Policy Experiment in India." *Econometrica* 72 (5): 1409–43.

Chaudhury, Nazmul, Jeffrey Hammer, Michael Kremer, Karthik Muralidharan, and F. Halsey Rogers. 2006. "Missing in Action: Teacher and Health Worker Absence in Developing Countries." *Journal of Economic Perspectives* 20 (1): 91–116.

Cheema, Ali, and Bilal Siddiqui. 2008. "Colonial Village Institutions, Path Dependence and Public Good Provision: Do Peasant Republics Serve Better than Feudal Estates?" Work in progress, Lahore University of Management Sciences, Lahore, Pakistan.

Das, Jishnu, and Asim Khwaja. 2005. "Bunching and Heterogeneity: Characterizing the Monopolistic Provision of Excludable Public Goods." Working Paper, Kennedy School of Government, Harvard University, Cambridge, MA.

Duflo, Esther, Rema Hanna, and Stephen Ryan. 2008. "Monitoring Works: Getting Teachers to Come to School." CEPR Discussion Paper DP6682, Centre for Economic Policy Research, London.

Engerman, Stanley L., and Kenneth L. Sokoloff. 2000. "Institutions, Factor Endowments, and Paths of Development in the New World." *Journal of Economic Perspectives* 14 (3): 217–32.

———. 2005. "Colonialism, Inequality and the Long-Run Paths to Development." NBER Working Paper 11057, National Bureau of Economic Research, Cambridge, MA.

Gallego, Francisco A., and Robert Woodberry. 2006. "Christian Missionaries and Education in Former Colonies: An Early Example of the Economics of School Choice?" Working Paper, MIT, Cambridge, MA. http://www.economia.puc.cl/ archivos_profes/63/ missionaries_jun13.pdf.

Habyarimana, James, Macartan Humphreys, Daniel Posner, and Jeremy Weinstein. 2007. "Why Does Ethnic Diversity Undermine Public Good Provision?" *American Political Science Review* 101 (4): 709–25.

India. 2001. *Census of India 2001: Village Directory Data,* Electronic Data Files. New Delhi: Office of the Registrar General.

Isaac, R. Mark., and James M. Walker. 1988. "Group Size Effects in Public Goods Provision: The Voluntary Contributions Mechanism." *Quarterly Journal of Economics* 103 (1): 179–99.

Iyer, Lakshmi. 2007. "Direct versus Indirect Colonial Rule in India: Long-Term Consequences." Working Paper, Harvard Business School, Cambridge, MA. http://www.people. hbs.edu/liyer/Iyer_colonial_dec2007.pdf.

Keefer, Philip, and Stuti Khemani. 2005. "Democracy, Public Expenditures, and the Poor: Understanding Political Incentives for Providing Public Services." *World Bank Research Observer* 20 (1): 1–27.

Khwaja, Asim Ijaz. 2009. "Can Good Projects Succeed in Bad Communities?" *Journal of Public Economics* 93 (7–8, August): 899–916.

Kremer, Michael, and Edward Miguel. 2007. "The Illusion of Sustainability." *Quarterly Journal of Economics* 112 (3): 1007–65.

Kremer, Michael, Nazmul Chaudhury, Jeffrey Hammer, Karthik Muralidharan, and F. Halsey Rogers. 2005. "Teacher Absence in India: A Snapshot." *Journal of the European Economic Association* 3 (2–3): 658–67.

Krishnan, Nandini. 2007. "Political Reservations and Rural Public Good Provision in India." Working Paper, Boston University, Boston. http://www.bu.edu/econ/ied/dp/papers/ Political%20Reservations%20and%20Rural%20Public%20Good%20Provision%20in %20India.pdf.

Ledyard, J. 1995. "Public Goods: A Survey of Experimental Research." In *Handbook of Experimental Economics,* ed. J. H. Kagel and A. Roth. Princeton, NJ: Princeton University Press.

Miguel, Edward. 2004. "Tribe or Nation? Nation-Building and Public Goods in Kenya versus Tanzania." *World Politics* 56 (3): 327–62.

Miguel, Edward, and Mary Kay Gugerty. 2005. "Ethnic Diversity, Social Sanctions and Public Goods in Kenya." *Journal of Public Economics* 89 (11–12): 2325–68.

Muralidharan, Karthik, and Michael Kremer. 2008. "Private-Public Schools in Rural India." In *School Choice International: Exploring Private Public Partnerships,* ed. Rajashri Chakrabarti and Paul E. Peterson. Cambridge, MA: MIT Press.

Muralidharan, Karthik, and Venkatesh Sundararaman. 2006. "Teacher Incentives in Developing Countries: Experimental Evidence from India." Working Paper, Harvard University, Cambridge, MA.

Olken, Benjamin. 2007. "Monitoring Corruption: Evidence from a Field Experiment in Indonesia." *Journal of Political Economy* 115 (2): 200–49.

Pakistan. 2007. *Pakistan Social and Living Standards Measurement Survey 2005–06.* Islamabad: Statistics Division.

Pandey, Priyanka. 2006. "Service Delivery and Capture in Public Schools: How Does History Matter and Can Mandated Political Representation Reverse the Effects of History?" Working Paper, South Asia Human Development Department, World Bank, Washington, DC.

PROBE Team. 1999. *Public Report on Basic Education in India.* New Delhi: Oxford University Press.

Ramachandran, V. K. 1997. "On Kerala's Development Achievements." In *Indian Development: Selected Regional Perspectives,* ed. Jean Drèze and Amartya Sen. New Delhi: Oxford University Press.

Sri Lanka. 2006. *Statistical Abstract 2005.* Colombo: Department of Census and Statistics.

Sri Lanka, Ministry of Education. 2004. "Historical Overview of Education in Sri Lanka." Ministry of Education, Colombo. http://www.moe.gov.lk/modules.php?name=Content&pa=showpage&pid=2.

———. 2007. *School Census 2006: Preliminary Report.* Colombo: Department of Census and Statistics.

Tiebout, Charles M. 1956. "A Pure Theory of Local Expenditures." *Journal of Political Economy* 64 (5): 416–24.

Travancore State. 1901. *Travancore Administrative Report.* Travancore, India.

UNDP (United Nations Development Programme). 2007. *Human Development Report 2007/2008: Fighting Climate Change: Human Solidarity in a Divided World.* New York: UNDP.

World Bank. 2004. *World Development Report 2004: Making Services Work for Poor People.* Washington, DC: World Bank and Oxford University Press.

Comment on "The Political Economy of Public Service Provision in South Asia," by Lakshmi Iyer

ASHUTOSH VARSHNEY

Until the late 1980s, political economy was a subfield primarily populated by political scientists, with occasional participation by economists such as Mancur Olson (1965, 1982), on the one hand, and Kenneth Arrow (1970) and Amartya Sen (1981), on the other. Over the past decade or so, participation by economists has been much more vigorous. By now, the field of political economy has become a joint enterprise of the two disciplines of political science and economics.

Does that mean that the two fields agree on how to define, or identify, what is political? Although it would be too much to say that all political scientists (or, for that matter, all economists) define what is political, or identify the determinants of politics, in the same way, I as a political scientist, using Iyer's paper, would like to suggest how conceptions and determinants of politics can be quite different across disciplines. As a consequence, the explanations, too, might vary.

The central question in Iyer's paper is, why do some regions of a country succeed in obtaining public goods for their residents, while other areas within the same country lag behind? The public goods she primarily focuses on are education and health, although there are brief references to "public amenities" in general. In effect, her central question takes the following form: why, in India, do states like Kerala have a school for every village (and a literacy rate of more than 90 percent), while states like Bihar have provided schools to only 39 percent of their villages?

Before we examine Iyer's argument, let us ask, at what level should we examine variation in the provision of public goods? There are three easily identifiable units of analysis: states (or provinces), districts, and villages. With meticulous care and balance, Iyer has surveyed the literature explaining variation at the village level, and to some extent her analysis can be leveraged at the district level, but the paper does not adequately deal with variation at the state level. Her independent variables—group size, group influence, and group heterogeneity—can work well at the village level,

Ashutosh Varshney is a professor of political science at Brown University, Providence, RI.

Annual World Bank Conference on Development Economics 2009, Global

and also potentially at the district level, but their explanatory power weakens when we go up to the state level.

Is this simply a theoretical point, or one with actual empirical and explanatory significance? Health and education in India are state-level subjects. It is the state government that is primarily responsible for fiscal allocations for, and the administration of, primary and secondary education and primary health. The central government can be a partner, but it is not a decision maker. It follows that state-level variation in literacy and health will depend substantially, if not entirely, on how much the state government spends on education and health and on whether, and why, different states have different public expenditure profiles.

Indeed, if we examine the patterns of literacy and health in India, something more interesting than the state-level variation stands out. The four southern Indian states are systematically ahead of the northern part of the country (with the exception of a small northern state, Himachal Pradesh). One of the most interesting political-economy questions in India is why the South is so far ahead of the North in literacy and health.

To answer this question, one would have to survey two facets of political-economy literature that are not the focus of Iyer's analytical gaze: historical political economy and what might be called, for want of a better term, institutional political economy. Historical political economy deals with the long legacies of some transformative eras, or critical junctures, in politics. Institutional political economy deals with issues such as the impact of party systems. Let me turn to each briefly.

Historical Caste Dynamics in India's North and South

The historical political economy of India makes it very clear that caste dynamics constitute one of the most dramatic differences between India's South and North (Varshney 2000). Like race in the United States, caste is the dark underbelly of Indian politics, economy, and society. Skin color is not its primary basis, but the caste system resembles racial stratification in several other ways. Traditionally, castes were birth-based groups organized in a vertical hierarchy. The upper castes had the higher professions; the lower castes—now called the other backward classes (OBCs)—were peasants, service providers, and artisans; and the Dalits, the ex-untouchables, were at the bottom of the social scale and were restricted to menial jobs.

Caste differences were not simply professional. Lower castes also historically suffered humiliation and discrimination at the hands of the upper castes in a vertical Hindu social order. For centuries, they were looked down on; they were not allowed access to upper-caste temples, wells, schools, or village commons; their styles of dress and the architectural patterns of their homes had to be in keeping with their "station in life"; their children were viewed as fit only for menial jobs and not worthy of education; and their women were treated with disrespect. Upward mobility in the caste system was highly limited. Tradition, if violated, was enforced by coercion.

In southern India, the lower castes had already been mobilized into social movements during the last decades of British rule. In the 1950s and 1960s, they rose in politics, as well. By the late 1960s, all over southern India, upper-caste hegemony had been undermined, leading to a new political equilibrium in the 1970s. In this new equilibrium, the OBCs held the upper hand, and the upper castes accepted their junior role. In the North, such political reversal has of late been under way in two of the largest states, Uttar Pradesh and Bihar.

In short, the South went through a lower-caste revolution decades ago. Does that have an impact on health and literacy? As regards literacy, the impact is very clear. The lower-caste movements emphasized, among other things, two objectives—to quote a major southern leader of the movement, "respect yourself," and "educate yourself." (For a detailed discussion, see Rajendran 1974.) As a result, the rise of the lower castes, which constituted anywhere from 80 to 90 percent of the southern Indian population, lifted the average literacy rates for the southern Indian states enormously. (See Varshney 2005 on the further implications.) The rise of the lower castes began several decades later in northern India.

Party Politics, Health, and Education

Shall we conclude that caste dynamics is all that we need to look at—that states are locked into equilibria struck decades ago? Let me briefly turn to the institutional political-economy literature that is beginning to emerge and ask if party politics has a public goods impact. On the basis of a study of all states of India, Chhibber and Nooruddin (2004) note that the delivery of public goods varies significantly across Indian states, and they show that states with two-party competition provide more public goods than states with multiparty competition. This is so because in two-party systems political parties need the support of large social groups, whereas in multiparty systems the social base of the parties is smaller and political parties provide "club goods" to these smaller groups rather than public goods to larger social coalitions. I am not absolutely certain that the argument is correct, but at any rate Chhibber and Nooruddin have proposed an intriguing idea for further exploration.

Conclusion

To sum up, Iyer's remarkable survey of political-economy literature is confined to the village or to district-level variation. For state-level variation, which is an important aspect of public goods variation in India, we need to turn to a very different kind of political economy that conceptualizes politics not only in terms of historical drivers of politics but perhaps also in view of the nature of party politics in India.

References

Arrow, Kenneth. 1970. *Social Choice and Individual Values*. 2nd ed. New Haven, CT: Yale University Press.

Chhibber, Pradeep, and Irfan Nooruddin. 2004. "Do Party Systems Count? The Number of Parties and Government Performance in the Indian States." *Comparative Political Studies* 37 (2, March): 152–87.

Olson, Mancur. 1965. *The Logic of Collective Action.* Cambridge, MA: Harvard University Press.

———. 1982. *The Rise and Decline of Nations.* New Haven, CT: Yale University Press.

Rajendran, G. 1974. *The Ezhava Community and Kerala Politics.* Trivandrum, India: Academy of Political Science.

Sen, Amartya. 1981. *Poverty and Famines.* Oxford, UK. Oxford University Press.

Varshney, Ashutosh. 2000. "Is India Becoming More Democratic?" *Journal of Asian Studies* 59 (1, February): 3–25.

———. 2005. "Democracy and Poverty." In *Measuring Empowerment*, ed. Deepa Narayan. Washington, DC: World Bank.

Closing Remarks

ALAN GELB

This Annual World Bank Conference on Development Economics (ABCDE) is a historic one. It is a first for the African continent, and it combines the global and regional ABCDE conferences. It has brought together more than 500 participants to share insights about the process of development. We come from more than 60 countries, and 228 of us live in Africa and 61 in Asia, so we are very widely distributed.

Before proceeding, I would like again to thank the South African government, especially Treasury, for the wonderful support and fantastic organization that you have provided for this conference. I think that even if we forget some of the papers, presentations, and debates, we are going to remember the dinner last night, and the music, the dancing, and the poetry, for a very long time. It was really a great experience. Thank you very much, for all of us.

Actually, it was so good that I am sorry that we rotate the ABCDE—I would love to come back to Cape Town next year.

The conference, as you know, has been about people, politics, and globalization. As we convened here, South Africa's minister of finance, Trevor Manuel, observed that the global and continental commitments expressed in recent years have actually helped developing countries enter a higher growth path and that these countries have begun to reap the benefits of difficult economic policy decisions and of globalization. But he also pointed to the near-term impediments, including rapidly rising food and fuel prices and global economic turmoil, and he emphasized that new conditions require dynamic and innovative solutions from development economists. Indeed, such solutions have been a central feature of our discussions.

The World Bank's chief economist, Justin Lin, noted in the opening session that Africa has demonstrated robust growth in recent years—it is no longer a "hopeless continent," as the *Economist* labeled it back in 2000. The challenge will be to

Alan Gelb is a senior fellow at the Center for Global Development, Washington, DC. At the time of the conference, he was the director, Development Economics, World Bank.

Annual World Bank Conference on Development Economics 2009, Global
© 2010 The International Bank for Reconstruction and Development / The World Bank

maintain and strengthen this growth. The chief economist stressed that people are not simply the end of development; they are also the *means* of development, and it is important that they be given opportunities to work and to contribute to development. He pointed out that globalization provides very good examples of this—for example, in East Asia and China—but that it also poses new challenges for developing countries.

President Thabo Mbeki reminded us, on the first day of the conference, that rumors of the death of development economics are very premature, and he asked the conference to consider a number of questions that concern policy makers in Africa and elsewhere in the developing world. These questions include what steps to take in response to rising food and fuel prices, how Africa can take advantage of the commodity boom, what can be done to strengthen the development of human capital in the event of a global turndown that curtails exports and inward investment, and what measures to take to sustain the rhythm of development. During the past two and a half days, we have had 43 sessions, some 90 speakers in all, plus discussions, and a wonderful essay competition. It is not possible to cover all this in a single summary—unless, of course, you would like to stay another week in Cape Town, which many of us would. So I am going to be very brief in summarizing as best I can some of the themes that came up surrounding the first topic of the conference—people.

It is clear that human capital development is central to development, and this aspect was covered in sessions that included Minister Trevor Manuel; Michael Spence, the chair of the Growth and Development Commission; and Paul Schultz. Among other events, there was a comparative session on human capital development, which demonstrated that public health interventions can have positive effects on the lives of the poor and can lead to positive impacts on the economy. We heard some interesting reports about antiretroviral therapy, vitamin supplementation, and other examples that came up in the discussion, such as the successful HIV/AIDS program in Thailand. We need to learn from these cases and to share experiences.

Michael Spence's address on rethinking growth emphasized that health is not only a basic human right, but also a critical input for economic growth. There is, clearly, growing evidence, including at the micro level, that especially among the young, poor health and malnutrition have a detrimental effect on productivity and economic growth. This effect occurs through the channel of labor supply reduction but also through damage to cognitive development, which has a lasting effect on skills acquisition that cannot be easily reversed.

The challenge of measuring the impact of public health investments was also discussed. It might seem obvious that public health investment provides support for economic growth, but the devil is in the details. Costly investments in health today may yield improvements in growth only in 20 or 30 years' time, making it difficult to estimate the overall returns and, therefore, to budget accurately. Maximizing the gains from health investment and identifying appropriate interventions require a focus on equity, efficiency, and service delivery. (Failures in the last area are, unfortunately, all too common in the health sector.) The conference also examined the role of health policy concerning HIV/AIDS and its effect on economic growth. The interaction on this topic included a range of views on the relationship between poverty, wealth, and HIV infection. Some presentations dealt with the educational impact on children who lose their parents to HIV/AIDS. Understanding these aspects of the HIV/AIDS tragedy is important for ensuring effective policy.

A session on higher education and high-technology industries, organized by Devesh Kapur, was motivated in part by emerging evidence that the spectacular economic and social development that has taken place—particularly, perhaps, in the Far East—has occurred simultaneously with the rapid development and expansion of higher education. The session highlighted the important links between higher education and the development of high-technology industries. From an African perspective, it was agreed that poor outcomes in this area, which persist despite an expansion of university enrollment, relate in part to a lack of focus on science and technology. The difficulties in many developing regions, including Africa, in sustaining high-level academic communities—the core of the science and technology community—and the related issues were also noted.

One particular aspect of employment that received attention was the high incidence of youth unemployment in developing countries, especially in the countries of North Africa and in South Africa. It is interesting that at these two extremes of the continent, the issue of youth unemployment seems to be a particularly salient question. Clearly, if youth unemployment can be addressed, a source of tremendous economic growth and dynamism can be tapped. Alternatively, youth unemployment can be a source of social tension and conflict. Appropriate education and training policies are critical, especially for advanced education and vocational training. The youth employment issue was also brought up in the context of a global dichotomy: the average age of the population in advanced countries is increasing, and the developing world is becoming younger. The Commission on Growth and Development argued that the potential for work-related migration and labor mobility to address these issues deserves careful consideration in the years ahead.

Philanthropy and development share a long history, but the importance of this link has been mounting because of the growing size of private foundations. There was a debate on the roles of philanthropy, government, and nonprofit organizations. One view was that development is helped most when companies get involved and contribute their technical expertise rather than simply make donations.

We all know that politics is a key driver of development and that it can help or hinder inclusive economic growth and the policies that support economic activity. Indeed, the issue of politics pervaded many sessions that were not explicitly about that topic. The findings of the Commission on Growth and Development also highlighted the critical importance of the political leadership's taking a long view and acting in the interests of all citizens rather than of a small, select group.

A comparative session organized by Robert Bates addressed many interesting political-economy questions, such as whether government spending is really redistributional. That discussion brought up some interesting differences between rich and poor countries—for example, that social spending is more likely to be redistributive in rich than in poor countries.

Who receives public goods? What have we learned from experience in India? At the micro level, the village level, group size, group interests, and group influence appear to be important. But it was also suggested that at the provincial level there is a historical and an institutional dynamic and that, in certain respects, the North of India lags the South by 50 years. Some very interesting thoughts emerged about the relationship between transfers of political power and implications for development.

The session also considered the analytics of political transitions—for example, in South Africa and Sri Lanka—and the trade-offs for elites between productivity gains from empowering the poor and the loss of potential power. A clear understanding of when these transitions are going to be productive and when they are going to be destructive is important from many points of view. This exchange was supplemented by a focus on crime and poverty that included a discussion of the negative consequences associated with police corruption, an assessment of job creation issues in northern and southern Africa, and, again, an emphasis on the importance of politics in ensuring that public expenditures are allocated in ways that maximize benefits for the poor. This issue was discussed in the context of poverty reduction strategies and Heavily Indebted Poor Countries (HIPCs).

Bassma Kodmani of the Arab Reform Initiative underlined the political challenges and new opportunities for democracy in the Middle East. Her plea for a political approach to reform in the Arab states highlighted that grassroots movements are becoming more confident about expressing discontent around social and political issues such as water, land, and food and that their interest in democratic reform is converging with the concerns of more elite social strata seeking parliamentary and judicial reform.

India—the other major low-income part of the world, in addition to Africa—offers a remarkable reform story. Sunil Kant Munjal, the chairman of Hero Corporate Services, spoke about India's reforms and the role played by political consensus in this success. India provides a very concrete example of the importance of shared and balanced growth, labor market reform, and balanced government intervention. Reaffirming the presentation of the Commission on Growth and Development, we note that the call is for better government rather than for less government. We also looked at the role of governments and the public sector in the Southern African Development Community (SADC) and in Africa more broadly. In this area, as in others, this ABCDE helps us to learn from comparative experience.

Closing Remarks

FUNDI TSHAZIBANA

There is no question that the reality of the world that we will all leave to our children will be vastly different as a result of processes that we have come to identify as globalization—in particular, the integration of the world in a way that would have seemed impossible a couple of decades ago. At the beginning of this conference, someone asked me whether globalization was a topic that was worth exploring further. In fact, one of the things we have noted is that there are always new facets to globalization and that new opportunities—and new threats—present themselves all the time.

The three Fs—food prices, fuel prices, and financial market turmoil—were strong themes from the opening session and have remained at the center of the conference and of many of our deliberations. These factors threaten to undermine global growth and stability. There is a clear need for national policies in these areas, supported by multilateral factors. Food prices and food security were addressed throughout the conference, and there was a parallelization that focused on the importance of national, regional, and international responses to offset the effects on welfare and to support increased productivity in agriculture and bolster food supply. There was also quite a dynamic debate on financial market turmoil, which emphasized that the financial crisis we face at the moment is different in that it originated in the developed world. Given strong economic growth and resilience, emerging markets are a vital part of the solution to the prevailing financial market crisis. Economic growth in developing economies is projected to be four times that of high-income economies in 2008. Globalization is also evidenced by the internationalization of banking, which heightens the risk of transmitting financial shocks worldwide. Some 40 percent of domestic banking assets are now owned by foreign banks, and the number of banks from the south is growing.

Several factors have helped improve emerging-market resilience to financial crises. These include prudent macroeconomic policies, as practiced in a number of countries,

Fundi Tshazibana is director for economic policy at the National Treasury of South Africa.

Annual World Bank Conference on Development Economics 2009, Global
© 2010 The International Bank for Reconstruction and Development / The World Bank.

including countries in Sub-Saharan Africa; a reduction in public debt; and accumulation of foreign reserves.

Despite the challenges, globalization provides significant opportunities for furthering human development. Indeed, accessing high external demand and maximizing the import of knowledge are among the commonalities linking the 13 countries identified in the Commission on Growth and Development as experiencing high and sustainable growth in the post–World War II period. It is perhaps in this context that the advantages of globalization are best considered.

There was also robust discussion in the area of trade and investment. In a session organized by Anthony Venables of Oxford University, we looked at how trade and investment affect economic development. It was argued that part of the divergence in economic performance between Africa and Asia over the past several decades reflects Africa's fragmentation into many economies, which imposes a wide range of costs on African citizens by limiting the benefits of spillovers, preventing manufacturing from exploiting the potential for large-scale economies, and skewing production toward small-scale manufacturing and agriculture.

The topic of deep integration raises questions concerning how regional integration is best used to achieve economic development. Southern African economic integration would be supported by greater attention to harmonization of institutions and policies across the region. There was also a supposition put forward that the relatively disappointing performance of African manufacturing trade stemmed from the fact that African indigenous firms tend to be less productive than nonindigenous ones. This raised the question of how to accelerate the growth of indigenous African firms. It was argued that substantial growth in trade flows would likely follow trade liberalization if accompanied by complementary policies to lower costs associated with trade-related infrastructure and institutions.

The underperformance of Sub-Saharan African export-oriented manufacturing was a recurring theme in the trade discussion and was taken up in a session on industrialization in least-developed countries. A discussion on infrastructure, productivity, and growth concluded that although infrastructure enhances growth, public infrastructure priorities should be country specific and complemented by sound economic policy. Perspectives on foreign direct investment (FDI) included a discussion of whether the determinants of FDI and the benefits for host economies differ according to whether such investment comes from the North or the South. We also had a robust discussion of migration, which is a highly visible aspect of globalization. In a comparative session, it was argued that both remittances and foreign aid support development through improvement of child health outcomes but that the overall effect is weak once medical brain drain is taken into account. Jean-Paul Azam suggested that one motivation for foreign aid was to reduce migration pressures. The threat that brain drain poses to human capital development in developing countries was also flagged as a limitation on reaping the benefits of globalization.

The conference, finally, took up the interlinkages of issues related to climate change, which touched on our themes of people, politics, and globalization.

ECO-AUDIT
Environmental Benefits Statement

The World Bank is committed to preserving endangered forests and natural resources. *People, Politics, and Globalization* is printed on recycled paper made with 50-percent postconsumer fiber. The Office of the Publisher follows the recommended standards for paper usage set by the Green Press Initiative, a nonprofit program supporting publishers in using fiber that is not sourced from endangered forests. For more information, visit www.greenpressinitiative.org.

Saved:
- 16 trees
- 5 million BTUs of total energy
- 1,537 pounds of net greenhouse gases
- 7,404 gallons of waste water
- 450 pounds of solid waste

green press
INITIATIVE

Themes and Participants for the

ANNUAL WORLD BANK CONFERENCE ON

DEVELOPMENT ECONOMICS

Seoul, Republic of Korea

"LESSONS FROM EAST ASIA AND THE

GLOBAL FINANCIAL CRISIS"

June 22–24, 2009

Industrial Policy and Development
Social Capital, Institutions, and Development
Financial Crisis and Regulation
The Road Ahead to a Sustainable Global Economic System
Innovation and Competition

Jeung-Hyun Yoon • Justin Lin • Il Sakong • Anne O. Krueger • Simon Johnson • Olivier Blanchard • James Robinson • Ha-Joon Chang • Karen R. Polenske • Bert Hofman • Partha Dasgupta • Masahiko Aoki • Wonhyuk Lim • Mariano Tommasi • Yung Chul Park • Joshua Aizenman • Jaime Jaramillo-Vallejo • Jong-Wha Lee • Stijn Claessens • Giovanni Zanalda • Yoon Je Cho • Jeromin Zettelmeyer • Philip Lane • Sungchul Chung • Jan Svejnar • Jean-Jacques Dethier • Alan Gelb • Young Geol Lee

Look for publication of the proceedings from this conference in November 2010 under the title **Annual World Bank Conference on Development Economics 2010, Global: Lessons from East Asia and the Global Financial Crisis** (ISBN 978-0-8213-8060-4).

www.ingramcontent.com/pod-product-compliance
Lightning Source LLC
Chambersburg PA
CBHW080602270326
41928CB00016B/2898